Cambridge International AS & A Level
Complete Psychology
Third Edition

Craig Roberts

Seth Alper
Susan Bantu

Great Clarendon Street, Oxford, OX2 6DP, United Kingdom

Oxford University Press is a department of the University of Oxford. It furthers the University's objective of excellence in research, scholarship, and education by publishing worldwide. Oxford is a registered trade mark of Oxford University Press in the UK and in
certain other countries.

© Oxford University Press 2022

The moral rights of the author[s] have been asserted

First published in 2022

Second edition published in 2016

First edition published in 2014

All rights reserved. No part of this publication may be reproduced, stored in a retrieval system, or transmitted, in any form or by any means, without the prior permission in writing of Oxford University Press, or as expressly permitted by law, by licence or under terms agreed with the appropriate reprographics rights organization. Enquiries concerning reproduction outside the scope of the above should be sent to the Rights Department, Oxford University Press, at the address above.

You must not circulate this work in any other form and you must impose this same condition on any acquirer

British Library Cataloguing in Publication Data
Data available

978-1-38-203396-1

10 9 8 7 6 5 4 3 2 1

Paper used in the production of this book is a natural, recyclable product made from wood grown in sustainable forests.

The manufacturing process conforms to the environmental regulations of the country of origin.

Printed in the UK by Bell and Bain Ltd, Glasgow

Acknowledgements

The publisher and authors would like to thank the following for permissions to use photographs and other copyright material:

Anat Shoshani et al: Reprinted by permission from Springer Nature: Journal of Happiness Studies, "Positive Psychology at School: A School-Based Intervention toPromote Adolescents' Mental Health and Well-Being" by Anat Shoshani et al, Copyright 2013.

Andrade, J: "What does doodling do?" *Applied Cognitive Psychology*, 2010, John Wiley & Sons, Copyright © 2009 John Wiley & Sons, Ltd. Reprinted by permission.

Atalay, A S, Bodur, H O and Rasolofoarison, D: "Shining in the Center: Central Gaze Cascade Effect on Product Choice", Journal of Consumer Research, vol.39, no.4, pp.848–66, 2012, by permission of Oxford University Press.

Auty, S and Lewis, C: Table from "Exploring children's choice: the reminder effect of product placement". *Psychology & Marketing*. Vol. 21, No. 9. John Wiley and Sons Reproduced by permission.

Baer RA, Smith GT, Lykins E, et al: "Construct Validity of the Five Facet Mindfulness Questionnaire in Meditating and Nonmeditating Samples". *Assessment*. 2008;15(3):329-342. doi:10.1177/1073191107313003. Reprinted by permission of Sage Publication.

Baron-Cohen, S., Wheelwright, S., Hill, J., Raste, Y. and Plumb, I: The "Reading the Mind in the Eyes" Test Revised Version: A Study with Normal Adults, and Adults with Asperger Syndrome or High-functioning Autism. *Journal of Child Psychology and Psychiatry*, 2001, John Wiley & Sons. Copyright © 2001 John Wiley & Sons, Ltd. Reprinted by permission.

Becker et al: Reprinted from 'Tough package, strong taste: The influence of packaging design on taste impressions and product evaluations. Food Quality and Preference, 22:17-23, © 2010 with permission from Elsevier.

Blackwell et al: Reproduced in Bray "Consumer behaviour theory: approaches and models", 2001, Bournemouth University: http://eprints.bournemouth.ac.uk/10107/1/Consumer_Behaviour_Theory_-_Approaches_%26_Models.pdf. Reproduced with permission of Cengage Learning.

Blaszczynski, A, and Nower, L: "Imaginal Desensitisation: A Relaxation-Based Technique for Impulse Control Disorders". Journal of Clinical Activities, Assignments & Handouts in Psychotherapy Practice, vol.2, no.4, pp.1–14, 2003. Reprinted by permission of Taylor & Francis Ltd.

Blau, G.T. & Boal, K. T: "Conceptualizing how job involvement and organizational commitment affect turnover and absenteeism", *Academy of Management Review*. Vol. 12 No. 2, April 1987.

Borda Mas, M., López Jiménez, A.M. and Pérez San Gregorio, M.A: "Bloodinjection Phobia Inventory (BIPI): Development, reliability and validity". *Anales de Psicologia*. 2010, Vol. 26, No. 1. Reprinted by permission.

BPS Code of Human Research Ethics, April 2021, Lead author Professor John Oates © 2021 The British Psychological Society, Pages 9, 10-11, 15, 21, 23 and 26.

BPS Guidelines for psychologists working with animals, British Psychological Society, March 2020. © 2020 The British Psychological Society. 'Working with animals in psychology' p.5-10.

Brudvik, C, Moutte, S D, Baste, V and Morken, T: "A comparison of pain assessment by physicians, parents and children in an outpatient setting". *BMJ: Emergency Medicine Journal*, 34(3): 138–44, 2016. Reproduced with permission of the BMJ Publishing Group Ltd.

Budzynski, T. H. and Stoyva, J.M: "An instrument for producing deep muscle relaxation by means of analog information feedback". *Journal of Applied Behavior Analysis*. Vol. 2, No. 4, 1969. Reproduced by permission of John Wiley & Sons.

Chapman LK, DeLapp RCT: "Nine Session Treatment of a Blood–Injection–Injury Phobia With Manualized Cognitive Behavioral Therapy: An Adult Case Example". *Clinical Case Studies*. 2014;13(4):299-312. doi:10.1177/1534650113509304. Reprinted by permission of Sage Publication.

Chung, K F and Naya, I: Reprinted from 'Compliance with an oral asthma medication: a pilot study using an electronic monitoring device', in Respiratory Medicine, vol.94, no.9, pp.852–58, 2000, with permission from Elsevier.

Ciceri et al: "A Neuroscientific Method for Assessing Effectiveness of Digital vs. Print Ads", Andrea Ciceri, Vincenzo Russo, Giulia Songa, Giorgio Gabrielli, Jesper Clement, Journal of Advertising Research Apr 2019, 10.2501/JAR-2019-015; DOI: 10.2501/JAR-2019-015. Copyright © 2019 ARF. All rights reserved. Used by permission.

Claypoole, V L and Szalma, J L: Reprinted from 'Computers in Human Behavior' 94: 25–34, "Electronic Performance Monitoring and sustained attention: Social facilitation for modern applications", © 2019 with permission from Elsevier.

Cuadrado, I, Morales, J F and Recio, P: "Women's access to managerial positions: an experimental study of leadership styles and gender". The Spanish Journal of Psychology, 11(1): 55–65, 2008. reproduced with permission from Cambridge University Press.

Dayan, E. and Bar-Hillel, M: Table from p. 334 "Nudge to nobesity II: menu positions influence food orders". *Judgment and Decision Making*. Vol. 6, number 4. Reprinted by permission of E. Dayan and M. Bar-Hillel.

Del Campo et al: "Decision making styles and the use of heuristics in decision making". Journal of Business Economics, 86:389-412, 2016. Reprinted by permission from Springer Nature.

Dogu U, Erkip F: "Spatial Factors Affecting Wayfinding and Orientation: A Case Study in a Shopping Mall". *Environment and Behavior*. 2000;32(6):731-755. doi:10.1177/00139160021972775. Reprinted by permission of Sage Publication.

Fagen, A, Acharya, N and Kaufman, G E: "Positive Reinforcement Training for a Trunk Wash in Nepal's Working Elephants: Demonstrating Alternatives to Traditional Elephant Training Techniques". Journal of Applied Animal Welfare Science, 17(2): 83–97, 2014. Reprinted by permission of Taylor & Francis Ltd.

Fox, D K, Hopkins, B L and Anger, W K: "The Long-term Effects of a Token Economy in Safety Performance in Open Pit Mining", in Journal of Applied Behavior Analysis, vol.20, no.3, pp.215–24, 1987. Reproduced by permission of John Wiley & Sons.

Freeman et al: "Can virtual reality be used to investigate persecutory ideation?" The Journal of Nervous and Mental Disease, 191(8): 509–14, 2003. Reproduced by permission of Wolters Kluwer Health, Inc. and Copyright Clearance Center.

Gansberg, M: "37 who saw murder didn't call the police: Apathy at stabbing of Queen's woman shocks Inspector", The New York Times, 27 March 1964, copyright © The New York Times 1964. All Rights reserved. Used by permission of PARS International Corp and protected by the Copyright Laws of the United States. The printing, copying, redistribution, or retransmission of this content without express permission is prohibited.

Gil, J. et al: "The differentiating behaviour of shoppers: clustering of individual movement traces in a supermarket". Proceedings of the 7th International Space Syntax Symposium, 2009.

Gold, et al: "Rotating shift work, sleep, and accidents related to sleepiness in hospital nurses". *American Journal of Public Health*. Vol. 82 No. 7 1992. Used by permission.

Contents

Introduction 5

1	Research methods for AS Level............ 8	13	Milgram... 94
2	Issues and debates for AS Level 33	14	Perry et al.. 102
3	Approaches to psychology 35	15	Piliavin et al..................................... 110
4	Dement and Kleitman 37	16	Exam centre: AS Level 118
5	Hassett et al.................................... 44	17	Research methods for A Level........... 126
6	Hölzel et al 51	18	Issues and debates for A Level 128
7	Andrade.. 57	19	Clinical psychology......................... 130
8	Baron-Cohen et al 62	20	Consumer psychology 173
9	Pozzulo et al 67	21	Health psychology........................... 228
10	Bandura et al................................. 74	22	Psychology and organisations........... 276
11	Fagen et al 82	23	Exam centre: A Level....................... 319
12	Saavedra and Silverman 90		Index 322

Introduction

This book has been written as a companion to support you throughout your Cambridge International Examinations Psychology AS and A Level (9990 syllabus).

The book is divided into two parts: one for the AS Level and one for the A Level. The part for the AS Level will guide you through all of the 12 core studies and all of the research methods, issues, debates and evaluations. The part for the A Level will guide you through the two options you have chosen to study (from the four available). There are a range of activities throughout the book to get you thinking psychologically, which are ideal preparation for the examinations.

Author

Craig is a freelance tutor and author of psychology textbooks. He has been teaching for over 27 years and is a very experienced examiner with a number of national and international examination boards.

Acknowledgements

There are so many people to thank that have been part of the process of not just this edition of the book but the previous ones too. My family and friends have always been so supportive, especially when times get tough. Thank you Javi for always being there no matter what. Thanks also to Gingerella, my cat, for sitting on all important paperwork I needed whilst writing this edition! Thanks to Susan and Seth for being involved in this edition of the book wholeheartedly. Also, thanks to Oliver and Emily at OUP for commissioning me again to write a book with the publisher.

I also need to thank many Modern Pentathletes who have supported my Modern Pentathlon Research & Statistics venture with open arms and open minds, before and during the writing of this book. In particular, major thanks go to Alexandre Dällenbach, Charles Fernandez, Pavlos Dakoutros, Yaroslav Radziuk, Danilo Fagundes, Fabian Leibig, Buğra Űnal, Gustav Gustenau, Ilya Palazkov, Pavlo Zvedeniuk and Cristobal Rodriguez for being extra supportive and always being happy to chat. Also, a shout out to James Tzanoudakis who presents and commentates for Modern Pentathlon World Cups for his support.

A portion of the royalties I receive for this book will go towards my supporting Modern Pentathletes around the world and also supporting entrepreneurs via Lend With Care to help people get a start in life.

Dedication

To all teachers of Cambridge Psychology whom I have had the pleasure of meeting and training with.

AS Level

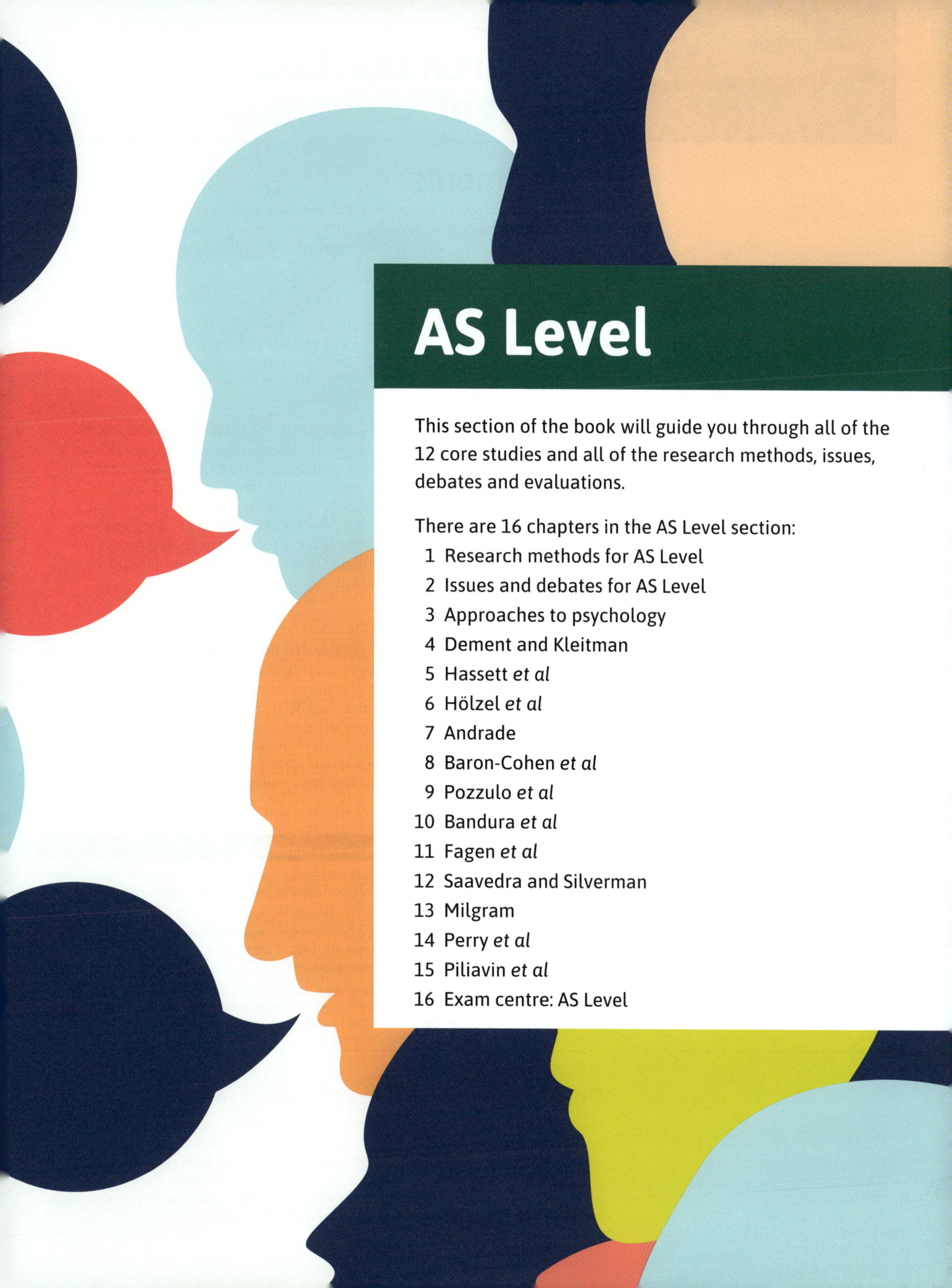

This section of the book will guide you through all of the 12 core studies and all of the research methods, issues, debates and evaluations.

There are 16 chapters in the AS Level section:
1. Research methods for AS Level
2. Issues and debates for AS Level
3. Approaches to psychology
4. Dement and Kleitman
5. Hassett *et al*
6. Hölzel *et al*
7. Andrade
8. Baron-Cohen *et al*
9. Pozzulo *et al*
10. Bandura *et al*
11. Fagen *et al*
12. Saavedra and Silverman
13. Milgram
14. Perry *et al*
15. Piliavin *et al*
16. Exam centre: AS Level

1 Research methods for AS Level

Experiments

An experiment is one of several research methods used in psychological research. The aim is to identify the effect that one variable has on another variable. Therefore, the concept behind the experimental method is that of cause and effect.

Laboratory

These take place in a situation or environment that is artificial to the participants in the study. There are two main types of variable that need to be considered when running any experiment.

Independent variable

The independent variable (IV) is the variable that the psychologist chooses to manipulate or change. This represents the different conditions that are being compared in any study. These usually form the experimental condition and the control condition. To make sure that only one factor is being changed in an experiment, the IV is divided into two groups. One group, called the control, is exposed to all of the experiment but does not get whatever is being tested or changed in the experiment. Essentially, it is used as a comparison group. At the same time, the experimental condition gets all of the experiment plus the one variable being tested by the experiment.

Dependent variable

The dependent variable (DV) is the variable that the psychologist chooses to measure. It is always hoped that the IV is directly affecting the DV in an experiment. The psychologist will attempt to control as many other variables as possible to try to ensure that it is the IV directly affecting the DV. There are different types of variable that can affect the DV as well that have to be controlled if possible. One type is called participant variables. These are the traits and behaviours (eg level of intelligence, prejudices or any previous experiences) that participants bring to the study that may affect the DV. There is usually an attempt at a standardised procedure.

For more on these two main types of variable, and other examples, see pages 18–19.

Strengths of laboratory experiments	Weaknesses of laboratory experiments
Laboratory experiments have high levels of standardisation and so can be replicated to test for reliability. As laboratory experiments have high levels of control, researchers can be more confident it is the IV directly affecting the DV.	As laboratory experiments take place in an artificial setting, it is said that they can lack ecological validity. (See more on ecological validity on page 27.) Many laboratory experiments make participants take part in tasks that are nothing like real-life ones, so the tasks lack mundane realism. (See more on mundane realism on page 27.) Participants usually know they are taking part in an experiment and they may respond to demand characteristics as something about the set-up indicates the aim of the experiment. (See more on demand characteristics on page 27.)

Field

These are experiments that take place in the participants' own natural environment rather than in an artificial laboratory. The researcher still tries to manipulate or change an IV while measuring the DV in an attempt to see how the IV affects the DV. There is an attempt to control other variables that could affect the DV. One type of these is called situational variables. These are variables from the setting that might affect the DV (eg the weather or time of day).

Strengths of field experiments	Weaknesses of field experiments
As field experiments take place in a realistic setting, it is said that they have ecological validity. As participants will not know they are taking part in a study, there will be few or no demand characteristics, so behaviour is more likely to be natural and valid.	Situational variables can be difficult to control, so sometimes it is difficult to know whether it is IV affecting the DV. It could be an uncontrolled variable causing the DV to change. As participants will not know they are taking part in a study, there are issues with breaking ethical guidelines. These include the issues of informed consent and deception.

Evaluations of all experiments on validity, reliability and ethics

	Laboratory experiments	Field experiments
Validity (see pages 26–27)	These experiments have high internal validity because controls mean the researcher can be confident it is the IV directly affecting the DV. They have low external validity as it may be difficult to apply the findings to a real-life situation.	These experiments have lower internal validity as the researcher can control some variables but not all of them. There is stronger external validity than in laboratory experiments due to the 'field' setting of the study.
Reliability (see page 28)	These have high levels of reliability because controls and standardised procedures allow for full replication.	These have medium levels of reliability as some elements of the study are controlled with some standardised procedures but full replication may be difficult.
Ethics (see pages 21–26)	It is usually easy to gain informed consent. Deception can be dealt with through a full debrief. Participants know that they are in a study, so can withdraw at any time.	Researchers can gain informed consent from participants, but it is not always possible. Participants may not know that they are part of a study, which can make debriefing difficult and sometimes impossible. (Also, if participants do not know they are in a study their right to withdraw is invalidated.)

Notes: Internal validity refers to whether it is the IV directly affecting the DV (and not some other variable or variables). External validity refers to the extent to which the findings of the study can be applied to real-life settings and to other people outside the sample.

Experimental design

Researchers who choose to use an experiment have to decide on an experimental (participant) design. This refers to how they allocate participants to the varying conditions of their experiment.

Independent measures

This is when a participant only takes part in one level of the IV. If the IV is naturally occurring (eg gender or age) then a researcher must use this type of design. In a true independent measures design, participants are randomly allocated to one level of the IV (so they get an equal chance of being placed in any level of the IV).

Strengths of independent measures	Weaknesses of independent measures
As participants only take part in one condition they are less likely to guess the aim of the study, therefore reducing the potential effects of demand characteristics. As participants only take part in one condition there are no order effects that can reduce the validity of findings. (See below for examples of order effects.)	There may be a problem with participant variables affecting the DV rather than the IV – even by chance, all people of a certain personality might form one condition and all people with a different personality might form the other condition – so it could be personality affecting the DV rather than the IV. More participants are required for this type of design compared to repeated measures.

Matched pairs

This is when participants are matched on a variable researchers wish to *control* for in the study. Examples of variables they may match participants on include gender, age, and ethnicity. A good source of participants for this type of design is *identical twins* (monozygotic twins) as many variables are already matched genetically. Once participants are matched, each member of the pair takes part in one level of the IV.

Strengths of matched pairs	Weaknesses of matched pairs
Participant variables are controlled for and eliminated as the pairs of participants have been matched on them; therefore the psychologist can be more confident it is the IV affecting the DV rather than participant variables.	It can be a study in itself to find participants who are matched on all of the variables the psychologist has chosen. This is very time consuming. There may be one or two participant variables that are overlooked with the initial matching and these could affect the DV rather than the IV – we cannot control every participant variable.

Repeated measures

This is when a participant takes part in all of the levels of the IV. This cannot be used if the IV is naturally occurring (eg a participant cannot be a male and a female at the same time). Researchers should use counterbalancing, which is sometimes called an ABBA design. For example, 50% of participants do level A then level B of the IV and the other 50% do level B then A.

Strengths of repeated measures	Weaknesses of repeated measures
Using repeated measures eliminates any effect of participant variables as all participants take part in all conditions, therefore they are controlled. Fewer participants are needed for this type of design than the number needed for independent measures design.	As all participants take part in all conditions, there is a chance of demand characteristics affecting the study – participants might work out the aim of the study and behave in a way to fulfil that rather than showing their true behaviour. Order effects can affect the findings of the study and reduce its validity. These are some examples. • Practice effect – participants get better at a task when they complete a similar one or the same one more than once. • Fatigue effect – the more tasks participants do the more tired they might become. • Boredom effect – repeating similar tasks can bore participants.

Evaluation of experiments: use of experimental and control conditions

Scientific research wants to establish cause and effect wherever possible. In psychological experiments, the experimental group are those participants who are exposed to the IV. The control (or comparison) condition consists of participants who are *not* exposed to the IV. Wherever possible, participants should be randomly assigned to either condition in an attempt to reduce the impact of participant variables. This can only be done if the IV allows the control condition to *not* be exposed to it.

Self-reports

Questionnaires

Technique: paper and pencil/online

Paper and pencil questionnaires are those printed on paper (so they are physical objects) and are completed by participants using a pen or pencil. They may have to circle choices for closed questions or write answers to open questions. Online questionnaires are those that are filled in online. A link to the questionnaire is clicked, questions appear on the screen and participants may have to select responses for closed questions or type answers to open questions. They can be set up so only one question appears on the screen at a time and the participant clicks on a continue button to show the next question.

Strengths of paper and pencil/online	Weaknesses of paper and pencil/online
People tend to believe that printed questionnaires are more anonymous (compared to an online survey) which should lead to more honest, valid responses.	The mechanism of printing and distributing questionnaires can be costly, especially if a large sample is required. However, online questionnaires can reduce this cost dramatically.
A large volume of questionnaires can be distributed at the same time to increase the chances of a large volume of responses to use in the data analysis. This may increase generalisability. This is true for both paper and pencil, and online questionnaires.	The process of collecting and logging all responses from paper and pencil questionnaires is labour intensive and sometimes the handwriting/typing skills of respondents can be difficult to understand. This could reduce validity.

Question format

When a study uses a questionnaire, it is asking participants to answer a series of questions in the written form. A psychologist can use a variety of question types in a questionnaire-based study.

- **Likert scales** are statements (eg 'Owning a pet is good for your psychological health') that participants read and then state whether they 'Strongly agree', 'Disagree', etc with the statement.
- **Rating scales** are questions or statements where the participant gives an answer in the form of a number (eg 'On scale of 0–10, how happy are you today? Answer based on the scale 0 = not at all happy and 10 = very happy).'
- **Open-ended** questions or statements allow participants to develop an answer and write it in their own words, as an answer, for example 'Tell me about a happy childhood memory.'
- **Closed questions** are questions that can be answered 'yes' or 'no' or instructions with a set amount of options, for example 'Pick the emotion that best describes how you feel today: happy, sad, cheerful, moody.' Participants choose which answer best fits how they feel.

Strengths of questionnaires	Weaknesses of questionnaires
Participants may be more likely to reveal truthful answers in a questionnaire as it does not involve talking face to face with someone.	Rather than giving truthful answers, participants may give socially desirable answers because they want to look good. This lowers the validity of the findings.
A large sample of participants can answer the questionnaire in a short time span, which should increase the representativeness and generalisability of the findings.	If the questionnaire has a lot of closed questions, participants might be forced into choosing an answer that does not reflect their true opinion.

Interviews

These are similar to questionnaires but answers are given in the spoken not written form. Interviewers ask a series of questions using the types highlighted above. They may record the interview so they can go back and transcribe exactly what participants said. Depending on what the psychologist is studying, there are three main types of interview.

Structured

Structured interviews use set questions. Each participant will be asked the same questions in the same order.

Unstructured

Unstructured interviews involve the interviewer having a theme or topic that needs to be discussed. The interviewer may have an initial question to begin the interview but each subsequent question is based on the response given by the participant.

Semi-structured

Semi-structured interviews involve certain questions that must be asked of participants. However, the interviewer can ask them in a different order and/or ask other questions to help clarify a participant's response.

Strength of interviews	Weaknesses of interviews
If the interview has a lot of open questions participants will reveal more of the reasons why they behave in a certain way or have a certain opinion. Interviews provide rich qualitative data and an interviewer can gain additional data such as body language, tone of voice, emotions, and eye contact.	Participants might be less likely to give truthful answers in interviews (maybe due to social desirability) as they are actually face to face with the interviewer and might not want to be judged. Interviews are time consuming in comparison to questionnaires as a researcher has to interview multiple participants one at a time. There could also be interviewer bias when interpreting the large amounts of verbal data.

Interview technique (telephone or face to face)

Telephone interviews are conducted over the telephone with the researcher reading out questions and the participant speaking their answers. Therefore, the researcher and participant cannot see each other, only hear each other. A face-to-face interview follows the same idea of a researcher reading out questions and the participant speaking his or her answers, but both are in the same room engaging, like we do when having a conversation. However, with the advancement of technology you no longer *need* to be in the same room as you can conduct face-to-face interviews over the internet and social media platforms.

Strength of telephone interviews	Weakness of telephone interviews
There tends to be a better *response rate* when a telephone interview is used compared to a face-to-face interview when the focus is on socially sensitive or personal thoughts and behaviours.	People are actually less likely to *report* unhealthy behaviours in a telephone interview compared to a face-to-face interview.
Strength of face-to-face interviews	**Weakness of face-to-face interviews**
This type of interview makes it easier for respondents to clarify any of their answers or ask for clarification of any questions being asked. This should improve validity.	Reporting of socially undesirable behaviours can also be less for a face-to-face interview due to potential embarrassment or fear of being judged by the interviewer.

Open and closed questions

Open and closed questions are covered on page 11.

Case studies

According to Shaughnessy and Zechmeister, a case study is '… an intensive description and analysis of a single individual' (1997: 308). As with correlations (see pages 15–16), case studies are not a unique research method, they simply use other research methods in a quest for drawing a conclusion (eg naturalistic observation, interviews, or questionnaires). Variables are not systematically controlled or altered as in single-case experimental designs. Case studies are simply in-depth detailed analyses of individuals or close-knit groups of people as in a family unit.

Sometimes case studies form longitudinal studies. This type of study extends over a period of time. The researcher studies the same individual or unit of individuals for a fixed amount of time (eg five years). This allows for an analysis of the development of behaviour over a time period. Of course, longitudinal studies do not have to be exclusively about one person or unit of individuals. They can involve following a cohort (group) of people for the purposes of analysing the development of behaviour.

Strengths of case studies	Weaknesses of case studies
As researchers are focusing on one individual (or unit of individuals) they can collect rich, in-depth data that has details – this makes the findings more valid.	As researchers are focusing on one individual (or unit of individuals), the case may be unique. This makes generalisations quite difficult.
Participants are usually studied as part of their everyday life, which means that the whole process tends to have ecological validity.	As participants are studied in depth, an attachment could form between them and the researcher that could reduce the objectivity of the data collection and analysis of data. This could reduce the validity of the findings.

Observation

This research method involves observing people or animals and their behaviours. There are many different types of observation, as described below. However, there are some elements that are core to observations in general. Prior to observing, the psychologist must create a behavioural checklist (called an ethogram if observing non-humans). This checklist must name each behaviour that the psychologist is expecting see. In addition, a picture of the behaviour happening and a brief description of that behaviour is useful. This makes sure that if there is more than one observer, they are looking for the same behaviours. The checklist must be 'tested' before the main observation to ensure that all potential behaviours are covered and the observers can use the checklist successfully. This is called a pilot observation. Additional behaviours may be added to the checklist after this process. An example of one of these can be found under structured observations.

In observations there are two ways in which an observer can 'sample' behaviours.

1. Time sampling: behaviours are recorded in specified time intervals. Three types can be used.

    - Instantaneous scan: the behaviour that is being shown by the person being observed is recorded at the start of each set time interval. For example, every 10 seconds whatever behaviour being shown by a child in the playground is recorded.

    - Predominant activity scan: the observer records the most frequent behaviour shown by the person being observed in a set time period (eg in a 10-second period).

    - One-zero scan: the observer records whether each behaviour happened (a 1) or did not happen (a 0) within the time period set. Frequency of that behaviour is not recorded, just whether it happened or not.

2. Event sampling: every time a behaviour is seen in the person being observed it is tallied. A set time period is decided upon before recording begins.

Strengths of observations in general	Weaknesses of observations in general
If participants are unaware that they are being observed then they should behave 'naturally'. This increases the ecological validity of the observation.	If participants are aware that they are being observed then they may not behave 'naturally' but show more socially desirable behaviours. This reduces the validity of findings.
As behaviours are 'counted' and are hence quantitative, the process is objective and the data can be analysed statistically with minimal bias.	It may be difficult to replicate the study if it is naturalistic as many variables cannot be controlled. This reduces the reliability of the study.

Overt or covert

Observation can be overt or covert. The difference is that:

- overt observation is when participants know who the researcher is and that they are being observed
- covert observation is when participants do not know that a researcher is in the group observing them.

Participant or non-participant

Participant observations are when the researcher becomes a part of the group the researcher wishes to observe. The researcher can be overt or covert about this. The researcher interacts with participants and takes notes on behaviours, participants' comments, and any other relevant information.

Strengths of participant observations	Weaknesses of participant observations
Usually, the participants being observed are in a real-life setting so there is increased ecological validity.	There are ethical problems as the informed consent of those being placed into the group has not been sought or given.
As observers become involved with the group they are more likely to understand the motives and reasons for behaviours. This increases the validity of findings.	The presence of an outsider (the observer) can initially change the behaviours of the group members. This lowers the validity of findings.

Non-participant observations are when the researcher is 'away' from the people or animals being observed. This can also be an overt or covert process. The researcher does not interact with any of the participants.

Strengths of non-participant observations	Weakness of non-participant observations
Participants' behaviour will not be affected by knowing they are being observed because the observers are out of sight.	It can be difficult to make detailed observations and to produce qualitative data that allows understanding as to why the behaviours are occurring.
Researchers' observations are more likely to be objective as they are detached from the people they are observing.	

Structured or unstructured

Structured observations are those where the observers have created a behavioural checklist in order to code the behaviour they are observing. For example, if researchers were interested in aggressive and affiliative play in children they would construct a behavioural checklist similar to the one below.

Name of behaviour	Diagram	Description
Hitting		When one person purposively makes physical contact with another (eg hand to arm) – not accidental.
Hugging		When two people place their arms around each other in a non-aggressive way.

The observers can then tally how many times a behaviour occurs during the time period set aside to observe. They can use time or event sampling as outlined on page 13.

Strength of structured observations	Weakness of structured observations
The coding system (via the behavioural checklist) allows objective quantitative data to be collected. This can then be analysed statistically.	The sampling of observed behaviour tends to be restrictive (eg time sampling) and does not give an idea of the reasons why the behaviours are occurring.

Unstructured observations are when observers note all the behaviours they can see in qualitative form over a period of time. No behavioural checklist is used as the observers simply record what is happening in real time.

Strength of unstructured observations	Weakness of unstructured observations
These types of observations can generate in-depth, rich qualitative data that can help explain why behaviours are occurring.	Observers may easily be drawn to noticeable or eye-catching behaviours that may not fully represent all the behaviours occurring during the observation period.

Naturalistic or controlled

Naturalistic observations take place in a person's or animal's own natural environment.

Strengths of naturalistic observations	Weaknesses of naturalistic observations
As participants are unaware that they are being watched, they should behave more naturally, removing the chances of demand characteristics affecting their behaviour.	There is very little control over extraneous variables, which makes it difficult to draw cause-and-effect conclusions about the observed behaviours.
As the observation takes place in a natural setting for participants, there are increased levels of ecological validity.	Replication may be difficult as there cannot be a totally standardised procedure due to possible extraneous variables. This makes it difficult to test for reliability.

Some observations take place in a controlled setting. For example, during an experiment in a laboratory room the observers could be behind a one-way mirror so they cannot be seen observing.

Strengths of controlled observations	Weaknesses of controlled observations
As the set-up is controlled, the observers can be more confident about what is causing any of the behaviours shown by participants.	Carrying out the observations in an artificial setting can easily influence participants' behaviour. For example, children may be anxious in an environment that is different from their usual environment.
There is less risk of extraneous variables affecting participants' behaviour.	As the setting is artificial, the findings may lack ecological validity.

Correlations

Correlations do not constitute a separate research method as such because other research methods are used to gain the data. Correlational designs look for relationships between the measures collected from other research methods (eg questionnaires or observations). Correlations can be defined as the relationship between two measured variables.

There are three broad categories that results of correlational studies can fall into: positive, negative or no correlation.

- A *positive correlation* takes the form that if one variable increases, the second variable is also likely to increase. For example, there may be a positive correlation between people's height and their shoe size in that we expect a taller person to have larger feet. As one variable increases, so does the other.

- A *negative correlation* takes the form that if one measured variable increases, the other measured variable decreases. For example, there may be a negative correlation between the number of therapy sessions a person has and the number of depressive symptoms the person exhibits – we expect that as the number of therapy sessions increase, the number of exhibited depressive symptoms decreases. As one variable increases, the other decreases.

- *No correlation* refers to the situation where no definite trend occurs and the two measured variables do not appear to be related to each other. For example, if we attempted to correlate the circumference of people's heads and then rated them on a 'big-headedness scale', such as how much they liked to talk about their achievements and boost their ego, we would probably find no correlation.

Strengths of correlations	Weaknesses of correlations
Correlations are good for showing the relationship between two variables. Further research, such as experiments, can then be conducted to establish cause and effect between the variables.	There are issues of causality. If a correlation is reported in a study, researchers do not know whether variable A is causing a change in variable B or whether variable B is causing a change in variable A. There could also be a third variable causing changes in both A and B that has not been measured.
Correlations do not require any manipulation (researchers simply look at the relationship between two measures) so correlations can be used where experiments are either unethical or impractical.	Correlations are restricted to research where measurements are quantitative so cannot be used to investigate why behaviours are occurring.

Strength of correlations

Inferential statistical tests can be used on data collected for correlations. One such test is the Spearman's Rank Order Correlation Coefficient. This test analyses the data and produces a number that indicates the strength of a correlation. The number ranges from -1 (perfect negative correlation) to $+1$ (perfect positive correlation). If the number generated by the test is negative then the correlation is negative and if the number generated by the test is positive then the correlation is positive. The size of the number indicates the actual strength of the correlation. The higher the score, the stronger the correlation. For example, a $+0.75$ correlation is stronger positive correlation than a $+0.35$ correlation.

Operational definitions of co-variables (measured variables)

An operational definition refers to how a measure or an observation has an action, process, or procedure (these are the operations). Therefore, an operational definition is outlining an action, a process, or a procedure that reflects the behaviour, thought, etc that is being measured or observed. An example would be happiness. The operational definition could be the results on a test designed to measure happiness, smiling at other people, or the release of serotonin in the brain. For correlations, the co-variables will need an operational definition that creates a numerical value or there would be no way that they could be analysed to see whether there is a correlation.

Longitudinal studies

This is when the same set of participants is followed over a longer period of time to examine areas such as developmental changes. They may repeat similar tasks once per year, for example. Therefore, these types of studies do not directly manipulate any variables.

Strengths of longitudinal studies	Problems with longitudinal studies
These studies allow analysis of how behaviour develops over time (eg throughout childhood) and long-term effects (eg of life events on development). Individual differences between people in the study are controlled as the same people are tracked over a set amount of time. Therefore, findings are more likely to be valid.	Not all participants will want to be followed for the length of the study and will drop out. This is called 'participant attrition'.
	This can reduce the sample size and then the generalisability and/or validity of the study as time progresses.
	Psychologists could become attached to participants and be subjective in their analysis of the data.

Experiments with longitudinal designs

These types of studies are experimental, so there has to be some form of IV manipulation to see the effects that has on the DV. The longitudinal part refers to a gap in time between a first recording of the DV (or baseline measure) and at least a second recording of the DV. The time gap can be days, weeks, or even months depending on what the IV manipulation is. These are often used in clinical psychology settings to see whether following a specific therapeutic treatment is successful over time.

Strengths of longitudinal designs	Problems with longitudinal designs
There is a baseline measurement that allows for a direct comparison of DV measures over time. This can allow an assessment if an intervention, for example, is working and/or when it began to work. These studies can yield rich and detailed qualitative data that provides a holistic view about the behaviour under study.	Participant drop out can be an issue, especially with generalisability. Those who remain to the end may be qualitatively different from those who dropped out, which can affect representativeness. Studies could be limited to a smaller sample in many cases because it is difficult to follow up on large samples for far too long.

Methodological concepts

Aims and hypotheses

Aim

The aim is written before a study is run. It is a statement that tells people what the purpose of a study is. It does not predict the outcome of the study (a hypothesis does this) but merely states what the study is about. It can be written as a question. There are examples of aims for the 12 core studies you need to learn for your AS Level.

Hypothesis

A hypothesis predicts the findings of a study. It is also written before the study is run. An experimental hypothesis always contains the IV and DV (fully operationalised). A correlational hypothesis will always have both measured variables operationalised. There are two main types of experimental or alternative hypotheses, as highlighted below.

Directional (one-tailed)

A directional, or one-tailed, hypothesis predicts a significant difference or correlation and also the direction of results. Here are two examples.

- Females will be able to spell more words correctly (out of 25 words) compared to males.
- There will be a positive correlation between the amount of hours spent revising for an AS Level Cambridge International Psychology examination and the final score a student achieves.

Non-directional (two-tailed)

A non-directional, or two-tailed, hypothesis still predicts a difference or correlation but not the expected direction of results. Here are two examples.

- There will be a difference in the number of words spelt correctly (out of 25 words) by females compared to males.
- There will be a correlation between the amount of hours spent revising for an AS Level Cambridge International Psychology examination and the final score a student achieves.

Null

A null hypothesis is necessary if we are going to use inferential statistical tests to examine whether we have found a significant difference or a significant correlation. These tests calculate how far the actual findings have deviated from chance. Here are two examples.

- Any difference in the number of words spelt correctly (out of 25 words) of females compared to males will be due to chance.
- Any correlation between the amount of hours spent revising for an AS Level Cambridge International Psychology examination and the final score a student achieves will be due to chance.

Variables

Independent variable

The IV is the variable that researchers choose to manipulate or change. This represents the different conditions that are being compared in any study. For example, if a researcher wants to investigate memory in school children, then the variable that requires changing is age. Therefore, age is the IV. However, the IV requires some form of operationalisation. To do this, the researcher must clearly define what the different conditions are. For the memory in school children example, the operationalised IV could be: level 1 = five to six years old; level 2 = seven to eight years old.

Dependent variable

The DV is the variable that researchers choose to measure. It is always hoped that the IV is directly affecting the DV in an experiment. Also, the DV needs some form of operationalisation. To achieve this, researchers must clearly define how they will measure. Taking the example above of investigating memory in school children, the operationalised DV could be the amount of items that a child remembers after being shown a tray of objects containing a maximum of 25 objects.

Operational definition + operationalise IV/DV

We have already introduced what an operational definition means on page 16. The process of creating an operational definition is called *operationalisation*.

Controlling of variables

Controlling variables and standardisation of procedure

Obviously, any researcher would not want any variable to affect the DV except the IV. Therefore, researchers will find ways to control variables that could potentially do this. These are discussed below.

A standardised procedure is one where all participants follow the same order of events within a study. The only subtle difference would be which level of the IV a participant is exposed to. Aspects such as standardised instructions, standardised materials and a standardised location all form part of a standardised procedure. The more a procedure is standardised, the more likely it is that another researcher could replicate the study and test for reliability.

In contrast, when a researcher attempts to control variables, it is to strengthen the cause–effect relationship between the IV and the DV. Of course, standardising a procedure adds to this strengthening as it eliminates other variables that could have a direct or indirect effect on the DV.

Extraneous variables

These are variables that can influence the relationship between the IV and DV. They can affect the outcome of an experiment but they are not the variables of interest. Therefore, they add error to the experiment.

Uncontrolled variables

These are variables that cannot be controlled by a researcher. Examples are forces of nature, the weather, or other aspects of the environment. Uncontrolled variables can have an impact on a study, for example by affecting the DV in an experiment or changing people's behaviours during an observation. These variables can lower the validity of findings.

Participant variables

Variables that the participant brings to the study can affect the DV rather than the IV. Examples of participant variables include prejudices, previous experiences with a similar study or task, level of intelligence, gender, and personality.

These are some ways of helping to control participant variables.

- Participants can be randomised to each level of the IV. It is hoped that, by chance, these types of variables will 'balance' themselves out across the levels.

- Repeated measures can be used where possible. If all participants take part in all levels of the IV then their participant variables are effectively controlled for.

Situational variables

Variables that the situation brings to the study can affect the DV rather than the IV. Examples of situational variables are noise, temperature, lighting, and the weather.

Ways of helping to control situational variables include the following.

- The situation where the study takes place can be standardised. For example, the temperature and noise levels can be controlled.

- If using repeated measures, researchers can ensure that counterbalancing is used.

- A double-blind technique can be used. This is when the researcher does not know the full aim of the study and simply follows a standardised procedure.

Types of data

Quantitative

Quantitative data is in the numerical form and researchers can perform statistical analyses on it. Anything in the form of a number is quantitative data.

Strengths of quantitative data	Problems with quantitative data
As the data are numerical, it allows easier comparison and statistical analysis to take place (eg the average score of two different groups of participants can easily be compared).	As the data are numerical, they miss out on valuable information. If the answer is simply yes/no or on a rating scale we do not know why participants chose the answers that they did.
As the data are numerical, analysis is objective and scientific – there is only minimal chance of researchers miscalculating the data and drawing invalid conclusions.	This approach can be seen as reductionist as researchers are reducing complex ideas and behaviours to a number or percentage.

Qualitative

Qualitative data take the form of descriptions via words, sentences, and paragraphs. These data are rich in detail and can contain participants' explanations of their answers to questions asked.

Strengths of qualitative data	Problems with qualitative data
The data collected are in-depth responses in the words of participants so they are rich and in detail and represent what participants believe. Therefore, it can be argued that this approach is not reductionist. As the data come directly from participants we can understand why each participant thinks, feels or acts in a certain way.	The interpretation of the data could be subjective as we are dealing with words rather than numbers – a researcher could misinterpret what the participant was meaning to say or be biased against some of the participant's views. There may be researcher bias: the researcher might only select data that fits into the hypothesis or aim of the study. This cannot be done with quantitative data.

Subjective and objective data

Subjective data is usually collected via self-reports as it is information from the viewpoint of a participant, a patient, a researcher, etc. It can take the form of feelings, concerns, viewpoints, attitudes, and perceptions about something or someone. Objective data is usually collected via scientific machinery and includes brain scans and observations. The data are directly measurable and observable.

Here are some examples from the core studies that you will be learning at AS Level.

- Subjective data – in the study by Fagen *et al* (elephant learning), the idea of a pass was judged solely by the trainer when she thought that the elephant had successfully performed a full trunk wash, for example. The recorded data was based on her viewpoint only.
- Objective data – in the study by Hölzel *et al* (mindfulness and brain scans) an MRI scan was used to directly measure brain grey matter density. This was directly measurable and observable.

Subjective data

Strengths of subjective data	Problems with subjective data
This data is excellent when investigating people's feelings, perception, concerns, etc about something, as it allows the person to explain and clarify anything. It allows for a deeper understanding of whatever is being investigated.	The data can be biased in a number of ways. There could be recall bias from participants themselves, where what they recall is not necessarily factual; or from social desirability bias, where participants answer in a way to make themselves look and feel good. The latter can also be seen in observers, where they only record certain behaviours, especially those that are expected or predicted.

Objective data

Strengths of objective data	Problems with objective data
There is a reduction in bias as the data has been collected using scientific measures that are much less likely to be misinterpreted.	Objective data does not always give 'the full picture' about a person. For example, if we are measuring fitness using a pedometer, we are provided with a number of steps but there is no information about intensity, frequency of steps, or type of activity leading to steps being counted.

Sampling of participants

Sample and population

Participants are the people who choose to take part in a study. They form the sample of participants whom the study will be conducted on. It is hoped that these people represent a wider, target population (TP). The researcher must have a TP.

This is the group of people a researcher studies in the same way in the hope that the findings can generalise to and be representative of that TP. For example, if a psychologist wants to investigate memory in school children then the researcher's TP might be children from five to eight years old. There are different sampling techniques that psychologists can use to help recruit their participants from the TP.

Opportunity sampling

This technique involves the researcher recruiting participants who happen to be around at the time the researcher needs participants. Once the correct number has been chosen and those participants have completed the study, no more participants are asked.

Strength of opportunity sampling	Weakness of opportunity sampling
Large numbers of participants can be obtained relatively quickly and easily because this method involves using people who are around at the time of the study.	A researcher is unlikely to gain a wide variety of participants to allow for generalisation because this technique draws in one type of person in the main.

Random sampling

Random sampling involves every participant in the TP having an equal chance of being chosen. If the TP is small then potential participants can be numbered and, for example, chosen from a hat. If the TP is large, all potential participants can be numbered then a random number generator can be used to select the sample.

Strength of random sampling	Weakness of random sampling
The researcher can generalise to the TP with more confidence. This is because the sample is more likely to be representative of the TP.	Obtaining details of the TP from which draw the sample (eg lists of people in the TP) may be difficult. You cannot guarantee a representative sample as with random sampling, eg all chosen participants could be of one gender. With both techniques a researcher may find a 'perfect' sample but may still have the problem that the participants will not take part in the study.

Volunteer (self-selecting) sampling

This technique involves the researcher advertising for participants. It is frequently used in universities to recruit participants for a range of studies. Therefore, for this technique participants choose whether they want to participate or not.

Strength of volunteer sampling	Weakness of volunteer sampling
People are more likely to participate if they have already volunteered so the drop-out rate should be lower, making generalisations potentially stronger.	Using this technique a researcher is unlikely to gain a wide variety of participants to allow for generalisation. Instead, the group will consist only of the type of people who will volunteer to take part in research or in a particular study.

Ethics

Guidelines for the use of humans

The British Psychology Society (BPS) updated some of its guidelines in 2021. Formerly the *Code of Ethics and Conduct*, the BPS guidelines are now called the *Code of Human Research Ethics*. Both sets of guidelines can be found at www.bps.org.uk/news-and-policy/bps-code-human-research-ethics. This code is a substantive update of the 2014 guidelines.

There are various ethical guidelines that a researcher has to consider when designing and running any study. The main aspects are highlighted below, and the guidance is that given by the BPS.

Minimising harm (and maximising benefit)

Value statement

Psychology researchers should seek to maximise the benefits of their work at all stages, from inception through to dissemination and application. Psychologists should consider all research from the standpoint of the research participants and any other persons, groups or communities who may be potentially affected by the research, with the aim of maximising potential benefits and avoiding potential risks to psychological wellbeing, mental health, personal values, privacy or dignity.

Harm to research participants must be minimised. Where risks arise as an unavoidable and integral element of the research, robust risk assessment and management protocols should be developed and complied with. Normally, the risk of harm should be no greater than that encountered in ordinary life, i.e. people should not be exposed to risks greater than or additional to those to which they are exposed in their normal lifestyles.

Risk can be defined as the potential physical or psychological harm, discomfort or stress to human participants that a research project may generate. This is an important consideration in psychological research, where there is a wide range of potential risks. These include risks to the participant's self-esteem, personal social status, privacy, personal values and beliefs, and personal relationships, as well as the adverse effects of the disclosure of illegal, sexual or deviant behaviour. Research that carries no physical risk can nevertheless be disruptive and damaging to research participants (both as individuals or whole communities/categories of people).

It can be difficult to determine all potential risks at the outset of a piece of research. However, researchers should endeavour to identify and assess all possible risks and develop protocols for risk management as an integral part of the design of the project, and ensure that appropriate levels of ethics review are sought. The following research would normally be considered as involving more than minimal risk:

- Research involving vulnerable groups (such as children aged under 16; those lacking mental capacity; or individuals in a dependent or unequal relationship, or who have prior experience of psychological or physical harm or adversity in its broadest sense);
- Research involving potentially sensitive topics (such as participants' sexual behaviour; their legal or political behaviour; their experience of violence; their gender or ethnic status);
- Research involving a significant and necessary element of deception;
- Research involving access to records of personal or confidential information (including genetic or other biological information);
- Research that might open access to potentially sensitive data through third parties;
- Research that could induce psychological stress, anxiety or humiliation or cause more than minimal pain (e.g. repetitive or prolonged testing);
- Research involving invasive interventions (such as the administration of drugs or other substances, vigorous physical exercise or techniques such as hypnosis) that would not usually be encountered during everyday life;
- Research that may have an adverse impact on employment or social standing (e.g. discussion of an employer, discussion of commercially sensitive information);
- Research that may lead to 'labelling' either by the researcher (e.g. categorisation) or by the participant (e.g. 'I am stupid', 'I am not normal');
- Research that involves the collection of human tissue, blood or other biological samples.

Some research may pose risks to participants in a way that is legitimate in the context of that research and its outcomes. For example, research to reveal and critique fundamental economic, political or cultural disadvantage and exploitation may involve elements of risk. Further, some research may be considered legitimate if the longer-term gains outweigh the short-term immediate risks to participants (provided that these risks are minimal and neither have lasting effects nor induce prolonged personal discomfort).

Valid consent including informed consent

Researchers should ensure that every person from whom data are gathered for the purposes of research consents freely and voluntarily to participation, having been given sufficient information to enable them to make an informed choice. They should be free during the data gathering phase to withdraw or modify their consent and to ask for the destruction of all or part of the data that they have contributed within agreed and consented limits.

The way in which consent is sought from people to participate in or otherwise contribute data for research should be appropriate to the research topic and design, and to the ultimate outputs and uses of the analyses. It should recognise in particular the wide variety of data types, collection and analysis methods, and the range of people's possible responses and sensitivities. The principle of proportionality should apply, such that the procedures for consent are proportional to the nature of participation and the risks involved. For example, for data from existing datasets where consent was properly gained in the initial collection and this consent covers the uses of data proposed, no further consent will normally be needed. For de-identified at-source, non-sensitive data, consent may usually be considered to have been given by the act of participation or by ticking a box, for example. Nevertheless, the risks involved in some research where data are de-identified at the point of collection, for example, web-based research on sensitive topics such as sexual behaviours, will require carefully prepared prior information and clear consent processes. While written consent, as described below, will be the usual approach, other methods, such as audio-recorded verbal consent or implied consent (for example, in choosing to input responses to an anonymous online survey on a non-sensitive subject), may be preferable if based on a careful consideration of the research context. It is always important that consent should be documented in an auditable record.

Informing participants

Consent is not valid unless it is given from an informed perspective. Giving potential participants necessary and sufficient information about the research in an understandable form is crucial to giving them an adequate basis for deciding whether or not participate. This requires careful thought about the most appropriate means to use, which might include oral, pictorial, audio, or video media as well as or instead of a textual information sheet. Format is also important; it can be paper but digital formats are also common. Whatever the chosen medium, information must be accessible and portable.

It is important that people are addressed politely, respectfully and, where appropriate, compassionately. It is recommended that at least one pilot test of the processes for informing and debriefing participants be carried out with a person naïve to the research and with a literacy/understanding level at the lower end of the range expected in the planned research sample. In certain circumstances the aims of the research may be compromised by giving full information prior to data collection. In such cases, it should be made clear that this is the case in the participant information and the means by which the withheld information will be given at the conclusion of data collection should be specified. The amount of information withheld and the delay in disclosing the withheld information should be kept to the absolute minimum necessary. The information given to potential participants for them to keep should normally offer a clear statement of all those aspects of the research that are relevant for their decision about whether or not to agree to participation. The following list offers a series of headings for consideration. Not all of these will be relevant in specific cases.

- The aim(s) of the project.
- The type(s) of data to be collected.
- The method(s) of collecting data.
- Confidentiality and anonymity conditions associated with the data including any exceptions to confidentiality, for example, with respect to potential disclosures.
- Compliance with the Data Protection Act (2018).
- The time commitment expected from participants.
- The right to decline to offer any particular information requested by the researcher.
- The opportunity to withdraw from the study at any time with no adverse consequences.
- The opportunity to have any supplied data destroyed on request (up to a specified date).
- Details of any risks associated with participation.
- If appropriate, a statement that recompense for out-of-pocket expenses and payment for time and inconvenience associated with participation will be given, normally without specifying the amount or nature of such payment beyond the reimbursement of incurred expenses such as travel costs.
- The name and contact details of the Principal Investigator.
- The name and contact details of another person who can receive enquiries about any matters which cannot be satisfactorily resolved with the Principal Investigator.
- Details of any insurance indemnity for the research.
- Any debriefing that is planned.
- How the data will be owned, stored and used, and future uses including in open datasets.
- A privacy notice.
- Planned outcomes and potential benefits of the research.
- How the results of the research will be made available to participants.

Sufficient time should be given for potential participants to absorb and consider the information given about the research and what is expected of their participation before they are asked to make a decision regarding participation. There should also be adequate opportunity given for potential participants to ask questions and have them answered.

Assuring valid consent

The consent of participants in research, whatever their age or competence, should always be sought, by means appropriate to their personal characteristics. Special safeguards need to be in place for research with vulnerable populations and persons with specific vulnerabilities. Vulnerable populations include children, persons lacking capacity, those in a dependent or unequal relationship, people with learning or communication difficulties, people in care, people in custody or on probation, people who have suffered physical or psychological trauma and people engaged in illegal activities, such as drug abuse. Researchers should be aware of the risk of stigmatisation and ensure that this Code's Principle of Respect for the Autonomy and Dignity of Persons is fully upheld. Psychologists should ensure that participants from vulnerable populations where understanding be more difficult are given ample opportunity to understand the nature, purpose and anticipated outcomes of any research participation, so that they may give consent to the extent that their capabilities allow. Methods that maximise the ability of vulnerable persons to give informed consent and that respect their agency should be used whenever possible.

Where children are concerned, there is no one-size-fits-all approach to putting in place ethically sound protocols for ensuring that they participate freely and voluntarily in research with an appropriate understanding of what their participation involves. Much depends on the ages of the children and their developmental levels, as well as the specific demands of research projects. Best practice is for researchers to engage in early planning of their consent procedures, and piloting where appropriate, to ensure that the target population characteristics have been well understood and have informed the planning.

Informing consent

The developmental age of a child, particularly in respect of literacy level as well as reasoning and decision-making capacities, is a crucial consideration when planning how best to inform the child about the research, so that their consent decision is validly informed. The information given must be sufficiently comprehensible and clear that the child knows what they are agreeing to. Best practice is to check texts and scripts for age-appropriate literacy level and to pilot with the target age group.

For younger children, the use of pictograms or other forms of graphic communication is worth considering. Similarly, the response mode to questions seeking agreement could make use of smiley/sad face icons to be circled rather than tick boxes.

Any paper-based consenting process should normally be supplemented by a scripted verbal introduction and a clear invitation to the child to ask any questions that they want to about what participation would entail.

Provision of information does not have to be paper-based. Researchers should consider the use of other media such as short films and animations which can be provided in digital formats. In some cases a simple oral explanation is sufficient. It should always be borne in mind that a signature on a consent form is not in itself consent – it is a record of it. A similar record could be made elsewhere including the researcher's field notes. The main concern is that, unlike adults, a single information text will not be suitable for children of all ages; it is likely to be necessary to have two or three versions covering appropriate age ranges.

Right to withdraw

Participants should be given the ultimate right to withdraw from research without penalty. This can be at any point during the research, even at the end when the participant has completed all tasks but still decides that their data cannot be used in the analyses.

(Lack of) deception

Deception or covert collection of data should only take place where it is essential to achieve the research results required, where there are no alternatives, where the research objective has strong scientific merit and where there is an appropriate risk management and harm alleviation strategy.

The experience of deception in psychological research may have the potential to cause distress and harm and can make the recipients cynical about the activities and attitudes of psychologists. However, since there are very many psychological processes that are modifiable by individuals if they are aware that they are being studied, stating the research focus to a participant in advance of the collection of data would make some psychological research impossible. There is a difference between withholding some of the details of the hypothesis under test and deliberately falsely informing the participants of the purpose of the research, especially if the information given implies a more benign topic of study than is in fact the case. This *Code of Human Research Ethics* expects all psychologists to seek to supply as full information as possible to those taking part in their research, recognising that providing all of that information at the start of a person's participation may not be possible for methodological reasons. If the reaction of participants when deception is revealed later in their participation is likely to lead to discomfort, anger or objections from the participants then the deception is inappropriate. If a proposed research study involves deception, it should be designed in such a way that it protects the dignity and autonomy of the participants.

Where an essential element of the research design would be compromised by full disclosure to participants, the withholding of information should be specified in the project protocol that is subjected to ethics review and explicit procedures should be stated to prevent any potential harm arising from such withholding.

Studies based on observation in natural settings must respect the privacy and psychological wellbeing of the individuals studied. Unless those observed give their consent to being observed, observational research is only acceptable in public situations where those observed would expect to be observed by strangers. Additionally, particular account should be taken of local cultural values and of the possibility of intruding upon the privacy of individuals who, even while in a normally public space, may believe they are unobserved.

Confidentiality

Participants in psychological research have a right to expect that information they provide will be treated confidentially and, if published, will not be identifiable as theirs. In the event that confidentiality and/or anonymity cannot be guaranteed, the participant must be warned of this in advance of agreeing to participate.

The duty of confidentiality is not absolute in law and may in exceptional circumstances be overridden by more compelling duties such as the duty to protect individuals from harm or alerting authorities to evidence of terrorist activity. Where a significant risk of such issues arising is identified in the risk assessment, specific procedures to be followed should be specified in the protocol.

Privacy

A researcher should make it clear that participants have the right to ignore any questions or aspect of a study that they do not want to answer or engage in. This protects individuals' privacy. Also, studies should try to refrain from making people reveal personal details that they would not reveal in their everyday lives.

Debriefing

When the research data gathering is completed, especially where any deception or withholding of information has taken place, it is important to provide an appropriate debriefing for participants. In some circumstances, the verbal description of the nature of the investigation will not be sufficient to eliminate all possibility of harmful after-effects. For example, following an experiment in which negative mood was induced, it would be ethical to induce a happy mood state before the participant leaves the experimental setting.

It may the case that some participants do not take up the offer of debriefing or other information, nevertheless this should be offered when appropriate.

Ethical guidelines as used in psychological research in relation to animals

In March 2020, the BPS published an updated version of their 'Guidelines for Psychologists Working with Animals'. You can download the document from www.bps.org.uk/news-and-policy/bps-guidelines-psychologists-working-animals.

Minimising harm (and maximising benefit)

Psychologists work with animals for a variety of reasons. The most obvious use is in research, including studies where animals are the primary subjects, for example there has been some growth in studies of the cognitive capacities of different species (e.g. dogs and horses). In studies of this kind, the primary beneficiary is likely to be the animal species in question. Historically invasive studies of 'animal models' (of which humans are the intended beneficiary) and of the neural substrates of normal behaviour have commanded most attention in the general media. Animals (or simulations of their behaviour) are also still sometimes used in practical teaching within psychology degree programmes. However, these do not exhaust the possible ways in which psychologists, in their professional capacity, may work with animals. For example, there is increasing use of animals in various forms of psychological therapy with people, or to advise on therapy for animals whose behaviour appears disordered in some way. Psychologists may also find themselves involved in the training and use of animals for commercial purposes. Many psychological studies involve no more than the observation of the animals but even observational studies can have unintended consequences; some research questions cannot be answered adequately without more invasive studies; and all studies of captive animals necessarily involve keeping animals in confinement. Studies of free-living animals in their natural habitat may involve disruption of their environment, habituation to humans, brief capture for marking or attachment of a tracking or telemetry device.

Our recommendations are general in scope, since the diversity of species and techniques used in psychology preclude giving specific details about appropriate animal care and treatment. Thus members of the Society are reminded of their general obligation to avoid or at least minimise discomfort to living animals. It should be noted that permission to perform procedures regulated under the 1986 Act will not be granted unless the researcher can justify the harms caused to the animals in relation to the likely benefits of the research. In addition, when permission to perform a regulated procedure is requested, the researcher is also required to demonstrate that consideration has been given to replacing animals with non-sentient alternatives whenever possible, reducing the number of animals used to the minimum consistent with the scientific objectives, and refining procedures to minimise suffering (The Three Rs: Russell & Burch, 1959), and to apply these 3Rs principles throughout the licensed programme of work. Psychologists who work with animals should, therefore, keep abreast of new developments in animal welfare, with new ways of reducing the numbers of animals required for the procedures, and with refining the procedures so as to enhance the welfare of the animals concerned and improve the quality of scientific data derived from them.

Replacement

Much psychological study requires an intact behaving organism. However, alternatives such as video records from previous work or computer simulations may also be useful. Both can be especially helpful in teaching contexts; see Stricklin *et al.* (1995) and Hull (1996). Two specific examples of these approaches are the video material of free-living rats that is a part of the 'Ratlife' project and a simulation of rat behaviour in operant learning procedures. General advice on computer simulations for teaching can be obtained from the Higher Education Psychology Network, formerly known as LTSN. InterNICHE provides a large database of alternatives to animal use for educational purposes.

Species

Psychologists should choose a species that is scientifically and ethically suitable for the intended use. Choosing an appropriate subject species usually requires knowledge of that species' natural history and some judgement of its level of sentience. Knowledge of an individual animal's previous experience, such as whether or not it was bred in captivity, is also important. When the use involves regulated procedures, and when a variety of species can be used, the psychologist should employ the species which, in the opinion of the psychologist and other qualified colleagues, is likely to suffer least whilst still attaining the scientific objective, and must justify their choice in any Project Licence application. Moreover, the animal model chosen should be one that is effective and efficient in producing the anticipated benefit. The use of non-human primates will always require particularly careful consideration because of their high level of sentience.

Different strains of commonly-used laboratory rodents have very different physiological and behavioural characteristics that may make them more or less suitable for psychological research. In addition, the amount of variation between individuals may be greater in outbred than in inbred strains. As a consequence, the use of inbred strains may reduce the numbers of animals that are required, although it may reduce the generality of the results that are obtained.

Numbers

Researchers working under the 1986 Act are legally required to use the smallest number of animals sufficient to accomplish the research goals, and this principle should be generally applied. The aim of minimising the number of animals used in an experiment can be achieved by appropriate pilot studies, reliable measures of behaviour, good experimental design and the appropriate use of statistical tests. In 1996, the American Psychological Association's Task Force on Statistical Inference was published, giving guidance on the importance of taking statistical power into account when designing experiments.

Procedures: pain, suffering and distress

See the section on minimising harm (and maximising benefit) on page 25.

Procedures: housing

Caging conditions should take into account the social behaviour of the species. Caging in isolation may be stressful to social animals; overcrowding may also cause distress, and possible harm through aggression. Because the degree of stress experienced by an animal can vary with species, age, sex, reproductive condition, rearing history, depression of the immune system, temperament and social status (Abbott et al, 2003; Palanza et al, 2001), the natural behaviour of the individual animals concerned and their previous social experience must be considered in order to minimise such stress. Guidance documents associated with the Animals (Scientific Procedures) Act 1986 – such as the code of practice for the housing and care of animals bred, supplied or used for scientific purposes – specify minimum standards for the housing of laboratory animals. Depending on the data collection requirements, home cage testing should be considered to reduce potential stress on the animals. Automated cages in which the animals both live and are tested are increasingly sophisticated (e.g. 'IntelliCages' for behavioural and cognitive phenotyping in the home cage, and the Home Cage Analyser (HCA) for continuous 24/7 recording and analysis of individual animal behavior when socially housed in a standard laboratory cage).

Procedures: reward, deprivation and aversive stimuli

It is not always necessary to provide all species of animals with ad libitum food intake, and, in some cases, this may even be considered harmful; deprivation, on the other hand, can cause distress to animals (Claasen, 1994). Some levels of deprivation are regarded as regulated procedures under the Animal (Scientific Procedures) Act 1986, but others are not. Thus, when arranging schedules of deprivation the experimenter should consider the animal's normal eating and drinking habits and its metabolic requirements; a short period of deprivation for one species may be unacceptably long for another. When using deprivation or aversive stimulation, the investigator should ascertain that there is no alternative way of motivating the animal that is consistent with the aims of the experiment, and that the levels of deprivation used are no greater than necessary to achieve the goals of the experiment (Prescott et al, 2010). Alternatives to deprivation include the use of highly preferred foods and other rewards which may motivate even a sated animal.

Validity

Types of validity

There are several types of validity that may concern a psychologist conducting research. Validity generally concerns itself with looking at whether the study measured what it was supposed to measure. Table 1.1 highlights some of the main types of validity.

Subjectivity and objectivity

When researchers run a study, they need to think about what data will be collected and then how to analyse it and draw appropriate conclusions. One aspect that may affect the conclusions drawn is subjectivity or objectivity.

Subjectivity refers to analysing data by judging it from your own personal opinion and feelings. Qualitative data, when analysed, has to have some degree of subjectivity as there are no statistics associated with it. An example would be interpreting a dream someone told you about. You can attempt to interpret it using symbols or your knowledge of the person but this analysis would simply be based on your personal opinion. Someone else may give a completely different analysis based on his or her opinion. Therefore, when you are interpreting data from your own perspective, you are being subjective.

Table 1.1 Types of validity

Type	Description
Ecological	Ecological validity has been the subject of great debate. There are two strands that psychologists analyse to make an overall judgement on levels of ecological validity in a study.
	• The environment in which the study is set is the first consideration. If it is artificial and not truly reflecting a real-life situation then a study is said to have low ecological validity. If it mirrors a real-life situation then it is said to have high ecological validity.
	• Behaviour is the second consideration when analysing ecological validity. Some psychologists argue that the level ecological validity is simply 'the degree to which the behaviour of the subjects in the laboratory corresponds to their behaviour in the natural environment'. (Breakwell *et al* 1995: 221). According to this view, ecological validity is more to do with the behaviour of the participant than the setting itself.
	It may be worth noting that the term 'mundane realism' is increasingly used in psychology. This tends to refer to the reality of the task set for participants in any study. For example, the task of reading a word list then trying to recall the words is not something commonly done in everyday life. The task would have low mundane realism. However, an activity such as reading social media and then having a conversation about how you felt is something many people do in everyday life. A task reflecting this would have high mundane realism.
Criterion	Criterion validity is a way of assessing the validity of a task by comparing the results with another measure. There are two main types of criterion: concurrent and predictive.
	• A concurrent criterion is used when a new test and its results are compared to a standard measure that already exists for that behaviour or skill. An example would be when developing a new intelligence test. Researchers might ask: Are results from the new test similar to those gained from well-established measures such as the Weschler Adult Intelligence Scale or the Stanford-Binet Test? If so, the new measure would be said to have high concurrent validity. If not, it would be said to have low concurrent validity.
	• A predictive criterion is a test used to see whether a prediction can be made of what is likely to happen in the future. Using the example of an intelligence test, it could be used as a predictor for academic success. People could take the intelligence test and have their scores recorded. Then they could sit AS Level Cambridge International Psychology examinations and have their results compared to the original intelligence test scores. If the A grade students scored highest on the intelligence test whereas the E grade students scored the lowest, then the intelligence test is said to have some predictive validity. If there is no pattern then it is said to have low predictive validity.
Construct	This looks at whether a test or task given in a study reflects any theoretical constructs it was based on. Using an intelligence test as an example again, the questions used and range of factors being tested must be justified in terms of what a theory expects a person to show in terms of intelligent behaviours or responses.
Population	This refers to how well the sample used in the study can be extrapolated to the target population and then the population as a whole.

Objectivity refers to analysing data based on fact with no need to use personal judgements. This means that all potential sources of bias are minimised. For example, let's say participants are asked to complete a task as quickly as possible. Participant A completes it in 20 seconds whereas participant B completes it in 40 seconds. From an objective perspective, participant A is faster; in fact twice as fast. This conclusion is based on fact and no personal opinions are needed.

> **Challenge yourself**
>
> Find out about internal validity and why it is useful in psychological research.

Demand characteristics

Hayes defined demand characteristics as 'those aspects of a psychological study (or other artificial situation) which exert an implicit pressure on people to act in ways that are expected of them' (2000: 369). Therefore, they are the features of a study that somehow inform the participants about the true aim and this influences their behaviour independently of the IV. While Hayes noted the implicit nature of the 'pressure' when a repeated measures design is used, the characteristics can be explicit if the tasks only differ on one crucial aspect.

Generalisability

This is about the extent to which results or the findings from a study can be transferred to situations or people who were not originally studied. These can take the following forms.

- Population validity: can the findings be transferred to the TP from which the sample has been drawn from or those not represented in the sample?
- Ecological validity: can the findings be transferred to situations away from the situation or setting the study took place in?

Reliability and replicability

Reliability

Reliability generally concerns itself with consistency over time and whether replicating a study would produce similar results. There are several types of reliability, as highlighted below.

Inter-rater or observer

This is a test of the consistency between observers when watching the same behaviours shown by the same participants. Independent observers are briefed to observe the behaviours of the same participants. This usually happens as a pilot study before the real data collection. A time period for the observation is agreed, as well as the recording method (eg the observation may be continual as in time sampling or observers might record what the participant was doing at, say, 10 seconds, 20 seconds, 30 seconds, etc). After the task, the two observers' records are compared for consistency. One crude way of doing this is simply to compare the two in terms of the frequency of different behaviours shown to see if they are approximately the same. A more objective way is to conduct correlational analyses on the data to see the strength of the correlation between the two (or more) observers' records. However, the correlation only shows the degree of similarity, overall, between the observers' records. It does not tell us that they recorded the frequency of exactly the same behaviours. One way around this could be to train observers by having them watch pre-recorded sequences of behaviours so that they can replay an event and agree whether the behaviour was shown or not.

Test-retest reliability

This is a test of consistency of a questionnaire-based measure (eg an attitude). When a questionnaire is devised using techniques that generate quantitative data, a test-retest reliability analysis can be conducted to test whether the questionnaire is a reliable measure. Researchers would follow these steps.

1. Create a questionnaire that generates numerical data.
2. Allow a group of participants to complete the questionnaire.
3. After a set time frame (usually greater than two weeks), get the same participants to complete the same questionnaire.
4. Correlate the overall scores for the two time points and see whether a positive correlation occurs. This can even be assessed question by question but it is usually on total scores. If a strong positive correlation occurs then the questionnaire is said to be a reliable measure.

Replicability

Replicability is an important concept in psychology for it is a scientific subject. A psychological research paper must give the readership enough detail about the study so it can be replicated (repeated). Details can include the sampling technique, experimental design used, psychometric scales used, questionnaire scales used, the exact order of the procedure, and all other materials used in the study.

Data analysis

Present and interpret data in tables

Both raw data and analysed data can be presented in tables to help a reader understand what data has been collected and what it means. Tables can be used to effectively summarise the main results of a study.

> **Test yourself**
>
> Find examples from the AS Level core studies where data has been presented as a table in this book.

Measures of central tendency

A measure of central tendency (sometimes called a measure of average) represents how data clusters around a central point in the data set. It is supposed to represent a typical score from the collected data.

Mean

The mean is usually called the average but there are another two types of average that we will look at here (see below). The mean is also called the arithmetic mean. To calculate this we must complete the following procedure.

1. Add up all of the scores we have collected to form our data set.
2. Divide this total by the number of scores that we have just added up.

Median

This measure of average is the middlemost score. That is, when data has been placed in rank order from the smallest number to the largest number (including every repetition of a score), the median is the score that lies in the middle of the data set. To calculate a median, follow these steps.

1. Rank the data from the smallest number to the largest number.
2. Eliminate one score from the lowest end of the ranked data and one score from the highest end of the ranked data (called a pair of scores).
3. Continue eliminating these pairs of scores until either one or two scores are left. If there is an odd number of scores left in the data set you should be left with just one number. This is the median. If there is an even number of scores left in the data set you should be left with two numbers. In this case, you must complete step 4 below.
4. Add up the two remaining numbers and divide the total by 2. This is the median.

Mode

This measure of average is the most common score in the data set. Therefore, on inspecting the data set you can discover the mode by seeing which score or value is represented the most times. If two scores are equally represented then we call the distribution of scores bi-modal. If there are three modes then it is tri-modal, and so on. The best way of calculating the mode is to draw up a frequency table and see which score has the highest frequency, for example as shown in Table 1.2.

From the frequency column we can easily conclude that the modal shoe colour for this data set is black.

When is it most appropriate to use each measure of average?

Each particular measure of average and measure of dispersion cannot be used on any data collected. That is, the mode, median and mean for the data are not simply calculated and all reported on every occasion (this also applies to the measures of dispersion). Table 1.3 shows that the type of measure of average and measure of dispersion used depends on the type (level) of data collected.

Calculating the mean: an example

We measured the height of ten people and the results were as follows (in centimetres):

158   163   165   165
165   168   170   170
170   175

First, we add up all of the scores:

158 + 163 + 165 + 165 + 165 + 168 + 170 + 170 + 170 + 175 = 1669

Next, we divide the total score by the number of scores, which is 10.

$\frac{1669}{10}$ = 166.9. The mean height is 166.9 centimetres.

Calculating the median: an example

The following are questionnaire scores generated from a Likert-type scale:

11   13   13   13   15   17   17   17   18
19   19

The median is 17. Now, recalculate with an extra score:

11   13   13   13   13   15   17   17   17
18   19   19

The two remaining numbers are 15 and 17. If we now execute step 4, we get:

15 + 17 = 32. We then divide this by 2 to get $\frac{32}{2}$ = 19.

The median score is 16.

Table 1.2 Frequency table for males' choice of shoe colour

Shoe colour choice in males	Frequency
Brown	10
Green	15
Blue	18
Black	27
White	17
Red	4

Table 1.3 Measure of average appropriate for different levels of data

Level of measurement	Appropriate measure of average
Nominal: categories of data (eg favourite subject)	Mode
Ordinal: numerical data on a scale devised by the researcher (eg a happiness index)	Median
Interval/ratio: numerical data measured on a universal scale (eg height, weight)	Mean

Table 1.4 Results of males and females solving a maze

Females	Males
Mean = 68.4 seconds	Mean = 69.3 seconds
Standard deviation = 3.9 seconds	Standard deviation = 10.4 seconds

Challenge yourself

People were asked what their favourite colour was. Their answers were blue, red, black, blue, green, pink, green, red, red, red, blue, black, yellow, blue, green, green, pink, blue, blue, brown.

From this data set, draw a bar chart.

What does your bar chart show?

Measures of spread

A measure of spread (sometimes called a measure of dispersion) gives an index of how spread the data is around a measure of central tendency.

Range

This measure of spread is used in conjunction with the median but can be used with any continuous data. It is the simplest to calculate, as follows.

1. Rank the data from the smallest to the largest number (as for calculating the median).
2. Subtract the smallest number from the highest number then add 1.

This is used when the data is at least ordinal.

Standard deviation

This measure of spread is used in conjunction with the mean. This measure is the spread of data around the mean point. It is the most stringent measure of dispersion as it uses all the data in the calculation.

It is easier to interpret a standard deviation if you have two or more data sets to compare. For example, say that you have timed males and females on their ability to solve a maze. Your results are shown in Table 1.4.

The means are similar so, on average, females and males solve mazes in roughly the same time. However, the standard deviation is telling us that the results for females have less spread around the mean than the results for males. This is because, for the results for females, the standard deviation is smaller. Many of the females would have completed the maze around the mean time of 68.4 seconds. However, for the males the data set is much more spread out. Therefore, there were some males who were much slower than the 69.3 seconds average to solve the maze but there were some males who solved it much faster.

This measure of spread is normally used when the data is interval/ratio.

Understand the meaning of measure of spread

A measure of spread gives information about the range of scores attained by participants in a study. It helps to see whether certain groups of participants were scoring roughly the same or whether there was wide variation between participants in that group. Therefore, when calculating any measure of spread, a higher score means that the participants' scores were spread widely across the group whereas a smaller score means that their scores were more consistent as a group.

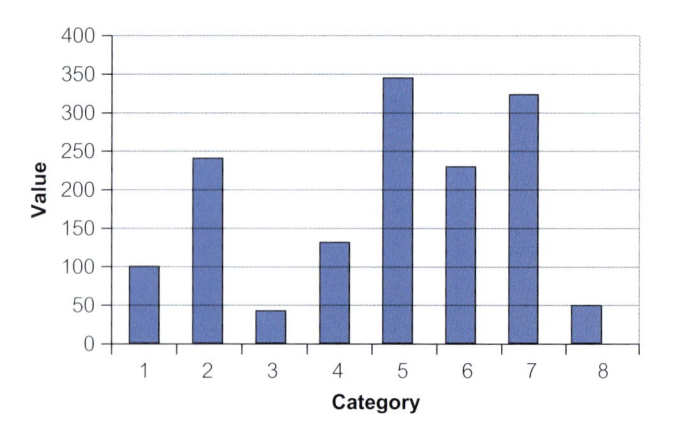

Plotting data

Bar chart

A bar chart is usually used for nominal data (results in named categories) or for plotting the average scores for groups of data collected. The x-axis (horizontal axis) should always have the categories of data while the y-axis (vertical axis) should always have the frequency of occurrences or the average value that is to be represented.

To plot a bar chart follow these steps.

- Enter the categories of data collected (eg favourite animal, or a score on a happiness scale) along the x-axis.
- On the y-axis, write the frequency that each category was recorded.
- Ensure that there are gaps between each bar because the bars represent *separate* categories.

Histogram

A histogram is usually used when the data is continuous (on a numerical scale) and is plotted on the x-axis (horizontal axis). The y-axis (vertical axis) should always be used for the frequency of occurrences.

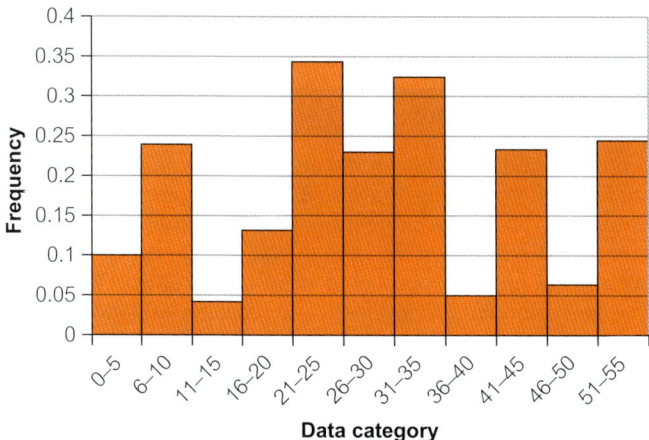

To plot a histogram follow these steps.

- Choose an appropriate width for each bar along the x-axis. Try to keep them exactly the same; for example, if you are entering the speed of completing a task use 1–5 seconds (s), 6–10 s, 11–15 s, 16-20 s, and so on.
- On the y-axis, enter the frequency at which data fell within the width of each bar on the x-axis.

Scattergraph

Sometimes scattergraphs are referred to as scatterplots or scattergrams. They are used for plotting correlations, the relationship between two numerical measures. From these, it is clear what type of correlation has been found. The x-axis (horizontal axis) should represent one of the numerical measures and the y-axis (vertical axis) should represent the other.

To plot a scattergraph, in the example below of participants' scores in two psychology tests, these steps would need to be followed.

- Enter the participant's first score along the x-axis.
- Enter the participant's second score along the y-axis.
- Each cross placed on the scattergraph represents a participant's pair of scores, so find a participant's score on the x-axis and then move up to that person's score on the y-axis and place a cross.

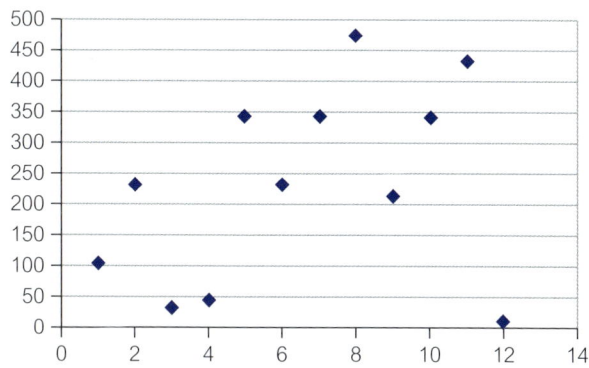

The golden rules of plotting data

The following are guidelines that should be applied every time data is to be plotted.

- Tabulate the data either as a frequency tally chart or where each participant's score on one variable for the scattergraph is next to the score on the other variable.
- Choose an appropriate graph for the type of data you have and the information that you are intending to get across to the reader with the graph.

Research methods for AS Level

Challenge yourself

People were timed how quickly they could write a text message to a friend. The results were given as times in seconds. The results were: 10, 12, 5, 32, 17, 15, 17, 12, 6, 44, 18, 22, 21, 15, 13, 12, 11, 10, 8, 37, 22, 22, 22, 20, 17, 11, 12.

From this data set, plot a histogram.

What does your histogram show?

Challenge yourself

The following scores are from two tests completed by students of psychology. The first test was on cognitive psychology and the second test was on biological psychology. The scores are percentages and are presented as cognitive/biological. The scores were: 76/44, 88/67, 44/44, 55/32, 88/78, 21/7, 55/33, 50/50, 79/55, 42/65, 33/12, 76/67, 60/40, 93/52, 77/65, 66/60, 10/17, 58/49, 76/42, 45/35.

- Plot a scattergraph from this data set.
- What does your scattergraph show?

- Label the axes fully and clearly. For example, if you are representing age groups on the x-axis, state whether the age is in years or months.

- Give the graph an appropriate title. Anyone should be able to read the title and know what the graph is representing.

- Interpret the graph as part of the data analysis. Graphs are not just to fill the space in a report, they should be used as part of your report.

> **Challenge yourself**
>
> Now that you have a much better understanding of research methods and how to collect data, you may want to try the following. The list contains different studies that need designing and it is your job to design each one using the information in this chapter. The research method has been chosen for you but you need to decide on things such as sampling, IV and DV, ethics, experimental design, and controls where appropriate. Make sure that you comment on how valid and reliable your study will be.
>
> 1. Design a laboratory experiment to test whether people are better at remembering a word list when it is read to them compared to when they read it themselves.
>
> 2. Design a field experiment to test whether people are more likely to help another person in need who is carrying a pet animal (eg a cat) compared to carrying a bag of shopping.
>
> 3. Design a questionnaire study to investigate gender differences in perceptions of reality television programmes.
>
> 4. Design an interview study to investigate cultural differences in health eating.
>
> 5. Design a case study to examine why a child has a phobia of windows.
>
> 6. Design an observation (you choose the type) to test whether children are more playful before or after lunch.
>
> 7. Design a correlational study to test whether there is a relationship between the number of hours studied for an examination and the result gained in that examination.

Issues and debates for AS Level

The application of psychology to everyday life

Some people argue that if studies and ideas from psychology cannot be used in everyday life then they are not useful. All psychologists have to consider this before they complete a study. Once a study has been published, other psychologists may evaluate its usefulness. This can be positive or negative.

A study may only have been conducted on one sex so it may not be useful in explaining the behaviour of the opposite sex. The extent to which something is useful is debating how the findings can be used (or not used) in everyday life.

Strength of conducting useful research	Problems with conducting useful research
The main advantage is that it is can be used to improve human behaviour in some way. For example, if we find a better way to treat a mental illness then it is useful to society as a whole.	Studies might be unethical to gain more valid results. Studies need to be high in ecological validity to be of more use to society but this can be quite difficult if they are conducted in a laboratory, for instance.

Individual and situational explanations

Individual explanations account for behaviours using factors from within the person (called dispositional factors, such as personality). Situational explanations account for behaviours using factors from the external environment (situations that people find themselves in).

Strengths of this debate	Problems with this debate
The findings can be very useful to society as a whole. If we find out which behaviours are down to individuals and which are down to the situations we find ourselves in, then we can help explain human behaviour more clearly. If psychologists find that there is an interaction between both sides of the debate then this is useful too.	It is not always easy to separate out individual and situational factors. Studies might be unethical to gain more valid results. Studies need high ecological validity to be of more use to this debate but this can be difficult if they take place in a laboratory, for instance.

Nature versus nurture

Nature refers to behaviours that are thought to be hardwired into people pre-birth (innate or genetic). Nurture refers to behaviours that are thought to develop through the lifetime of the person. Therefore, nature tends to be based on biological factors whereas nurture tends to be based on social and psychological factors.

Strengths of this debate	Problems with this debate
The findings can be very useful to society as a whole. If we find out which behaviours come from nature and which from nurture, we can help to explain behaviour more clearly. If there is an interaction between both sides of the debate this is useful too.	It is not always easy to separate out what is nature and what is nurture. If behaviour is seen to be purely down to nature (genetics) this can be very socially sensitive. Sections of society could use this to undertake a 'eugenic' movement to get rid of people with 'inferior genes'. This is clearly unacceptable. Studies might be unethical in order to gain more valid results.

The use of children in psychological research

There are specific rules about using children in psychological research.

- Children aged under 16 cannot give their own informed consent to take part in a study.
- Children aged under 16 must get parental permission to participate in studies or *loco parentis* permission (eg someone who looks after them in a nursery or school).

There are other issues that may surround the use of children in research that are not linked to ethical concerns. These include the following.

- There must be use of appropriate language to ensure that children used as participants in research *understand* what they are doing.
- Some psychologists believe that children are *less* susceptible to demand characteristics.
- Children may get bored quicker and tired faster than adults so this needs to be considered when designing tasks in studies.

The use of animals in psychological research

There are ethical guidelines and rules for using animals in psychological research. The main ones are as follows.

- The law – psychologists must work within the law about protecting animals.
- Number of animals – this should be a kept to the minimum amount to make statistical analysis meaningful.
- Social environment – social species should be kept together and non-social species kept apart.
- Caging – housing in cages should not lead to overcrowding and increased stress levels.

Strength	Weaknesses
We can conduct research on animals that we cannot do on humans for ethical reasons.	Due to the differences in physiological and psychological 'make-ups' of animals and humans it can be difficult to generalise from animal studies to human behaviour.
	It can be expensive to house animals and they need proper care compared to humans who can participate in and leave a study at will.

See pages 25–26 for more in-depth coverage of ethical guidelines in relation to the use of animals in psychological research.

Approaches to psychology   3

There are many different ways in which psychologists try to explain human and animal behaviour. The approaches that psychologists use form the discipline of psychology. However, these approaches differ widely from each other. This chapter will cover how psychologists use these different approaches to try to explain behaviour. There are four approaches that you are expected to know about. This section looks at each in turn, highlighting their general assumptions, the main research methodology they use and which studies from AS Level fit into each approach.

Biological

Physiological psychologists are interested in how our biology affects our psychology. They look, for example, at the roles that genetics, brain function, hormones, and neurotransmitters have on our behaviour. Many physiological psychologists believe that our behaviour can be explained more by biological mechanisms than psychological mechanisms. However, others believe that there may be an interaction between the two. Areas of interest include origins of mental disorders, treatments of mental disorders, sleep, circadian rhythms, and localisation of brain function (that is, which parts of the brain are responsible for different behaviours).

The AS Level studies that are listed in the Cambridge International syllabus under this section are:

- Dement and Kleitman (sleep and dreams)
- Hassett *et al* (monkey toy preferences)
- Hölzel *et al* (mindfulness and brain scans).

The main research methods used in this approach are laboratory experiments and brain scanning techniques.

These are the two main assumptions that you are expected to know.

- Behaviour, cognitions, and emotions can be explained in terms of the working of the brain and the effect of hormones, genetics, and evolution.
- Similarities and differences between people can be understood in terms of biological factors and their interaction with other factors.

Cognitive

Cognitive psychologists are interested in how we process information. They look into how we input information, then how we process that information and finally how we retrieve and/or use it. Some cognitive psychologists believe that the brain works like a computer following the procedure of input–process/storage–output. Areas of interest include memory and forgetting, perception, language, and attention.

The AS Level studies that are listed in the Cambridge International syllabus under this section are:

- Andrade (doodling)
- Baron-Cohen *et al* (eyes test)
- Pozzulo *et al* (line-ups).

The main research method used in this approach is laboratory experiments.

These are the two main assumptions that you are expected to know.

- Information is processed through the same route in all humans: input – process – output, in a similar way to how information is processed by a computer.

- People have individual differences in their cognitive processing such as with attention, language, thinking, and memory. These processes can also help to explain behaviour and emotion.

Learning

Behaviourist psychologists are interested in ways in which humans and animals learn. They look into general laws that can apply to all species and how the experiences we have mould our behaviour over time. The three main areas within this perspective are:

- learning by the consequences of our behaviour (operant conditioning)
- learning through association (classical conditioning)
- learning through observation, imitation, and modelling (social learning).

Strict behaviourism follows the idea that we should 'observe the observable' and not examine mental processes, as they cannot be directly seen. Behaviours can be directly seen, so we have objective measures of behaviour. Areas of interest include behaviour modification, therapies for mental health disorders, therapies for prisoners, and development of behaviours such aggression.

The AS Level studies that are listed in the Cambridge International syllabus under this section are:

- Bandura *et al* (aggression)
- Fagen *et al* (elephant learning)
- Saavedra and Silverman (button phobia).

The main research methods used in this approach are laboratory experiments and observations.

These are the two main assumptions that you are expected to know.

- We all begin life as a blank slate. Experiences and interactions with the environment shape our behaviour and these changes are directly observable.
- We learn through the processes of operant conditioning, classical conditioning, and social learning. This can be understood using the stimulus-response model.

Social

Social psychologists are interested in how we 'work' in the social world. They look at how individuals interact with each other and how we interact in groups. Therefore, they look at the individual as an individual but also as a group member to see how this affects behaviour. They also examine how the role of culture and society affects our behaviour. Areas of interest include prejudice, obedience, and conformity.

The AS studies that are listed in the Cambridge International syllabus under this section are:

- Milgram (obedience)
- Perry *et al* (personal space)
- Piliavin *et al* (subway Samaritans).

The main research methods used in this approach are questionnaires and interviews.

These are the two main assumptions that you are expected to know.

- Behaviour, cognitions, and emotions are influenced by social contexts, social environments, and groups.
- Behaviour, cognitions, and emotions are influenced by the actual, implied, or imagined presence of others.

Dement and Kleitman (1957)

Background

The topics of sleep and dreaming are clearly hard to investigate because the participant is necessarily asleep and so cannot communicate with the researcher. Even when participants are awake, only self-report data can be obtained about dream content, and these alone might not be valid, as they are subjective. The study of sleep and dreaming became more scientifically rigorous with the invention of physiological techniques to measure brain activity that indicated dreaming (the electro-encephalograph, or EEG) and allowed the electrical recording of eye movements (the electro-oculogram, or EOG) rather than their direct observation. These techniques were used by Dement and Kleitman to trace the cyclical changes that occur in brain activity and eye movements during a night's sleep. The cycle alternates between a stage in which there are eye movements and several stages during which there are none.

An electro-encephalograph (EEG) detects and records tiny electrical charges associated with nerve and muscle activity. The EEG machine produces a chart (an encephalogram) that shows brain waves. These change with the frequency and amplitude (ie the 'height', which indicates the voltage) of electrical output from the brain over time. In REM sleep, the EEG is relatively low voltage, high amplitude. In contrast, nREM sleep has either high-voltage and slow (low-amplitude) waves, or frequent 'sleep spindles', which are short-lived high-voltage, high-frequency waves.

Modern EEG machines are entirely computerised, whereas Dement and Kleitman's EEG had continuously running paper. The faster the paper moved, the more detail could be recorded. The paper was usually moving at 3 or 6 millimetres per second, although a faster speed of 3 centimetres per second was used for detailed analysis.

To remember the meaning of EEG it can help to break the word down into:

- electro (electric)
- encephalo (in head)
- graph (writing).

The same EEG electrodes and machine can also be used to record eye movements. The output – called an electro-oculogram (EOG) – indicates the presence or absence of eye movements, their size and their direction (horizontal or vertical).

The psychology being investigated

Sleep and dreaming

In the dream or rapid eye movement (REM) sleep stage, our eyes move under the lids (hence 'rapid eye movement'). In Aserinsky and Kleitman's (1955) study, participants woken from this stage were more likely to report a vivid, visual dream than participants woken from non-rapid eye movement (nREM) sleep. It is possible to separate nREM sleep into stages 1 to 4, where 1 is the lightest and 4 the deepest.

REM sleep resembles wakefulness in some ways: our eyes move, we often experience vivid (if bizarre) thoughts in the form of dreams, and our brains are active. However, in other ways it is very different from wakefulness: we are quite difficult to wake up, we are fairly insensitive to external stimuli, and we are paralysed. As REM sleep presents these contradictions, it is also known as paradoxical sleep.

Dreams are a subjective experience for many. They can form both coherent and incoherent stories based on the imagery experienced by the person who is asleep. There are many ideas as to what dreams could be, ranging from them having unconscious meanings, being the result of random firing of neurons, to us resolving cognitive and emotional problems that we currently experience in our waking state.

> **Ask yourself**
>
> Do you remember your dreams? Are there always certain types of dreams you remember?

Ultradian rhythms

These types of biological rhythms are those that last less than 24 hours. Therefore, the sleep cycle, which has four non-REM stage and one REM stage, repeats itself every 90 minutes when someone is allowed to sleep without interruption.

Aim

Overall aim: to investigate dreaming in an objective way by looking for relationships between eye movements in sleep and the dreamer's recall.

There were three specific aims.

1. To test whether dream recall differs between REM and nREM sleep.
2. To investigate whether there is a positive correlation between subjective estimates of dream duration and the length of the REM period.
3. To test whether eye-movement patterns are related to dream content.

Method

This study included several laboratory investigations with different designs. Three specific approaches were used to test the three aims above.

1. To test whether dream recall differs between REM and nREM sleep. Participants were woken either from REM or nREM sleep, but were not told which stage of sleep they had been in prior to waking. They confirmed whether they had been having a dream and, if so, described the content into a recorder.
2. To investigate whether there is a positive correlation between subjective estimates of dream duration and the length of the REM period. Participants were woken following either 5 or 15 minutes in REM sleep. They were asked to choose whether they thought they had been dreaming for 5 or 15 minutes. Longer REM periods were also tested. Again, they gave a report of dream content and the number of words in the dream narrative was counted.
3. To test whether eye-movement patterns are related to dream content – whether these patterns represent the visual experience of the dream content or whether they are simply random movements arising from the activation of the central nervous system during dream sleep. The direction of eye movements was detected using electrodes around the eyes (EOG). Participants were woken after exhibiting a single eye-movement pattern for longer than one minute. Again, they were asked to report their dream.

Participants

Nine adult participants were used in this study (seven male and two female). Four of these were mainly used to confirm the data obtained from the five others, who were studied in detail.

Design

The researchers carried out three studies as experiments.

- Study 1 was a natural experiment in a laboratory setting. The levels of the IV were REM sleep/nREM sleep and the DVs were whether a dream was reported and, if so, the detail.

- Study 2 was a true experiment, with each participant being tested in both conditions (ie using repeated measures). The data were used in both experimental and correlational designs.
    - Experimental analysis – the levels of the IV were waking after 5 or 15 minutes, and the DV was the participant's choice of 5 or 15 minutes.
    - Correlational analysis – the two variables were the participant's time estimate and the number of words in the dream narrative.
- Study 3 was a natural experiment conducted in a laboratory (the IV of eye-movement pattern type could not be manipulated by the researchers). The DV was the report of dream content.

Procedure

The five participants studied in detail spent between 6 and 17 nights in the laboratory and were tested with 50–77 awakenings. The four participants used to confirm the findings stayed only one or two nights and were awoken between four and ten times in total. Each participant was identified by a pair of initials. Table 4.1 shows a summary of what each participant went through.

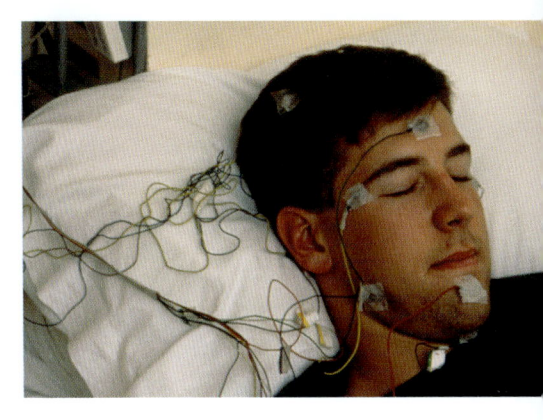

Figure 4.1 Participants in these experiments slept in a sleep laboratory attached to an EEG monitor

Table 4.1 *Instances of dream recall following awakenings from REM and nREM sleep*

Sleep stage	REM-sleep awakenings		nREM-sleep awakenings	
Number of times participants reported the presence or absence of a dream (DV)	Dream recall	No recall	Dream recall	No recall
	152	39	11	149

Source: Dement and Kleitman (1957: 340)

Test yourself

Outline how the three studies in this research were designed.

During the daytime prior to arrival at the laboratory, each participant ate normally (excluding drinks containing alcohol or caffeine). Participants arrived at the laboratory just before their normal bedtime and were fitted with electrical recording apparatus. This included electrodes attached near the eyes (to record eye movements) and on the scalp (to record brain waves). Once participants were in bed in a quiet, dark room, wires from the electrodes (which fed to the EEG in the experimenter's room) were gathered into a 'pony tail' from each participant's head, to allow the person freedom of movement. The EEG ran continuously through the night to monitor participants' sleep stages and to inform the researchers when participants should be woken up. They were woken by a doorbell that was loud enough to wake them from any sleep stage. This meant that the researcher did not have to enter the room to wake participants, and so they were all treated in exactly the same way. The doorbell was rung at various times during the night and participants indicated whether they had been dreaming prior to being woken and, if so, described their dream into a voice recorder. They then returned to sleep (typically within 5 minutes). Occasionally, the researcher entered the room after a participant had finished speaking in order to ask questions. When the narrative was analysed, what was described was considered to be a dream only if there was a coherent, fairly detailed description of the content (ie vague, fragmentary impressions were not scored as dreams). In terms of awakenings, 21% occurred in the first two hours of being asleep, 29% in the second two hours, 28% in the third and the remaining 22% in the fourth.

The patterns of REM and nREM wakings differed between the participants. The participants with the initials PM and KC were determined randomly to eliminate any possibility of an unintentional pattern. WD was treated in the same way, although he was told that he would be woken only from dream sleep. DN was woken in a repeating pattern of three REM followed by three nREM awakenings. The waking of IR from REM or nREM was chosen by the researcher.

Results

Quantitative and qualitative data were gathered in response to studies 1 and 2. Only qualitative data were gathered for study 3.

Study 1

Does dream recall differ between REM and nREM sleep?

Participants described dreams often when woken in REM but rarely from nREM sleep (although there were some individual differences). This pattern was consistent over the night. When awakened from nREM, participants tended to describe feelings (eg pleasantness, anxiety, detachment) but this did not relate to specific dream content.

Waking pattern did not affect recall. Specifically, WD was no less accurate despite being misled, and DN was no more accurate even though he might have guessed the pattern of awakenings. When participants were woken in high-voltage, slow-wave periods (as shown by the EEG) they often looked bewildered. They tended to state that they must have been dreaming but could remember nothing about their dream.

Table 4.2 Number of dreams recalled following awakenings from nREM sleep immediately after, or much longer after, an REM stage

	Time of waking after REM stage	
	Within 8 minutes	After 8 minutes
Number of awakenings conducted	17	132
Number of dreams recalled	5	6
Percentage of occasions on which dreams recalled	29	5

When woken from nREM sleep, participants returned to nREM and the next REM stage was not delayed. The only exception tended to be when a participant was woken in their final REM phase of the night. They then went back into REM after the awakening.

So, REM and nREM sleep differ as the vivid, visual dreams are reported only from awakenings during, or a short time after, REM sleep.

Study 2

Are subjective estimates of dream duration related to the length of the REM period?

Initially, the researchers tried to wake participants after various REM durations to ask them to estimate these durations. Although participants' responses were not wildly wrong, the task was too difficult. When asked instead whether they had been in REM sleep for 5 or 15 minutes, the participants responded more accurately. They were 88% and 78% accurate respectively for 5- or 15-minute REM durations. Table 4.3 shows the results for the five main participants.

Table 4.3 Results of dream-duration estimates after 5 or 15 minutes of REM

S	5 minutes		15 minutes	
	Right	Wrong	Right	Wrong
DN	8	2	5	5
IR	11	1	7	3
KC	7	0	12	1
WD	13	1	15	1
PM	6	2	8	3
Total	45	6	47	13

Source: Dement and Kleitman (1957: 343)

Although most of the participants were highly accurate (with only 0–3 incorrect responses), one was not. Participant DN frequently found he could recall only the end of his dream, so it seemed shorter than it actually was. Therefore, he consistently underestimated dream duration, often choosing 5 minutes instead of 15. This meant he was accurate on short REM estimates (making only two errors over ten awakenings), but inaccurate after 15 minutes' of REM (making five errors over ten awakenings).

Using REM periods over a range of durations, narratives from 152 dreams were collected. However, 26 of these could not be used as they were too poorly recorded for accurate transcription. For the remaining dreams (15–35 per participant) the number of words in the dream narrative was counted. Even though this was affected by how expressive the participant was, a significant positive correlation was found between REM duration and number of words in the narrative. The r values varied between 0.40 and 0.71 for different participants (all were significant at $p < 0.05$).

Dream narratives for very long durations (eg 30 or 50 minutes) were not much longer than those for 15 minutes. The participants did report, however, that they felt as though they had been dreaming for a long time, suggesting that they could not recall the early part of the dream.

Study 3

Do eye-movement patterns in REM sleep represent the visual experience of the dream?

The researchers found that participants' narratives were not sufficiently accurate to be matched exactly to the changes in eye-movement patterns over the length of an REM-sleep period. Instead, participants were woken after periods of specific eye-movement patterns (vertical, horizontal, both or little movement). A total of 35 awakenings were analysed further.

Three of the nine participants showed periods of predominantly vertical eye movements, and each was allied to a narrative about vertical movement. In one, the participant dreamed about standing at the foot of a tall cliff, using a hoist (a kind of winch or pulley). The participant reported looking up at climbers at various levels on the cliff, and down at the hoist machinery. In another dream one participant was climbing up a series of ladders and looking up and down while climbing. In a third dream a participant was playing basketball, shooting at the net and looking up to see if he had scored then looking down to pick up another ball. A single dream followed predominantly horizontal movements – the participant reported dreaming about two people throwing tomatoes at each other.

On ten occasions participants were woken after little or no eye movement. They reported either watching something in the distance or staring with their eyes fixed on a single object. In two cases the participants had been dreaming about driving. Their eyes had been very still, then made several sudden movements to the left just before being woken up. One participant reported a pedestrian standing on the left who hailed him as he drove by, and the other had been startled by a speeding car appearing to his left as he arrived at a junction.

Twenty-one awakenings followed mixed eye movements. In these instances, participants reported looking at people or objects nearby rather than far away (eg people fighting or talking to a group of other people).

The researchers also recorded the eye movements of people when they were awake (including the 5 original participants and 20 naïve ones). These findings confirmed that, when awake, our eyes are relatively stable when we are focused on objects in the distance, and show movements of similar amplitude to when we are dreaming of viewing nearby objects (ie many small but frequent and predominantly horizontal movements). Few vertical movements were recorded except when the researcher threw a ball in the air for participants to watch (and when they blinked).

Other results suggested that REM periods lasted from 3–50 minutes with an average of around 20 minutes. The amount, pattern and size of REM phases varied from period to period. The REM periods were at fairly regular intervals but individually specific. For example, participant DM averaged 1 REM phase every 70 minutes, WD 1 every 75 and KC 1 every 104. The average for the entire group was 1 REM phase every 92 minutes.

> **Test yourself**
>
> Outline four different results from this study.

Conclusion

Dement and Kleitman drew three main conclusions from this research, one in relation to each study.

1. Dreams probably (although not certainly) occur only during REM sleep, which occurs regularly throughout each night's sleep. Dreams reported when woken from nREM sleep are ones from previous REM episodes. As the REM phases are longer later in the night, dreaming is more likely at this time. Earlier research found that dreams did not occur every night. This study suggests three possible explanations for this difference.

   (a) If previous recordings were not continuous, they may have failed to catch instances of dream sleep in every participant (if short REM periods occurred between sampling intervals).

   (b) Equipment might not have detected small eye movements.

   (c) Participants in whom no dreaming was identified might have had dreams that led to few eye movements, such as those about distant or static objects.

2. It is often believed that dreams happen in an instant. If the length of REM periods is proportional to subjective estimates, this would help to confirm that the two are related and would provide some information about the rate at which dreaming progresses. The finding that the length of an REM period and its estimation by the participant are very similar shows that dreams are not instantaneous events but rather they are experienced in 'real time'.

3. Eye movements during REM sleep correspond to where, and at what, the dreamer is looking in the dream. This suggests that eye movements are not simply random events caused by the activation of the central nervous system during dream sleep, but are directly related to dream imagery. Furthermore, they correspond in amplitude and pattern to those we experience when awake.

Summary

Research method (main)	Experimental
Other technique(s)	Observations, interviews and correlations
Sample	Nine adult participants
Sampling technique	Opportunity
Experimental design	Repeated measures
IV	Study 1: the levels of the IV were REM sleep/nREM sleep
	Study 2: the levels of the IV were waking after 5 or 15 minutes
	Study 3: the IV of eye-movement pattern type
DV	Study 1: whether a dream was reported and, if so, the detail
	Study 2: participants' choice of 5 or 15 minutes
	Study 3: the report of dream content
Quantitative data	As above
Qualitative data	Narrative of the dreams

Evaluation

Evaluation	General evaluation (laboratory experiments)	Related to Dement and Kleitman
Strength	Laboratory experiments have high levels of standardisation and so can be replicated to test for reliability.	This study had a standardised procedure including pre-study levels of caffeine and alcohol, the doorbell sound, the EEG monitoring. This means that other researchers could easily replicate this study to test it for reliability.
Strength	As laboratory experiments have high levels of control, researchers can be more confident it is the IV directly affecting the DV.	The high level of control, so that all participants experienced the same conditions (eg the EEG monitoring and how data were recorded plus the pre-study levels of caffeine and alcohol) mean that for each part of the experiment, the researchers could confidently conclude cause and effect (eg that dream recall is affected by stage of sleep).
Weakness	As laboratory experiments take place in an artificial setting, they can lack ecological validity.	Participants had to sleep in an unusual environment (a laboratory) with electrodes on their head (EEG monitor) which is, of course, an artificial setting for them. Therefore, the study has low ecological validity.
Weakness	In many laboratory experiments particpants' tasks are not like real-life ones, so lack mundane realism.	Being woken up and asked to recall dream content or estimate dream length is not a normal activity for people. Therefore, the study lacks mundane realism.

Other evaluation points include the following.

- Generalisability: only five people were studied in detail with four more used to confirm the findings. This could make it difficult to generalise. The small sample may not represent a wide cross-section of society in terms of how we dream and what we dream about.
- Reductionism: the findings are all based around biological mechanisms affecting our dreaming state. This could be seen as reductionist as psychological mechanisms could also affect dream content.
- Ethics – confidentiality: only the participants' initials were published, to ensure that specific dreams could not be linked to individuals.
- Ethics – protection: as the participants were sleeping in an unnatural situation it may have altered their normal sleep patterns. The person's ability to concentrate at work or at home next day could have been affected. There was no chance to ensure a normal sleeping night before the study ended.
- Self-reports: the researchers could not be certain that, when woken, participants reported exactly what they experienced in their dreams. Due to changes in brain chemistry, memories for dreams can disappear quickly once someone is in the waking state. Some participants may have 'filled in the gaps' to make their dream a coherent story rather than reporting it exactly. This could reduce the validity of the findings.

Challenge yourself

Evaluate this study on the use of correlations and the use of independent groups.

Challenge yourself

Identify two other applications to everyday life this study could have. Explain who would benefit from these applications.

Issues and debates

The following table discusses the Dement and Kleitman study in terms of the core issues and debates for AS Level.

Application to everyday life	The study could identify when participants were entering REM or nREM sleep. The EEG monitor that did this could help sleep scientists to identify whether a person has a disorder based around REM sleep. A person complaining of poor sleep could come into a sleep laboratory and be wired up to an EEG. The person's brain wave patterns could be monitored to see whether they were typical or atypical.
Individual and situational explanations	The **individual** side of the debate is supported by participants having different successes at estimating dream duration. This may be down to an individual factor such as memory. The **situational** side of the debate is supported by participants being in the laboratory, which have caused some of the strange dreams reported, such as the tomato fight.
Nature versus nurture	The study could be considered to be relevant to the nature-nurture debate as it is believed that the experience of REM and n-REM sleep are universal and therefore due to nature. All participants in the study experienced both types of sleep and also the majority of dreaming took place during REM sleep. This also suggests that dreaming during REM sleep could be due to nature. However, there were individual differences between participants and this could be as a response to the environment as some of the participants had very disturbed sleep, possibly due to the uncomfortable environment of the sleep laboratory. This shows that environmental factors can also affect sleeping patterns.
The use of children	Not applicable
The use of animals	Not applicable

5 Hassett et al (2008)

Background

Sex differences in toy choice in humans is quite marked. Boys tend to interact with masculine-type toys and girls tend to interact more with feminine-type toys. Boys also tend to play more with toys that are seen as being stereotypically male. Girls tend to play with a range of feminine and masculine toys. Some psychologists believe this is because of the societal ideas of expected masculine and feminine gender roles. Other psychologists believe that it is not whether the toy is seen as being masculine and feminine; it is about the features of the toys that cause sex differences in toy choice. These features fulfil the needs of children, such as manipulation or cradling.

Another viewpoint is that some biological mechanism(s) affect toy choice and play behaviours. Exposure to prenatal hormones has been shown to affect toy preferences in humans. Girls with congenital adrenal hyperplasia (CAH), which causes increased adrenal androgens, show toy preferences more in line with boys than girls. Even when CAH girls are encouraged by their parents to play with female-typical toys, they still play with, and show a preference for, masculine toys.

However, any research conducted on humans makes it very difficult to separate out biological processes and socialisation processes due to ethical reasons. One previous study using vervet monkeys had only recorded the amount of play with a variety of toys available. This had shown that male vervets spent similar amounts of time playing with both masculine and feminine toys while female vervets spent more time playing with the feminine toys. Hassett et al argued that this was not a methodologically strong study as the vervet monkeys were never given a choice of toy, so preference was not directly measured. The Hassett et al study gave monkeys a choice.

> **Ask yourself**
>
> Are all toys easy to categorise into being 'male' and 'female' toys? Make a list of at least five toys that you feel are 'male', five toys that you feel are 'female' and five toys that are 'gender neutral'.

The psychology being investigated

Sex differences

This refers to investigating different behaviours shown by males and females across species. These are focused on the biology that may cause the differences (sex is biological whereas gender is psychological). Biological factors that may cause these differences include hormones, neurotransmitters, and brain function.

Socialisation

This refers to a social process that can cause or change an organism's behaviour. It is the process that happens when an individual adjusts to a group (including peers, family, society, etc) and its rules and the behaves in a way that is being seen as correct by that group. Therefore, socialisation is how our experiences with others and their views of the world affect the course of our behaviour.

Play

Play appears to be important across many species. Play involves activities that appear to be consciously chosen by an organism for enjoyment, be it individually or as part of a group. Play can help develop social skills, cognitive processing, and emotional development. Some mammals use it as a safe way to improve co-ordination for hunting or as part of a social hierarchy.

The role of hormones

Hormones play a significant role in the development of organisms. Testosterone (the 'male' hormone) is linked to muscle growth, aggression, libido, and the production of red blood cells, among others. Oestrogen (the 'female' hormone) is linked to the female reproductive cycle and the modulation of emotional behaviours. These can have a direct effect on the behaviour of an organism.

> **Ask yourself**
>
> Do you think that hormones can directly affect behaviour in humans? Find out about how three different hormones affect behaviour in humans.

Aims

- To investigate sex differences in toy preferences of rhesus monkeys.
- To see if socialisation processes, or biological mechanisms affect sex-stereotypical toy choice in rhesus monkeys.
- To see if there are sex differences in toy choice of rhesus monkeys compared to human children.

Method

Participants

The sample of rhesus monkeys was chosen from a social group of 135 that had lived for over 25 years at the Yerkes National Primate Research Center Field Station. The group had a typical social structure for a troop of monkeys. Fourteen monkeys were not included in the study as they had been exposed to hormonal treatments prenatally. Also, 39 monkeys aged 0–3 months could not be reliably identified so were excluded from the study. This meant that the sample used in the study consisted of 61 females and 21 males. The participating monkeys were kept in their natal group in 25-metre by 25-metre outdoor compounds with an indoor space that was temperature-controlled for comfort. Water was always available, and they were fed on monkey chow (a mixture of biscuits and minerals) twice per day. Once per day they were also fed fruit and vegetables. The study was conducted in accordance with rules set out by the NIH Guide for the Care and Use of Laboratory Animals. The monkeys were already involved in environmental enrichment at the Yerkes Center.

The social rank and the age of all eligible participants were also coded after previous behavioural observations that had recorded rank behaviours such as grooming. Table 5.1 shows the distribution of rank by sex of monkey.

Table 5.1 The distribution of rank by sex of monkey

	Rank				
	No rank or Ranks 1–3	Ranks 4–8	Ranks 9–13	Ranks 14–16	Total
Males in the group	3	4	6	8	21
Males used in analysis	1 (33%)	3 (75%)	3 (50%)	4 (50%)	11 (52%)
Females in the group	8	15	17	21	61
Females used in analysis	6 (75%)	6 (40%)	4 (24%)	7 (33%)	23 (38%)

Source: Hassett et al (2008: 14)

Figure 5.1 Rhesus monkeys were the participants in this study

Table 5.2 The distribution of age by sex of monkey

	Age				
	Juvenile 1–4 years	Subadult 5–7 years	Adult 8–12 years	Elderly 13+ years	Total
Males in the group	12	7	0	2	21
Males used in analysis	8 (67%)	2 (29%)	0	1 (50%)	11 (52%)
Females in the group	23	12	14	12	61
Females used in analysis	10 (43%)	5 (42%)	3 (21%)	5 (42%)	23 (38%)

The percentage (%) represents the percentage of that rank or age group that was used in the final data analyses.

The higher the rank number, the higher the rank status in the group.

Materials

Hassett *et al* did not categorise the choices of toy by 'traditional gender assignment'. Instead, they decided to use specific object properties. Table 5.3 shows these categories.

Table 5.3 Description of each category of toy

Category	Description	Toys used
Wheeled (masculine)	Sizes ranged from 16 cm to 46 cm, and all had six wheels.	Car, truck, shopping cart (trolley), wagon, dump truck, construction vehicle
Plush (feminine)	Sizes ranged from 14 cm to 73 cm, and all were soft to touch.	Armadillo, Winnie-the-Pooh, Raggedy-Ann, Scooby-Doo, turtle, teddy bear, koala bear hand puppet

Procedure

Before each trial, the monkeys had to be in the indoor part of the enclosure. Then, one wheeled and one plush toy were placed in the outdoor area, ten metres apart. The left or right placement for the toys was counterbalanced across all trials. The monkeys were then allowed to go into the outdoor area. There was a separate camera recording each toy and how any monkey interacted with it. At the end of each trial, the toys were removed from the outdoor area. Each individual monkey was identified on the videotape for every trial by two observers who worked together to achieve reliability and validity. Each trial lasted for 25 minutes. There were seven trials in total. One trial had to be stopped after seven minutes as one of the plush toys got destroyed. Table 5.4 shows the behaviours that were coded by the observers.

Figure 5.2 A dump truck was a wheeled category toy and a teddy bear was a plush category toy used in this study

Table 5.4 Interactions with plush and wheeled objects coded from videotaped trials

Behaviour	Description
Extended touch	Placing a hand or foot on toy
Hold	Stationary support with one or more limbs
Sit on	Seated on the toy or a part of the toy
Carry in hand	Moving with toy in hand and off the ground
Carry in arm	Moving with toy in arm and off the ground
Carry in mouth	Moving with toy in mouth and off the ground
Drag	Moving the toy along the ground behind the animal
Manipulate part	Moving, twisting or turning a part

Table 5.4 (continued)

Behaviour	Description
Turn entire toy	Shifting 3D orientation of toy
Touch	Brief contact using hands or fingers
Sniff	Coming very close to the toy with the nose
Mouth	Brief oral contact – no biting or pulling
Destroy	Using mouth or hands to bite or tear toy
Jump away	Approach, then back away from toy with a jumping motion
Throw	Project into air with hands

Every instance of behaviour was tallied to give a total frequency. If a behaviour was continuous, duration was recorded. As the monkeys participated in different numbers of trials, these data were divided by the number of trials, so a mean frequency and duration was calculated per monkey. If a monkey showed fewer than five total behaviours, it was not used in the analysis. This was true for 3 males and 14 females. Therefore, the final sample used for data analysis was 11 males and 23 females.

Results

Table 5.5 shows the mean frequency and duration of interactions by sex of monkey.

Table 5.5 The mean frequency and duration of interactions by sex of monkey

Type of toy	Sex of monkey	Frequency Mean (sd)	Duration (mins) Mean (sd)
Wheeled	Male	9.77 (8.86)	4.76 (7.59)
	Female	6.96 (4.92)	1.27 (2.20)
Plush	Male	2.06 (9.21)	0.53 (1.41)
	Female	7.97 (10.48)	1.49 (3.81)

The main results were as follows.

- Males significantly preferred wheeled toys compared to plush toys.
- Females showed *no* significant preference for plush toys compared to wheeled toys.
- Males and females showed no significant difference in the frequency of interactions of wheeled toys compared to plush toys.
- Males showed significantly lower frequency of play with plush toys compared to females.
- Males' duration of interaction was significantly longer with wheeled toys compared to plush toys.
- Females' duration of interaction was *not* significantly different between plush toys and wheeled toys.

A 'magnitude of preference' score was calculated for all monkeys. This was for both frequency and duration. For males this was total frequency/total duration with wheeled toy *minus* total frequency/duration with plush toy. For females, this was total frequency/duration with plush toy *minus* total frequency/total duration with wheeled toy. These are the main results from this analysis.

- Males had a significantly higher frequency 'magnitude of preference' score compared to females.
- Males also had a significantly higher duration 'magnitude of preference' score compared to females.

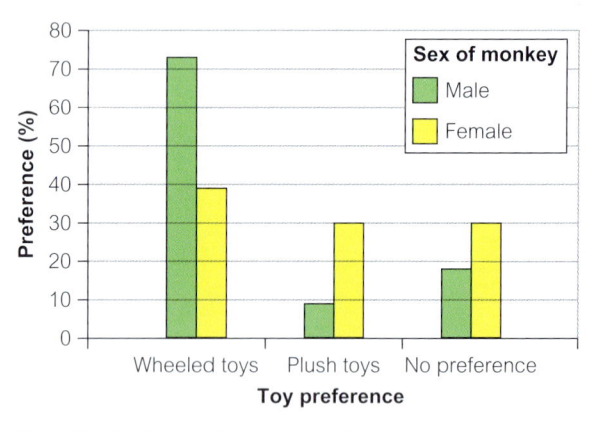

Figure 5.3 Preference for each type of toy

- Overall, males showed a significantly higher preference for the wheeled toys (seen as masculine) than females showed for the plush toys (seen as feminine).

Other key results included the following.

- When the data were combined for both sexes, rank and frequency of interaction were significantly positively correlated for both types of toys.
- For females, rank significantly correlated with frequency of interaction for both types of toys. This was not seen for males.
- For females, rank significantly positively correlated with duration of play with plush toys but not for wheeled toys. The correlations for males were not significant.
- Age did *not* affect frequency or duration of interaction with both types of toys.

Figure 5.3 shows the percentage preference for each type of toy.

Test yourself

On index cards write out all of the key results – one per card. Then, on index cards, write out the opposite to all key results. Mix up all of the index cards and have two piles – one for the correct results and ones for the incorrect results! See if you can sort them.

Comparison to human children

Data from this study was compared to that reported in a study by Berenbaum and Hines (1992). Figure 5.4 shows this comparison.

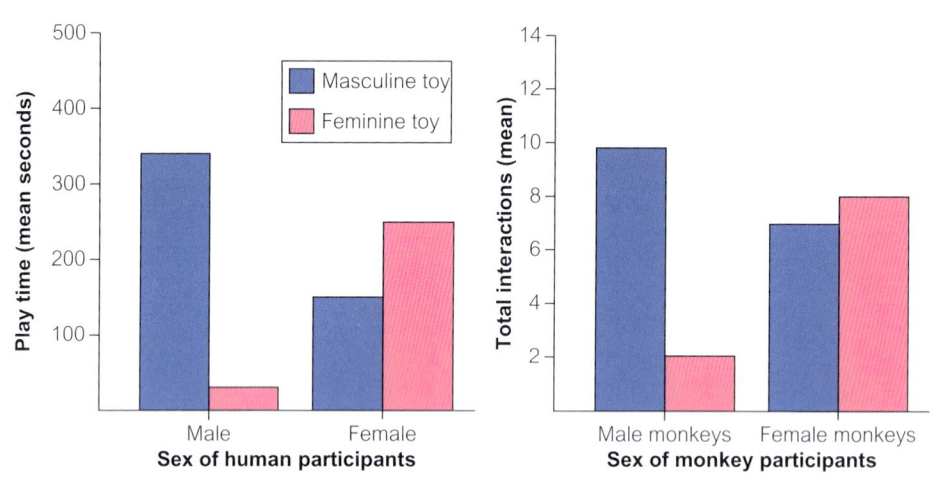

Figure 5.4 The play time (humans) and interaction times (monkeys) of male and female participants across the two studies

As can be seen, there is a very similar pattern of results for monkeys as compared to children.

Conclusion

Toy preference in monkeys appears to reflect behavioural and cognitive biases influenced by hormones, which in turn are affected by some social processes or pressures to form observable sex differences.

Summary

Research method (main)	Experimental
Other technique(s)	Observation
Sample	21 male and 61 female rhesus monkeys
	(11 male and 23 female rhesus monkeys qualified for data analyses)
Sampling technique	Opportunity
Experimental design	Independent measures
IV	Sex of monkey (female or male)
DV	Frequency of interaction with toys (wheeled and plush)
	Duration of interaction with toys (wheeled and plush)
	Magnitude of preference score (wheeled and plush)
Quantitative data	As above
Qualitative data	–

Evaluation

Evaluation	General evaluation	Related to Hassett et al
Strength	Laboratory experiments have high levels of standardisation and so can be replicated to test for reliability.	Hassett et al had a standardised procedure, including where the toys were placed in the outdoor area and the toy chosen for use in the study. This means another researcher could easily replicate this study to test for reliability.
Strength	Laboratory experiments have high levels of control so researchers can be more confident it is the IV directly affecting the DV.	There were many controls, such as pre-rating of the rank of each monkey and the selection of toys to represent masculine and feminine, so Hassett et al could be confident that it was the sex of monkey affecting the toy choice, frequency of interaction and duration of interaction with the toys.
Weakness	In many laboratory experiments participants take part in tasks that are nothing like real-life ones, so the tasks lack mundane realism.	The task of being given a forced toy choice and then being observed as to how the chosen toy is interacted with for a specified amount of time was not a usual task for these monkeys in everyday life. Therefore, the study can be said to be low in mundane realism.
Weakness	As the sampling technique was opportunity, it is unlikely to gain a wide variety of participants to allow for generalisation.	All participants were from one troop in one enclosure at the Yerkes Center. These were the only rhesus monkeys available at the time of the study as it was conducted in one location. Therefore, it may be difficult to generalise the findings to other rhesus monkey groups in captivity that may have different group dynamics, or to how wild troops choose objects to play with in real-life settings. Also, some monkeys were not used in the data analysis due to low levels of interaction so these are not represented in the final results.

Other evaluation points include the following.

- Use of more than one observer: there were two observers who reviewed the videotape evidence for toy choice and toy interaction behaviours. While inter-observer reliability tends to have two observers working independently and then comparing observations, here the two observers worked together. Any differences would have been discussed by the two observers to ensure correct identification of: each individual monkey, each monkey's toy choice, and which behaviours matched the behavioural checklist. This means that both reliability and validity were strengthened for this study.
- Use of structured observation: the coding system (via the behavioural checklist) allows objective quantitative data to be collected. This can then be analysed statistically. Having the behavioural checklist with each behaviour being named (eg sit on, sniff, turn entire toy) with a one sentence description ensured that the data collected was as objective as possible (see Table 5.4). The videotaping of all trials also ensured that the coding of behaviours was objective, and counts were agreed upon by the two observers – plus a third observer could have been

Challenge yourself

Evaluate this study in terms of the use of an independent measures design and the use of quantitative data.

used to validate the coding. This meant that the data could be compared across the sex of monkey to look for significant differences in toy choice and duration of interaction.

Issues and debates

The following table discusses Hassett *et al* in terms of the core issues and debates for AS Level.

Application to everyday life	The results might be useful for companies that design and manufacture toys. To increase sales, 'boy' toys need to have wheels on them while 'girl' toys can be more varied, including using plush (soft) fillings but also other types of materials.
	In addition, this study can be useful in helping the rehabilitation of rhesus monkeys who have been rescued from the wild. To help social bonding through play, zoos could provide wheeled toys for males to play with and a range of different toys for females to play with to help improve bonding and cohesion within a troop. Some vulnerable monkeys may want to use the toys for comfort (especially plush ones) so these should be provided for monkeys to use and play with.
Individual and situational explanations	Both sides of the argument can be seen in this study. In terms of **individual**, some monkeys were not used in the final data analyses as they showed too few choices of and interactions with any of the toys. Some individual monkeys were not interested in toys or play that involved the toys. In terms of **situational**, the monkeys had been placed in a scenario that was novel and potentially exciting as they had never seen the toys before. The situation the monkeys found themselves in encouraged toy choice and interactions with the toys and played a role in what toys the monkeys chose and how they played with them.
Nature versus nurture	The study is centred around the debate of nature versus nurture. The results point towards **nature** being the main factor behind toy preference in rhesus monkeys (and in the comparison study, the human children). This is because the findings showed that without any known socialisation period, the male monkeys chose the masculine-type toys more often whereas the females chose a range of toys. As this was a similar result to the study with the children, it can be argued that there are common biological mechanisms affecting the behaviours of males and females. However, as both the male and female rhesus monkeys did not all play exclusively with masculine-type or feminine-type toys, some may argue that **nurture** still plays a role (although with a smaller impact compared to nature). There may still be some aspects of upbringing and societal pressures that drive some rhesus monkeys and children to play with gender-type toys, maybe through psychological mechanisms such as social learning or operant conditioning.
The use of children	No children were directly used in this study. It was data from another study that was used to compare the preferences of rhesus monkeys to that of children.
The use of animals	The study was conducted in accordance with rules set out by the NIH Guide for the Care and Use of Laboratory Animals. The monkeys were already involved in environmental enrichment at the Yerkes Center. They had access to a varied diet and lived in social groups, which happens with wild rhesus monkeys.

Hölzel et al (2011)

Background

Prior to the study by Hölzel *et al* there had been around 30 years of mindfulness meditation being used in therapies for people with anxiety problems, depression, substance abuse, eating disorders, and chronic pain. The neural mechanisms that might be part of the practice of mindfulness meditation had been researched by conducting neuroimaging studies. Hölzel *et al* provided an overview of only six studies that measured either cortical thickness or grey matter density. All six studies found significant differences between participants in the mindfulness meditation group compared to a control group. Each study found that different parts of the brain showed increased density, but two localised areas were found to be affected in more than one study: the hippocampus and the right anterior insula. The former processes learning, memory, and elements of emotional control while the latter plays a crucial role in the process of awareness in general. Therefore, it was no surprise to see previous studies showing these differences. However, these studies had mainly been cross-sectional (one point in time) so there was no way of knowing whether there were already differences between groups *before* each study was conducted. The study by Hölzel *et al* used a longitudinal design to track changes across all participants over time.

> **Ask yourself**
>
> What evidence do you know about that claims that some form of activity actually changes the brain? Research and try to find at least two examples. Do the claims have validity?

The psychology being investigated

Mindfulness

Mindfulness meditation is a human ability to be fully aware of who we are, where we are, and what we are doing. It is a skill to not become overwhelmed by everything that might be happening around us, physically and/or psychologically. Hölzel *et al* define it as '…the development of awareness of present-moment experience with a compassionate, non-judgemental stance' (2011: 2).

Localisation of function

Localisation of function refers to how different parts of the brain perform specific functions. For example, our hippocampus is the part of the brain that deals with learning, memory, some emotional control, and spatial navigation. The amygdala is a different part of the brain and helps in the processing of fearful and threatening stimuli.

Therefore, this study by Hölzel *et al* investigates how mindfulness meditation may affect localisation of function in the brain via changing actual brain density. There has been evidence that increased brain volume or density is linked to increased performance abilities.

Aim

To investigate the potential long-term effect of a mindfulness-based stress reduction programme on brain grey matter density.

Method

Participants

Participants recruited for the experimental group were from those enrolled on Mindfulness-Based Stress Reduction (MBSR) courses held at the Center for Mindfulness at the University of Massachusetts Medical School. They had either been referred to the programme by their physician (doctor) or had referred themselves. They also had to meet the following criteria. They must:

- be psychologically and physically healthy
- not be taking any prescribed medication
- have had no meditation classes in the previous six months
- have had no more than four meditation classes in the last five years
- have nothing to prevent a magnetic resonance imaging (MRI) brain scan (eg having a metallic implant, claustrophobia)
- have a commitment to attend all eight of the MBSR lessons
- have a commitment to complete the compulsory daily homework
- be right-handed.

A total of 18 participants were part of the experimental group. However, due to some discomfort with the first MRI scan, two participants did not return for the second MRI scan. Each participant who completed the study was given a discounted MBSR course fee. Table 6.1 shows the characteristics of the experimental group compared to the control group.

Table 6.1 The characteristics of the experimental group compared to the control group

Experimental group	Control group
n = 16 (2 withdrew between sessions)	n = 17
6 males and 10 females	11 males and 6 females
Mean age = 38.0 years	Mean age = 39.0 years
13 Caucasians, 1 Asian, 1 African American, 1 multi-ethnic	Majority Caucasian with at least 1 Hispanic, 1 Asian and at least 1 African American
Average 17.7 years of education	Average 17.3 years of education

The study was ethically approved by the Massachusetts General Hospital and the University of Massachusetts Medical School. All participants gave written informed consent.

Procedure

The MBSR Program consisted of eight weekly group meetings that lasted 2.5 hours. In the sixth week of the course, participants had one full day (6.5 hours). There were three elements to the programme.

- Body scan – the aim was the get the participant to feel the body 'as a complete whole'. This was achieved by being guided through the body, being made aware of any sensations felt.
- Mindful yoga – this included gentle stretching exercises through slow movement, coordinated with breathing patterns. Participants were encouraged to appreciate the limits of their body.
- Sitting meditation – this included awareness of the sensation of breathing before moving on to other senses such as taste and sound. Later in the MBSR

course, the emphasis switched to awareness meditation which is based around anything that comes into a person's consciousness.

Participants in the experimental group were given audio recordings of 45-minute mindfulness exercises (comprising the three components above). This was created to be used at home. Participants were also taught how to practice mindfulness informally while engaged in everyday tasks such as eating and walking. When the participants came to class, any questions about the exercises were clarified.

Outcome measures

There were two measures taken for all participants – a self-report and a brain scan.

Self-report

This was the Five Facet Mindfulness Questionnaire (FFMQ). It is a 39-item scale designed to measure the following five factors of mindfulness.

1. Observing – this measures ability to attend to or notice both external and internal stimuli such as emotions or smells.
2. Describing – this measures the ability to note or mentally label the stimuli from the Observing factor.
3. Acting with awareness – this measures the ability to attend to your own current actions.
4. Non-judging of inner experience – this measures the ability to stop judging your own cognitions, emotions, and sensations.
5. Non-reactivity to inner experience – this measures the ability to allow thoughts to simply come and go without allowing them to have full attention given to them.

Table 6.2 shows one item per factor of the FFMQ.

Table 6.2 Example Items for Mindfulness Facets

Facet	Example item
Observing	I notice the smells and aromas of things.
Describing	I am good at finding words to describe my feelings.
Acting with awareness	I find myself doing things without paying attention. (R)
Nonjudging of inner experience	I think some of my emotions are bad or inappropriate and I should not feel them. (R)
Nonreactivity to inner experience	I perceive my feelings and emotions without having to react to them.

NOTE: R = reverse-scored item (higher scores represent higher levels of mindfulness).
Source: Baer et al (2008)

Each item on the FFMQ is rated on a 5-point Likert scale with 1 = never or very rarely true and 5 = very often or always true.

Brain scan (MRI)

The brain scan was produced using MRI. All participants were scanned twice. For the MBSR participants this was conducted two weeks before participation in the programme and then after the programme. For the control group, this was approximately two months apart.

The research team could analyse the whole brain but also regions of interest (ROI). The two main ROIs were the hippocampus and the insula. The main analysis was based around voxel-based morphometry. This technique measures concentration of brain tissue.

Figure 6.1 Mindful yoga is part of the Mindfulness-Based Stress Reduction (MBSR) Program used in this study

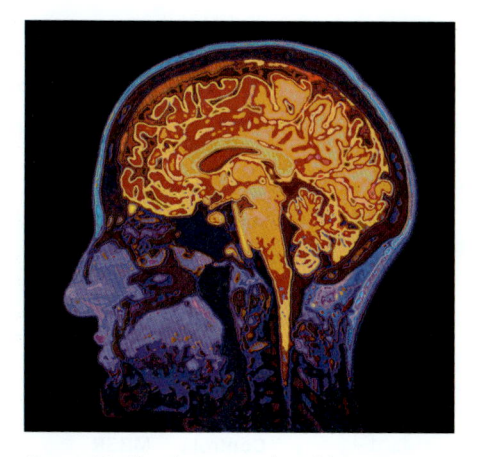

Figure 6.2 The picture produced from an MRI scan

Results

The amount of mindfulness practice is highlighted in Table 6.3.

Table 6.3 *The amount of mindfulness practice*

MBSR component	Average time (range)
Engaged in formal homework	22.6 hours
Body scan practice	699 minutes (335–1002 minutes)
Mindful yoga	327 minutes (103–775 minutes)
Sitting meditation	332 minutes (0–755 minutes)

From the FFMQ, an analysis of all five sub-scales was reported. For three of the sub-scales there was a significant increase in scores in the MBSR group compared to the control group. These were the acting with awareness, observing, and non-judging of inner experience. It should be noted that data was only available for 14 participants per group.

Body scan, yoga, and sitting measures were not significantly correlated to each other. Also, the amount of homework practice and changes in FFMQ scores were not significantly correlated with changes in grey matter density.

For the ROIs, only one area showed a significant result. This was the left hippocampus. While there was no significant difference between the MBSR and control groups before the study, there was a significant increase in grey matter concentration for this region for the MBSR group, post study. This was not found for the insula ROI.

When whole-barin analysis was conducted, four regions showed increased grey matter concentration in the MBSR group. These were the:

- posterior cingulate cortex
- temporo-parietal junction
- lateral cerebellum
- cerebellar vermis/brainstem.

Figures 6.3 to 6.7 show these changes as bar charts.

> **Challenge yourself**
>
> Find out about brain regions listed here explain what functions each has in relation to actions, behaviours and cognitions they control and process. Why would the MBSR Program be good for someone who has problems with each of these regions of the brain?

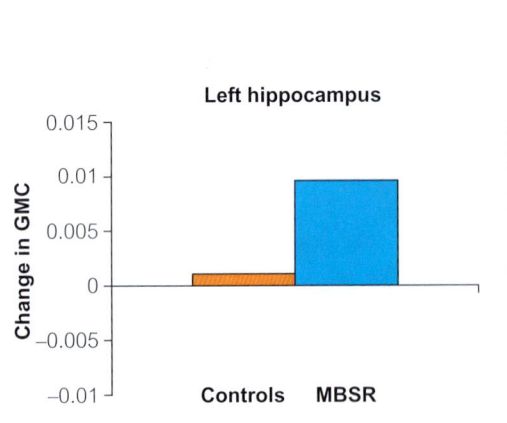

Figure 6.3 *Left hippocampus*

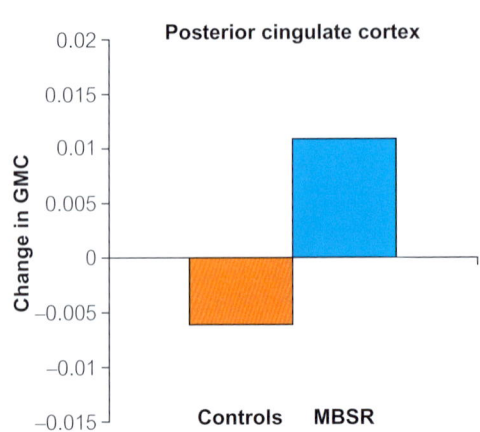

Figure 6.4 *Posterior cingulate cortex*

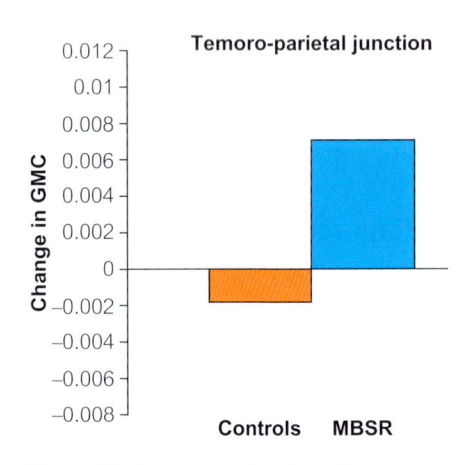

Figure 6.5 *Temporo-parietal junction*

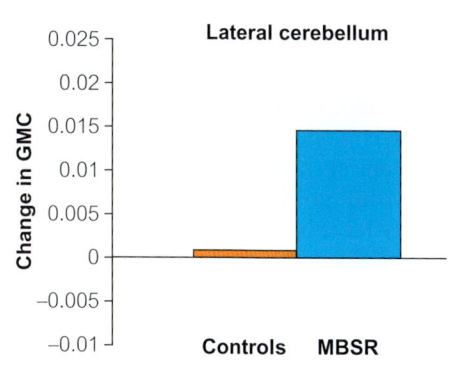

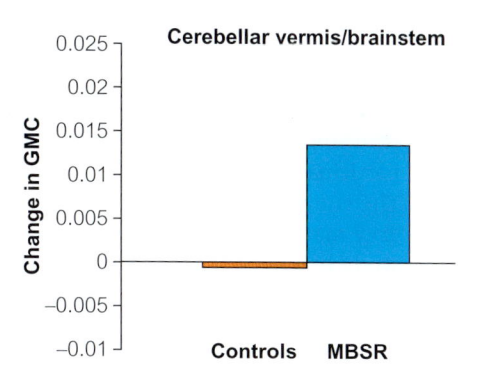

Figure 6.6 Lateral cerebellum

Figure 6.7 Cerebellar vermis/brainstem

Conclusion

There was a longitudinal change in brain grey matter concentration as a result of the eight-week MBSR Program. Participating in mindfulness activities can increase brain grey matter concentration. Hölzel *et al* concluded that 'the adult nervous system has the capacity for plasticity, and the structure of the brain can change in response to training ... (and) increased grey matter results from repeated activation of a brain region' (2011: 9).

Summary

Research method (main)	Experimental using a longitudinal design
Other technique(s)	Self-reports; brain scans
Sample	16 participants in the MBSR group (originally 18 but two withdrew); 17 participants in the control group
Sampling technique	Not mentioned in the study, but as the people were enrolled on the MBSR course, it *could* be volunteer.
Experimental design	Independent measures
IV	MBSR + control group
DV	FFMQ (five sub-scales); voxel-based morphometry scores
Quantitative data	As above
Qualitative data	–

Evaluation

Evaluation	General evaluation	Related to Hölzel *et al*
Strength	Experiments have high levels of standardisation and so can be replicated to test for reliability.	Hölzel *et al* had a standardised procedure including the contents of the MBSR Program and examining specific regions of interest. This means another researcher could easily replicate this study to test for reliability.
Strength	Experiments have high levels of control so researchers can be more confident it is the IV directly affecting the DV.	As there were many controls including the criteria for participation, the regions of interest and mean age of participants, Hölzel *et al* could be confident that it was the mindfulness programme itself that was causing a change in brain grey matter density.
Weakness	With questionnaires, participants may give socially desirable answers as they want to look good rather than giving truthful answers – this lowers the validity of findings.	The completion of the FFMQ before and after the programme might have made some participants rate differently based on wanting to look good (as if the programme had worked) rather than it being a valid reflection of the programme itself.
Weakness	If the questionnaire has a lot of closed questions, then participants might be forced into choosing an answer that does not reflect their true opinion.	The five-factor scale used on the FFMQ may not have a choice that truly reflected a participant's feelings towards one or more of the statements. This could lower validity of findings.

Other evaluation points include the following.

- Ethics: informed consent was taken from all participants across both groups. However, two participants withdrew after feel discomfort during the MRI scanning and they could have experienced psychological stress, so not every participant left the study in the same psychological state that they entered in. The study did show that participants in the MBSR group had increased brain grey matter concentration, but this could only have been known after the study had been completed. The results did not give individual participant data for reasons of privacy, but did all participants have this increase? What if a decrease had been found? Could it have been reversed?

- Quantitative data: as the data are numerical, it allows easier comparison and statistical analysis to take place. For example, the scores on the FFMQ could be directly compared pre- and post-MBSR Program to show quantifiable changes in aspects such as acting with awareness or non-judging. Also, as the data are numerical, the process is objective and scientific – there is only minimal chance of psychologists' miscalculating the data and drawing invalid conclusions. The voxel-based morphometry scores, which measured density of brain grey matter, is a scientific way of quantifying density as it is computer based.

> **Challenge yourself**
>
> Evaluate this study in relation to the use of an independent measures design, the sample of participants used, and the use of a longitudinal design.

Issues and debates

The following table discusses Hölzel *et al* in terms of the core issues and debates for AS Level.

Application to everyday life	The results might be useful for people who are experiencing memory problems. They could be enrolled on an MBSR-style programme to help them increase brain density in the hippocampus, which could lead to a more efficient memory system.
Individual and situational explanations	Both sides of the argument can be seen in this study. In terms of **individual**, the participants had a wide range of times engaged in the different parts of the MBSR Program. Therefore, there may be some personality types that engage in the programme more or less successfully. In terms of **situational**, the process of engaging in the MBSR Program did affect brain grey matter density compared to the control group who did not engage in any mindfulness techniques. Therefore, the situation of being in the MBSR Program had an effect on the brain.
Nature versus nurture	The **nature** side of the debate could be supported by the resultant increase in grey matter density in the left hippocampus. The **nurture** side of the debate could be supported by the fact that it was the experience of MBSR training that had an effect on the participants' brain structure.
The use of children	Not applicable
The use of animals	Not applicable

Andrade (2009)

Background

People have been known to daydream frequently when presented with something boring. In turn, this leads to them not paying full attention to the task at hand. It is quite common for people to doodle (draw abstract or concrete symbols, patterns, figures, etc) in ways not linked to the primary task. Prior to this study it was not known whether the act of doodling impairs attention processes by taking away resources from the primary task or whether it actually aids concentration towards the primary task, additionally maintaining arousal. It is common in research on attention to set participants dual tasks to monitor performance, then see which cognitive processes are needed to complete these tasks (or which processes contribute to participants failing to complete them). However, Andrade notes that if the effects of boredom are overlooked, then we cannot form any solid conclusions. Could it be that doodling actually aids concentration?

The psychology being investigated

Attention

This refers to our mental ability to concentrate. It can be about focusing on a task and trying to exclude other stimuli that could interfere with the concentration. Think about the examinations you will take to get your AS Level Cambridge International Psychology. You will focus all of your attention on each examination for 1 hour 30 minutes while ignoring any other stimuli in the examination room. Attention can also be about being prepared for information being directed at you, for example, 'paying attention' to an important message. We can also 'divide our attention' by attempting to focus on more than one message at the same time. Finally, we can show 'selective attention' where we focus on one message while at the same time ignoring a competing message.

Memory

This refers to our ability to store information that has been processed, then locate it and retrieve it at a later date to use it. One idea about memory is that we have sensory memory that lasts for less than a second and it allows us to process information from our senses. Material that is attended to is then processed into short-term memory. This holds around 7±2 items of information for around 30 seconds. If this information is rehearsed, it then transfers to long-term memory where it can be stored indefinitely and retrieved when needed.

> **Ask yourself**
>
> What do you try to do when you know you have to concentrate on something? List all the behaviours you show that you think help you to pay attention more efficiently.

Aim

To test whether doodling aided concentration in a boring task.

Method

Participants

Forty members of an Applied Psychology Unit participant panel at the University of Plymouth (UK) were used. They had volunteered for a different study but were recruited via opportunity sampling – once their original study had been conducted, the researcher approached them to ask if they would spend another five minutes taking part in this study. They were from the general population and aged 18–55. They were paid for participating. They were randomly assigned to either the control group (n = 20: 18 females and 2 males) or the doodling group (n = 20: 17 females and 3 males).

Design

The researcher recorded a mock telephone message using a cassette recorder. A fairly monotonous voice was used. The average speaking rate was 227 words per minute. The recording was played at a 'comfortable' volume to listen to. The script included eight names of people who would be attending a party alongside the names of three people and one cat who would not attend. In addition, eight place names were mentioned. The full text appears in the original research paper.

Procedure

As participants were asked to take part in this research just after they had completed a study they had volunteered for, they were already thinking about going home. It was hoped that this would enhance the boredom of the task.

Participants were placed in one of two groups: the doodling condition or a control group. Those in the doodling condition were asked to use a pencil to shade different shapes that were 1 centimetre in diameter on a piece of A4 paper. There were ten shapes per row. Each row alternated between squares and circles. There was a left-hand side margin of 4.5 centimetres so that participants could write down any target information. Participants in the control group were given a piece of lined paper and a pencil.

Participants were led into a quiet and visually dull room. All participants were tested individually. The following instructions were read out (Andrade 2009: 2–3):

"I am going to play you a tape. I want you to pretend that the speaker is a friend who has telephoned you to invite you to a party. The tape is rather dull but that's okay because I don't want you to remember any of it. Just write down the names of people who will definitely or probably be coming to the party (excluding yourself). Ignore the names of those who can't come. Do not write anything else."

Participants in the doodling condition were told that it did not matter how neat they were when shading their doodle or how quickly they did it. They were told that doing the shading was just to relieve the boredom of the listening task. They listened to the tape, which lasted 2.5 minutes, and wrote down the names as requested. As soon as the recording finished, the researcher collected participants' sheets and talked to them for about one minute. This included apologising for misleading them about the imminent memory test. Half of the participants were then asked to recall as many names as they could of the people who would attend the party, then the places mentioned. The other half did the reverse – they gave place names then names of people attending the party. During the debriefing after the task participants were asked whether they had suspected that they were going to be given a memory test.

> **Test yourself**
>
> Draw a flow diagram that shows how the participants were recruited and how the study was run.

Results

Those in the doodling group shaded a mean of 36.3 shapes (range 3–110). One of the participants failed to doodle so was replaced. None of the participants in the control group doodled. Only three participants in the doodling condition and four in the control group suspected a memory test. All claimed that they had then actively tried to remember the information for the test. Table 7.1 shows the correct noting down of the eight people who were going to attend the party.

Table 7.1 Correct names noted during the memory test

Condition	Average number of correct names written down	Number of false alarms
Doodling	7.8 (SD = 0.4)	1
Control	7.1 (SD = 1.1)	5

If a response indicated a plausible mishearing (eg a participant had heard the name Greg instead of Craig), it was scored as being correct. New names not similar to the ones given, names of people who could not attend or responses such as 'sister' were recorded as false alarms.

Each participant was given a monitoring performance score. This was calculated as the number of correct names written down minus the number of false alarms. A total of 15 participants in the doodling group and 9 in the control group scored maximum. Monitoring performance was significantly higher in the doodling condition (mean = 7.7, standard deviation (SD) = 0.6) than in the control condition (mean = 6.9, SD = 1.3), with p = 0.01.

In terms of recall, each participant generated a names score and a places score. These were scored in the same way as the monitoring performance score except that if a plausible mishearing was presented it had to be the same in the monitoring and recall phases. Table 7.2 shows these scores.

Table 7.2 Mean correct recall, false alarms, and memory scores (correct minus false alarms) for names and places for the control and doodling groups (standard deviation)

		Group	
		Control	Doodling
Names (monitored information)	Correct	4.3 (1.3)	5.3 (1.4)
	False alarms	0.4 (0.5)	0.3 (0.4)
	Memory score	4.0 (1.5)	5.1 (1.7)
Places (incidental information)	Correct	2.1 (0.9)	2.6 (1.4)
	False alarms	0.3 (0.6)	0.3 (0.4)
	Memory score	1.8 (1.2)	2.4 (1.5)

Source: Andrade (2009: 3)

Overall, participants in the doodling condition recalled a mean of 7.5 pieces of correct information (names plus places) compared to 5.8 recalled by participants in the control condition. Overall, monitored names were recalled more than places (p < 0.001). Recall was significantly better for participants in the doodling condition than for those in the control condition (p = 0.02). When participants who had suspected a test were removed from the analysis, there was still a significant difference (p = 0.01).

> **Challenge yourself**
>
> Plot the results of this study as a bar chart.

Conclusion

Andrade concluded: 'Participants who performed a shape-shading task ... concentrated better on a mock telephone message than participants who listened to the message with no concurrent task' (2009: 4). This was seen in both the monitoring performance task and the recall task. However, it was not clear whether the doodling led to better recall because doodlers happened to notice more of the target information or whether it actually aided memory recall by encouraging some deeper processing of the telephone message.

Summary

Research method (main)	Experimental
Other technique(s)	–
Sample	40 people from an Applied Psychology Unit participant panel at the University of Plymouth (UK)
Sampling technique	Opportunity (but originally participants had come as volunteers for a different study)
Experimental design	Independent groups
IV	Doodling and control
DV	Mean correct recall, false alarms and memory scores
Quantitative data	As above
Qualitative data	–

Evaluation

Evaluation	General evaluation (laboratory experiments)	Related to Andrade
Strength	Laboratory experiments have high levels of standardisation and so can be replicated to test for reliability.	This study had a standardised procedure including the rate of speaking and the same dimensions of paper for those in the doodling group. This means other researchers could easily replicate this study to test for reliability.
Strength	As laboratory experiments have high levels of control, researchers can be more confident it is the IV directly affecting the DV.	As there were many controls (eg the script and the length of time participants were talked to by the researcher before the recall test), Andrade could be confident that it was the doodling itself that was causing a change in the recall rates.
Weakness	In many laboratory experiments participants take part in tasks that are nothing like real-life ones, so the tasks lack mundane realism.	Listening to a tape recording and then having an unexpected recall test is not a usual task for people in everyday life. Therefore, the study could be low in mundane realism.

Other evaluation points include the following.

- Generalisability – as the sample was from a volunteer participant panel:
  - the participants may be qualitatively different from other people (they may be more motivated than others to perform in a study)
  - the results may not reflect the population as a whole: that is, the effects of doodling may only be applicable to the sample.
- The use of independent measures: as different participants were used in the doodling and non-doodling conditions, participant variables may have affected some of the results. People in the doodling group may already happen to doodle a lot when they concentrate on tasks. Also, participants in that group may have just had a better memory compared to those in the non-doodling group. These possible issues reduce the validity of the findings.

Ethical issues are as follows.

- This study does not cause psychological harm as doodling is an everyday activity that is done by many people. In addition, the quality of the doodling was not judged by the experimenters so the participants should not have felt judged in any way. Participants in the doodling condition were told "It doesn't matter how neatly or how quickly you do this—it is just something to help relieve the boredom".
- There was some deception in the study as the participants were told they would not be expected to remember any of the information on the tape-recorded message. However, when it was over they were given a surprise

> **Challenge yourself**
>
> Evaluate this study on demand characteristics and the use of quantitative data.

memory test. The researchers did apologise for this test and did give a full debrief at the end of the study. This is a justifiable breach of the issue of deception as it was necessary for the study to be completed successfully and would not have affected the participants in the study.

Issues and debates

The following table discusses the Andrade study in terms of the core issues and debates for AS Level.

Application to everyday life	The results of this study might be useful for students when they are revising for examinations. If students have a podcast to listen to or are reading notes, it could be useful for them to doodle at the same time.
Individual and situational explanations	Both sides of the argument can be seen in this study. In terms of **individual** explanations, participants may have used a similar strategy before or have a personality type that requires extra stimulation when processing information (eg some may be extroverts). In terms of **situational** explanations, the process of doodling in the given situation could have caused the improvement in recall rather than it being due to the individual: that is, the act of doodling is what helps people retain information.
Nature versus nurture	The **nature** side of the debate may be supported by biological differences in how memory is processed in the brain (STM and LTM) and some people may, as a result, recall information better than others. The **nurture** side of the debate may be supported by some of the participants being better than others in recalling information due to experience or exposure (eg places they have been to or heard of, or names they have experienced before).
The use of children	Not applicable
The use of animals	Not applicable

> **Challenge yourself**
>
> Identify two other applications to everyday life this study could have. Explain who would benefit from these applications.

8 Baron-Cohen *et al* (2001)

Background

In 1997 a 'Reading the mind in the eyes' test was developed to assess a concept called theory of mind. This refers to the ability to attribute mental states to oneself and other people. This test appeared to discriminate between adults with Asperger syndrome (AS) and high-functioning autistic (HFA) adults from control adults. The two former groups scored significantly worse than the control group on the test, which asked participants to look at a pair of eyes on a screen and choose, from a forced choice of emotions, which emotion the eyes best conveyed. However, the researchers were not happy with elements of the original version and wanted to 'upgrade' their measure to make it better. The problems and solutions are outlined in the design section.

The psychology being investigated

Theory of mind

The main idea of the eyes test is to investigate theory of mind. The theory of mind refers to our ability to attribute mental states such as desires, beliefs, intentions, and emotions to ourselves and others around us. It also refers to how we use this knowledge to explain and predict the actions of other people. That is, we can use the knowledge to understand that people may have different ideas and hold different emotions from us. It is believed that many people on the autistic spectrum do not have a theory of mind.

In addition, the researchers were also attempting to make the measure a more valid test of theory of mind.

Social sensitivity

This is about our ability to identify, perceive, and understand social cues in social contexts to aid social interactions. It also involves being socially respectful to others. This differs depending on the social context you find yourself in. Cultural, social, and situational norms also affect levels of social sensitivity. For example, in a business meeting it is seen as not being socially sensitive if you dominate the conversation and interrupt other people all of the time. However, when with friends it may not matter if you interrupt as it is a totally different social context.

> **Ask yourself**
>
> How do you read the emotion that is conveyed by another person's face? What do you look for?

Aims

1. To test a group of adults with AS or HFA on the revised scale of the eyes test. This was to check whether the same deficits seen in the original study could be replicated.

2. To test a sample of normal adults to see whether there was a negative correlation between the scores on the eyes test and their autism spectrum quotient (AQ).

3. To test whether females scored better on the eyes test than males.

Method

Design

As covered in the 'Background' section above, there were problems with the original version of the eyes test that needed rectifying. Table 8.1 highlights what these problems were and how the researchers redesigned the questionnaire in an attempt to overcome them.

Initially, the 'correct' word and the 'foils' were chosen by the first two authors of this study: Simon Baron-Cohen and Sally Wheelwright. The words were then piloted on eight judges – four male and four female. For the correct word and its foils to be used in the new eyes test, five of the eight judges had to agree with the choice. Also, if more than two judges picked a foil over the correct word, these items were replaced: a new correct word was generated with suitable foils and retested. The data from groups 2 and 3 (see below) were merged as they did not differ in performance. This was also used as a check that the correct words had some form of consensus – at least 50% of this group had to select the correct word and no more than 25% had to select a foil for it to be included in the final version of the eyes test. From the original 40 pairs of eyes, 36 passed these tests and were used.

The research method is a natural experiment as the IV is naturally occurring (the four groups of subjects used).

Table 8.1 Problems with the original study and changes made to overcome

Original problems	New design element (if applicable)
Forced choice between two response options meant just the narrow range of 17–25 correct responses (out of 25) to be statistically above chance. The range of scores for parents of those with AS were lower than normal but again there was a narrow range of scores to detect any real differences.	Forced choice remained but there were four response options. There were 36 pairs of eyes used rather than 25 – this gave a range of 13–36 correct responses (out of 36) to be statistically above chance. This meant that individual differences could be examined better in terms of statistics.
There were basic and complex mental states so some of the pairs of eyes were 'too easy' to identify (eg happy, sad) and others 'too hard' so it made comparisons difficult.	Only complex mental states were used.
There were some pairs of eyes that could be 'solved' easily because of eye direction (eg noticing or ignoring).	These were deleted.
There were more female than male pairs of eyes used in the original test.	The new study used an equal amount of male and female pairs of eyes.
The possible two responses were always 'semantic opposites' (eg happy versus sad), which made choosing between them too easy.	Semantic opposites were removed and the 'foil choices' (those that were incorrect) were more similar to the correct answer.
There may have been comprehension problems with the choice of words used as the forced choice responses.	A glossary of all terms used as the choices on the eyes test was available to all participants at all times.

Test yourself

Outline two problems with the original version of the 'Reading the mind in the eyes' test and describe how the research team tried to overcome them.

Participants

Four groups of participants were used.

1. In group 1 there were 15 males with either AS or HFA. They were recruited via a UK National Autistic Society magazine or support group. They had all been formally diagnosed.

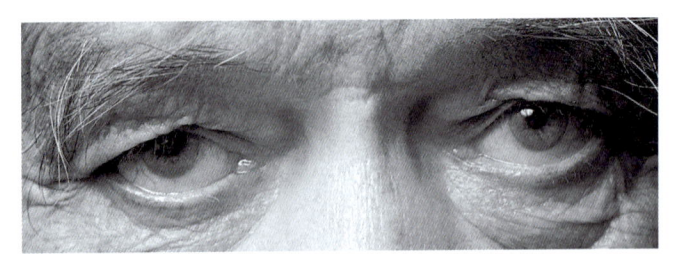

Figure 8.1 A male pair of eyes used in the test

2. There appeared to be a broad range of people in group 2. This group consisted of 122 normal adults recruited throughout adult community and education classes in Exeter or in a public library in Cambridge.

3. Participants in group 3 were all assumed to have a high intelligence quotient (IQ), as the group consisted of 103 normal adults (53 male and 50 female) who were all undergraduates at Cambridge University (71 in sciences and 32 in other subjects).

4. Group 4 consisted of 14 randomly selected adults who were matched for IQ with group 1.

Procedure

All participants, irrespective of group, completed the revised version of the eyes test. Each participant completed it individually in a quiet room. Participants in group 1 were asked to judge the gender of the person in each image. Groups 1, 3, and 4 completed a questionnaire to measure their AQ. All participants were asked to read through a glossary of terms used in the test and indicate any they were unsure of. They were reassured that they could refer to the glossary at any time during the test. It was a paper and pencil task. They could also view the slides at their own pace.

Results

Table 8.2 shows the scores gained in the new eyes test and the AQ of each group.

Test yourself

Outline two differences between the different sets of participants used in this study in terms of their performance in the eyes test.

Table 8.2 Mean and standard deviation (in parentheses) scores for the new eyes test and AQ by group

Group	Eyes test means (SD)	AQ means (SD)
AS/HFA adults	21.9 (6.6)	34.4 (6.0)
General population	26.2 (3.6)	N/A
Students	28.0 (3.5)	18.3 (6.6)
Matched	30.9 (3.0)	18.9 (2.9)

Source: Baron-Cohen et al (2001: 245)

In the eyes test the AS/HFA group performed significantly worse than the other three groups. In general, females scored better than males. Unsurprisingly, the AS/HFA group scored significantly higher on the AQ than the other groups. The correlation between the eyes test and AQ was negative. The distribution of scores for the eyes test (all groups merged) formed a normal bell curve.

Conclusion

The revised version of the eyes test could still discriminate between AS/HFA adults and controls from different sections of society as it replicated previous findings. The new eyes test appeared to overcome the initial problems of the original version and the research team stated '... this therefore validates it as a useful test with which to identify subtle impairments in social intelligence in otherwise normally intelligent adults' (Baron-Cohen *et al* 2001: 246).

Summary

Research method (main)	Experimental
Other technique(s)	Questionnaire (survey)
Sample	15 males with either AS or HFA
	122 normal adults recruited throughout the adult community
	103 normal adults (53 male and 50 female) who were all undergraduates at Cambridge University
	14 randomly selected adults who were matched for IQ with group 1
Sampling technique	Opportunity and volunteer
Experimental design	Independent groups
IV	Four groups of participants (see sample above)
DV	Scores on the eyes test and AQ
Quantitative data	As above
Qualitative data	–

Evaluation

Evaluation	General evaluation	Related to Baron-Cohen et al
Strength	Comparisons can be useful as people's results are being compared on the same, standardised scale.	The revised eyes test was used for all participants. This means that all comparisons between the groups have some validity as they were compared on the same set scale using the same questions, etc.
Strength	As the measures are standardised, they are reliable because they can be used again and again to see whether they give similar results.	The revised eyes test can be used by other researchers to see whether they can replicate findings and test for reliability. Even though an older version of the eyes test was used in the original study, the new study did find reliable results in terms of performance of AS/HFA adults (there were low scores in both studies).
Weakness	There may be issues with validity. Is the test actually measuring the behaviour it is supposed to be measuring? Some psychologists, for example, believe that an IQ test does not measure intelligence. Instead they believe it measures someone's ability to complete an IQ test.	Some psychologists might query whether the revised eyes test is still actually measuring theory of mind traits or just the ability to complete the eyes test.
Weakness	There are further issues of validity using self-report measures with participants. Participants can misunderstand the questions, give socially desirable responses, etc.	The participants did have a one in four chance of just guessing the correct answer on the eyes test and this lowers the validity of the study. The researchers addressed the issues of misunderstanding by providing a glossary of definitions of the words used in the eyes test for the participants to read. However, it is possible that even with the definitions the participants still did not understand the words used.

There could be some evaluation based around usefulness.

- The main strength is that such a study can be used to improve human behaviour in some way. As the results show that AS/HFA adults appear to lack a theory of mind, psychologists could now create therapies (or training) to help these people improve their social communication and social emotional skills to help them integrate better into society.

- A weakness of the eyes test is that it does not take into account the 'full picture' of understanding emotions – in reality there are subtle cues such as body language alongside other facial cues that can help people to understand the emotions of others. A study that assessed the same aspects as the eyes test but using a full face or a moving image with verbalisation might be even more useful to assess theory of mind.

- Ethics – protection: as the participants in the AS/HFA group scored poorly on the eyes test, completing it may have caused them stress. If they did not understand the emotions portrayed in the eyes the test may have been too difficult, perhaps causing distress.

Challenge yourself

Identify two other applications to everyday life this study could have. Explain who would benefit from these applications.

Issues and debates

The following table discusses the Baron-Cohen *et al* study in terms of the core issues and debates for AS Level.

Application to everyday life	Schools and educators could use the findings of this study to help AS/HFA students. These students could have extra support in helping them to understand emotions and how to read them in faces. This could help them to cope with everyday situations that involve emotions.
Individual and situational explanations	The **individual** side of the debate is supported by clear individual differences between the AS/HFA group and other groups, which shows that the AS/HFA group appear to lack a theory of mind. The **situational** side of the debate is supported by being provided with a glossary may have made it easier for Ps to understand the words that were complex. This may have improved the scores on the eyes test.
Nature versus nurture	The idea of whether AS/HFA can be attributed to nature or nurture is a long-standing debate with psychologists, but this study does not add to the debate.
The use of children	Not applicable
The use of animals	Not applicable

Pozzulo et al (2011)

Background

In everyday life, there are many instances of crimes being committed where the only eyewitness is a child or group of children. Eyewitness accounts are used extensively in courts in the process of convicting criminals. However, there appears to be a qualitative difference in the accuracy of these accounts from children compared to accounts from adults. When the culprit is in a line-up where the eyewitness is asked to choose who they saw, there are minimal differences between adults and children in terms of accuracy. However, when the culprit is *not* in the line-up, children are much more likely to still choose someone from the line-up (an innocent person) compared to adults. Adults are more likely to state that no one in this type of line-up is the culprit. Prior to this study, the reason for this error was not well documented. It was assumed that both social and cognitive factors play roles in the incorrect choice of person in a line-up that did not contain the culprit.

> **Ask yourself**
>
> Find an example of crime where a person has been wrongly committed based on eyewitness testimony using a line-up. How did it happen?

The psychology being investigated

Eyewitness testimony

This refers to the information provided by an individual or group based on what they can recall from observing an incident that is usually criminal in nature. This could include information about the person or people involved in the incident, what happened during the incident or details about the crime scene. Eyewitnesses tend to be interviewed using both open and closed questions or on a questionnaire. The subsequent information may then be used in a court of law to help prosecute. There is a debate in psychology surrounding whether the information provided by eyewitnesses is valid and/or reliable. One problem may be eyewitnesses producing false positive responses.

False positive responses

This refers to when a person selects something (eg a person in a line-up) that is not accurate but the person believes it is.

Aims

- To investigate if cognitive and/or social factors affect correct identification and false positive responses in a line-up.
- To investigate correct identification and false positive responses in a line-up in relation to the familiarity of the target.

Method

Participants

There were 59 young children aged from four to seven years recruited from kindergarten classes in three private schools in Eastern Ontario, Canada. The mean age of the group was 4.98 years. There were 21 females and 38 males.

There were 53 adults (age range 17–30 with a mean of 20.54 years) recruited from the Introductory Psychology Participant Pool in an Eastern Ontario university. There were 36 females and 17 males.

Experimental design

The design involved both independent measures and repeated measures. The independent measures part involved a comparison between the young children and the adults. However, all participants took part in the identification of human faces and cartoons plus identifying from target-present and target-absent line-ups, which is the repeated measures part.

Materials

Table 9.1 contains all of the materials that were used in this study.

Table 9.1 Materials used in the study

Material	Description
Demographic and cartoon watching form	Every participant completed a form requesting their age, gender, primary language, ethnicity, number, and ages of children in the household, and the amount of time spent watching cartoons per week including how much time watching *Dora the Explorer* and *Go Diego Go* (as these were the target cartoon characters in the study). The adult participants completed the form themselves, but the children had their forms completed by a parent or guardian.
Human face targets	These were two Caucasian university student 22-year-olds, one female and one male. Each student was filmed completing an everyday task for a six-second video clip. For the female this was brushing her hair and for the male it was putting on a coat and leaving his house. Each video had an approximately three-second close-up of the student's face. The videos were filmed in colour. There was no sound.
Human face foils	Both human targets were photographed wearing a different outfit from the one they wore in the video clip. The foils were selected from a pool of 90 female and 90 male faces. The foils chosen had to have similar facial structure, hair length, and hair colour to that of the target. Four foils were chosen for each target by a panel of three raters. The final photographs showed the face, neck, and top of shoulders. All of the photographs were black and white.
Cartoon target	One female and one male cartoon character were chosen. For the female, this was Dora the Explorer talking to an audience. For the male, this was Go Diego Go putting on a pair of gloves for safety. Each clip lasted for six seconds. Each video had an approximately three-second close-up of the character's face with no other character visible. The video clips were in colour. There was no sound.
Cartoon foils	The foils were selected from readily available cartoon images on the internet. The foils chosen had to have similar facial structure, hair length, and hair colour to that of the target. A short list of approximately ten cartoon characters was prepared and three raters judged these characters on similarity to the target. The four cartoon characters that received the highest similarity ratings were used as the cartoon foils. These were cropped to show only the face from the top of the shoulders upwards. This was to reduce any distinctive clothing being seen. All foils were present in black and white to reduce the often-vibrant colours used in cartoon clothing. This was to reduce the clothing being used for recognition of the characters, rather than the face.
Line-up presentation	For each target, a line-up was presented. In the line-up were four photographs plus a silhouette used to represent an absent target. All of the photographs and silhouette were presented at the same time. Target-present line-ups contained three foils and the target. Target-absent line-ups contained four foils. Each target line-up was randomised. Every participant watched four videos in a random order. They were then shown a line-up.
Instructions for line-up identification	"Please look at the photos. The person/cartoon from the video may or may not be here. If you see the person/cartoon please point to the photo. If you do not see the person/cartoon, please point to this box (instructor pointed to silhouette)' (Pozzulo et al 2011:4).
Line-up administrators	These were three females used with the child participants. Previous research had shown than type of clothes affects children's behaviour in choosing people from a line-up. The administrators wore professional-casual clothes such as a blouse and smart trousers. These were chosen to reduce the any sense of them being seen an authoritative figure by the children. The administrators looked 'neat' rather than overly formal.
Free recall descriptions	Participants were asked an open-ended question to describe everything and anything they could remember about the video clip. A researcher recorded what each child said while the adults recorded their own response. This task was also used as a filler between video and line-up choice and it usually lasted approximately two minutes.

Figure 9.1 The two cartoon faces used on this study: Dora The Explorer and Go Diego Go

Procedure

Children

The parent or guardian of each child was given a consent form and the Demographic and Cartoon Watching form. Each school was then visited by three female experimenters and a female facilitator. Children were invited to participate only if they had completed forms. The research team was introduced to the eligible participants as from the local university conducting a project on watching television and playing computer games. It was made clear to the children that they could change their minds and not participate in the project and that they would not get into trouble for doing so. The research team then engaged the children in craft activities before the actual study started. The children were told that they would be watching some brief video clips. They were also told to pay attention to each video clip because afterwards they would be asked some questions about it and shown some pictures. All participants were monitored for any signs of stress, fatigue, and anxiety as a result of being in the study.

The experimenter played the first video clip (randomly chosen) once the child was comfortable. After the video clip the child was asked one open-ended question, for example, "What did the cartoon character look like?". After the child had responded, he or she was asked at least two non-specific open-ended questions like "Do you remember anything else?". The line-up was then displayed. The child was then read the 'Instructions for line-up identification' (see Table 9.1). Once the child had given a response, the same procedure was repeated for the other three video clips. After all of the four video clips had been watched and the child had chosen a response from the line-up, the child was thanked and given a small gift for participating (eg a colouring book).

Adults

Each adult was introduced to the study and asked to complete the consent form. The adults were told that the study was investigating memory and that they would be watching some brief video clips. They were also told to pay attention to each video clip because afterwards they would be asked some questions about it and shown some pictures. After the first video, each adult was given a sheet asking the same free recall questions as the children were asked. The remainder of the procedure was the same as for the child participants except that the adults recorded their line-up choice on a matching sheet. After all of the four video clips had been watched, the adults completed the 'Demographic and cartoon watching form'. The adult participants were then debriefed and thanked for their participation.

> **Test yourself**
>
> Write a description of each of the materials on one side of an index card. On the other side write the name of that material. Either get someone to read out the description and you have to name it, or the person reads out the name and you must describe how that material was created for this study.

Results

Data were analysed by age, target-present/target-absent, and human/cartoon faces.

Target-present line-ups

Table 9.2 shows the identification rates split by age and type of stimulus. The data is given as a percentage (%).

Table 9.2 Identification rates split by age and stimulus

	Children			Adults		
	Target chosen	Foil chosen	False rejection	Target chosen	Foil chosen	False rejection
Cartoons: Dora	100	0	0	100	0	0
Cartoons: Diego	97	0	3	89	0	11
Human: female	24	38	38	46	0	54
Human: male	21	45	34	85	15	0

These were the key results.

- Children had a 23% correct identification rate for human faces.
- Children had a 99% correct identification rate for cartoon faces.
- Adults had a 66% correct identification rate for human faces.
- Adults had a 95% correct identification rate for cartoon faces.
- Both children and adults were significantly more accurate identifying cartoon faces compared to human faces.
- There was no significant difference between children and adults when correctly identifying a cartoon face.
- Children produced a significantly lower correct identification rate for human faces compared to adults.

Target-absent line-ups

Table 9.3 shows the correct rejection rates split by age and type of stimulus. The data is given as a percentage (%).

Table 9.3 Correct rejection rates split by age and stimulus

	Children		Adults	
	Correct rejection	Incorrect identification	Correct rejection	Incorrect identification
Cartoons: Dora	80	20	96	4
Cartoons: Diego	67	33	92	8
Human: female	47	53	72	28
Human: male	43	57	67	33

These were the key results.

- Children had a 45% correct rejection rate for human faces.
- Children had a 74% correct rejection rate for cartoon faces.
- Adults had a 70% correct rejection rate for human faces.
- Adults had a 94% correct rejection rate for cartoon faces.

- Both children and adults were significantly more accurate in correctly rejecting cartoon faces compared to human faces.
- Children produced a significantly lower correct rejection rates for human faces *and* cartoon faces compared to adults.

The important difference in rates across all conditions between the children and adults can be related back to the aims of the study. As the children could identify Dora and Diego in virtually 100% of cases when these cartoon characters were present in a line-up shows that children used cognitive skills of attention and memory to help with the correct identification. However, their poorer performance on target-absent line-ups to correctly reject a line-up (by choosing the silhouette) that did not contain the same target cartoon characters or humans means that some social pressure is affecting cognitive ability. That is, the social demands of being asked to choose from a line-up (even though they had been told the target may not be in the line-up) is a powerful force. Therefore, children's memories for potential culprits of crime should be taken as being valid but only if the culprit is in the line-up. Where the culprit may not be present in a line-up, other techniques should be used to aid the children's memory for a criminal event.

Conclusion

Pozzulo *et al* concluded that '… children are likely to make an error in target-absent condition due to an expectation to the "social demands" to make a selection rather than due to faulty memory' (2011: 7).

Summary

Research method (main)	Laboratory experiment
Other technique(s)	Self-reports (questionnaires and interviews)
Sample	59 children aged four to seven years
	53 adults aged 17 to 30 years
Sampling technique	It is not known which technique was used to recruit the child participants.
	While the adults had volunteered to be part of the Participant Pool, it is not known how they were recruited for this study from that Pool.
Experimental design	Independent groups (for the children versus adult groups)
	Repeated measures (for the human/cartoon and target-present/absent parts of the study)
IV	Age (children and adults)
	Type of face/degree of familiarity (human [not familiar] and cartoon [familiar])
	Type of line-up (target-present and target-absent)
DV	Correct identification rate for target-present
	Correct rejection rate for target-absent
Quantitative data	As above plus number of foils chosen and false rejection rates
Qualitative data	Free recall about the content of each video clip

Evaluation

Evaluation	General evaluation	Related to Pozzulo et al
Strength	Laboratory experiments have high levels of standardisation and so can be replicated to test for reliability.	Pozzulo et al had a standardised procedure including the Instructions for Line-up Identification and clothing worn by the line-up administrators. This means another researcher could easily replicate this study to test for reliability.
Strength	Laboratory experiments have high levels of control, so researchers can be more confident it is the IV directly affecting the DV.	As there were many controls, such as the choice of human target faces and the length of time the close-up was shown, Pozzulo et al could be confident that it was the age/familiarity/line-up type that was affecting correct identification/rejection rates.
Weakness	In many laboratory experiments participants take part in tasks that are nothing like real-life ones, so the tasks lack mundane realism.	The task of having to watch a six-second clip of an unknown human face and then try to spot the person in a line-up (and he or she might not even be there) is not a usual task that people carry out in everyday life. Therefore, the study can be said to be low in mundane realism.
Weakness	For a repeated measures design, order effects can affect the findings of the study and reduce its validity. Order effects include: practice effect (getting better at a task when you complete a similar one for the second time); fatigue effect (the more tasks you do the more tired you might become); and boredom effect (repeating similar tasks can bore participants).	Even though Pozzulo et al counterbalanced the four tasks, there could still be some practice effect occurring. That is, completing four very similar tasks might have meant that participants tried harder on the later tasks – by then they knew what was going to happen; they had viewed other clips and had become better at finding ways to remember the face. This could reduce some validity of findings.

Other evaluation points include the following.

- Quantitative data: as the data are numerical, it allows easier comparison and statistical analysis to take place. For example, the correct identification rates and correct rejection rates could be calculated and compared across age of participant, familiarity of face, and type of line-up. It was clear that adults had a higher successful rejection rate in target-absent line-ups compared to children (around 70% compared to around 45%). Also, as the data are numerical, the process is objective and scientific – there is only minimal chance of psychologists miscalculating the data and drawing invalid conclusions. The percentage choice of each face is objective and allows direct comparisons leading to valid conclusions.

- Ethics: (informed) consent had been given by the parent or guardian for the child participants. The adults had already pre-consented to taking part in studies as they were part of the Participant Pool. There could have been some degree of psychological stress involved in the study, more so for the children as the findings showed that social pressures were affecting their cognitive ability. The idea of not knowing if a face in the line-up was or was not in the video clip could be psychologically stressful. However, the study only began for children once they were comfortable, and a facilitator played with them between each trial to ensure that they were happy.

- Use of repeated measures: a strength is that this type of design eliminates any effect of participant variables as all participants take part in all conditions; therefore, they are controlled. As a result, elements such as the participants' usual cognitive ability to remember faces is controlled for.

Issues and debates

The following table discusses Pozzulo *et al* in terms of the core issues and debates for AS Level.

Application to everyday life	The results from the study are useful for the criminal justice system. They can be used to improve the way in which children are questioned by people in authority about what they saw when witnessing a crime. For example, questions should only be asked where there is a correct answer available, especially when this involves selecting people from a line-up. Additionally, some credence can be placed on eyewitness accounts by children involving people they know: they are excellent at identifying known cartoon characters in a line-up and this could be extrapolated to known human faces (the study used faces that the children were not familiar with).
Individual and situational explanations	Both sides of the argument can be seen in this study. In terms of **individual**, there were differences in the false positive responses in children, especially for human faces. Over one-third of trials saw a child falsely reject a face from a line-up and in around one-fifth of trials a child did choose the correct face from a line-up. Therefore, there may be individual differences in the way that children process faces and memories for events. In terms of **situational**, the scenario of being asked to choose a face from a line-up when it was not there appeared to make children incorrectly choose a face in over 50% of trials. This also happened in around 30% of trials for adults. The expectation of the target person being in the line-up affected their choices, probably due to the social pressures of questioning.
Nature versus nurture	Not applicable
The use of children	There are always issues surrounding the use of children in research and the subsequent real-world application of findings. This study clearly shows that children can be heavily influenced by adults asking questions about information that is presented to them when none of the information contains a correct answer. Also, we cannot be sure that the children did fully understand and comprehend the questions being asked, as their language skills had not been measured before the study.
The use of animals	Not applicable

> **Challenge yourself**
>
> Think of two other real-world applications for this study. Make sure that you write down what the real-world application is and how it will be achieved.

10 Bandura *et al* (1961)

Background

This study is concerned with the tendency of children to imitate adult social behaviour, specifically aggression. Learning behaviour by imitating others is called observational learning. Several studies had already demonstrated that children are influenced by witnessing adult behaviour. However, previous studies had tended to show children repeating adult behaviour in the same situation and in the presence of the adult who modelled the behaviour. Although this suggests that children identify with adult models, it does not show whether they will go on to repeat the observed behaviour in other situations and without the adult present. One purpose of the study, therefore, was to test whether children will reproduce observed behaviour in a new situation and in the absence of the model.

This study is also concerned with the learning of gender-specific behaviours. Previous studies had shown that children are sensitive to gender-specific behaviours. For example, children see their parents as preferring gender-stereotyped behaviours. Aggression is a good example of a gendered social behaviour, being associated with masculinity.

A further purpose of this study was to investigate whether boys were more likely to imitate aggression than girls, and whether they would be more likely to imitate male than female models.

The psychology being investigated

Social learning theory

Social learning theory is being tested by the researchers in this study. To learn something in this way, someone has to go through four stages.

1. Attention. Observers must pay attention to the behaviour(s) of a role model. The role model could be the observer's parent or even a character on television. The role model must have some features that attract the observer. These can be individual factors linked to the observer only or general traits such as being friendly. The idea is that a same-sex model might have more of the relevant characteristics to be observed.

2. Retention. Observers must store the observed behaviour(s) in their long-term memory so that the information can be used again. This could be when the observer wants to imitate the observed behaviour.

3. Reproduction. Observers must feel capable of imitating the retained, observed behaviour. If they do, they may attempt to imitate the behaviour. If they do not, they may observe some more or choose never to attempt to imitate the behaviour.

4. Motivation. If observers experience vicarious reinforcement they are more likely to imitate the observed behaviour. This is when the role model has been rewarded for performing the observed behaviour so it increases the chances that an observer will get rewarded too if he or she imitates it. Vicarious punishment can also happen where the role model gets punished for the observed behaviour. As a result, the observer is less likely to want to imitate the behaviour.

Therefore, social learning is about learning through observation and imitation. It is also 'learning by proxy', which means learning indirectly through others.

Aggression

This is any *behavioural* act that has the intention to harm another living organism. Examples include hitting, throwing objects, fighting, and biting. It can also be a *verbal* act that is also intended to hurt them psychologically. Examples include shouting horrible things, swearing, and name calling.

> **Ask yourself**
>
> Do you think that watching aggressive media makes someone aggressive? Are there other factors that might make someone aggressive?

Aim

Overall aim: To investigate observational learning of aggression.

The following are specific aims.

1. To see whether children would reproduce aggressive behaviour when the model was no longer present.
2. To look for gender differences in learning of aggression.

Method

Participants

There were 72 participants: 36 male and 36 female. All were selected from the nursery school of Stanford University. Ages ranged from 37 months (just over 3 years) to 69 months (5 years and 9 months). The mean age was 52 months (4 years and 4 months).

Design

This was a laboratory experiment, using a matched groups design. The effect of three IVs was tested. These were:

- the behaviour of the model – aggressive or non-aggressive
- the sex of the model
- the sex of the children.

There were eight conditions plus a control group. The children in each condition were matched for their aggression levels so that this did not become a confounding variable. This was achieved by the researcher and a nursery teacher independently rating 51 of the children on a scale of 0 to 5 for attributes such as physical aggression, verbal aggression, aggression towards inanimate objects, and aggressive inhibition. Very good agreement between the two raters was achieved ($r = +0.89$). Table 10.1 gives details of the conditions in the study.

Table 10.1 Conditions

Condition	Model	Sex of model	Sex of children	n
1	Aggressive	Male	Male	6
2	Aggressive	Male	Female	6
3	Aggressive	Female	Male	6
4	Aggressive	Female	Female	6
5	Non-aggressive	Male	Male	6
6	Non-aggressive	Male	Female	6
7	Non-aggressive	Female	Male	6
8	Non-aggressive	Female	Female	6
Control	None	N/A	Males and females	24

Procedure

The experiment was conducted as follows.

- An aggressive model was shown to 12 boys and 12 girls. Six boys and six girls saw aggression modelled by a same-sex model, while the rest saw aggression modelled by an opposite-sex model.

- A non-aggressive model was shown to 12 boys and 12 girls. Six boys and six girls saw non-aggression modelled by a same-sex model, while the rest saw non-aggression modelled by an opposite-sex model.

- A control group of 12 boys and 12 girls did not see a model display any behaviour, aggressive or otherwise.

- One male and one female were the role models and one female researcher conducted the study for all participants.

There were three stages.

1. Modelling the behaviour. Each child was brought individually to the experimental room. Just before entering the room, the child met the model, who was in the hallway. The researcher invited the model to come into the room and join in a game. This activity lasted for ten minutes. The child was then led to a corner of the room that looked like a play area. Once he or she was seated, the researcher showed how the child could design a picture using potato prints and stickers. The potato prints were all geometric shapes and the stickers were objects such as animals and flowers. These were chosen as previous studies had shown that children took an interest in them.

    Once the child was settled, the researcher took the model to an opposite corner of the room. This contained a small chair and table, a toy set, a mallet, and a five-foot inflatable 'Bobo' doll. The researcher explained that these were things for the model to play with. When the model was seated, the researcher left the room.

    In the non-aggressive conditions, the model assembled some of the toys in a quiet manner, ignoring the Bobo doll. In the aggressive conditions, the model began by assembling the toys. However, after around one minute, the model started being aggressive towards the Bobo doll. So that the test would show that participants may well be imitating specific aggressive behaviours, the model showed a range of these. The model punched the doll; however, this is an act a child may do without witnessing the model. The model also raised the doll, picked up a mallet and struck the doll on its head then tossed the doll into the air and kicked it around the room. This sequence of physically aggressive acts was repeated around three times. In addition, the model also shouted verbal aggressive responses such as intentions to "sock him in the nose", "hit him down", "throw him in the air", "kick him" and "Pow!". A further two non-aggressive comments were spoken: "He keeps coming back for more" and "He sure is a tough fella". At the end of ten minutes, the researcher returned to the room, told the child to go to another games room and then said goodbye to the model.

2. Aggression arousal. All of the children were subjected to mild aggression.

    After seeing the model in the previous room, the child entered a games room that had some attractive toys in it. These included a fire engine, a locomotive, a spinning top, a doll set, and a fighter plane. The child was told that these were for him or her to play with. However, soon after the child had begun to get involved in play with the toys (usually after around two minutes), the researcher explained that these were actually her very best toys. She stated that she did not let just any child play with them and that she was going to keep these toys for other children. The child was told that he or she could play with the toys in the next room. Both the child and researcher then entered the experimental room. It should be noted that the researcher remained in the room for stage 3 as the child might refuse to be alone, but she never interacted with the child; instead, she busied herself with paperwork in the corner of the room away from the child.

3. Testing for delayed imitation. The experimental room contained toys that could allow each child to show imitative and non-imitative aggression. There were other toys that should elicit other non-aggressive forms of play. The aggressive toys included a three-foot Bobo doll, a mallet, a peg board, two dart guns, and a tether ball hung from the ceiling, with a face on it. The non-aggressive toys included a tea set, crayons, colouring paper, a ball, dolls, toy bears, cars, trucks, and plastic farmyard animals. All of the toys were placed in the same location for every child.

The child spent around 20 minutes in the experimental room. The child's behaviour was rated on a pre-determined checklist of categories by judges through a one-way mirror. The session was divided into five-second intervals via an electronic timer. Therefore, each child had 240 behaviours recorded.

The male model rated the behaviours for all 72 children. Apart from the children he had been a model to, he never knew which condition that child was in. To assess inter-observer reliability, half of the children were observed by a second researcher who scored the children independently from the male model observer. The correlation between the two observers was greater than $r = +0.90$.

Table 10.2 shows the categories used in the observation stage of the study.

Table 10.2 Checklist for categories of behaviour

Category	Examples of behaviour in the category
Imitative physical aggression	The child: hits the Bobo doll with a mallet; sits on the doll; punches the doll on its nose; kicks the doll; tosses the doll in the air
Imitative verbal aggression	repeats any of the phrases: "sock him", "hit him down", "kick him", "throw him in the air", "Pow!"
Imitative non-aggressive verbal responses	repeats the phrases: "He keeps coming back for more" or "He sure is a tough fella"
Mallet aggression	hits an object other than the Bobo doll with the mallet
Sits on the Bobo doll	lays the Bobo doll on its side and sits on it, but does not show aggression towards it
Punches the Bobo doll	strikes, slaps, or pushes the Bobo doll aggressively
Non-imitative physical and verbal aggression	shows any physical aggression towards objects other than the Bobo doll; makes any hostile remarks except those in the imitative verbal aggression category
Aggressive gun play	shoots the darts or aims the gun and fires imaginary shots at objects in the room.

Results

Quantitative data was recorded. This showed significant differences in levels of imitative aggression between the group that witnessed aggression and the other two groups. This was true of physical and verbal aggression. To a lesser extent this was also true of partial imitation and non-imitative aggression. Significantly more non-aggressive play was recorded in the non-aggressive model condition. All the results are shown in Table 10.3.

Table 10.3 Results showing the mean aggressive scores for all conditions across all categories of behaviour

	Experimental groups				Control group
Response category	Aggressive		Non-aggressive		
	F model	M model	F model	M model	
Imitative physical aggression					
Female subjects	5.5	7.2	2.5	0.0	1.2
Male subjects	12.4	25.8	0.2	1.5	2.0
Imitative verbal aggression					
Female subjects	13.7	2.0	0.3	0.0	0.7
Male subjects	4.3	12.7	1.1	0.0	1.7
Mallet aggression					
Female subjects	17.2	18.7	0.5	0.5	13.1
Male subjects	15.5	28.8	18.7	6.7	13.5
Punches Bobo doll					
Female subjects	6.3	16.5	5.8	4.3	11.7
Male subjects	18.9	11.9	15.6	14.8	15.7
Non-imitative aggression					
Female subjects	21.3	8.4	7.2	1.4	6.1
Male subjects	16.2	36.7	26.1	22.3	24.6
Aggressive gun play					
Female subjects	1.8	4.5	2.6	2.5	3.7
Male subjects	7.3	15.9	8.9	16.7	14.3

Source: Bandura et al (1961: 578)

Table 10.4 Differences between the groups based solely on the behaviour of the model

Response category	Aggressive compared to non-aggressive model	Aggressive model compared to control	Non-aggressive model compared to control
Imitation of physical aggression	Yes. Aggressive.	Yes. Aggressive.	No
Imitation of verbal aggression	Yes. Aggressive.	Yes. Aggressive.	No
Imitation of non-aggressive verbal responses	Yes. Aggressive.	Yes. Aggressive.	No
Mallet aggression	Yes. Aggressive.	No	Yes. Control.
Sits on the Bobo doll	Yes. Aggressive.	No. Aggressive showed more but p = 0.059	No
Punches the Bobo doll	No	No	No
Physical and verbal non-imitative aggression	Yes. Aggressive.	No	No
Aggressive gun play	No	No	No

Table 10.4 shows the significant differences between the groups based solely on the behaviour of the model. Each cell states whether a difference was significant, which group displayed more of the response category and gives the p value.

Table 10.4 clearly shows that participants who observed an aggressive model performed significantly more aggressive behaviours:

- in six of the eight response categories compared to the non-aggressive model
- in three of the response categories compared to the control.

The control group only showed significantly more aggressive behaviour for mallet aggression than the non-aggressive model. This was mainly due to the girls showing much more of this behaviour in the control group.

The researchers also reported these results.

- Around one third of the children in the aggressive conditions repeated the model's non-aggressive verbal responses. No child in the other two conditions did this.
- In the aggressive conditions, boys reproduced more imitative physical aggression than girls. There were no differences in terms of verbal aggression.
- Boys who witnessed a male aggressive model showed significantly more physical imitative aggression, more verbal imitative aggression, more non-imitative aggression and more gun play than girls who witnessed a male aggressive model.
- Girls who witnessed a female aggressive model showed more imitative verbal aggression and non-imitative aggression than boys who witnessed a female aggressive model. However, the results were not significant.
- Apart from the mallet aggression, there were no significant differences between the non-aggressive model conditions and the control group. However, this appeared to be masking some important findings. Compared to the control group, those who witnessed a non-aggressive male model (irrespective of their sex) performed *less* imitative physical aggression, *less* imitative verbal aggression, *less* mallet aggression, *less* non-imitative physical and verbal aggression, and punched the Bobo doll *fewer* times.
- Girls spent significantly more time playing with the dolls and tea set and more time colouring than boys. Boys spent significantly more time playing with the guns.
- Children in the non-aggressive conditions engaged in significantly more non-aggressive play with dolls than was seen in the other two groups.
  - Children who had observed non-aggressive models spent more than twice as much time sitting quietly (not playing with any toys) than children who had observed the aggressive model.

In summary, the key overall results were as follows.

- Children who had witnessed an aggressive model were significantly more aggressive themselves.
- Overall, there was very little difference between aggression in the control group and that in the non-aggressive modelling condition.
- Boys were significantly more likely to imitate aggressive male models. The difference for girls was much smaller.
- Boys were significantly more physically aggressive than girls. Girls were slightly more verbally aggressive.

> **Test yourself**
>
> Outline the sample used in the study and get someone to ask you for specific results.

Conclusion

Witnessing aggression in a model can be enough to produce aggression by an observer. Children selectively imitate gender-specific behaviours. Boys are more likely to imitate physical aggression, while girls are more likely to imitate verbal aggression. As the boys but not girls were more likely to imitate aggression in a same-sex model, it could be concluded – although only cautiously – that children selectively imitate same-sex models.

Summary

Research method (main)	Experimental
Other technique(s)	Controlled observation
Sample	There were 72 participants: 36 male and 36 female. All were selected from the nursery school of Stanford University.
Sampling technique	Opportunity
Experimental design	Matched groups independent measures
IV	The behaviour of the model – aggressive or non-aggressive; the sex of the model; the sex of the children
DV	Amount of behaviour observed in eight categories
Quantitative data	As above
Qualitative data	Any comments noted from the children

Evaluation

Evaluation	General evaluation (laboratory experiments)	Related to Bandura et al
Strength	Laboratory experiments have high levels of standardisation and so can be replicated to test for reliability.	This study had a standardised procedure including the amount of time participants watched a model for the layout of the room and which toys were available for each child. Therefore, other researchers could easily replicate this study to test it for reliability.
Strength	As laboratory experiments have high levels of control, researchers can be more confident it is the IV directly affecting the DV.	As the controls were high for both parts of the study (eg time watching the model, priming before entering the observation room), the researchers could be confident that it was the actions of the model that caused the children to show aggressive and non-aggressive behaviour.
Weakness	As laboratory experiments take place in an artificial setting, it is said that they can lack ecological validity.	The set-up was artificial because, especially for the first stage, the child was in an unfamiliar setting for children. As a result, it could be argued that the findings were low in ecological validity.
Weakness	In many laboratory experiments participants take part in tasks that are nothing like real-life ones, so the tasks lack mundane realism.	Some of the tasks expected of the child were not usual (eg sitting watching an adult play with some toys and not being involved in the play). Therefore, aspects of the study could be low in mundane realism.

Other evaluation points include the following.

- Quantitative data: this enabled clear comparisons of all groups to see the effect the model was having on behaviour. Therefore, conclusions could easily be drawn. However, we do not know *why* the children were acting in the ways they did as no qualitative data were collected to explore this.
- Ethics – protection: the children displayed aggressive behaviour and this may have continued *after* the study had ended. The children did not leave the study in the same physical or psychological state in which they entered it.

> **Challenge yourself**
>
> Evaluate this study in terms of the use of observations and the sampling technique used.

Issues and debates

The following table discusses the Bandura *et al* study in terms of the core issues and debates for AS Level.

Application to everyday life	The finding of this study could be used by television networks to ensure that programmes are appropriate for children. This could include ensuring that aggressive acts in a programme are limited or, alternatively, encouraging pro-social behaviour. The findings are useful for parents too. They can pick and choose which television programmes their children should watch if they know that children may imitate what they see.
Individual and situational explanations	The **situational** side of the debate is supported here. Children had been matched on **individual** levels of aggression already yet there were differences in imitated behaviours. Therefore, the situation that children found themselves in caused the imitated aggressive behaviours.
Nature versus nurture	Similar to the point above, children had already been matched on their levels of aggression, so the environment they found themselves in caused the imitated behaviours. Therefore, the nurture side of the debate is supported here. Also, as the boys were generally more aggressive, this supports the **nature** side of the debate as boys have higher levels of testosterone, the hormone linked to aggressive behaviour.
The use of children	Some psychologists have noted that the children may have been distressed by watching the aggressive acts. They may have been psychologically harmed by witnessing the acts and by being frustrated with not being able to play with the 'best' toys. Therefore, they left the experiment in a different psychological state from when they entered it.
	Some psychologists believe that children are less susceptible to demand characteristics than adults. In this study it was hoped that the children were showing their real behaviours when playing with the Bobo doll as they had not worked out the purpose of the study.
The use of animals	Not applicable

> **Challenge yourself**
>
> Identify two other applications to everyday life this study could have. Explain who would benefit from these applications.

11 Fagen et al (2014)

Background

Some of the main traditional training methods for elephants tended to focus on punishment or the use of aversive stimuli. It also included unlimited contact between the handlers and the trainers using free contact. However, more contemporary methods are beginning to be used with a management system that has protected contact between the handler and the elephant (improving keepers' safety too) and is based around positive reinforcement/rewards.

Secondary positive reinforcement (SPR) training attempts to be a more humane way of training elephants. A distinctive sound 'marker' acts as secondary reinforcer, which is consistently followed by a primary positive reinforcer, usually food. Once the animal understands the conditioned relationship between the sound marker and reward, the marker can be used more precisely to show the animal the exact time it is performing the correct behaviour (as taking out a treat and giving it to an animal takes time but a sound marker is instant).

Positive reinforcement allows a handler or trainer to prompt behaviour that is motivated by something pleasant rather than by fear, and just as importantly, is voluntary. This has many benefits such as increased control and problem-solving abilities for the animal plus safer conditions for a handler or trainer. Likewise, using positive reinforcement is useful when attempting to get animals to accept and be part of crucial veterinary procedures that can include discomfort and stress. Voluntary willingness to do this by the animal can make the whole procedure less stressful and it is less likely to lead to an animal needing anaesthesia or some form of sedation.

There have been several studies showing SPR to be effective in training non-human primates, bongos and nyalas (types of antelope), and giant pandas. However, prior to this study there had been no studies testing the efficacy of SPR training with elephants.

Fagen *et al* noted one situation where the SPR method might be very useful: the collection of sputum (thick mucus from the lungs) from an elephant for tuberculosis (TB) testing. Estimations range from 11% to 25% of captive elephant populations in places such as India and Nepal testing positive for TB. There may even be some evidence of zoonotic (animal to human) transmission of TB, so it is crucial to be able to safely test elephants. The best way to achieve this is to test for the bacteria that causes TB in a sample of sputum from the elephant using a procedure referred to as a trunk wash. Prior to this study, researchers had reported that it was very difficult to acquire good-quality trunk-wash samples for TB testing.

Figure 11.1 *Elephants were used as the sample in this study*

Psychology being investigated

Operant conditioning

This is a type of conditioning based around the idea of learning by consequences. The organism needs to be directly involved in the process for it to be conditioned. The consequences are based around reinforcement and punishment. Reinforcements increase the probability of repeating a behaviour while punishments decrease the probability of repeating a behaviour.

Reinforcement (positive, negative, primary, secondary)

There are different types of reinforcement (and punishment), as highlighted in Table 11.1.

Table 11.1 The different types of reinforcement and punishment used in operant conditioning

	Positive This is defined as the addition of something.	**Negative** This is defined as the removal of something.
Reinforcement This is defined as increasing the probability of repeating the behaviour.	**Positive + Reinforcement** This refers to the **addition** of something **nice** to **increase the probability** of that behaviour being repeated.	**Negative + Reinforcement** This refers to the **removal** of something **aversive** to **increase the probability** of that behaviour being repeated.
Punishment This is defined as decreasing the probability of repeating the behaviour.	**Positive + Punishment** This refers to the **addition** of something **aversive** to **decrease the probability** of that behaviour being repeated.	**Negative + Punishment** This refers to the **removal** of something **nice** to **decrease the probability** of that behaviour being repeated.

There are also two *types* of reinforcer.
1. Primary reinforcer. These fulfil a direct biological need. An example would be a treat for a dog or sweets for a child.
2. Secondary reinforcer. These have no *intrinsic* value to the organism, but they can be 'exchanged' for a primary reinforcer *or* they become associated with a primary reinforcer. Examples include clicker training for dogs (using a click sound made by a device) or offering money to a human.

> **Challenge yourself**
>
> Give examples for all four cells in Table 11.1 based on real-world behaviour.

Shaping

This is a technique that utilises the idea of operant conditioning, specifically the reinforcement part, to refine the behaviour of an organism. When an organism is attempting to learn a new behaviour there will be variation in the quality of attempts. The attempts that are the better ones (that bring the organism closer to the overall goal) are rewarded. Ultimately rewarding these better attempts *shapes* the behaviour and means the organism is more likely to keep repeating the ones closest to the final goal.

Behavioural chaining

This also uses the principles of operant conditioning with a focus on reinforcement. This follows the idea of creating 'strings of behaviours' so that they are performed in succession. There are two main types of behavioural chaining.
1. Forward chaining – the first behaviour in a sequence is rewarded and once this is mastered, the second behaviour is rewarded. Now the first and second behaviours have to be performed correctly in order to gain the reward. This is then repeated with the third, fourth, etc behaviours in a sequence. So, the primary reinforcer is only given after the final part of the current sequence being taught has been shown.
2. Backward chaining – the final behaviour in a sequence is rewarded first and then the trainer works backwards. The primary reinforcer is only ever given after the final behaviour in the sequence has been shown. So, the organism needs to perform the behaviours preceding the final one correctly in order to attempt the final one, and if successful it gains a primary reinforcer.

Aim

To investigate whether using secondary positive reinforcement training would be effective on elephants in Nepal to participate, voluntarily, in a trunk wash to aid tuberculosis (TB) testing.

Method

Participants

Five female elephants were used in this study. They were housed in the same stable in Nepal. Four of the elephants were five to seven years old and had been born in the stable, the fifth was over 50 years old. The elephants were selected by staff at the stable using the following criteria.

- They had a docile nature.
- They were not pregnant and did not have a current calf.
- They had a willing mahout (handler).
- Prior to the study, they had been trained using traditional methods.
- They had never been exposed to SPR training methods.

Training

An SPR method was used in this study. The primary reinforcer was chopped bananas. The secondary reinforcer was a short whistle blow. All training was conducted in morning or afternoon sessions when the elephant was leg chained. Due to mahout unavailability, not all elephants were trained in every session. However, no elephant went more than two days without some training. Also, if an elephant clearly did not want to participate then she skipped that session. Elephants indicated they did not want to participate by walking to the other side of the stalls or away from the trainer, for example. Mahouts were always present for each training session and were instructed not to communicate with their elephant during this time.

The sequence of behaviours that formed a successful trunk wash that needed to be taught to the elephants was as follows.

1. Place the end of the trunk in the hand of the trainer.
2. Allow the trainer to insert saline or plain sterile water into the trunk.
3. Lift the trunk up so the liquid went into the base of the trunk.
4. Hold the liquid in the base of the trunk.
5. Lower the tip of the trunk into a collection device.
6. Blow out the sample of liquid.

This had to be in succession, so no liquid missed the collection device, and the elephant did not swallow the liquid. The idea of this sequence is based around the elephant being active and not passive.

Initial training consisted of four techniques.

1. Understanding the reinforcers – the trainer had to get the elephant to understand the connection between the primary and secondary reinforcer. This was achieved by repeatedly pairing the whistle blow with a banana reward.
2. Capture – this is when the elephant spontaneously performs a behaviour necessary for the trunk wash, and this gets 'captured' by rewarding it repeatedly with the primary and secondary reinforcer.
3. Lure – this is when the elephant is tempted into a necessary position to complete the trunk wash by the strategic placement of a reward. The necessary position is then rewarded immediately.
4. Shaping – as described on page 83.

Test yourself

Write the name of the trained behaviour on one set of cards and then the description of each trained behaviour on another set of cards. Shuffle them then try to match the name with the description.

Table 11.2 shows the descriptions used for all trained behaviours.

Table 11.2 Descriptions of trained behaviours

Behavior	Description
Trunk here	The distal end of the trunk is placed gently on top of the outstretched palm of the trainer, with the ventral aspect of the trunk in contact with the trainer's palm.
Trunk up	The distal end of the trunk is held upward either in a loose curl with the dorsal aspect of the tip of the trunk in close contact with the elephant's own forehead or is held diagonally up and outward with a completely straight trunk. The exact height or angle of the trunk is not measured.
Bucket	The distal end of the trunk is gently placed inside a bucket.
Blow	The elephant gives a strong, sharp exhale through the trunk.
Steady	The elephant holds the trunk still with the trunk held in the position previously requested (trunk here, trunk down, or trunk out). The elephant can move its feet, ears, head, tail, and body slightly as long as the trunk remains still in the previous position requested.
Syringe	The elephant holds the trunk still in the trunk-here position to have the distal end of a catheter tip syringe placed inside the nostril of the trunk and up to 60 mL of saline or water instilled into the trunk.
Blow into bucket	The elephant places the distal end of the trunk in the bucket and gives a strong, sharp exhale through the trunk.
Trunk down	The trunk is held in a relaxed position with the trunk hanging loose toward the ground.
Trunk out	The trunk is held stretched straight outward, approximately parallel to the ground.
Targeting	The elephant moves such that the centre of the forehead makes contact with the end of a targeting stick placed at the height of the forehead.

Source: Fagen et al (2014: 18)

Five of the behavioural tasks from Table 11.2 were the focus of the training.

1. Trunk here: initially used the lure technique. When successful, shaping was used with the reward only given when the underside of the tip of the trunk was gently placed in the palm of the hand of the trainer.

2. Trunk up: initially used the lure technique. This was important for those elephants who were attempting to drink the liquid. The lure part differed depending on the size of the elephant. If the elephant was short enough, the trainer held banana pieces a few inches above the forehead of the elephant, so the elephant had to raise her trunk to reach the reward. If the elephant was taller, the trainer's arm was fully extended above the trainer's head with the banana in his or her hand. Again, the elephant would have to raise her trunk to reach the reward. After this was successful, the position of the trunk was shaped for increasing height.

3. Bucket: initially used the lure technique. Once successful and the elephant could retrieve the banana from the bottom of the bucket, the behaviour was marked (with the whistle) and rewarded.

4. Blow: initially used the capture technique. The capture was the natural exhale of the elephant. This was then shaped to be more forceful.

5. Steady: this only happened once the elephant had learned whichever behaviour(s) needed to be held steady. Shaping was then used to increase the time in 'steady'. The steady behaviours were then reinforced with the marker (whistle) and the banana given after the whole steady behaviour had been performed.

A verbal cue was paired with each behaviour only after the elephant had completed it. Each cue was monosyllabic that had no meaning in English or Nepali. Each sound was distinctive.

Three other tasks, namely targeting, trunk down, and trunk out, were introduced to the elephants but this was quickly stopped as none of these tasks appeared necessary for the trunk wash to be performed.

Once each elephant was able to perform the five behaviours consistently correctly, behavioural chaining was used. The procedure for the behavioural chaining was as follows.

- The elephant was rewarded for blows made towards any part of the bucket. This was then shaped so that rewards only occurred with blows aimed at the centre of the bottom of the bucket.
- Separate behaviours were paired in a range of combinations and were practised in multiple behavioural sequences, working towards the full trunk wash.
- The trainer used a marker (the whistle) at appropriate *stages* of the sequence, but the primary reinforcer of banana was only ever given at the end of a correct *sequence*.
- The final stage was to chain together the full trunk wash sequence of trunk here (short steady), trunk up (long steady), bucket, then blow.

The final part of the training involved introducing the elephant to the syringe and saline liquid. This was done via a step-by-step procedure paired with a reward to decrease the likelihood of a negative experience with the syringe. Each elephant was rewarded when staying in the position for trunk here when the syringe was in view. Repeated rewards were given for holding this position with the syringe getting closer and closer to the tip of the trunk until it touched it. This regime was continued with the syringe slowly touching the outside of the trunk tip, then touching the inside of the nostril, until finally the syringe tip was in the nostril. Once this had been successful, increasing amounts of liquid were inserted into the trunk using the syringe. It began with a single drop then increased in small amounts (between 1 and 15 mL) until reaching the 60 mL necessary for a trunk wash.

All five elephants began with a 0.9% saline liquid medium. When training they were moved to plain water. Once this transition was successful, each elephant was offered water at the start of any training session to reduce the probability of drinking the liquid, which would mean the trunk wash could not happen. One elephant preferred saline over the plain water and would continue to drink the saline even when offered water before training. She was moved over to water as the liquid medium and after this happened her success rate improve rapidly.

Overall training plans were tailored to each individual elephant due to different rates of learning.

Ethical considerations

The husbandry conditions were not altered for this study.

- The elephants were able to graze in the jungle with their mahouts from 5am to 7am and then from 10.30am to 4pm.
- For the remainder of the day and during the night each elephant was leg-chained to posts in an open stall. These were usually placed on both legs. The chain was between 6 foot and 8 foot long and was slack enough to allow easy movement around the post.
- The elephants' diet was mainly fresh grass and dhana (a mixture of grain, nutritional supplements, and grass).
- The elephants had access to water only when they were grazing.

Data collection

A research assistant timed every training session to the nearest minute. This started when the first verbal cue was offered by the trainer and ended when the elephant had responded to the final verbal cue offered by the trainer. This was the 'session time'.

Figure 11.2 *The final part of the full trunk wash was to blow the liquid into the bottom of a bucket for collection and testing*

For each training session, a research assistant would tally the total number of times an elephant was given a verbal cue for a specific behaviour. This was recorded as the 'number of offers' for each behaviour. Offers were still counted even before the verbal cue had been associated with a specific behaviour.

The 'performance tests'. began after training session 10. These tests were then given after every five subsequent training sessions. They only began after session 10 to allow the elephants time to learn and potentially master that behaviour. When it was time for a performance test, all behaviours that the elephant had been taught were tested. A pass score was 80%. If the elephant had not been taught a specific behaviour then that was recorded as 0%. To register a pass, the elephant had to perform the behaviour of sufficient quality to function in a trunk wash. However, this was subjectively determined by the trainer. This was also the case for a sequence of behaviours that were tested. A pass was awarded if the elephant completed the sequence successfully in at least 80% of attempts. If a pass was awarded, then the entire sequence was given a score between 80% and 100% and each individual behaviour within that sequence was given a score of 90% (the median between 80 and 100). However, if an elephant did not pass on a sequence, each individual behaviour *within that sequence* or a shorter sequence of behaviours was tested to determine where the fail occurred.

The behaviours for steady and trunk down were tested separately. The steady behaviour required three positions when tested: trunk up, trunk down, and trunk here. However, the trunk down was not a necessary part of the trunk wash sequence so it could not be given a default pass as part of a sequence. This is why it was also tested separately.

Overall training was recorded as 'complete and concluded' when the elephant had a pass rate of 80% or more for the full sequence of a trunk wash, irrespective of the animal's pass rate scores for trunk down and steady behaviours.

Results

The four juvenile elephants all successfully passed the full sequence of a trunk wash. The adult elephant did not pass. Table 11.3 summarises this.

Table 11.3 *The number of sessions it took for each elephant to pass the trunk wash test and the mean duration of each training session per elephant*

	Session number when passed the full trunk wash	Mean duration of training sessions (minutes)
Elephant 1	30	12.42
2	25	10.29
3	35	13.27
4	35	11.11
5	Never passed	N/A

All elephants passed all individual task tests with only the following exceptions.

- Elephants 2 and 4 never passed their separate steady tests.
- Elephant 5 (the adult) never passed her blow, syringe, and steady tests.

Figure 11.3 shows the degree of difficulty experienced for each specific task. This was measured by the number of offers needed before each elephant first passed the performance test.

The task for trunk here required significantly more offers compared to both the bucket and blow tasks. Therefore, the task for trunk here was the most difficult of the behaviours to master in the sample.

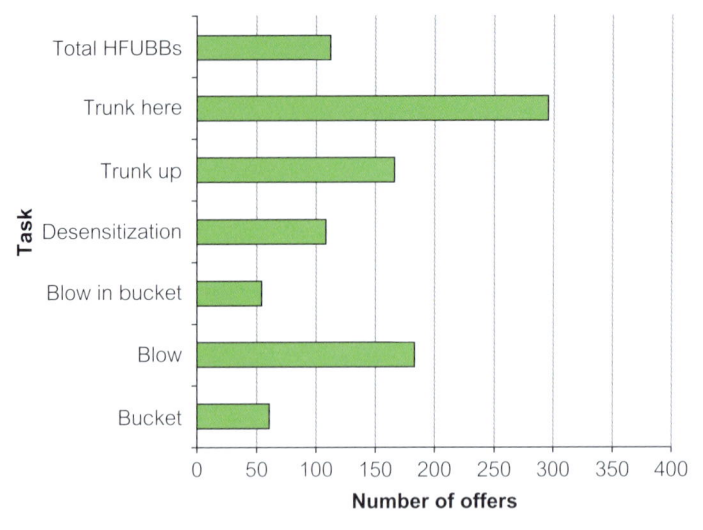

Figure 11.3 The degree of difficulty experienced for each specific task

Figure 11.4 shows the total amount of time in training for each elephant.

The mean time in training for all elephants was 378 minutes and 367 minutes for the four elephants who successfully passed the full sequence for the trunk wash.

Figure 11.5 shows the mean correct pass score by number of sessions.

As can be seen, the passing rate increased over time from around 37% in session (the first time they had performance tests) to 89% in session 35.

The research team offered potential reasons why elephant 5 (the adult) did not complete the training. These included significant distractions from a baby elephant that came into the test area to steal from the reward bucket, and the adult's condition: some visual impairment and trunk weakness, and a foot abscess.

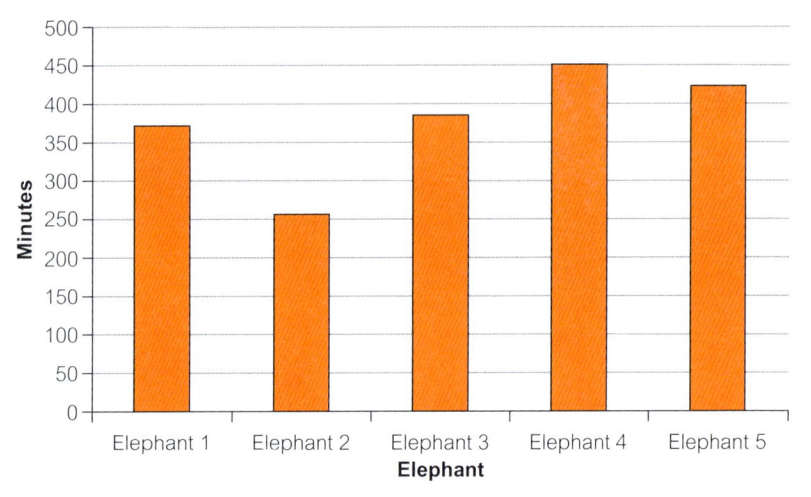

Figure 11.4 The total amount of time in training for each elephant

Conclusion

Fagen *et al* concluded that '… it is feasible to effectively train juvenile, free-contact, traditionally trained elephants in Nepal to voluntarily and reliably participate in a trunk wash using only secondary positive reinforcement techniques' (2014: 1). Also, positive reinforcement using shaping and behavioural chaining can teach elephants to successfully engage in a voluntary full trunk wash to help test for TB. In addition, secondary positive reinforcement techniques could be a very useful tool in the captive management of other species, especially through voluntary participation in health-related behaviours.

Challenge yourself

What are the strengths and weaknesses of using elephants as participants in this study?

Summary

Research method (main)	Observation
Other technique(s)	Secondary positive reinforcement
Sample	Five female elephants
Sampling technique	Opportunity
Experimental design	Not applicable
IV	Not applicable
DV	Not applicable
Quantitative data	Session times (measured in minutes) Number of offers Number of training sessions needed to successfully complete each task Number of test passes
Qualitative data	–

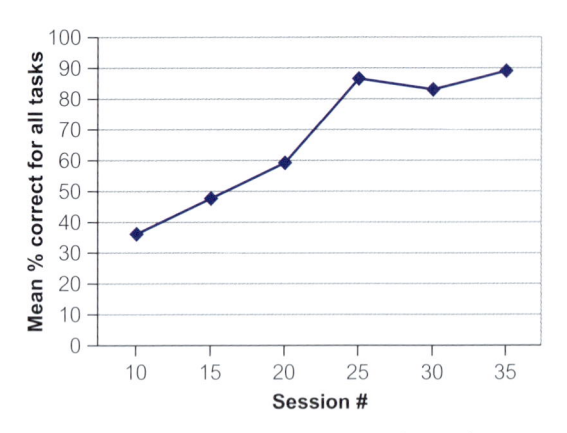

Figure 11.5 The mean correct pass score by number of session

Evaluation

Evaluation	General evaluation	Related to Fagen et al
Strength	The coding system used in structured observations (via the behavioural checklist) allows collection of objective quantative data, which can then be analysed statistically.	Direct comparisons could be made via the number of offers needed to pass a performance test to assess how difficult a task was. For example, the task for trunk here needed an average of around 300 offers while total HFUBBs (here, fluid, up, bucket, blow) needed an average of around 110.
Strength	Standardisation of the procedure of a study allows other researchers to replicate the study and test it for reliability.	Fagen et al had a standardised procedure including the behavioural checklist and definitions for things such as trunk here plus the SPR training regime. This means another researcher could easily replicate this study to test for reliability.
Weakness	Measurement of outcome variables can be subjective and affected by the motivations of the observer and trainer if they are directly involved in data collection.	To pass a test, the behavioural responses needed to be 'of sufficient quality to function in a trunk wash' which was subjectively determined by the trainer. The trainer could not have been using the exact same criterion for every single behavioural response made by all elephants. There was no checking of these nor were the sessions recorded to ensure some form of inter-observer reliability and a check on validity.
Weakness	It is unlikely to gain a wide variety of participants to allow for generalisation as the study used opportunity sampling.	The four juvenile and one older adult elephant were chosen from those who happened to be available for training at one elephant centre in Nepal. All were female. Therefore, it may be difficult to generalise the success to male elephants or age groups older than juveniles as there may be something unique about the four female elephants who passed the full trunk wash. In addition, it may be difficult to generalise to African elephants; these were not represented in the sample.

Other evaluation points include the following.

- Ethics: as well as the aspects of the study already described under 'Ethical considerations' on page 86, the elephants were housed in their usual place. Rewards (bananas) were used in addition to their usual diet, so they were not food deprived in such a way as to make the banana very desirable.
- Distractions during training: the researchers noted a range of distractions at different times during the training and testing. These included other animals in the jungle surrounding the elephants, tourists taking photographs, and that the afternoon sessions were quite close to the usual feeding time. These may have affected the validity of findings as it may have taken some elephants longer to master a behavioural response.

Issues and debates

The following table discusses Fagen et al in terms of the core issues and debates for AS Level.

> **Challenge yourself**
>
> Think of one other real-world application based on this study that could be used with humans. Remember to write about what the application is and how it could be achieved.

Application to everyday life	Secondary positive reinforcement techniques could be a very useful tool in the captive management of other species, especially through voluntary participation in health-related behaviours. Examples could include disease testing in primates and other mammals, so the animal provides the sample voluntarily rather than researchers having to sedate or anaesthetise.
Individual and situational explanations	Both sides of the argument can be seen in this study. There were **individual** differences in the performance and training times seen in the elephants. Elephant 2 appeared to be faster at passing tasks once trained while elephant 5 never completed the final trunk wash. In terms of **situational**, the process of engaging in SPR training allowed four of the elephants to successfully complete a voluntary full trunk wash. If this situation had never happened to them then they would not have been able to achieve this without rewards and encouragement.
Nature versus nurture	The **nurture** side is supported here, as the elephants were engaging in SPR protocols that help to develop and sustain learned behaviours. The techniques of luring, capturing, and giving primary reinforcers are all about learning new behaviours over time.
The use of children	Not applicable
The use of animals	See the ethical considerations part of the procedure on page 86.

12 Saavedra and Silverman (2002)

Background

There has been a lot of research by psychologists and psychiatrists into the causes and treatment of phobias. However, the role of disgust within phobias has received little attention. Disgust could interact with the fear a phobic stimulus produces to increase avoidance behaviour of that stimulus. During something called evaluative learning, the person perceives or evaluates a previously neutral object or event in a negative way (see below). Prior to this study there had been very few studies into evaluative learning in children with a specific phobia.

The psychology being investigated

Evaluative learning

Evaluative learning is the key concept under investigation in this case study. It is a form of classical conditioning which is learning by association. With this type of learning, a person comes to perceive (evaluate) a previously neutral object or an event negatively. Therefore, the individual negatively evaluates the object or event without anticipating any threat or danger. As a result, the negative evaluation elicits a feeling of disgust rather than fear. This differs from classical conditioning (expectancy learning) as it means that the person is being cognitively active by thinking about disgust and consequences rather than being a potentially passive organism.

Operant conditioning

See page 82 from Fagen *et al.*

Classical conditioning

This is learning by association. There are three stages as highlighted below.

Pre-conditioning

Pre-conditioning
| Unconditioned Stimulus UCS | → | Unconditioned Response UCR |
| Neutral Stimulus NS | → | No response |

A biological relationship needs to already exist between an unconditioned stimulus (UCS) and an unconditioned response (UCR). A neutral stimulus (NS) should not cause any response in the organism.

Conditioning
| Unconditioned Stimulus UCS | + | Neutral Stimulus NS | → | Unconditioned Response UCR |

Conditioning

This is when the UCS is repeatedly paired with the NS to produce the UCR.

Post-conditioning
| Conditioned Stimulus CS | → | Conditioned Response CR |

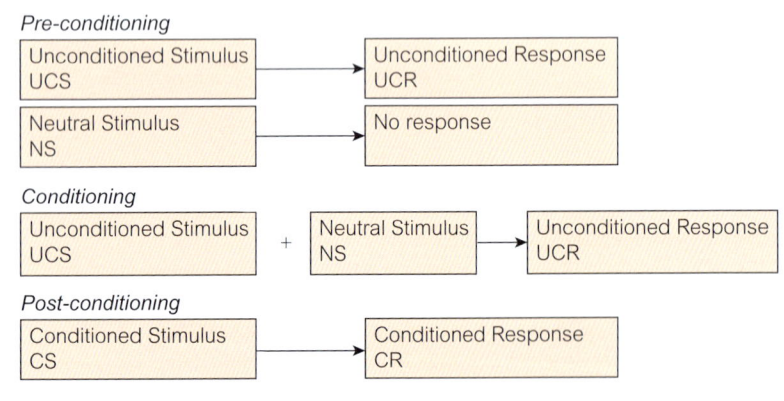

Figure 12.1 How a phobia may be formed using classical conditioning

Post-conditioning

The NS becomes a conditioned stimulus (CS) to produce a conditioned response (CR).

Figure 12.1 shows these stages as a diagram.

See pages 157–158 for an example of how a phobia may form via classical conditioning.

Phobias

A phobia is an irrational fear of an object, situation, place, feeling, animal, etc. See pages 157–162 for more examples of phobias and how they may be caused.

> **Ask yourself**
>
> List all the ways you can think of that could cause someone to develop a phobia.

Aim

There were two main aims.

1. To investigate the causes of a button phobia in a child.
2. To attempt to treat a child's phobia of buttons via targeting both disgust and fear responses.

Method

Participant

The participant was a 9-year-old Hispanic-American boy. He was part of the Child Anxiety and Phobia Program at Florida International University. The boy and his mother gave informed consent to participate in the assessment and treatment procedures of the programme. Subsequent to the follow-up process, the mother provided written consent for details of the study to be published. From the data presented to the researchers from the boy and mother (via the Anxiety Disorders Interview Schedule for DSM-IV Child and Parent versions), the boy met the DSM-IV criteria for a specific phobia of buttons.

Design and procedure

The therapy

The child was treated with an exposure-based treatment programme that tackled cognitions and behaviour. The treatment used was based on the mother providing positive reinforcement if the boy successfully completed a gradual exposure to buttons. The treatment sessions lasted about 30 minutes with the boy alone and 20 minutes with the boy and the mother. Before the first session the boy devised a disgust and fear hierarchy using a distress rating from 0–8 via a 'feelings thermometer'. Table 12.1 shows details for ratings 2–8. He was to have four sessions of behavioural exposure to the buttons using this hierarchy.

After the behavioural exposure it was planned to have seven sessions looking into the boy's disgust imagery and cognitions with a view to help him to change these over time. The sessions involved him exploring what he found disgusting about buttons alongside the researchers using self-control and cognitive strategies with him to change these thoughts.

Table 12.1 Types of buttons and distress rating scale on the feelings thermometer'

Feelings thermometer rating	Type of button(s)
2	large denim-jean buttons
3	small denim-jean and clip-on denim-jean buttons
4	large plastic buttons – coloured and clear
5	hugging his mother when she wears large plastic buttons and medium, coloured plastic buttons
6	medium, clear plastic buttons
7	hugging his mother when she wears regular medium plastic buttons
8	small plastic buttons – coloured and clear

Results

The phobia began when the boy was five years old. In an art class he ran out of buttons to paste onto a posterboard he was creating. He went to the front of the class to get more buttons from a large bowl on the teacher's desk. His hand slipped and all of the buttons in the bowl fell on him. He said this was very distressing and since then he has avoided buttons. Initially, this avoidance did not present any real difficulties in everyday life but as time progressed it became a problem. Aspects of life such as having difficulty dressing himself, being preoccupied with button thoughts at school affecting his concentration, and not touching his school uniform became more frequent. There was no evidence of any other stressors or events that coincided with his onset of the phobia and he did not meet the criteria for a diagnosis of obsessive–compulsive disorder.

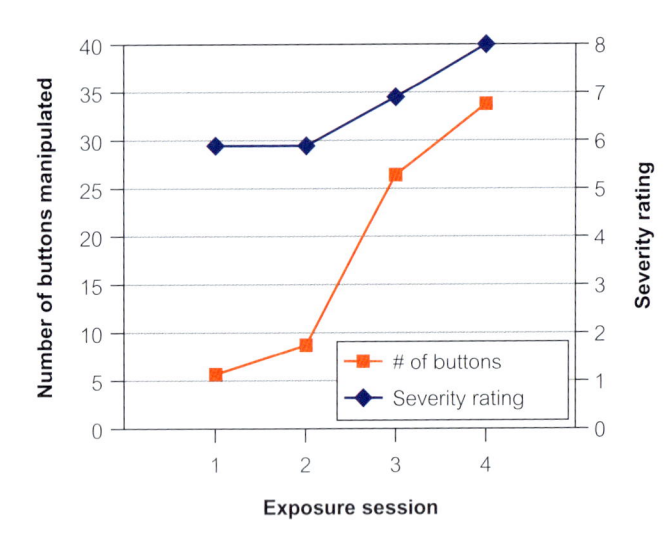

Figure 12.2 Ratings of distress relative to manipulation of buttons in treatment exposure sessions
Source: Saavedra and Silverman (2002: 1378)

By session 4, the boy had successfully completed all in vivo exposure tasks up to those with the highest distress ratings. Even though he could handle more and more buttons, his distress increased dramatically from session 2 to 3 and then from 3 to 4 (see Figure 12.2).

In session 4, the boy's subjective ratings that had been 6 or 7 prior to the treatment were now higher. Even though the behavioural element was progressing, his distress kept increasing.

At the beginning of the seven sessions looking at disgust imagery and cognitions, the boy stated that he found buttons to be disgusting upon contact with his body and that they emitted unpleasant odours. He successfully followed the treatment regime of imagining buttons falling on him, stating how they looked, felt, and smelled, and explaining why. The imagery sessions progressed from using larger to smaller buttons and involved cognitive restructuring. These techniques appeared to help the boy. Two key results are worth noting.

- In a session where he had to imagine hundreds of buttons falling on him, before the cognitive restructuring, he rated the experience as 8 on a 0–8 scale. This rating decreased to a 5 midway through the session and ended up as 3 by the end.

- In a session where he had to imagine hugging his mother who was wearing a shirt with many buttons, the distress ratings went from 7 down to 4 then to 3.

He was followed up 6 and 12 months after treatment and at both times he did not meet the DSM-IV criteria for a specific phobia anymore. Also, he could wear clear plastic buttons on his school uniform shirt.

Test yourself

List three key results from this study.

Conclusion

It would appear that disgust plays a key role in the development and maintenance of a phobia (in this case button phobia) but a mixture of behavioural exposure and, more so, cognitive restructuring helped to eliminate the feelings of disgust, even 12 months after treatment.

Summary

Research method (main)	Case study
Other technique(s)	Interviews, rating scales and observations
Sample	A 9-year-old boy
Sampling technique	Opportunity
Experimental design	–
IV	–
DV	–
Quantitative data	Distress ratings and severity ratings
Qualitative data	Questions about why the boy found buttons disgusting

Evaluation

Evaluation	General evaluation (case study)	Related to Saavedra and Silverman
Strength	When researchers focus on one individual (or unit of individuals) they can collect rich, in-depth data that has details. This makes the findings valid.	The researchers focused on just one person (the boy). He was assessed using DSM-IV. His feelings were assessed throughout the intervention. Therefore, a lot of data was collected to help understand the boy's phobia and how best to treat it, and this added validity to the findings.
Strength	The participant is usually studied as part of his or her everyday life, which means that the whole process tends to have some ecological validity.	It could be argued that the study has some ecological validity as the boy was in therapy and the assessment followed what could happen in a therapeutic setting.
Weakness	Generalisations are difficult when researchers focus on one individual (or unit of individuals) because the case may be unique.	The researchers only studied one individual. He could be a unique case, which would make generalising difficult as he may not represent any other person who has a button phobia.

The 'Use of children' section in 'Issues and debates' below can be used for evaluation purposes. Other evaluation points include the following.

- Ethics – informed consent: this was taken from the boy (who wanted the therapy) and from his mother. This allowed the therapy to happen and the account to be published in a journal.

- The ratings given by the child are subjective and there is no way of knowing whether he was telling the truth about his fears. He may have been giving lower fear and disgust ratings to get out of the therapy rather than there being a true reduction (however, this is probably not the case as he chose to undergo therapy).

Issues and debates

The following table discusses the Saavedra and Silverman study in terms of the core issues and debates for AS Level.

> **Challenge yourself**
>
> Identify two other applications to everyday life this study could have. Explain who would benefit from your applications.

Application to everyday life	The findings of this study showed that the intervention therapy was a success. This means that it could be implemented with other phobic children or even adults. Using exposure-based treatment can help decrease phobias in people so could be used more often.
Individual and situational explanations	The **individual** side of the debate is supported by the boy having a rare phobias of buttons and all of his experiences may be unique to him. The **situational** side of the debate is supported by the therapies helping him recover with the aid of the therapist and his mother giving him positive reinforcement.
Nature versus nurture	The process in which the boy acquired the phobia relates to nurture as it was an experience in the classroom that the boy identified as being the cause of the phobia. It is unlikely that a button phobia has gone through the process of preparedness transmission. (This process involves evolutionary ancestors passing down genetic information to make an individual 'naturally' scared of certain stimuli that are dangerous and this is triggered when the person comes into contact with that stimulus.) The procedure of the therapy was set up so the boy had to unlearn his phobia, therefore also suggesting that the phobia is based around nurture rather than nature.
The use of children	The child was put under distress in order to complete the intervention so psychological harm happened and this goes against ethical guidelines. However, informed consent was taken from both the child and his mother and it would have been made clear that he would have to be exposed to buttons as part of the therapy intervention.
	Children may get bored and tired faster than adults so this needs to be considered when designing tasks in studies. The entire therapy procedure would have been designed to counteract this for the boy so that the sessions were applicable to a child.
The use of animals	Not applicable

13 Milgram (1963)

Background

Most of the time we are told that obedience is a good thing. If your teacher tells you to get your book out or to answer a question, you might not want to do it but you probably accept that the most socially appropriate behaviour is to obey. You probably also accept that your teacher has the right to give you an instruction of this kind. However, what if you were ordered to do something that caused harm or distress to another person? This type of obedience, in which people obey orders to cause harm, is called destructive obedience. Social psychologists such as Milgram have been particularly interested in destructive obedience.

As the member of a European Jewish family that had left Europe for the United States, Milgram was profoundly affected by the atrocities committed by Nazi Germany against Jewish people and other minority groups. One of the key features of the Nazi atrocities was the extent to which people displayed destructive obedience. Many ordinary people obeyed orders that led to the systematic mass murder of minority groups, including Jews, Romanies, Communists, trade unionists, and people with disabilities.

Early psychological research into the Holocaust focused on the idea that something distinctive about German culture or personality led to the high levels of conformity and obedience necessary for genocide to take place. This is known as the dispositional hypothesis. While Milgram was interested in this idea, he was also interested in the social processes that take place between individuals and within groups.

The psychology being investigated

Obedience

This is when we *behave* in a certain way in response to the demand(s) of an authority figure. An example would be following the orders of a person perceived to be in authority.

Social pressure

These are pressures that come from other individuals or groups that have a direct influence on how we feel and/or how we behave.

The idea that we can explain events such as the Holocaust by reference to the social pressures operating in the situation, rather than the characteristics of the individuals involved, is called the situational hypothesis. This is what Milgram was testing.

Subsequent to this study he produced his agency theory. This is when we have two psychological states in certain situations.

- Agentic state: when we give up our free will to serve as an 'agent to authority'.
- Autonomous state: when we act on our own free will and choose whether to, for example, be obedient or not.

Milgram believed that from a young age we are socialised to be obedient to authority figures. He also believed that we experience moral strain. This is when, during the agentic state, we go along with the demands of the authority figure even though we know this is wrong and do not agree with it.

> **Ask yourself**
>
> Why do you think the Holocaust happened? Can you think of any modern-day examples of such an atrocity?

Aim

Overall aim: To investigate how obedient people would be to orders from a person in authority that would result in pain and harm to another person.

Specific aim: To see how large an electric shock a participant would give to a helpless man when ordered to by a scientist in his laboratory.

Method

Participants

A newspaper advertisement was used to recruit 40 men aged 20–50.

Public Announcement

WE WILL PAY YOU $4.00 FOR ONE HOUR OF YOUR TIME

Persons Needed for a Study of Memory

*We will pay five hundred New Haven men to help us complete a scientific study of memory and learning. The study is being done at Yale University.

*Each person who participates will be paid $4.00 (plus 50c carfare) for approximately 1 hour's time. We need you for only one hour: there are no further obligations. Your may choose the time you would like to come (evenings, weekdays, or weekends).

*No special training, education, or experience is needed. We want:

Factory workers	Businessmen	Construction workers
City employees	Clerks	Salespeople
Laborers	Professional People	White-collar workers
Barbers	Telephone workers	Others

All persons must be between the age of 20 and 50. High school and college students cannot be used.

*If you meet these qualifications. Yale University, New Haven. You will be notified later of the specific time and place of the study. We reserve the right to decline and application.

*You will be paid $4.00 (plus 50c carfare) as soon as you arrive at the laboratory.

TO:

PROF. STANLEY MILGRAM, DEPARTMENT OF PSYCHOLOGY, YALE UNIVERSITY, NEW HAVEN, CONN.
I want to take part in this study of memory and learning. I am between the ages of 20 and 50. I will be paid $4.00 (plus 50c carfare) if I participate.

NAME (Please Print)...
ADDRESS..
TELEPHONE NO... Best time to call you...
AGE... OCCUPATION... SEX..................................
CAN YOU COME:
WEEKDAYS.. EVENINGS.................................... WEEKENDS..

Figure 13.1 Advertisement used to recruit participants for Milgram's study
Source: Milgram (1974, 1997, 2005). Obedience to Authority. Pinter & Martin, London

The sample was therefore mostly a volunteer sample. Participants were from a range of backgrounds and held a range of jobs: 37.5% were manual labourers, 40% were white-collar workers and 22.5% were professionals. All were from New Haven, Connecticut, USA. The breakdown of the sample is shown in Table 13.1.

Table 13.1 Distribution of age and occupation types

Occupation	20–29 years	30–39 years	40–50 years	Percentage of total (occupations)
Workers, skilled and unskilled	4	5	6	37.5
Sales, business and white collar	3	6	7	40.0
Professional	1	5	3	22.5
Percentage of total	20	40	40	

Note: Total n = 40
Source: Milgram (1963: 372)

Design

Milgram described his original study as a laboratory experiment but this is not strictly correct. Technically, it might more accurately be called a controlled observation. The results from this condition then served as a baseline for a number of variations in follow-up studies, at least 17 of which happened. Obedience was operationalised as the maximum voltage given.

Procedure

Participants were promised $4.50 for their time and it was made clear that payment was for turning up to the study, and was not conditional on completing the procedure. When each participant arrived at Yale University he was introduced to a man he believed to be another participant (called Mr Wallace; in fact, he was a confederate). The two men were then briefed on the supposed purpose of the experiment, which was described to them as to investigate the effect of punishment on learning. The experimenter was a 31-year-old biology teacher. His manner during the study was to be impassive with a somewhat stern appearance. He wore a grey technician's coat. Mr Wallace was a 47-year-old Irish-American accountant. He had been selected for the role because he was mild-mannered and likeable.

Milgram had devised a 'pre-text' to justify why electric shocks were being used. After a general introduction about punishment and learning, the following standardised text was read to the naïve participant and the confederate.

> But actually, we know very little about the effect of punishment on learning, because almost no truly scientific studies have been made of it in human beings.
>
> For instance, we don't know how much punishment is best for learning – and we don't know how much difference it makes as to who is giving the punishment, whether an adult learns best from a younger or an older person than himself – or many things of that sort.
>
> So in this study we are bringing together a number of adults of different occupations and ages. And we're asking some of them to be teachers and some of them to be learners. We want to find out just what effect different people have on each other as teachers and learners, and what effect punishment will have on learning in this situation.
>
> (Milgram 1963: 373)

The naïve participant and the confederate were told that one of them would play the role of teacher and one the role of the learner. They drew slips of paper from a hat to allocate the roles, but this was rigged: the naïve participant was always the teacher and the confederate was always the learner. They were then immediately taken to another room where the learner (Wallace) was strapped into a chair. It was explained that the strapping was to prevent excessive movement while being shocked. An electrode was attached to Wallace's wrist with a paste to 'avoid blisters and burns'. Both Wallace and the participant were shown the electric shock generator. This had a row of switches, each labelled with a voltage, rising in 15-volt intervals from 15 volts up to 450 volts. They were told that the shocks could be extremely painful but not dangerous and were each given a 45-volt shock to demonstrate.

A wall between the participant and Wallace meant that the participant could hear but not see Wallace. The participant read out word pairs to test Wallace on his recognition of which words went together. Each time Wallace made a mistake, the experimenter ordered the participant to give a shock. The shock got larger by 15 volts for each mistake. Wallace did not receive shocks, but there was no way for the participant to know this. When the participant pressed one of the switches, a bright red light corresponding to it lit up.

An electric buzzing sound was heard as it happened. Then, an electric blue light labelled 'voltage energiser' flashed and a dial representing a voltage meter moved to the right.

Milgram conducted a preliminary run. Prior to this study he had noted that a procedure of reading words and giving a shock required some practice. This involved the participant being given ten words to read to the confederate. Three of these were answered correctly by Wallace; the rest of his answers were incorrect. Therefore, the participant had to administer seven shocks (up to 105 volts). Virtually all participants mastered the procedure during this preliminary run. After this, they began the 'real' trial and were told that if they got to the bottom pairing on the list they were to start the list again.

At certain voltage levels, Wallace would give a pre-determined set of responses based on the ratio of three wrong answers to one correct one. In this study, there was no vocal response at all from Wallace until the shock had reached 300 volts. At this point he would pound on the wall, which could be clearly heard by the participant. From this point on, every time the participant read out the word, no answer would appear on the four-way panel. When this happened, the experimenter instructed the participant that an absence of response was to be treated as an incorrect answer and a shock should be administered. The participant was told to allow a five- to ten-second response time. If no answer was given during that time, the participant should count this as an incorrect response. Wallace repeatedly pounded the wall when the 315-volt button was pressed. However, after this voltage, he never responded to a word list, nor was he ever heard from again.

At any point, the participant could have protested and turned to the experimenter for advice on whether he should continue giving the shocks, or simply refuse to continue. Therefore, the researcher created a series of standardised prods for the experimenter to say in an attempt to force the participant to continue. These were as follows.

- Prod 1 – experimenter says "Please continue" or "Please go on."
- Prod 2 – experimenter says "The experiment requires that you continue."
- Prod 3 – experimenter says "It is absolutely essential that you continue."
- Prod 4 – experimenter says "You have no other choice, you must go on."

The prods were always used in sequence listed. If the participant refused to continue after prod 4, the experiment was terminated. The experimenter would always read the prod out in a firm but not impolite manner. Each time a participant tried to stop, the sequence was started again. There were two special prods as follows.

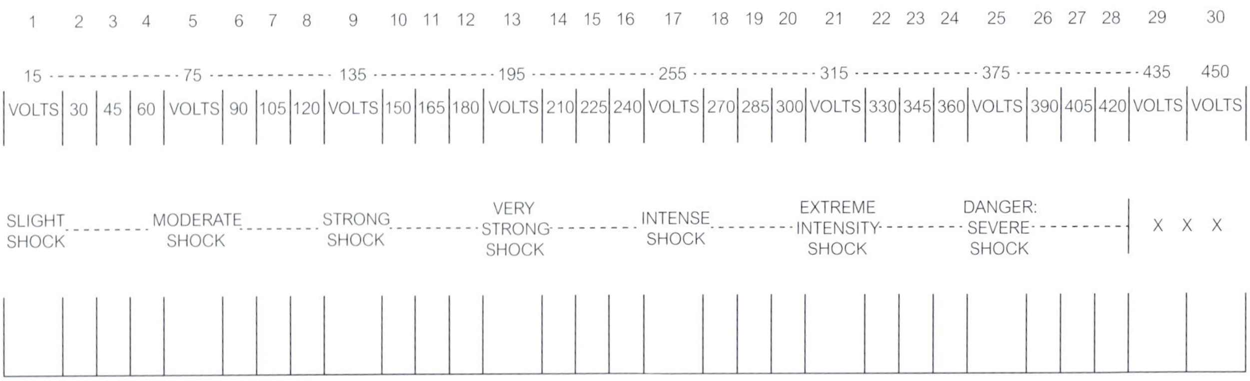

Figure 13.2 Diagram of the control panel used in the experiment.
Source: Milgram (1974, 1997, 2005). Obedience to Authority. Pinter & Martin, London

- If the participant asked whether the shocks could cause permanent injury the response was: "Although the shocks may be painful, there is no permanent tissue damage, so please go on." Then the usual prods were used if necessary.

- If the participant stated that he felt the confederate did not want to continue the response was: "Whether the learner likes it or not, you must go on until he has learned all the word pairs correctly. So please go on." Then the usual prods were used if necessary.

Each participant was considered to have completed the procedure either when he refused to give any more shocks (called a defiant participant), or when he reached the maximum voltage on the shock machine (called an obedient participant). Most of the trials were recorded and some photographs were taken through a one-way mirror. Notes were taken if any unusual behaviour was seen, and another observer took objective notes of any behaviours shown. The latency and duration of shocks was also measured. Participants were then interviewed and de-hoaxed. During their interview they were asked to rate on a scale of 0–14 how painful the last few shocks they gave were, then asked open-ended questions and given projective tests (designed to reveal hidden emotions and internal conflicts). They were told that the shocks were not real, that Wallace was unharmed, and that the real purpose of the study was to investigate obedience. It was the intention that each participant would leave the laboratory in a state of wellbeing.

> **Test yourself**
>
> Try to get the procedure down to eight 'vital parts' that are essential for you to understand what the participants had to do.

Results

Preliminary notions

Before Milgram conducted this study he asked 14 Yale University seniors (all psychology majors) to read a detailed description of what the study entailed. They were asked to plot a distribution of obedience for '100 Americans of diverse occupation, and ranging in age from 20 to 50 years' (Milgram, 1963: 375). All of them stated that 0–3% of a sample would give the 450-volt shock. The mean was 1.2%. Informally, Milgram also asked colleagues how high a shock they thought participants would give to a learner. The general consensus was that very few subjects would go beyond a 'very strong shock' on the generator.

Participants accept situation

Virtually all of the participants appeared convinced that they were administering shocks to Wallace. One of the questions asked post-experiment was: "How painful to the learner were the last few shocks that you administered to him?" (Milgram 1963: 375). They had to respond on a 14-point scale ranging from 1 = not at all painful to 14 = extremely painful. The modal score was 14 with the mean being 13.42.

Signs of extreme tension

Many of the participants exhibited signs of nervousness, especially when giving the larger shocks. Qualitative data was gathered in the form of the comments and protests participants made during the procedure, and in the form of observations of their body language. Most participants showed signs of tension during the procedure. Signs included groaning, sweating, biting lips, and stuttering. Fourteen giggled nervously. Three had seizures and for one of these the procedure was stopped. One observer commented (quoted in Milgram 1963: 377):

> "I observed a mature and initially poised business man enter the laboratory smiling and confident. Within 20 minutes he was reduced to a twitching, stuttering wreck, who was rapidly approaching the point of nervous collapse."

When interviewed after the experiment, participants who had giggled went to great lengths to explain that they were not sadistic and that the laughter did not indicate that they enjoyed shocking the victim.

Distribution of obedience scores

Table 13.2 shows the levels of shock as described on the generator and the number of participants who administered each level as their maximum shock.

Table 13.2 Shock levels administered by participants

Voltage	Verbal description on the shock generator	Number of participants who gave this as their maximum shock
0–285	Slight shock, Moderate shock, Strong shock, Very Strong shock, Intense shock	0 at every voltage level
300	Intense shock	5
315	Extreme intensity shock	4
330	Extreme intensity shock	2
345	Extreme intensity shock	1
360	Extreme intensity shock	1
375	Extreme intensity shock	1
390	Danger: Severe shock	0
405	Danger: Severe shock	0
420	Danger: Severe shock	0
435	Danger: Severe shock	0
450	Danger: Severe shock	26

No participant stopped before shock level 20 (300 volts). Remember that at 300 volts, Wallace would pound on the wall and then never answer again. A total of 14 participants were classed as defiant (35% of the sample) and 26 as obedient (65% of the sample). An example of the behaviour shown by a defiant participant is shown in this quote:

> "I think he's trying to communicate, he's knocking ... Well, it's not fair to shock the guy ... these are terrific volts. I don't think this is very humane ... Oh I can't go on with this; no, this isn't right. It's a hell of an experiment. The guy is suffering in there. No, I don't want to go on. This is crazy."
>
> (Milgram 1963: 375–376)

Even when under extreme stress, many of the participants continued to give Wallace shocks. Some did express a reluctance to do so (especially beyond the 300-volt level) and showed similar behaviours to those who defied; yet they continued. There were mixed behaviours shown by those reaching the 450-volt level: some mopped their brows, others went straight for a cigarette, yet others remained calm throughout the whole procedure.

Test yourself

How generalisable are the results? How easy would it be to replicate this study? Why?

Conclusion

Milgram drew these main conclusions from this study.

- People are much more obedient to destructive orders than we might expect, and in this case considerably more than psychology students suggested in their estimates. In fact, the majority of people are quite willing to obey destructive orders.
- People find the experience of receiving and obeying destructive orders highly stressful. They obey in spite of their emotional responses. The situation triggers a conflict between two deeply ingrained tendencies – to obey those in authority, and not to harm people.

Results supported the situational hypothesis rather than the dispositional (individual) hypothesis.

Summary

Research method (main)	–
Other technique(s)	Controlled observations, interviews and questionnaires
Sample	40 men
Sampling technique	Volunteer
Experimental design	–
IV	Not applicable
DV	The percentage of participants who went to each voltage level was the key outcome measure, rather than a DV.
Quantitative data	As above
Qualitative data	Noted behaviours and quotes from participants

Evaluation

Evaluation	General evaluation (laboratory experiments)	Related to Milgram
Strength	Laboratory experiments have high levels of standardisation and so can be replicated to test for reliability.	This study had a standardised procedure including the drawing of lots to be teacher or learner, the timing of when scripted responses were heard and stating that the shocks were going up in 15-volt increments. Therefore, other researchers could replicate this study to test it for reliability. Ethical guidelines may now stop this, but a study by Slater did replicate it.
Strength	As laboratory experiments have high levels of control, researchers can be more confident it is the IV directly affecting the DV.	As there were so many controls (eg having a 'test' shock, receiving the prods at a certain time in the same order and the shock generator being the same for everyone), the researcher could conclude with confidence that it was the situation that the participants were placed in that caused the obedience levels.
Weakness	As laboratory experiments take place in an artificial setting, it is said that they can lack ecological validity.	Sitting in a laboratory in front of a shock generator is not an everyday setting that people find themselves in. Therefore, in, so the study lacks ecological validity.
Weakness	In many laboratory experiments participants take part in tasks that are nothing like real-life ones, so the tasks lack mundane realism.	Having to give an electric shock to somebody who gets a word-pair wrong is not a task that people come across in everyday life. Therefore, the study is low in mundane realism.

The study can also be evaluated in terms of ethics. However, always take into consideration that strict ethical guidelines only came into place in 1973, so we are retrospectively criticising this study. Also, Milgram's preliminary notion findings did not predict what actually happened in the study.

General evaluation (ethics)	Related to Milgram
Deception	Participants thought that they were giving Wallace a real electric shock each time. Also, they were told that it was a study about memory and not obedience.
Debriefing	At the end of the study all was revealed to participants so they left knowing that they had not harmed Wallace. They were also followed up six months later to check whether they were having any psychological issues.
Right to withdraw	The prods given by the experimenter made it difficult for participants to withdraw from the study – they kept being convinced to continue even though some wanted to leave.

Other points that can be used to evaluate the study include the following.

- Usefulness: the study did highlight that the situation may make people behave in the way that they do rather than it being individual (dispositional). This is useful as Milgram was attempting to see (in relation to the atrocities committed during the Holocaust) whether 'Germans were different' and he did not find this. All of this could begin to help explain other atrocities so we can then find ways to stop them happening.

Challenge yourself

Identify two other applications to everyday life this study could have. Explain who would benefit from these applications.

Issues and debates

The following table discusses the Milgram study in terms of the core issues and debates for AS Level.

Application to everyday life	The findings of this study have been used extensively to explain why humans engage in destructive obedience. For example, ordinary people who became part of the Nazi movement in the 1930s followed out destructive orders in the Second World War from higher authority figures. Genocide, as was seen in Rwanda and the former Yugoslavia, can also be explained by the findings of this study: people will follow the orders of authority figures when placed in certain morally straining situations.
Individual and situational explanations	The **situation** that the participants found themselves in could explain the obedience rates shown. For example, it was a prestigious university, and there was always a man in a technician's coat standing behind participants. The sample was taken from the local community from a wide range of occupations, to make sure that **individual** factors would not play a role in obedience levels. The **individual** side is supported as not all participants went to 450 volts so there may have been a type of personality trait that made some of them stop at 300 volts. The **situational** side is supported by the prods given by the experimenter to try to make the participants continue to give higher voltage shocks.
Nature versus nurture	There is some evidence for **nurture** as Milgram argued that people are socialised to be obedient, based on life experiences. Therefore, they obeyed the experimenter as it was expected of them due to this socialisation.
The use of children	Not applicable
The use of animals	Not applicable

14 Perry et al (2015)

Background

Humans use interpersonal distance (personal space) to regulate social interactions in any situation. Hall (1963) introduced the idea of *spatial zones* that dictate what activities and relationships happen within them but also what input our senses have to process. Table 14.1 shows these spatial zones.

Table 14.1 The four types of spatial zones by distance

Distance	Unusual activities and relationships	Input to the senses
Intimate (0.0–1.5 feet [0.0–0.45 metres])	Contact is intimate (eg comforting another or having sex). Physical sports such as judo and wrestling allow invasion of the intimate zone.	Touch is the basic mode for communication. We are intensely aware of other sensory information, such as smell and heat emitted from another person.
Personal (1.5–4.0 feet [0.45–1.2] m)	Friends are allowed to get within this zone, especially those who are close to us. Your usual everyday interactions will trespass into this zone too.	Speech is the key source of sensory input from others (more so than touch). However, research has shown vision to be a key source of sensory input too.
Social (4.0–12.0 feet [1.2–3.66] m)	People we do not really know personally, but whom we meet quite regularly, are allowed in this zone. Business-like contacts are also allowed to enter this zone.	Sensory input from other people is now rather minimal. Vision is less crisp, speech is still easily processed but touch is now impossible.
Public (more than 12 feet [3.66 metres] away)	This is for formal contact (eg for someone giving a public speech).	Sensory input is usually only from speech. Non-verbal communication takes over as a main source of information.

Interpersonal distance (personal space) can be affected by culture, social experiences, personality traits, and individual differences. Aspects such as social anxiety or being forced to be further away than usual (seen during the Covid-19 pandemic with social [physical] distancing) affect our interpersonal distance (personal space) experiences too and this can affect friendships and intimate relationships that people have.

An area of the brain called the amygdala appears to play a role in interpersonal distance (personal space) in humans. People who have lesions in part of their amygdala show quite a dramatic reduction in the need for interpersonal distance (personal space) compared to pre-lesion. Interestingly, part of the amygdala is regulated by oxytocin, a type of social hormone. Oxytocin appears to play a large role in social behaviour and social cognition in humans. Some research has shown it to promote pro-social behaviour and also approach behaviours. However, for the latter, this can be affected by social cues linked to context and individual experiences. This was shown by Scheele *et al* (2012) who reported that the administration of oxytocin increased the preferred interpersonal distance (personal space) between a participant and an attractive woman. However, this effect was only seen in male, monogamous participants when a female experimenter was present and not a male experimenter! The oxytocin had no effect on male participants who were single.

This led to the idea of a social salience hypothesis. Perry *et al* (2015) describe this as: '… if oxytocin increases attention to social cues, it should have widely varying effects on downstream cognition and behaviour, depending on the interpersonal context (such as in the presence of an attractive woman for men in a relationship), as well as on how an individual perceives social situations and tends to react in different interpersonal settings. For example, one person may find a social setting comforting and enjoyable, whereas another may find it intimidating or threatening. Social saliency may therefore have opposite consequences for different individuals' (2015: 4).

Finally, empathy can affect how we process social cues, which in turn can affect our interpersonal distance (personal space) experiences. Therefore, our level of empathy may 'cloud' the effects of oxytocin on interpersonal distance (personal space).

This study attempted to control for empathy to see if oxytocin did affect interpersonal distance (personal space) in humans.

Psychology being investigated

Interpersonal distance (personal space)

As far back as 1937, psychologists were discussing personal space. Bell *et al* (1996) defines it as '… a portable, invisible boundary surrounding us, into which others may not trespass. It regulates how closely we interact with others, moves with us, and expands and contracts according to the situation in which we find ourselves' (1996: 275). Therefore, it is like a bubble that surrounds us and changes depending on the people around us and the situations we find ourselves in.

Social hormones

Social hormones are ones that help in the regulation and perception of social interactions in humans and other mammals. They appear to help in the positive feelings of social interactions between humans and coordinate the cause and effect of these interactions. One such hormone is oxytocin – see the 'Background' section for a fuller description of its role in social interaction.

Empathy

This refers to the ability to share someone else's emotional state by imagining what it would be like to be in that situation. You may never have directly experienced the situation for yourself, but you are able to understand what the feelings could be like. It refers to us being able to understand the feelings of others. We can do this by trying to adopt the perspective of the other person, imagine what it feels like for them, or feel some level of distress or concern for them.

> **Ask yourself**
>
> Is there a distance where you feel comfortable or uncomfortable when you are next to someone or when someone approaches you? Are there different scenarios where this distance changes? If so, why?

Aim

To investigate whether oxytocin affects interpersonal distance (personal space) in people who are seen as having stronger empathic skills.

Method

Participants

A total of 54 male participants formed the sample. All of them were undergraduate students at the University of Haifa, Israel. The age range was 19 to 32 years (mean 25.29; sd 2.74). Five of the participants were left-handed. All of the participants had normal or corrected-to-normal vision. None of them reported a history of neurological or psychiatric disorder. This information was obtained via an interview with each participant. Either course credit or a payment was given to all participants. Written consent was gained from the participants and the study had ethical approval from the Hadassah Medical Center and the University of Haifa.

As the study was trying to control the potential effects of empathy, the research team wanted a high empathy group and low empathy group *before* the main study. They achieved this by asking the participants to complete the Interpersonal Reactivity Index (IRI). After this, participants who were half a standard deviation above the mean formed the high empathy group and those who were half a standard deviation below the mean formed the low empathy group. Table 14.2 shows the features of the two groups.

Table 14.2 The features of the two groups of participants

Group	IRI score	n	Mean age in years (sd)
High	≥40	20	23.9 (2.5)
Low	≤33	20	25.9 (3.0)

Design

Administration of oxytocin

Participants attended the study twice, one week apart, on the same day and at the same time. They signed an informed consent form. They were then randomly assigned to either the oxytocin condition or the placebo (saline solution) condition. The conditions were counterbalanced across time points. The participant applied three drops of either solution into each nostril. This part of the procedure was double-blind so neither the participant nor the experimenter knew which condition the participant was in. Participants were observed for any type of side effect before proceeding. No instances of side effects were reported.

Empathy assessment

If no side effects were seen from the administration of oxytocin or saline, each participant then completed an online version of the IRI. This is a 28-item questionnaire measuring four components of empathy: fantasy, perspective-taking, empathic-concern, and personal distress. An example for each component is shown in Figure 14.1.

Fantasy:

16. I sometimes try to understand my friends better by imagining how things look from their perspective.

1	2	3	4
Does not describe me well			Describes me well

Perspective-taking:

28. I often have tender, concerned feelings for people less fortunate than me.

1	2	3	4
Does not describe me well			Describes me well

Empathic concern:

20. Occasionally I am not very sympathetic to my friends when they are depressed.

1	2	3	4
Does not describe me well			Describes me well

Personal distress:

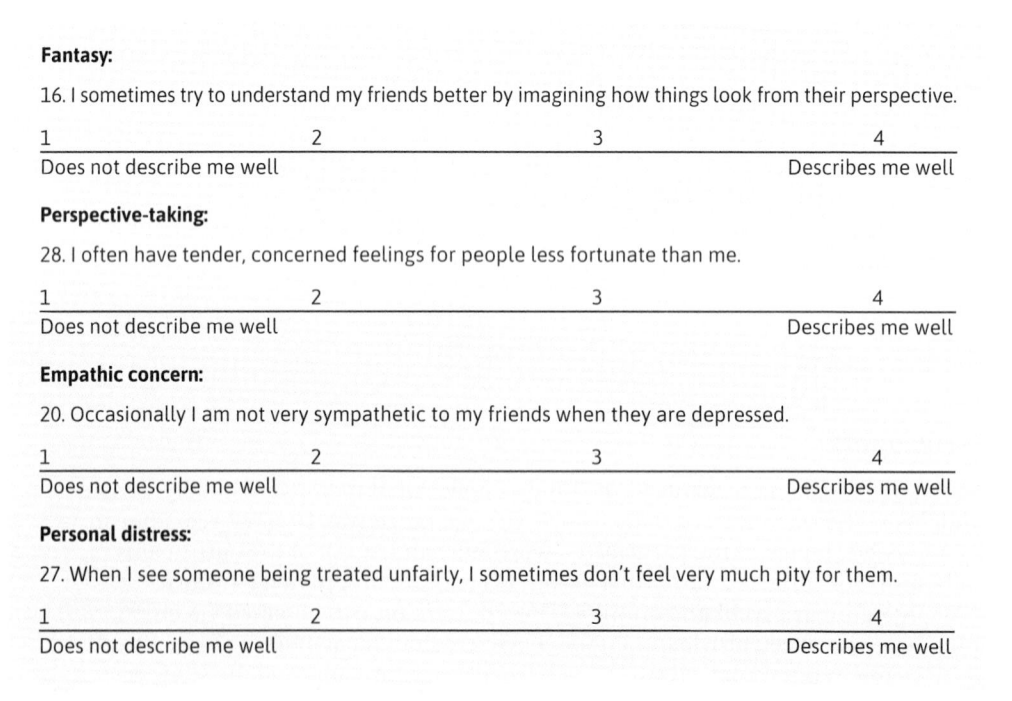

27. When I see someone being treated unfairly, I sometimes don't feel very much pity for them.

1	2	3	4
Does not describe me well			Describes me well

Figure 14.1 Some of the items used to assess empathy
Source: Davis et al (1980)

After the participants had completed the IRI they were asked to wait 45 minutes. This was to allow oxytocin to reach a plateau level in the central nervous system of those in the oxytocin condition. During this time, the participants were put in a quiet room with magazines to read, to limit social interactions. Once the 45 minutes had elapsed, each participant began one of the experiments. The order of these experiments was counterbalanced.

Experiment 1: Using the Comfortable Interpersonal Distance (CID) scale

This was a computerised, modified version of the original CID, which was a pencil-and-paper way of measuring interpersonal distance (personal space). The procedure was as follows.

1. The participant was shown the name of the approaching figure for one second. This was either a stranger, a friend, an authority figure, or a rolling ball.

2. Then, a fixation point appeared for 0.5 seconds.

3. A still picture of a circular room was shown with a figure in the centre. A figure was shown approaching the centre from one of eight entrances. This was shown for one second.

4. The participant had already been told to imagine himself being the figure in the centre. He was told to press the spacebar to indicate when he would like the figure to stop approaching him.

5. The animation of the figure approaching the participant lasted for a maximum of three seconds. The animation either stopped at this point (as both figures had collided) or when the participant had pressed the spacebar.

6. Each of the four figures appeared at each of the eight entrances on three different occasions during the experiment. This meant each figure had 24 trials.

The responses from each participant were calculated as a percentage of the distance remaining between the centre figure and the approaching figure. Therefore, a 0% score would be the two figures colliding and 100% would mean the participant pressed the spacebar immediately.

Experiment 2: Choosing rooms

All participants were told that they would be asked to sit in a room with another participant to discuss some personal topics with them. They were told that they would be shown two pictures of rooms that looked very similar, but they had to choose which one they would like to use for the discussion. In addition to this, participants were told that a computer program would calculate an average room based on all of their choices that would be set up in reality two weeks after the experiment for the 'discussion part' of the study. However, in reality this discussion never happened and after two weeks all participants were told about the real purpose of experiment 2.

The pictures were colour and depicted two very similar rooms to choose from. Each room always had two chairs, a table to one side of the room, a plant on the other side of the room, a closet, a lamp, and a clock. A pair of pictures differed on one of the following:

- the distance between the chairs (ranged from 20 cm to 140 cm in 20 cm intervals)

- the distance between the chair and the plant (200 cm to 320 cm in 20 cm intervals)

- the angle that the chairs faced each other (0° [both facing forward], 45° or 90° [directly facing each other])

- the angle of the table to the plant (0°, 45° or 90°).

Each of the distances was compared with every other possible distance. The three remaining variables (the other 'distance' measure and the two angles) were always the same in both pictures but chosen randomly. This meant that 84 pairs of pictures were shown to each participant. This was done twice, so each participant chose from 168 pairs. Figure 14.2 shows examples of the pairs of rooms.

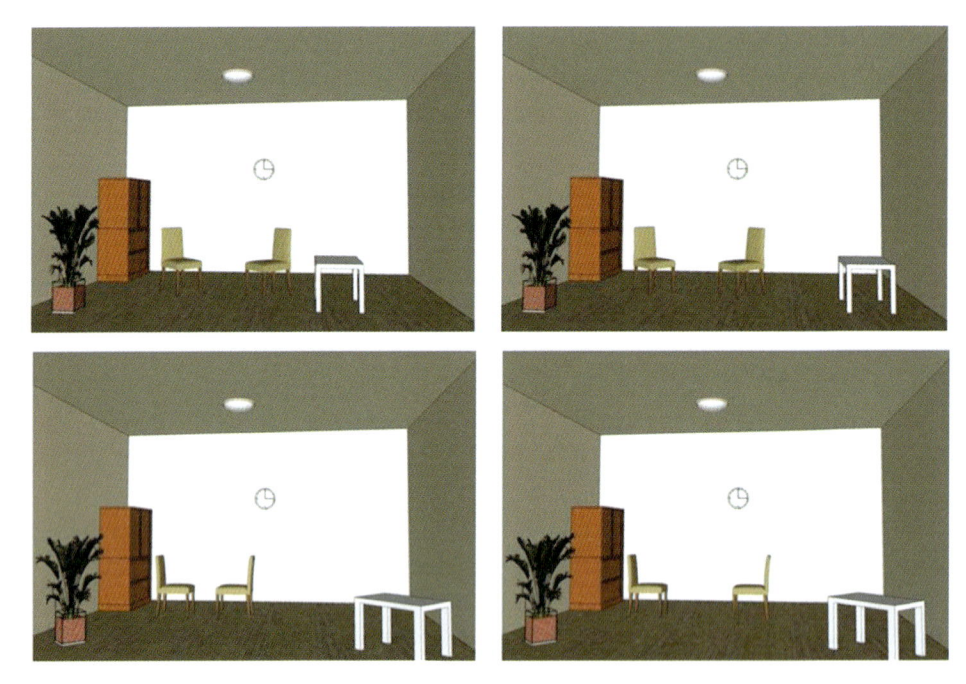

Figure 14.2 *Examples of the stimuli used in the choosing rooms experiment. The top two pictures depict rooms that differ only in the distance between the table and the plant, whereas the bottom two pictures depict rooms that differ only in the distance between the chairs. Simulated distances in top pictures: chairs at 60 cm distance at 45° each; table and plant at 260 cm distance (left) and 320 distance (right), at 90° each. Bottom pictures: chairs at 40 cm distance (left) and 100 cm distance (right), at 90° each; table and plant at 320 cm distance and an angle of 45° each.*

The procedure for each trial was as follows.

1. A fixation point appeared on the screen for 0.5 seconds.
2. Two rooms were then shown on screen (using the combinations described earlier) for two seconds.
3. The participant then was asked to choose the left or right picture as a preference.

For each participant an average preference was calculated for:

- preferred distance between the two chairs
- preferred distance between the table and the plant
- preferred angle for each furniture pairing.

Predictions

Experiment 1: those in the high empathy group would choose closer distances in the oxytocin condition compared to the low empathy group. Also, when in the oxytocin condition, participants will choose closer distances with people they know (a friend, an authority figure) compared to a stranger or a ball.

Experiment 2: the preferred distances and preferred angles would be affected by both oxytocin and empathic level of the participant (high empathy versus low empathy).

> **Test yourself**
>
> Write out all of the different steps of the procedure for experiment 1 and experiment 2. Have each on a separate index card. Shuffle *all* of the cards then place them in the correct order for both experiments.

Results

Experiment 1: using the Comfortable Interpersonal Distance (CID) measure

Table 14.3 shows the mean percentage distance remaining by treatment condition (oxytocin versus placebo) and condition (four approaching figures).

Table 14.3 The mean percentage distance remaining by treatment condition

	High empathy placebo	High empathy oxytocin	Low empathy placebo	Low empathy oxytocin	Overall
Friend	11.028	8.486	14.000	16.318	12.460
Ball	20.956	14.418	18.630	26.806	20.200
Authority	33.920	30.554	35.178	36.826	34.120
Stranger	38.552	39.734	40.136	40.836	39.820

Note: Numbers are mean percentage distance. The smaller the score, the less distance between the two figures was chosen.

Using the overall figures in Table 14.3, each pairing was significantly different to the rest except for friend versus ball. The interaction of empathy and treatment did not reach significance, but it did follow the trend of high empathy plus oxytocin decreased the mean distance between self and other compared to placebo, whereas low empathy plus oxytocin increased the mean preferred distance compared to placebo. Figure 14.3 shows this.

There was a significant three-way interaction between treatment, condition, and empathy. When analysed further, a main significant result only happened with the high empathy group. Table 14.4 shows these significant differences within the high empathy group.

> **Challenge yourself**
>
> Plot the data from Table 14.3 as a bar chart.

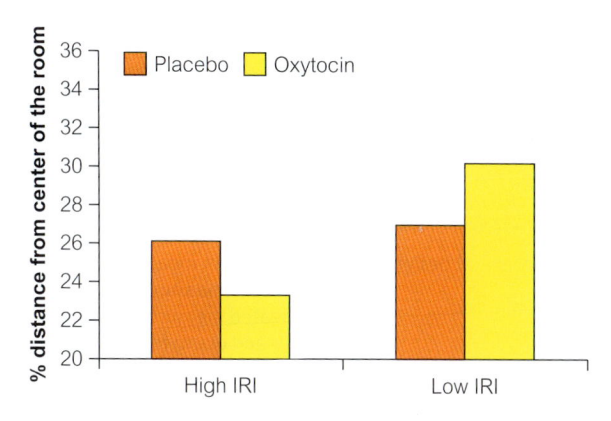

Figure 14.3 Results of the CID experiment: the interaction between high and low IRL groups and treatment is close to significant. Although OT decreased the mean distance from self to other in the high empathy group, it had an opposite effect in the low empathy group, increasing the preferred distance between self and other.

Table 14.4 The significant differences within the high empathy group

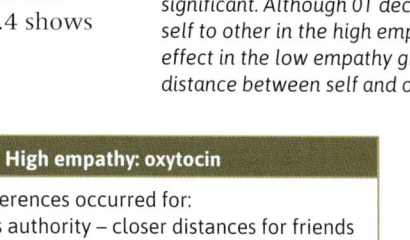

High empathy: placebo	High empathy: oxytocin
Significant differences occurred for: • friend versus authority – closer distances for friends • friend versus stranger – closer distances for friends	Significant differences occurred for: • friend versus authority – closer distances for friends • friend versus stranger – closer distances for friends • ball versus stranger – closer distances for the ball • ball versus authority – closer distances for the ball

Experiment 2: choosing rooms

A significant result was reported for chair distances. Participants in the high empathy group chose significantly closer chair distances with oxytocin compared to those in the low empathy group with oxytocin. No other comparisons reached statistical significance. However, within the high empathy group, there was a trend towards oxytocin decreasing interpersonal distance (personal space) compared to a placebo. Figure 14.4 shows the average preferred chair distance by treatment and empathy.

To show that both experiments were testing the same effect, there was a moderate positive correlation found between average distance in the placebo treatments in experiment 1 and the average chair distance chosen in placebo treatments in experiment 2.

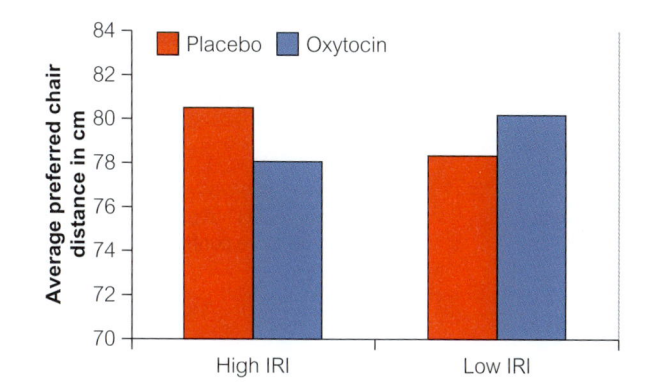

Figure 14.4 Results of choosing rooms experiment: a significant interaction was found between the high and low empathy groups and treatment. Although OT decreased the mean distance between chairs in the high empathy group, it had no significant effect in the low empathy group.

Conclusion

Perry *et al* concluded that: '… the enhancement of social cues following oxytocin administration may have opposite effects on individuals with different empathic abilities' (2015: 3). That is, people with high empathic abilities tend to have smaller zones of interpersonal distance (personal space), particularly when oxytocin levels are elevated. In addition, people with low empathic abilities tend to have larger zones of interpersonal distance (personal space) especially when oxytocin levels are elevated. Overall, there appears to be some support for the social salience hypothesis.

Summary

Research method (main)	Laboratory experiment
Other technique(s)	Self-report
Sample	54 male participants but only 40 used in main experiments split equally into high empathy and low empathy groups
Sampling technique	–
Experimental design	Independent measures (empathy group: high or low) for both experiments Repeated measures (treatment: oxytocin and placebo; condition: friend, ball, authority, or stranger) for experiment 1 Repeated measures (treatment: oxytocin and placebo; condition: preferred distance between two chairs and between chair and plant) for experiment 2
IV	Empathy (high or low) Treatment (oxytocin or placebo) For experiment 1 condition (friend, ball, authority, or stranger) For experiment 2 condition (distance between chairs; distance between chair and plant; angles of chairs; angle of table to plant)
DV	Experiment 1: preferred distance chosen when figure approached; measured as the percentage distance remaining between the two figures Experiment 2: preferred choice of one picture from two picture choices; chair distance in cm; chair to plant distance in cm
Quantitative data	As above
Qualitative data	–

Evaluation

Evaluation	General evaluation	Related to Perry *et al*
Strength	Experiments have high levels of standardisation and so can be replicated to test for reliability.	Perry *et al* had a standardised procedure including the forced-choice pictures of rooms in experiment 2 and the amount of time allowed to stop the figure approaching in experiment 1 (three seconds). This means another researcher could easily replicate this study to test for reliability.
Strength	Experiments have high levels of control so researchers can be more confident it is the IV directly affecting the DV.	As there were many controls, including splitting the sample into high and low empathy groups and ensuring that all participants experienced placebo and oxytocin, Perry *et al* could be confident that it was the combination of empathy and oxytocin that was affecting interpersonal distance (personal space).
Weakness	With questionnaires, participants may give socially desirable answers as they want to look good rather than giving truthful answers – this lowers the validity of findings.	The completion of the IRI before and during the study might have made some participants rate differently based on wanting to look good (and in this case, being more empathic) rather than it being a valid reflection of the participants' themselves.
Weakness	If the questionnaire has a lot of closed questions, then participants might be forced into choosing an answer that does not reflect their true opinion.	The 4-point scale used on the IRI may not have a choice that truly reflected a participant's feelings towards one or more of the statements. This could lower validity of findings.

Other evaluation points include the following.

- Sample: the sample consisted of only male students. This could make generalisability difficult especially to populations not represented in the sample (eg females). Females are known to be more naturally empathic, in general, than males so there is no way we can conclude that oxytocin affects interpersonal distance (personal space) in highly empathic females. They could react differently from males.

- Quantitative data: this allows direct comparisons to be easier across conditions. Therefore, the percentage distance remaining can be averaged across the four treatments (high empathy – oxytocin; high empathy – placebo; low empathy – oxytocin; low empathy – placebo) and compared objectively to see how each is affected by condition in experiment 1 (friend, stranger, etc).

- Ethics: participants gave written and informed consent and when the two-week personal discussion did not happen, the purpose of the study to see how empathy and oxytocin affects interpersonal distance (personal space) was revealed, which is a form of debriefing. However, measurement of invasion of interpersonal distance (personal space) can be psychologically stressful even on a screen as the participants had to imagine the invasion and we do not know what they were actually thinking. Also, the two-week period between ending experiment 2 and knowing you are going to have a personal discussion with someone could also be psychologically stressful.

> **Challenge yourself**
>
> Think of two other real-life applications based on the study by Perry et al. Make sure that you write about what the application is and how it will be achieved.

Issues and debates

The following table discusses Perry et al in terms of the core issues and debates for AS Level.

Application to everyday life	The results might be useful in the recruitment of people whose jobs involve being close to other people so they would not mind having their interpersonal distance (personal space) invaded. Screening could happen beforehand to see which applicants are the most empathic and used as part of the selection process. In addition, people who are highly empathic can be encouraged to eat foods that promote the production of oxytocin (eg avocados or mushrooms) so they feel even less stressed having their interpersonal distance (personal space) invaded as part of the job.
Individual and situational explanations	Both sides of the argument can be seen in this study. In terms of **individual**, the participants were placed into two groups: high empathy and low empathy, which can be considered a personality trait or part of a behavioural repertoire that is individually based and even affected by hormones (which have different levels in different people). In terms of **situational**, the process of having to choose when to stop one of the figures in experiment 1 or choosing a favourite room layout in experiment 2 is driven by being able to understand the situation that is being presented. The differing figure situations presented in experiment 1 did cause differences in the amount of interpersonal distance (personal space) people wanted. The situation was also causing some of the differences seen between participants.
Nature versus nurture	Some people may argue that **nature** is being supported here to an extent as oxytocin is biological (a hormone) that is natural in every human with an intact pituitary gland. However, some people may argue that the study supports **nurture** as the people were basing their stop judgements in experiment 1 and their favoured room layout in experiment 2 on experiences they have had rather than because of a hormone or being empathic.
The use of children	Not applicable
The use of animals	Not applicable

15 Piliavin et al (1969)

Background

This study is concerned with bystander behaviour. Bystanders are people who witness events and have to choose whether to intervene or not. There has been a lot of debate over 'have-a-go heroes' who put themselves at risk to intervene and attempt to stop crimes taking place. Most of the time bystanders can help without putting themselves at risk. However, surprisingly often we do not choose to act to help people in need.

The Kitty Genovese murder

Psychological research into bystander behaviour was triggered by a murder that took place in New York in 1964. Read the excerpts from the *New York Times* article describing the incident.

---

37 Who Saw Murder Didn't Call the Police; Apathy at Stabbing of Queens Woman Shocks Inspector

by Martin Gansberg

For more than half an hour 38 respectable, law-abiding citizens in Queens watched a killer stalk and stab a woman in three separate attacks in Kew Gardens. Twice the sound of their voices and the sudden glow of their bedroom lights interrupted him and frightened him off. Each time he returned, sought her out and stabbed her again. Not one person telephoned the police during the assault; one witness called after the woman was dead.

That was two weeks ago today. But Assistant Chief Inspector Frederick M. Lussen, in charge of the borough's detectives and a veteran of 25 years of homicide investigations, is still shocked. He can give a matter-of-fact recitation of many murders. But the Kew Gardens slaying baffles him – not because it is a murder, but because the "good people" failed to call the police.

This is what the police say happened beginning at 3:20 A.M. in the staid, middle-class, tree-lined Austin Street area: Twenty-eight-year-old Catherine Genovese, who was called Kitty by almost everyone in the neighborhood, was returning home from her job as manager of a bar in Hollis. She parked her red Fiat in a lot adjacent to the Kew Gardens Long Island Railroad Station, facing Mowbray Place.

Miss Genovese noticed a man at the far end of the lot, near a seven-story apartment house at 82–40 Austin Street. She halted. Then, nervously, she headed up Austin Street toward Lefferts Boulevard, where there is a call box to the 102nd Police Precinct in nearby Richmond Hill. She got as far as a street light in front of a bookstore before the man grabbed her. She screamed. Lights went on in the 10-story apartment house at 82–67 Austin Street, which faces the bookstore. Windows slid open and voices punctuated the early-morning stillness.

Miss Genovese screamed: "Oh, my God, he stabbed me! Please help me! Please help me!" From one of the upper windows in the apartment house, a man called down: 'Let that girl alone!' The assailant looked up at him, shrugged and walked down Austin Street toward a white sedan parked a short distance away. Miss Genovese struggled to her feet. Lights went out. The killer returned to Miss Genovese, now trying to make her way around the side of the building by the parking lot to get to her apartment. The assailant stabbed her again. "I'm dying!" she shrieked. "I'm dying!"

Windows were opened again, and lights went on in many apartments. The assailant got into his car and drove away. Miss Genovese staggered to her feet. A city bus, Q-10, the Lefferts Boulevard line to Kennedy International Airport, passed. It was 3:35 A.M. The assailant returned. By then, Miss Genovese had crawled to the back of the building, where the freshly painted brown doors to the apartment house held out hope for safety. The killer tried the first door; she wasn't there. At the second door, 82–62 Austin Street, he saw her slumped on the floor at the foot of the stairs. He stabbed her a third time—fatally.

Source: *New York Times*, 27 March 1964

Some of the details of the story as it was reported at the time have since been challenged. Given the layout of the block, it would not have been possible for anyone to have seen the whole incident, so each person would have seen just fragments of the event. Also, the area was not actually as quiet as the article implies – one neighbour said that rows between couples leaving a local bar were common late at night. Given these facts, we cannot be sure that 37 people really saw, correctly interpreted, and chose to ignore the murder. However, the Genovese murder captured the public imagination and stimulated psychological research into bystander behaviour.

1. How could you explain these events according to the individual and dispositional hypotheses?
2. What do you think you would have done?

The psychology being investigated

Bystander apathy

This refers to when people who are witnessing a situation that requires help have a tendency *not* to help others or intervene. The example of Kitty Genovese shows this. Bystander apathy is a result of pressures such as diffusion of responsibility or pluralistic ignorance. Pluralistic ignorance is when people think they feel or think differently from other members of a group, but this is an error. This happens when others in the group setting are behaving in the same way. For example, we decide not to help when we see someone collapse on the street as no one else is helping. We believe that others must think that helping is an inappropriate decision under the circumstances.

Diffusion of responsibility

Latane and Darley (1968) proposed that the key issue in deciding whether we help or not is whether we see it as our personal responsibility to do so. One reason why groups of people do not help individuals in need is that responsibility is shared equally among the group so that each person has only a small portion of responsibility. Latane and Darley called this idea 'diffusion of responsibility'. In a series of laboratory experiments they demonstrated that the more people who are present in an emergency, the less likely people are to help.

> **Ask yourself**
>
> What factors would make you more or less likely to help someone who is obviously in trouble and asking for help?

Aim

The researchers wanted to extend early studies of bystander behaviour in several key ways. They had two aims.

1. To study bystander behaviour outside the laboratory, in a realistic setting where participants would have a clear view of the victim.
2. To see whether helping behaviour was affected by four variables: the victim's responsibility for being in a situation where they needed help, the race of the victim, the effect of modelling helping behaviour, and the size of the group.

Method

Participants

An estimated total of around 4450 passengers travelled in the trains targeted by the researchers. These were all regarded by the researchers as 'unsolicited participants'. An average of 43 people were present in each carriage in which the procedure was conducted. An average of eight were in the immediate or 'critical' area. The racial mix of passengers was estimated as 45% black and 55% white.

Design

The study was a field experiment carried out on trains on the New York subway. The trains chosen for use were those running 11am and 3pm during the period of 15 April to 26 June 1968. One particular stretch of track was targeted where there was a 7.5 minute gap between two stations. A single trial was a non-stop ride between 59th Street and 125th Street.

Procedure

The procedure involved a male experimenter faking collapse on a train between stops, in order to see whether he was helped by other passengers. Figure 15.1 shows the layout of the adjacent and critical areas of the subway car.

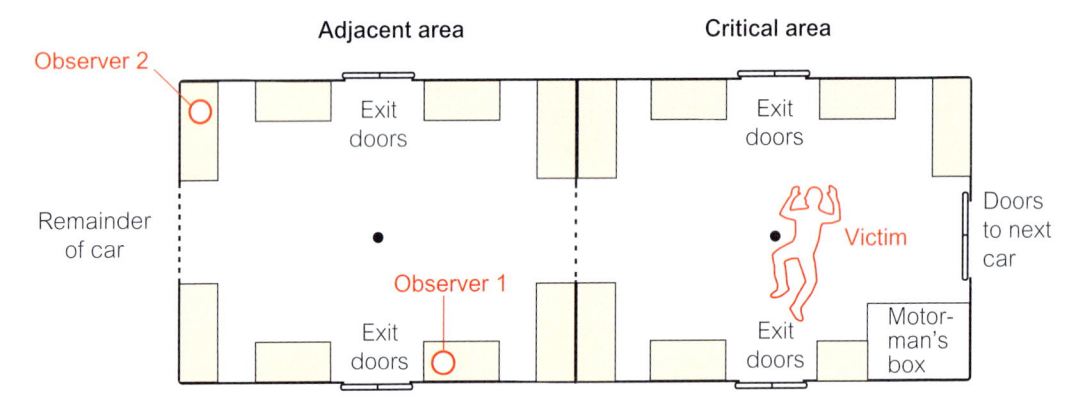

Figure 15.1 *Layout of adjacent and critical areas of the subway car*
Source: Based on Piliavin et al (1969: 291)

Four IVs were manipulated in the procedure. They were:

- victim's responsibility: operationalised as carrying a cane (ill – low responsibility) or smelling of alcohol and carrying a bottle wrapped in a paper bag (drunk – high responsibility)
- victim's race: operationalised as black or white
- presence of a model: operationalised as whether a male confederate; either close to or distant from the victim; helped after 70 or 150 seconds
- number of bystanders: operationalised as how many people were present in the vicinity.

For this study, four different teams were used to collect data over 103 trials. Each team consisted of four Columbia General Studies students – two males and two females. In each team the two males played the roles of victim and model helper. Each male taking the role of victim took part in both conditions used: drunk and ill. In one of the teams, the victim was black. The two females recorded the results.

For each trial, a team boarded the train using different doors. The female confederates sat outside of the critical area and recorded all data covertly. The male model and the male victim stood. The victim always stood next to a metal pole in the critical area. Shortly after the train had passed the first station (usually after around 70 seconds), the victim staggered and collapsed. Until any help was given to him, he lay on the floor looking at the ceiling.

If the victim received no help by the time the train got to the next station, the model helped him back onto his feet. At the stop, the team got off the train. The team then boarded the next train going in the other direction and repeated the procedure. Between six and eight trials were completed on a single day.
All trials on a given day used the same victim condition (eg drunk).

The victim

All victims were males aged 26–35. Three of them were white and one was black. All dressed identically in Eisenhower jackets, old trousers and no tie.
For 38 of the trials, the victim would smell of alcohol and carried a bottle of it in a brown bag. For the remaining 65 trials, the victims appeared to be sober but carried a black cane.

The model

Four males, aged 24–29, and identically dressed in casual clothes, took the role of models of helping behaviour. Four model conditions were applied to both apparently drunk and ill victims.

- Critical area – early: the model stood in the critical area and helped after 70 seconds.
- Critical area – late: the model stood in the critical area and helped after 150 seconds.
- Adjacent area – early: the model stood in the adjacent area and helped after 70 seconds.
- Adjacent area – late: the model stood in the adjacent area and helped after 150 seconds.

Whenever the model had to give assistance to the victim, he would help him into a sitting position and stay with him for the rest of the trial.

The DV – helping – was measured in terms of:

- time taken for first passenger to help
- total number of passengers who helped.

For each trial, one of the observers noted the race, sex, and location of every person in the critical area. She also counted the total number of people in the subway car and recorded the total number of people who gave help, alongside their race, sex, and location. The other observer recorded the race, sex, and location of every person in the adjacent area. She also recorded the time taken for the first person to help. In addition, she recorded the amount of time it took someone to help after the model had gone to help the victim. Both of the observers recorded the comments of people in the subway car. They also attempted to get comments from the person sitting next to them.

The researchers noted that in the end there were more cane trials than drunk trials and that these were not evenly distributed across the race of the victim. Teams 1 and 2 (both white victims) began on day 1 with the cane condition. Teams 3 and 4 (one white and one black victim) began with the drunk condition. They were supposed to alternate each day. On day 4, team 2 did not do as instructed and ran cane trials instead of drunk trials as the victim did not like playing the drunk man.

> **Test yourself**
>
> Outline four controls used in this study. How were the participants recruited? What ethical issues are problems for this study?

Results

These were some of the findings of the study:

> 'The victim with the cane received spontaneous help, that is, before the model acted, on 62 of the 65 trials. Even the drunk received spontaneous help on 19 of the 38 trials.'
>
> (Piliavin *et al*, 1969: 292).

Table 15.1 shows the results of trials where help was given.

Table 15.1 Percentage of trials on which help was given, by race and condition of victim, and total number of trials run in each condition

Trials	White victims		Black victims	
	Cane	Drunk	Cane	Drunk
No model	100%	100%	100%	73%
Number of trials run	54	11	8	11
Model trials	100%	77%	–	67%
Number of trials run	3	13	0	3
Total number of trials	57	24	8	14

Source: Piliavin *et al* (1969: 292)

The differences cannot be attributable to the number of people in the carriage as the mean number for the cane trials was 45 and for the drunk trials it was 40. There was an expectation that the time taken to help spontaneously would be long (based on previous research). This was certainly not the case for the cane condition as on only 3 of the 65 trials did the model initiate help. The model was less likely to initiate help for the drunk victim.

Table 15.2 shows the data broken into two groups: trials where help was given before 70 seconds has elapsed (when the model would initiate help) and trials where help was only given after the 70 seconds had elapsed.

Table 15.2 Time and responses to the incident

Trials in which help was offered:	Total number of trials		% of trial on which 1+ persons left critical area		% of trials on which 1+ comments were recorded		Mean number of comments	
	White victim	Black victim	White victim	Black victim	White victim	Black victim	White victim	Black victim
Before 70 sec.								
Cane	52	7	4%	14%	21%	0%	.27	.00
Drunk	5	4	20%	0%	80%	50%	1.00	.50
Total	57	11	5%	9%	26%	18%	.33	.18
After 70 sec.								
Cane	5	1	40%	–	60%	–	.80	–
Drunk	19	10	42%	60%	100%	70%	2.00	.90
Total	24	11	42%	64%	96%	64%	1.75	.82

Source: Piliavin *et al* (1969: 293)

It is clear that there was more spontaneous help for the cane victim than the drunk victim. When the victim was in the drunk condition, significantly more people left the critical area after 70 seconds (especially if the drunk victim was black). Also, significantly more comments were recorded from participants after 70 seconds (especially if the drunk victim was white). In 60% of the 81 trials where a victim received help, it was from more than one 'good Samaritan' participant irrespective of condition or race of victim. However, we do not know if the additional helpers were there to help the victim or give support to the first person who helped.

On average, 60% of participants in the critical area were male. However, of the 81 spontaneous first helpers, 90% were male. Therefore, men were significantly more likely to help than women ($p < 0.001$). In addition, of the 81 first helpers, 64%

were white but this did not differ significantly from the 55% expected based on the racial distributions in the subway car. There were 65 trials where spontaneous help was given to white victims. In these cases, 68% of the helpers were white. This was a significant result ($p < 0.05$). In the 16 trials where spontaneous help was given to black victims, 50% of these helpers were white. Table 15.3 shows the distribution of helpers broken down by race of helper and victim.

When the victim was drunk there was mainly same-race helping. The researchers noted that this '… interesting tendency toward same-race helping only in the case of the drunk victim may reflect more empathy, sympathy, and trust toward victims of one's own racial group' (Piliavin *et al*, 1969: 294). One reason why less help was given to the drunk victim is that the situation is potentially more dangerous than the cane situation and people may feel blame, fear and disgust towards the drunk victim.

It should also be noted that in 21 of the 103 trials, a total of 34 participants left the critical area to move away from the victim. This was seen more when the victim was drunk. In addition, they were much more likely to leave in trials where no one helped in the first 70 seconds. Even though it did not reach significance ($p < 0.08$), participants were more likely to leave the critical area if the victim was black. However, this could be because there were more trials run when the black victim was drunk compared to being in the cane condition.

Table 15.3 Spontaneous helping of cane and drunk by race of helper and race victim

Race of helper	White victims			Black victims			All victims		
	Cane	Drunk	Total	Cane	Drunk	Total	Cane	Drunk	Total
Same as victim	34	10	44	2	6	8	36	16	52
Different from victim	20	1	21	6	2	8	26	3	29
Total	54	11	65	8	8	16	62	19	81

Source: Piliavin et al (1969: 294)

Qualitative data that was recorded came mainly from female participants with comments such as "It's for men to help him", "I wish I could help him. I'm not strong enough" and "You feel so bad that you don't know what to do."

Finally, there appeared to be no evidence for diffusion of responsibility occurring. Table 15.4 shows the mean latency times for helping as a function of the number of males in the critical area.

Table 15.4 The number and percentage of trials where help was given to the victim

No. males in critical area	Cane			Drunk		
	White victim	Black victim	Total	White victim	Black victim	Total
1–3						
M	16	12	15	–	309	309
4–6						
M	20	6	18	155	143	149
7 and up						
M	3	52	9	107	74	97

Also, Piliavin *et al* calculated speed of response in hypothetical and natural groups of three and seven people. Figure 15.2 shows this.

Larger groups responded *faster* than smaller groups which goes against diffusion of responsibility happening.

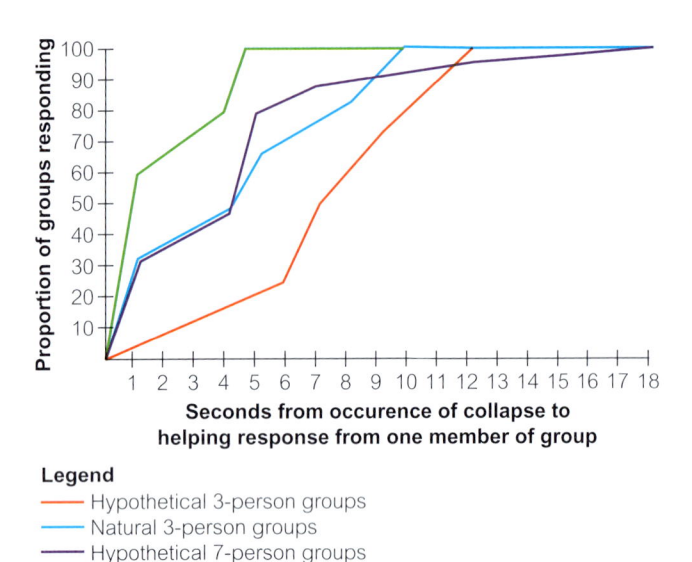

Figure 15.2 *Cumulative proportion of groups producing a helper over time (cane trials, white victims, male helpers from inside critical area)*

Legend:
— Hypothetical 3-person groups
— Natural 3-person groups
— Hypothetical 7-person groups
— Natural 7-person groups

Conclusion

Piliavin and his colleagues admitted that the situation they set up was unusual in that their participants were trapped in a carriage with a collapsed person and therefore could not simply walk away as they could normally. Based on this study, the following occurs in this situation.

- A person who appears to be ill is more likely to receive help than a person who appears to be drunk.
- Men are more likely to help another man than women are.
- People are slightly more likely to help someone of their own ethnic group, especially when that person appears to be drunk.
- There is no strong relationship between size of group and likelihood of helping. The small correlation between group size and helping behaviour is positive rather than negative. Therefore, there is no support for diffusion of responsibility.
- The longer an incident goes on, the less likely people are to help (even if help is modelled), the more likely people are to leave the area, and the more likely they are to discuss the incident.

Summary

Research method (main)	Field experiment
Other technique(s)	Observations
Sample	An estimated total of around 4450 passengers
Sampling technique	Opportunity
Experimental design	Independent groups
IV	• Victim's responsibility: operationalised as carrying a cane (ill – low responsibility) or smelling of alcohol and carrying a bottle wrapped in a paper bag (drunk – high responsibility). • Victim's race: operationalised as black or white. • Presence of a model: operationalised as whether a male confederate; either close to or distant from the victim; helped after 70 or 150 seconds. • Number of bystanders: operationalised as however many people were present in the vicinity.
DV	The amount of people who helped the victim, the speed it took people to help the victim
Quantitative data	As above
Qualitative data	Comments made from the passengers who witnessed the events

Evaluation

Evaluation	General evaluation (field experiments)	Related to Piliavin et al
Strength	As field experiments take place in a realistic setting, it is said that they have ecological validity.	The setting was a subway train which is not artificial: travelling on these trains is a real situation that many people find themselves in daily. Even the event is something that could easily happen, so the study has ecological validity.
Strength	As participants do not know they are taking part in a study, there will be few or no demand characteristics so behaviour is more likely to be natural and valid.	As the setting is natural and no one was aware that the whole situation was staged, there was very little chance that anyone would have shown behaviour to fit the aim of the study. Therefore, the behaviour shown by participants was natural and so valid.
Weakness	Situational variables can be difficult to control so sometimes it is difficult to know whether it is the IV affecting the DV. It could be an uncontrolled variable causing the DV to change.	The positioning of people in the carriages could not be controlled for, and this is just one such example of an uncontrolled aspect. People may not have noticed the incident or may have ignored it (eg if they were reading) so it may not have been the type of victim affecting helping levels.
Weakness	As participants do not know they are taking part in a study, there are issues with breaking ethical guidelines such as guidelines relating to informed consent and deception.	Participants did not know they were taking part in a study – they were deceived; obviously, informed consent could not be taken from them prior to the collapse. This goes against ethical guidelines (although formal guidelines were not established at the time of the study).

Other evaluation points include the following.

- Usefulness: the study told us that type of victim can affect how long a person takes to help or whether a person helps at all. This could be used to educate people that in an emergency we should help others no matter who they are because the longer it takes to help, the more likely it is that the person will suffer more in the long term (especially if medical attention is required).
- Generalisability: it would be difficult to generalise past the sample itself as participants were all urban dwellers who were (presumably) used to travelling on a subway train. People in urban areas are more used to deindividuating (losing their sense of identity) and feeling 'anonymous' whereas people who live in rural areas of even a different city might act differently.
- Ethics – deception: as participants did not know that they were being presented with a fake event, they believed that what they were witnessing was real, so they were deceived. Also, they did they not know they were part of a study.
- Ethics – informed consent: participants did not know they were part of a study, so they could not give their permission to be used in it.
- Ethics – protection: witnessing someone collapse can be a distressing (and some people did leave the scene quickly); participants were not protected from experiencing psychological stress.

Figure 15.3 What makes people help or not help people in need?

Challenge yourself

Identify two other applications to everyday life this study could have.

Explain who would benefit from these applications.

Issues and debates

The following table discusses the Piliavin et al study in terms of the core issues and debates for AS Level.

Application to everyday life	The findings of this study can be used to educate people about bystanders' intervention. To try to break stereotypes, children could be educated about helping others no matter who those in need are.
Individual and situational explanations	The results clearly show a situational effect as there was variation in who was helped and when. The subway train and types of victim formed the situation that participants found themselves in and this then caused certain behaviours such as helping or not helping. However, an individual effect might have an influence – as the sample was large and varied it might have been a certain personality type that was making people help or not help.
Nature versus nurture	Not applicable
The use of children	Not applicable
The use of animals	Not applicable

16 Exam centre: AS Level

Paper 1

Biological approach

Dement and Kleitman (sleep and dreams)

1. One technique that was used to collect the data was a physiological measure.

    (a) Identify the physiological measure used in this study. [1]

    (b) Describe the function of the physiological measure in (a). [2]

    (c) Outline **one** weakness of physiological measures in psychological research. [3]

2. This study was useful application to real-life situations. Describe **one** way the findings in the study **can** be applied to real life and **one** way the findings in the study **cannot** be applied to real life. [5]

3. Explain how **two** results in this study support the nature side of the nature-nurture debate. [8]

Hassett et al (monkey toy preferences)

4. (a) Describe the sample used in this study. [2]

    (b) Describe **two** animal ethics that were followed in this study. [4]

5. Describe the procedure from when the animals in this study were released into this outdoor area to when the trial ended. [5]

6. Explain how **one** result in this study **supports** gender differences in toy preferences and how one result **does not** support gender differences in toy preferences. [8]

Hölzel et al (mindfulness and brain scans)

7. (a) Identify **two** measures used to collect data in this study. [2]

    (b) The participants were instructed to practise guided mindfulness exercises using audio recordings at home. Describe **one** weakness for the study based on the instruction given. [2]

8. Describe the sample used in this study and explain **one** way in which the sample is generalisable and **one** way it is not generalisable. [5]

9. Explain **one** similarity and **one** difference between this study and one other study in the biological approach. Do not refer to the sample in your answer. [8]

Cognitive approach

Andrade (doodling)

10. (a) Identify the sampling technique used to recruit the participants in this study. [1]

    (b) Outline **one** strength of the sampling technique used to recruit the participants in this study. [2]

    (c) Outline **one** conclusion made about memory and concentration in this study. [2]

11. (a) Describe the psychology being investigated in this study. [5]

    (b) Outline **one** strength of this study in terms of reliability. [2]

12. Explain how **two** results from this study support the assumptions in the cognitive approach. [8]

Baron-Cohen et al (eyes test)

13. (a) State **three** changes that were made on the revised version of reading the mind in the eyes test. [3]

    (b) Explain why the AS/HFA group performed worse than other groups on reading the mind in the eyes test. [2]

    (c) Outline **one** conclusion made from this study. [2]

14. Peter is a new teacher in high school who wants to find out what interventions he can put into place for students who have problems understanding other people's emotions and reacting to them appropriately. He is seeking information on how Baron-Cohen participants for the theory of mind. Outline the information that you would give to Peter, following your understanding of the study by Baron-Cohen *et al* (eyes test). [5]

15. Evaluate the study by Baron-Cohen *et al* (eyes test) in terms of **two** strengths and **two** weaknesses. One of your evaluative points must be about the laboratory-based research method. [10]

Pozzulo et al (line-ups)

16. (a) Outline **one** prediction made in this study. [2]

    (b) Describe how **one** finding in this study supports the prediction made in (a) above. [2]

17. Describe the procedure in this study from when the experimenter played the first video (human or cartoon) to when the child made the identification from the line-up. [5]

18. Evaluate this study in terms of **one** strength and **one** weakness of using children in psychological research. [8]

Learning approach

Bandura et al (aggression)

19. (a) Give **one** example of physically aggressive behaviour recorded by the observers. [1]

    (b) Outline **one** result on the physical aggression in this study. You must include data. [2]

    (c) Outline one prediction made about aggressive behaviour in this study. [2]

20. Explain the nature and nurture debate in psychology, using this study. [5]

21. Explain what psychologists have learned about the social learning theory using **two** results from this study. [8]

Fagen et al (elephant learning)

22. (a) Identify **two** behavioural tasks the elephants in this study were trained to perform. [2]

    (b) Describe how **one** of the behavioural tasks in (a) above was performed by the elephant. [2]

23. Describe how the data collection procedure was controlled in this study. [5]

24. Explain **two** ways this study supports the nature and/or nurture side of the nature-nurture debate. [8]

Saavedra and Silverman (button phobia)

25. (a) State **two** avoidance behaviours reported by the mother and the 9-year-old boy prior to being treated for his phobia. [2]

    (b) One ethic in psychological research is informed consent. Explain how this ethic was raised in this study. [2]

26. (a) Describe **one** assumption of the learning approach using any study in the approach. [2]

    (b) This study has real-world applications in gaining knowledge and understanding on how to treat different aspects of a phobia. Describe **one** real-world application of this study. [4]

27. Explain **one** similarity and **one** difference in methodology between the study by Saavedra and Silverman (button phobia) and Fagen *et al* (elephant learning). [8]

Social approach

Milgram (obedience)

28. This study used a 'learner' and a 'teacher':

    (a) Outline what the 'teacher' was expected to do when the 'learner' gave an incorrect response. [2]

    (b) Explain how **one** vocalisation made by the 'teacher' was indicative of the tension he felt while giving shocks to the learner. [2]

29. Asenath and Jasmine are having a conversation about this study. Asenath believes that there could be individual factors that could explain the behaviour of the 'teacher' while Jasmine believes the behaviour by the 'teacher' was largely due to situational factors. Explain why both Asenath and Jasmine could be correct in their arguments. [5]

30. Evaluate this study in terms of **two** strengths and **two** weaknesses. One of your evaluative points must be about the observation method. [10]

Perry et al (personal space)

31. (a) Identify **two** characteristics of the sample used in experiment 1 in this study. [2]

    (b) Explain how **one** of the characteristics in (a) above was useful to this study. [2]

32. Describe the procedure in this study from the point the participants completed the online questionnaire to when they pressed the spacebar in experiment 1. [5]

33. Evaluate this study in terms of two strengths and two weaknesses. One of your evaluative points must be about the use of controls. [10]

Piliavin et al (subway Samaritans)

34. (a) Outline the participants who were recruited in this study. [2]

    (b) Describe **two** features that made the procedures in this study look real. [4]

35. Daniel wants to replicate this study study in a shopping mall and wants to know more about how the study was conducted on the New York subway. Suggest **two** improvements Daniel could make in his study to obtain a better understanding of helping behaviour. [5]

36. Explain **one** ethical similarity and **one** ethical weakness between the study by Piliavin *et al* (subway Samaritans) and the study by Milgram (obedience). [8]

Paper 2

Section A

1. From the study by Piliavin *et al* (subway Samaritans):

   (a) Briefly describe what is meant by a 'control' in psychological studies. [2]

   (b) Identify **two** controls in place within the procedure of the study. [2]

2. In the Hölzel *et al* study on mindfulness, data was collecting using a MRI brain scan.

   (a) Describe the purpose of the two MRI brain scans that were given to each participant. [2]

   (b) Suggest **one** strength of collecting data using these brain scans. [2]

3. In the Hassett *et al* study (monkey toy preference), trails were videotaped and later viewed by researchers, noting the behaviour of the monkey with the presented toys.

   (a) Identify **two** behaviours that were coded within the observations. [2]

   (b) Briefly explain how counterbalancing of the toys was used in the study. [2]

4. Describe **two** types of observations, using any two core studies as examples. [6]

5. For each type of hypothesis noted below, provide a brief definition and your own example related to time spent revising core studies and exam score:

   (a) directional (one-tailed) hypothesis. [2]

   (b) non-directional (two-tailed) hypothesis. [2]

   (c) null hypothesis. [2]

6. Describe **one** strength and **one** weakness of the case study methodology, using Saavedra and Silverman (phobias) as an example. [6]

7. Sarah wants to conduct a study to see whether her puppy learns the command of 'sit' faster when using crunchy or chewy treats during training. She plans to start her training using crunchy treats for the first two days and chewy then use treats for the next two days.

   (a) Suggest **one** problem with Sarah's plan for training her puppy. [2]

   (b) Suggest **one** alternative way to train the puppy to address the potential problem you mentioned in part (a). [3]

   (c) Explain why it would be better for Sarah to conduct her study with a wider sample of puppies. [2]

8. Kwame's school is planning to offer online (virtual) schooling next year for students. Kwame wants to conduct a study to investigate students' thoughts on in-person schooling compared to online or virtual schooling. He will use a questionnaire to collect data.

   (a) Suggest **one** closed-ended question that could be asked about thoughts on virtual schooling. [1]

   (b) Suggest **two** ways in which Kwame can notify his fellow students of the questionnaire. [4]

   (c) Suggest **one** strength of collecting data using a questionnaire. [2]

   (d) Suggest **one** reason why Kwame might want to use an interview rather a questionnaire. [2]

9. Neville wants to conduct a field study to see whether cars adhere to reduced speed limits in construction areas when using traffic cones compared to road signs with warning lights. He plans to conduct his study along a road that is in the business district of his city.

    (a) Operationalise the IV of Neville's proposed field study. [1]

    (b) Operationalise the DV of Neville's proposed field study. [1]

    (c) Suggest **one** strength of using a field study for Neville's proposed study. [2]

    (d) Suggest **two** reasons why using video cameras to collect data would strengthen the data collection in Neville's proposed study. [4]

Section B

10. Amelia believes that where her third-grade students sit in the classroom influences their reading test scores. Amelia believes that sitting in the front, the middle, and the back of the room will influence the test scores. She has already received permission from her students' parents/guardians to conduct a study throughout the term.

    (a) Describe how Amelia could conduct a field study to investigate whether where her students sit in the room influences their reading test scores.

    Do **not** describe sampling or ethical issues/guidelines in your answer. [10]

    (b) Describe one practical/methodological strength of the procedure you have described in your answer to part (a).

    Do **not** refer to sampling or ethics in your answer. [2]

    (c) Explain why the feature of the procedure you have identified in (b) is a strength.

    Do **not** refer to sampling or ethics in your answer. [2]

11. Dr Burrows believes that there is a correlation between secondary students' grades and the amount of sleep they receive each night. Dr Burrows plans to sample students, aged 14–17, from three local schools with permission from the Ministry of Education.

    (a) Describe how Dr Burrows could conduct a correlational study using a questionnaire to investigate a potential link between secondary students' grades and the amount of sleep received each night.

    Do **not** describe ethical issues/guidelines in your answer. [10]

    (b) Describe one practical/methodological strength of the procedure you have described in your answer to part (a).

    Do **not** refer to sampling or ethics in your answer. [2]

    (c) Explain why the feature of the procedure you have identified in (b) is a strength.

    Do **not** refer to sampling or ethics in your answer. [2]

12. Dr Hsu wants to investigate whether infants have an innate preference for certain colours. He plans to use a sample of infants aged 3–8 months, accompanied by their caregiver. To test the idea, Dr Hsu plans to use the same stuffed animal (a dog) in varying colours.

    (a) Describe how Dr Hsu can use a laboratory experiment to investigate whether infants have an innate preference for certain colours.

    Do **not** describe sampling or ethical issues/guidelines in your answer. [10]

    (b) Describe one practical/methodological strength of the procedure you have described in your answer to part (a).

    Do **not** refer to sampling or ethics in your answer. [2]

    (c) Explain why the feature of the procedure you have identified in (b) is a strength.

    Do **not** refer to sampling or ethics in your answer. [2]

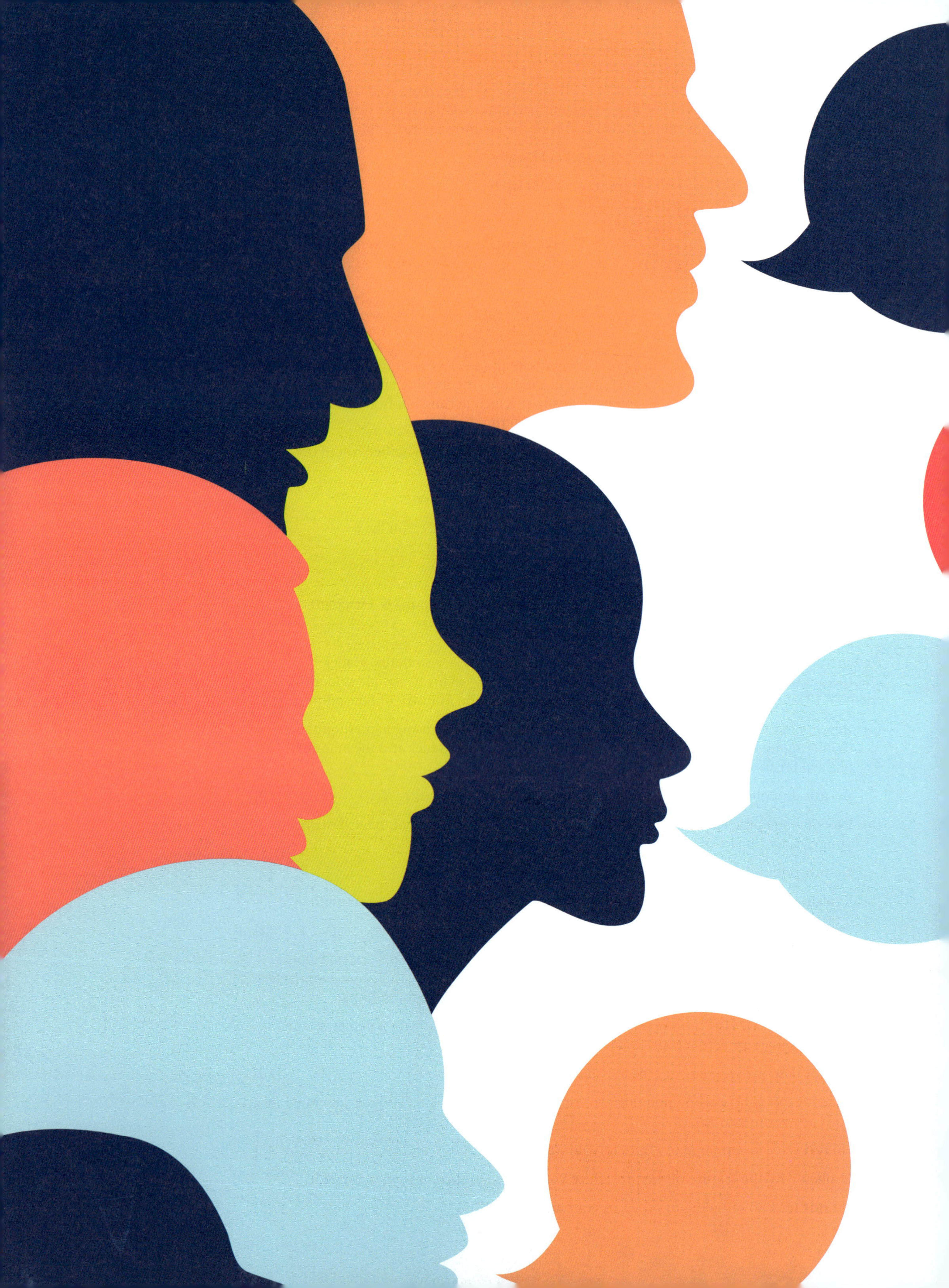

A Level

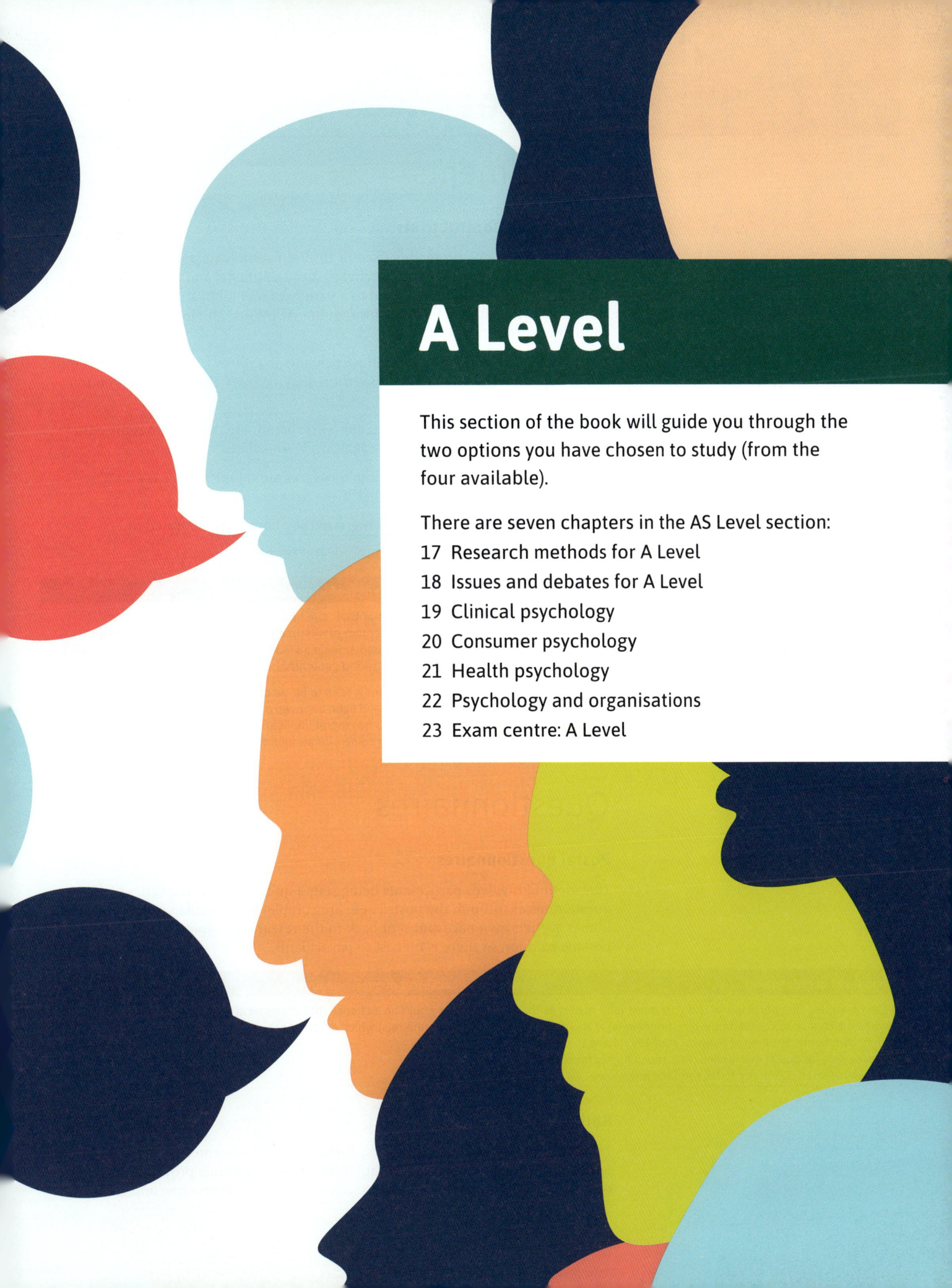

This section of the book will guide you through the two options you have chosen to study (from the four available).

There are seven chapters in the AS Level section:
17 Research methods for A Level
18 Issues and debates for A Level
19 Clinical psychology
20 Consumer psychology
21 Health psychology
22 Psychology and organisations
23 Exam centre: A Level

17 Research methods for A Level

Experiments

Randomised control trials

In psychology, these are mainly used in clinical psychology and health psychology. There are used to evaluate the effectiveness of treatments and techniques to help control or reduce symptoms linked to a variety of mental health disorders, or promotion of healthy behaviour through interventions. The main principles are as follows.

- There is a random allocation of participants to groups (usually an 'intervention group' and a 'control group', but there may be more than one intervention group).
- Inclusion and exclusion criteria for participation are decided (to reduce the effects of certain participant variables).
- Researchers who collect outcome measures are 'blind' to which group participants are in.
- Participants do not know which group they have been allocated to.
- There is a standardised procedure for the study.

Strengths of randomised control trials	Weaknesses of randomised control trials
The random allocation of people to conditions potentially overcomes selection bias and participant variables directly affecting outcome measures. The potential bias and participant variables should be evenly distributed across conditions meaning that validity is not compromised.	These types of trials can be logistically challenging. The management of multiple participants on multiple sites with long-term assessment can lead to participant drop-out which could affect validity and generalisability.
If the trial uses a 'blind' technique (so the researcher and/or participant does not know which group the participant is in) it improves credibility and decreases the potential effects of experimenter bias (including subjectivity).	If a treatment is seen to be successful, the participants in the control condition have been deprived of a treatment intervention just by chance. This has moral implications. Conversely, if a treatment shows severe side effects, then the experimental group are worse off.

Questionnaires

Postal questionnaires

This method involves participants being sent a questionnaire or a series of questionnaires through the post. These are completed by participants in their own homes at their own pace and sent back to the researcher, typically with return postage paid for, so there is no cost to participants.

Strengths of questionnaires	Weaknesses of questionnaires
It can be argued that participants will give more valid results as they have had a chance to complete the questionnaire(s) at their own pace in their own home. Studies (eg Hayashi *et al* 1999) have shown that response rate for postal questionnaires is much higher for socially sensitive research compared to face-to-face interviews.	There could be a chance that someone else completed the questionnaire(s) which decreases the validity of findings.

Rating scales

These are used as part of self-reports. Participants are presented with a question or have to read an item and then rate their answer on a scale provided. It can be important to choose the range of the scale used when constructing and/or using rating scales. Dawes (2008) reported that using a 5- or 7-point scale (for the same questions) produces a higher rescaled mean score of satisfaction compared to a 10-point scale. This could reduce the validity of overall scores in research measuring subjective thoughts, feelings, and attitudes.

Forced/fixed choice questions

These are used as part of self-reports. A participant is presented with a question or has to read an item and then chooses an answer from a range of potential answers that are already there. Sometimes an 'Other' option is given to allow participants to write their own answers if these are not covered by the available options.

Strengths of forced/fixed choice questions	Weaknesses of forced/fixed choice questions
This method produces quantitative data that can be statistically analysed so that different groups can be compared directly.	Some questionnaires do not have the 'Other' category, which could force participants to choose an option that does not truly reflect what they believe. This reduces validity of findings.

Psychometric tests

These are usually paper-and-pen tasks that literally mean 'measurement of the mind'. Examples are an intelligent quotient (IQ) test, an aptitude test, or a test to help with educational needs. They are standardised, so people's results can be compared to a 'norm' to see how intelligent they are or to what extent they have a particular personality.

Strengths of psychometric tests	Weaknesses of psychometric tests
As these tests are standardised on a large sample of people, they can be seen as being objective and scientific. Comparisons can be useful as people's results are compared on the same, standardised scale. As they are standardised, they are reliable measures – we can use them again and again to see if we get similar results.	There may be issues with validity. Is the test actually measuring the behaviour it is supposed to measure? For example, some psychologists believe that an IQ test does not measure intelligence, but instead measures someone's ability to complete an IQ test. If tests measure specific cultural knowledge rather than the behaviour they are supposed to measure, they will be seen as ethnocentric.

Hypotheses

See page 17 (AS Level) to read about how to write hypotheses.

A directional hypotheses is used when previous research is consistent or when a theory predicts a specific direction of results.

A non-directional hypothesis is used when previous research has shown conflicting results or there has been no previous research.

Validity

Temporal validity

This is a type of external validity. It refers to assessing a study based on its findings in relation to the progression of time. Factors that might have affected results when the study was conducted and published may, or may not, be relevant today. For example, by how much do the findings of Milgram (1963) apply to present times?

> **Challenge yourself**
>
> During your A Level course, find four studies that can be assessed on temporal validity. Argue why **two** of the studies **do show** temporal validity and then why **two** studies **do not show** temporal validity.

18 Issues and debates for A Level

For the examination you need to know about a series of issues and debates surrounding psychology and psychological research. Four of these have already been covered at AS Level. They are:

- the application of psychology to everyday life
- individual and situational explanations
- nature versus nurture
- the use of children in psychological research.

At A Level, there are four more issues and debates that need to be covered.

Cultural differences

This is typically referred to as cross-cultural differences. The American Psychological Association noted that a great deal of psychological research is WEIRD (Western, Educated, Industrialised, Rich, Democratic) and this only represents a certain sector of the global population. Some reviews have stated that over 90% of psychological research happens in North America. A culture needs to have some form of organised system linked to shared meanings and experiences. A culture is not the same as someone's nationality or the country they live in. There can be several distinct cultures within the borders of one country, one area, and even one city. Therefore, when assessing studies on 'cultural differences' ensure that you know something about the culture of the participants (eg: is it collectivist or individualist? Are there social norms unique to the area the participants were recruited from? What are the beliefs and values of the group of participants?).

> **Ask yourself**
>
> During your A Level course, see how many studies look at cross-cultural differences rather than nationality differences. Have you learned something new from these studies about different cultures? Also, make notes on the differences between race, ethnicity, nationality, and culture.

Reductionism versus holism

Reductionism is when a psychologist believes that a complex behaviour can be explained by reducing it to one single cause or a series of component parts. For example, a researcher might state that some aspect of personality is caused only by biological mechanism. This could easily overlook social and psychological factors that could also be affecting personality. It is the opposite of holism, which is when research examines all possible angles to explain a single behaviour or set of behaviours.

Holism occurs when an approach or a theory is seen as being a unified whole that simply cannot be explained by its constituent individual features or characteristics.

> **Test yourself**
>
> Explain two strengths and two weaknesses of conducting cross-cultural research. Use examples.

Strength of reductionism	Weakness of reductionism
It allows research to be conducted that can analyse a specific area or behaviour in depth, to investigate how it affects humans.	It overlooks other factors that could be affecting the behaviour of people.
Strength of holism	**Weakness of holism**
It allows psychologists to assess multiple factors that might be contributing to a behaviour, action or problem.	It may over-complicate explanations for behaviours, actions or problems by over-looking single factors that might be the cause.

Determinism versus free will

Determinism is the idea that people's actions and thoughts are totally determined by external and internal mechanisms operating on them. That is, people's behaviours and cognitions are caused (determined) by factors that make them predictable. For example, a researcher may believe that depression is caused by neurochemistry or another researcher might believe that aggression is caused by observation and imitation. Belief in determinism is the opposite to belief in free will, which argues that individuals choose their own behaviour and thoughts. Determinism is therefore about how factors outside of the individual are causing behaviours to occur (environmental determinism) or from within the individual (biological determinism).

Strength of determinism	Weakness of determinism
It allows research to take place that is focused and can unearth whether a single factor is causing a particular outcome. This can help to generate further research to see whether it is just that factor that is the cause, or a combination of factors.	It ignores the idea of free will (when people choose their own behaviours and thoughts based on a variety of factors). Soft determinism does state that people choose their own pathway in life, but also that their behaviour is still subject to either biological or environmental pressures. Determinism does not allow for free will and sees it as an illusion therefore removing personal responsibility can lead to labelling.
Strength of free-will	**Weakness of free-will**
There is evidence that individuals who have a strong internal locus of control (belief that they themselves have a high degree of control of their behaviours, thoughts, and actions) are more mentally healthy (eg Khumalo and Plattner, 2019).	Pre-cognitive decision-making (eg Knutson et al 2007) shows that free will could be an illusion. The brain appears to make a decision before we *consciously* recognise we have made that decision, making it feel as if it was our free will choosing when it was not.

Idiographic versus nomothetic

The idiographic approach to psychology aims to describe and understand a single case. The approach intends to focus on an individual's traits and characteristics showing how unique every individual is.

The nomothetic approach to psychology aims to establish general 'laws' about behaviour that can be applied to all people. The approach intends to find universally valid laws that characterise the 'average person'.

Strength of idiographic	Weakness of idiographic
This approach can have a focus on the individual, so tends to use the case study research method to understand thoughts, feelings, and behaviours. This means that a wealth of data can be collected to help explain individual experiences.	This approach is generally seen as being unscientific and unable to fulfil one of the general laws of science: explain the most variation (in thoughts, feelings, and behaviours, in this area) in the fewest number of possible variations. Having unique therapies, for example for every individual with a mental health issue, is too time consuming and resource consuming.
Strength of nomothetic	**Weakness of nomothetic**
This approach is generally seen as being scientific as it tends to use experimental methods and quantitative methods of data collection. This can allow for direct comparisons between groups, establish cause and effect, and show that general laws can apply to certain aspects of human behaviour.	This approach ignores individual differences and individual experiences that may be at conflict with a general group law.

19 Clinical psychology

For this option, you will need to know terms used in:

- biological explanations (eg genetic)
- biological measures (eg blood tests)
- biological treatments (eg drugs)
- psychological explanations (eg cognitive)
- psychological therapies (eg systematic desensitisation).

19.1 Schizophrenia

19.1.1 Diagnostic criteria for schizophrenia

Symptoms can be split into positive and negative.

- Positive refers to the *addition* of certain behaviours. For example, hallucinations, delusions of grandeur, or of control and insertion of thoughts are all positive.
- Negative refers to the *removal* of certain behaviours. For example, poverty of speech, withdrawal from society and flattening of mood are all negative.

ICD-11 diagnostic criteria for schizophrenia

The essential features of schizophrenia are listed below. To indicate schizophrenia, there has to be *two* of the listed symptoms for most of the time for at least one month. One of the symptoms *must* come from the first four on this list.

- Persistent delusions – these can be grandiose (being grand or impressive) or persecutory (patients thinking someone intends to harm them).
- Persistent hallucinations – these are mainly auditory.
- Disorganised thinking – if severe, the person's speech may become very incoherent.
- Experiences of influence, passivity, or control – feeling that thoughts are not controlled by oneself.
- Negative symptoms – these include flattening of emotion, alogia (paucity of (very little) speech), avolition (lack of motivation), asociality (not social), and anhedonia (inability to feel pleasure).
- Disorganised behaviour that impedes goal-based activities.
- Psychomotor disturbance – these include catatonia, agitation, posturing, waxy flexibility, negativism, mutism, and stupor.
- The symptoms are not caused by organic problems or substance abuse including when on treatment for substance abuse.

The World Health Organization stresses that there must be cultural considerations where some of the behaviours above are typical for a particular culture or group of people.

> **Challenge yourself**
>
> Find two real-life case studies of people being diagnosed with schizophrenia or living with schizophrenia.

Types of delusions and investigating delusions

KEY STUDY: Freeman et al (2003)

Context, main theories, and explanations

The use of virtual reality (VR) in clinical psychology is based around the assumption that people will react in the same way in a VR setting as they would in the real world. Using VR has been successful in treating a range of phobias. However, there has been limited exploration as to whether avatars (the people you meet and interact with in VR sessions) can trigger persecutory ideation. As VR environments and avatars can be controlled, this tool could be useful to clearly identify what triggers persecutory ideation in patients diagnosed with schizophrenia. Persecutory ideation is when a person has distorted beliefs that mean they cannot recognise what is reality and what is not reality.

Aim and hypotheses

The aim of this exploratory study was to investigate whether people without any mental health disorder diagnosis have thoughts of persecutory ideation in a VR setting. The researchers also wanted to investigate whether there are any cognitive factors that can predict persecutory ideation in a VR setting.

Design

Participants

A total of 24 participants were recruited. All had no history of mental illness. It was a volunteer sample from University College London. Twenty-one participants were students and there was an equal number of males and females. Consent was taken from all participants, but nothing was revealed about the task being linked to persecutory thoughts.

Procedure

All participants were allowed some time to explore the VR setting. Once they had got used to the VR equipment, participants were instructed to explore the room (a library, but it was never referred to as this) and form some impressions of the avatars in there with them, including what they may think about the participant. A total of five avatars were used in the study.

Figure 19.1 *The scenario: virtual people in the library*

Sometimes the avatars showed potentially ambiguous behaviour such as smiling, chatting to each other, or looking around the room or at the participant. After five minutes, the participant was told to leave the VR setting. The participants were in two groups: one half completed a set of measures before *and* after the VR experience. The other half completed the same measures but *only* after the VR experience. This was to account for the possibility that the idea of persecutory thoughts being tested was primed from the measures.

Measures

Six measures were taken.

1. The Brief Symptom Inventory (BSI) was used. This measured a range of symptoms including paranoid ideation of the last seven days.
2. The Paranoia Scale was used.
3. The Spielberger State Anxiety Questionnnaire was completed.
4. VR-Paranoia was measured. The research team created a measure of the feelings of paranoia in a VR setting. It measures VR-Persecution, VR-Reference, and VR-Positive feelings.
5. A semi-structured interview and observer rating of persecutory ideation took place. The participants were asked about their experiences in the VR setting. It was video recorded, and an observer then watched it to rate whether there were any signs of persecutory ideation.
6. A sense of presence questionnaire was completed. This measured how immersed the participant felt in the VR setting.

Results, findings, and conclusions

Table 19.1 shows the mean scores on the VR-paranoia measurement. It can be seen that participants assigned positive views towards the avatars the most. However, there were examples of participants feeling some level of persecution.

Table 19.1 Scores on the VR-Paranoia Questionnaire

	Mean	SD	Minimum–maximum scores
VR-Persecution	2.3	2.2	0–7
VR-Reference	4.0	2.6	0–10
VR-Positive	6.0	4.1	0–13
VR-Total score	12.3	4.6	5–23

In addition, Table 19.2 highlights some of the comments made by participants about the avatars.

Table 19.2 A selection of comments made about the avatars (each comment is from a different participant)

Positive	Negative
"Friendly people just being friendly and offering a smile"	"They were very ignorant and unfriendly"
"People were nicer than real people"	"Sometimes appeared hostile, sometimes rude"
"Part of a game (flirting but being shy)"	"It was their space: you're the stranger."
"It was nice when they smiled, made me feel welcome."	"They were telling me to go away"
"They looked friendly – that was my overall impression"	"The two women looked more threatening"
"I smiled and chuckled"	"Some were intimidating"

Table 19.3 shows the correlations between some of the measures to investigate what predictors there were for persecutory ideation in a VR setting.

Table 19.3 Correlations between persecutory ideation, interpersonal sensitivity, and anxiety (n = 24)

Measure	1	2	3	4	5
1. VR-Persecution					
2. Paranoia Scale	.156				
3. BSI – Paranoia	.368	.729**			
4. BSI – Inter. sensitivity	.562**	.506*	.652*		
5. BSI – Anxiety	.443*	.276	.488*	.490*	
6. Spielberger Anxiety	.173	.574*	.337	.473*	.326
*p, .05; ** p, .01					

Source: (all three tables above) Freeman *et al* (2003: 511; 512)

Therefore, this study does provide evidence that people attribute mental states to avatars in a VR setting, and so will be useful when exploring what triggers persecutory ideation in patients diagnosed with schizophrenia.

Main discussion points

- This study provides evidence that people attribute mental states to avatar in a VR setting. This means that people think that avatars have intentions towards them. Nearly all of these were benevolent but there were some individuals that showed some persecutory intentions. The main predictor of persecutory ideation in this study was interpersonal sensitivity. This now needs to be tested on a clinical sample to see if this is also the main predictor.
- The research team noted that the VR setting shows promise to begin to understand persecutory ideation in a 'safe setting' that may be of some use with clinical samples.

Evaluation

- The sample used was a non-clinical sample. The argument could be that, while this findings are of interest in terms of the use of VR, there is no way of knowing whether it would work in the same way with a clinical sample. Patients diagnosed with persecutory ideation issues may not be able to cope with a VR setting or willingly participate in VR 'therapy'.
- The sample used was small and very specific. Participants were students and staff in a prestigious London-based university so this may not necessarily represent the general public and definitely does not represent a clinical sample. Therefore, there may be limited generalisability and applicability.
- The procedure used in the study was clear and standardised. The situation used in the VR setting and all of the measures were clearly outlined, so other researchers can replicate the study to test for reliability.
- The study *may* have good application in a therapeutic setting. Using VR to understand the persecutory thoughts of people diagnosed with schizophrenia and related disorders could be the way forward to create better treatment regimes and therapies for these patients.

19.1.2 Explanations of schizophrenia

Biological explanations

Genetic

One argument centres on whether there is an inherited (genetic) component to schizophrenia. Many reviews have taken place, but those conducted by Gottesman and Shields appear to be the ones quoted the most in the field. This review looked at adoption, twin and family studies to see whether there was a potential genetic component to schizophrenia.

With studies of twins, researchers can examine monozygotic twins (MZ: identical) and dizygotic twins (DZ: non-identical) to test whether a genetic component is seen because the monozygotic twins share all of their genetic material. Therefore, if the prevalence of schizophrenia is higher in monozygotic twins (when both twins have been diagnosed with schizophrenia) this could point towards a genetic component. Five twin studies formed the review and the results are shown in Table 19.4.

The difference between the pairwise concordance rate and probandwise concordance rate is highlighted by Gottesman and Shields as: '… the pairwise rate expresses the degree of concordance as the percentage of all pairs in which both twins are schizophrenic, given a specified sample of twin pairs with at least one twin schizophrenic. The probandwise rate is the percentage of independently ascertained schizophrenic twins (the probands) who have a schizophrenic co-twin' (1976: 372).

> **Challenge yourself**
>
> Look at the issue and debate tracker table on page 137. Create similar issue and debate commentaries for individual and situational explanations, idiographic versus nomothetic, case studies, and generalisations from findings.

Table 19.4 *Concordance in recent twin studies. Concordance rates are presented without age corrections.*

	N pairs and probandwise concordance		
	MZ	DZ	Country
Cannon et al, 1998	67: 40/87 (46%)	186: 18/195 (9%)	Finland
Franzek and Beckmann, 1998	14: 11/14 (79%)	12: 2/12 (18%)	Germany
Cardno et al, 1999	43: 21/50 (42%)	58: 1/57 (2%)	UK
Kläning et al, 2016	13: 7/16 (44%)	31: 1/31 (3%)	Denmark

Representative twin studies of schizophrenia. DZ pairs are all same-gender except for inclusion of opposite-gender in Danish sample.

Note: Standard errors for small numerators will be large.

Source: Personal Communication, © I.I. Gottesman, May 20, 2016 and used by permission

The overall results do point towards a potential genetic component to schizophrenia as the probandwise rates calculated for monozygotic twins is 35–58% whereas for dizygotic twins it is 9–26% so there is no overlap between the rates. The general population rate is around 1.1%. However, none of the rates are 100% which would mean a definite genetic cause. Gottesman and Shields concluded that, even though the data points towards some form of genetic component, the external environment must play a part in the onset of schizophrenia.

They also examined adoption studies and found a trend of an increased rate of biological relatives having schizophrenia if their adopted children were also diagnosed. This was between 12.1% and 18.8% for the studies reviewed.

> **Test yourself**
>
> Explain one further weakness of the genetic argument for schizophrenia.

Strengths	Weakness
The study was a thorough review of the field, which allowed for a somewhat objective analysis of the field at that time.	As there were different studies used, it might be difficult to 'truly' compare them in a review as they may have used different criteria to diagnose schizophrenia. This might mean the review is unreliable in that aspect.
The results could have been used to help understand the potential causes of schizophrenia.	

Biochemical (the dopamine hypothesis)

The main idea of the dopamine hypothesis is that dopaminergic systems in the brain of people with schizophrenia are overactive. That is, their dopamine receptors are oversensitive rather than it being a higher level of dopamine that is causing their symptoms. However, there is evidence for both.

- When people experience amphetamine psychosis it resembles certain types of schizophrenia. This is caused by an excess of dopamine.
- Drug treatment (eg prescribing phenothiazines) does help to treat some of the symptoms of schizophrenia but these drugs can bring about symptoms similar to Parkinson's disease, which is caused by *low* levels of dopamine.

Lindström *et al* (1999) used a PET scan to test the dopamine hypothesis. Ten people with schizophrenia and ten healthy controls were injected with a radioactively labelled chemical called L-DOPA. This is used in the production of dopamine. The PET scan could trace its usage in all participants. The L-DOPA was taken up significantly faster in people with schizophrenia, pointing towards them producing more dopamine.

Psychological (cognitive) explanation

Cognitive (Frith, 1992)

Frith (1992) noted that people with schizophrenia might have a deficient 'metarepresentation' system – the system that makes people able to reflect on thoughts, emotions, and behaviours. It could also be linked to theory of mind (see page 62) as it controls self-awareness and how we interpret the actions of others. These are characteristics that are lacking in some people with schizophrenia. Also, those showing more negative symptoms might have a dysfunctional supervisory attention system. This system is responsible for generating self-initiated actions. In one study, Frith and Done (1986) reported that when participants were asked to do things such as name as many different fruits as possible, or generate as many designs for something as possible, those with schizophrenia (with negative symptoms predominant) had great difficulty in managing this.

Frith (1992) also examined a central monitoring system. This allows us to be able to understand and label actions that we do as being controlled by ourselves. Frith had noticed that in some people with schizophrenia inner speech may not be recognised as being self-generated. Therefore, when they hear 'voices' it is their own voice but they are unaware that it is themselves producing inner speech and believe it is someone else.

Johnson et al (2013) tested the cognitive abilities of 99 people with schizophrenia and 77 healthy controls on a battery of cognitive tests. It was seen that people with schizophrenia performed worse across all cognitive tests including those for working memory (which involves tasks such as dealing with inner speech) and that this might be the core determinant of overall cognitive impairment in people with schizophrenia.

> **Test yourself**
>
> Explain at least one strength and one weakness of the cognitive explanation for schizophrenia. Use research examples in your answer.

> **Challenge yourself**
>
> To what extent do you feel that schizophrenia is based in nature rather than nurture? Justify your answer.

> **Challenge yourself**
>
> Look at the issue and debate tracker table on page 137. Create similar issue and debate commentaries for nature versus nurture, reductionism versus holism, determinism versus free will, and idiographic versus nomothetic.

19.1.3 Treatment and management of schizophrenia

Biological treatments

Biochemical: biochemical treatment centres on using drugs to alleviate the symptoms of schizophrenia

Davison and Neale (1997) noted that, from the 1950s onwards, drugs classed as phenothiazines were commonly used to treat schizophrenia. They were effective as they block dopamine receptors in the brain. However, many had 'extrapyramidal side effects' that resemble symptoms of neurological diseases such as Parkinsonian-type tremors, dystonia (muscular rigidity), dyskinesia (chewing movements) and akasthesia (the inability to keep still). Second-generation antipsychotics were developed to also block dopamine receptors but produce fewer side effects and there are now third-generation antipsychotics that reportedly produce even fewer side effects.

Contemporary research still shows the effectiveness of antipsychotics in treating schizophrenia. Sarkar and Grover (2013) conducted a meta-analysis on 15 randomised controlled studies testing the effectiveness of antipsychotics on children and adolescents diagnosed with schizophrenia. It was seen that both first- and second-generation antipsychotic drugs were superior to the placebo in alleviating symptoms. Second-generation drugs were superior overall with chlozapine being the most effective of all drugs. Extrapyramidal side effects were seen more in first-generation antipsychotics while side effects that affected metabolism were seen more often in second-generation drugs.

> **Ask yourself**
>
> What do you know about first-, second-, and third-generation drugs? Find out information about all three, including possible side effects.

Ehret *et al* (2010) noted that a third-generation drug called lurasidone had been shown to be effective in four separate clinical trials, reducing both positive and negative symptoms. Noted side effects had only been nausea, vomiting, and dizziness. The researchers noted that drugs such as clozapine were now showing more metabolic dysfunction side effects plus bone marrow toxicity so newer drugs needed to be developed.

Atypical antipsychotics do not usually cause movement-related side effects and, in theory, should produce fewer overall side effects. Longer-term issues such as tardive dyskinesia (abnormal facial, tongue, and mouth movements) are also lessened using atypical antipsychotics as these drugs do not increase the production of prolactin (which happens with typical antipsychotics).

Electro-convulsive therapy (ECT)

ECT is basically a procedure where a person receives a brief application of electricity to induce a seizure. Early attempts at this were not pleasant but nowadays patients are anaesthetised and given muscle relaxants. Electrodes are fitted to specific areas of the head and a small electrical current is passed through them for no longer than one second. The seizure may last up to one minute. The patient regains consciousness in around 15 minutes. There will always be debate about whether ECT should be used for any mental health issue as clinicians and psychologists are divided on the severity of the therapy and the longer-term side effects. ECT is now mainly used for depression (see page 143), but there has been research conducted on the use of ECT with people with schizophrenia.

Zervas *et al* (2012) conducted a review of the use of ECT in schizophrenia. They looked at four issues: symptom response, technical application, continuation/maintenance ECT and its combination with medication. It would appear that ECT can be quite effective for people with catatonic schizophrenia and in reducing paranoid delusions. There was also evidence that it may improve a person's responsiveness to medication. Lengthier courses worked well with people with catatonic schizophrenia. When combined with medication, ECT worked better than when only ECT was used.

Strengths	Weakness
There is evidence to suggest that ECT can be effective in helping to treat schizophrenia.	There are ethical issues in the use of the technique and long-term effects are still largely unknown.

Psychological therapy

Cognitive behavioural therapy (CBT)

CBT aims to change or modify people's thoughts and beliefs and also change the way that they process information. A therapist will challenge irrational and faulty thoughts as well as behaviours that are not helping. Patients may be set tasks outside the face-to-face therapy to help challenge faulty thoughts and beliefs. For schizophrenia, the intention of CBT would be to help patients make sense of the psychotic experiences and reduce the negative effects of the condition plus any distress they may be feeling. Patients may also be given help to understand that views, thoughts, and interpretations are not facts, then given help to deal with assessing them.

CBT (Sensky *et al*, 2000)

Sensky *et al* (2000) tested the potential usefulness of CBT for persistent symptoms of schizophrenia that were resistant to medication. Patients were recruited if they fitted the following criteria. They:

- were aged 16 to 60 years

- had a diagnosis of schizophrenia according to both the ICD and DSM
- had symptoms that had persisted for at least six months
- had showed no improvement for being on medication (with no evidence of poor adherence)
- did not abuse alcohol or drugs.

There were 90 qualifying participants, who were randomly assigned to one of two groups, which were:

- a manualised CBT specifically developed for schizophrenia
- a 'befriending' intervention.

Both of the interventions were delivered by experienced nurses. The patients were assessed at baseline, after treatment (lasting up to nine months) and at a nine-month follow-up. An assessor who was blind to the study rated a selection of therapy sessions for quality.

Both interventions did result in a significant reduction in both negative and positive symptoms of schizophrenia alongside depression scores on the Comprehensive Psychiatric Rating Scale. However, at the nine-month follow-up, those who had received CBT continued to improve whereas the befriending group did not.

Therefore, it would appear that CBT is effective at reducing the symptoms of schizophrenia in those who have previously been resistant to antipsychotic medication.

Strengths	Weakness
There was a long-term follow-up that showed the therapy to still be having a positive effect on clients.	Some of the outcome measures were from questionnaires so results could be more subjective than objective, potentially lowering the validity of findings.

Bechdolf *et al* (2005) assessed the effectiveness of CBT versus group psychoeducation on re-hospitalisation and medication compliance up to 24 months after treatment. A total of 88 patients were randomly assigned to either group and they received 8 weeks' therapy. When followed up six months later, the CBT group were less likely to be hospitalised and be taking their medication.

At 24 months post-treatment, the CBT group had had 71 fewer days in hospital than the psychoeducational group. In a further study, Bechdolf *et al* (2010) analysed the data collected from their first study but on quality of life measures taken at six months post-treatment. Both groups reported improved quality of life but there was no significant difference between the two treatment groups.

Challenge yourself

Create similar issue and debate tracker commentary for idiographic versus nomothetic, experiments, and ethics.

	Issue and debate tracker
Longitudinal studies	These types of studies allow for a long-term assessment of the validity of treatments for schizophrenia. This allows clinicians to understand how long a treatment regime should last for (and continue to work) but also if there are any long-term side effects, especially with drug treatments. There is always debate as to 'how long is long'. A lot of studies appear to follow-up 6–12 months post-treatment intervention. This, of course, could be down to the cost of continuing a study and collating results. There is also an attrition rate that requires examining in these types of studies. There may be something qualitatively different in patients that complete a long-term treatment package compared to those who do not, making generalisations sometimes debatable.
Generalisations from findings	Some of this has been covered above in relation to attrition rates. Also, as many patients have co-morbidity (so not only having a diagnosis of schizophrenia but other mental health disorders), it may mean that generalisations are limited due to smaller samples sizes. However, statistical tests on data do take into account sample size, meaning that some results are showing a positive effect of treatment and could be generalised to other patients about to begin their own treatment regime. In many studies there are also some patients that do not respond to the treatment regime, meaning that overall results have some limited generalisability.

19.2 Mood (affective) disorders: depressive disorder (unipolar) and bipolar disorder

19.2.1 Diagnostic criteria for mood (affective) disorders

ICD-11 diagnostic criteria for depressive disorder (unipolar)

There are two main types of depressive disorder in ICD-11.

- Single episode–this is when the patient has a history of one depressive episode in the absence of ever having one before. A depressive episode is defined as a reduced interest in daily activities for a period of at least two weeks. Other symptoms have to be present, such as difficulty in concentrating, feeling worthless, excessive or inappropriate guilt, a sense of hopelessness, recurrent thoughts of death or suicide, changes in appetite and sleep patterns, and reduced energy, or fatigue.

- Recurrent episode – this is when a patient has a history of at least two depressive episodes separated by at least a few months without any other significant disturbance of mood.

ICD-11 diagnostic criteria for bipolar disorder

There are two types of bipolar disorder.

Bipolar type I disorder
This list gives the diagnostic criteria for bipolar type I disorder.

- There is occurence of one or more manic or mixed episodes.

- A manic episode involves euphoria, irritability, expansiveness, increased activity than typical, subjective experience of having increased energy, rapid speech, flight of ideas, increased sense of self-esteem, decreased need to sleep and rest, being easily distracted, impulsive behaviour, and reckless behaviour.

- A mixed episode involves the presence of manic episodes and the presence of depressive episodes. These can occur simultaneously or alternate rapidly (within the same day, or day by day).

- Diagnosis *must* include altered state consistent with the above and be present for most of the day for *at least* two weeks.

Bipolar type II disorder
This list gives the diagnostic criteria for bipolar type II disorder.

- There is occurrence of one or more hypomanic episodes and *at least* one depressive episode.

- A hypomanic episode involves a persistent mood state that lasts for several days that includes elevation of mood *or* increased irritability with increased activity *or* subjective experience of having increased energy, plus increased talkativeness, rapidly changing thoughts, increased sense of self-esteem, decreased need to sleep and rest, being easily distracted, impulsive behaviour, and reckless behaviour.

- The hypomanic symptoms *must* be a marked change from the person's typical mood, level of energy, and general behaviour but *not* severe enough to impair daily functioning.

- A depressive episode involves depressed mood or decreased interest in typical daily activities that are seen for most of the day, nearly every day for *at least* two weeks. Other symptoms include changes to appetite and sleep patterns, psychomotor agitation or retardation, fatigue, feelings of worthlessness, excessive guilt, feelings of hopelessness, difficulty in concentrating, and suicidal thoughts.

- There *must* be no history of manic or mixed episodes.

Measure of depression

The Beck Depression Inventory

This measure of depression is a 21-item questionnaire that covers a range of factors seen as being symptoms of depression. These include past failure, self-dislike, crying, loss of interest, irritability, and tiredness or fatigue. Each statement has a 4-point scale to choose from. The points are totalled up and the higher the points, the higher the depression levels of the individual.

Strengths	Weakness
The scale has been validated and is a long-standing measure of depression. Therefore, the result produced when a person completes it should be an accurate representation of that individual's current level of depression.	This measure of depression relies on the self-report of the individual. As the person may well be depressed, the views given as answers to the statements may not be how the person is truly feeling. Depressed people can have distorted cognitions about the world and themselves.

	Issue and debate tracker
Quantitative and qualitative data	The diagnostic guidelines from ICD-11 appear to utilise both types of data. The checklist can be used to see how many of the symptoms a person is presenting but also there must be an element of listening and observing the person to generate qualitative data to support whether the person is presenting the symptom(s) or not. For example, with either of the bipolar disorders, examples of reckless behaviour or rapid speech need to be recorded qualitatively to then help with the quantitative assessment of number of symptoms. Also, the Beck Depression Inventory generates a quantitative score and there are various cut-off points to show the level of depression shown by any patient who completes it.
Psychometrics	These types of measures tend to have had reliability and validity tests performed on them to make sure that they are measuring what they intend to measure and that they are stable over time. The Beck Depression Inventory allows a meaningful comparison across groups of people so then aspects of depression can be discussed using standardised scores and descriptions. These can be seen as valid measures for depression. This is the only example in this section that uses psychometrics.

> **Challenge yourself**
>
> Create similar issue and debate commentaries for individual and situational explanations, cultural differences, and validity.

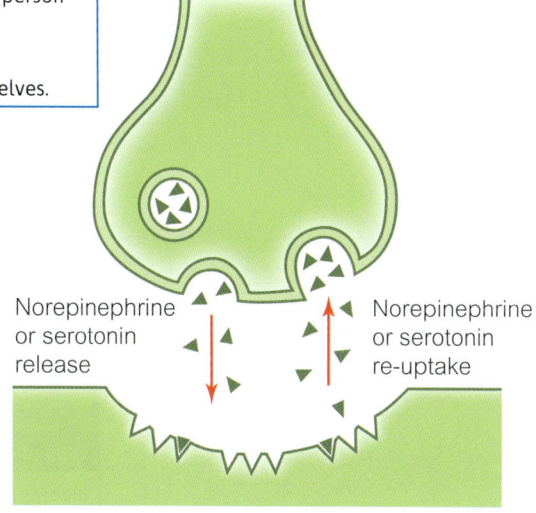

19.2.2 Explanations of mood (affective) disorder: depressive disorder (unipolar)

Biological explanations

Biochemical

In terms of a biochemical cause, there are two neurotransmitters that have been investigated: norepinephrine and serotonin. Low levels of both of these may well be a cause of depression. Davison and Neale (1998) highlighted how certain drugs block the re-uptake of these neurotransmitters so that more of them can be used in the postsynaptic neuron. This is shown in Figure 19.2.

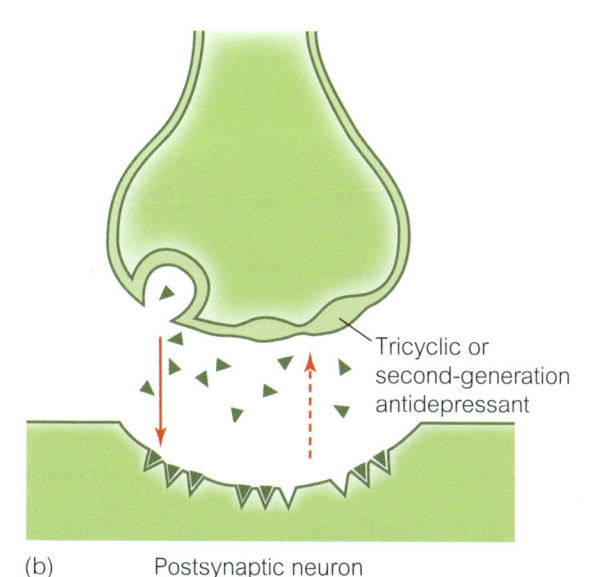

Figure 19.2 (a) When a neuron releases norepinephrine or serotonin from its endings, a re-uptake mechanism begins to recapture some of the neurotransmitters before the postsynaptic neuron receives them.
(b) Antidepressant drugs called tricyclics block this re-uptake process allowing more norepinephrine or serotonin to reach the postsynaptic neuron.

Genetic

The genetic argument follows the idea that depression may well run in families and be encoded in genetics.

One way of testing the idea that depression may run in families is to conduct twin studies using monozygotic (MZ: identical) and dizygotic (DZ: non-identical) twins. McGuffin *et al* (1996) examined 214 pairs of twins where at least one of them was being treated for depression. They reported that 46% of MZ and 20% of DZ twins of the patients also had a diagnosis of depression. This hints at a part-genetic component for depression but a drawback is that twins tend to be brought up together and treated in the same way so we cannot rule out environmental influences.

Following on from this, Silberg *et al* (1999) wanted to assess whether it was genetics, the environment or a combination of the two that could be causing depression. A total of 902 pairs of twins completed psychiatric interviews to assess levels of depression alongside data about life events and from parents. In general, females were diagnosed more often with depression than males. This was more marked when life events were negative. However, there were individual differences seen among the females, and those who were diagnosed with depression after a negative life event were more likely to have a twin who was also diagnosed with depression. Therefore, it would seem both genetics and the environment interact to cause depression.

Earlier studies had also shown a part-genetic component of depression. Bertelsen *et al* (1977) reported that the genetic component varied depending on the type of depression. Table 19.5 records this.

Table 19.5 *Genetic component and type of depression*

Type of depression	Percentage chance for MZ twins	Percentage chance for DZ twins
Bipolar disorder	80	16
Severe depression (three or more episodes of depression)	59	30
Depression (fewer than three episodes of depression)	36	17

Therefore, the strongest evidence for a genetic component comes from bipolar disorder, then severe depression, followed by depression.

KEY STUDY: Oruč *et al* (1997)

Context and main theories/explanations

There has been some belief that all types of depressive disorder have an element of genetic causation. Various 'disturbances' in serotonin (5-HT: 5-hydroxytryptamine) transmission appear to play a role in depression and suicidal tendencies. Some antipsychotic drugs such as clozapine are a 5-HT antagonist (binds or blocks a receptor) with an affinity to 5-HT2c receptors. These receptors help to control our appetite and as loss of appetite is a major diagnostic feature for depression, it was hypothesised that there may be a link. Also, the serotonin transporter protein (5-HTT) may also play a role as low density could be a marker for depression. This study examines the role of all of these in bipolar disorder (not unipolar depression).

Aim and hypotheses

To investigate the role of 5-HT2C receptors and 5-HT transporter genes in bipolar (depressive) disorder.

Design

In Croatia, Oruč *et al* (1997) analysed the DNA of 42 patients (females n = 25; mean age 31.7 years) diagnosed with bipolar type disorder and compared it to 40 healthy controls. All of the bipolar type patients had undertaken a clinical interview with a trained physician to ensure that they met the criteria for bipolar disorder. As part of the interview, they completed a validated Croatian translation of the Lifetime Version of the Schedule for Affective Disorders and Schizophrenia.

Results, findings, and conclusions

Of the 42 patients diagnosed with bipolar type disorder, 16 had a positive family history. Within the control group no participant had a positive family history for bipolar type disorders. They were assessing DNA polymorphisms in the serotonin receptor 2c (5-HTR2c) and serotonin transporter (5-HTT) genes. There were no significant differences between the two groups. However, when the data was analysed by gender, an association was discovered. Females were more likely to show both polymorphisms, indicating that these variations in genetics could help to explain why females are more susceptible to bipolar disorder.

Main discussion points

- It is doubtful that because this pathway was seen in people with bipolar disorder it can explain unipolar depression. Recent research has reported weak associations between 5-HTR2c receptors and unipolar depression. For example, Ochi *et al* (2019) reported no association between any 5-HT receptor genes and unipolar depression improvement when taking antidepressants. However, in a meta-analysis of six studies, Zhang *et al* (2020) concluded that carriers of the S allele of 5-HTTLPR are more vulnerable to depression. The sample was based on people with coronary heart disease so it may have limited generalisability. It should be noted that in this study by Oruč *et al* it was patients with the C allele who produced higher bipolar depressive scores (when compared to those with the S allele). However, nothing was significantly different between those with or without bipolar disorder.

Evaluation

- The measurements are objective, meaning that the findings are more likely to be valid. Genetic analyses do not require a subjective judgement, so any alleles detected are correct.
- The procedure used in the study was clear and standardised. The genetic analysis and how the sample was recruited with specific criteria were clearly outlined, so other researchers can replicate the study to test for reliability.
- The results may be culturally specific (and therefore biased) as all of the sample were from Croatia. This may make generalisation difficult beyond the sample.

Psychological explanations

Cognitive processes (Beck, 1979)

Beck (1979) was interested in examining the irrational thought processes involved in depression. He believed that there were three factors that make people cognitively vulnerable to depression. The three factors in Beck's inventory are called the cognitive triad. The inventory consists of:

- negative view of self
- negative view of the world
- negative view of the future.

These three factors can interact with each other to make a person depressed. They will also 'change' the way information is processed as they become an 'automatic' way of thinking. That is, when information is being processed it is affected by all three factors so the information will be processed in a 'negative way'. People may simply overestimate the negative aspects of a situation, meaning they will conclude that whatever happens, something bad will come of it. Depressives may also have negative self-schemas (packets of information about themselves) that have developed since childhood by having negative experiences and/or overly critical parents, peers, or teachers. All new information that is processed will become negative as the mechanisms are all negative. As a result, depression develops.

> **Test yourself**
>
> Explain at least one strength and one weakness of the belief that cognitive processes can explain depression.

Learned helplessness or attributional style

Learned helplessness is about individuals becoming passive because they feel they are not in control of their own life. This is caused by unpleasant experiences that they have tried to control in the past (unsuccessfully). This gives people a sense of helplessness which in turn leads to depression. The idea was based on Seligman's (1974) research on dogs. The dogs received electric shocks that they could not escape from (so they experienced lack of control) and it did not take long for them to stop trying to escape. They all became passive and appeared to accept the painful situation they were in. When in future trials there was an opportunity to escape, the dogs still did not try to do this. This is the sense of helplessness that depressives will feel if they cannot escape situations that are negative and out of their control. In addition, attribution theory could also explain depression. Weiner *et al* (1971) noted three levels of attribution that can affect people's views of their own behaviour:

1. internal (personal) or external (environmental)
2. stable or unstable
3. global or specific.

Table 19.6 gives an example of how the different attributional schemata can be used to explain why someone failed a psychology examination.

Table 19.6 Using attributional schemata to explain examination failure

	Internal		External	
	Stable	**Unstable**	**Stable**	**Unstable**
Global	"I lack general intelligence for exams."	"I am really, really tired today."	"Exams are an unfair way to test my ability."	"It's an unlucky day."
Specific	"I lack the ability to pass psychology exams."	"I am fed up with studying psychology."	"The psychology exam was really unfair as it had questions I did not know the answers to."	"My psychology exam had 13 questions, which is unlucky."

Challenge yourself

To what extent do you think that abnormal affect disorders are more related to nurture than nature? Justify your answer.

Challenge yourself

Look at the issue and debate tracker table on page 139. Create similar issue and debate commentaries for nature versus nurture, reductionism versus holism, determinism versus free-will, experiments, and reliability.

Learned helplessness or attributional style (Seligman *et al*, 1988)

Seligman *et al* (1988) assessed 39 unipolar depressives and 12 bipolar depressives for signs of learned helplessness and attributional style. They all completed the Attributional Style Questionnaire at the beginning of their cognitive therapy, at the end of their therapy and one year later. The questionnaire asks participants to make causal attributions for 12 hypothetical events (both good and bad). They then rate each cause on a 7-point scale for internality, stability, and globality.

The results were as follows.

- A pessimistic explanatory style for negative (bad) events correlated significantly with severity of depression at all three time points. Explanatory style improved by the end of the therapy, as did depressive symptoms for the unipolar group.
- The pattern was also seen in bipolar depressives but the significant results were not as strong.

This study suggests that it is explanatory style (attributional style) that requires changing in depressive patients via cognitive therapy to help them improve their mental health.

Strengths	Weakness
The study has good application as a therapist can assess clients for types of learned helplessness.	The measures taken were from questionnaires, which could cast doubt on the validity of findings as people may not have been honest when completing them (and as they were all diagnosed with depression, responses may have been affected).

19.2.3 Treatment and management of mood (affective) disorders

Biological treatments

Antidepressants

Two examples of antidepressants that are commonly used are as follows.

- Selective serotonergic re-uptake inhibitors (SSRIs) – see Figure 19.2 to see how re-uptake inhibitors work. Possible side effects include fatigue, headaches, and insomnia.

- Monoamine oxidase inhibitors (MAOIs) – these work by inhibiting monamine oxidase (this breaks down neurotransmitters such as norepineprhine and serotonin) which means more serotonin and norepinephrine is available in the synapse. Possible side effects include hypertension (which is potentially fatal), dizziness, and nausea.

Rucci *et al* (2011) tested the effectiveness of SSRIs versus interpersonal psychotherapy on suicidal thoughts in a group of 291 outpatients with major depression. Participants were randomly assigned to either treatment regime and suicidal ideation was measured using a questionnaire. The 231 patients who had shown no suicidal ideation pre-study were analysed and 32 of these did exhibit suicidal ideation during the treatment. For those on SSRIs, the time taken for these thoughts to emerge was much longer than in the psychotherapy group. Therefore, SSRIs may reduce suicidal thoughts in people with major depression.

Electro-convulsive therapy (ECT)

See page 136 for a description of the procedure for administering ECT.

Nordenskjold *et al* (2013) tested the effectiveness of ECT with drug therapy compared to drug therapy alone. A total of 56 patients were randomly assigned to either 29 treatments of ECT alongside drug therapy, or drug therapy alone. The researchers measured relapse of depression within one year of completing treatment. In the group of patients just on drug therapy 61% relapsed within the year compared to just 32% of patients who had ECT and drug therapy.

There have been several meta-analyses testing the effectiveness of ECT. Dierckx *et al* (2012) reviewed the field in terms of whether response to ECT differs in bipolar disorder patients versus unipolar depressed patients. A total of six studies formed their analysis. The overall remission rate was nearly 51% for unipolar and over 53% for bipolar disorder. The data covered over 1000 patients. Overall, the data were encouraging as they showed similar efficacy rates for the two types of depression.

Psychological therapies

Cognitive restructuring (Beck, 1979)

The idea of this therapy follows Beck's cognitive triad approach to the potential causes of depression (see page 141). It is a six-stage process.

1. The therapist explains the rationale behind the therapy and what its purpose is.
2. Clients are taught how to monitor automatic negative thoughts and negative self-schemata.
3. Clients are taught to use behavioural techniques to challenge negative thoughts and information processing.
4. Therapist and client explore how negative thoughts are responded to by the client.

> **Test yourself**
>
> Explain at least one strength and one weakness of using drugs to help treat depression.

> **Test yourself**
>
> Explain at least one strength and one weakness of using ECT to help treat depression. Make sure one of your points is about ethics.

> **Challenge yourself**
>
> Design a longitudinal study to investigate the effects ECT has on people with depression.

5. Dysfunctional beliefs are identified and challenged.
6. The therapy ends with clients having the necessary 'cognitive tools' to repeat the process by themselves.

Hans and Hiller (2013) conducted a meta-analysis on the effectiveness of CBT on adults with unipolar depression. A total of 34 studies formed the analysis and they had to assess the effectiveness of individual or group CBT as well as drop-out rates. The studies also had to have at least a six-month follow-up. It would appear that outpatient CBT was effective in reducing depressive symptoms and these were maintained at least six months after the CBT ended. The average drop-out rate was 24.63%. This was reported as being quite high by the researchers but they also noted that better-quality effectiveness studies are needed to assess how good CBT truly is with depressive patients.

Rational emotive behaviour therapy (REBT) (Ellis, 1962)

Ellis (1962) stated that rationality consists of thinking in ways that allow us to reach our goals; irrationality consists of thinking in ways that prevent us from reaching our goals. The idea behind the therapy follows an ABC model.

- **A**ctivating event – this is a fact, behaviour, attitude or an event.
- **B**eliefs – the person holds beliefs about the activating event.
- **C**ognitive – this is the person's cognitive response to the activating event as well as emotions.
- **D** – disputation or challenge of the irrational or limiting beliefs is required for mental change to take place. Reviewing, challenging and eschewing the current beliefs sets the person up for future success.

  To achieve point D, there are three key kinds of disputes that can be used.
  - Empirical or scientific dispute – where is the proof or basis for the belief, feelings or thought pattern?
  - Functional dispute – is the belief supporting some other, potentially unconscious goals?
  - Logical dispute – does the belief system follow common sense? Is there any generalisation or other thought pattern influencing these beliefs?

- **E** – this is the effect of challenging the self-defeating belief system. Psychologists often call this cognitive restructuring, as new mental patterns and habits are created. An example would be: a presenter gains more confidence as presentations become more fluid and get more positive feedback. This in turn improves the presenter's self-belief and creates a positive cycle of change.

Using the example from Table 19.6, failing a psychology examination would be the A. The B that might follow could be "I am a failure" or "I hate it when I do not pass an exam" and then the C would be depression.

Szentagotai et al (2008) examined the effectiveness of REBT, CBT, and drug therapy for the treatment of a major depressive episode. A range of outcome measures were taken based on a questionnaire that tested three main depressive thoughts: automatic negative thoughts, dysfunctional attitudes, and irrational beliefs. A general measure of depression was also taken. There were 170 participants randomly assigned to either the REBT (n = 57), CBT (n = 56) or drug therapy (n = 57) groups. In terms of depressive symptoms, there were no significant differences between the three groups but the REBT groups had an average score significantly lower than the drug therapy group. In terms of the three main depressive thoughts, all three treatments appeared to decrease these immediately post-treatment and then at follow-up.

Sava et al (2008) compared REBT, CBT and the use of prozac in a sample of depressives. The participants were split into the three treatment groups and all had 14 weeks' therapy. All participants completed questions based on the

> **Test yourself**
>
> Explain at least one strength and one weakness of using cognitive restructuring to help treat depression. Make sure one of your points is about ethics.

> **Challenge yourself**
>
> Look at the issue and debate tracker table on page 139. Create similar issue and debate commentaries for application to everyday life, individual and situational explanations, reductionism versus holism, determinism versus free will, and generalisations from findings.

Beck Depression Inventory (see page 139) prior to the therapy and then at 7 and 14 weeks post-therapy. There were no significant differences between the three groups in terms of scores on the inventory but REBT and CBT cost less for the same outcomes so these are preferred treatments.

19.3.1 Diagnostic criteria for impulse control disorders

19.3 Impulse control disorders

ICD-11 diagnostic criteria of impulse control orders

Kleptomania

These are the diagnostic criteria for kleptomania.

- There is recurrent failure to control any strong impulses to steal.
- There is no clear motive to steal.
- Increasing feelings of tension and emotional arousal prior to engaging in theft are experienced.
- A sense of pleasure, excitement, relief, and/or gratification during the act of theft is experienced.
- A sense of pleasure, excitement, relief, and/or gratification after the act of theft is experienced.
- The behaviour *cannot* be explained by intellectual impairment or any co-morbid disorder or substance intoxication.

Pyromania

These are the diagnostic criteria for pyromania.

- There is recurrent failure to control strong impulses to set fires.
- Multiple acts (or attempts) are made to set fire to property or other objects where the motivation is not monetary gain, revenge, sabotage, etc).
- There are increasing feelings of tension and emotional arousal prior to engaging in fire setting.
- A sense of pleasure, excitement, relief, and/or gratification during the act of fire setting is experienced.
- A sense of pleasure, excitement, relief, and/or gratification after the act of fire setting is experienced.
- The behaviour *cannot* be explained by intellectual impairment or any co-morbid disorder or substance intoxication.

Gambling disorder

These are the diagnostic criteria for gambling disorder.

- A pattern of persistent or recurrent gambling behaviour (online or offline) is formed.
- Impaired control over gambling (frequency onset, context, duration, etc) is shown.
- Increasing priority is given to gambling so it takes precedence over other daily activities.
- There is continuation or escalation of gambling even in the face of negative consequences.

- Gambling results in significant stress and/or impairment to family life, personal, social, educational, and/or occupational areas of functioning.
- These behaviours and consequences seen over a period of at least 12 months.
- If symptoms are severe, it can be for less than 12 months.

Measures of impulse control disorders

Kleptomania Symptom Assessment (K-SAS)

- The K-SAS (see page 147) is a 12-item questionnaire that is aimed at evaluating kleptomania symptoms.
- The questions use a variety of techniques such as Likert-type scales and closed questions to help evaluate how severe each case is.
- The higher the score generated, the more severe the symptoms.

> **Challenge yourself**
>
> Look at the issue and debate tracker table on page 148. Create similar issue and debate commentaries for idiographic versus nomothetic, questionnaires, case studies, quantitative and qualitative data, and objective and subjective data.

19.3.2 Explanations of impulse control disorders

Biological: dopamine

Dopamine has been linked to addiction and impulse control disorders because when it is released in the body it gives us the feelings of pleasure and satisfaction. Once these feelings become a desire, we then repeat behaviours that cause the release of dopamine and the cycle continues with repetitive behaviours. More specifically, when someone experiences an activity that is pleasurable, dopamine is released in the nucleus accumbens, which is sometimes called 'the brain's pleasure centre'. The sooner that an activity gives a sense of reward, the faster the nucleus produces dopamine and it produces higher levels. The entire 'reward circuit' in the brain includes sources of motivation and memory alongside pleasure. Any addictive behaviour stimulates the same circuits within the brain, overloading it with dopamine. Vroon *et al* (2010) reported that when participants were given a dopamine agonist (it activates dopamine receptors), impulsive choice increased, reaction times became faster and participants showed fewer decision conflicts compared to a control group. One drawback is that participants had Parkinson's disease so whether this can be related to people with impulse control disorder needs investigating. Koep *et al* (1998) observed gambling behaviour where PET scans were done on participants as they played competitive video games. They were to be paid large amounts of money for winning. The scans showed an increased release of dopamine as the risk level went higher. The closer the individual was to winning, the more the brain increased the level of pleasure and excitement.

> **Challenge yourself**
>
> To what extent do you feel that the dopamine hypothesis is deterministic? Justify your answer.

Kleptomania Symptom Assessment (K-SAS)

The following questions are aimed at evaluating kleptomania symptoms. Please **read** the questions **carefully** before you answer.

1) If you had urges to steal during the past WEEK, on average, how strong were your urges? Please circle the most appropriate number:

   None — 0　Mild — 1　Moderate — 2　Severe — 3　Extreme — 4

2) During the past WEEK, how many times did you experience urges to steal? Please circle the most appropriate number.
   1. None
   2. Once
   3. Two or three times
   4. Several to many times
   5. Constant or near constant

3) During the past WEEK, how many hours (add up hours) were you preoccupied with your urges to steal? Please circle the most appropriate number.

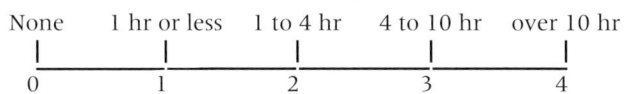

   None — 0　1 hr or less — 1　1 to 4 hr — 2　4 to 10 hr — 3　over 10 hr — 4

4) During the past WEEK, how much were you able to control your urges? Please circle the most appropriate number.

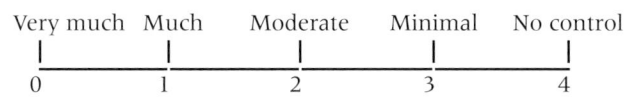

   Very much — 0　Much — 1　Moderate — 2　Minimal — 3　No control — 4

5) During the past WEEK, how often did thoughts about stealing come up? Please circle the most appropriate number.
   1. None
   2. Once
   3. Two to four times
   4. Several to many times
   5. Constantly or nearly constantly

6) During the past WEEK, approximately how many hours (add up hours) did you spend thinking about stealing? Please circle the most appropriate number.

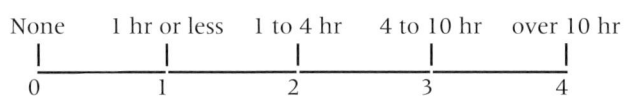

   None — 0　1 hr or less — 1　1 to 4 hr — 2　4 to 10 hr — 3　over 10 hr — 4

7) During the past WEEK, how much were you able to control your thoughts of stealing? Please circle the most appropriate number.

   Very much — 0　Much — 1　Moderate — 2　Minimal — 3　No control — 4

8) During the past WEEK, on average, how much tension or excitement did you have shortly before you committed a theft? If you did not actually steal anything, please estimate how much anticipatory tension or excitement you believe you would have experienced if you had committed a theft. Please circle the most appropriate number.

   None — 0　Minimal — 1　Moderate — 2　Much — 3　Very much — 4

9) During the past WEEK, on average, how much excitement and pleasure did you feel when you successfully committed a theft? If you did not actually steal, please estimate how much excitement and pleasure you believe you would have experienced if you had committed a theft. Please circle the most appropriate number.

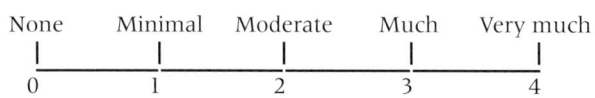

   None — 0　Minimal — 1　Moderate — 2　Much — 3　Very much — 4

10) During the past WEEK, how much emotional distress (mental pain or anguish, shame, guilt, embarrassment) has your stealing caused you? Please circle the most appropriate number.

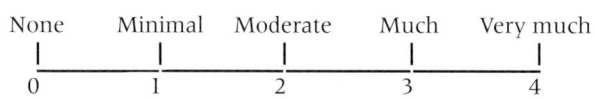

    None — 0　Minimal — 1　Moderate — 2　Much — 3　Very much — 4

11) During the past WEEK, how much personal trouble (relationship, financial, legal, job, medical or health) has your stealing caused you? Please circle the most appropriate number.

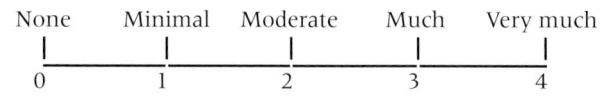

    None — 0　Minimal — 1　Moderate — 2　Much — 3　Very much — 4

12) During the past WEEK, how many times did you steal? Please circle.
    1. None
    2. Once
    3. Two or three times
    4. Several to many times
    5. Daily or almost daily

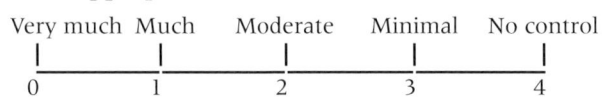

Figure 19.3 Kleptomania Symptom Assessment (K-SAS)
Source: Grant (rev. E. Corsale, MA, MFT and S. Smithstein, Psy.D.)

Psychological

Behavioural: positive reinforcement

This follows the idea of rewards. When an action is followed by a pleasurable outcome, the person is more likely to engage in that behaviour again. For example, if an addictive behaviour or impulse control behaviour is followed by a positive outcome (eg feeling a sense of arousal when setting fire to a house or winning on a fruit machine), the person is likely to repeat the behaviour.

This can then be linked to the 'reward' of a dopamine release within the brain (see page 146). Therefore, the release of dopamine is the outcome of engaging in an impulse control disorder behaviour, increasing the probability that the person will engage in that behaviour again.

Cognitive: feeling-state theory (Miller, 2010)

Miller (2010) introduced the feeling-state theory for impulse control disorders. The main idea is based around state-dependent memories. Impulse control disorders are created when positive feelings, linked to certain objects, activities or events, form these state-dependent memories. This combination of feelings and objects, activities, or events form a 'feeling-state' in the individual. Miller defines this feeling-state as '… the entire psycho-physiological arousal of the body and its connections with the memory of a specific behaviour. In other words, the feeling-state is a unit that is composed of the feelings (sensations, emotions, and thoughts…) associated with the behaviour plus the memory of the behaviour itself' (2010: 4). Miller uses the example of a gambler – the thoughts or feelings of 'I'm a winner!' combined with the memory of the event could easily create a gambling compulsion, especially if the two are linked several times. However, there can be many feeling-state links that can contribute to an impulse control disorder.

Figures 19.4 and 19.5 illustrate Miller's theory.

> **Test yourself**
>
> Explain at least one strength and one weakness of the feeling-state theory.

> **Challenge yourself**
>
> Create similar issue and debate commentaries for application to everyday life, reductionism versus holism, and determinism versus free will.

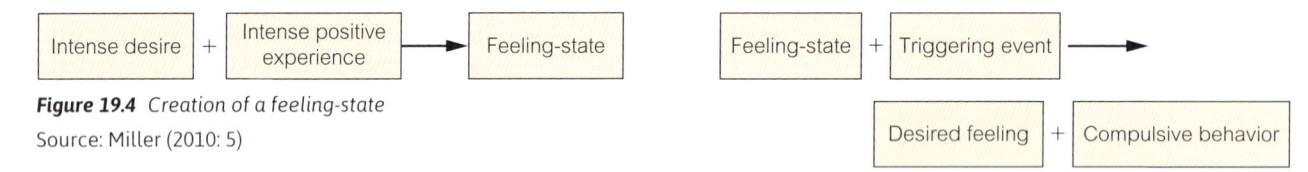

Intense desire + Intense positive experience → Feeling-state

Figure 19.4 Creation of a feeling-state
Source: Miller (2010: 5)

Feeling-state + Triggering event →
Desired feeling + Compulsive behavior

Figure 19.5 Activation of the compulsive disorder
Source: Miller (2010: 5)

	Issue and debate tracker
Nature versus nurture	This can be seen by the biological explanations (nature) versus the psychological explanations (nurture). Dopamine levels are biological (nature) but positive reinforcement and cognitive pathways are psychological and develop over time (nurture). However, there is an argument that the environment affects brain growth and neurochemistry, meaning that it can be very difficult to separate nature from nurture when it comes to impulse control disorder. It may well be a complex interaction of the two sides of this debate as can be seen with the debate about dopamine and rewards interacting.
Individual versus situational explanations	Individual explanations can be based around individuals' internal mechanisms in terms of how their biological make-up causes dopamine to affect their impulse control disorder. There may well be clear individual differences. In addition, positive reinforcement may not work the same for everyone as there are different types of reinforcer (money, praise, etc). Finally, people have their own cognitive pathways that have been moulded by internal mechanisms and experiences, again meaning that there may be clear individual differences between people with impulse control disorders. However, the situation that people find themselves in can also affect impulse control disorders. Some people who have pathological gambling have a family history of addictive behaviours and this situation has been observed and becomes part of a person's psychology.

19.3.3 Treatment and management of impulse control disorders

Biological treatments

KEY STUDY: Grant *et al* (2008)

Context

Grant *et al* (2008) acknowledged that opiate antagonists had shown some positive outcomes when used to help treat pathological gambling. However, no study had attempted to examine why individual differences occur in the outcome.

Main theories/explanations

Pathological gambling diagnostic criteria are on pages 145–146.

Aims and hypotheses

To investigate the clinical variables related to treatment outcomes of opiate antagonists on pathological gambling. To utilise any significant findings to generate a treatment algorithm for pathological gambling.

Design

Participants

A total of 284 participants (48.2% women) with a diagnosis of pathological gambling formed the sample group. They had already participated in one of two double-blind placebo-controlled trials (one was 16 weeks of nalmefene and the other was 18 weeks of naltrexone). All participants had been diagnosed using criteria from the Diagnostic and Statistical Manual of Mental Disorders (DSM-IV) via a structured clinical interview. All had to score above 5 on a second measure of gambling (South Oaks Gambling Screening) and they must have gambled within two weeks of the study. All trials were conducted in the United States.

Outcome measures

A 'positive' response to the treatment was measured as a 35% reduction in scores on a scale measuring pathological gambling symptoms. The primary outcome measure was the Yale Brown Obsessive Compulsive Scale Modified for Pathological Gambling. An independent researcher, who did not know which group any patient was in, administered this measure. Measures of anxiety, depression, and family history were also taken.

Results, findings, and conclusions

The strongest factor associated with a positive response was a positive family history of alcoholism. Those who were on the highest dosage of drug who had more intense urges to gamble were also more likely to show a positive response. For those receiving the placebo, those who were younger were more likely to show a positive response. No other variables were significant.

Main discussion points

- The idea of a potential algorithm for customising treatment could not be created as there was only one predictor variable that reached significance. However, it does mean that when beginning a treatment regime with a patient, if there is a family history of alcoholism then the use of opiate antagonists should be the first part of the treatment. To a lesser degree, higher doses may be administered to those with higher levels of gambling urges.
- The researchers note that more thorough research using neuroimaging and genetic analyses should give a more complete understanding of the results of this present study.
- There may be a genetic pathway for gambling disorder due to the family history link found in this study. This needs exploring further.

Evaluation

- Pathological gambling is a chronic condition, and it may require a long-term therapy. The two studies used in this statistical review did not follow-up after 18 weeks post therapy so there may have been more predictor variables that were significant in the longer term.
- There may be some difficulty in generalising from this study. There were many patients excluded who had co-morbidity, so it is not known if these pathological gamblers respond better or worse to opiate antagonists.
- The studies used a double-blind procedure so there were no experimenter effects that could have affected the outcome measures. Therefore, the findings should be valid.
- The outcome measures were collected via questionnaires, so we cannot be sure that the participants were telling the full truth. This may reduce the validity of findings.

Psychological (cognitive behavioural) therapies

Covert sensitisation (Glover, 1985)

Glover (1985) reported on a case study of a female kleptomaniac who was treated using covert sensitisation. The 56-year-old female had been shoplifting for 14 years, mainly for 'non-purposive' goods. For example, she stole baby shoes although she did not have a baby to give them to. She tended to wake every morning and think about stealing and, even though she felt a strong resistance to these thoughts, would give into them during her lunch break.

She wanted therapy, and on initial interview appeared very motivated to treat her kleptomania. She did not want to use imagery of her being caught or apprehended for stealing as she had tried to use that herself and it was never successful. She and the therapist debated what imagery should be used as part of the covert sensitisation therapy. They agreed on using the imagery of vomiting and nausea to be paired with the process of stealing goods. The four sessions worked as follows.

- In the first three sessions she had to imagine herself approaching something in a supermarket that she would steal. The closer she got to the product she was wanting to steal, the more nausea she had to imagine.
  She then had to imagine vomiting as she picked up the product. Finally, she had to imagine other shoppers watching her as she vomited.

- In the final session, she had to continue feeling more nauseous as she approached the product but imagine it all stopping once she put the product back on the shelf and left the supermarket.

- Muscle relaxation techniques were used during all sessions. She was also interested in self-hypnosis so this was also used in sessions three and four.

- After each session she was asked to complete homework of rehearsing the imagined scenes several times per day. When she had to go shopping she was asked to make a list of specific items to buy and not take her usual shopping bag, which she always used for shoplifting.

The therapy lasted eight weeks, as each session happened fortnightly.
She reported that her thoughts of shoplifting decreased over time but she did relapse twice, stealing minor items from four different shops. There were follow-up sessions every three months and during these it became apparent that she was finding it easier to go shopping alone and not steal. At a final 19-month follow-up session she appeared more confident and cheery and had only relapsed once. She believed that the covert sensitisation using the nausea imagery had helped her overcome the kleptomania.

Strengths	Weakness
The case study has real-world application: therapists can choose to use convert sensitisation to help other people overcome kleptomania.	As it was a case study it may be difficult to generalise the actual procedures to other kleptomaniacs. The woman in this example said that she could visualise the scenes very clearly and this helped. Other people may not be able to do this so it might not be an appropriate treatment for them.

Imaginal desensitisation (Blaszczynski and Nower, 2002)

Blaszczynski and Nower (2002) reported on the role of imaginal desensitisation for helping people with impulse control disorders including pathological gambling, kleptomania, and compulsive buying. The technique allows clients to be taught brief progressive muscle relaxation methods. According to Blaszczynksi and Nower, there should be six steps used in a 'treatment sequence'.

1. Initiating the urge – clients must begin to re-enact, mentally, a scene where they begin to have the urge to engage in some impulsive behaviour such as gambling. As this is happening, brief relaxation instructions are given to help the client relax.

The following is a sample script for conducting Progressive Muscle Relaxation (PMR) for use in the office or on tape.

> Make yourself comfortable in a chair. Close your eyes and clear your mind of any thoughts or images and focus attention on your breathing … [pause] … Take a deep breath and let it out slowly … [pause] …. Just breathing easily and gently now, no effort, breathing as you normally would. Now, as you breathe out, I want you to say to yourself, 'relax.'
>
> Source: Blaszczynski and Nower (2002: 11)

2. Planning to follow through on the urge – clients must then visualise the 'trip' to the place where the impulsive behaviour usually takes place such as a bingo hall or a favourite shop. Again, relaxation instructions are read out as this is happening.

3. Arriving at the venue – clients must then imagine, in detail, what it feels like to arrive at the venue where they are going to engage in their compulsive behaviour. As with the other steps, brief relaxation instructions are given.

4. Generating arousal and excitement with the behaviour – this allows clients to imagine a certain scenario where they are getting ready to fully engage in the impulsive behaviour. In the example of gambling, this may include them choosing their favourite roulette wheel or fruit machine and imagining getting money ready to use. As usual, brief relaxation instructions are given.

5. Having 'second thoughts' about the behaviour – this is when clients are asked to imagine looking around the venue and seeing people who look discouraging. Clients also must become aware of how they feel if they lose or are caught. Brief relaxation instructions are read out again.

6. Decreasing the attractiveness of the behaviour – in this final step, clients have to imagine all of the negative outcomes that could possibly happen as a result of engaging in the impulse control behaviour. They must then visualise themselves walking away from the venue having not engaged in the impulsive behaviour.

Alongside this, each client completes a Trigger Monitoring Table so that these behaviours can be used during the visualisation sessions. Figure 19.6 shows an example.

The recommendation is for clients to do some of this at home too. Successful interventions are based on about 15 sessions spread over one week.

> **Challenge yourself**
>
> Look at the issue and debate tracker table on page 148. Create similar issue and debate commentaries for application to everyday life, reductionism versus holism, idiographic versus nomothetic, interviews, and generalisations from findings.

Strengths	Weakness
It has good application as therapists can use the techniques to help clients control their impulses better.	It relies on people being able to visualise (rather than actually behaving) and some clients may not be able to do this well, so the technique might not be good for everyone with impulse control issues.

The following is a table designed to identify situations that trigger your urges to engage in troublesome behaviours. Whenever you encounter a stressor or other situation that makes you want to [behaviour], please note that situation on the sheet below. In addition, indicate on a scale of "1" to "10," with "1" being "lowest" and "10" being "highest," the various feelings you felt upon initially encountering the situation. In addition, write a brief quote of the thought(s) that went through your head when you had those feelings. Finally, identify on the same scale the feelings you experience when you first thought of [behaviour] as a way of dealing with the situation.

Trigger Monitoring Table

Situation	Feelings before planning the behaviour Scale 1 (low)–10 (high)	Thoughts before planning the behaviour	Feelings when planning the behaviour
"Coworkers leaving at the end of a work-day"	Lonely = 8 Anxious = 5	"I don't want to go home again alone"	Excited = 10 Happy = 8

Figure 19.6 Example Trigger Monitoring Table
Source: Blaszczynski and Nower (2002: 10)

19.4 Anxiety disorders and fear-related disorders

19.4.1 Diagnostic criteria for anxiety disorders and fear-related disorders

Diagnostic criteria (ICD-11) of anxiety disorders and fear-related disorders

Generalised anxiety disorder

These are the diagnostic criteria for generalised anxiety disorder.

- Marked symptoms of anxiety are seen on the majority of days on one month.
- There is either general apprehension (free-floating anxiety) or excessive worry about everyday events such as family, health, work, etc.
- Muscular tension, motor restlessness, physiological over-activity (sympathetic autonomic), nervousness (subjective), concentration issues, irritability, and disturbance of sleep are experienced.
- There is significant distress or impairment to family life, personal, social, educational, and/or occupational areas of functioning.
- The anxiety *cannot* be explained by an underlying health condition or due to substances affecting the nervous system.

Agoraphobia

These are the diagnostic criteria for agoraphobia.

- Marked and excessive fear/anxiety happens in response to situations where escape may be difficult or where help may not be available if needed. This can be, for example, when the person is on public transport, in crowded areas, or outside the home alone.
- The consistent anxiety is due to the fear or certain negative outcomes such as panic attacks or showing some physical symptoms.
- Fear/anxiety provoking situations are actively avoided or only entered into with a trusted companion or simply endured with high level of fear and anxiety.
- Symptoms have to last for several months.
- There is significant distress or impairment to family life, personal, social, educational, and/or occupational areas of functioning.

Specific phobia

These are diagnostic criteria for specific phobia.

- Marked and excessive fear/anxiety happens in response to, or anticipation of, one or more specific objects or situations. These have to be out of proportion to the actual danger posed.
- The phobic objects and situations are actively avoided or simply endured with high level of fear and anxiety.
- Symptoms have to last for several months.
- There is significant distress or impairment to family life, personal, social, educational, and/or occupational areas of functioning.
- Exclusions include body dysmorphic disorder and hypochondriasis.

Measures of anxiety and fear-related disorders

Generalised Anxiety Disorder Assessment (GAD-7)

This is a seven-item questionnaire used to measure the severity of generalised anxiety disorder. The higher the score out of 21 generated, the more severe the generalised anxiety disorder.

PLEASE PRINT IN BLACK PEN

| Patient's Full Name | Date of Birth | NHS Number |

Generalised Anxiety Disorder Assessment (GAD-7)

This easy to use self-administered patient questionnaire is used as a screening tool and severity measure for generalised anxiety disorder.

In the past 2 weeks how often have you been bothered by any of the following problems:

1. Feeling nervous, anxious or on edge?
- [ ] Not at all
- [ ] Several days
- [ ] More than half the days
- [ ] Nearly every day

2. Not being able to stop or control worrying?
- [ ] Not at all
- [ ] Several days
- [ ] More than half the days
- [ ] Nearly every day

3. Worrying too much about different things?
- [ ] Not at all
- [ ] Several days
- [ ] More than half the days
- [ ] Nearly every day

4. Trouble relaxing?
- [ ] Not at all
- [ ] Several days
- [ ] More than half the days
- [ ] Nearly every day

5. Being so restless that it is hard to sit still?
- [ ] Not at all
- [ ] Several days
- [ ] More than half the days
- [ ] Nearly every day

6. Becoming easily annoyed or irritable?
- [ ] Not at all
- [ ] Several days
- [ ] More than half the days
- [ ] Nearly every day

7. Feeling afraid as if something awful might happen?
- [ ] Not at all
- [ ] Several days
- [ ] More than half the days
- [ ] Nearly every day

Total =   /21

The GAD-7 score is calculated by assigning scores of 0, 1, 2 and 3 to the response categories of "not at all", "several days", "more than half the days", and "nearly every day" respectively, and adding together the scores for the seven questions.

Scores of 5, 10 and 15 are taken as the cut-off points for mild, moderate and severe anxiety, respectively.

| Assessor Name Signature | Date Time | Designation |

Figure 19.7 Generalised Anxiety Disorder Assessment (GAD-7) version 1 (March 2012)

The Blood-injection Phobia Inventory (BIPI)

The Blood-injection Phobia Inventory (BIPI) is a questionnaire that initially had 50 items on it that covered a range of situations related to blood and injection phobias. They were:

- 32 situations related to blood, injections and the dentist
- 5 situations related to animal blood
- 4 situations related to the colour red
- 5 situations about agoraphobia to see whether it produces a similar phobic response
- 4 situations about social anxiety to see if whether produces a similar phobic response.

The BIPI also measures:

- the frequency of symptoms, on a scale ranging from 0 = Never to 3 = Always, of a patient's different type of reactions to the situations (cognitive, physiological, behavioural)
- situational anxiety as well as anticipatory anxiety.

Further explanation of the BIPI is given below, and an excerpt is shown in Figure 19.8.

> **Items of the proposed version of the BIPI**
>
> Below is a list of situations where you can find yourself and that could create distress, tension, etc. to you. The objective is to evaluate the different reactions that occur to you in each of the described situations.
>
> The task is to rate from 0 to 3, the frequency of each symptom. Use the following scale:
>
> 3 = Always   2 = Almost always   1 = Sometimes   0 = Never

Respondents are given the following instructions. Read each of the situations shown on the left side, and then score from 0 to 3 each symptom that is listed in the top of the page.

> **Test yourself**
>
> Explain at least one strength and one weakness of using psychometric measures to measure anxiety disorders.

> **Challenge yourself**
>
> Look at the issue and debate tracker table on page 164. Create similar issue and debate commentaries for questionnaires, psychometrics, subjective and objective data, validity, and reliability.

Items of the proposed version of the BIPI

Blood-injection Phobia Inventory (BIPI)

Symptoms+		Situations	1. When I see an injured person after an accident, bleeding in the road or on TV.	2. When I see blood on my arm or finger after pricking myself with a needle.	3. When I get an intravenous injection.	4. When I see a laboratory tube with blood.	5. When I hear a conversation about blood.	6. When I think I have to accompany a relative to have a blood test or to cure an open wound.	7. When I see another person getting an intramuscular injection.	8. When I describe to another person an experience or situation involving blood.	9. When I think that the nurse has to insert the needle in my vein to extract my blood.	10. If I see an operation or surgical intervention.	Score total symptom
Cognitive responses	I don't think I will be able to bear the situation.												
	I think that "something bad is going to happen to me."												
	I perceive that not much time will go by before I get dizzy.												
	I feel I confused, disoriented.												
	I think people will notice how distressed I feel.												
	I don't think I'll know how to react.												
	I remember past experiences and anticipate panic.												
	I think I'm going to faint.												
	I must get out of here before I make a fool of myself.												
	I think I should have avoided the situation, because this feeling is nothing new to me.												
Physiological responses	My heartbeat speeds up.												
	My palms or armpits sweat.												
	My muscles start to tense.												
	I feel that I am getting dizzy.												
	I breathe more quickly.												
	I feel a cold sweat all over my body.												
	I feel more blood pumping in my body.												
	I feel my face is hot.												
	I get pale.												
	I faint.												
	I feel a lump in my throat.												
	I feel stomach discomfort.												
Behavioural responses	I avoid going. I avoid it.												
	My legs and/or hands shake.												
	I escape from the situation immediately.												
	I shift around in my seat nervously, etc.												
	My words don't come out fluidly or my voice is uneven.												
	Score total situation												TOTAL

Figure 19.8 Excerpt from the BIPI

Source: Borda Mas, López Jiménez and Pérez San Gregorio (2010: 69–70)

19.4.2 Explanations of fear-related disorders

Biological explanations

Blood and injection phobias (Öst, 1992)

Öst (1992) investigated two groups of patients who had been diagnosed with a 'simple phobia' via DSM: blood phobic patients (n = 81) and injection phobic patients (n = 59). Participants in each group were asked whether they had a first-degree relative who had the same phobia. In the blood phobic group, 61% of participants reported this, compared to only 29% of patients in the injection phobic group.

The pattern continued when participants were asked about whether they would faint in their phobic situation: 77% of the blood phobic group reported this compared to 48% in the injection phobic group. However, there were no differences between the two groups regarding:

- history of actually fainting in the phobia situation
- age of onset
- marital status
- occupational status
- age at which they received treatment.

Overall, there were more similarities than differences between the two groups and Öst believed that the blood and injection phobia should not be seen as separate. Also, due to the large percentage of people who had a first-degree relative with the same phobia, Öst believed that the cause may well be genetic.

Could it be that we are pre-programmed to fear certain objects that may be potentially harmful? That is, are there certain objects or things that we are expected to be frightened of so we are biologically prepared to fear them? This theory could help us to explain fears that are not totally irrational (eg fear of snakes – they can be dangerous). Seligman (1971) proposed the idea that we have evolved to be frightened of fear-relevant stimuli. So, we fear objects and things that might be of a survival threat in evolutionary terms (Mineka and Öhman, 2002). We have fear-relevant stimuli such as snakes that we may be 'prepared' to fear. We also have fear-irrelevant stimuli such as flowers that we are not 'prepared' to fear.

Psychological explanations

Behavioural (classical conditioning)

Classical conditioning is all about learning through association. It is a form of conditioning where the organism (be it human or animal) associates an unconditional stimulus with a neutral stimulus. After repeated associations, the organism then responds to the neutral stimulus (now called a conditioned stimulus) without having the unconditional stimulus present anymore. Figure 19.9 shows what happens in classical conditioning.

In their study of Little Albert, Watson and Rayner (1920) were interested in two aims.

> '1. Can we condition fear of an animal (e.g. a white rat) by visually presenting it and simultaneously striking a steel bar?
>
> 2. If such a conditioned emotional response can be established, will there be a transfer to other animals or objects?' (Watson and Rayner, 1920).

> **Challenge yourself**
>
> What else might be causing the blood and injection phobias in this study other than genetics? Justify your answer.

> **Test yourself**
>
> Explain at least one strength and one weakness of a biological explanation for phobias. Make sure one of your points is about nature versus nurture.

At approximately nine months of age, Little Albert was presented with a range of stimuli (eg a white rat, a rabbit, a dog, a monkey). Albert showed no fear towards any of the objects. When Albert reached 11 months and 3 days old, the experimental procedure began to test the first aim. Albert was presented with a white rat again and as before he showed no fear. However, as Albert reached out to touch the rat, Watson struck an iron bar immediately behind Albert's head. Albert 'jumped violently and fell forward, burying his face in the mattress' (1920: 4).

Albert tried to approach the rat again but as soon as he got close the iron bar was struck. After the two associations of the rat and loud noise the rat was taken away.

Seven days later, the researchers wanted to see whether his experience with the loud noise had made Alfred fearful of white rats. He was very wary around the rat and did not really want to play with it or touch it. When he did reach for it the loud noise was made, the same as in the previous week. This was done five times during the session. So, in total, Albert experienced the loud noise and white rat occurring together on seven occasions. Finally, the rat was presented by itself and Albert began to cry and crawled away rapidly. This was the first time he had cried during the study in response to the rat.

Over the next month Albert's reactions to a range of objects were observed. He was still fearful of the white rat. He showed negative reactions to a rabbit being placed in front of him and a fur coat (made from seal skin). He did not really like cotton wool but the shock was not the same as it was with the rabbit or fur coat. He even began to fear a Santa Claus mask.

His experiences can be explained via the mechanisms of classical conditioning, as shown in Figure 19.9.

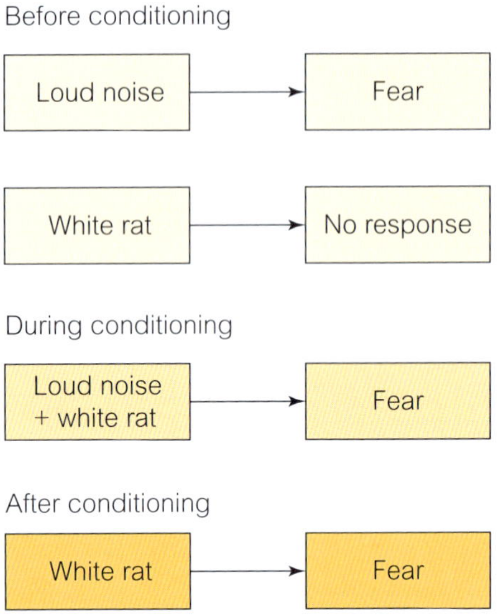

Before conditioning

Loud noise → Fear

White rat → No response

During conditioning

Loud noise + white rat → Fear

After conditioning

White rat → Fear

Figure 19.9 *Classical conditioning of Little Albert*

Classical conditioning may be able to explain why we form some of our phobias.

- *Generalisation* occurs when we produce a conditioned response to a stimulus that is *similar* but not the same as the conditioned stimulus. For example, we may produce a fear response to wasps. We could *generalise* this fear to other flying insects such as bees and hornets.

- *Extinction* occurs when the conditioned stimulus no longer produces the conditioned response. This could be because the conditioned stimulus has no longer been paired with the unconditional stimulus. So, for example with a person who fears wasps, over time the conditioned response of fear disappears in the presence of the conditioned stimulus of the wasp.

Psychodynamic

Freud was the first psychodynamic psychologist who attempted to explain how people acquire a phobia. A phobia is a defence against any anxiety produced by any repressed impulses from the id. This fear is then transferred to an object, person or situation that has some sort of 'symbolic' connection to the anxiety. The person then becomes fearful of that, rather than the repressed id impulses. This avoidance means the person can function psychologically by not having to focus mental energy onto the repressed conflicts he or she is having.

Freud used the case study of Little Hans to show how this can happen. When Hans was 4 years old, he developed a phobia of horses. Specifically, he was afraid that a white horse would bite him. When reporting this to Freud, Hans' father noted that the fear of horses seemed to relate to their large penises. At around the same time as the phobia of horses developed, a conflict developed between Hans and his father. Hans had been in the habit for some time of getting into his parents' bed in the morning and cuddling his mother. However, his father began to object to this. Hans' phobia worsened to the extent that he would not leave the family house.

> **Test yourself**
>
> Explain at least one strength and one weakness of a behavioural explanation for phobias.

> **Test yourself**
>
> Explain at least one strength and one weakness of a psychodynamic explanation for phobias. Make sure one of your points is about temporal validity.

Freud interpreted the case as an example of the Oedipus Complex. More specific details are as follows.

- Horses represented Hans' father. White horses with black nosebands were the most feared because they resembled the moustached father. Horses also made good father symbols because they have large penises.
- The anxiety Hans felt was really castration anxiety triggered by his mother's threat to cut off his 'widdler' and fear of his father caused by his banishing Hans from the parental bed.

The 'children fantasy' represents a relatively friendly resolution of the Oedipus Complex. In this fantasy Hans replaces his father as his mother's main love object, but the father still has a role as grandfather.

> **Challenge yourself**
>
> Look at the issue and debate tracker table on page 164. Create similar issue and debate commentaries for nature versus nurture, determinism versus free will, case studies, longitudinal studies, and validity.

19.4.3 Treatment and management of anxiety disorders and fear-related disorders

Behavioural therapy

Systematic desensitisation (Wolpe, 1958)

If we look at the case of Little Albert again (see pages 157–158), it can be clearly seen that the conditioned stimulus of the white rat elicited the conditioned response of fear. The phobia had been learned.

Systematic desensitisation works on the idea that the phobia can then be unlearned. The end point should recondition the patient so that the conditioned stimulus (which will be the phobic stimulus) produces a conditioned response of relaxation and not fear.

In the systematic desensitisation therapy developed by Wolpe (1958), the first step is to teach patients relaxation skills so that they understand what it feels like to have relaxed muscles. This should enable patients to recreate this feeling in a variety of situations including when confronted with their phobic stimulus.

Second, the patient produces an anxiety or fear hierarchy to work through with the therapist. A simple hierarchy, for use by a person fearful of snakes, would be as follows.

1. This is the least anxious situation – looking at a cartoon snake in a children's book.
2. The person looks at a picture of a real snake in a book.
3. The person watches a snake on a wildlife programme.
4. A snake is in the same room as the person but in a cage.
5. The snake is in the same room as the person and out of the cage.
6. The person is within three feet of the snake.
7. The person touches the snake.
8. This is the most anxious situation – the person lets the snake go around his or her neck.

Stage 1

Spider (CS) → Fear (CR)

Relaxation technique (UCS) → Calmness (UCR)

Stage 2

Spider (CS) + Relaxation technique (UCS) → Calmness (UCR)

Stage 3

Spider (CS) → Calmness (CR)

CS: conditioned stimulus;
CR: conditioned response;
UCS: unconditioned stimulus;
UCR: conditioned response

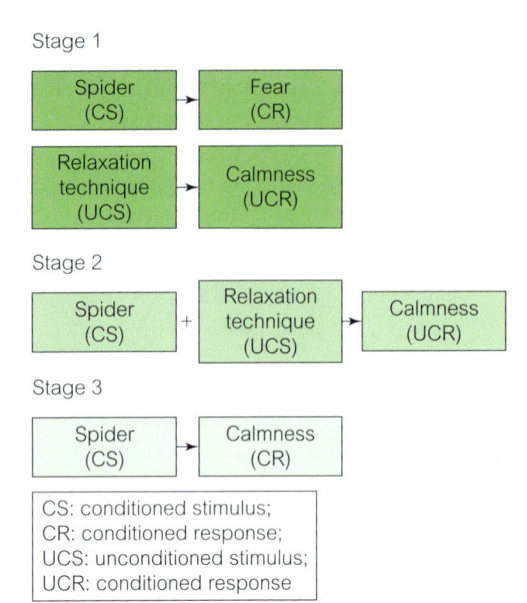

Figure 19.10 *Principles of classical conditioning linked to systematic desensitisation*

> **Test yourself**
>
> Explain at least one strength and one weakness of systematic desensitisation as a treatment for phobias. Make sure one of your points is about long-term effectiveness.

Strengths	Weakness
There was a long-term follow-up procedure to show that the positive effects of the CBT lasted.	Some of the outcome measures were using self-report scales so some of the participants may not have told the truth (they may have given socially desirable answers) and this could reduce the validity of the findings.

Patients can only move to a higher stage of the hierarchy once each stage has been successfully completed; that is, the patient is showing signs of relaxation in relation to a specific stage on the hierarchy (eg for stage 2 above it would be when looking at a book; for stage 7, when touching the snake).

Figure 19.10 shows the principles of classical conditioning linked to systematic desensitisation. In the conditioning phase there are competing responses of fear and relaxation. This is called reciprocal inhibition whereby it is impossible to experience both emotions at the same time. The idea is to promote the relaxation response more than the fear response. If the patient is feeling more fear than relaxation then that stage of the hierarchy is stopped until the patient feels relaxed again and is willing to have another go.

There have been many studies that support the use of systematic desensitisation to treat phobias and fears. One example is the study by Zettle (2003), which showed that systematic desensitisation can be applied to people who fear mathematics. Twenty-four college students underwent treatment for six weeks (split between systematic desensitisation and a different therapy) and had to rate their anxieties towards mathematics before, during and after the treatment. Anxiety decreased markedly for those who completed their systematic desensitisation even though their mathematics ability never changed.

Psychological therapy

Cognitive behavioural therapy (CBT)

See page 136 for a description of how CBT works. There have been numerous studies assessing the effectiveness of CBT in relation to phobias.

CBT (Öst and Westling, 1995)

Öst and Westling (1995) tested the effectiveness of using CBT against using applied relaxation (AR) to treat panic disorder. The patient group (n = 38) had all been diagnosed with panic disorder using the Diagnostic and Statistical Manual of Mental Disorders (DSM). All of the patients were assessed via an independent rater, self-report scales, and observations before and after treatment as well as at a one-year follow-up. All patients had an individual session (CBT or AR) each week for 12 weeks.

Both of the treatment groups showed large improvements at the end of treatment and at the one-year follow-up. There were no significant differences between the two groups but the results did favour CBT. At end of treatment, 65% of the AR group and 74% of the CBT group were panic-free and after one year this was 82% for the AR group and 89% for the CBT group.

Andrews *et al* (2011) tested out the effectiveness of face-to-face versus internet-based CBT for people with social phobias. The researchers randomly assigned 70 participants to either group. Both groups made significant progress relating to symptoms and disability measures. However, the total amount of time that the therapist was required differed markedly: 18 minutes for the internet-based CBT whereas it was 240 minutes for the usual CBT. Therefore, internet-based CBT would be more cost-effective in areas where healthcare budgets are limited.

Clinical psychology

Applied tension

KEY STUDY: Chapman and DeLapp (2013)

Context

Blood-injection-injury (BII) phobia is unique in terms of its treatment. BII patients have an increased susceptibility to fainting in the presence of phobic stimuli. Therefore, treatment has to include both techniques to help them cope with the fear but also techniques to allow them to remain conscious when exposed to phobic stimuli.

Main theories/explanations

Page 153 highlights the diagnostic criteria for a specific phobia using ICD-11. Additionally, the Diagnostic and Statistical Manual of Mental Disorders [DMS-IV] highlights a phobia as being an excessive and unreasonable fear triggered by the presence or the anticipation of seeing a specific object or situation. BII is specific in terms of it being a fear of exposure to blood or certain medical-related procedures. This could be fear of having surgery, being shot with a gun, or injuring themselves resulting in an open wound. In addition, patients may also have disgust sensitivity.

CBT is described on page 136.

Aim and hypotheses

To help treat a person who has BII phobia using CBT.

Case history

This case study centres around a 42-year-old white male. He was self-referred because of his BII phobia. For confidentiality, he was referred to as 'T'. He had been unable to receive medical care due to severe panic attacks. It was also difficult for him to help his two children, one of whom regularly attended hospital. T could not observe any medical procedure that his children needed. T described several incidents that formed his case history, including the following.

- His mother would joke that T was susceptible to heart problems.
- He was exposed to incidents that involved death and dying. For example, he spent a great deal of his childhood with this grandparents. His grandmother regularly listened to an ambulance dispatch scanner that reported on local emergencies throughout the day.
- T was the only other person there when his grandfather died of cancer and also witnessed his uncle die of cancer and his aunt die of lupus (an autoimmune condition).
- He was always fearful of crowds in his youth.
- He had a routine medical examination after graduating. He believes that the physician exaggerated the importance of health, the actual medical examination, plus eating habits. He remembers having high blood pressure after this event.
- He would experience panic attacks just at the thought of going to see a physician.
- He was recently given anti-anxiety drugs to help him cope with medical visits.

Assessment of T

T had a clinical interview and completed a range of self-report questionnaires, including:

- the Beck Anxiety Inventory
- the Beck Depression Inventory
- the Quality of Life Satisfaction Questionnaire
- the Fear Survey Schedule 11 – this measures fear towards a number of objects on a 0 (none) to 6 (terror) scale
- the Blood-Injection Symptom Scale – this is a 17-item scale that measures severity of BII phobia.

Table 19.7 summarises events that contributed to T's BII phobia.

Table 19.7 Fear acquisition form

Phobia	Traumatic experiences	Observational learning	Informational transmission
Doctor visits	1. Grandfather died of cancer and T was with him	Grandmother and scanner	Mother's comments while watching "20/20"
	2. Watched uncle die of lupus		
Medical procedures/blood	1. Passing out while getting blood drawn	The movie "Last Man Standing"	Doctor said my problems were "cardiac in nature."
	2. Panic attack at doctor's office during routine checkup		

Source: Chapman and DeLapp (2013: 6)

Treatment, results, findings, and conclusions

The initial self-reports clearly showed that T scored in the 'severe' range for anxiety with 'minimal' depression. He was in good physical health even though he did not endorse that when asked (he self-described it as 'fair'). The treatment had nine planned sessions with accompanying homework. The sessions involved CBT and applied muscle tension.

Sessions 1 and 2

These involved more assessments about fear acquisition, psychoeducation, and the importance of T self-monitoring his BII phobia. They also discussed the strengths and weaknesses of using CBT. T also completed a Fear Acquisition Form plus other forms asking about phobias and bodily sensations. For the latter he had to rate different sensations on a scale of 0 to 100. Table 19.8 shows these.

Table 19.8 Bodily sensations

Sensation	Fear of sensations (0-100 scale)	Comments
Racing heart	95	"The heartbeat causes me to lose control"
Hot flashes or cold chills	60	"Other people will notice"
Chest tightness	50	NA
Dizziness, unsteadiness, fainting	45	"I turn as white as that door" (points finger); "I look bad." "I feel sick"
Shortness of breath	30	NA

Source: Chapman and DeLapp (2013: 7)

At the end of session 2, T reported that he now had a significant insight into his BII phobia.

Session 3

After recapping the previous sessions, a discussion about cognitive restructuring and exposure therapy happened. This involved explaining the cognitive restructuring (misinterpretation, misinformation, sensation feeling, etc) and thinking errors (eg catastrophising). During the previous week T had felt 'panicky' at a barber shop but assessed the situation for danger and quickly calmed down.

Session 4

Again, the first part of the session was a recap. Some of T's current beliefs were challenged by the therapist and new patterns of thinking were suggested. For example, he had an old association of a doctor's office = fear and anxiety = I will surely die. A new association was proposed of doctor's office = fear and anxiety = I will not die. T also created an exposure hierarchy of ten situations, assigning each a score from 0 to 100 on the Subjective Unit of Discomfort Scale (SUDS). Table 19.9 shows this exposure hierarchy.

Table 19.9 Exposure hierarchy with SUDS by treatment session

Situations	Initial SUDS (0-100)	Treatment session
Getting a physical or stress test	100	9
Getting blood pressure taken at CVS (a local pharmacy) or Wal-Mart	90	9
Getting blood pressure by a nurse	85	9
Taking blood pressure myself	75	9
Getting a phlebotomy	70	8
Seeing someone get a phlebotomy in person	55	8
Taking my own blood sugar	55	7
Wife taking my blood sugar	50	6
Seeing someone get a phlebotomy in a video	50	6
Wrapping a tourniquet around my arm and touching my veins	45	5

Source: Chapman and DeLapp (2013: 8)

Session 5

The applied tension and exposure preparation was introduced. The procedure is given below (Chapman and DeLapp, 2013: 9).

'1. Find a comfortable chair. Begin by tensing the muscles of your arms, torso, and legs;

2. Hold tension for 10 to 15 s, release tension for 20 to 30 s, repeat 5 times;

3. You can practice measuring your blood pressure after this procedure to notice that this increases your blood pressure;

4. Practice this exercise 5 times per day during the next week; and

5. Use this exercise during exposure to "fainting items" following the first week of successful practice'.

Sessions 6 to 9

T discussed anything that had happened each week that involved tackling the BII phobia. The hierarchy was used and T began to work up it with success, either face-to-face or watching videos. All instances of this are covered in depth in the journal paper. After completing session 9, T successfully measured his blood pressure in public and by a nurse. He did not even need to use applied tension to help cope with the situations. "I've never felt better in my life" he said. He then discontinued the treatment.

Follow-up

At four months post-treatment, T reported that he had several doctor's appointments coming up. He also felt that he had overcome his BII phobia. At a ten-month post-treatment contact, he was still fine. At 12 months post-treatment, T completed several of the questionnaires. His anxiety score had dropped dramatically. He stated that he only had four sensations when exposed to BII stimuli: feeling anxious, heart pounding, feeling nauseous, and sweating, but he could control these.

Main discussion points

- The treatment techniques used in the study increased self-efficacy and an ability to learn new tasks to help tackle the phobia. Therefore, things such as psychoeducation, objective recordings, exposure for a sufficient (but limited) time, and applied tension are techniques that appear to work well with this BII phobic patient.

- Only nine sessions were needed to help T, taking significantly less time than other published treatment regimes. Customising sessions to the individual could also explain the success in a short time period.

Evaluation

- The procedure used in the study was clear and standardised. The treatment regime, including all techniques and measures, were clearly outlined so other researchers can replicate the study to test for reliability, or use it on a different specific phobia.

- This was a case study of one individual male with BII phobia. There may be something unique about his clinical history or his commitment to the treatment. Therefore, it may be difficult to generalise the nine-session treatment to other people with BII phobia, or with other specific phobias.

> **Challenge yourself**
>
> Create similar issue and debate commentaries for self-reports, longitudinal studies, and generalisations from findings.

Issue and debate tracker	
Case studies	Case studies allow an in-depth analysis of an individual or a unit of people. A wealth of data can be collected to ensure that all available potential causes of a phobia are known so then appropriate treatments and therapies can be made available. In the example reported by Chapman and DeLapp (2013), there was one individual male with BII phobia. There may be something unique about his clinical history or his commitment to the treatment regime that made him atypical. Therefore, it may be difficult to generalise the nine-session treatment to other individuals with BII phobia or individuals with other types of specific phobia.
Idiographic versus nomothetic	Many phobias are labelled in the same way (eg agoraphobia, button phobia) but the causes can be idiographic, meaning that some treatments and therapies have to be customised. The case reported by Chapman and DeLapp showed this as other people may have the same phobia, have a similar pathway, but require a different treatment regime. However, there are some nomothetic aspects to the treatment of a phobia. Systematic desensitisation works on the same principle for all patients with a phobia; it is just that the hierarchy of fear is idiographic. The way that a patient works up the hierarchy is nomothetic – a general law based on classical conditioning.

19.5 Obsessive-compulsive disorder (OCD)

19.5.1 Diagnostic criteria for obsessive-compulsive disorder (OCD)

ICD-11 diagnostic criteria for obsessive-compulsive disorder

Obsessive-compulsive disorder (OCD)

These are the diagnostic criteria for OCD.

- Persistent obsessions (thoughts) or compulsions (actions) or both are present.
- The person has obsessions that are repetitive and persistent thoughts, impulses, and urges that are intrusive and unwanted.
- Compulsions are repetitive behaviours that can include repetitive mental acts that the person feels they need to perform as a result of an obsession. These can be followed with rigid rules or to achieve a sense of overall 'completeness' as a person.
- The person has to show that they are attempting to neutralise the obsessions with compulsions.
- Both obsessions and compulsions must be time-consuming. This is defined as taking up more than one hour per day.
- There is significant distress or impairment to family life, personal, social, educational, and/or occupational areas of functioning.

Common obsessions and common compulsions

There are many common obsessions that people with OCD experience. These include intrusive and persistent thoughts, doubts, worries, images, etc. They are unwanted and somewhat disturbing and can easily affect the person's life. This makes them very difficult to ignore.

There are also many common compulsions that people with OCD experience. These are the repetitive physical behaviours and actions (or mental repetition) that are performed over and over again. They may include:

- excessive washing of hands
- checking that items in the house are displayed in the 'correct order'
- checking that light switches are off and that electrical plug sockets are off
- mentally counting to a certain number as it 'neutralises' the obsessional thought.

Case study

Rapoport (1989) reported on a boy called Charles in his book *The Boy who Couldn't Stop Washing*. At the age of 12, Charles began to wash obsessively. For some time he managed to keep this action under control but then spent more and more of his school day washing. Eventually, he washed so often that he had to leave school. The ritual was always the same: he would hold the soap in his right hand and put it under a running tap for one minute. He would then transfer the soap to his left hand away from the tap for another minute. He would repeat this for about one hour. He would then wash for about another two hours before getting dressed.

At first, his mother discouraged him but, seeing how upset Charles became, she began to clean items in the house with alcohol. She stopped people from visiting as they had 'germs' and it would upset Charles.

Rapoport wanted Charles to have an EEG but the boy refused. Charles found stickiness to be 'terrible' like a 'disease'. He had drug therapy and his symptoms disappeared for around one year. He developed a tolerance for the drug, but then he engaged in his OCD behaviour in the evening only, so as not to disrupt his day.

Measures

Maudsley Obsessive-Compulsive Inventory (MOCI)

The Maudsley Obsessive-Compulsive Inventory (MOCI) is a 30-item scale. It has two major sub-scales and two minor ones:

- major: Checking and Cleaning
- minor: Slowness and Doubting.

Each of the 30 items is answered with 'True' or 'False'. Some of the items are reversed and some of them feature on more than one of the sub-scales. The total number of items for each sub-scale are:

- Checking – 9 items
- Slowness – 7 items
- Cleaning – 11 items
- Doubting – 7 items.

A practitioner can calculate an overall score and a score for each sub-scale to help individuals pinpoint the main features of their OCD. Here are some examples.

1. I frequently have to check things (e.g. gas or water taps, doors, etc.) several times.	TRUE	FALSE
2. My hands do not feel dirty after touching money.	TRUE	FALSE
3. I do not stick to a very strict routine when doing ordinary things.	TRUE	FALSE
4. I tend to get behind in my work because I repeat things over and over again.	TRUE	FALSE

Source: Hodgson and Rachman (1977: 395)

Strengths	Weakness
The scale went through rigorous validity and reliability testing to ensure that it does measure OCD symptoms and that it is consistent over time.	The questionnaire relies on a patient's honesty. Patients may not want to admit to certain behaviours and thoughts when completing a questionnaire, so the overall score may not be a true representation of the OCD symptoms.

The Yale-Brown Obsessive Compulsive Scale (Y-BOCS)

The Y-BOCS is a very popular measure used in many studies. There are two parts to the measurement and it is used as a semi-structured interview technique.

- The symptom checklist is a list of 67 symptoms for OCD and the interviewer notes whether each symptom is current, past or absent (in the latter case it is not recorded). This helps the interviewer determine whether a group of clustered symptoms exists (the list is divided into groups such as aggressive obsessions, sexual obsessions, contamination obsessions, checking compulsions, ordering compulsions, and cleaning or washing compulsions). An example is shown in Figure 19.11.

Symptom checklist

CLEANING/WASHING COMPLUSIONS			
	Current	Past	Examples
43. Excessive or ritualised hand washing	☐	☐	Washing your hands many times a day or for long periods of time after touching, or thinking you have touched, a contaminated object. This may include washing the entire length of your arm.
44. Excessive or ritualised showering, bathing, tooth brushing, grooming or toilet routine	☐	☐	Taking showers or baths or performing other bathroom routines that may last for several hours. If the sequence is interrupted the entire process may have to be restarted.
45. Excessive or ritualised cleaning of household items or other animate objects	☐	☐	Excessive cleaning of faucets, toilets, floors, kitchen counters or kitchen utensils.

2. INTERFERENCE DUE TO OBSESSIVE THOUGHTS

0 = None.
1 = Mild, slight interference with social or occupational activities, but overall performance not impaired.
2 = Moderate, definite interference with social or occupational performance, but still manageable.
3 = Severe, causes substantial impairment in social or occupational performance.
4 = Extreme, incapacitating.

Q: How much do your obsessive thoughts interfere with your social or work (or role) functioning? Is there anything that you don't do because of them? [If not currently working, determine how much performance would be affected if the patient were employed.]	☐ 0 ☐ 1 ☐ 2 ☐ 3 ☐ 4

Figure 19.11 Excerpt from the Y-BOCS symptom checklist and an example question

- The Y-BOCS itself consists of 19 items that the interviewee completes during the interview based on responses and observations. An excerpt, including an example question, is shown in Figure 19.11.

As you can see, there is a part-script for this question alongside how to score it. The scores are transferred to a grid that measures obsessions, compulsions, and other aspects of the condition.

A person is given an obsessions score out of 20 and a compulsion score out of 20. Then nine other items are noted on the 1–4 scale for severity.

There is also a children's version of the scale.

	Issue and debate tracker
Quantitative and qualitative data	The diagnostic guidelines from ICD-11 appear to utilise both types of data. The checklist can be used to see how many of the symptoms a person is presenting but also there must be an element of listening and observing the person to generate qualitative data to support whether the person is presenting the symptom(s) or not. For example, incidences and types of obsessive thoughts (content of) or compulsive behaviours (types of) need to be recorded qualitatively to then help with the quantitative assessment of number of symptoms. Also, the MOCI and Y-BOCS generate a quantitative score and there are various cut-off points to show the level of OCD shown by any patient who completes it.
Psychometrics	These types of measures tend to have had reliability and validity tests performed on them to make sure that they are measuring what they intend to measure and that they are stable over time. Both the MOCI and Y-BOCS allow for a meaningful comparison across groups of people so then aspects of OCD can be discussed using standardised scores and descriptions. These can be seen as valid measures for OCD. When studies are conducted, there can be a direct comparison across samples and across different types of therapies and treatments.

19.5.2 Explanations of OCD

Biological explanations: biochemical and genetic

In terms of a neurological explanation, OCD is quite complex. There appears to be an interaction between certain areas of the brain such as the orbitofrontal cortex, the anterior cingulate cortex, the striatum, the thalamus, the caudate nucleus, and the basal ganglia. These structures all communicate in the brain and deal with our 'primitive' emotions such aggression, sexuality, and bodily functions. Usually these circuits activate after certain activities. For example, after someone goes to the toilet it gives the person an urge to wash his or her hands. However, once the hand washing has been completed, the circuit activity dies down and the person continues with the next task. This does not appear to happen in people with OCD; the circuits do not 'die down' enough which leads to complications in communication between these areas of the brain. This then stimulates the person to keep having the urge to wash his or her hands constantly. As these parts of the brain are 'primitive' there is no reasoning that can take place: once it fires, the action has to be thought about and then acted upon. Therefore, the rational parts of the brain act upon the primitive urges, causing obsessions and compulsions.

There is some evidence to suggest that OCD could be genetic. Ozomaro *et al* (2013) noted that the SLITRK1 gene appears to be linked to some aspects of OCD. The researchers examined 381 individuals with OCD and 356 control participants. They discovered three novel variants on this gene present in seven of the OCD individuals and concluded that the SLITRK1 and variants need more research but currently they appear linked to OCD.

> **Test yourself**
>
> Explain at least one strength and one weakness of using the Y-BOCS to measure OCD. Make sure one of your points is about its usefulness, using evidence.

> **Challenge yourself**
>
> Create similar issue and debate commentaries for case studies, interviews, and validity.

> **Challenge yourself**
>
> Research the functioning of the parts of the brain mentioned above.

Humble *et al* (2011) wanted to test whether the neuropeptide oxytocin was correlated with OCD symptoms as previous studies had hinted at this. Even though the researchers were testing whether SSRIs affect oxytocin, the main result they reported was that, at baseline, levels of oxytocin were positively correlated with OCD symptoms as measured by the Y-BOCS.

Those with early onset OCD had the highest levels of oxytocin. Finally, reduced levels of serotonin may be linked to OCD and the drugs used in the studies do affect serotonin levels (see the section on treatment of OCD on pages 169–170).

Strengths	Weakness
The measures taken to test this idea are objective and scientific, which means that they are more likely to be valid.	The idea is reductionist as it does not take into account other factors that may cause OCD such as cognitions or psychodynamic ideas.

Psychological explanations

Cognitive (thinking error)

The cognitive aspect of this is linked to the obsessive thoughts that OCD individuals have. It would appear that these thoughts increase with levels of stress. In an everyday situation most people can learn to control these but people with OCD tend to have thoughts that are more vivid and elicit greater concern. Psychologists believe that this could be due to childhood experiences that have taught these people that some thoughts are dangerous and unacceptable and this has affected their information-processing networks. When new information is being processed, it is affected by these processing networks and generates anxiety and stress that can only be alleviated with compulsive behaviours.

Behavioural (operant conditioning)

The behavioural aspect is linked to the compulsions that people perform during OCD. Psychologists consider it to be a learned behaviour that is being reinforced by the consequences of performing the compulsions. For example, if a compulsive behaviour ends in a favourable outcome (eg reductions of anxiety or hands are now free of germs) then this is positive reinforcement. As we know, positive reinforcers increase the probability of repeating that behaviour again. For example, if the end goal of a compulsion is to have arranged clothes in some form of order and this reduces anxiety and also fulfils the compulsion to have things in order, then two reinforcement mechanisms are working here: negative (removal of anxiety) and positive (clothes are now arranged in order).

Psychodynamic

OCD is caused by instinctual forces (driven by the id in the unconscious) that are not under full control due to traumatic experiences in the anal stage of psychosexual development. The person with OCD is therefore fixated in the anal stage. It is the battle between the id's desires and the superego's morals that can cause OCD as the ego (and its defence mechanisms) fail to control either. Obsessive thoughts may be generated by the id (eg to be messy and out of control) but the ego uses defence mechanisms to counteract this by making the person behave in a way that is completely opposite to that (eg being neat and orderly). This defence mechanism is called reaction formation. For example, if a child has a traumatic experience while potty training (eg if the child is harshly treated for being messy) then the obsessive thoughts of being neat and tidy re-emerge in adolescence and adulthood. The person develops OCD as a result because any thoughts of being messy cause great anxiety because of those early unresolved traumatic experiences.

> **Test yourself**
>
> Evaluate all three psychological explanations for OCD. Make sure you outline at least one strength and one weakness.

> **Challenge yourself**
>
> To what extent do you feel that the cause of OCD is more nature than nurture? Justify your answer.

> **Challenge yourself**
>
> Look at the issue and debate tracker table on page 167. Create similar issue and debate commentaries for individual and situational explanations, nature versus nurture, reductionism versus holism, determinism versus free will, and idiographic versus nomothetic.

19.5.3 Treatment and management of OCD

Biological treatments: SSRIs

Selvi *et al* (2011) studied the effects that two 'extra' drugs had on OCD patients who had not responded successfully to just taking SSRIs (see page 139 on how re-uptake inhibitors work). The initial part of the study assessed 90 patients with OCD to assess that just taking SSRIs did not work on reducing symptoms. The researchers chose 41 patients from this part of the study and randomly assigned them to either the risperidone (n = 21) or aripiprazole (n = 20) group. They were then given these drugs too for eight further weeks. The researchers measured success by a patient having a 35% or more reduction in scores on the Y-BOCS. In the aripiprazole group 50% of participants did reduce their scores by at least this, as did 72.2% of the risperidone group. Therefore, risperidone appears to be more effective at treating OCD when SSRIs fail by themselves.

Another study by Askari *et al* (2012) examined the effectiveness of using granisetron in conjunction with fluvoxamine (an SSRI). Participants were people aged 18–60 who were diagnosed with OCD via DSM-IV-TR. They were randomly assigned to either a granisetron or placebo group. They received 1 milligram of their 'drug' every 12 hours for 8 weeks. All patients were assessed using the Y-BOCS at baseline then at weeks two, four, six, and eight. Outcomes were measured in the following ways.

- A partial response was a minimum 25% reduction in Y-BOCS scores.
- A complete response was a minimum 35% reduction in Y-BOCS scores.
- Remission was scoring 16 or less on the Y-BOCS.

By week eight, 100% of the granisetron group had scored a complete response and 90% had met the remission criterion. Only 35% of patients in the placebo group managed the same. There were no differences in the tolerance levels of both groups to the 'drugs'. Therefore, it would appear that the additional drug helped people with OCD reduce their symptoms.

> **Test yourself**
>
> Explain at least one strength and one weakness of drug therapies for OCD. Make sure one of your points is about ethics.

Psychological therapies

Exposure and response prevention (Lehmkuhl *et al*, 2008)

Lehmkuhl *et al* (2008) reported on a case study of a 12-year-old boy with autism who was also diagnosed with OCD. The researchers used exposure and response prevention (ERP) to help the boy with his OCD. ERP programmes for OCD usually have three components.

1. Information is gathered about any symptoms.
2. ERP is initiated and led by a therapist.
3. There is generalisation and relapse training.

The therapy also involves gradual exposure, in vivo, to the feared stimuli based on a hierarchy of fear. The response prevention involves the patient blocking or refraining from engaging in any rituals during the exposure to the feared stimuli.

Jason (a pseudonym) was a 12-year-old boy who had been diagnosed with high functioning autism since he was 2 years old. At age 11 years 9 months he began developing ritualistic behaviours that were based around fears of contamination (overuse of hand sanitisers, avoidance of items such as door knobs, and repeatedly checking the expiration dates on food). The symptoms began to interfere with everyday functioning. For example, at school his teachers noticed that he would not turn the pages of a book or sit comfortably in his chair. Jason went through ten 50-minute therapy sessions over a period of 16 weeks. The entire procedure was adapted to take into account his autism.

- The first two sessions ran as follows. The first session introduced Jason to the therapy and allowed him to construct his hierarchy of fear to work with. He had difficulties in identifying his obsessional thoughts. In session two, the therapist exposed Jason to situations based on his hierarchy of fear in the hospital. For example, he had to touch elevator buttons and door handles repeatedly until he habituated to the anxiety.

- For the next six sessions, each session began with a review of any homework set for Jason. This might have included giving out papers in class or using contaminated items at home. The researchers also reviewed Jason's use of coping statements when he felt distressed.

- In the penultimate session, Jason and his parents told the therapist that they felt there had been a significant decrease in Jason's distress levels and number of symptoms linked to his OCD. He was participating in many more classroom activities too. The final session was used to answer any remaining questions that Jason or his parents had about the treatment and what to do after the treatment phase had ended.

Jason had completed the Children's Y-BOCS at pre- and post-treatment. The initial score was 18 (showing moderately severe OCD) but this had reduced to a score of 3 immediately after session ten (normal range). This score was maintained at a three-month follow-up meeting. Therefore, it would appear that ERP was successful in helping Jason with his OCD.

Strengths	Weakness
As this was a case study, in-depth information was recorded, meaning that the data are rich and should be valid.	As it was a case study, generalisation may be difficult as Jason may be a unique case for whom the therapy worked.

Clinical psychology

Cognitive behavioural therapy (CBT)

KEY STUDY: Lovell et al (2006)

Context

It has been estimated that over $8m of direct and indirect costs to the economy in the United States comes from OCD. Therefore, ways to be able to treat and manage it should reduce this overall cost. Different types of treatments are available, but little research has been conducted based on the *method* used to *deliver* treatment. Costs, accessibility, and the patient's available time are all factors that require evaluation to introduce a more efficient and cost-saving treatment for OCD.

Main theories/explanations

The diagnostic guidelines for OCD can be found on page 164. An overview of exposure and response prevention (ERP) used for OCD can be found on page 169.

Aim and hypotheses

To investigate the effectiveness of a telephone-delivered CBT compared to face-to-face delivery using patients diagnosed with OCD.

Design

Participants

Participants were recruited from two outpatient treatment units in Greater Manchester, UK. To be asked to participate in the study, each patient had to fulfil certain criteria. These were: an official diagnosis of OCD with it being the main presenting problem at the unit, a score over 16 on the Yale-Brown Obsessive Compulsive Scale (Y-BOCS), and age 16–65. Patients were not asked if they presented any of the following: a diagnosis of obsessional slowness, brain disease, substance misuse, severe depression, of if they were already having medical treatment for depression or anxiety. Figure 19.12 shows how participants were chosen.

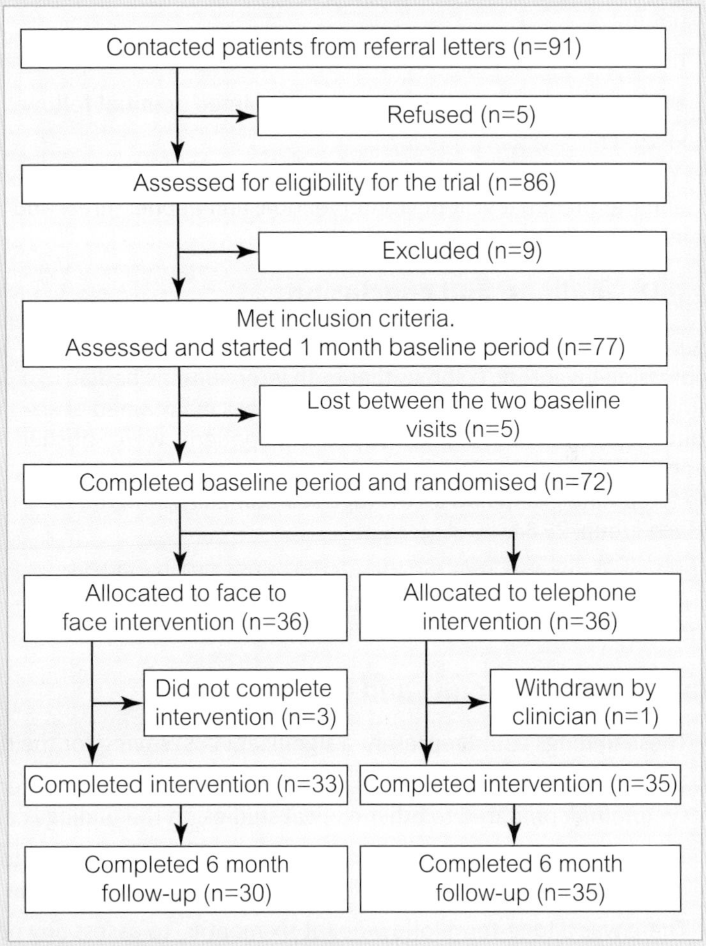

Figure 19.12 Flow of participants through the trial
Source: Lovell et al (2006: 2)

Interventions

Participants were randomly assigned to one of two conditions.

1. Face-to-face – these were ten, one-hour sessions on an individual basis with a therapist. During the sessions there was graded Yale-Brown Obsessive Compulsive Scale (Y-BOCS), which aims to reduce anxiety via repeated exposures. Patients would create a hierarchy of fear to use in the sessions. There was at least one hour of homework per week.
2. Telephone – the first session was face to face; it was exactly the same as the face-to-face therapy intervention. After that, there were eight session of 30 minutes conducted via telephone. All tasks were the same as for the face-to-face intervention, but half the time.

There were two therapists, one per unit, who delivered both types of interventions. They followed a treatment manual, and they were both monitored regularly.

Outcome measures

Participants completed a range of self-reports. They were:

- the Yale-Brown Obsessive Compulsive Scale (Y-BOCS), a ten-item questionnaire where each item is scored from 0 to 4 by the patient
- the Beck Depression Inventory
- a client satisfaction questionnaire (completed at initial follow-up only).

The outcome measures (except satisfaction) were completed at baseline, at an initial visit post-intervention, and at one, three, and six months post-intervention.

Results, findings, and conclusions

Figure 19.13 shows the scores from the Y-BOCS and Beck Depression Inventory. It shows that both interventions had an immediate impact on OCD scores, and this was maintained at six-month follow-up. It would also appear that patients were satisfied by both interventions. The satisfaction score ranged from 0 to 32. The telephone group had an average score of 28.74, and the face-to-face group, 29.84.

Therefore, it appears that telephone-delivered CBT for OCD is equivalent to face-to-face sessions in terms of reducing OCD outcome measures and patient satisfaction.

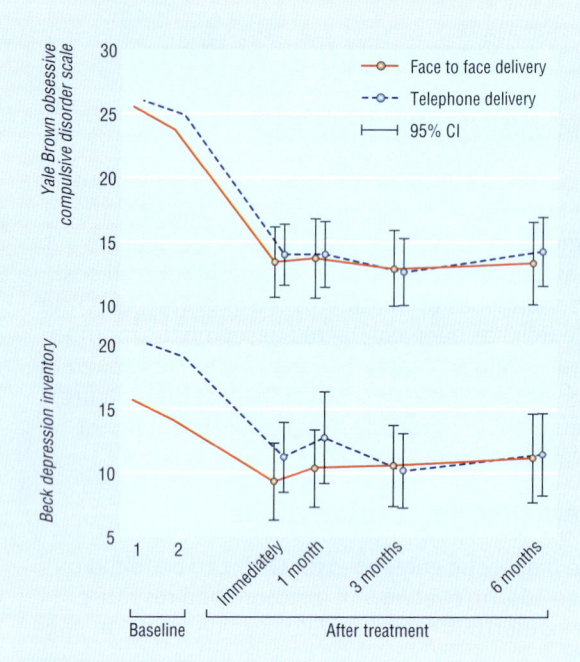

Figure 19.13 Scores for the Y-BOCS and Beck Depression Inventory from first baseline visit to six months of follow-up

Source: Lovell et al (2006: 3)

Main discussion points and evaluation

- These findings could represent a significant cost saving for the delivery of CBT for OCD without a reduction in quality.
- The research team reported that the sample used were no different, in terms of demographics and severity of OCD symptoms, compared to other clinical studies, so the findings can be generalised.
- There was no control group to compare the two interventions to. There was also no other type of treatment used as a comparison group to see if CBT *per se* over the telephone is the most effective treatment regime for OCD.
- There was a long-term follow-up (at six months) to assess any potential longer-term benefits of the interventions. Some may argue that this is still not 'long term enough'.
- The procedure was clear and standardised. The recruitment process and the treatment manual and measures taken were all clearly outlined so other researchers can replicate the study to test for reliability.

Challenge yourself

Design a study that tests the effectiveness of two different treatments for OCD.

Challenge yourself

Look at the issue and debate tracker table on page 167. Create similar issue and debate commentaries for individual and situational explanations, cultural differences, use of children in research, case studies, and reliability.

Consumer psychology

20.1.1 Retail store design

20.1 The physical environment

Types of store exterior design

Different types of store interior can be used to try to tempt consumers into a store. They include these features.

- Storefront – this refers to the exterior features of a store that can give consumers a positive impression of the store depending on colour, art, architecture, etc. Some larger companies may pay less attention to this as their 'brand' is enough to get consumers to enter the store.

- Window displays – these are also an external cue where products that are on sale in the store are displayed in windows that passing consumers can see. Displays could include pictures of models, mannequins dressed in designer clothes, or a bedroom set-up. They are a way of communicating to consumers what the store can offer them as the store has direct control over what is displayed.

- Landscaping – this can be both external and internal to the store. The use of nature imagery, flowers, and other vegetation can bring about a more positive judgement of a store, especially in urban areas. It can elevate mood and even make consumers spend more money and see the store as being of better quality than rivals that do not use landscaping.

Landscaping and window displays (Mower *et al*, 2012)

Mower *et al* (2012) wanted to test the effects of landscaping and window displays on consumer behaviour. They predicted that both would have a positive influence on consumers' moods, liking of the external environment, and patronage intentions.

An online survey was created. An opportunity sample of 180 American college students (mean age of 20.4 years; 94% female) were allocated to one of four conditions, as shown in Table 20.1.

Table 20.1 The four conditions for participants

Condition	Landscaping	Window displays
1	Present	Present
2	Present	Absent
3	Absent	Present
4	Absent	Absent

Each participant read a description of a store, so the study used an independent measures design. Participants had been asked to imagine that they had to go and purchase a new pair of jeans for school. The physical structure and colour of the store descriptions remained the same for all four conditions. For landscaping-present conditions, the description included aspects of vegetation such as oversized planters, the colour of flowers in them, how ivy was draping over a pot, etc. For window display-present conditions, a clear description of a mannequin wearing a fashionable outfit set in front of a modern backdrop was used. Pleasure and arousal were measured using six items based Mehrabian and Russell's ideas (see page 179 for a description of this model). There was a one-item measure for both the landscaping and liking the window displays. Patronage was measured using three items and tested aspects such as the likelihoods of recommending the store to someone else, returning to the store, and purchasing from the store.

These were the main results.

- Both landscaping and window displays did not affect perceptions of pleasure and arousal.

- Both landscaping and window displays had a positive impact on liking the external environment and patronage intentions. However, there was no interaction effect.

- Respondents liked the external environment and reported higher patronage intentions when landscaping was present compared to no landscaping. The same was true for window displays.

- A measure of mood was also taken as to investigate whether that has a mediating effect. It was reported that pleasure, arousal, and patronage were significantly linked to liking.

It was concluded that both landscaping and window displays can have a positive effect on the liking of a store and levels of patronage. Stores need to focus more on using both to attract and maintain a solid consumer base.

Strength	Weakness
The use of independent measures means participants only take part in one condition, so they are less likely to guess the aim of the study therefore reducing the potential effects of demand characteristics. Therefore, they would not be aware that it was landscaping and window display information that was being manipulated and could be more likely to give valid responses.	The study used stories without pictures as the materials. This means that the perception of the store was subjective to the participant and might not clearly reflect their behavioural intentions if they actually observed the store. This might mean that the results lack some validity as the respondents might act differently when they see the store – it might not be congruent with their imagined idea of what the store could look like.

Types of store interior design

Store layout and interior design can be crucial in terms of whether shoppers enjoy the experience of shopping and so buy more products. A study by Vrechopoulos *et al* (2004) focused on store layout used in grocery retail in the UK and Greece, where three main types of store layout are used. These are:

- grid store layout
- freeform store layout
- racetrack store layout.

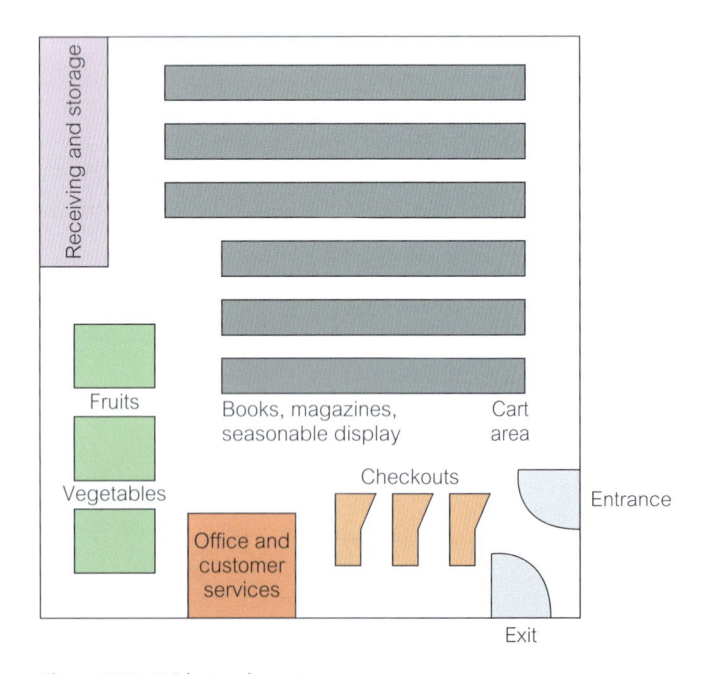

Figure 20.1 *Grid store layout*
Source: Levy and Weitz (2001) reproduced in Vrechopoulos *et al* (2004: 14)

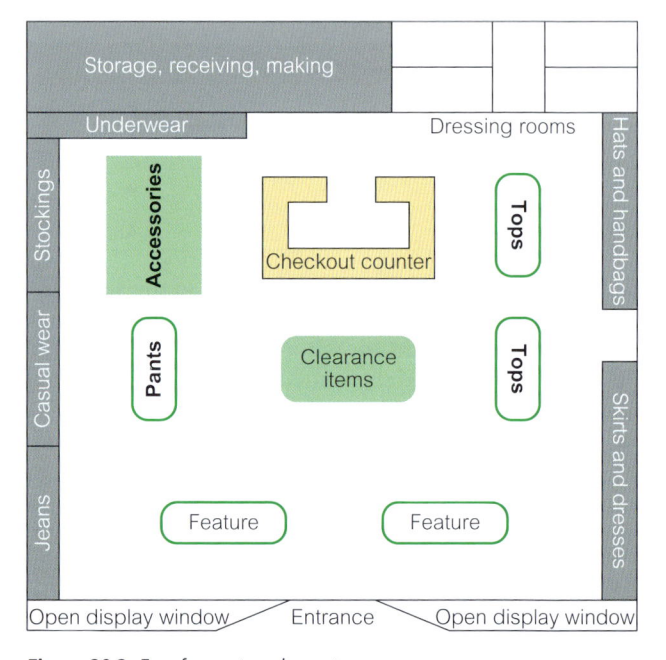

Figure 20.2 *Freeform store layout*
Source: Levy and Weitz (2001) reproduced in Vrechopoulos *et al* (2004: 14)

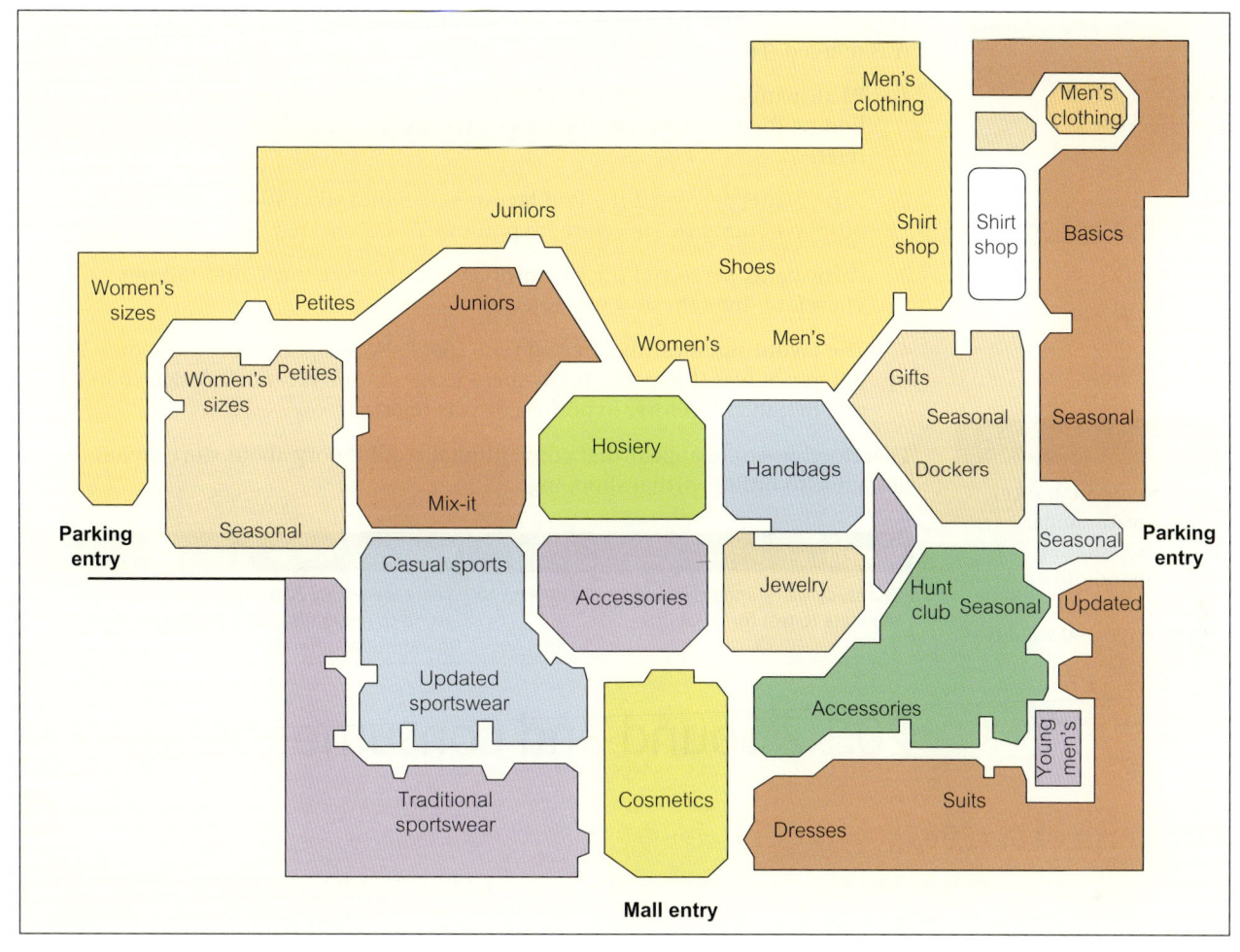

Figure 20.3 *Racetrack store layout*
Source: Levy and Weitz (2001) reproduced in Vrechopoulos et al (2004: 15)

To test which layouts affect shopping behaviour, this study used a virtual store layout giving participants certain tasks to complete. Four main hypotheses were tested.

1. Consumers perceive the grid layout as more useful for conducting planned purchases than freeform or racetrack layouts.

2. Consumers perceive virtual stores using freeform layout as easier to use than stores employing the grid or racetrack layouts.

3. The racetrack layout offers more entertainment for consumers during the shopping activity.

4. Consumers spend more shopping time in the freeform layout.

The three different store designs were created into virtual stores. Real customers were given tasks to perform in just one of them, hence the design was independent measures. The same experiment was run in the UK and in Greece. There were 60 participants per country, split equally between the three design layouts. Each participant was given a budget of £20 (UK) or 12 000 drachma (Greece) to make purchases in the stores. Any product that was purchased by a participant was subsequently purchased 'for real' and delivered to the participant. There were many internationally known brands in the stores (eg Pringles®, Heineken®) and also some local produce. The sample was drawn from internet shoppers and experienced internet users. A stratified sample was drawn to cover the main occupations of academics, students, employees, business executives, and researchers from Brunel and Athens universities. DVs included time spent in the shop and questionnaires that measured aspects such as perceived usefulness, ease of use, and entertainment.

There was no statistical difference between the UK and Greek participants so data was merged. The main results were as follows.

1. Participants perceived the freeform layout as significantly more useful in finding their shopping as the other two designs. Therefore, hypothesis 1 was rejected.

2. Participants perceived the grid layout as significantly easier to use than the other two designs. Therefore, hypothesis 2 was rejected.

3. Participants perceived the freeform layout to be the most entertaining. Therefore, hypothesis 3 was rejected.

4. The layout significantly affected time spent shopping. However, the only key difference was that participants spent longer in the racetrack design than in the grid design. Therefore, hypothesis 4 was rejected.

Therefore, it would appear that conventional retail theory about store layout does not apply to online virtual shopping.

> **Challenge yourself**
>
> Look at the issue and debate tracker table on page 179. Create similar issue and debate commentaries for questionnaires, quantitative and qualitative data, objective and subjective data, and ecological validity.

Strength	Weakness
The study was standardised so would be easy to replicate to test for reliability.	There were only 20 participants per layout group so generalisability may be an issue due to individual differences.

20.1.2 Sound and consumer behaviour

KEY STUDY: North *et al* (2003)

Context

Previous research had shown that playing classical music increases a consumer's intention to purchase, more so than pop music or no music. For example, Areni and Kim (1993) showed that people were willing to buy more expensive wine when classical music was being played. Music can also affect our perception of an establishment. Playing classical music made people feel a student cafeteria was more upmarket (North and Hargreaves, 1998). However, there had been little research into the effects of music on purchasing in restaurants.

Main theories/explanations

Music could well affect neural networks and human cognition, but specific pathways were not analysed in this current study.

Aim and hypotheses

North *et al* (2003) wanted to investigate the effects of different types of music on spending in a restaurant.

The main hypothesis was 'Playing classical music would lead to customers spending more money in a restaurant compared to playing pop music.'

Design

Participants

A total of 393 customers who ate in a restaurant were participants in the study. Gender was balanced and no-one knew that they were taking part in a study. During the study, 142 participants were exposed to pop music (in 49 parties), 120 to classical music (in 44 parties) and 131 to no music (in 48 parties).

Materials

Two CDs were prepared for each condition. No single piece of music was repeated. The research team analysed the tempi of both CDs and there was no significant difference.

Experimental design

The field experiment used an independent measures design. Each condition lasted for six nights and was counterbalanced across days of the week. All lighting, temperature, menu, and decoration was the same for all 18 evenings. The DV measures were spending on starters, main courses, desserts, coffee, bar drinks, wine, total amount spent on food, total amount spent on drink, and total overall spend. The restaurant served *a la carte* food at prices above market average. Each participant provided one data point for the condition they were in. This was calculated by taking the mean for each party for every DV measure.

Procedure

The restaurant was in a Grade II listed building, located in a small town in Leicestershire, UK. The study took place over three consecutive weeks and did not coincide with any school or public holidays. The experimenter was able to collect the data while working as a waitress in the restaurant.

Results, findings, and conclusions

These were the main significant results.

- Starters, coffee, total food bill, and total spend: people spent significantly more when classical music was played compared to both pop and no music.
- The remainder: people did spend more on *all other* DVs (except wine) in the classical music condition compared to the other two, but they were not statistically significant.

Main discussion points

- This study has implications for restaurants in terms of what music they play and how this could increase profits.
- Explanation one for the results: classical music was 'synergistic' with the restaurant – the music matched the restaurant style.
- Explanation two for the results: the participants simply preferred classical music, and this directly affected spending. However, there was no measure of musical preference taken.
- Explanation three for the results: classical music promotes a form of upmarket perception of the restaurant and therefore people eating there feel they can spend more. This is called congruent behaviour.

Evaluation points

- Independent measure design was used, so individual differences may be playing a role in affecting the DVs. North *et al* did not collect data about musical preference or affluence and these could have been key participant variables affecting spending power.
- The study was clearly standardised to allow other researchers to replicate the study to test for reliability. For example, the length of CD, music choices, and how spending power was measured were clearly outlined in the study.
- The research method was a field experiment. There were many controls put in place (decoration, menu, etc), which meant that the research team could be more confident it was the IV (music type) that was affecting the DV (spending). Also, the study has ecological validity as it was in a real-life setting of a restaurant with music playing in the background.

Background noise focusing on how sound and noise affect the perception of food

Woods *et al* (2010) investigated the effects of auditory background noise on the perception of 'gustatory food properties' (eg sugar and salt levels), food crunchiness, and food liking. They ran two experiments.

Experiment 1

A total of 48 students (39 female) from Manchester University in the UK volunteered to participate in the study. The age range was 19–39 years. Five participants were smokers and five reported mild symptoms of a common cold. While being recruited, participants were told that the study involved assessing foods on different attributes. All gave informed consent to take part. The food stimuli were:

- savoury: Pringles® Original Salted Crips (crunchy) and Cathedral City® Mini Mild Cheese (soft)
- sweet: Sainsbury's Nice Biscuits (crunchy) and Sainsbury's All Butter Mini Flapjacks (soft)
- distractor: Carr's® Water crackers (these are neither salty nor sweet).

Participants were given bite-sized pieces of all of the food samples. During the trials, participants wore headphones that presented them with white noise that was either 45–55 decibels (quiet) or 75–85 decibels (loud). For baseline ratings, no noise was played. A repeated measures design was used as all participants ate and rated all food types under the different sound conditions. They had to sit with their eyes closed. A researcher held a paper plate containing one of the foods and made it touch the participant's fingers to let the participant know that the trial had started. Participants rated saltiness, sweetness, and liking (given in a random order) on a labelled magnitude scale with responses measured to the nearest millimetre. Each participant went through 25 trials. After each food was consumed, the participant took a sip of water. To control for other individual differences, scores were generated by subtracting the baseline rating from the quiet or loud ratings given.

Statistical analysis showed that level of sound did affect people's perceptions of sweetness and saltiness. Both of these were rated lower in the loud condition compared to the quiet condition. There was no effect of 'hardness' on perceptions; background noise affected ratings for both crunchy and soft food.

Experiment 2

A total of 34 students (19 female) from Manchester University in the UK volunteered to take part in this experiment. Their ages ranged from 20 to 49 years and none of them had food allergies. The study was run in the same way as experiment 1 but this time the researchers were also testing whether liking of background noise also has an effect on perception of sugar and salt levels. The food stimuli were:

- sweet: berry and caramel flavoured rice cakes
- savoury: salt and vinegar flavoured plus Marmite® flavoured rice cakes
- distractor: organic rice cakes, cream and chive flavoured rice cakes, sweet chilli rice cakes and softened rice cakes.

Again, a repeated measures design was used with sound (no sound, quiet sound, loud sound) and food type (savoury, sweet) as the main factors. Measures this time were flavoursomeness, crunchiness, and liking, again all based on labelled magnitude scales.

Sound had a significant effect on crunchiness. In the loud condition, participants rated their food as significantly crunchier than in the quiet condition. There was no effect of noise on flavoursomeness. In the loud condition, there was a correlation between liking of food and liking of the background noise for the Marmite® stimuli only.

Therefore, the main conclusions were:

- perception of saltiness and sweetness diminished when the food samples were eaten in the presence of loud music
- food was perceived to be crunchier if eaten while listening to loud music
- the effect of noise on the liking of food correlated with liking of the particular noise.

Strength	Weakness
The procedure for the study was standardised so it can be replicated and tested for reliability.	The sample sizes for each study were small, meaning that individual differences may affect the generalisabilty of findings.

Test yourself

For the strength and weakness of Woods *et al* (2010), note two aspects of the study that were standardised and explain why a small sample size makes generalisability difficult.

Challenge yourself

Look at the issue and debate tracker on the next page. Create similar issue and debate commentaries for reductionism versus holism, determinism versus free will, and generalisations from findings.

	Issue and debate tracker
Individual and situational explanations	The **situation** of either listening to classical music (North et al, 2003) or of having background noise playing or not (Woods et al, 2010) affected the behaviour of the participants. In the North et al study participants did spend more when classical music was playing and in the Woods at el study participants rated sweetness and saltiness as lower in the loud condition. Woods et al controlled for **individual** explanations as they used a repeated measures design but North et al did not measure musical preference in the participants so some individual music preference may have affected some of the spending.
Validity	North et al has **ecological validity** as the setting was a real restaurant that typically played music. Woods at el (2010) does not have **ecological validity** as participants wore headphones in a laboratory setting. However, due to the controls and repeated measures design there was a high degree of **internal validity**.

20.1.3 Retail atmospherics

Model of effects of ambience: Mehrabian and Russell's pleasure-arousal-dominance (PAD) model

The pleasure-arousal model (normally referred to as the pleasure-arousal-dominance or PAD model; Mehrabian and Russell, 1974; Mehrabian, 1996) looks at individual differences in temperament. There is a key difference that this model is based on, described below.

- Emotional states are those that are short-lived and vary dramatically across situations such as being in a favourite store.
- Temperament refers to those elements of a personality that are stable over time and situation.

This model is based around three main personality traits.

- State pleasure–displeasure: these traits are positive versus negative affective states such as relaxation and love versus cruelty and boredom.
- State arousal–non-arousal: these traits are based around levels of arousal such as concentration and alertness versus sleep and boredom.
- State dominance–submissiveness: these traits are based around aspects such as feeling in control versus not feeling in control at all.

All of these can be measured on a personality scale and an individual's overall profile is then plotted on a triangular graph to see how much of each PAD the person has.

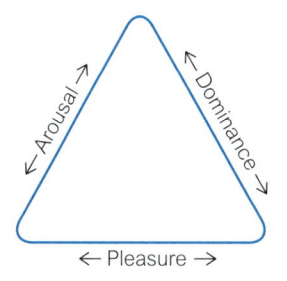

Figure 20.4 Three faces of emotion: a representation of the pleasure–arousal–dominance emotional state
Source: Mehrabian (1996: 264)

Challenge yourself

Explain how you think each of the PAD dimensions might predict how someone will react to a new store opening in your local mall.

Effects of odour on shopper pleasure-arousal-dominance

Chebat and Michon (2003) wanted to test the effects of ambient scents in a shopping mall. They tested a variety of hypotheses (11 in total) to assess how scents in a Canadian shopping mall affected people's perceptions. Data were collected over two consecutive weeks. In the first week, there was no odour control in the mall but in the second week a light citrus scent was vaporised in the mall's main corridor. Ten diffusers emitted the citrus smell for three seconds every six minutes. The scent was of a concentration to be noticed but not bother people. Participants were asked to complete a questionnaire about their shopping trip. A total of 145 people completed the questionnaire after being exposed to the scent and 447 formed the control group. Measures taken included pleasure, arousal, mall perception, perception of product quality, and overall spending. The main findings included the following.

- The scent appeared to have a mediating effect on mood, which in turn positively affected perception of the shopping environment and product quality.
- Mood by itself contributed little to overall spending.

- Consumer spending is more likely to occur via cognitive processes than by mood alone.

Therefore, retailers ought to consider using light scents to entice shoppers into their stores as it gives the area a sense of quality.

The effects of crowding on shopper pleasure-arousal-dominance

In a series of studies, Machleit *et al* (2000) examined whether perceived crowding affects consumers' satisfaction levels while shopping. The points below relate to two of these studies. For the first study, 722 undergraduate and postgraduate marketing students completed a retrospective survey. They were asked to complete it after their next shopping trip (irrespective of whether they bought anything or not). They had to name the store, shopping centre or mall they had visited and then answer questions as follows.

- They were asked to rate perceived crowding on a Likert-type scale. Human crowding and spatial crowding were both measured.
- Satisfaction was measured via items on a 7-point scale.
- Emotions were measured in two different ways: using ten emotion types as noted by Izard where participants rate adjectives; then via pleasure and arousal questions (based on semantic differentials).
- Participants were asked about prior expectations of crowding. For example, when they went shopping were they expecting more or fewer shoppers than usual?
- Their intolerance of crowding was investigated.

Results (from study 1 only)

- Increased perceptions of crowding resulted in decreased positive feelings and increased negative feelings. The effect was stronger for spatial crowding compared to human crowding.
- Perceived human crowding did not significantly affect feelings of arousal.
- If the shopper found the store to be spatially crowded, the excitement of shopping decreased.
- Feelings of surprise significantly increase when the shopper experiences human crowding.
- The strongest negative emotions linked to spatial crowding were anger, disgust and contempt.
- Higher levels of perceived crowding (both human and spatial) were correlated to lower levels of satisfaction.
- Females tolerate crowding more than males (although this was not statistically significant).

Therefore, it would appear that both spatial and human crowding affect a shopper's experiences.

Strength	Weakness
There was a large, diverse sample so generalisability beyond the sample is likely to be possible.	Measures were taken using questionnaires, meaning the results could be more subjective than objective and so casting doubt on their validity.

> **Challenge yourself**
>
> The owners of a shopping mall want your help. They are trying to get more consumers to visit their mall and need to know the best ways in which to do this. Write a report for them, based on psychology evidence, which may help them increase the number of consumers who visit.

> **Challenge yourself**
>
> Explain why a larger sample could improve generalisability and also why the questionnaires used might be subjective.

> **Challenge yourself**
>
> Look at the issue and debate tracker table on page 179. Create similar issue and debate commentaries for application to everyday life, questionnaires, quantitative and qualitative data, and objective and subjective data.

20.2.1 Environmental influences on consumers

Wayfinding in a shopping mall (Dogu and Erkip, 2000)

Dogu and Erkip (2000) reported on a case study of the Karum Shopping Mall in Turkey. They analysed the spatial layout of the mall and used questionnaires to gather data from consumers about the mall. The focus of this description of the questionnaire case study will be on signage and 'You are here' maps. In terms of signage, the researchers noted the following.

- Only 'WC' and 'Exit' were written in English and were placed at intersections throughout the mall. The remainder of signage was based on pictographs (a pictorial symbol for a word or phrase).

- Door numbers were confusing. Those on the ground floor were numbered from 1 to 100. However, those on the second floor were not all in the 200s. Some had numbers in the 300s. This was repeated on the third floor (some had 400+ as the shop number). Also, the numbers were not in order as some of the shops had been divided into two *after* the original numbers had been assigned per shop.

- The 'You are here' map and directory for all shops was placed in an area that was difficult for shoppers to notice (see Figure 20.6). Dogu and Erkip noted that the system for the directory was confusing for shoppers and followed a bureaucratic hierarchy rather than one that was 'shopper friendly'.

20.2 The psychological environment

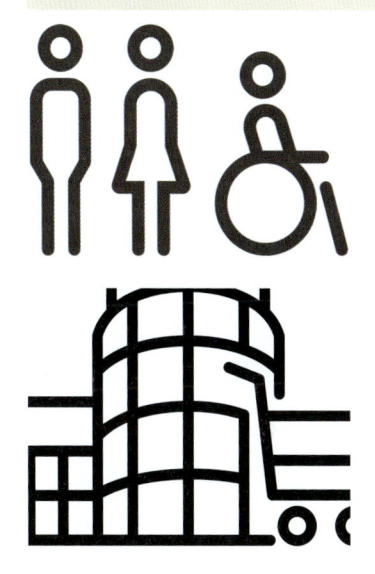

Figure 20.5 *Examples of pictographs used in signage*

Figure 20.6 *The 'You are here' map and directory at the entrance*
Source: Dogu and Erkip (2000: 745)

A questionnaire was handed out to 78 female and 76 male shoppers using a quota sampling technique (based on sex). There were three sections to it.

1. The first section included questions about participants remembering how they got into the mall today, knowledge about the layout of the mall, and how confident they were to direct a stranger to a location within the mall.

2. This section included questions about indoor routes around the mall. The participants were asked questions about how useful signage was, including the 'You are here' map.

3. The final section included questions measured how attentive the participants were to architectural information within the mall, such as symmetry, landmarks, how corridors intersected, and lighting.

Upon completion of all questionnaires, each participant was asked to point out the direction of a randomly chosen shop within the mall.

Table 20.2 shows the key result about signage and the 'You are here' map.

Table 20.2 Evaluation of signage and 'You are here' maps in Karum

Item evaluated	Males	%	Females	$	Total	%
Signage						
Is sufficient	31	40.78	30	38.46	61	39.62
Is not sufficient	45	59.22	48	61.54	93	60.38
Total	76	100	78	100	154	100
You-Are-Here Maps						
Are sufficient	19	25	30	38.46	49	31.81
Are not sufficient	57	75	48	61.54	105	68.19
Total	76	100	78	100	154	100

Source: Dogu and Erkip (2000: 747)

As can be seen, both signage and 'You are here' maps were classed as not sufficient by the majority of participants. Other reported results included the following.

- Participants who stated that they found wayfinding easy in general, tended to report that the signage was sufficient.
- A large number of participants did not notice any signage.
- Nearly half of the participants claimed that there were no 'You are here' maps in the mall.
- Reasons for the signage being seen as 'not sufficient' included these phrases: difficult to understand, placed carelessly, confusing floor plans, a lack of emphasis.

Strength	Weakness
The study has ecological validity as it took place within the mall itself. Participants had already chosen to visit the mall for either browsing or purchasing. They were engaged in real-life behaviour in a real-life setting of a mall in Turkey.	As it was a case study of one mall, all findings about how signage and 'You are here' maps can be used may be unique to the Karum Shopping Mall and no others. There may be something about the choice of signage and positioning of the 'You are here' maps that makes this mall unique and so any recommendations based on this finding may not be generalisable to other shopping malls.

Shopper behaviour focusing on spatial movement patterns

Gil *et al* (2009) tested shopper movement patterns in a supermarket. They focused on three questions.

1. How and to what extent does the spatial configuration of store layout have an impact on shoppers' behaviour?
2. Do any of the groups of shoppers express distinctive use of space or distinctive shopping behaviours?
3. Can we identify distinctive movement patterns of shoppers? If so, are those patterns associated with certain groups of shoppers?

The researchers collected data from over 480 customers by interviewing them and tracking their movements around a supermarket. This data was then used to profile shoppers based on their demographics and behaviour in the supermarket. Participants were approached just before they entered the supermarket. Details of their basic demographics were taken and they then were given a coloured tab to wear so they could be identified on exit (and followed easily via CCTV footage). On exit, they were interviewed about the aim of their trip, satisfaction, money spent, whether they had a list, etc.

The researchers identified four movement cluster patterns across the participants. These are shown in Figure 20.7.

Short trip (32)

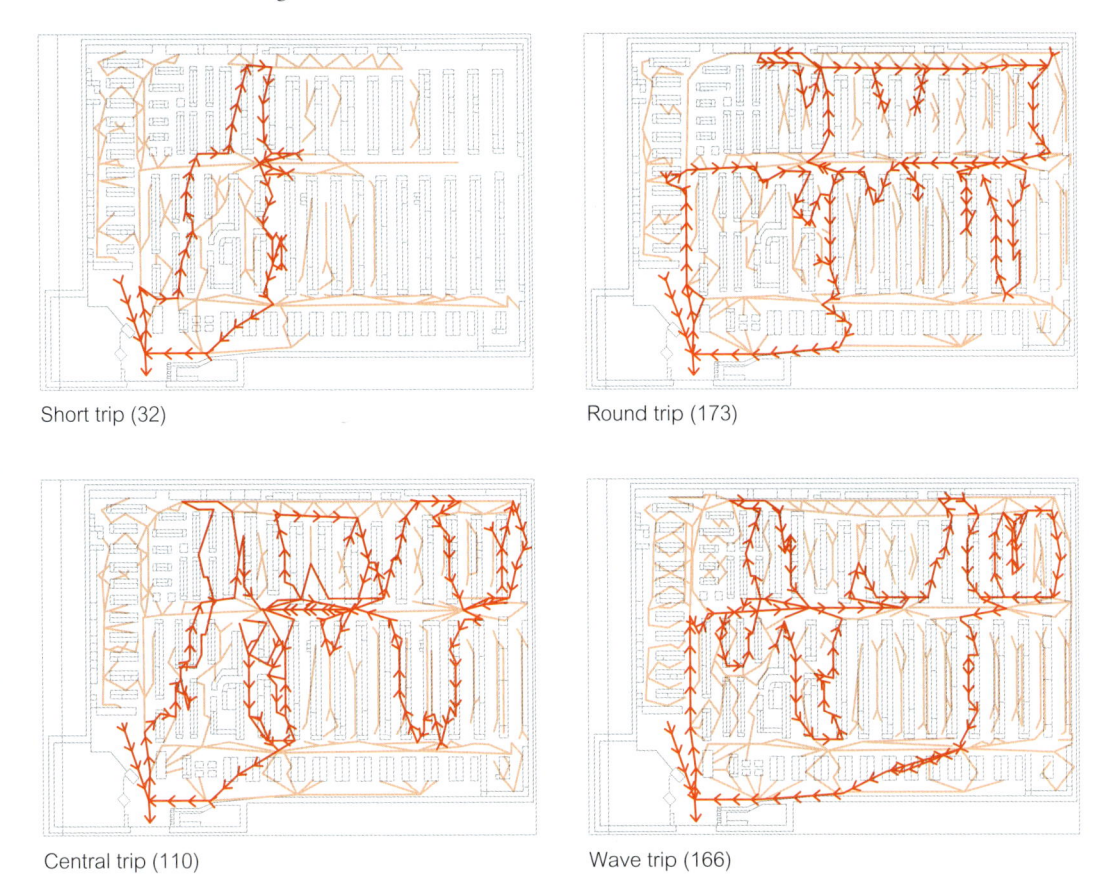

Round trip (173)

Central trip (110)

Wave trip (166)

Figure 20.7 *Plans representing each of the four movement pattern clusters*
Notes: For each movement pattern cluster, the 'medoid' is identified, that is the most representative trace of the cluster closest to its centre. Each plan shows the combined level of movement from all traces in the cluster with varying intensity, overlaid with the medoid, where the arrows indicate the direction of movement.
Source: Gil *et al* (2009: 036:6)

The researchers then created 'shopper DNA' profiles based on 12 different attributes. These are shown in Table 20.3.

Table 20.3 *Shopper profile attributes*

Attributes	0	1	2	3	4	5	6
Gender	Male	Female					
Age group	–	18–24	25–34	35–44	45–54	55–64	65 and over
Group size	–	Alone	Two	Three	Four	Five	Six or more
Carrier type	None	Basket	Shallow trolley	Deep trolley			
Frequency of visit	–	First time	Regularly	Occasionally			
Shopping mission	–	Main	Top-up	Tonight	For now	Non-food	
Shopping list	–	Yes	No				
Attitude to promotions	–	Always	Familiar	Familiar	Never		
Satisfaction	–	Very satisfied	Satisfied	Neither	Dissatisfied	Very dissatisfied	
Shopping duration	–	<10 min	<20 min	<30 min	<45 min	45 min or more	
Walking speed	–	Slow	Medium	Fast			
Duration of interactions	–	Short	Medium	Long			

Source: Gil *et al* (2009: 036:7)

From these attributes, four distinct 'shopper DNA' profiles were reported, as shown in Figure 20.8.

Short trip (32)

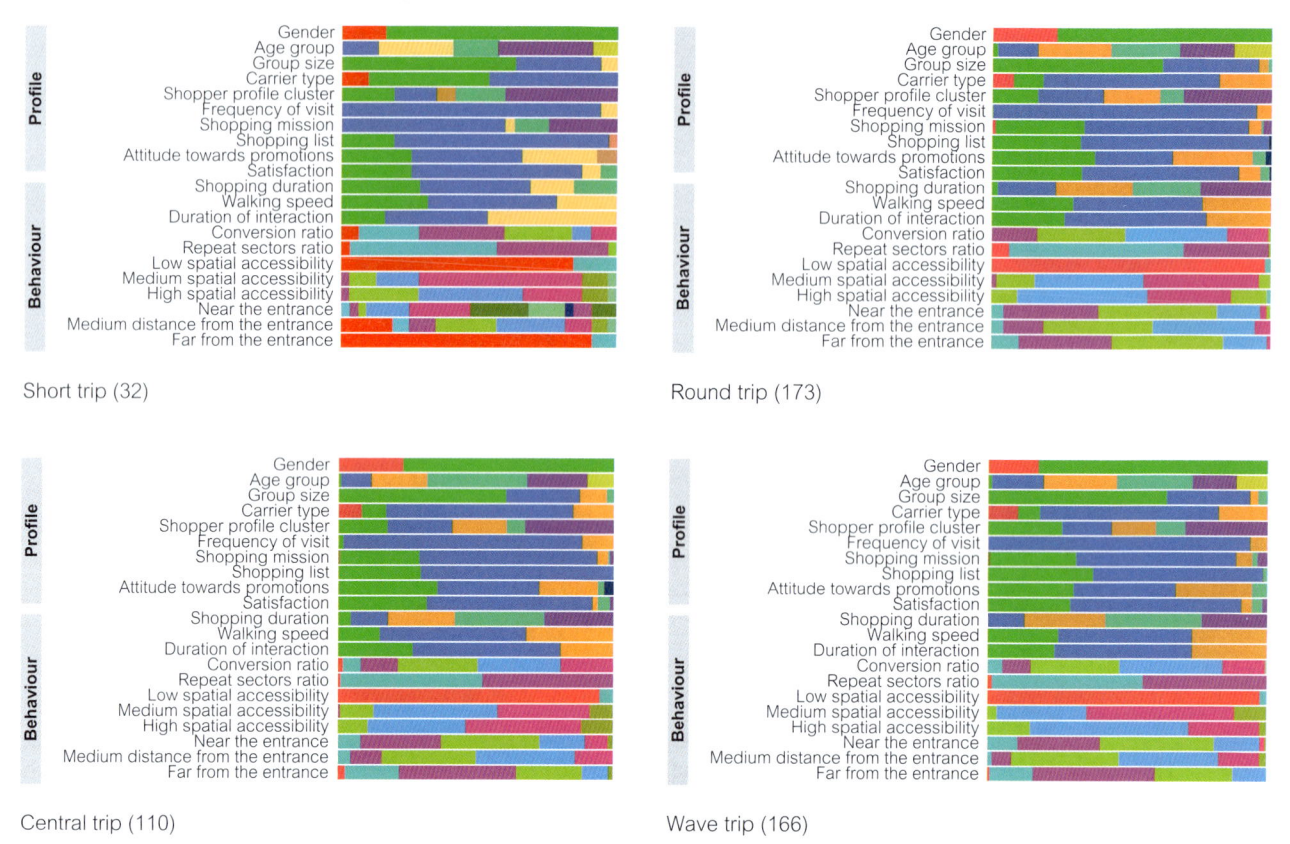

Round trip (173)

Central trip (110)

Wave trip (166)

Figure 20.8 *'Shopper DNA' profile of each movement pattern cluster. Each band represents the percentage share of shoppers with a particular attribute according to the researchers' classification, apart from the 'short trip' cluster, that has unique share of carrier types, shopping mission and shopping duration.*

Source: Gil et al (2009: 8)

As shown in Figure 20.9, the researchers also analysed data to produce five different types of shopper based on movement habits.

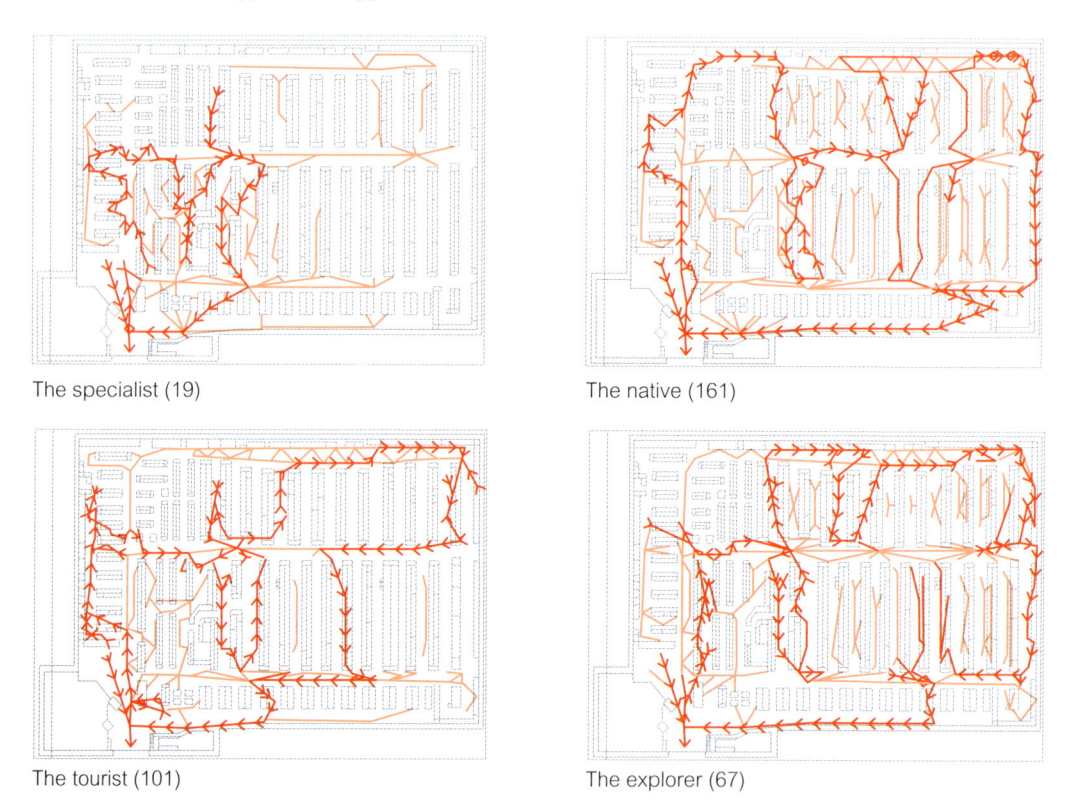

The specialist (19)

The native (161)

The tourist (101)

The explorer (67)

Consumer psychology

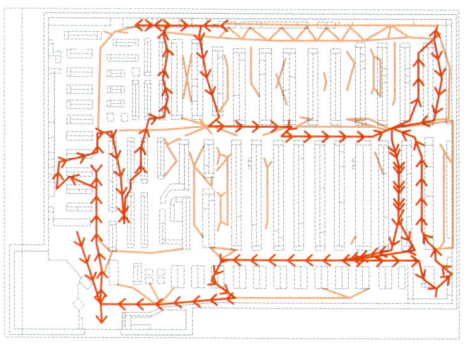

The raider (113)

Figure 20.9 *Plans representing each of the five spatial behaviour types, with the level of movement from all traces in the cluster displayed with varying intensity, overlaid by the 'medoid', with the arrows indicating the direction of movement*

Source: Gil et al (2009: 036:10)

Test yourself

Explain at least one strength and one weakness of the study by Gil *et al*.

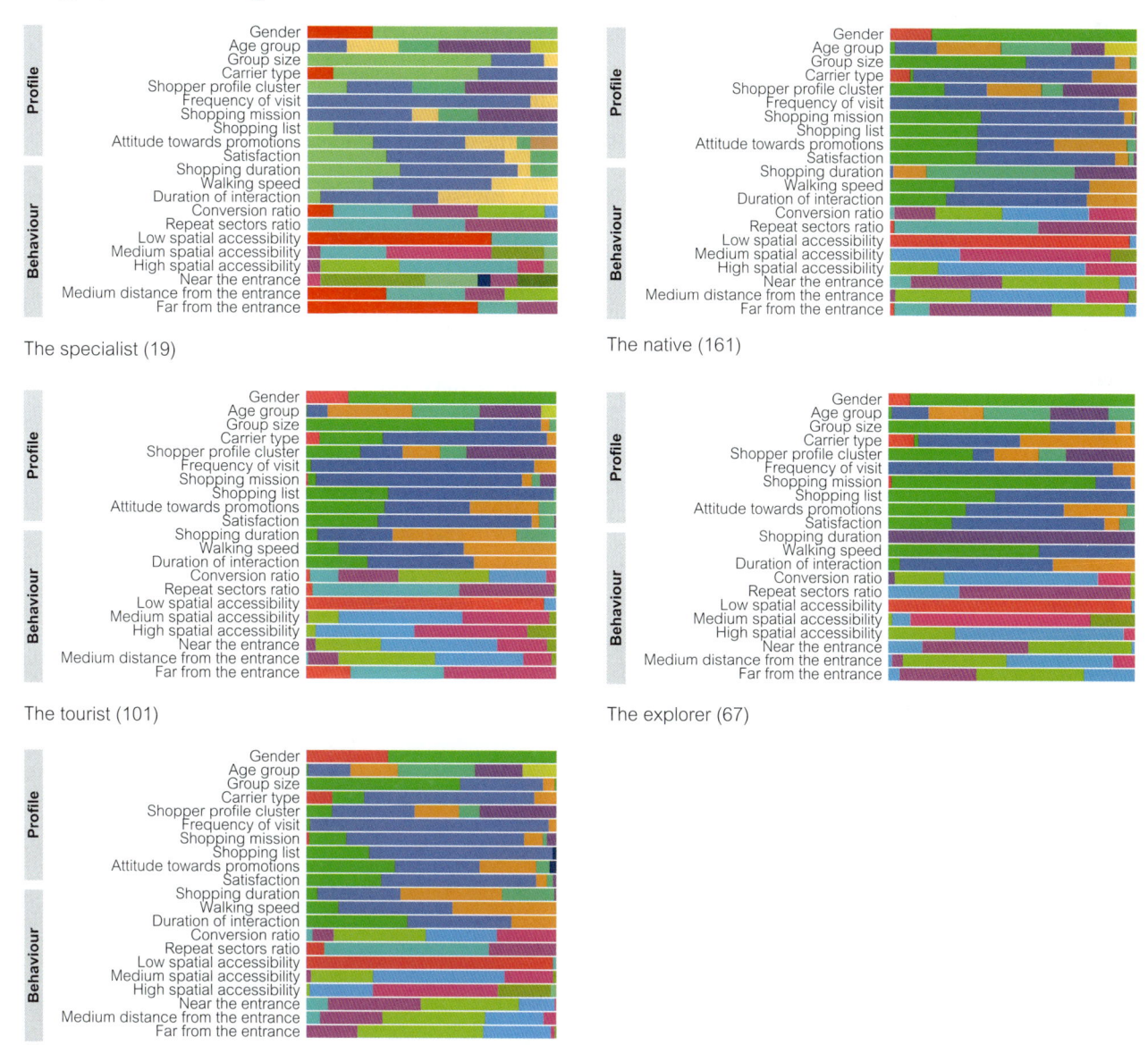

Finally, the researchers produced 'shopper DNA' profiles for these five types of shopper, as shown in Figure 20.10.

The specialist (19)

The native (161)

The tourist (101)

The explorer (67)

The raider (113)

Figure 20.10 *'Shopper DNA' profile of each spatial behaviour cluster*

Source: Gil et al (2009: 036:12)

185

> **Challenge yourself**
>
> Look at the issue and debate tracker table on page 195. Create similar issue and debate commentaries for reductionism versus holism, idiographic versus nomothetic, questionnaires, generalisations from findings, and reliability.

The researchers concluded that '… distinct clusters of shopping strategy defined in terms of characteristic search trail through the store, and that these correlate with specific shopper profiles' (Gil *et al*, 2009: 036:1).

20.2.2 Menu design psychology

Menu design focusing on the features of menu design that have positive and negative impacts

Pavesic (2005) noted common mistakes restaurants make with their menu designs.

- There is inadequate management commitment to menu design: the managers of a restaurant do not treat their menu design with the same diligence as other capital investment in their business. Investment in an eye-catching design is cost-effective.

- The menu is hard to read. This may be because the font size is too small, font colours make the menu difficult to read or pages have too much text.

- Prices are overemphasized. For example, all the prices are in the same column so customers can easily compare them and go for the cheapest option.

- The menu represents poor salesmanship because it fails to emphasise the products the restaurant wants to sell.

- There is poor use of space on the menu. This might include not utilising the front and back covers for generic information (eg opening times, address, and the history of the restaurant). Pavesic collected over 1000 restaurant menus and noted that around 25% have no identifying feature that links them to a specific restaurant.

- The menu is incongruent: it does not match the décor of the restaurant or what the restaurant is selling in terms of quality of food.

- The menu is too large. The size of the menu needs to take into account the size of the table. A very large menu is awkward to handle.

Pavesic also noted that, on average, a customer will look over a menu for only 109 seconds so any message needs to be portrayed in such a way that a customer quickly notices offers, prices, meal deals, etc. Pavesic noted typical eye movements over a menu that are quite 'standard' in customers. This is shown in Figure 20.11.

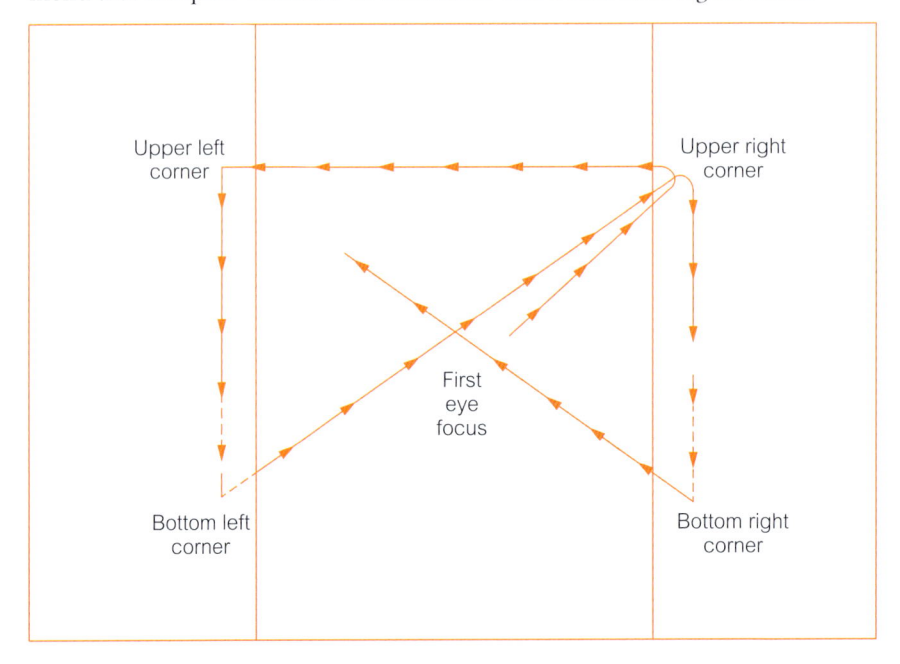

Figure 20.11 *Typical eye movement over a three-panel, two-fold menu*
Source: Pavesic (2005: 40)

Pavesic stated that 'eye magnets' can be used to stop this standard pattern happening by having sections of the menu that look different from the rest to catch people's attention. He proposed that these sections are used sparingly so not to diminish their effectiveness. He noted two other design features that are effective: highlighting or using arrows, and using borders or graphics. Examples are shown in Figures 20.12 and 20.13.

Figure 20.12

Figure 20.13

Strength	Weakness
The study has good application as restaurants can improve their menu designs as a result.	The study reflects only Pavesic's views on menu design so is subjective.

The effect of primacy and recency and menu item position on menu item choice

Dayan and Bar-Hillel (2011) conducted two studies that examined the effect on food orders of manipulating the position of foods on a restaurant menu.

Study 1

A total of 240 students from Hebrew University, Jerusalem, Israel (aged 19–35 years; 52% female) were recruited from around the campus. They were randomly assigned to one of four conditions:

1. baseline menu
2. mirror menu: a reverse of the base menu
3. inside-out baseline menu: formed by turning the middle items of the base menu to the extremes and the extremes to the middle
4. inside-out mirror menu: a reverse of the inside-out base menu.

The menus had four appetisers, ten entrées, six soft drinks and eight desserts. Table 20.4 shows the format of each menu.

Table 20.4 Item order in the four menus: A = appetisers, E = entrées, S = soft drinks, D = desserts

Baseline menu:	A1, A2, A3, A4 E1, E2, E3, E4, E5, E6, E7, E8, E9, E10
	S1, S2, S3, S4, S5, S6 D1, D2, D3, D4, D5, D6, D7, D8
Mirror menu:	A4, A3, A2, A1 E10, E9, E8, E7, E6, E5, E4, E3, E2, E1
	S6, S5, S4, S3, S2, S1 D8, D7, D6, D5, D4, D3, D2, D1
Inside-Out base:	A2, A1, A4, A3 E5, E4, E3, E2, E1, E10, E9, E8, E7, E6
	S3, S2, S1, S6, S5, S4 D4, D3, D2, D1, D8, D7, D6, D5
Inside-Out mirror:	A3, A4, A1, A2 E6, E7, E8, E9, E10, E1, E2, E3, E4, E5
	S4, S5, S6, S1, S2, S3 D5, D6, D7, D8, D1, D2, D3, D4

Source: Dayan and Bar-Hillel (2011: 334)

Each participant was given the menu and asked to choose one item from each category. Figure 20.14 shows the findings. It shows that, especially for appetisers, participants chose items from the 'extremes' of the list over those in the middle irrespective of the menu they were given.

Study 2

The research team noted that for study 1 the choices were made under controlled conditions. They wanted to test the results of study 1 in a real café in Tel Aviv. This study focused on three categories from the real menu: coffee with alcohol, soft drinks, and desserts. There was a baseline menu that the café already used and then an inside-out baseline menu was also produced. These menus alternated daily for 15 days. The researchers analysed 459 baseline menu purchases and 492 inside-out baseline menu purchases. The findings are shown in Figure 20.15.

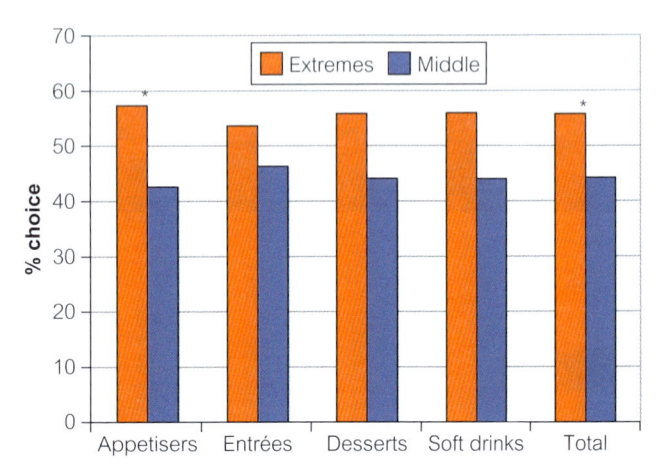

Figure 20.14 The mean percentage of choices made when an item was on the top or bottom versus in the middle of its food category, sorted by category type

* indicates $p < .05$, two tailed

Source: Dayan and Bar-Hillel (2011: 335)

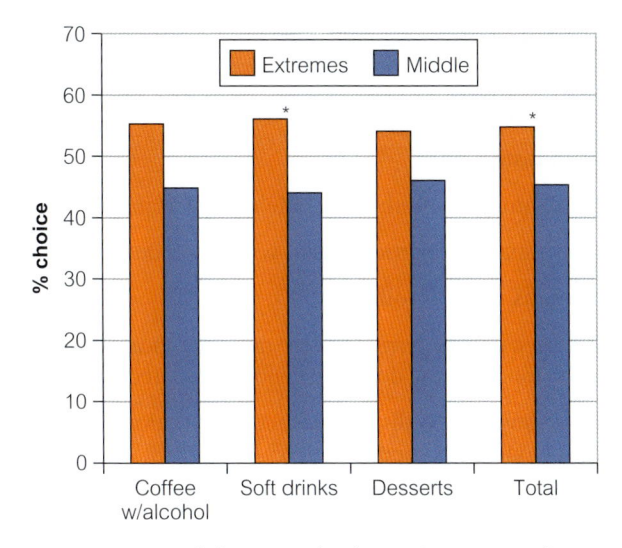

Figure 20.15 *The mean percentage of choices made when an item was on the top or bottom versus in the middle of its food category, sorted by category type (study 2)*

* indicates p <.05, two tailed

Source: Dayan and Bar-Hillel (2011: 340)

Strength	Weakness
The procedure was standardised so the study can be replicated and tested for reliability.	The sample was from one university so generalising beyond the sample may be difficult.

The effect of food name on menu item choice

Wansink *et al* (2005) tested whether descriptions of food on a menu affected perceptions of that food after eating it. The idea was that labelling food items with a 'richer' description could affect how people perceive the food in terms of taste and quality. In this study, the researchers tested a range of hypotheses to see whether favourable descriptions of food affected post-consumption sensory ratings, evaluations of the food eaten, and comments about the food.

A cafeteria in a major US university was used as the setting. Six of the most popular dishes consumed on its menu were chosen and their descriptions were manipulated. The descriptions were altered slightly so that during any one lunch session, two of the foods had a regular or basic label, two had a more descriptive label, and two were not offered. These were the labels (Wansink *et al*, 2005: 7).

- 'Traditional Cajun red beans with rice' versus 'Red beans with rice'
- 'Succulent Italian seafood filet' versus 'Seafood filet'
- 'Tender grilled chicken' versus 'Grilled chicken'
- 'Homestyle chicken Parmesan' versus 'Chicken Parmesan'
- 'Satin chocolate pudding' versus 'Chocolate pudding'
- 'Grandma's zucchini cookies' versus 'Zucchini cookies'.

Anyone who selected one of the target foods was handed a one-page questionnaire by the person at the cash register. A total of 140 participants were given a questionnaire and 98% completed it. The age range of participants was 23–74 years.

Challenge yourself

Design a menu, based on what you have learned so far, for a new restaurant that offers a three course meal with five starters, five main dishes, and five desserts. Justify all of your design decisions.

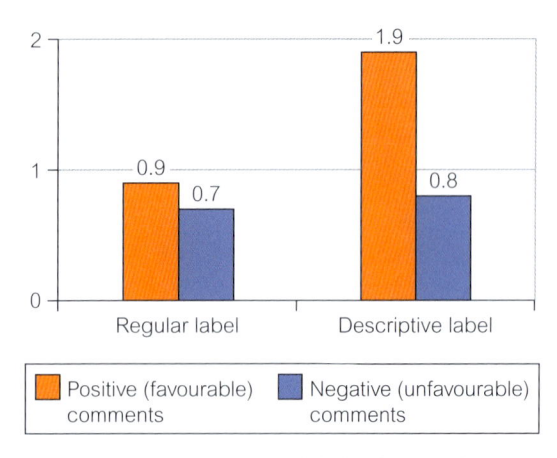

Figure 20.16 *How descriptive labels influence the valence of open-ended feedback*
Source: Wansink et al (2005: 18)

These three crucial items were included on the 9-point Likert scale that was used.

1. The items were appealing to the eye.
2. The item tasted good.
3. After finishing this menu item, I felt comfortably full and satisfied.

There was also space for participants to write any comments about the food.

The main results were as follows.

- For the three crucial items, all were rated significantly higher on average when the food had the descriptive label compared to the regular name.
- People believed their dish contained more calories on average if the descriptive label had been used.
- Those who ate food when the label was descriptive generated significantly more positive comments about the food (see Figure 20.16).

It would seem that a simple task of adding a few descriptive words to a dish on a menu can positively affect how diners perceive the food.

> **Challenge yourself**
>
> Look at the issue and debate tracker table on page 195. Create similar issue and debate trackers commentary for field experiments, objective and subjective data, generalisations from findings, and validity.

20.2.3 Consumer behaviour and personal space

Personal space

Bell *et al* (1996) define personal space as a '… portable, invisible boundary surrounding us, into which others may not trespass. It regulates how closely we interact with others, moves with us, and expands and contracts according to the situation in which we find ourselves' (1996: 275).

Hall (1963) distinguished between zones of personal space, which he called 'spatial zones', based around interpersonal relationships we may have. (See page 102, Perry *et al* core study from AS Level for a description of these zones.)

Overload, arousal and behaviour constraint

Overload theory suggests we maintain an optimal personal space in situations. This prevents us from being bombarded with too much sensory information. Overstimulation needs to be avoided or it can be quite difficult to cope with that situation. This is because we are too busy trying to process all of the information at once.

Arousal theory suggests that we get aroused when people invade our personal space. We try to make sense of this sudden arousal and this then dictates how much space we require. An example would be a first date. We may feel good or we may feel nervous. Both of these situations will arouse us. However, if we feel good we may require less personal space than if we feel nervous.

Behaviour constraint theory suggests that we all require a level of personal space or we feel that our behavioural freedom has been taken away. This can happen when people get too close to us.

Consumer psychology

KEY STUDY: Robson *et al* (2011)

Context

Previous research had shown that nearly two-thirds of people found that tables that are too close to each other made for a negative dining experience. There had been plenty of research examining personal space when designing and managing a restaurant, but little had been conducted investigating the preferences of diners and their behaviours.

Main theories/explanations

Halls' zones of personal space were explored in this study. See page 102 for a full description.

Aim and hypotheses

Robson *et al* (2011) wanted to investigate how personal space may affect people's comfort while dining in a restaurant. The study examined whether 'reduced' (tight) table spacing had an influence on diners' attitudes and preferences.

Design

The study used a web-based questionnaire. The first part of the survey gathered demographic information alongside any experiences respondents may have had in the restaurant business. The second part of the survey measured emotional, intentional, and anticipated behavioural reactions to one of three images of tables for two placed at distances of 6, 12, or 24 inches away from each other. It was based on a banquette style of seating which is an upholstered bench that is against the length of a wall. This can be seen in Figure 20.17.

Figure 20.17 *Example of visual prompt (6-inch table spacing shown)*
Source: Robson et al (2011: 255)

The questions asked were designed to investigate three different dining scenarios:

1. business purposes
2. friendship meeting
3. romantic date.

The distances were based on Hall's zones of personal space. As there were three distances and three scenarios, there were nine conditions that participants were randomly allocated to. The questionnaire had 32 statements that used a 7-point Likert scale with 1 = strongly disagree to 7 = strongly agree. Twelve of these statements were from the Stress Arousal Check List. The other items covered things such as perceived control, physical and sensory privacy, goal blocking, and general comfort. All of these items had been pretested with a different opportunity sample of 282 participants to give the measure psychometric properties. This did reduce the number of items directly related to seating to eight from the original 16.

A total of 1013 completed questionnaires were used in the analyses. Participants were recruited to represent a diverse national sample provided by a professional sampling company via a web link. It is not clear if the actual technique used was volunteer (the people were in a pool) or opportunity (the questionnaire was sent out to openly accessible email addresses or websites so people happened to be there when recruitment took place). Table 20.5 gives some of the key demographics of the sample.

Gender	n	%
Male	461	45.5
Female	537	53.0
No response	15	1.5
Age (years)		
Under 21	62	6.1
21-35	234	23.1
36-50	319	31.5
>50	391	38.6
Ethnicity		
White	821	81.1
Black	74	7.3
Hispanic (any race)	44	4.3
Asian	33	3.3
Other	37	3.7
No response	4	0.4

Table 20.5 Demographics of survey respondents
Source: Robson et al (2011: 256)

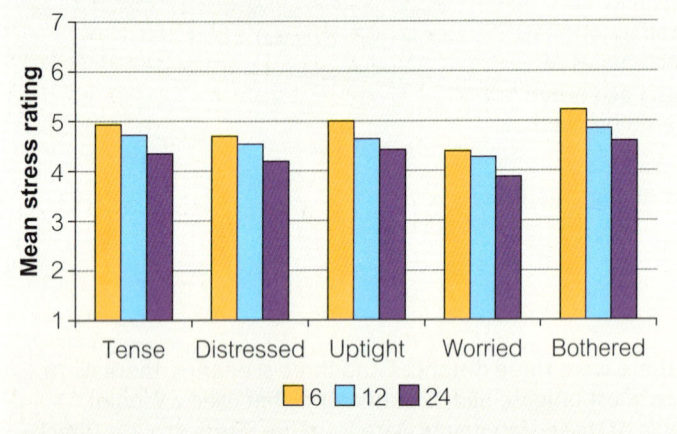

Figure 20.18 Comparison of survey items by table spacing: stress

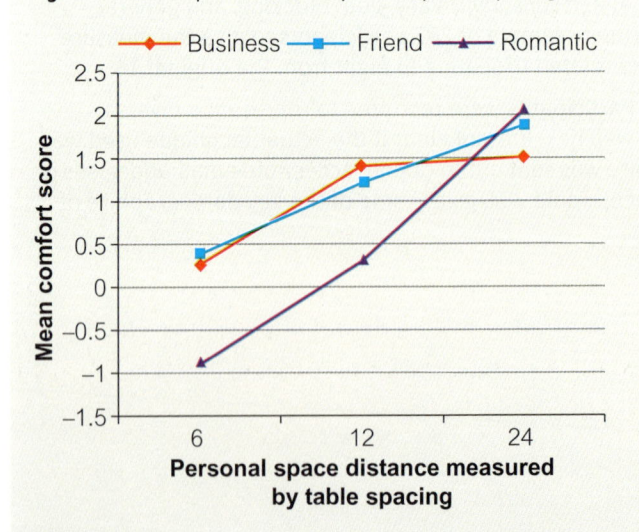

Figure 20.19 Comfort ratings by table spacing and scenario

Results, findings, and conclusions

These were the key results.

- For pleasure, stress, control, and comfort there was a significant difference between these ratings and distances in the expected direction.
- Close table spacing made respondents feel less private, less likely to have a positive meal experience, and more dissatisfied with the table given to them.
- When imagining sitting only six inches from the next table, people were concerned about disturbing others or being overheard during a meal.
- Figures 20.18 and 20.19 show the results for the stress measures.
- Figure 20.18 shows comfort ratings by scenario.
- It would seem that table distances and reasons for dining do affect the quality of experiences when dining in a restaurant.
- Female respondents felt significantly more stress, less control, and greater discomfort than men at all distances. Men felt more aroused than women at all distances.
- In terms of ethnicity, the scores for arousal and stress were very similar across all groups. However, control and comfort scores did show some differences. For example, Asian respondents felt more in control at 6 and 24 inches compared to all other groups. Hispanic respondents felt more control and comfort when the distance was 12 inches compared to all other groups.

Main discussion points

- The use of banquettes in restaurants may not be the best choice of seating, especially if the restaurant wants to attract more couples to dine there. In addition, people may spend less when experiencing banquette seating as they are likely to be in the restaurant for a shorter time due to increased stress and negative experiences.
- However, a greater turnaround of tables may mean *more* customers, so more meals may be served, leading to increased revenue. However, the restaurant would have to find a way of getting these customers back on a regular basis.

Evaluation points

- The feelings experienced while simply looking at table spacing may not be well correlated with *actually* feeling stress, lack of comfort, lack of control, etc. Therefore, there has to be some caution attached to the validity of findings as no behavioural measure was taken. Respondents might think they would feel discomfort but, in reality, they may enjoy a meal at six inches spacing if they are enjoying the company or food.
- As the study was a web-based survey, there is no way of verifying the validity of demographics of the sample or that the survey was taken seriously by all participants. This could reduce both the validity of findings and the application of those findings to real-life restaurants.
- The use of an independent measures design means that certain participant variables might be affecting the results. We do not know how each person would feel in *all nine scenarios*. It might be that the one scenario that the participants were assigned too was not one they were familiar with or was one that they had previous negative experience of, which is not reflective of how they would respond to the other eight scenarios.
- The measures were tested for psychometric properties so it can be argued that the measures used had validity and reliability.

Defending place in a queue

Milgram *et al* (1986) assessed how people defend their place in a queue. Prior to the study the researchers had noted three distinguishing features of a queue.

- It regulates the sequence in which people are served in shop or gain access to services.
- The order of a queue has a distinctive spatial format.
- Maintenance of the queue depends on a 'shared knowledge of the standards of behaviour appropriate to that queue' (Milgram *et al*, 1986: 683).

The researchers created an experiment that studied queue intrusions in 129 waiting lines, mainly at a railroad ticket counter. The queues were of an average length of six people (excluding confederates). The confederate always calmly approached a point between the third and fourth person in a queue and remarked in a neutral tone: "Excuse me, I'd like to get in there". Before anyone could respond the confederate entered the queue at that point. If the confederate was asked to leave the queue the person did so, otherwise he or she would remain there for one minute before leaving voluntarily. Three female and two male intruders were used. The number of intruders varied too: either one or two. 'Buffers' were also used – these were confederates who occupied a position between the point of intrusion and the next naïve queuer.

There were six experimental conditions, as shown in Figure 20.20.

The main results were as follows.

- Physical action (eg tugging a sleeve, putting hands on shoulders) occurred in 10.1% of queues.
- Verbal objections were quite common. Examples included "Excuse me, you have to go to the back of the line", "No way! The line's back there. We've all been waiting and have trains to catch", "Are you making a line here?!" This happened in 21.7% of queues.

Challenge yourself

Design a study using a self-report technique that investigates spacing at restaurant tables.

```
Head  −2 −1 0 +1 +2 +3 +4 +5   End
             |
          Intrusion
           point
```

Figure 20.20
Source: Milgram *et al* (1986: 684)

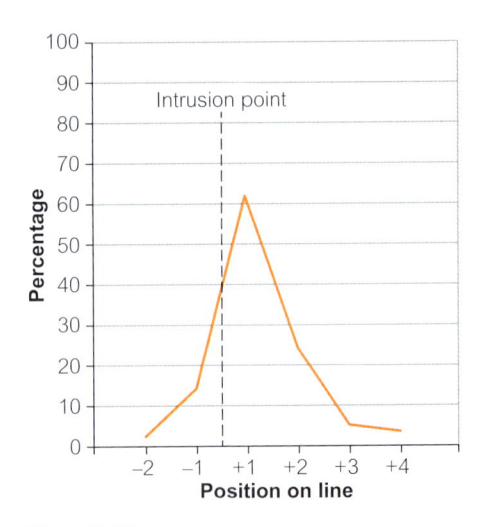

Figure 20.21
Source: Milgram et al (1986: 686)

- In 14.7% of queues, non-verbal objections occurred, such as hostile stares and gestures.

Table 20.6 Objections to intrusions in six experimental conditions

Condition	No. of lines	No. of intruders	No. of buffers	No. of lines in which objections occurred	% of lines in which objections occurred
1	22	1	0	12	54.0
2	24	1	1	6	25.0
3	20	1	2	1	5.0
4	23	2	0	21	91.3
5	20	2	1	5	25.0
6	20	2	2	6	30.0

Source: Milgram et al (1986: 685)

Figure 20.21 shows the percentage of people objecting according to their position in the line.

Table 20.7 shows the effects of the buffers on objections.

Table 20.7 Spatial distribution of responses to intrusions: percentage and number of persons objecting according to position in line

Condition	Position in line						
	% − 2	% − 1	I	% + 1	% + 2	% + 3	% + 4
1	4.5 (1/22)	22.7 (5/22)		36.4 (8/22)	14.3 (2/14)	0.0 (0/9)	0.0 (0/7)
2	0.0 (0/22)	12.5 (3/24)		Buf	16.7 (4/24)	0.0 (0/15)	0.0 (0/9)
3	0.0 (0/18)	5.0 (1/20)		Buf	Buf	0.0 (0/20)	0.0 (0/18)
4	4.3 (1/23)	21.7 (5/23)		86.9 (20/23)	43.5 (10/23)	9.1 (2/22)	0.0 (0/20)
5	0.0 (0/18)	10.0 (2/20)		Buf	20.0 (4/20)	0.0 (0/15)	0.0 (0/4)
6	0.0 (0/18)	10.0 (2/20)		Buf	Buf	15.0 (3/20)	11.8 (2/17)
Total	1.7 (2/121)	14.0 (18/129)		62.2 (28/45)	24.7 (20/81)	5.0 (5/101)	2.7 (2/75)

Note: The figures in parentheses show the exact number of persons for each position on which the percentage figures are based. I = intrusion point.

Buf = buffer (a confederate who passively occupied a position between the point of intrusion and the next naïve queuer).

Source: Milgram et al (1986: 685)

Therefore, we can conclude that people will object to an intrusion within a queue, but these objections are limited to mild physical action, verbal objections or non-verbal gestures, most often from people immediately behind the person who has intruded.

Strength	Weakness
The study has some ecological validity as it took place in a natural setting.	Some of the verbalisations may not have been recorded correctly.

Challenge yourself

Explain why the study had ecological validity and why incorrect recording of verbalisation could be a problem in relation to validity.

Challenge yourself

Create similar issue and debate commentaries for individual and situational explanations, and observations.

	Issue and debate tracker
Ethics	The act of having your place in a queue invaded could have caused **psychological stress** in participants (Milgram *et al*, 1986). Also, just imagining different table spacing (Robson *et al*, 2011) can also cause some levels of **psychological stress**. None of the researchers explicitly stated that they attempted to reverse any potential psychological stress caused to participants.
Quantitative and qualitative data	Both studies collected **quantitative data**, meaning that direct comparisons could be measured between groups of participants. In the Robson *et al* study this was the measure of stress across distances and scenario. In the Milgram *et al* study an example was the number of times an objection was made. Milgram *et al* also collected **qualitative data** in the form of the actual objections people said, meaning that we know why people were objecting to the intrusion.

20.3.1 Consumer decision making

20.3 Consumer decision making

Models of consumer decision making: utility, satisficing, prospect

- The utility model proposes that consumers make decisions based on the expected outcomes of their decisions. Consumers are viewed as rational humans who can estimate outcomes to maximise their wellbeing.

- The satisficing model proposes that consumers get to approximately where they want to go and then stop any decision making. For example, when trying to find a new apartment potential buyers might simply evaluate possibilities that are a certain distance from a desired location and then stop.

- The prospect model proposes two main elements involved in decision making: value and endowment. The value relates to potential gains and losses of purchase, while the endowment refers to when an item is perceived as being more precious if you own it rather than someone else.

Strategies of consumer decision making

Table 20.8 Compensatory, non-compensatory, and partially compensatory strategies for decision making

Type of strategy	Strategy	Description
Compensatory	Linear	Each attribute of product can be measured on a scale. Each attribute is given a weight dependent on its relative importance to the consumer. The highest value product is then chosen.
	Additive difference	The consumer compares all products attribute by attribute. The consumer focuses on differences. A total difference is calculated so that the consumer can then purchase the best alternative.
	Image theory	Decisions are potentially a two-part process. The first part is a compatibility test where any product that does not meet the minimum accepted 'value' in terms of quality is eliminated. If only one alternative is left then that is more likely to be purchased. However, if more than one alternative is left, the consumer uses a profitability test. This tends to be based on the previous two compensatory strategies outlined above.
Non-compensatory	Satisficing	Each product has a minimum acceptable value, placed on it by the consumer. The first alternative to meet this value is purchased.
	Lexicographic	A consumer determines the relative importance of each attribute related to a product. Every alternative is assessed via the attribute seen as being the most important. The product that is ranked highest on the most important attribute is chosen. However, if there are two or more alternatives with the same score, those are re-assessed with the second most important attribute, and so on until there is a clear 'winner'.
	Recognition	Consumers select the best alternative based solely on familiarity. This is usually based on a company's trustworthiness.
Partially compensatory	Majority of conforming decisions	Two products are compared across all relevant attributes and the winner is retained. This is then pitted against another product and another winner is declared. The last product is then purchased.
	Frequency of good and bad features	All products are assessed simultaneously across all relevant attributes and the one that has the largest number of good features is purchased.

> **Challenge yourself**
>
> Design a study using a self-report technique that tests the three models above.

Decision-making strategies in internet shopping

Internet shopping is continually changing as consumers look for the best price or for discounts. There are several decision-making strategies that consumers use when internet shopping. Jedetski *et al* (2002) looked at the six compensatory and non-compensatory strategies outlined on page 191. The study had four predictions.

1. Consumers would use compensatory decision-making strategies when purchasing a product from the internet when the website allows for alternatives to be compared.

2. Consumers would use non-compensatory decision-making strategies when purchasing a product from the internet when the website does not allow for alternatives to be compared.

3. Consumers would use compensatory decision-making strategies when purchasing a product from the internet when there are fewer than 30 alternatives.

4. Consumers would use non-compensatory decision-making strategies when purchasing a product from the internet when there are more than 100 alternatives.

The experiment used a 2×2 design (CompareNet and Jango websites; fewer than 30 alternatives and greater than 100 alternatives). The CompareNet website allowed for direct comparisons between alternatives based on criteria chosen by the consumer. The Jango website did not allow direct comparisons. Answering machines and baby monitors were chosen for the fewer than 30 alternatives while golf clubs and toasters were chosen for the greater than 100 alternatives. A volunteer sample of 24 participants was randomly assigned to one of the four conditions. The sample was evenly split by gender and the majority were younger than 30 years old, regularly used the internet, and had purchased products online before.

Before searching for products, each participant had to read a document that described the six compensatory and non-compensatory decision-making strategies and were tested to ensure that they understood each one. Then the participants were shown how to use whichever website had been assigned to them. They were then asked to choose an alternative from whichever products had been assigned to them. They also had to speak out loud their decision-making processes. At the end of the task, they had to complete a questionnaire that allowed them to indicate which of the six decision-making strategies they thought they had used.

Tables 20.9 and 20.10 show the main results by decision-making strategy.

Table 20.9 Compensatory and non-compensatory strategies by website and number of alternatives

	CompareNet	Jango	<30	>100
Compensatory	31	17	30	18
Non-compensatory	17	31	18	30

Table 20.10 Decision strategies by website

Website	CompareNet	Jango	Total
Linear model	8	1	9
Additive difference	6	4	10
Image theory	17	12	29
Satisficing	3	14	17
Lexicographic	12	11	23
Recognition	2	6	8
Total	**48**	**48**	**96**

Source: (both tables above) Jedetski *et al* (2002: 76)

The results followed all predictions overall, except for the Lexicographic non-compensatory strategy which was used slightly more with CompareNet rather than Jango.

Therefore, in conclusion, consumers do use a range of compensatory decision-making strategies when internet shopping on a website that allows a customised comparison across alternative products. Also, consumers do use a range of non-compensatory decision-making strategies when internet shopping on a website that does not allow direct comparisons between alternatives.

Challenge yourself

Create similar issue and debate commentaries for reductionism versus holism, determinism versus free will, and application to everyday life.

Strengths	Weaknesses
The sampling technique was volunteer so the participants may have been more motivated to engage in the task and more likely to verbalise their thought processes.	The study has low temporal validity as it was conducted in 2002 using two websites that no longer exist. More recent comparison websites might do the comparisons for the consumer rather than the consumer being in control of criteria of assessments.
	The participants had to read about the six strategies before engaging in the website task. This may have given some participants a new and different way of making a decision that did not reflect their usual decision-making strategy. This could lower the validity of findings as it may not be a true representation of how each participant *typically* makes decisions in relation to shopping on the internet.

	Issue and debate tracker
Idiographic versus nomothetic	All of the models of consumer decision making, in addition to the strategies used by consumers to help with decision making, are **nomothetic** as they show how consumers can be grouped together to form a 'general' law from that model or strategy. Jedetski et al (2002) also showed this when participants were having to actually choose products to buy – there were several general laws of behaviour that represent the average consumer who uses any of the strategies tested. There was no real evidence for an **idiographic** approach being relevant here as no strategy was unique to just one consumer.

20.3.2 Choice heuristics

Availability and representativeness

A heuristic is a 'mental shortcut' that allows us to make a series of decisions quickly. There are two main types.

- Availability – this shortcut helps us to make a quick decision based on how easy it is to bring something to our consciousness. It relies on how easily and quickly we can find information to help us make a judgment on our shopping. For example, if we have just heard that there has been a recall on a product made by Sony, we might not go and buy a different Sony product as a result.

- Representativeness – this shortcut helps us to make a decision based on comparing available information with a mental 'prototype' (sometimes stereotype) we have about a product. For example, we might have a prototype that all Apple products are excellent so we use this to help us make a decision about purchasing other Apple products even if we have never bought, say, a laptop before.

Heuristics can be influenced by both situational factors such as time pressure and how information is presented, and individual factors such as intelligence and personality.

The following are all types of heuristics.

- Recognition: this is based around making decisions based on just one piece of information, the recognition cue, while discarding all other information. If consumers have to make a quick decision about two products, they are more likely to choose (and purchase) the one they recognise.

- Take-the-best: this is based around a consumer having several criteria (or cues) to base a decision on. They are ranked in order of validity to the consumer. When presented with two alternatives, the consumer will assess the products on the cue ranked highest and work down each cue until a difference is found and then the decision to buy the 'winning' product happens.

- Anchoring: this is based around consumers making decisions based around one particular reference point called an 'anchor'. Once the anchor is set, any subsequent decision made by the consumer could change from what would have happened *without* the anchor point. For example, a consumer sees a necklace priced £2000, which she really likes. She then finds another necklace that costs £350, which she also really likes. As a result, the second necklace is perceived as being 'cheap'. However, if the consumer had only seen the £350 necklace then she may not have perceived that as being cheap. The anchor price of £2000 has affected her decision making.

Point of purchase decision including multiple unit pricing and suggestive selling

Wansink *et al* (1998) investigated what makes consumers buy a certain amount of units. The researchers used a series of field and laboratory experiments.

Study 1

The aim of the first study was to test whether supermarket multiple-unit pricing increased sales. An example of multiple-unit pricing is 'On sale – 6 for $3' whereas an example of single-unit pricing is 'On sale – 50 cents each'. This study was conducted over a one-week period. In 86 different stores, 13 products were put on sale using either single-unit or multiple-unit pricing. Sales were recorded and any increase in sales from baseline was noted.

Table 20.11 The impact of multiple-unit pricing on supermarket sales

Product	Level of discount	Form of price expression	Percentage change in unit sales		
			Single unit	Multiple unit	p-value
Bathroom tissue	15%	1/50¢ versus 4/$2.00	+57	+97	.02
Candy	9%	1/50¢ versus 2/$1.00	+24	+25	n.s.
Cereal (Breakfast)	33%	1/$1.99 versus 2/$3.98	+133	+137	n.s.
Cookies	44%	1/$1.67 versus 2/$3.34	+306	+372	.01
Frozen dinners	12%	1/$2.49 versus 2/$5.00	+33	+70	.003
Frozen dinners	20%	1/$2.50 versus 2/$5.00	+133	+195	.0001
Frozen entrees	26%	1/$1.25 versus 2/$2.50	+133	+156	.02
Paper towels	31%	1/75¢ versus 2/$1.50	+403	+565	.001
Soap (3-bar packs)	15%	1/$1.99 versus 2/$3.98	+48	+30	n.s.
Soft Drinks (2 liters)	17%	1/$1.49 versus 2/$3.00	+33	+66	.01
Soup (Canned)	20%	1/$1.33 versus 3/$4.00	+200	+248	.01
Soup (Canned)	17%	1/50¢ versus 2/$1.00	+108	+112	n.s.
Tuna (Canned)	18%	1/65¢ versus 2/$1.30	+36	+66	.004
	21%		+125%	+165%	.0001

Source: Wansink *et al* (1998: 73)

Overall, multiple-unit pricing increased sales by, on average, 32% in all stores. For 12 of the products, multiple-unit pricing increased sales. Nine of these were significant increases compared to the single-unit figures.

Study 2

The aim of the second study was to test whether high purchase-quantity limits increased sales. Three supermarkets in Sioux City, Iowa, USA, ran an offer over three consecutive evenings. The offer was a (modest) 12% discount on Campbell's® soup (which made the price 79 cents per can rather than 89 cents). However, on each evening a different limit was imposed on the number of cans consumers could buy.

On the first evening there was no limit on the amount of cans a person could purchase.

On the second evening, each customer could only buy four cans.

On the third evening, each customer could only buy 12 cans.

The supermarkets used were all of a similar size and had a similar shopper volume. A total of 914 shoppers passed the display and the researchers simply noted how many cans consumers placed in their basket or trolley. Those with no purchase limits bought 3.3 cans on average, compared to 3.5 cans when the limit was 4 cans, and 7 cans when the limit was 12 cans.

The bar charts in Figure 20.22 show the frequency of purchasing across the three conditions.

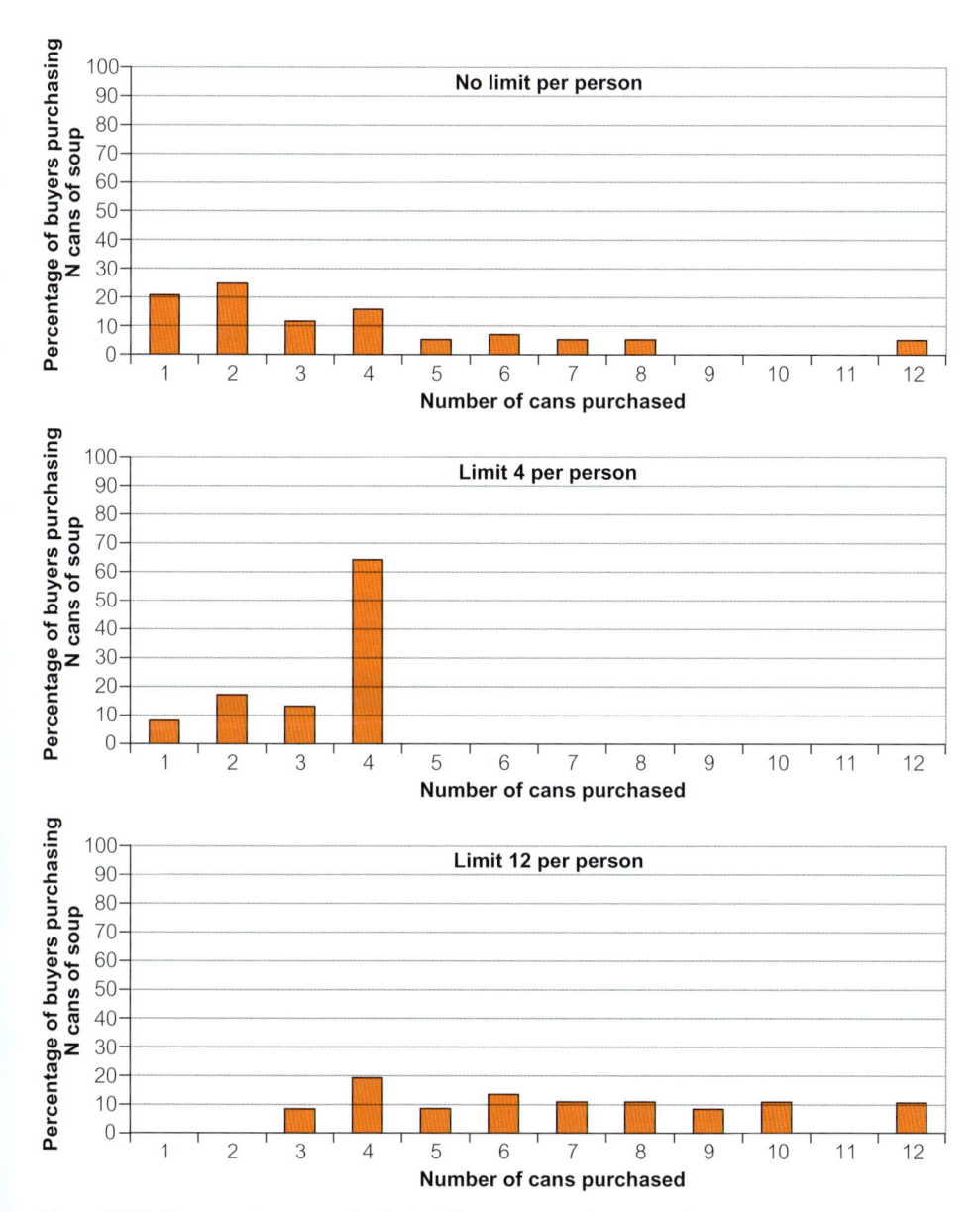

Figure 20.22 *How purchase-quantity limits influence canned soup purchases*
Source: Wansink et al (1998: 75)

Figure 20.23 The impact of suggestive selling anchors and discounts
Source: Wansink et al (1998: 76)

Studies 3 and 4

These studies examined 'selling anchors' to see whether they affected purchasing. One hundred and twenty undergraduates were offered six well-known products at one of three price levels:

an actual convenience store price

a 20% discount

a 40% discount.

In addition, participants were given one of two selling claims (called 'anchors'). For example:

'Snickers® bars – buy some for your freezer.'

'Snickers® bars – buy 18 for your freezer.'

Figure 20.23 shows the results. It shows that when a specific anchor was used, sales increased across all discount levels.

In the final study, it was found that using an 'expansion anchor' (eg 'This has 101 uses!') increased sale intentions across a range of purchase-quantity limits.

Overall, from their studies the researchers concluded the applications shown in Table 20.12.

Table 20.12 Executing and improving anchor-based promotions

	Anchor-based promotions			
	Multiple-unit pricing	**Purchase-quantity limits**	**Suggestive selling**	**Expansion anchors**
Executions	3 for $1.97	Limit of 12 per person	Grab 6 for studying	101 uses!
	12 for the price of 10	Limit of 1 per visit	Buy 8 and save a trip	Buy a month's worth
	Baker's dozen for $2.99	4 per person per day	Buy 12 for your freezer	Buy for all your friends
Implementation considerations	Discounts of 10–20 per cent can increase sales while protecting margins.	Very low limits increase purchase incidence; high limits increase purchase quantities.	Anchor-based sales suggestions may work without a corresponding sales promotion.	Advertisements, packages, and POP materials can increase purchase quantities by stimulating thoughts of new uses.
	The larger and more expensive the product, the lower the suggested number should be.	To avoid truncating sales, set limits of at least two times higher than the typical quantity bought on deal.	Suggestive selling can be most effective with familiar, inexpensive items, such as snacks and drinks.	Expansion anchors can be used in advertising campaigns and without a sales promotion.

Source: Wansink et al (1998: 79)

Challenge yourself

Next time you visit a supermarket, note real-life examples of the techniques mentioned in the study.

Strength	Weakness
The study has good application as shop owners can use the findings to increase their sales.	The study only took place in one supermarket in the United States, so generalisability beyond the study may prove difficult.

Applying heuristics to decision making

Before the study by del Campo *et al* (2016) there had been little research about which heuristics consumers use when making decisions about purchasing.

The study by del Campo *et al* (2016) investigated the use of heuristics in decision making. The researchers used several questions based around the use of recognition and take-the-best types of heuristics and whether time pressure affects how we make consumer purchasing decisions. Participants were from Austria and Spain. The researchers used a mixture of sampling techniques. Participants volunteered but were then asked to send the questionnaire link to people they knew (a sampling technique known as snowball sampling). The Austrian sample consisted of 143 participants (64.3% female) and the Spanish sample consisted of 128 participants (51.6% female).

Consumer psychology

Price: **only 2.99 Euro**
Raising: free-range
Quality Grade: A
Country of Origin: Austria
Shelf Life: 2 weeks
Quantity: 6 eggs
"Take-the-best" stimulus

Price: 3.19 Euro
Raising: free-range
Quality Grade: A
Country of Origin: Austria
Shelf Life: 2 weeks
Quantity: 6 eggs
"Recognition" stimulus

Price: 3.19 Euro
Raising: free-range
Quality Grade: A
Country of Origin: Austria
Shelf Life: 2 weeks
Quantity: 6 eggs
"Emotional" stimulus

Price: **3.10 Euro**
Raising: free-range, **with additional information** on raising of chicken
Quality Grade: A/ **extra large**
Country of Origin: Austria, **of guaranteed origin**
Shelf Life: 2 weeks
Quantity: 6 eggs
Additional information: GM-free, salmonella-free, animal rights tested, free of toxins, hygiene programme
"Cognitive" stimulus

Price: 3.19 Euro
Raising: barn/deep litter
Quality Grade: B
Country of Origin: Austria
Shelf Life: 2 weeks
Quantity: 6 eggs
"Filler" stimulus

Figure 20.24 *Stimulus material for Austria (in Spain, Country of Origin was indicated as Spain)*
Source: del Campo *et al* (2016: 397)

Participants were given an online task of buying eggs from a variety of choices, each one representing a different heuristic (or no heuristic as a control). Figure 20.24 shows the five choices given to participants with all of the information provided.

The experiment used an independent measures design with participants being randomly assigned to either a time pressure (choose within 40 seconds of being presented with the five choices) or no time pressure. A measure of decision-making style was completed by all participants but the focus on the results presented here will be about the role of heuristics. The main result can be seen in Figure 20.25.

Challenge yourself

Look at the issue and debate tracker table on page 197. Create similar issue and debate commentaries for application to everyday life, individual and situational explanations, experiments, quantitative and qualitative data, and objective and subjective data.

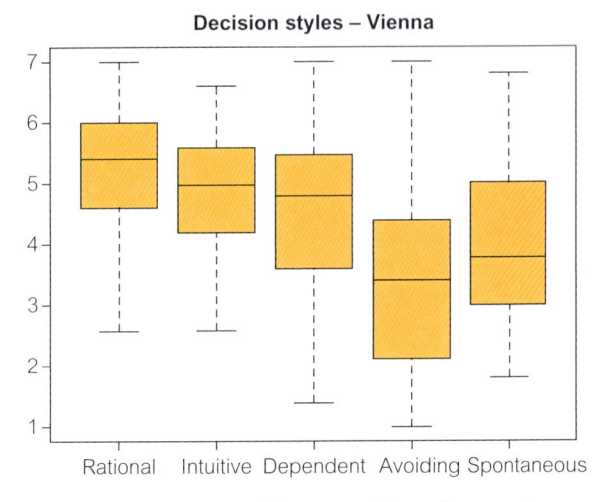

Figure 20.25 Distribution of decision making style scores for subjects in Madrid (top) and Vienna (bottom)

For both samples of participants, applying a time pressure made participants less likely to choose the 'cognitive' product but more likely to choose the 'take-the-best' and 'recognition' products. Participants from Austria chose 'cognitive' and 'recognition' products more often than participants from Spain. Participants from Spain chose 'take-the-best' products more often than participants from Austria.

In conclusion, it would appear that under time pressure consumers use different heuristics to choose a product (in this case six eggs) compared to when there is no time pressure involved in their decision making. In particular, the 'take-the-best' and 'recognition' types of heuristics are used more frequently when there is limited time to make a purchase decision.

Strength	Weakness
The study was clearly standardised to allow other researchers to replicate it, to test for reliability. For example, the five choices of eggs (pictures and descriptions) and the procedure for both time pressure and no pressure are described clearly by the researchers means that other psychologists can replicate the study to test for reliability across other cultures.	The task itself has low mundane realism and may not predict what would happen in a real-life consumer decision-making situation. Participants only had to choose *without* the actual act of buying the eggs. In a supermarket, the participants may not use the same heuristics as shopping online, so the study may lack some real-life validity.

20.3.3 Mistakes in decision making

Thinking fast and thinking slow; system 1 and system 2

Shleifer (2012) reviewed the work of Kahneman and the idea of system 1 and system 2 thinking.

- System 1 involves thinking fast. People who are system 1 thinkers are intuitive, automatic, unconscious and effortless thinkers. They answer questions quickly through recognising resemblances and using associations.
- System 2 involves thinking slow. People who are system 2 thinkers are conscious, slow, controlled, deliberate, effortful, suspicious and lazy.

Most people use system 1 thinking patterns but certain circumstances may make them use system 2. Shleifer highlighted this with an example from Kahneman.

> 'An individual has been described by a neighbor as follows: "Steve is very shy and withdrawn, invariably helpful but with very little interest in people or in the world of reality. A meek and tidy soul, he has a need for order and structure, and a passion for detail." Is Steve more likely to be a librarian or a farmer?'
>
> (Shleifer, 2012: 3)

Shleifer notes that virtually everyone would choose librarian because associative memory links the 'tale' to the job. System 1 thinking prevails. However, system 2 rarely engages even though it might be useful in this scenario. People do not take the time to assess facts such as: there are five times as many farmers in the United States as there are librarians; there are far more male farmers than male librarians.

Challenge yourself

Design a study that tests whether a person is a system 1 or a system 2 thinker.

Choice blindness, preferences and defending a choice

KEY STUDY: Hall et al (2010)

Context

Previous research had shown that people are not the best at noticing changes when subtle manipulations are used. For example, people could be asked to choose what they feel is the most attractive face from a pair. However, if they are distracted and then shown the face they *did not originally choose*, only about one-quarter of people will detect that the change happened. However, most research was conducted in a laboratory so very little was known about whether the same would happen in a naturalistic setting.

Main theories/explanations

Choice blindness refers to when people fail to recognise that something they have just tasted or smelt (as in this present study) has been changed.

Aims and hypotheses

Hall *et al* (2010) investigated the phenomenon of choice blindness in a naturalistic setting. The research team had the following expectations.

- The larger the difference in likeability scores for each pair of jam/tea should correlate with higher degrees of detection.
- Giving an incentive would motivate people to increase their attention to any decision making.
- The second tasting of the manipulated sample could distort the original memory of any discrepancy between the two options. As a result, participants would state that they found it more difficult to differentiate the two samples.
- If a person had a lingering doubt about the manipulation, they should record lower levels of confidence in their choice of favourite jam/tea.

Design

This was a field experiment using a questionnaire and an interview to collect the data.

Participants

A total of 180 consumers (118 female) at a supermarket in Lund, Sweden were the participants in the study. Their ages ranged from 16 to 80 years with a mean of 40.2 years. They were recruited as they passed a tasting venue that was set up like an 'independent consultant' within the supermarket.

Procedure

The stand was set up in one of the outer aisles of the supermarket away from product labels, stimulating odours, and noise. For each participant the order of presentation, the type of manipulation, and which pairs of jam/tea they tasted was randomised.

Three pairs of jams and three pairs of teas were used in the study. Independent participants had already rated the pairs for similarity on a 10-point scale so that the pairs were are towards the mid-point of 5 for 'difference' (the scale was 1 for very different to 10 for very similar). The pairings were:

- jam: blackcurrant/blueberry; ginger/lime; cinnamon-apple/grapefruit
- teas: apple pie/honey; caramel and cream/cinnamon; Pernod (anise)/mango.

Participants were told that the 'taste test' was for a quality control study. The procedure is shown in Figure 20.26.

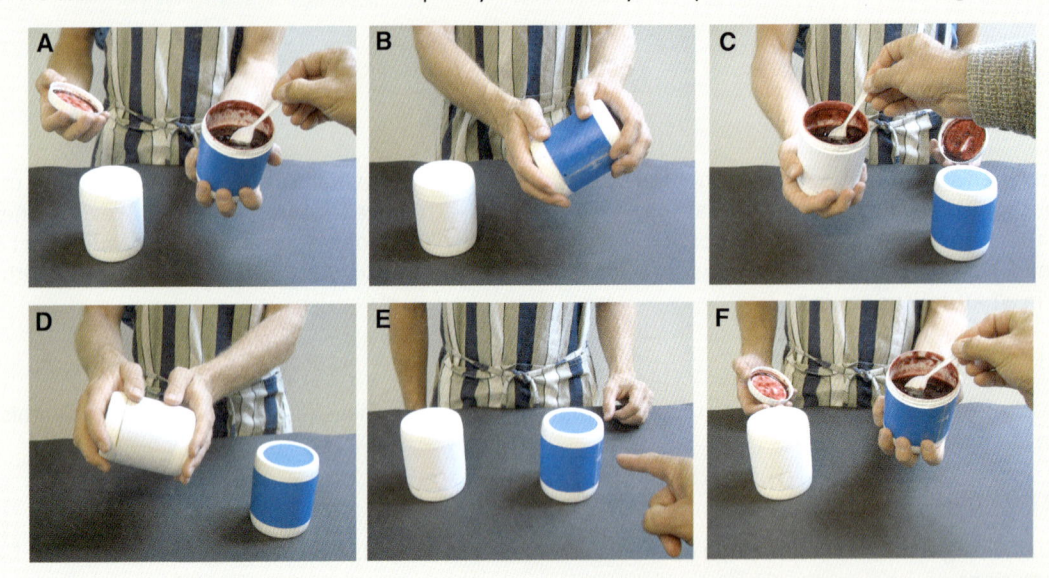

Figure 20.26 A step-by-step illustration of a manipulated choice trial in the jam condition. (A) The participants sample the first jam. (B) The experiment secures the lid back on and flips the jar upside down while putting it back on the table. The jar looks normal, but it is lidded at both ends, and with a divider inside, containing one of the included samples at each end. (C) The participants sample the second jam. (D) The experimenter performs the same flipping manoeuvre for the second 'magical' jar. (The participants indicate which jam they prefer. (F) The participants sample the chosen jam a second time, but since the containers have been flipped they now receive the alternative they did not prefer.

Source: Hall et al (2020: 55)

Each participant sampled a pair of jams and a pair of teas. After tasting the jams and then smelling the teas, the participants had to rate each on a 10-point scale from 'not at all good' to 'very good'. Once they had tasted the second of each pairing, they were asked which they preferred on the same scale. They were then offered a second taste or smell of their 'preferred option'. However, this was always the opposite of what they had said they preferred. After they had sampled their supposed preferred option they were asked if they had felt anything was odd or unusual. They had to indicate on a different 10-point scale how easy they felt it was to discriminate between the two tastes (very difficult to very easy). Finally, another 10-point scale was used by participants to measure how confident they were in their preferred choice (very unsure to very certain).

Their responses were noted and if they had detected something *had* changed then this was classified in one of three ways.

1. Concurrent detection. This was when the participants immediately noticed that they had not got their preferred option.
2. Retrospective detection. This was when the participants either before or after debriefing noticed the manipulation.
3. Sensory-change detection. This was when the participants noticed some subtle change (even if they did not consciously notice the manipulation) by saying that it was sweeter/weaker/stronger, etc.

Non-manipulated trials also took place as a control. To test the role of incentives on detection, half of the participants were offered their chosen sample to take home with them.

At the end of the study, each participant was asked to give consent for their data to be included in any analysis. Particpants were also debriefed about the true aim of the study being about choice blindness.

Results, findings, and conclusions

The rates of detection for each pairing are shown in Figure 20.27.

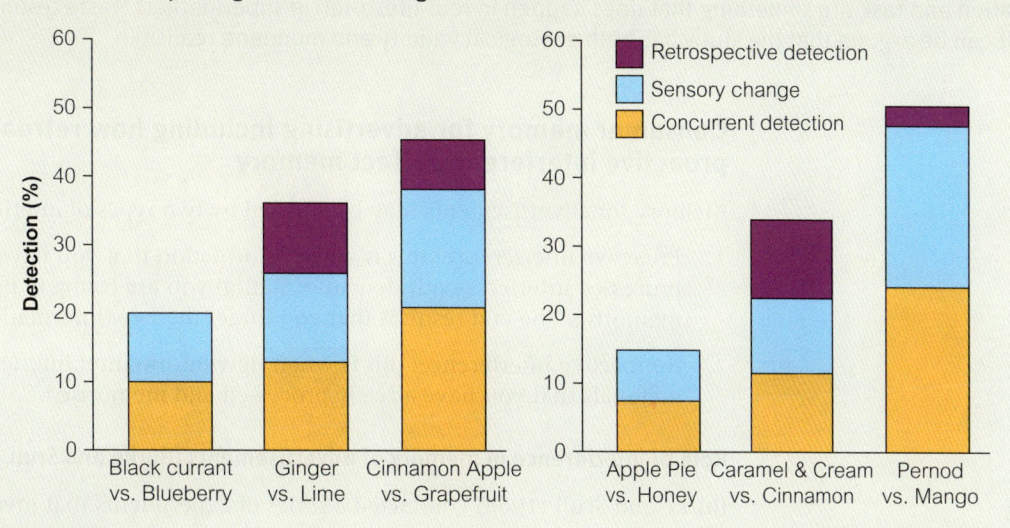

Figure 20.27 *The data is divided into detection type (retrospective detection, sensory-change, concurrent detection), pair (three stimuli pairs), and modality (A for jam and B for tea).*
Source: Hall et al (2020: 58)

The rates of detection by type for jam and tea are shown in Table 20.13.

Table 20.13 *Detection rates for jam pairings and tea pairings*

	Concurrent detection	Retrospective detection	Sensory change
Jam pairings	14.4	6.2	12.4
Tea pairings	13.8	6.9	11.5

Note: Numbers are percentage of trials.

Overall, no more than one third of all manipulation trials were detected by the participants (33.3% for jam and 32.2% for tea). Therefore, in the majority of cases, the participants were blind to the manipulation that had happened and could not detect it. Also, in around two-thirds of the trial where detection happened, it was not a conscious reaction. Overall confidence of choice did not differ between jam and tea trials.

The role of incentives was not supported; in fact, it had the opposite effect. Those given a sample to take home performed significantly worse in the tea trials than those not given an incentive (19.6% detection compared to 46.3%). There was no significant effect of incentive on jam trials.

In conclusion, there are considerable levels of choice blindness for the taste and smell of consumer goods.

Main discussion points

- Some participants may not have noticed the differences because the decision was of great importance to their everyday lives. However, the research team did rate attractiveness scores for both products and they were high, plus the amount of tea and jam consumed is high in Europe so the decision could have had high importance to some of the consumer participants.
- The lower rates of detection in those who were given an incentive could be explained as the people became more obedient to the study, wanted to be less critical to gain the reward, or were less willing to report just in case they did not receive their incentive. However, the research team thought it may be the reverse: people who were not going to receive a gift were happy to report differences as it had no consequence.

Evaluation points

- The study was clearly standardised to allow other researchers to replicate the study to test for reliability. For example, the 'magic jar' was reported and explained, plus how to perform the manipulation.

- The sample was only from one area of Sweden so the results may be culturally biased and may not apply to other nationalities or to people who do not consume much jam or tea.
- Both the location and task are something that does happen in real-life, often in supermarkets. Taste testing events are common so it can be argued that the study has both ecological validity and mundane realism.

Consumer memory for advertising including how retroactive and proactive interference affect memory

Memory for advertisements may be affected by two types of interference.

1. Proactive interference: this is when information that you have already processed interferes with new information you are trying to process or memorise. The end result is that you forget the new information.

2. Retroactive interference: this is when new information interferes with materials that you have already processed and memorised.

Role of interference in memory of advertisements (Burke and Srull, 1988)

Burke and Srull (1988) conducted a series of experiments that investigated the role of interference in consumer memory for advertisements.

Experiment 1 investigated retroactive interference on consumer advertisement recall. The volunteer sample consisted of 144 students enrolled on an introductory psychology class and received course credit for participation. Experiment 2 investigated proactive interference on consumer advertisement recall with a different 144 student participants. The procedure for both experiments is shown in Table 20.14.

Table 20.14 Procedure for Burke and Srull (1988) experiments 1 and 2

Experiment 1: retroactive interference	Experiment 2: proactive interference
Participants were told that the study was about assessing the reliability of copytesting used in advertising research.	
For both experiments, participants were randomly assigned to one of two conditions.	
1. Brand purchase likelihood condition: participants were told they would review a selection of magazine advertisements with the aim of indicating their likelihood of purchasing the advertised brands. 2. Advertisement interest condition: participants were told that they would review of selection of magazine advertisements with the aim of rating their interest value for each one.	
Participants viewed 12 one-page advertisements for branded goods. The brands and goods were chosen to be relatively unfamiliar to the participants. They could read and judge each advertisement at their own pace. Once participants had read the advertisement, they pressed the space bar on their keypad and a question appeared (the type of question depended on which condition they were in), asking them to either rate their likelihood of purchase *or* their interest value.	
Three of the advertisements were chosen as the 'target advertisements' that would later be tested for recall (lawn tractor, car stereo, and a tent). These advertisements appeared in positions **three**, **five**, and **seven**. The advertisements were randomly assigned to these three positions, counterbalanced across participants.	Three of the advertisements were chosen as the 'target advertisements' that would later be tested for recall (lawn tractor, car stereo, and a tent). These advertisements appeared in positions **six**, **eight**, and **ten**. The advertisements were randomly assigned to these three positions, counterbalanced across participants.
'Context advertisements' were used to promote interference with the target advertisements in three different ways. 1. Varied-product context: the advertisement was from a different brand and in a different product class compared to the three target advertisements. 2. Same-product context: the advertisement promoted a different brand but in the same product class as a target advertisement. 3. Same-brand context: the advertisement promoted the same brand and same product class as a target advertisement but it would be a different model.	
Context advertisements appeared in positions **ten** and **eleven**. The seven advertisements that were not 'context' or 'target' were randomised.	Context advertisements appeared in positions **two** and **three**. The seven advertisements that were not 'context' or 'target' were randomised.

After seeing all 12 advertisements, participants had to complete a questionnaire about reading and television viewing habits. After this, a surprise recall test about the three target advertisements was given. Participants were presented with the brand name, model, and product class for one target advertisement as a time. They had to verbally report any information they could recall. They were given two minutes to complete this for each target advertisement. Each response was transcribed.

Two judges who did not know about the aim of the study independently scored each transcription. This was done by comparing the response from the participant to a list of all informational elements in that target advertisement. The recall score for each target advertisement was the total number of matches.

The main results were as follows.

- Retroactive interference: recall scores were lower when participants subsequently looked at an advertisement from the same-product or same-brand contexts compared to a varied-product context. There was also an interaction with judgement task. Those in the advertisement interest condition scored lower on recall in the same product and same brand contexts. This interaction was not seen in the brand purchase likelihood condition.

- Proactive interference: recall scores were lower when participants saw an advertisement from the same product or same brand contexts before the target advertisements compared to a varied product context. There was no interaction effect with judgement task.

In conclusion, retroactive and proactive interference can lower recall of seen advertisements when there are same product or same brand advertisements competing in a magazine.

> **Challenge yourself**
>
> Look at the issue and debate tracker table on page 197. Create similar issue and debate commentaries for individual and situational explanations, determinism versus free will, experiments, interviews, and reliability.

Strength	Weakness
The study was clearly standardised to allow other researchers to replicate the study to test for reliability. For example, the position of the 'context' advertisements and how the qualitative recall data was converted into quantitative recall data are described clearly by the researchers, which means that other psychologists can replicate the study to test for reliability across other media, for example.	The task itself has low mundane realism and may not predict what would happen in a real-life advertising recall situation. Being presented with 12 advertisements for products you are unfamiliar with or have little interest in and then asked to recall what you know about three of them is not an everyday task.

20.4.1 Packaging and positioning of a product

20.4 The product

Gift wrapping including beliefs of giver and recipient

Porublev *et al* (2009) conducted a qualitative study on people's perceptions of gift wrapping. Prior to the study, little research had been conducted on this topic but the researchers were aware of certain trends that had appeared in the literature.

- People believe that a gift should be wrapped.
- A gift should look like a gift.
- An unwrapped gift is often called a 'naked gift'.

> **Ask yourself**
>
> Do you always wrap presents for people when you give them a gift? Why do you do this? How do you feel when you receive a gift that is *not* gift wrapped?

The team used grounded theory for data collection and performed interpretative techniques for the analysis. Three methods of data collection were used.

- Observation of a Christmas gift wrap stall was carried out.
- There were in-depth interviews with 20 Australian participants who were 25–35 years old.
- Projective workshops were organised. At these workshops participants, in pairs, were asked to wrap two gifts: one for someone they were close to and one for an acquaintance. All discussions that took place were noted.

Most of the participants preferred to receive a gift that was wrapped. This was based on the 'expectation of what a gift should look like'. These are examples of some of the qualitative findings:

> "I prefer wrapped. I like the reveal. I think all gifts are good, don't get me wrong, I like a gift under any circumstances, but it does mean somebody's taken a little bit of extra time and put extra thought into it"
>
> (Tammy).
>
> "I'd be more embarrassed by a gift that was unwrapped than no gift at all"
>
> (Katya).
>
> "People have always received gifts that are wrapped and therefore I think a lot of people would do it without even thinking about it... it's a tradition in our society where you give me a gift there's an expectation that you'll wrap it therefore signifying that it is a gift"
>
> (Martin).
>
> Source: Porublev *et al* (2009: 4)

During the projective workshops, 24 gifts were wrapped. All of them looked like 'traditional' gifts with ribbons and bows. Figure 20.28 shows some examples.

Figure 20.28 *A sample of the gifts wrapped in the projective workshops*
Source: Porublev *et al* (2009: 5)

There were certain expectations about the use of gift wrap in the process of gift exchange. Gift wrapping makes it easier for gift exchange to occur as the giver and receiver can fulfil their roles without any confusion.

Strength	Weakness
Qualitative data were collected so the researchers had rich, in-depth data to analyse, potentially increasing the validity of findings.	The sample consisted of just 20 Australians so generalisability may be an issue.

Food package design and taste perceptions

KEY STUDY: Becker *et al* (2010)

Context

Consumers will often base their shopping choices on the visual appearance of a product. This could be product size, product shape, colour of packaging, etc. These can have a direct and indirect effect on how we perceive the quality of the product and even its taste.

Main theories/explanations

Many ideas were investigated in this study, including the following.
- Design of packaging and evaluation of its content – consumers do make links between different senses. A study showed that just adding 15% yellow colour to the can of 7-Up made people experience a taste that was more 'lemony' even though the actual drink was typical 7-Up (lemon and lime).

- Product shape and its potency – there has been a relationship between how angular a product shape is and impressions of potency: more angular = more potent.
- Shape and colour – there appears to be a noticeable interaction between shape of product and colour in terms of attractiveness and liking. Stimuli that are easily processed are liked more.
- Sensitivity to design – how consumers categorise and ultimately evaluate a product is based on a combination of level of interest, level of sensitivity to design decisions, and their expertise.

Aims and hypotheses

One aim of this study was to investigate the influence of food packaging on the impression of taste. Another was to investigate the influence of food packaging on consumer evaluation of a product.

Four hypotheses were tested in the study.

'H1. An angular, as opposed to a rounded, packaging shape will lead consumers to experience the product taste as more intense.

H2. A highly saturated, as opposed to a lowly saturated, packaging color will lead consumers to experience the product taste as more intense.

H3. Shape–color congruency (an angular shape combined with a highly saturated color or a rounded shape combined with a lowly saturated color) will lead to a more positive overall product attitude compared to shape–incongruency (an angular shape combined with a lowly saturated color or a rounded shape combined with a highly saturated color).

H4. The predicted effects of design features on the taste experience and overall product evaluations are more pronounced for consumers with a sensitivity to design compared to those indifferent with respect to product design' (Becker et al, 2010: 18–19).

Design

Pre-test

The researchers conducted a pre-test to investigate packaging shape and packaging colour manipulations. Three pairs of packaging shape were shown to 20 participants who had to rate them on a 12-item potency construct (eg bland, rebellious, or impressive). They rated each product shape on a 7-point scale from 'not at all' to 'very much so'. Figure 20.29 shows these pairings. A different set of 20 participants then rated two pairs of colours, all lemon-greenish. The same 12-item potency construct was used.

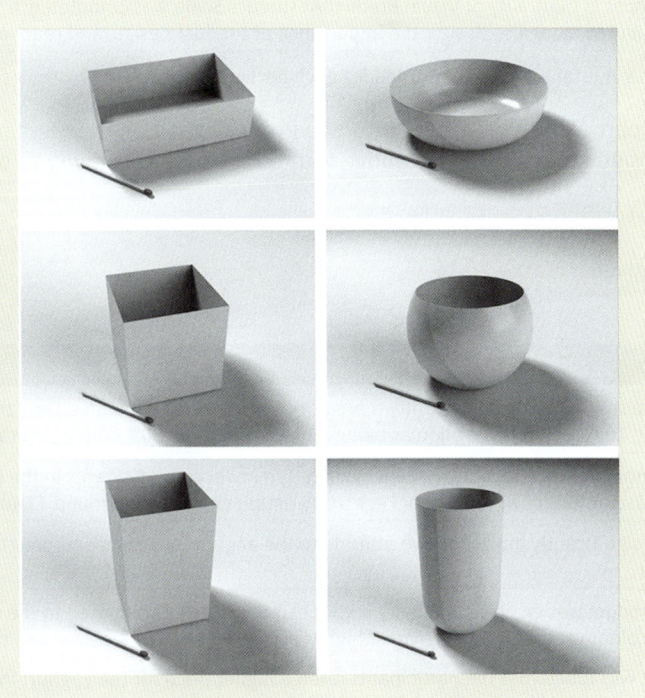

Figure 20.29 Shape variants (pre-test)
Source: Becker et al (2010: 19)

From this, the researchers could construct four lemon yoghurt product variations to use in the main study. Overall, the design was multifactorial (2 × 2 × 2) with packaging (angular or rounded), colour saturation (low: 50% or high: 100%) and sensitivity to design (low or high) being analysed.

Main study

Participants

The sample consisted of 151 customers from a German supermarket. They volunteered for the study and were not told the aim. There were 74 males and 77 females, with an age range of 15 to 81 years (mean age = 30.7 years).

Procedure

Each participant was asked if he or she would like to participate in a taste test in the entrance hall of the supermarket. The product was a 'new brand of yoghurt'. Participants viewed one of the four package designs shown in Figure 20.30. This viewing was on a laptop screen for 20 seconds with a 360° angle. After viewing they were asked to taste test the lemon yoghurt. The sample was the same for all participants. After finishing the taste test, each participant had to complete a range of questionnaires on a computer.

Measures

Participants completed the five measures shown in Table 20.15.

Figure 20.30 Stimulus materials (main study)
Source: Becker et al (2010: 20)

Table 20.15 The five measures used in the study

Measure	Description
Manipulation check	This was a single item. They had to indicate to what extent they agreed with 'this product package strikes me as potent'. It was the same 7-point scale as the pre-test.
Taste intensity*	They rated the yoghurt on three adjectives: sharp, bitter, and mild. High scores indicated a strong taste.
Product evaluation*	They rated the product on three statements about superiority, an eye-catching product, and a high-quality product.
Price expectation	They were asked to name a price for the yoghurt in Eurocents.
Sensitivity to design*	The Individual Differences in Centrality of Visual Product Aesthetics Scale was completed. It is an 11-item scale that assesses a person's ability to recognise design, the importance of product design, and reactions towards product design.

*The same 7-point scale as the pre-test was used. A total score was recorded for each participant by averaging their score across items.

From the sensitivity to design measure, participants were split into two groups based on the median. Those below the median formed the low sensitivity to design group and those above formed the high sensitivity to design group.

Results, findings, and conclusions

The main results for each measure are given in Table 20.16.

Table 20.16 Main results by measure

Measure	Result
Manipulation check	Angular packages were seen as being significantly more potent than round packages. Only those in the high sensitivity to design group perceived 100% colour saturation as being more potent than 50% colour saturation.
Taste intensity	Shape and colour did not directly affect taste intensity directly. However, participants in the high sensitivity to design group rated a higher taste intensity when the package was angular compared to round. Figure 20.31 shows this.
Product evaluation	Participants showed a significantly more positive attitude to the angular product compared to the round product. There was no effect of colour.
Price expectation	Overall, the angular product was given significantly higher estimated price compared to the round product. There was a tendency for the 50% colour saturation to be given a higher price than the 100% colour saturation.
	With further analysis it was found that the participants rated a higher price for the yoghurt in the angular packaging *because* that type of packaging has a more potent impression on consumers.

One conclusion was that product package design (and to some extent colour saturation) affects consumers' perception of taste and price but only in those who are sensitive to design decisions. A more general conclusion was that shape of product (and its curvature) does affect how consumers evaluate products and their expectation of price.

Main discussion points

- The expected result for colour product evaluations did not follow the expected prediction. This might have been because the colour difference between high and low was very subtle. However, this could be due to the product used here (yoghurt).

- The study can now provide some practical guidelines for the design of some consumer products. Designers should base new products entering a competitive market on package design rather than colour saturation to have the maximum effect. Low colour saturation is less typical across many products so this could be used to make the product appear more 'exclusive'.

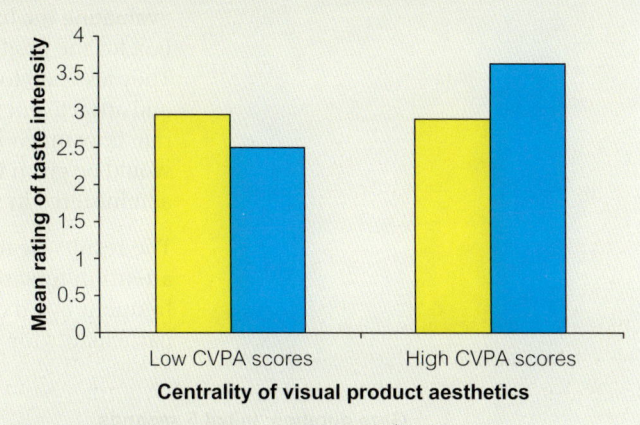

Figure 20.31 *Interaction between packaging shape and sensitivity to design*

Evaluation

- The study was a field study, as taste testing does happen within a supermarket environment and the study pre-manipulated two IVs and a further one after completion of a questionnaire. Therefore, the study can be said to have some ecological validity as well as mundane realism.

- The median split to make the high and low sensitivity to design groups meant that there were some very similar participants in both groups. For example, if the median score was 3.5 then is there a real difference in sensitivity to design of a participant scoring 3.4 and one scoring 3.6?

- The pre-test allowed a more objective choice of packaging and colour saturation based on factual information from a group of participants rather than a subjective feeling from Becker *et al*.

Attention and shelf position

Atalay *et al* (2012) wanted to investigate the effect of gaze on product choice. More specifically, they wanted to assess whether consumers tend to choose the option in the centre of an array of products. The idea of 'horizontal centrality' was under investigation. This is when an option is chosen that is located in the centre of a horizontal line of products such as items in a vending machine. The focus on this central product is given the term 'central gaze cascade effect'. The researchers ran three studies to test these effects. Two of their studies are reported here.

Study 1A

The idea was to use eye-tracking equipment to see how consumers look at products before choosing. The products used were vitamins and meal replacement bars. A pre-test was conducted to remove any potential extraneous variables with the fictitious brands that the study would use. Brand names were chosen that were not similar to any already on the market. Colour choice was tested via a readability assessment and a final three colours were chosen that did not differ statistically on readability.

This study used 67 undergraduates from HEC Paris, France. They gained extra credit for participation. Four participants had to be eliminated due to technical difficulties with the eye-tracking device. This left 63 (54% female) to form the final sample.

The eye-tracking device allowed participants a degree of head movement and also let them wear glasses or contact lenses if necessary. Each participant was presented with a planogram (a 3 × 3 matrix design). Each brand was placed in a column. There were three variants of each brand, counterbalanced for each participant. The brand names were Priorin, Aplecin, and Labrada for the vitamins and Bega, Niran, and Salus for the meal replacement bars.

Participants were asked to review each product array on the screen as if they were in a shop and press the enter key when they were ready to make a choice. As soon as the enter key was pressed, the visual display disappeared. Once this happened, participants were asked to choose what they would purchase and then complete a questionnaire evaluating the brands. The choice had to also be recorded by participants checking a box for the position of the product they would have bought from the 3 × 3 design. They also had to rate, on a scale of 1–9, quality of each brand, popularity of each brand and attractiveness (higher ratings were always more favourable). They then had to rate how much market share each brand probably had and how much shelf space each would be given in a store if they were the store manager. Finally, a memory test was administered in which participants had to try to recall the brand names.

The results clearly showed that horizontal centrality had an impact on visual attention towards the products. Those in the horizontal centre received more frequent eye fixations and they were looked at for longer. The real-time gazes of participants for the first and last five seconds of gazing are shown in Figure 20.32.

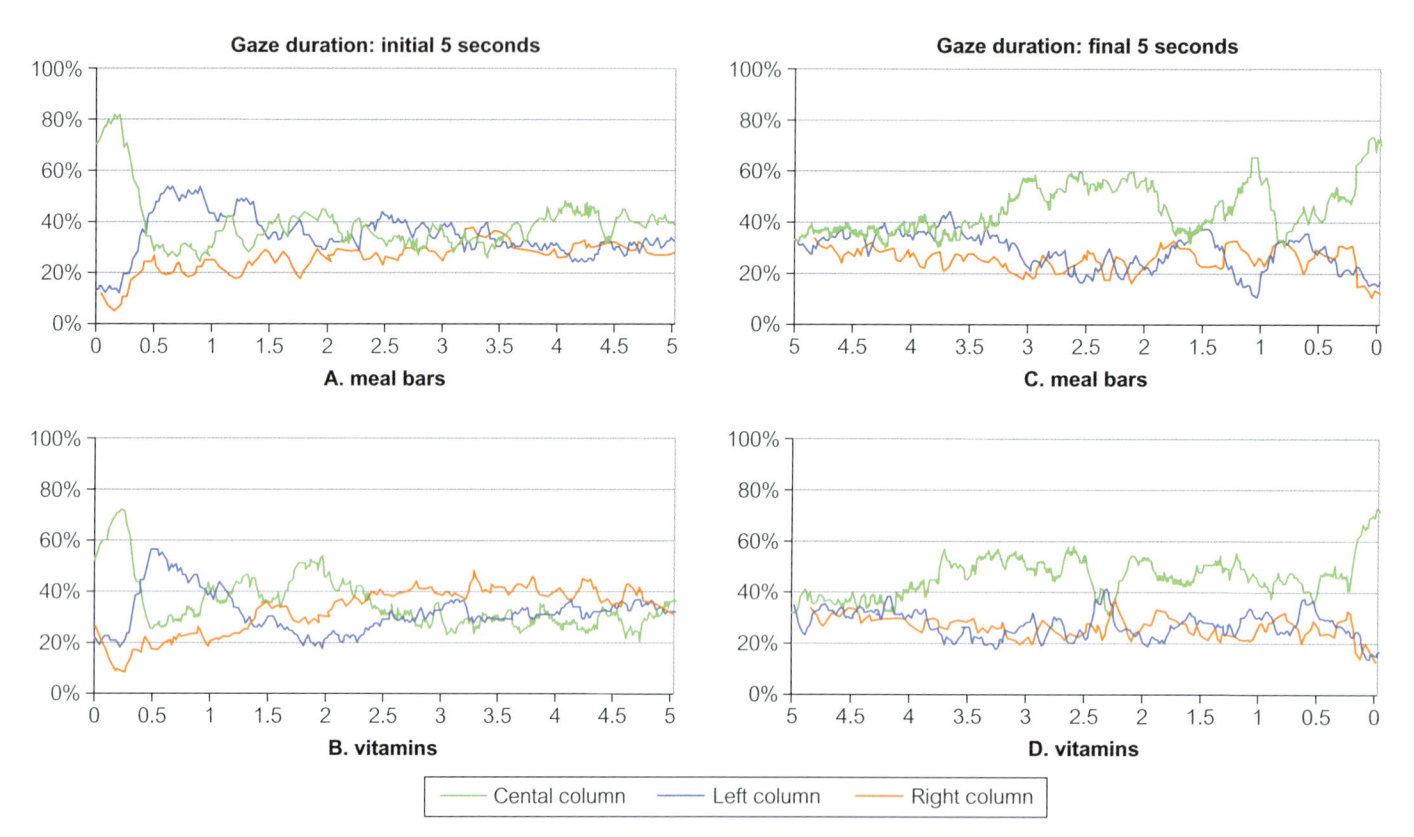

Figure 20.32 *Likelihood of looking at each column during the initial and final five seconds*
Source: Atalay et al (2012)

Of the overall gazing time, the central column receives the majority of gaze time initially and towards the end.

Study 1B

This smaller study was conducted to see whether the central gaze cascade effect was due to the horizontal centrality of the brand or the centrality of the computer screen. This study simply extended on study 1A by shifting the planograms to be off-centre on the computer screen (either left or right). Another 64 participants were used in this study (57% female). Participants in the study still fixated more on the central column, showing that the central gaze cascade effect was due to the horizontal centrality of the brand.

Study 2

This study examined the role of central gaze cascade in a more real-world setting. The sample consisted of 84 undergraduates from Concordia University. They received extra credit and had an average age of 22.21 years. Females represented 51.2% of the sample.

Three fictitious brands of energy drink (Cebion, Niran, and Viba) were presented on a horizontal shelf to participants. Each had a feature attribute (high intensity, endurance, or recovery) and these were randomised across the three brands per trial. The horizontal shelf had filler products within the 'central gaze' of the participant so that the three branded bottles of energy drink were to the left of the participants' visual field or to their right. During each trial, participants had to focus on the filler products that were central on the shelf. They were then asked to choose one of the energy drinks. The results showed that even when participants could not move to have the three choices in their 'actual central gaze', they still chose the energy drink that was in the centre of the choice of three.

> **Test yourself**
>
> Explain what controls Atalay *et al* had to ensure causality and explain why cultural differences might reduce the generalisability of the results.

> **Challenge yourself**
>
> Create similar issue and debate commentaries for reductionism versus holism, determinism versus free will, and objective and subjective data.

Strength	Weakness
The researchers employed many controls so they could be confident it was the IV directly affecting the DV.	The findings may be biased as they only used participants from a small area in France. Other nationalities may not show the same effects.

	Issue and debate tracker
Generalisations from findings	Findings from all studies may be limited due to the samples used. Porublev *et al* (2009) only used participants from Australia, *et al* (2010) only used participants from Germany, and Atalay *et al* (2012) only used participants from France. This may make it difficult to generalise to other nationalities due to different customs or shopping habits. Consumers from other countries may wrap gifts in completely different ways or perceive colours in a different way.
Validity	In terms of **external validity**, the study by Porublev *et al* has high levels as it was questioning people about actual gift wrapping. The Becker *et al* study also had high levels as the scenario was an everyday setting of a German supermarket and product evaluations are typical. However, the study by Atalay *et al* has low levels as the studies were controlled; even the final study on a real shelf was controlled as it restricted participants' views of a trio of energy drink bottles. The study by Atalay *et al*, however, does have high levels of **internal validity** as there were many controls to help ensure that centrality affected choice.

20.4.2 Selling the product

Sales techniques: customer focused, competitor, or product focused

Within consumer psychology, there appear to be two main techniques used to help sell a product.

Customer-focused technique

The focus here is on a dialogue between someone who is selling a product and a potential customer. Even before talking about the product, a customer-focused salesperson will get to know potential customers first (eg their background and desires linked to the product) to show a genuine interest into why they wish to purchase. As a result, there is no standard sales pitch for all potential customers, but instead a tailored approach that makes individual customers feel that the salesperson knows something about them. According to Dale Carnegie, there are four main qualities of customer-focused salespeople.

- They will ask more questions about the customer.
- They will use a customised approach to selling rather than a 'one technique fits all' approach.
- They are more interactive with the customer.
- They will generate more sales as a result.

Figure 20.33 shows the pathway that salespeople are likely to take if they adopt a customer-focused approach. Each stage is clearly necessary for a sale to be deemed a success and a product purchased.

Customer decision process

Approach → Interest ↔ Need awareness → Information → Evaluation → Decision

Engagement ↔ Need development → Demonstration → Vaildation → Handling positive feedback ↔ Handling resistance → Close

← Probing →

Customer-focused selling process

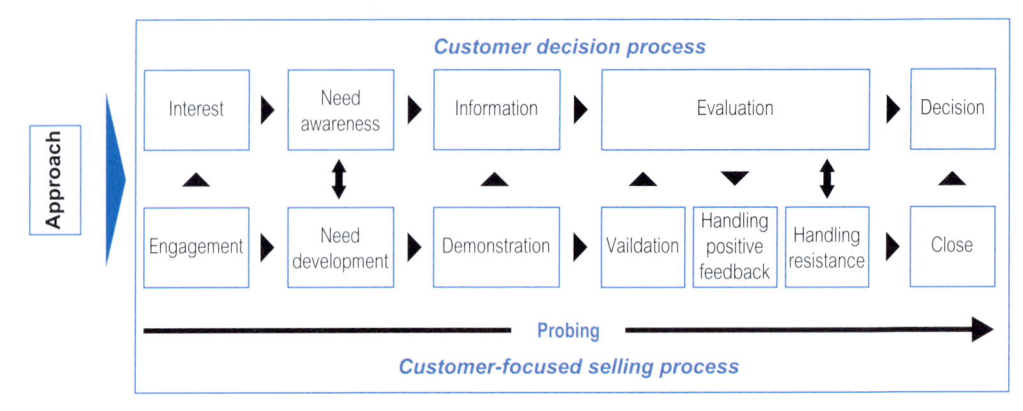

Figure 20.33 Customer-focused selling model

Competitor-focused or product-focused technique

This approach follows a model involving features, advantages, and benefits (the FAB model).

- Features – this aspect should focus on the unique selling point (USP) of the product. The salesperson needs to highlight what features makes this product different from other similar products on the market.

- Advantages – these can form part of the USP or can be highlighted separately. The salesperson needs to highlight what advantages the product has over competitors' products.

- Benefits – again, these may be described as part of the USP or separated out for more impact. The salesperson needs to tell the customer all of the benefits of the product in comparison to anything else on the market.

Technical information must be kept to a minimum – unless the customer asks about it – otherwise the customer may feel overwhelmed by the amount of information and not purchase. If a team of salespeople are going to be used to launch a product, their manager should get them all involved. For example, each member of the team should think of one example of FAB, then all of these ideas can be merged into one 'company policy' approach so that all salespeople are selling in the same way.

Interpersonal influence techniques: 'disrupt-then-reframe'

Kardes *et al* (2007) wanted to test the effectiveness of the 'disrupt-then-reframe' (DTR) technique on consumer behaviour. DTR follows the idea of confusing consumers with a disruptive message and then reframing the message to reduce the ambiguity caused. A series of experiments were conducted.

Experiment 1

A total of 147 participants (104 females) were randomly assigned to either a DTR condition or a reframe-only control condition. A salesperson in a supermarket approached potential participants about purchasing a box of candy.

- For the DTR condition the salesperson would say: "The price is now 100 eurocents (*two-second pause*)… that's 1 euro. It's a bargain!"

- For the reframe-only condition the salesperson would say: "The price is now 1 euro. It's a bargain!" (Kardes *et al*, 2007).

The number of boxes of candy sold was recorded. Overall, 54% of participants bought at least one box of candy. However, there was a significant difference between the two groups. In the DTR group, 65% of participants bought some candy compared to 44% in the reframe-only group.

> **Challenge yourself**
>
> Watch a series of commercials that last for more than three minutes (which are sometimes called infomercials). List all of the uses of the FAB model, and how many times each commercial uses each aspect. Compare this to use of the FAB model in the short commercials (usually lasting 10–15 seconds) that are shown between programmes.

Experiment 2

Another study was conducted where the participants were asked to pay 3 euros to become a member of a group. The sample was 155 participants (59% female). They were randomly assigned to the DTR condition or the reframe condition.

- For the DTR condition, the following script was used: "You can now become a member for half a year for 300 eurocents (*two-second pause*) that's 3 euros. That's a really small investment!"

- For the reframe only condition, the script was: "You can now become a member for half a year for 3 euros. That's a really small investment!"

Overall, 22% of the participants agreed to join the group. Analysis of each condition showed that 30% of participants in the DTR condition wanted to join but only 13% of those in the reframe condition wanted to. This was statistically significant.

It would appear that DTR works effectively for the sales of goods but also to get people to spend money on non-tangible items such as membership of a group.

Strength	Weakness
A large sample was used for both studies, so generalising beyond the sample is a possibility.	An independent groups design was used, so individual differences may account for some of the changes in the DV, rather than the IV itself.

Cialdini's six ways to close a sale

Cialdini uses these six 'persuasive' ways to close a sale.

1. Liking – this is based around the idea that if you want to influence a consumer to make a sale, make friends with the consumer. There are three pathways to this. The first is similarity. To close a sale, find some commonality between yourself and the consumer. Consumers are more likely to buy if they feel that you, as a seller, like them. The second is compliments. Praise can be used towards consumers by paying them a compliment about the type of product they are wanting to purchase, for instance. The consumer should appreciate your effort. The third is cooperative endeavours. Find a common goal for you and the consumer. For example, you could say "Yes, let's find the best deal for you as I can see what discounts I can use".

2. Reciprocity – this refers to the assumption that we can exchange ideas, etc for our mutual benefit. This could take the form of giving an 'added extra' to secure a sale or a free trial. The seller has given something beneficial so then the consumer returns the 'benefit' by purchasing the product.

3. Social proof – this is based around the idea of testimonials for other peers; in this case, other consumers. Therefore, a company can utilise independent ratings or ratings from platforms such as Amazon to show a consumer that lots of other consumers like the product after buying it. This is even more compelling when the reviews are from consumers very similar to us.

4. Commitment and consistency – this is based on the idea that it takes a series of small commitments to build a relationship between seller and consumer. Examples of small commitments include turning up for a meeting, making sure something is linked to the consumers' personal values (like a charity donation of their choice), giving a free trial for the product, or changing part of a contract. All of these have to show consistency, otherwise the consumer may not buy. Once commitment has been shown by seller and consumer, both parties are more likely to be consistent with their commitments.

5. Authority – this is not about being dictatorial. It is about being perceived as an 'authority' about a product (sometimes called an expert). Sellers can use expert testimonials or have examples of times when they sold the product and it got very positive reviews or feedback. If a seller has comprehensive knowledge of the product offered for sale, the consumer feels 'safe in this knowledge' as it has come from an authority expert.

Challenge yourself

Look at the issue and debate tracker table on page 213. Create similar issue and debate commentaries for application to everyday life, cultural differences, determinism versus free will, idiographic versus nomothetic, and field experiments.

6. Scarcity – this is about using scarce supply or exclusivity in your favour as a seller. If a product is in short supply a seller can use this as a selling point to consumers via fear of missing out (FOMO). Also, if an organisation has exclusivity of a product, this can be used to explain to a consumer that this particular produce or deal cannot be found anywhere else.

20.4.3 Buying a product

Buyer decision making (Blackwell *et al*, 2001)

This model is part of the cognitive approach to consumer behaviour. The model proposes a seven-point decision process that consumers go through each time they decide to purchase a product or not to purchase it.

1. Need recognition: consumers need to recognise that they may need or want a product.
2. Internal information search: does the consumer have a memory for a similar product? If so, was it a good or bad product?
3. External information search: what products are available that fulfil the consumer's current needs?
4. Evaluation of alternatives: are there any alternative products that serve the same purpose?
5. Purchase: (buying the product).
6. Post-purchase reflection: how well has the product performed?
7. Divestment: getting rid of the product when it is no longer useful or is broken.

The model can be seen in Figure 20.34.

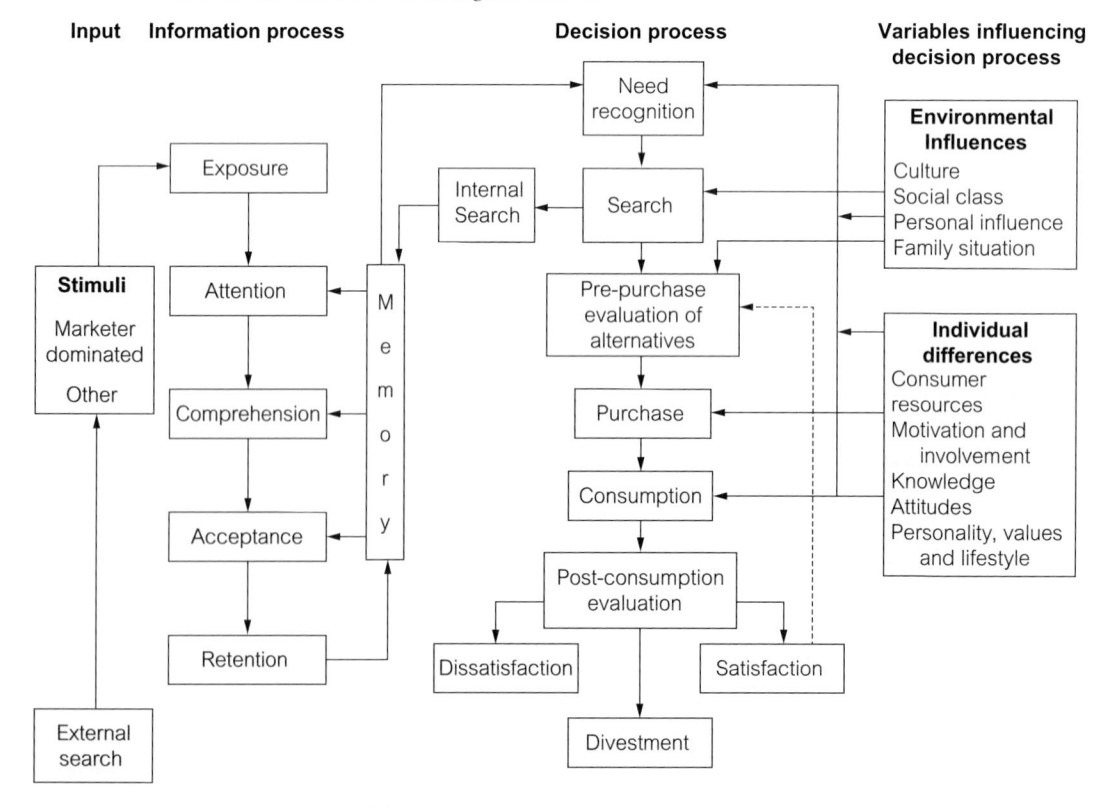

Figure 20.34 *Consumer decision model*

Source: Blackwell *et al* (2001) reproduced in Bray 'Consumer behaviour theory: approaches and models', Bournemouth University: http://eprints.bournemouth.ac.uk/10107/1/Consumer_Behaviour_Theory_-_Approaches_%26_Models.pdf

Strength	Weaknesses
The model has good real-world application as manufacturers and companies can use it to ensure that consumers pass through the seven stages to improve sales.	Some psychologists believe that there is no evidence that consumers process information in a linear way as predicted by the model. The model ignores other factors such as the roles of culture on decision making, or when people are buying a product for the first time so cannot conduct the internal information search.

Deciding where to buy and reasons for choice

There can be many factors that affect where a consumer decides to purchase goods. This was investigated in a study by Sinha *et al* (2002), involving an exploratory interview using a structured questionnaire. An opportunity sample of 247 respondents (shoppers) were interviewed after exiting stores in Ahmedabad, India. A range of stores selling different types of produce were used.

Shoppers were asked for up to three reasons why they chose to purchase from that store. This is summarised in Table 20.17.

Table 20.17 Reasons for purchase

Reason	Given as first reason	Given as second reason	Given as third reason	Total
Convenience	37.65	21.39	22	29.23
Merchandise	31.98	32.37	21	30.00
Ambience	7.69	9.83	14	9.62
Service	6.48	21.39	27	15.38
Patronage	8.10	5.78	6	6.92
Referral	3.64	5.20	8	5.00
Others	4.45	4.05	2	3.85

Note: All figures are the percentage reason given as first, second, third, and then overall total

Only 40% of shoppers could provide three reasons for their store choice. Around 70% could provide two reasons. This indicates that most shoppers only have one or two key reasons to visit a store. Convenience was the primary reason for store choice when purchasing groceries such as fruit and vegetables, products from a chemist, lifestyle products, and cigarettes. Merchandise was the primary reason for store choice for durables, books/music, apparel, and accessories. Results about primary store choices and images linked to patronage are shown in Table 20.18.

Table 20.18 Summary of results: primary store choice, image perception, and patronage

Type of store	Primary store choice reasons	Image perception and patronage
Grocery store	Proximity (close by) and patronage – if shoppers have been buying from the store for a long time, then distance is not a factor. This indicates loyalty.	Convenience and brand spread were the largest factors. Ambience and facilities do not affect perception or patronage.
Durables	Merchandise, referral, and ambience are important. Offering discounts helps. A wide variety of products is better, especially when the shopper can touch the products.	The level of customer service was important.
Chemist	There is compulsion to buy, with little importance given to merchandise or level of service.	The same points apply as for grocery stores.
Book/Music/ Accessories	Ambience is important. Lighting, displays, and the store looking good and well maintained are strong reasons.	Shopping for these products is perceived as being a leisure activity. Inside, the store has to be perceived as being of good quality.
Apparel	Shoppers value merchandise and ambience in these types of stores. Shoppers tend to prefer exclusive or branded stores. The ranges of products in terms of number and price are also important.	Store design, ambience and visual merchandising are important.

Other findings included the following.

- Convenience and merchandise were the primary reasons for store choice across all age groups interviewed.

- Males tended to choose convenience as the primary reason for store choice while females chose merchandise. Men showed a slightly higher tendency to use ambience as a reason for store choice, whereas females showed a similar tendency towards patronage.

    Males tended to buy 'grab-and-go' products, whereas females would look at the spread of brands or gather more information about a product before choosing a store then buying.

In conclusion, both convenience and merchandising are the primary reasons for store choice across a range of stores, but type of product being sold, ambience, and patronage are other key reasons for store choice.

Strength	Weakness
The shoppers were interviewed directly after purchase so it can be argued that they would provide valid reasons for store choice.	The sample was from one area in India so it may be difficult to generalise to other parts of India or other countries that have a different geographical layout/store accessibility, such as large malls in the United States or shopping centres in the UK.

Post-purchase cognitive dissonance

Cognitive dissonance (a theory proposed by Festinger, 1957) refers to a feeling of mental (cognitive) discomfort that is a consequence of having two (or more) conflicting beliefs, attitudes, values, or behaviours. As a result, we will change one of those beliefs, attitudes, values, or behaviours to reduce the discomfort so we can restore a 'cognitive balance'.

Nordvall (2014) investigated whether cognitive dissonance can be linked to consumer behaviour when grocery shopping. Previous research had examined cognitive dissonance in high involvement shopping such as buying a car or new laptop. Nordvall wanted to see whether cognitive dissonance would occur with low-involvement shopping, for example buying groceries such as lettuce, shrimp, and potatoes with the choice of organic or non-organic groceries.

One hundred undergraduates at a Swedish university (mean age 23 years) participated in the study. The task involved virtual shopping, was voluntary, and lasted for about 20 minutes. Participants were presented with a short text explaining that the simulation was about a typical everyday shopping trip to the grocery store. Fifty items (25 organic and 25 non-organic with no brand names) were presented individually on the screen. There were three stages to the study using the rate-choose-rate technique.

1. Rate (first): the 50 items were presented in a random order. Participants had to rate each item on how often they bought the item. This was on a 7-point scale ranging from 1 (never buy) through 4 (sometimes buy) to 7 (buy very often).

2. Choose (manipulation of dissonance): pairs of items were created based on similar ratings the participants had given to each item. A similar rating was defined as being ±2 points on the 7-point scale (eg an item rated 3 and an item rated 4 could form a pair, but an item rated 2 and an item rated 6 would not form a pair). The participants were told that it was time for them to fill their virtual shopping baskets. Pairs of items (one organic and one non-organic) were presented, and participants had to choose one to put into their basket. The idea of this was to potentially cause cognitive dissonance as participants had been forced to choose a good item and reject an equally good item. The discomfort felt should then result in participants giving a higher rating to the chosen good if they were asked to rate that item again.

3. Rate (second): the 50 items were presented again to the participants. The same 7-point rating scale was used. One difference was when an item was presented on the screen, participants were told whether they had chosen the item or rejected it. In addition, they had to choose from a list of ten motives for making their choice (they could choose as many motives as they wanted) covering things such as price, quality, appearance, and environmental issues.

Nordvall predicted that cognitive dissonance could be achieved in two ways, by:

- increasing the desirability of the chosen item from the pair
- lowering the desirability of the rejected item from the pair.

When the item chosen in a pair was non-organic, there was a significant increase in desirability at second rating for that non-organic item. However, there was a no significant lowering of desirability for the organic rejection; in fact it increased, too.

When the item chosen in a pair was organic, there was a significant decrease in desirability at second rating for the *rejected* non-organic item. However, there was a no significant increase of desirability for the chosen organic item; in fact it decreased, too.

Therefore, cognitive dissonance reduction was shown only when people forced-purchased non-organic items, by either: increasing their desirability for that item if it had been chosen instead of an organic item; or reducing their desirability for that item if they had rejected it in favour of an organic item.

> **Challenge yourself**
>
> Look at the issue and debate tracker table on page 213. Create similar issue and debate commentaries for reductionism versus holism, idiographic versus nomothetic, objective and subjective data, and validity.

Strength	Weakness
The study was clearly standardised to allow other researchers to replicate the study to test for reliability. For example, the choice of 25 products and the procedure for the first and second ratings of all items was described clearly by the researchers, which means that other psychologists can replicate the study to test for reliability across other types of products, for example.	The way desirability was rated may have been low in validity. Equating how often a person buys a product with desirability for that product may not be correct. There may be other factors such as price (which was reported in the study as the main factor for choosing non-organic items) that affect the ratings per item, rather than it being directly about desirability, which had been used as a measure of cognitive dissonance reduction.

20.5 Advertising

20.5.1 Types of advertising and advertising techniques

Yale model of communication including five features

Hovland *et al* (1953) conducted many studies at Yale University which helped to form a model of persuasive communication. There are three main stages in the process.

1. Attention – the message must grab people's attention. Sound and visual stimuli are the most effective so using television might be better than using leaflets or the radio.

2. Comprehension – for a message to be successful it must be understood by the recipient. Messages need to be clear and concise.

3. Acceptance – the overall message has to be accepted by the recipient for behaviour change to occur. The person does not have to believe the message but must accept it and behave according to it for it to be persuasive communication.

There are several factors that can affect any or all of the three stages above. These include the following.

- The communicator – a message is more persuasive if the communicator is attractive, is similar to the recipient and is likeable.

- The content – it is best to cause mild fear and it is best when the message is presented verbally *and* visually. A one-sided or two-sided argument needs to be considered too.

- The medium – for example, the communicator needs to choose whether a television campaign would work better than a radio or leaflet campaign. If the message is simple and straightforward then conveying it via television is best; if it is complicated it is best communicated via written media.

There are also five stages or factors that can affect the communication.

- The source – can the source be trusted, is it credible, and/or does the communication come from someone with any expertise?

- The message – is it a one-sided or two-sided message, does it have clarity, is it direct, and how vivid is it?

- The medium – is the message one-to-one communication, is it personal to you, what medium is being used (such as television or radio)?

- The target – who is the message primarily aimed at, could the audience be sympathetic or not, how much knowledge about the contents of the communication does the audience have?

- The situation – where will the message be finally received (such as at home), will it be spontaneous, or will the audience be prepared?

Advertising media including types of advertising media

There are many different types of advertising, including the following.

- Printed – these can be in a newspaper, in a magazine, or on a billboard.

- Television – these tend to appear in-between programmes or as a break within a programme. They are mainly visually driven.

- Internet – these can appear as banners on websites or from links sent to you via email.

- Smartphone – these Smartphone. These can be via social media platforms and apps.

A study by Ciceri *et al* (2019) investigated the effectiveness of digital versus printed advertisements. Previous research had investigated how to measure consumer responses to advertising, how memorising advertisements might be linked to visual attention, and how the brain responds to advertisements. Ciceri *et al* wanted to use eye-tracking equipment and an electroencephalograph (EEG) to measure reading behaviour and information memory in relation to viewing advertisements.

A stratified sample of 72 habitual newspaper readers (50% female; age range 23–55 years; mean age 38 years) participated in the study. All participants were right-handed and had no history of mental illness. A national Italian newspaper was the stimulus material. It was created in three different media (website, paper, and tablet) and contained 25 advertisements. All of these advertisements were identical and had the same proportional size depending on the media. For each of the three media, age and gender were matched, as shown in Table 20.19.

Table 20.19 Participants for each subgroup

	Subjects' age range	
	28–39	40–55
Males	6	6
Females	6	6

Source: Ciceri *et al* (2019: 6)

An independent measures design was used as participants only read from one media type. Each participant read the newspaper while wearing eye-tracking glasses and an EEG headset. The participants were told to read the newspaper at their own pace, but they could only read forward and could never go back to something they had read or seen. Each advertisement appeared in the same order irrespective of type of media. The session ended once the 25th advertisement had been seen. After viewing the newspaper, participants were given a distractor task for one hour. After this, they were given a memory recognition task. Fifty advertisements were shown to each participant for six seconds. Of these, 25 were ones they had already seen in the newspaper and the other 25 were new advertisements. Participants had to indicate by clicking on a computer screen either 'yes' or 'no' to indicate whether they had seen the advertisement in the newspaper.

The main results included these points.

- Participants in the web condition spent less time reading the advertisements and had the lowest memory performance score across the three conditions. Those who read the advertisements on the tablet spent the most time reading and had the best memory recognition performance (see Figures 20.35 and 20.36).

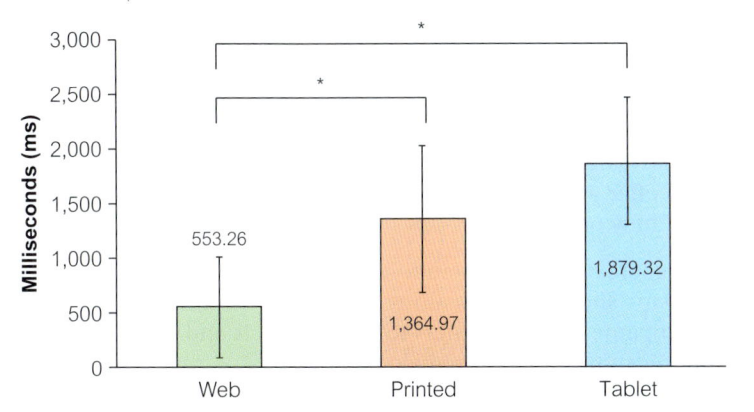

Note: Differences between tablet and web and between paper and web were statistically significant (p < .05).

Figure 20.35 *Mean values for fixation time on advertisements*

Source: Ciceri et al (2019: 8)

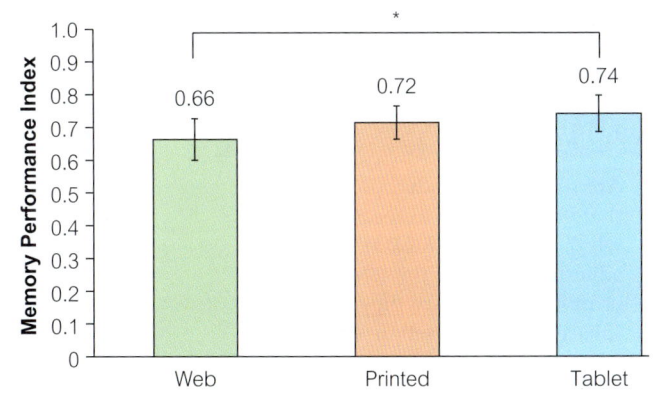

Note: Differences between tablet and web were statistically significant.

Figure 20.36 *Mean values for memory performance index*

Source: Ciceri et al (2019: 8)

- The EEG data were analysed using specific software that could detect different emotions that could be happening during the reading task. The one Ciceri *et al* focused on was 'frustration'. Participants in the 'tablet' condition had the highest frustration score followed by the 'printed' condition then the 'web' condition (see Figure 20.37).

Therefore, even though the participants in the printed and tablet conditions showed that they had the most unpleasant experiences while reading, it had no effect on their memory for the advertisements.

In conclusion, web-based advertising may be the best medium to reduce frustration in consumers when viewing advertisements, but it does not promote memory for advertisements. However, both printed and tablet advertising aid memory recognition of advertisements in consumers, despite the experience of seeing and reading them being quite frustrating. This is something consumer brands need to consider when launching an advertising campaign.

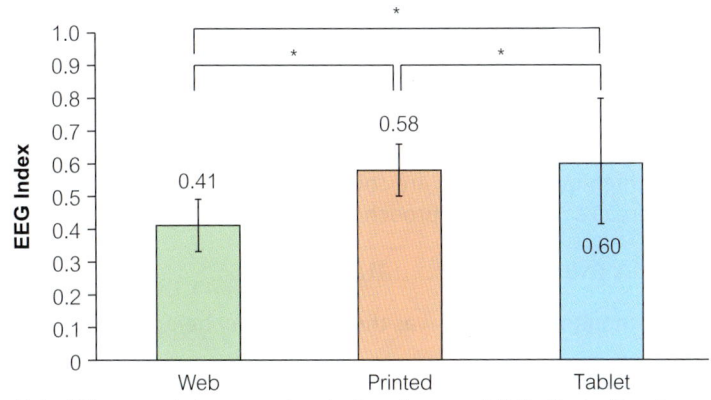

Note: Differences between each pair of media were statistically significant.

Figure 20.37 *Median values for the electroencephalography (EEG) frustration index*

Source: Ciceri et al (2019: 9)

Strength	Weakness
The study was clearly standardised to allow other researchers to replicate the study to test for reliability. For example, the procedure for reading the advertisements in each condition and how software produced an EEG frustration score were clearly outlined so the study can be replicated. The data collected from both the eye-tracking glasses and an EEG headset were objective and scientific. This allowed for valid and meaningful comparisons between the three conditions in terms of fixation time and frustration scores.	The study lacks both ecological validity and mundane realism. In terms of ecological validity, reading a newspaper while wearing eye-tracking glasses and an EEG headset is not something that occurs in everyday life so the action of being in this artificial set-up may reduce validity of findings. In terms of mundane realism, the participants were never allowed to go back to an article or advertisement that they were interested in. This task would not happen in reality, which may have affected some memory recognition scores.

Lauterborn's 4 Cs marketing mix model

1. Consumer wants and needs – products can only be sold to people who actually want to buy them so research into consumer needs is vital to success.

2. Cost to satisfy – this refers to the 'overall cost' of the product that actually satisfies the needs of the consumer. Lauterborn argued that the 'raw price' a product is sold at is irrelevant. All aspects need to be considered, such as the distance someone is willing to travel to buy the product; the ethical conscience a consumer has about buying or using the product; and what the product would mean to a consumer if he or she owned it, or bought it and consumed it (as with food products, for example).

3. Convenience to buy – this requires research. Consumers are ever changing and although many like to purchase online (so it is important for a company to have an easy-to-navigate website), they still go out of their homes to shop. A company needs to offer a variety of ways in which consumers can purchase its products (old and new ones).

4. Communication – a company has to listen to consumers when it is launching a product. The company should ask consumers what they want and what they need. Some companies ask consumers to trial products and write reviews. All communication should be a dialogue.

> **Challenge yourself**
>
> Look at the issue and debate tracker table on page 227. Create similar issue and debate commentaries for application to everyday life, objective and subjective data, generalisations from findings, and validity.

> **Ask yourself**
>
> Are there certain advertisements that you find easy to recall? If so, why? Also, take a look at some advertisements on the television or in magazines. Are they using a soft-sell or a hard-sell or both?

20.5.2 Advertising–consumer interaction

Advertising and consumer personality including self-monitoring

KEY STUDY: Snyder and DeBono (1985), study 3

Context

It is difficult for consumers to not be influenced by advertising. The promise of a better quality of life, time-saving devices, and high-quality goods are common themes used in advertising. A soft-sell approach tends to focus on the use of images whereas a hard-sell approach focuses more on inherent merit and quality of a product.

Main theories/explanations

Self-monitoring theory was the main theory being investigated here.

Aim and hypotheses

The aim of study 3 was to investigate the influence of self-monitoring on perception of advertising and subsequent consumption of a product.

Two hypotheses were tested.

1. High self-monitoring people are more likely to consume a product that is advertised with an appeal towards its image compared to a claim about the quality of the product.

2. Low self-monitoring people are more likely to consume a product that is advertised with a claim about the quality of the product compared to an appeal towards its image.

Design

This was an experiment using a telephone interview as a technique.

Participants

The sample consisted of 40 psychology undergraduates from the University of Minnesota, USA. They all received course credit for participating. They completed the self-monitoring scale and using a median split; half formed the high self-monitoring group and the other half formed the low self-monitoring group.

Procedure

An experimenter acted as a market researcher and telephoned participants to offer them a chance to participate in a test marketing study. The experimenter did not know which group the participant was in. The experimenter read a standardised script that contained information about the fake marketing research firm and that the product was a new shampoo.

The experimenter then read out information about the product. One message was based around the image of the shampoo and the other was based on the quality of the shampoo. The message was determined randomly.

- Image message – information was based around the brand being average for cleaning hair but above average for how it makes your hair look.
- Quality message – information was based around the brand being average for how it makes your hair look but above average on how well it cleans your hair.

The participant then had to answer two questions.

1. This focused on willingness to *use* the shampoo. Choices ranged from definitely not to definitely yes (with five choices overall). This was converted into an index of willingness by assigning one point for definitely not through to five points for definitely yes.
2. This focused on willingness to *try* the shampoo. Participants gave a percentage likelihood from 0% indicating not at all to 100% indicating definitely willing.

Each response was recorded per participant. The experimenter then answered any questions that the participant had and thanked the person for his or her time.

Results, findings, and conclusions

As there was a very strong correlation between the willingness to use the shampoo score and the willingness to try the shampoo, the researchers combined the scores to generate one 'willingness to use index'. Table 20.20 shows the main result:

Table 20.20 Willingness to use the product: study 3

	Type of message received	
Self-monitoring category	**Image**	**Quality**
High	.7626	–.7008
Low	–.9106	.9201

Source: Snyder and DeBono (1985: 592)

The results clearly supported both of the hypotheses.

Therefore, the conclusion to this study is that level of self-monitoring affects consumers' decisions to try a product based on its image or quality.

Main discussion points

- Self-monitoring does affect consumer decision making.
- High self-monitors prefer image-oriented advertisements, and they are willing to pay more for products that focus on image.
- Low self-monitors prefer quality-based advertisements, and they are willing to pay more for products that are perceived as being of high quality.
- The three studies can have an impact on how a company advertises a new product or an existing product. Which will generate more sales? Can both image and quality be merged in one advertisement to appeal to both high and low self-monitors?

Evaluation points

- The intention to use the shampoo might not be well correlated with *actually* using the product and this was not measured. Therefore, there has to be some caution attached to the validity of findings as no behavioural measure was taken.

- The measures taken were only one question for 'use' and one question for 'try'. For the use question, as it was fixed-choice, participants may have not had a descriptor that accurately reflected them. Also, for the try question, the percentage score assigned by each participant is subjective and makes it difficult to make objective comparisons, which is what Snyder and DeBono did. One participant's 33% could be very different from another participant's 33% in terms of why it is 33%, as they were not asked to explain their score.

- The study was clearly standardised to allow other researchers to replicate it to test for reliability. For example, the scripts used were all published and can be used word for word.

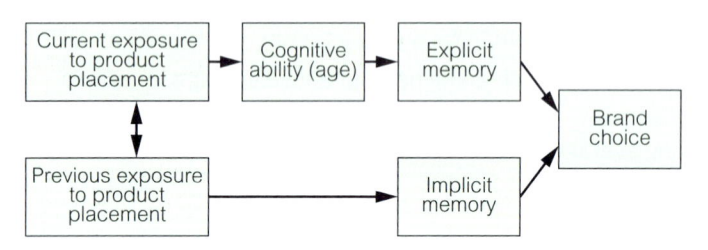

Figure 20.38 *Working model of the effect of product placement on choice in children*
Source: Auty and Lewis (2004: 701)

How product placement in films affects choice

Auty and Lewis (2004) wanted to understand the influence on children of branded products that appear on television and in movies. The researchers were interested in the role of explicit and implicit memory for product placements. The model they were testing is shown in Figure 20.38.

Participants were 48 students, who were 11–12 years old, from a secondary school in the UK, and 57 children aged 6–7. Prior permission to use the participants in the study had been obtained from their parents. Participants were then randomly assigned to one of two groups:

- Participants in the treatment group watched a clip lasting 1 minute 50 seconds from the film 'Home Alone' where the family were having a meal. Pepsi® could be seen throughout the clip and was also mentioned, by name, by the father.

- Participants in the control group watched a clip of Kevin, a child superhero, eat a macaroni and cheese microwave meal (with no brand mentioned or seen in the clip). He also drank a glass of milk.

The team who led the interviews with the participants (after the participants had watched the clip) were ex-students of each school. There were four cans of drink in the interview room (two Pepsi® and two Coke®). Participants in the treatment group were told that they could have a drink and then they would be asked some 'easy questions'. They were then asked to describe the clip they had seen in as much detail as possible. If a participant did not mention Pepsi® in the recall, then some general questioning was employed to see if he or she would mention a brand of cola.

Children in the control group went through the same procedure and if they did not recall the milk, they were prompted in the same way as the treatment group. Each interview lasted about five minutes. The results are shown in Table 20.21.

Table 20.21 Summary of the findings

Hypothesis	N =	Supported/ Not supported	X2	Significance (p =)
1 Children exposed to product placement in a film clip will choose a different brand when offered a choice on the same day from those who are not shown the branded film clip.	105	Supported	4.22	.040
2 (a) There will be a difference in recall of the brand shown in a product-placement film clip between cued processors (11–12-year-olds) and limited processors (6–7-year-olds).	52	Not supported	1.47	.225
2 (b) There will be a difference in the choice of brand between children who have correctly recalled the brand and those who do not recall the brand.	52	Not supported	0.07	.790
3 Children who have seen the film before will make a different choice of brand from those who have not, regardless of whether or not they have been exposed to the branded clip.	105	Not supported	0.16	.683
4 Among children who have seen the film before, those shown the brand in a film clip will choose a different brand from those who are not shown the branded film clip.	72	Supported	4.71	.030
5 Among children who have never seen the film before, those shown the brand in a film clip will choose a different brand from those who are not shown the branded film clip.	33	Not supported	0.31	.579

Source: Based on Auty and Lewis (2004: 702-703; 708)

As Table 20.21 shows, only two of the hypotheses were supported. For drink choice before the interview the split between Coke® and Pepsi® was 58:42 for the control group but 38:62 for the treatment group (in the UK the sales split is 75:25). Also, those who had been exposed to the clip before (irrespective of which condition they were in) chose Pepsi® more often (in a 33:67 split).

This led the researchers to propose a model of the effect of product placement on choice in children. Figure 20.39 shows this model.

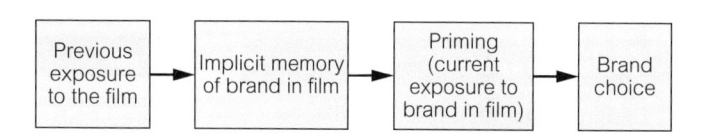

Previous exposure to the film → Implicit memory of brand in film → Priming (current exposure to brand in film) → Brand choice

Figure 20.39 *Suggested model of the effect of product placement on choice in children*

Source: Auty and Lewis (2004: 710)

Strength	Weakness
There was a standardised procedure, meaning that the study can easily be replicated and tested for reliability.	Only children were used in the study. We cannot generalise to adults because children and adults may perceive product placements in different ways.

Challenge yourself

Look at the issue and debate tracker table on page 227. Create similar issue and debate commentaries for application to everyday life, use of children in research (ethics), determinism versus free will, experiments, and interviews.

20.5.3 Brand awareness and recognition

Brand recognition in children

Fischer *et al* (1991) were interested to see if children as young as 3–6 years of age can recognise brand logos. The sample consisted of 229 children attending preschools in Augusta and Atlanta in the United States. The children were instructed to match logos with one of 12 products that appeared on a game board. In total, 22 logos were tested, covering a range of children's products, products for adults, and two cigarette brands. Other measures included having parents reporting the number of hours their children watched television each day and recording how often the children asked for products by their brand name.

Across all of the products, logo recognition was highly associated with the age of the child. For children's brand, cigarette brands and adult brands recognition rates increased by age. Therefore, the older the child, the more likely they were to recognise logos from all product categories, even cigarette brands!

The research team compared the recognition rates for the Disney Channel logo and Old Joe the Camel (for Camel cigarettes). For the children aged three, four or five, there was a significant difference in the recognition rates. The Disney Channel logo has significantly higher recognition rates for these ages compared to the Old Joe the Camel logo. However, for six-year-olds there was not such significant difference.

Race and gender had no effect on logo recognition. For the 6-year-old children, there was no significant difference in logo recognition between the two logos. However, for all of the younger ages, children were more likely to recognise the Disney Channel logo than the Camel cigarettes logo.

It would appear that very young children can recall and recognise brand logos, which is a useful application for advertisers and product developers. As the older children quite easily recognised tobacco-related logos, this could be useful for health campaigns.

> **Challenge yourself**
>
> Design a study that tests brand recognition in adults.

Strength	Weakness
The procedure was standardised so the study could easily be replicated to test for reliability.	Some of the measures relied on parents giving details about their children's behaviour (eg number of hours of television watched), but the parents may have given socially desirable data, making some of the findings potentially lacking in validity.

Brand awareness, brand image, and effective slogans

Kohli *et al* (2007) created a seven-point procedure for writing effective slogans.

1. Keep your eye on the horizon.

   The researchers recommend that advertisers have a long-term view about where they want the product to be. Slogans that are created today need to 'stand the test of time' so using language that might date should be avoided. The researchers note that the BMW slogan 'The Ultimate Driving Machine' is a good example.

2. Every slogan is a brand positioning tool, and it should position the brand in a clear manner. The positioning can be based on features of the product or the benefits of buying the product. Slogans can be simple. The researchers note one from Excedrin® (a 'painkiller' that uses the slogan 'The Headache Medicine').

3. Link the slogan to the brand.

   The researchers note that the level of incorrect slogan recall is very high. Therefore, advertisers should include the brand name in the slogan.

4. Please repeat that.

   According to the researchers, repetition of the slogan in any advertisement leads to better recall. Therefore, advertisers should not just use the slogan once.

5. Jingle, jangle.

   Jingles can enhance memorability of a product in the short term, so they should be used.

6. Use slogans at the outset. Slogans are a fundamental component of brand identity. Therefore, when a business is advertising new products from an 'old' company, a slogan should be used immediately to establish brand identity during the campaign and beyond.

7. It's okay to be creative.

    Keeping it simple may not be the most effective strategy as this involves shallow processing and the consumer may well forget the advertiser's efforts. The researchers use the example of Vicks NyQuil® that uses a complex slogan of 'The Nighttime, Sniffling, Sneezing, Coughing, Aching, Stuffy Head, Fever, So You Can Rest Medicine'.

    Source: The seven points above are based on Kohli *et al* (2007).

	Issue and debate tracker
Use of children in research	There are always potential issues of children **misunderstanding** what is expected of them in a study and not giving valid responses. Therefore, in the study by Fischer *et al* (1991), the children may have seen it as a game to match without necessarily knowing they were meant to be doing it correctly all of the time. Also, gaining **informed consent** can be problematic as even though the child cannot give direct consent, the parents may not necessarily know fully what the study entails to be able to give it on behalf of their child. This study involved tobacco products being identified, which may have stopped some parents from giving that consent. Also, children may not know they have the **right to withdraw** and just stayed in the study even though they did not want to.
Experiments	The study by Fischer *et al* could show some level of **cause and effect** as brand recognition appeared to be influenced by the age of the children. Product categories and logos were controlled to help establish some cause and effect. It also means that the experiment can be directly replicated as there was a standardised procedure across all ages of children with the game of matching logos to products. This means it can be tested for reliability.

Challenge yourself

Find the advertisements for at least five different products that do not have a slogan. Create a slogan for each one.

Challenge yourself

Create similar issue and debate commentaries for application to everyday life, and determinism versus free will.

21 Health psychology

21.1 The patient–practitioner relationship

21.1.1 Practitioner and patient interpersonal skills

Non-verbal communication

McKinstry and Wang (1991) wanted to investigate whether the way in which doctors dress affects what a patient thinks of them. A total of 475 patients (67% female) attending 30 doctors took part in the study. Five different locations in Lothian, Scotland were used. Participants were asked to look at eight different photographs, shown in Figure 21.1.

Participants were then asked: 'Which doctor would you feel happiest about seeing for the first time?' They scored each example on a scale of 0–5. They were also asked to rate the confidence in the ability of each of the doctors in the photographs, alongside whether they would be unhappy seeing any of them. The final section of the questionnaire enabled participants to answer closed questions about doctors' dress codes in general and to give their attitudes towards different styles of dress.

The results are show in Table 21.1.

Ask yourself

When you visit a doctor, what skills do you expect the doctor to show that make you feel more confident that he or she is giving you the best possible treatment?

Table 21.1 Scores for doctors in different styles of dress

| Acceptability score | Number of patients ||||||||
| | Male doctor wearing: ||||| Female doctor wearing: |||
	White coat	Suit	Tweed jkt	Cardigan	Jeans	White coat	Skirt	Trousers
5	183	238	141	76	60	263	222	104
4	122	116	120	77	44	118	194	86
3	75	46	182	96	58	56	42	166
2	47	48	22	147	76	25	13	65
1	39	19	4	31	154	7	2	20
0	9	8	6	48	83	6	2	34

Source: McKinstry and Wang (1991: 276)

The following results were statistically significant.

- The doctor in a smart suit was the most popular.
- The doctor in a cardigan and casual trousers scored significantly higher than the doctor in jeans.
- The informally dressed female doctor scored significantly lower than the other two female doctors.
- Older patients were more likely to give high scores to the male doctor in a white coat or a formal suit.
- Older patients were more likely to give higher scores to the female doctor in a white coat.

Of the sample, 41% (n = 194) answered yes to the question: 'Do you think you would have more confidence in the ability of one of these doctors (based on their appearance)?' Participants' main choices were:

- male: suit (n = 84), white coat (n = 74), tweed jacket (n = 22), jeans (n = 9), cardigan (n = 4)
- female: white coat (n = 94), skirt (n = 65), trousers (n = 13).

Health psychology

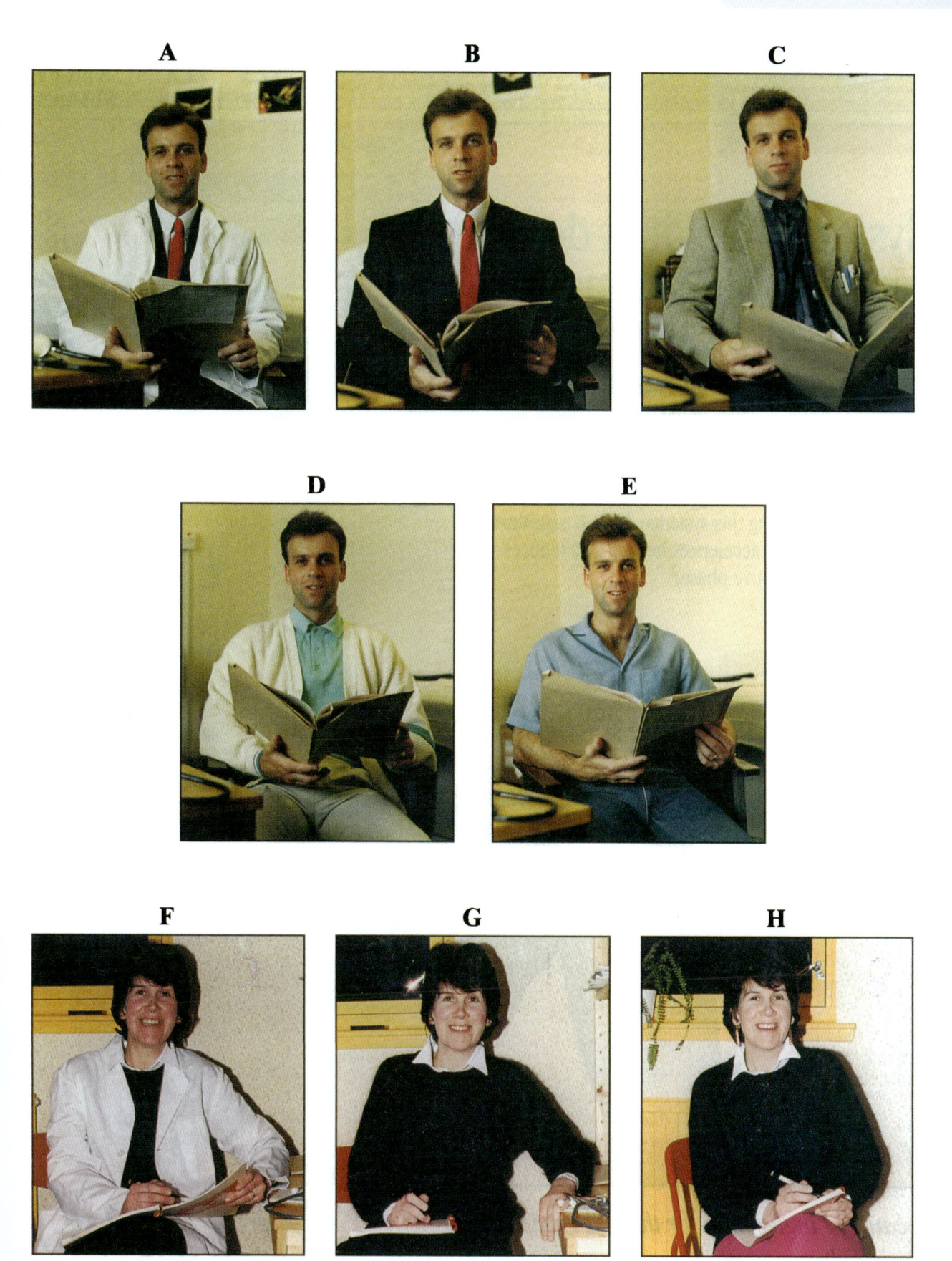

Figure 21.1 Photographs used in the study
Source: McKinstry and Wang (1991: 270)

Table 21.2 Patients' responses to questions about specific items of doctors' dress

Patients:	Percentage of respondents (n = 475)
believe male doctors should usually wear:	
white coat	15
suit	44
tie	67
would object to male doctor:	
wearing jeans	59
wearing an earring	55
having long hair	46
believe female doctors should usually wear:	
white coat	34
skirt (rather than trousers)	57
would object to female doctor:	
wearing jeans	63
wearing lots of jewellery	60

(n = total number of respondents)
Source: McKinstry and Wang (1991: 277)

> **Challenge yourself**
>
> To what extent do you feel the findings from the study are culturally biased? Justify your answer.

> **Challenge yourself**
>
> Compare the percentage scores for the two groups with the doctors' expectations. What conclusion would you make?

The final set of results is shown in Table 21.2.

Table 21.2 shows that most participants thought a male doctor should wear a tie, and a female doctor a skirt. Jeans appear to be too informal and prompted the most objections from participants, regardless of whether a male or female doctor was wearing them.

Strength	Weakness
A large, diverse sample was used in the study, making it easier to generalise beyond the sample.	The judgment was only based on appearance so could be seen as being reductionist: (several other factors also affect patients' judgments of their doctor).

Verbal communications

Verbal communications are based around the speech used by a doctor to try to gain access to relevant information about a patient's condition and then the potential treatment. Medical jargon is one potential hindrance when it comes to verbal communications between doctor and patient.

McKinlay (1975) examined the comprehension of medical terminology in sample of participants who were using a maternity service in Aberdeen, Scotland. A total of 87 families were used in the study and were interviewed about the use of maternity services 4 times in an 18-month period. The fourth interview collected data on the comprehension of medical terminology used by doctors. A total of 13 words were chosen that could be misunderstood. Each word was read out and then used in the context of a sentence. An example was:

> 'Rhesus: Doctors sometimes, while examining a woman who is expecting, say she's "rhesus positive". What are they talking about?' (McKinlay 1975: 10).

The responses were transcribed verbatim and two independent doctors scored them on the following scale.

- Score A: the patient did not recognise the word or understand it.
- Score B: the patient had an incorrect understanding of the word.
- Score C: the patient recognised the word but did not understand it.
- Score D: the patient had a good idea what the word meant.

One year after the transcripts were scored, a separate group of doctors rated each of the words on what they expected patients to understand. Patients were split into two groups for analysis: those who used the maternity services regularly ('utilisers') and those who were 'underutilisers'. When scoring a participant's transcript, the two doctors did not know which group the participant was in.

The main results are shown in Table 21.3.

For nearly all of the 13 words, the utiliser group had a higher percentage for score D than the underutiliser group. Therefore, it would appear that people using medical services regularly have a better understanding of medical terminology compared to people who don't use the services as much. In addition, the study showed that the doctors consistently underestimated the level of medical terminology comprehension in their patients.

Table 21.3 Distribution of comprehension of 13 words by two groups of patients and the comprehension expected by doctors (physicians). Results are given as percentages of the number of respondents, for each word.

	Underutilizers			Utilizers			Physicians		
	A: No Knowledge	B/C: Wrong or Vague	D: Adequate	A: No Knowledge	B/C: Wrong or Vague	D: Adequate	A: No Knowledge	B/C: Wrong or Vague	D: Adequate
Antibiotic	11.1	60.0	28.9	13.9	44.4	41.7	27.8	68.7	5.6
Breech	8.9	6.7	84.4	0.0	0.0	100.0	11.1	66.7	22.2
Enamel	8.9	40.0	51.1	8.3	30.6	61.1	27.8	44.4	27.8
Glucose	17.8	44.4	37.8	19.4	36.1	44.4	11.1	61.1	27.8
Membranes	24.4	31.1	44.4	11.1	25.0	63.9	50.0	50.0	0.0
Mucus	33.3	33.3	33.3	30.6	22.2	47.2	38.9	50.0	11.1
Navel	4.4	15.6	80.0	11.1	33.3	55.6	0.0	27.8	72.2
Protein	37.8	62.2	0.0	30.6	58.3	11.1	27.8	55.6	16.7
Purgative	57.8	28.9	13.3	72.2	13.9	13.9	16.7	44.4	38.9
Rhesus	13.3	75.6	11.1	11.1	86.1	2.8	55.6	38.9	5.6
Scanning	13.3	35.6	51.1	8.3	30.6	61.1	66.7	33.3	0.0
Sutures	48.9	6.7	44.4	50.0	11.1	38.9	61.1	33.3	5.6
Umbilicus	84.4	15.6	0.0	83.3	5.6	11.1	50.0	38.9	11.1
Total respondents	45 (100.0%)			36 (100.0%)			18 (100.0%)		

Source: McKinlay (1975: 6)

Strength	Weakness
The transcripts were scored independently with the doctors blind to which group each participant was in. This improves the validity of the study (as the scoring was objective). It also improves the study's reliability (as the physicians agreed on which score category each transcript was given).	The sample was limited in terms of geography (Scotland) and type of participant (maternity service users). This could make it difficult to generalise findings to other cultures. It could also be difficult to generalise to people who use other specialist health services where their comprehension levels may be specific to their medical condition.

Challenge yourself

Create a similar issue and debate tracker commentary for idiographic versus nomothetic, questionnaires, and generalisations from findings.

	Issue and debate tracker
Experiments	Experiments attempt to allow researchers to establish some form of cause and effect. In the study by McKinstry and Wang (1991) there was an attempt to see whether the type of practitioner clothing (IV) affected the perception of the practitioner (DV). Aspects of the experiment were controlled in an attempt to make the relationship causal. The McKinlay (1975) study was experimental as people were placed in utiliser and underutiliser groups and these were compared to see how many words they knew the meaning for. Again, this was an attempt at a causal relationship.
Quantitative data	This type of data tends to be more objective and allows a direct comparison across groups of participants. In the McKinstry and Wang study one example was the acceptability score (on a 6-point scale) for each type of clothing. The numerical data allowed a direct comparison to be made across clothing types to see if one had higher or lower average acceptability scores. Also, in McKinlay, the number of participants who were rated score D could be compared to the other three ratings to show that utilisers understood more than underutilisers.

21.1.2 Patient and practitioner diagnosis and style

Practitioner diagnosis focusing on making a diagnosis (disclosure of information, false positive and false negative diagnosis) and presenting a diagnosis

Disclosure of information

For a diagnosis to occur, the patient does have to give some information to the doctor. However, as the doctor will have an array of patients who have their own styles of communication, reaching the correct diagnosis can sometimes be quite difficult.

Sarafino (2006) noted that the patient can hinder the communication when the patient:

- wants to criticise the doctor or becomes angry
- clearly ignores what the doctor is saying
- insists on more tests and medication when the doctor says there is no need
- wants a certificate for an illness that the doctor does not believe the patient has
- makes sexual remarks to the doctor.

The above can stop a consultation 'in its tracks'. A patient may show a real concern about a condition that is only minor or show no concern for a condition that is major. The doctor still needs to get the correct information out of the patient to make a diagnosis. Different patients will describe symptoms of the same illness in vastly different ways, which can also make it difficult for the doctor to make a reliable and valid diagnosis. Sarafino (2006) noted that this may be the case as patients simply interpret symptoms differently from each other (or have a different hierarchy of what they feel are the 'main symptoms' of an illness). Also, some patients may wish to 'play down' symptoms that may point towards a major illness. Finally, patients may not have the requisite vocabulary to describe accurately the symptoms they are feeling.

Type I and type II errors

There are occasions where a doctor will get something wrong. Errors are classified into two types.

1. Type I error. This is when the doctor diagnoses somebody to be healthy when the patient is actually physically or psychologically ill. Many believe this to be the most serious of the two errors as the patient does not get any treatment and the condition worsens.
2. Type II error. This is when the doctor diagnoses somebody as ill when in fact the patient is healthy.

Practitioner style

Doctor-centred and patient-centred styles (Byrne and Long 1976; Savage and Armstrong, 1990)

Byrne and Long (1976) analysed about 2500 recorded medical consultations across many countries and discovered two main 'styles'.

- The doctor-centred style meant that the doctor asked questions that were closed so that the patient could only answer 'Yes' or 'No'. When the patient attempted to expand on answers or tried to give more information, this was mainly ignored. It would appear that the doctor wanted to make the symptom–diagnosis link with no extra communication and everything was based on 'fact' rather than any discussion. Therefore, the patient was passive in the conversation.

- The patient-centred style meant that the doctor asked open questions so that the patient could explain and expand on answers. The doctor would try to limit the use of medical jargon to ensure that the patient understood the diagnosis and potential treatment. The doctor would encourage patients to express themselves how they wished and would ask for clarification as and when it was needed. Therefore, the patient was active in the conversation.

> **Challenge yourself**
>
> Look at the issue and debate tracker table on page 231. Create similar issue and debate commentaries for application to everyday life, individual and situational explanations, determinism versus free will, and validity.

KEY STUDY: Savage and Armstrong (1990)

Context and main theories/explanations

There has always been a debate about which consulting style is the best one for a general practitioner (physician) to use with patients. Some believe that a more sharing approach is good for a patient where the general practitioner allows the patient to be part of the decision-making process. However, others believe that a more traditional, directed, style is good. This involves the general practitioner making the patient feel better by being authoritarian and dominant. However, a lot of evidence appears to be anecdotal, so Savage and Armstrong wanted to change this.

Aim and hypotheses

Savage and Armstrong (1990) wanted to compare the effects of directing and sharing styles of consultation on patients' satisfaction with a consultation.

Design

Participants

A total of 359 patients were randomly selected from an inner London general practice to receive either a direct or a sharing style of consultation. Of these, four refused to participate and five were excluded. A further 30 did not complete the initial assessment and 110 did not complete the assessment one week later.

All participants were aged 16 to 75 years and had to present at least one symptom at consultation. If the condition presented was life threatening, they were not used in the study. Savage also excluded patients if he felt they would get upset by the study. Consent was obtained by signing a form that told patients their consultation would be audio recorded.

Design

Table 21.4 shows the differences in style.

An independent observer listened to a selection of 40 recordings of the consultations and confirmed all aspects of the each one was correct, and the style identified.

Measures

This was a questionnaire consisting of five items, completed by each participant immediately after the consultation (in the waiting room) and then again one week after.

Procedure

The location was a deprived inner-city practice. Participants were selected via a random number generator that selected four patients per surgery held by Savage. The duration of the study was four months.

Table 21.4 Examples of directing and sharing styles of consultation by general practioner during five parts of consultation

Part of consultation	Style of consultation	
	Directing	**Sharing**
Judgment on the consultation	"This is a serious problem" or "I don't think this is a serious problem"	"Why do you think this has happened?" "Why do you think this has happened now?"
Diagnosis	"You are suffering from ... "	"What do you think is wrong?"
Treatment	"It is essential that you take this medicine"	"What have you tried to do to help so far?" "What were you hoping that I would be able to do?" "Would you like a prescription?" "I think this medicine would be helpful; would you be prepared to take it?"
Prognosis	"You should be better in ... days"	"What do these symptoms or problems mean to you?"
Follow up and closure	"Come and see me in ... days" "I don't need to see you again for this problem"	"Are there any other problems?" "When would you like to come and see me again?"

Source: Savage and Armstrong (1990: 969)

Savage had a set of cards that randomly allocated a participant to the directing or sharing style. He did not know which style he was to use until the participant turned up and had presented their symptoms to him. There were five prompts on the chosen card to help Savage with the chosen style. At the end of the consultation the participant completed the measures.

Results, findings, and conclusions

Table 21.5 shows results from patients who were questioned immediately after their consultation.

Table 21.5 Effect of doctor's style of consultation on assessment of his understand of their problem by patients immediately after consultation. Figures are numbers (percentages) of patients (n = 320).

Assessment	Style of consultation		Significance
	Directing	**Sharing**	
I was able to discuss my problem well	130/157 (83)	132/154 (86)	NS
I received an excellent explanation	63/162 (39)	41/156 (26)	$x^2 = 5.7$; df = 1; p = 0.02
I perceived the general practitioner to have complete understanding	86/162 (53)	61/158 (39)	$x^2 = 6.8$; df = 1; p = 0.01
I felt greatly helpe	77/162 (48)	66/156 (42)	NS
I felt much better	45/162 (28)	48/155 (31)	NS

Source: Savage and Armstrong (1990: 969)

As can be seen, the directing style was perceived as giving a much better explanation and that the GP had a complete understanding of the problem.

The research team also compared patients' responses for those who completed a questionnaire immediately after the consultation and the same one a week later and found the following results.

- It was found that 45% of the directing style group but only 24% of the sharing style group felt they received an excellent explanation immediately after consultation. One week later these were 33% and 17% respectively.
- It was also found that 62% of the directing style group but only 37% of the sharing style group felt the GP had a complete understanding of their health issue immediately after the consultation. One week later these were 39% and 18% respectively.

It would therefore appear that a more direct style of consultation brings about more satisfaction in patients.

Main discussion points

- The findings contradict the subjective experiences of doctors who use a sharing style of consultation. The measures used were analysed by the research team and they were not worded in a way to cause a bias *against* the sharing style. The audio recordings were analysed, and the observer confirmed that Savage had shown the two styles differently and clearly. The chosen style was only adopted *after* participants had presented their problems, so the *entire* consultation was directing or sharing.
- The directing style was not seen as being more satisfying if the consultation was long, where the advice was the main treatment regime, for those who had a chronic illness, or for those who presented psychological illness as their reason for seeing the doctor.

Evaluation

- The procedure was clear and standardised. The recruitment process and the measures used by the researchers, how the consultation style was chosen, and the use of an independent observer mean that other researchers can replicate the study to test for reliability.
- The participants were from one inner-London practice, meaning that it might be difficult to generalise beyond the sample used. Communication style is different across many geographical areas and the sharing style might be more suited to a different practice. Therefore, the generalisability may be reduced. However, doctors are trained in a certain way (eg consultations are usually ten minutes maximum where a diagnosis and/or treatment has to be identified) so the style of consultation *could* be generalisable to lots of other practices in very different areas (eg a small practice in a rural area).

21.1.3 Misusing health services

Delay in seeking treatment (Safer et al, 1979)

Safer *et al* (1979) devised a model after interviewing many patients that tried to explain why patients delay seeking treatment. There are three stages to this.

1. Appraisal delay – this refers to the time taken for a person to interpret a physical symptom as a potential indicator of illness. This is affected by immediate sensory information – something bleeding or making a person experience major levels of pain will be interpreted much more quickly as 'something wrong' than a small pain, for instance.

2. Illness delay – this refers to the time taken between people recognising that they are ill and actually seeking some form of medical attention. This is affected by familiarity – a new and different symptom will create a faster reaction and help-seeking behaviour than an old symptom that re-occurs.

3. Utilisation delay – this refers to the time taken between deciding to seek medical attention and actually doing so. This is affected by a number of factors such as cost, how severe the pain is and whether the person feels that going to get help would cure the illness. People can easily ignore illnesses without immediate pain and therefore can have illnesses such as hypertension and cancer for more than, for example, three months before they decide to go and get medical attention and advice.

> **Challenge yourself**
>
> Explain at least one strength and one weakness of the health belief model. Make sure one of your points is about real-world application.

Alternative explanations for delay: the health belief model (Becker and Rosenstock, 1979)

The health belief model developed by Becker and Rosenstock (1979) attempts to predict when people will make rational health decisions. It assumes that people will change health-related behaviours in the following situations.

- Perceived vulnerability: if people believe that they are vulnerable to a health problem.
- Perceived severity: if people believe that the health problem can have serious consequences.
- Perceived benefits: if people believe that taking the necessary action can reduce any vulnerability to the health problem.
- Perceived barriers: if people believe that the costs of taking the necessary action are outweighed by the overall benefits.
- Cues to action: if people are confronted with factors that will make them want to change (eg reading about someone else in a similar position; feeling physically ill).
- Self-efficacy: if people believe that they can be successful in changing their behaviours to benefit their health.
- Modifying variables: these are factors such as upbringing or cultural norms that can have an effect on decision making.

Figure 21.2 shows how these factors interact.

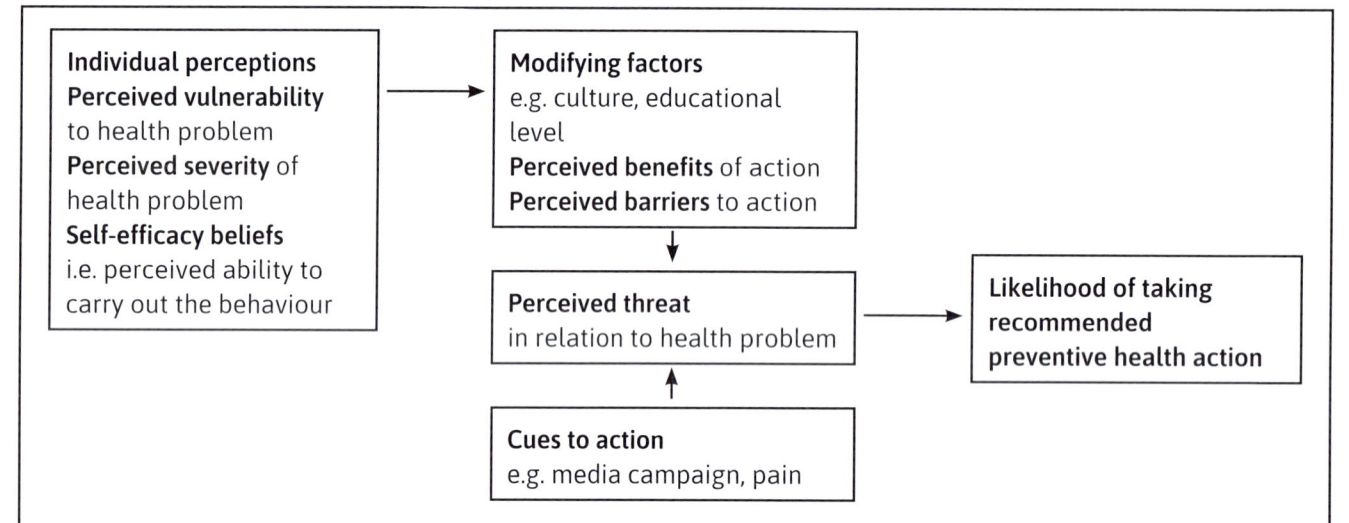

> **Challenge yourself**
>
> To what extent do you feel that the health belief model is deterministic? Justify your answer.

Individual perceptions
Perceived vulnerability to health problem
Perceived severity of health problem
Self-efficacy beliefs i.e. perceived ability to carry out the behaviour

Modifying factors
e.g. culture, educational level
Perceived benefits of action
Perceived barriers to action

Perceived threat in relation to health problem

Cues to action e.g. media campaign, pain

Likelihood of taking recommended preventive health action

The model assumes that people make rational decisions on health-related behaviours and that people are ready to change if they:
- believe they are vulnerable to the health problem in question (**perceived vulnerability**)
- believe the health problem has serious consequences (**perceived severity**)
- believe taking action could reduce their vulnerability to the health problem (**perceived benefits**)
- believe the costs of taking action (**perceived barriers**) are outweighed by the benefits (**perceived benefits**)
- are confronted with factors (e.g. pain in the chest or a television programme) that prompt actions (**cues to action**)
- are confident that they are able to be successful in the action (**self-efficacy**) – if people believe they can stop smoking or eat healthier, they are more likely to listen to health promotion messages).

At the individual level there are **modifying variables**, i.e. individual characteristics such as culture, education level, past experiences, and motivation that can influence people's perceptions.

Figure 21.2 *The health belief model* (Rosenstock et al, 1988)

Munchausen syndrome versus malingering

Malingering means that a person engages in many of the same activities as factitious disorders like Munchausen syndrome, but they do it for *personal gain*. People with Munchausen syndrome have a mental health condition.

Diagnostic features of Munchausen syndrome (essential and supporting features)

According to Folks and Freeman (1985), there appear to be three essential features of Munchausen syndrome.

'1. Recurrent, feigned, or simulated illness presented to a doctor

2. Peregrination. This refers to travelling or wandering around

3. Pseudologia fantastica. This refers to pathological lying with very exaggerated stories about themselves and their illness(es).'

Supporting features appear to focus upon actual evidence, such as:

'1. Tampering with test results to 'show' that they have the 'illness'

2. Inflicting symptoms on to themselves – this could be poisoning themselves or taking overdoses.'

Munchausen syndrome is an extreme form of factitious disorder accounting for about 10% of all factitious disorder case studies. A generic but typical case would involve patients who travel to different hospitals under different names and give a factitious history of their condition. They may simulate symptoms and in some cases eat contaminated food in order to vomit or produce blood. Many illnesses are claimed and the most common are fevers, infections, bleeding, and seizures. However, Turner and Reid state that these patients may go through medical procedures that do not show that they have a 'real illness' and many are then 'caught out' by inconsistencies in their self-reported medical histories.

Case studies: Munchausen syndrome

Aleem and Ajarim (1995) studied a 22-year-old female university student who had been referred to hospital with a potential immune deficiency. She had a painful swelling over her right breast for five days before admission. She also stated that she had previously had abdominal wall swellings that had needed medical attention on about 20 difference occasions. Her problems appeared to begin when she was 17 and suffering from amenorrhea. She had been prescribed oral contraceptives and after just a few months was showing symptoms of deep vein thrombosis. She was prescribed warfarin and was hospitalised to try to reduce the thrombosis.

Soon after this she began complaining of painful swellings in her groin. Assessment pointed towards hematoma. She had come from a supportive family. Her mother had died from breast cancer. The patient, while intelligent, lacked any real medical knowledge. The researchers' initial physical assessment revealed scarring from the previous swellings but results of a lot of other tests were 'normal'. An abscess had to be drained as it had failed to clear up with antibiotics. After four days of being hospitalised, the patient developed another breast lesion which became infected and needed to be surgically drained. Suspicion was now being raised by the doctors as there was no explanation for the abscess or lesions seen.

The patient underwent a psychiatric assessment but she did not know she was being assessed for potential Munchausen syndrome. She was very defensive in the assessment and 'extremely rationalizing her answers' and no other psychological issues were identified.

Finally, when she was not in bed one day, nurses found a syringe full of fecal material. When she returned to her bed, one of the other patients told her what the nurses had found. She became very hostile and angry, left the hospital immediately and was lost to the follow-up procedure. She was then officially diagnosed with Munchausen syndrome.

Strength	Weakness
As this was a case study, a lot of rich, in-depth qualitative data was collected so the findings should be valid.	As it was a case study, it may be difficult to generalise as the woman may have been unique.

In another case of Munchausen syndrome Zibis *et al* (2010) studied a 24-year-old woman who had been referred to a surgeon as she had extremely painful, stiff and swollen right hand and arm. She reported having had four previous operations on the same region. Four days into her treatment at the hospital she developed a 'fever temperature' that would not react well to any drug. However, diagnostic tests could not locate any infection or fever. It was discovered that she was preheating thermometers to take her own temperature and that she was often heard punching the wall at night (presumably with her right hand). She was also seen reading medical text books about hand diseases and amputations. The medical staff stopped her treatment. Her temperature dropped back to usual levels and 20 days after taking her cast off, her arm was free of any injury.

Faida *et al* (2012) reported a case of Münchausen syndrome involving a 40-year-old woman who had injuries to her right leg. She was complaining of arthritis of the right leg with headaches and ulcers. During her hospitalisation, her condition got worse and she could no longer walk on her right leg. Tests to examine why this could be the case showed nothing abnormal about the leg. When a standard x-ray was taken, it revealed that a sewing needle was embedded in her right calf. When the hospital staff questioned her about this she became very aggressive and denied any knowledge of it. She then attempted to jump out of the hospital window to escape but thankfully was stopped. Many of her symptoms resolved spontaneously after this incident.

> **Challenge yourself**
>
> Write up another case study of Munchausen syndrome. Compare it for similarities and differences to the Aleem and Ajarim case study.

> **Challenge yourself**
>
> Look at the issue and debate tracker table on page 231. Create similar issue and debate commentaries for reductionism versus holism, idiographic and nomothetic, interviews, case study, and generalisations from findings.

21.2 Adherence to medical advice

21.2.1 Types of non-adherence and reasons why patients do not adhere

Types of non-adherence

Failure to follow treatment, failure to attend appointments and problems caused by non-adherence

Clarke (2013) noted different types of adherence that we can reverse to discover different types of non-adherence, which are:

- not following short-term advice (eg to take three pills per day, five hours apart, for one week)
- failing to attend a follow-up interview or a referral appointment
- not wanting to make a lifestyle change (eg to reduce then quit smoking or take more exercise)
- not engaging in preventative measures linked to health (eg using contraception).

According to Sarafino (2006), up to 40% of a given population fail to adhere to the medical advice given to them. That is, two in five people do not follow their doctor's advice. In addition, the research showed the following.

- When medicine needs to be taken for short-term acute illness, the adherence rate climbs to 67%.
- For longer-term chronic regimes, the figure appears to be around 50%.
- People tend to adhere more just before or just after seeing a doctor.
- There appears to be very little adherence at all to any advice that involves a change in lifestyle.

Sarafino (2006) was quick to note that these are probably overestimates of non-adherence as the data are only based on people who were willing to take part in a study and then admit to non-adherence. Also, the data fails to appreciate the range of adherence as some patients will adhere to advice 100% of the time but others' adherence may vary markedly from illness to illness.

Problems caused by non-adherence

When patients don't adhere to their prescribed drug regimen, several problems can occur.

- They may not improve their health condition.
- They may become ill with a different health issue because they are not taking their drugs.
- Drugs that have not been consumed could be around the house for others to consume (eg a child may think the drugs are sweets).
- There are financial costs when patients don't turn up for follow-up appointments and/or through not turning up they may stop someone having an appointment who needs it.
- Producing drugs that are then destroyed incurs financial cost.

Explanations of why patients do not adhere

Rational non-adherence

There are patients who choose not to adhere to medical advice as it appears rational for them to do this. By this, we mean that they have conducted a cost-benefit analysis and it appears to them 'costly' to adhere to the treatment being given to them or asked of them. Laba *et al* (2012) wanted to try to understand rational non-adherence using a community sample of patients in Australia. The patients were given a discrete choice online survey that wanted to estimate the importance of eight medication factors with regard to non-adherence. The factors were:

- immediate medication harm
- immediate medication benefit
- long-term medication harm
- long-term medication benefit
- cost
- regimen
- symptom severity
- alcohol restrictions.

Six of the factors appeared to affect choice of adherence rationally in the sample. The two that did not were symptom severity and alcohol restrictions. Therefore, rational non-adherence is a complex interaction between the six remaining factors with an overall cost-benefit analysis by individual patients finally predicting whether they will adhere or not. It was noted that when a potential health outcome was framed in terms of 'side effects' the person quite rationally was more likely not to adhere than if a health outcome was framed in terms of 'therapeutic benefits'. Therefore, the way that the treatment is, essentially, 'sold to them' affects whether patients will adhere (as rational people do not want side effects but do want therapeutic benefits).

The health belief model can also explain why patients do not adhere. This model is covered on page 236.

> **Challenge yourself**
>
> Explain how the health belief model can explain why some patients *do* adhere to medical advice but some patients *do not* adhere to medical advice.

> **Challenge yourself**
>
> Look at the issue and debate tracker table on page 246. Create similar issue and debate commentaries for application to everyday life, individual and situational explanations, reductionism versus holism, idiographic versus nomothetic, and generalisations from findings.

21.2.2 Measuring non-adherence

Subjective measures: clinical interviews and semi-structured interviews

Clinical interviews

A clinical interview is essentially a dialogue between a psychologist and a patient. It is used to help diagnose the potential causes of pain and then come up with a plan of action to help to control or get rid of the pain. The psychologist will have a series of questions to ask the patient and will ask them when appropriate, as the situation will seem more like a conversation than an interview. The psychologist must ensure that all pre-set questions are asked but the order is not set because the psychologist will only ask questions based on the answers given by the patient. Therefore, the psychologist needs to be skilled in directing the interview by being able to ask the questions that will keep the dialogue going.

Strength	Weakness
This type of interview has good application as it allows psychologists to get a holistic view of the patients and find out all they need to know about the patients' health status. This will allow for more appropriate treatment to be given.	In clinical interviews psychologists rely on patients telling the truth and being able to describe their health experiences accurately.

For information on semi-structured interviews, see page 12.

Clinical and semi-structured interviews in the context of renal transplant (Butler *et al*, 2004)

Both a clinical interview and a semi-structured interview were used by Butler *et al* (2004). They were concerned about the non-adherence to immunosuppressants in patients who had undergone a renal (kidney) transplant. This type of non-adherence is one of the major causes of renal transplant failure. The study used 58 adults, recruited through random stratified sampling from 153 renal transplant recipients from a different study. There were three main outcome measures.

1. Electronic monitors were used to measure physiological adherence to immunosuppressants.

2. Assessment of health beliefs was measured using self-report questionnaires and a semi-structured interview. The questionnaires used included the Illness Perception Questionnaire and the Beliefs about Medicine Questionnaire. These were completed at home, but the participants also had a semi-structured interview about these topics.

3. Assessment of depression was measured using the Clinical Interview Schedule (CIS-R). It is based around ICD-10. It measures distress and psychiatric diagnosis.

The electronic monitors detected that 12% of the sample missed at least 20% of medication days and 26% had missed 10% of medication days. Half of the sample never missed their medication. From the questionnaires and semi-structured interview, the two main factors for non-adherence were beliefs about the medication and having a negative emotional impact to the renal transplant. When factors were eliminated from the analysis that had low numbers, other factors were seen to predict non-adherence. These included having a transplant from a live donor and having a low belief in the need for immunosuppressants.

> **Challenge yourself**
>
> Design a study using the self-report method that investigates reasons why people *do* adhere to medical advice.

Objective measures

Pill counting (Chung and Naya, 2000)

Chung and Naya (2000) tested compliance with treatment featuring an oral asthma medication using a device called TrackCap™. Ths study used 57 patients (32 male; age range 18–55 years). The treatment phase lasted 12 weeks. Participants were required to take 20 milligrams of zafirlukast twice a day. At the start of the study each participant was given 56 tablets, which was enough for three weeks' treatment with one week's supply spare. The tablets were dispensed in screw-top bottles fitted with a TrackCap™ mechanism. Patients were asked to return to the hospital every three weeks to have their medication replenished. They were told to remove only one tablet at a time then replace the cap immediately to stop moisture getting into the bottle. They did not know that the TrackCap™ was keeping a record. It worked as follows.

- Each removal of the TrackCap™ was taken to indicate a single medication use.
- It only recognised but did not accumulate multiple openings that occurred within one minute of each other.
- If the cap was left off the bottle for more than 15 minutes, it was recorded as one additional event.

A total of 47 patients completed the 12 weeks of the study. Compliance or adherence was calculated in three different ways.

Percentage TrackCap™ compliance was defined as:

$$\% \text{ Compliance} = 100 \times \frac{\text{Number of TrackCap}^{TM} \text{ events}}{\text{Number of prescribed tablets}}$$

Compliance also was estimated from returned tablet counts, with percentage compliance defined as:

$$\% \text{ Compliance} = 100 \times \frac{\text{Number of dispensed tablets minus number of returned tablets}}{\text{Number of prescribed tablets}}$$

TrackCap™ adherence was the degree to which patients followed dosing instructions precisely on a daily basis and was defined as:

$$\% \text{ Adherence} = 100 \times \frac{\text{Number of days with 2 TrackCap}^{TM} \text{ events at least 8 h apart}}{\text{Total number of days' dosing}}$$

The median adherence rate was 71% and the median compliance rate was 89%. Figures 21.3 and 21.4 show the distribution of days of full adherence and distribution of compliance levels.

Based on the tablet count method, the median compliance was 92%. Overall, the TrackCap™ system could be a way of measuring both compliance and adherence to a drug-based treatment programme for people with asthma.

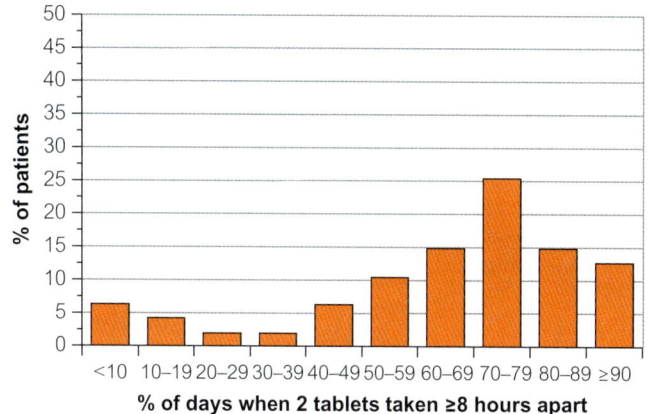

Figure 21.3
Source: Chung and Naya (2000: 855)

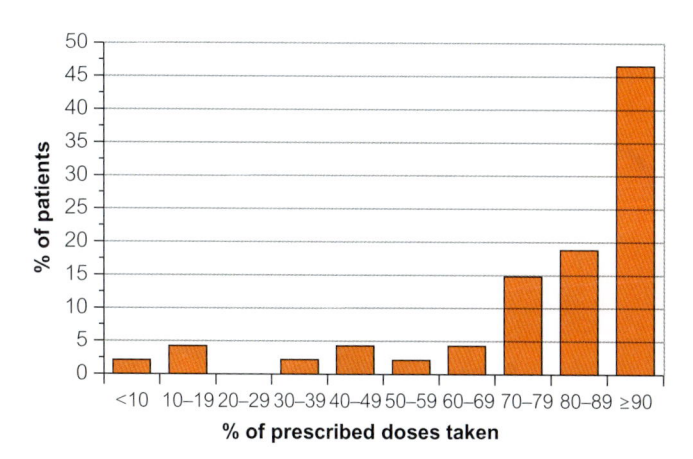

Figure 21.4
Source: Chung and Naya (2000: 855)

Strength	Weakness
The study has good application because the TrackCap™ system worked, so GPs could use it to measure how much a patient is adhering to a treatment regimen.	This system of measuring adherence is restricted to use with health conditions that require pills to be taken.

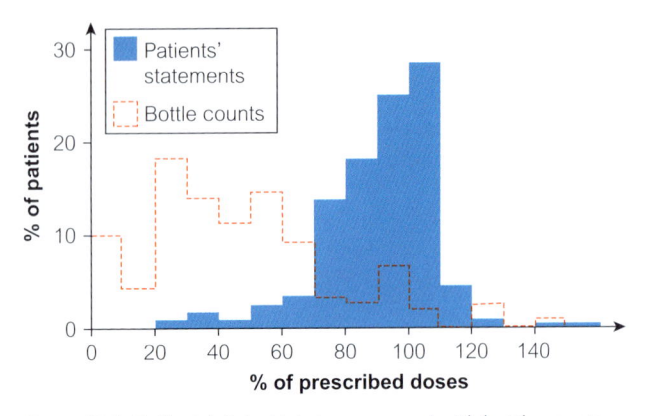

Figure 21.5 Patients' stated intake compared with bottle counts. The prescribed dose of 4 oz per day is 100% on the abscissa.
Source: Roth and Caron (1978: 363)

Challenge yourself

Explain at least one strength and one weakness of biological measures used to measure adherence. Make sure one of your points is about objectivity.

Challenge yourself

Look at the issue and debate tracker table on page 246. Create similar issue and debate commentaries for application to everyday life, idiographic versus nomothetic, quantitative and qualitative data, validity, and reliability.

Biological measures: blood and urine tests

Blood and urine tests are direct measures of adherence. These tests can detect biological markers to assess whether a drug has been taken.

Blood tests measure the amount of metabolised drug in a person. They can clearly show whether a drug has been taken. Some medications, however, are detected in the blood stream months after stopping taking the drug so the tests are not 100% accurate.

Urine tests can measure the amount of drug or medicine that has passed through the body and has been excreted. An example from Anderson (2018) showed that urine tests showed that 96% of patients who took a drug for preexposure human immunodeficiency virus (HIV) had detectable levels in their urine, showing adherence.

Roth and Caron (1978) used an element of biochemical analysis when examining the accuracy of patients' statements on the consumption of an antacid used to treat peptic ulcers. Patients were given 36 bottles of the antacid with measuring cups and told to take 1oz four times per day. A health professional visited to collect empty bottles and replenish the antacid. To validate the 'bottle count' as a measure of adherence, blood tests were taken to detect an inactive substance that had been placed in the antacid solution. On analysis, the mean actual intake by the sample of participants was 47% but their estimated intake was 89%. Figure 21.5 compares the patients' estimates with the amount of bottles of antacid consumed.

While patients believed they were consuming roughly the recommended doses of antacid, the bottle count (and blood analysis) told the doctors something very different.

21.2.3 Improving adherence

Improving adherence in children

Watt *et al* (2003) reported on a new asthma spacer called the Funhaler (see Figure 21.6). The study used a sample of 32 children (n = 10 males; age range 1.5–6 years; mean age 3.2 years; mean asthma duration 2.2 years). Questionnaires were completed after the use of the Breath-a-Tech (the current market leader in Australia for asthma drug dispensing) and the Funhaler.

The whistle and toy spinner (the toy element of the design) was designed to be away from the drug delivery system. In terms of adherence to the drug:

- 38% more parents medicated their child on the previous day using the Funhaler compared to those using the standard Breath-a-Tech method
- 60% more children adhered to the recommended dosage of four or more cycles of drug delivery with the Funhaler compared to the Breath-a-Tech method.

Therefore, it would appear that making delivery of drugs for children 'more of a game', by including fun as part of the procedure, improves adherence levels.

Figure 21.6 The Funhaler
Source: Watt et al (2003: 580)

Individual behavioural techniques: contracts, prompts, customising treatment

Contracts

These can be written or verbal agreements between a patient and a health professional. The patient commits to a set of behaviours and the health professional to a level of care related to a treatment regime. Bosch-Capblanch *et al* (2007) conducted a review of studies that had used contracts in this way. Of the studies reviewed, 15 reported that contracts did improve adherence, 6 reported better adherence from the *control group*, and 26 reported no difference between a contract group and a control group. Therefore, it appears that there is limited evidence that contracts work in improving adherence in health care settings.

Prompts

The key study by Yokley and Glenwick (1984) shows good examples of using prompts to increase adherence to treatment.

Customising treatment

Customising treatment means *not* using a 'one method fits all' technique when it comes to discussing health treatment. Patients and health care professionals can work out what is best for the patient. They can consider lifestyle, working hours, allergies to certain drugs, and exercise levels, among many other things.

> **Challenge yourself**
>
> To what extent do you feel that biochemical tests are the most effective measure of patient adherence? Justify your answer.

> **Challenge yourself**
>
> Use a search engine such as Google Scholar and find a study that has shown that customising treatment is effective.

Community interventions

KEY STUDY: Yokley and Glenwick (1984)

Context

Behavioural technology was something new in the 1980s, especially linked to health promotion. These included receiving prompts by post (it would, of course, be via text message, a secure website, or social media today). The use of the early types of behavioural technology had been successful in health promotions that involved smoking, nutrition, dental care, speeding, and wearing seat belts in cars.

Main theories/explanations

Some behavioural technology intervention techniques use the idea of operant conditioning in these two two ways.

- You follow the prompts that give health advice and reminders, and your health improves. This reinforcement via rewards means you are then more likely to follow the prompts next time.
- Some techniques have prizes to give away, for example cash or a luxury holiday. If you follow all prompts with proof of compliance with the health promotion, you are entered in a draw to potentially win the prizes.

Aim and hypotheses

To investigate the effectiveness and impact of four different behavioural technology interventions on immunisation rates in preschool children. The interventions were community based.

Design

Participants

A total of 1133 families with immunisation-deficient children were used in the study. They were found via medical records to verify that they had not been immunised against at least one of the following: diphtheria, tetanus, pertussis (whooping cough), polio, measles, mumps, or rubella.

Procedure

The children were randomly assigned to one of six groups.

1. General prompt (n = 195): they received a mailed prompt that contained general information about inoculation. It contained a standard immunisation schedule for the entire preschool age span.
2. Client-specific prompt (n = 190): they received a mailed prompt that told them which children needed which inoculations. It mentioned that the missing inoculations were going to be free of charge.
3. Specific prompt with increased public health clinic access (n=185): they received the same as the Client-specific prompt group but in addition received a second document about two different clinic sessions that were happening on a Wednesday night or on a Saturday. These sessions had the added incentive of enticing parents to sign their children up so they could go out for the evening or day and their children would be inoculated and looked after for free.
4. Specific prompt with monetary incentive (n = 183): they received the same as the Client-specific prompt but in addition received a second document about $175 in cash prizes if they brought their children to be inoculated.
5. Contact control (n = 189): they received a telephone call containing information about inoculation.
6. No contact control (n = 191): they received no contact during the study period.

Measures

The three main DVs were:

1. the number of children who received one or more inoculations at the clinic
2. the number of children who attended the clinic – this could be for any reason, not just for their inoculation(s)
3. the total number of inoculations received by the children.

These measures were taken at two weeks after the beginning of the intervention, then at two months and three months.

To test the reliability of the measures, 10% of the research record cards were examined against the original medical records. There was a 93% agreement rate.

Results, findings, and conclusions

Figure 21.7 shows the cumulative percentage of children who received one or more inoculations during the study period.

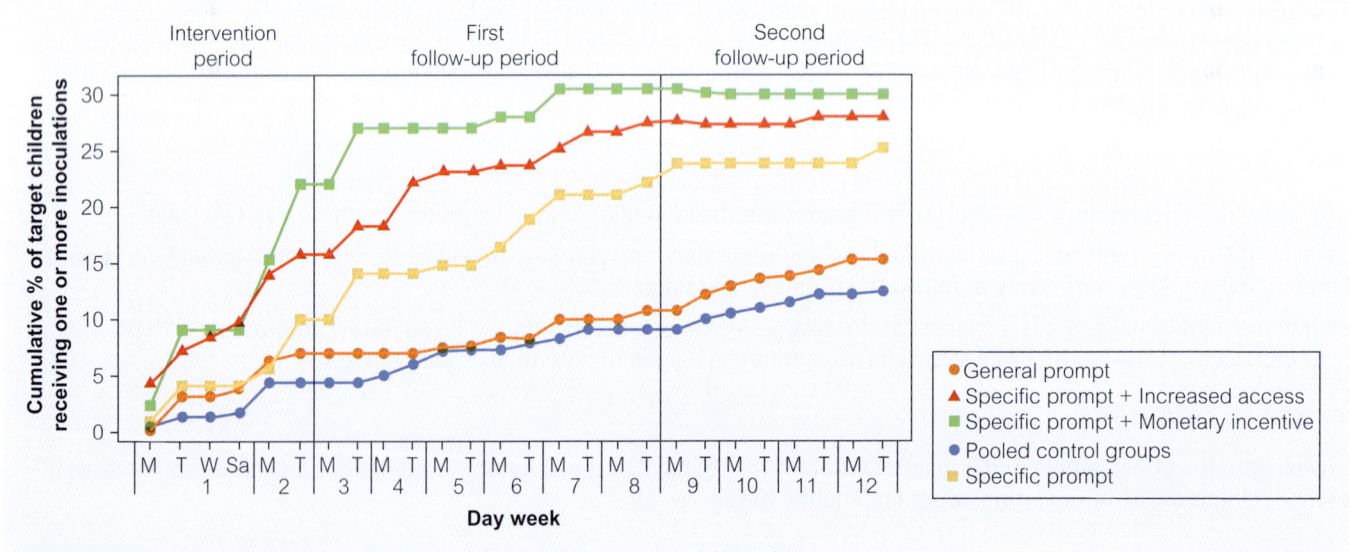

Figure 21.7 *Cumulative percentage of target children receiving one or more inoculations across time periods*

All intervention attempts (except the General prompt) produced evidence of improvement when compared to the control groups. The Specific prompt with monetary incentive group produced the largest effect, followed by the Specific prompt with increased public health clinic access group, the Specific prompt group, then the General prompt group. Therefore, it would seem that a relatively inexpensive approach to increasing immunisation is monetary incentives.

Table 21.6 shows the cost per child for each intervention.

Table 21.6 Cost/outcome results

Group	Cost per target child motivated to receive inoculation		
	After 2 weeks	After 2 months	After 3 months
GP	$8.10	$5.21	$3.64
SP	$5.86	$2.60	$2.27
SP + IA	$11.30	$6.46	$6.28
SP + MI	$9.46	$6.91	$6.91

Note. GP = general prompt, SP = specific prompt; SP + IA = specific prompt + increased access; SP + MI = specific prompt + monetary incentive.
Source: Yokley and Glenwick (1984: 322)

Main discussion points

- There was evidence of efficacy for all prompts except the single general prompt. This is useful for health intervention programme managers to know when deciding on how to use prompts in the community.
- Inoculation research using prompts can now follow a number of pathways. One includes choice of technology, as a computer would be more efficient than human personnel when choosing potential participants and initiating the letters to be sent as the prompts. The computer can standardise the letter and ensure that it is printed and sent when an inoculation is due.

Evaluation

- The study has a positive real-life application. The protocol and types of successful prompts can be used to improve immunisation rates for other diseases. It can also be used to improve take-up rates for vaccinations, including those for influenza and Covid-19. This will then increase the protection of more people against these viruses.
- As an independent groups method was used, we cannot rule out some individual differences causing a change in the DVs rather than the type of prompt. Certain individuals may, or may not, be better suited to one of the prompts available in the study but they may not have been placed in that group, meaning that their inoculation data might be lower than if a different, preferred, prompt had been used. This could reduce the validity of findings.
- The study has low temporal validity based on technology used. Many health centres can now use paperless ways of contacting patients, for example through text message or e-mail. The use of letters may not be applicable any more in certain regions of the world as other behavioural technology techniques are available that cost less and could be more effective. The study needs to now be replicated using modern technology.

	Issue and debate tracker
Experiments	As we know, experiments attempt to allow researchers to establish some form of cause and effect. In the study by Watt *et al* (2003) there was an attempt to see if the type of device (Funhaler or Breath-A-Tech) (IV) affected adherence to medication (DV). Aspects of the experiment were controlled in an attempt to make the relationship causal. The Yokley and Glenwick (1984) study was experimental as people were placed in different types of prompt groups and these were compared to see how children went for inoculation. Again, this was an attempt at a causal relationship. However, both studies were conducted in the field and there would have been many situational variables and participant variables that could not be controlled for. This could have had some impact on the DV in both studies.
Use of children in research	The Watt *et al* study used children as participants directly. Informed consent would have been taken by their parents as the children were not old enough to give it themselves. There are other issues surrounding the use of children in adherence research. The findings from the study that the Funhaler worked better meant that for a time those in Breath-A-Tech were not receiving the same level of treatment for their asthma. This could have moral consequences as being part of the study meant some children could have been worse off in terms of their health. The Yokley and Glenwick had an *indirect* use of children as they were not direct participants (the parents received the prompts) but as a consequence of their parents being in the study this affected their level of inoculation. This also has potential moral consequences.

Challenge yourself

Create similar issue and debate commentaries for questionnaires, validity, and generalisations from findings.

21.3 Pain

21.3.1 Types and theories of pain

Functions and types of pain

According to Sarafino (2006), pain can be a sensory and/or emotional discomfort which tends to be associated with actual tissue damage or threatened tissue damage including irritation. People's experiences of pain differ markedly but virtually every human being experiences pain in some form.

Acute pain refers to times when people experience temporary pain for about six months or less. They experience anxiety while the pain is there but this dissipates quickly once the pain begins to disappear. When pain lasts continually for more than a few months, it is referred to as *chronic pain*. People experiencing this will have high levels of anxiety and may well develop a sense of helplessness and depression. This is especially true if treatment is not helping. The pain interferes with daily life, thoughts and sleep patterns. For both of these types, the cause of the pain is physiological.

Phantom limb pain (PLP) is when an individual experiences the sensation of pain from a body part that no longer physically exists, for example an amputated arm or leg. As research has progressed this is no longer seen as being a psychological problem but more of a physiological problem centred on the spinal cord and brain.

The case of Alan (MacLachlan *et al*, 2004)

Treatments for PLP include a technique called mirror treatment and this was used in a case study of Alan (MacLachlan *et al*, 2004).

Mirror treatment for PLP follows a set procedure. The person experiencing PLP places their intact arm, for example, into a box. There is a mirror down the centre of the box so when it is viewed off-centre the reflection of the arm gives the impression that there are now two intact arms visible. However, there had been little research into using mirror treatment for PLP in legs until this case study.

Alan, when aged 32 years, was admitted to hospital to have fluid drained from his leg. However, the leg had to be amputated due to a bacterial infection. As he was very unwell and spent a great deal of time in intensive care, he only became aware of the amputation five weeks after it had happened. Alan's PLP began two days after he became fully conscious out of intensive care. He stated that it felt as if two of his toes were crossed. PLP progressed through the day from pins and needles to painful but bearable pain then severe pain. He reported that he felt a full phantom leg, but it was about two inches shorter than his real leg. He also reported that the phantom limb was in a cast.

The exercises that he had to do, the 'intervention procedure', consisted of ten repetitions of the following.

'1. Slowly straighten and then bend your legs at the knee at the same time.

2. Slowly straighten and then bend your legs at the knee alternately as if walking.

3. Point your feet upwards, and then point your feet downwards at the same time.

4. Turn your soles in towards each other and then away from each other at the same time.

5. Move your feet around in a circle to the left and to the right.

6. Lift your feet off the ground in a walking movement.

7. Point your toes upwards, and then downwards while trying to keep your ankle and foot still.

8. Clench and unclench your toes.

9. Spread your toes and then relax them.

10. Point up your big toes and point down the other toes, then reverse it so that your big toe is pointing down and you other toes are pointing up' (MacLachland *et al*, 2004: 902).

The entire protocol was as follows.

'*First five days:* daily morning + afternoon with one therapist at each session, with mirror.

Weekend: daily morning–afternoon on his own, with mirror.

Second five days: daily morning or afternoon with one therapist at each session, with mirror.

2–3 times daily on his own each day with mirror.

Weekend: 3–4 times daily on his own with mirror.

Third five days: 2–3 times daily on his own without mirror' (MacLachland *et al* (2004: 903).

Alan found the first two sessions very emotional as he saw his reflected leg for the first time. He reported that he only felt control over his phantom leg in the fourth session. The 'crossed toes' sensation began to diminish in week two and by the end of the third week he had minimal PLP and no sensation of crossed toes. Ratings of PLP and stump pain decreased throughout the entire protocol. It appeared that the mirror treatment for PLP was successful for Alan.

Strength	Weakness
This was a case study and focused on one individual with PLP. A great deal of data could be collected to increase the validity of the findings and also follow the course of PLP and mirror treatment in terms of whether the intervention was successful. The intervention procedure and entire protocol were clearly described so other patients with PLP in their leg can follow it and test it for reliability. It also, as a result, had good real-life application as it could be used with other PLP patients.	There may be something unique about Alan due to him only knowing about the amputation five weeks after it happened. Therefore, it may have some limited generalisability to people who know immediately that they have lost a limb (eg soldiers or people in an accident).

Theories of pain

Specificity theory (Descartes, 1664)

This was an early model of pain. It was predicted that we have a sensory system that is dedicated to pain. A series of neurons form a pathway to a dedicated pain centre in the brain. The more this pathway is used, the more intense is the pain experienced by the person. Therefore, according to this theory, pain is purely physiological and there are nerve centres in the brain that exclusively process this information. Some psychologists believe that they have evidence for certain fibres being exclusive to pain but others state that they cannot find them. There are sensory fibres in our skin that can detect heat, cold, and certain pressures but these can also detect pain so the exclusivity argument is now a weak one. A more comprehensive theory is gate control.

Gate control theory (Melzack and Wall, 1965)

Melzack and Wall (1965) proposed the idea of a gate control theory of pain. Pain is detected and still picked up by sensory signals but the spinal cord plays a key role in the experience of the actual pain. The spinal cord has a mechanism in it that acts just like a gate: it is either open or closed. If it is open the pain is experienced but the spinal cord can modulate the pain level by having the gate slightly open rather than fully open. There are three main factors involved in the gate-opening process.

- One factor is the amount of activity in pain fibres. The more 'noxious' the pain stimulus is, the more likely the gate will be opened (eg in someone with a severe cut).

- Another factor is the amount of activity in other peripheral fibres. These are called A-beta fibres. They carry information about 'low-level pain' (eg a scratch or a touch). When there is activity in these fibres the gate tends to close as the pain is low level and not dangerous.

- Messages from the brain are also a factor. Information such as excitement and anxiety can affect how much the gate is opened or closed.

Sarafino (2006) noted conditions that can open or close the gate in the spinal cord. The gate can be opened by:

- severe injury
- anxiety, worry, depression, etc
- focusing too much on the pain, plus boredom.

The gate can be closed by:

- medication
- positive emotions (eg laughing through happiness)
- rest and relaxation
- distraction from the pain.

> **Test yourself**
>
> Evaluate both theories of pain in terms of at least one strength and one weakness.

> **Challenge yourself**
>
> Look at the issue and debate tracker table on page 254. Create similar issue and debate commentaries for individual and situational explanations, nature versus nurture, reductionism versus holism, determinism versus free will, and case study.

21.3.2 Measuring pain

Subjective measures

The clinical interview is covered on page 240.

Self-report measures

Self-report measures are often obtained using questionnaires that allow the person experiencing the pain to rate how severe it is. Common examples are the use of a box scale, a verbal rating scale or a Likert-type scale. Examples of these are given in Figure 21.8.

Patients may also be asked to keep a pain diary, as shown in Figure 21.9, so the practitioner can monitor when the pain is happening and how the patient feels.

Box scale:

No pain | 0 | 1 | 2 | 3 | 4 | 5 | 6 | 7 | 8 | 9 | 10 | Worst pain possible

Verbal rating scale:

No pain   Some pain   Considerable pain   Worst pain possible

Likert-type scale:

The example questions below would be answered using the options of:

Strongly agree, Agree, Don't know, Disagree, Strongly disagree.

1. The pain usually gets worse at night.
2. Pain relief helps me control my pain.

Figure 21.8 Scales for recording pain – box rating, verbal rating, and Likert-type scales

PAIN DIARY FOR:

DATE: Did you change your medication today? If yes, describe:

Pain rating scale:

No pain | 0 | 1 | 2 | 3 | 4 | 5 | Unbearable pain

Time	Pain rating and body position	Activity at start of pain	What medication did you take and how much?	Pain rating after 1 or 2 hours	Comments/other problems
8.30 p.m.	5/ lower back pain	Leaned over and dragged dining chair away from table	Aspirin (2)	4 – helped a little	Could stand up better
11.00 p.m.	2/ lower back dull ache	Lying flat on back in the bed	Ibuprofen (2)	1 – helped	Trouble getting to sleep: got to sleep at around 2.00 a.m.

Figure 21.9 Example of a pain diary

Psychometric measures and visual rating scales

The McGill Pain Questionnaire (MPQ)

One standardised psychometric measure of pain is the McGill Pain Questionnaire (MPQ). This questionnaire comes in four parts.

1. A diagram of a body is presented to the patient, who simply has to mark where the pain is located around the body.
2. There are 20 sub-classes of descriptive words from which the patient has to choose a maximum of one per class. The further down the list in each sub-class the word is, the more points it scores so that an overall pain rating index can be calculated.
3. The patient has to describe the pattern of pain from three sub-classes of words and then produce some qualitative data about what things relieve but also increase the pain.
4. The final part asks the patient to rate the strength of the pain via six questions. The scores for the questions are added up to create a present pain intensity score.

Visual analogue scale

This type of scale attempts to measure a characteristic or attitude that is subjective. The aspect that is being measured is believed to be across a range of values (eg 0 to 100). Individuals simply make a mark in the visual analogue scale at the point they think represents their characteristic or attitude. The only descriptors given are at the left-hand and right-hand ends. Once the person has made the mark it is measured using a ruler. An example could be:

No pain — VAS — Pain as bad as it could possibly be

A visual analogue scale was used in the key study by Brudvik *et al* (2016) and is on the McGill Pain Questionnaire.

> **Test yourself**
>
> Explain at least one strength and one weakness of the MPQ. Make sure one of your points is about psychometrics.

Strength	Weakness
It allows a person the freedom to choose exactly where they think their pain is without any forced choices. This could improve validity.	It is still a subjective measure and would be difficult to directly compare the marks from different people as they will have different ideas of the two fixed end points.

KEY STUDY: Brudvik *et al* (2016)

Context

Prior to this study, it had been noted that children tend to receive less pain relief compared to adults for the same type of illness and injury. To be able to understand this, Brudvik *et al* wanted to identify which factors affect the handling of paediatric pain with a focus on how physicians and parents assess pain in children. The research team had noted that pain relief was not frequently part of treatment for fractures in accident and emergency departments when the patient is a child. There may be a range of factors that impact on the delivery of pain relief in children, including time constraints, reluctance to give strong painkillers, and potential side effects.

Aims and hypotheses

There were three main aims to this study.

1. To investigate how much agreement there is in pain intensity in children based on reports from the child, parents, and physicians.

2. To investigate differences in pain intensity given by children, parents, and physicians based on age of the child, the child's medical condition, and how severe the pain is.
3. To investigate whether the assessment of pain intensity affected the pain relief given to children.

Design

Participants

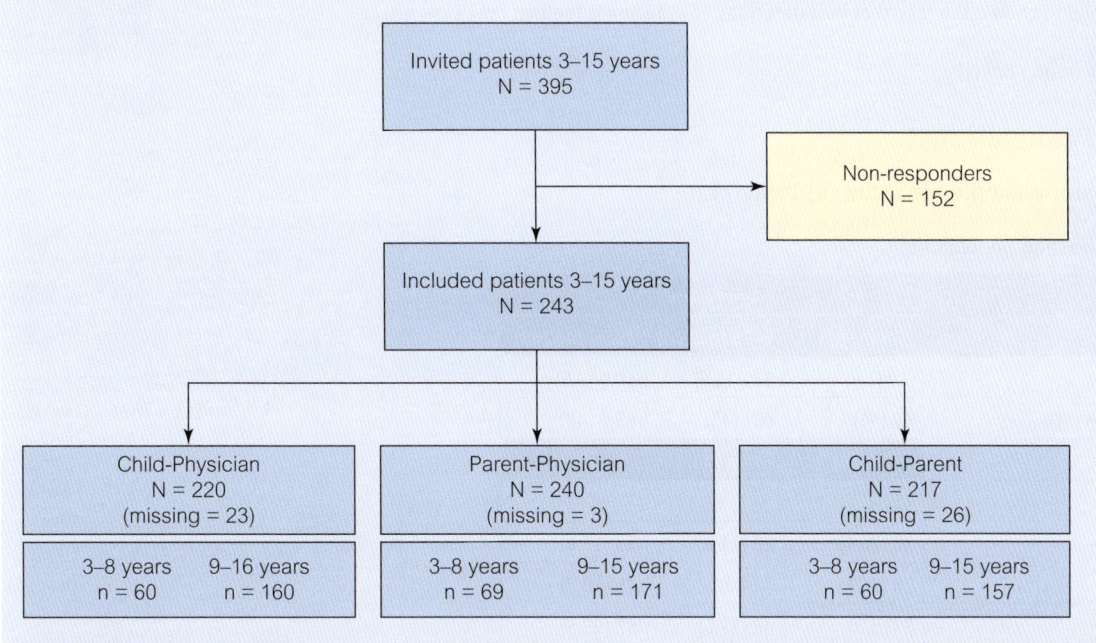

```
                    Invited patients 3–15 years
                            N = 395
                               │
                               ├──────────────► Non-responders
                               │                    N = 152
                               ▼
                    Included patients 3–15 years
                            N = 243
           ┌───────────────────┼───────────────────┐
           ▼                   ▼                   ▼
     Child-Physician     Parent-Physician      Child-Parent
         N = 220              N = 240             N = 217
      (missing = 23)        (missing = 3)      (missing = 26)

    3–8 years  9–16 years   3–8 years  9–15 years   3–8 years  9–15 years
    n = 60     n = 160      n = 69     n = 171      n = 60     n = 157
```

Figure 21.10 A flow chart showing the number of included patients, non-responders, and missing patients; and age distribution

Procedure

The emergency department used was in Bergen, Norway. Pain scoring is not mandatory in the department. However, 23% of participants had some experience of assessing pain in children less than nine years old and 69% had some experience for children aged nine or over. Therefore, all physicians and nurses were trained on using the pain scales and on helping children complete their own pain assessment. Each child and parent completed a written consent form before they were given the questionnaire to complete and engage in the consultation. The diagnosis for each child was classified as either infection, fracture, wounds, or ligament/muscle. The parent had to report whether the child had already taken painkillers. The physician had to record whether any painkillers were administered during the consultation.

Measures

Table 21.7 shows the measures used.

Table 21.7 The measures used in Brudvik et al (2016)

Group	Questionnaire(s)	Description
Children aged 3–8 years	Faces Pain Scale – Revised Wong–Baker Faces Pain Rating	See Figure 21.11 for the the Wong-Baker scale.
Children aged 9–15 years	Visual Analogue Scale Coloured Analogue Scale	This was a 100 mm line and the child had to mark where they felt their pain was. There were colours too, so the green end was no pain and the red end was 'worst thinkable pain'.
Parents	Numeric Rating Scale	Estimation of child pain on a scale of 0–10.
Physician and nurse	Numeric Rating Scale + others	Estimation of child pain on a scale of 0–10. Assessed whether child's pain reaction matched the diagnosis.

Source: Brudvik et al (2016: 140)

Explain to the child that each face is for a person who feels happy because he has no pain (hurt) or sad because he has some or a lot of pain. Face 0 is very happy because he doesn't hurt at all. Face 1 hurts just a little bit. Face 2 hurts a little more. Face 3 hurts even more. Face 4 hurts a whole lot, but Face 6 hurts as much as you can imagine, although you don't have to be crying to feel this bad. Ask child to choose the face that best describes how he/she is feeling.

Figure 21.11 Faces rating scale (Wong-Baker)

Results, findings, and conclusions

The characteristics of the study sample are shown in Table 21.8.

Table 21.8 Characteristics of the study population

Characteristics	Age (years)		
	3–8 (n=69)	9–15 (n=174)	Total (n=243)
Age in years, mean (SD)	5.9 (1.8)	12.4 (1.8)	10.6 (3.5)
Waiting time in minutes, mean (SD)	62 (56)	63* (45)	63.0 (48)
	n (%)	n (%)	n (%)
Diagnosis			
Infection	18 (26.1)	20 (11.5)	38 (15.6)
Wound	18 (26.1)	7 (4.0)	25 (10.3)
Fracture	9 (13.0)	48 (27.6)	57 (23.5)
Soft tissue, ligament or muscle injury	24 (34.8)	99 (56.9)	123 (50.6)
Concordance between medical condition and pain†			
Low	7 (10.1)	16 (9.2)	23 (9.5)
Some	24 (34.8)	57 (32.8)	81 (33.3)
High	38 (55.1)	101 (58.0)	139 (57.2)
Painkiller			
Parent‡	13 (18.8)	21§ (12.1)	34 (14.0)
Physician¶	5 (7.2)	16§ (9.2)	21 (8.6)

*One patient had missing waiting time.
†Physicians' perceived concordance between medical condition and pain.
‡Painkillers taken before consultation.
§One patient received painkillers from both parent and physician.
¶Painkillers administered by the physician during consultation.

Source: Brudvik et al (2016: 140)

The main results were as follows.
- Physicians assessed the child's mean pain to be lower than the child and parent estimations.
- Physicians significantly underestimated the pain levels of all children compared to the child and parent estimations.
- Physicians significantly underestimated the pain levels of all children in all diagnostic categories compared to the child and parent estimations.
- The assessment of pain was more consistent between physician and child as the pain estimations increased.

Brudvik et al concluded that child pain in an emergency department was very much underestimated by physicians. When a child cannot give a pain estimate, parental evaluations need to be considered. Analgesics are not given enough to children who are experiencing severe pain.

Main discussion points

- Physicians in an emergency department in Norway significantly underestimate levels of pain in children aged three years and above.
- While physician assessment of pain does improve when level of pain experienced increases, the research team state it is worrying that less than half of the sample received any pain relief.
- Physicians need to appreciate that they will probably underestimate pain in children. Using age-appropriate pain measures will help improve pain management in emergency departments.
- Pain management in an emergency department involving children is complex and requires thorough assessments from a physician, the child, and parent(s).

Evaluation

- The procedure used in the study was clear and standardised. The recruitment process and the measures used by the children, parents, and physicians were clearly outlined so other researchers can replicate the study to test for reliability.
- The study has good application. The findings can be used to improve the pain assessment and the delivery of pain relief in children who have fractures, wounds, etc in an emergency department. This could also improve the long-term care of children with health conditions that mean they experience a great deal of pain.
- Generalisability may be low. Even though the sample size was large it was only conducted in one emergency department in a Norwegian hospital. The way that consultation works here may be different from that in other hospitals and in other countries, so the findings about pain assessment and the delivery of pain relief may only apply to this emergency department. Other hospitals need to follow the same protocol to see whether it works elsewhere.

Behavioural/observational measures

The UAB Pain Behavior Scale

The University of Alabama at Birmingham (UAB) Pain Behavior Scale can be used by nurses to assess the degree of pain patients are in through observing their behaviour. The patient will be asked to perform several activities such as walking around, sitting down then standing up and the nurse rates each of these to give a total score of how much the pain is affecting the patient's behaviour. Figure 21.12 lists the parameters and shows the method of scoring some of them.

In addition, structured clinical sessions can be used and these can be tailored to the pain condition a patient has. Patients can be asked to perform a series of tasks linked to their pain (eg if it is lower back pain one of the tasks may be to tie their shoe laces). All of the tasks are recorded for observation. A trained observer then watches the recording and scores the patient so an overall pain score can be calculated.

Figure 21.13 shows some of the parameters of the UAB Pain Behavior Scale. The full list is: (1) vocal complaints verbal; (2) non-verbal complaints (groans, moans, gasps, etc); (3) down time (time spend lying down because of pain per day from 8.00 am to 8.00 pm); (4) facial grimaces; (5) standing posture; (6) mobility; (7) body language (clutching or rubbing site); (8) use of visible support equipment (brace, crutches, can, leaning on furniture, etc); (9) stationary movement (ability to stay still); (10) medication use.

Parameter	Points	Finding
verbal complaints	none	0
	occasional	0.5
	frequent	1
non-verbal complaints	none	0
	occasional	0.5
	frequent	1
down time	none	0
	0 to 60 minutes	0.5
	> 60 minutes	1
facial grimaces	none	0
	mild and/or infrequent	0.5
	severe and/or frequent	1
standing posture	normal	0
	mildly impaired	0.5
	distorted	1

Figure 21.12 The UAB Pain Behavior Scale

> **Challenge yourself**
>
> Create similar issue and debate commentaries for idiographic versus nomothetic, interviews, observations, and quantitative and qualitative data.

Total score = SUM for all 10 items

Interpretation: minimum score = 0; maximum score = 10

The higher the score, the more marked the pain-associated behaviour and the greater the level of impairment.

	Issue and debate tracker
Psychometrics	These types of measures tend to have had reliability and validity tests performed on them to make sure that they are measuring what they intend to measure and that they are stable over time. Both the McGill Pain Questionnaire and the Wong–Baker Scale have psychometric properties. These allow a meaningful comparison across groups of people so then pain can be discussed using standardised scores and descriptions. Both can be seen as valid measures of pain perception in adults (McGill) and children (Wong–Baker).
Generalisations from findings	Look at page 253 for an evaluation of the Brudvik et al (2016) study based on generalisations.

21.3.3 Managing and controlling pain

Patients can manage and control their pain levels in a variety of ways. These range from biological to cognitive and alternative techniques.

Biological treatment: biochemical

One of the main medical techniques used to control pain is the use of chemicals. Sarafino (2006) highlighted four main types available to patients.

- Peripherally active analgesics – these inhibit the production of certain neurochemicals that are produced as a result, for example, of tissue damage. Common examples of these drugs are aspirin and ibuprofen. Aspirin, for instance, reduces the experience of pain but also reduces inflammation that could be causing the pain.
- Centrally acting analgesics – these are good at reducing acute pain in the short term as they act directly on the central nervous system. Examples of these drugs are codeine and morphine.
- Local anaesthetics – these can be applied locally to the site of pain (or be injected) to give almost immediate relief. They block the nerve cells at the site of damage. An example of this type of drug is novocaine.
- Indirectly acting drugs – these are used for other conditions but can also help in pain management. For example, antidepressants can help reduce psychological aspects of depression but they can also help relieve pain.

Strength	Weakness
Techniques using chemicals are objective and biological and have been proven to work on organic pain.	There can be negative side effects.

Psychological treatments: cognitive strategies (attention diversion, non-pain imagery and cognitive redefinition)

A variety of cognitive strategies can be used to help alleviate and manage pain in patients. Cognitive behavioural therapy (CBT) can be used. The therapist needs to tackle the thinking behind the pain, the emotions involved with the pain, and the behaviour seen as a result of it. The therapist can use a variety of techniques for this. These include helping patients to reduce counterproductive strategies (eg changing strategies that are actually making the pain worse rather than better), giving them some skills training on how to cope, and training them to change their cognitions from negative to positive in terms of successful pain management.

Sarafino (2006) noted a range of other cognitive strategies that can be used with patients. These include the following.

- Attention diversion – this technique gets the patient to focus on something that is not linked to the pain in any way. This can include looking at a picture, singing a song, playing on a video console or having to focus on someone's voice. Distractors have to be relevant to the patient and be engrossing enough for that person. Hence, they have to be individually tailored.

- Non-pain imagery – this can be called guided imagery and involves patients creating a mental scene 'far removed' from the current state of pain. This could be a place that is pleasant (eg a beach) and the therapist has to guide patients through the scene to distract them from the pain. The therapist may ask about sights and sounds, for instance. The aim is to create a 'place' that cannot be linked to the pain being experienced.

Cognitive redefinition can also be used to help pain management. This is when patients can be told about what to expect, truthfully, about their pain but for them to redefine how they interpret their own pain experiences. When it comes to pain management, there are two ways that cognitive redefinition may help a patient.

- Coping statements – this technique allows patients to emphasise their own ability to tolerate pain. They may say to themselves "Come on, be brave, you can handle this!" or "This is going to hurt, but you are in control".

- Re-interpretative statements – this technique allows patients to help themselves negate any unpleasantness about their pain experiences. They may say to themselves "This is not the worst thing that will ever happen to me and it won't last long" or "Yes, this will hurt for a little while, but think of the long-term benefits".

Alternative treatments

- Acupuncture – this is an ancient Chinese practice of inserting special fine metal needles under the skin of the patient in areas chosen depending on the source of the pain. Once inserted, the needles are 'twirled' or stimulated electrically. There are reportedly hundreds of insertion points for the needles depending on what could be causing the pain or which area of the body is experiencing it.

- Transcutaneous electrical nerve stimulation (TENS) machines – these machines have electrodes that are placed either side of the source of pain. The TENS machine then sends a mild electrical current between the electrodes which, in theory, reduces the sensation of pain.

21.4.1 Sources of stress: the GAS model and effects of stress on health

Physiology of stress

The general adaptation syndrome (GAS) model (Selye, 1936)

Selye (1936) described the body's response to stress and began to explore the links between stress and illness. He induced stress in rats using stressors such as heat and fatigue. The rats showed the same physiological responses regardless of the nature of the stressor; they had enlarged adrenal glands and they developed stomach ulcers. Selye proposed that the body responded to any stressor by getting itself ready for action. This response has evolved to help the individual to deal with emergency situations such as fleeing physical danger. Selye identified three phases to the body's response to stress through which an individual passes if a stressor persists over time.

> **Challenge yourself**
>
> Find one study that supports psychological treatments for pain and one study that supports alternative treatments for pain.

> **Challenge yourself**
>
> To what extent do you feel that the best way to manage pain is through alternative treatments? Justify your answer.

> **Challenge yourself**
>
> Look at the issue and debate tracker table on page 254. Create similar issue and debate commentaries for application to everyday life, cultural differences, reductionism versus holism, determinism versus free will, idiographic versus nomothetic, and objective and subjective data.

21.4 Stress

1. Alarm reaction: the body's mechanisms for dealing with danger are activated. This reaction is based around the fight or flight mechanism in animals. Physiological reactions include respiration rate increasing, heart rate increasing, and blood pressure rising.

2. Resistance stage: the person struggles to cope with the stress and the body attempts to return to its previous physiological state. This happens if no more stress is experienced. However, the person is more vulnerable than before so if stress is experienced before returning to the previous state, the person will struggle to cope.

3. Exhaustion stage: if the stressor persists and the body cannot return to its previous state, physical resources become depleted, eventually leading to collapse.

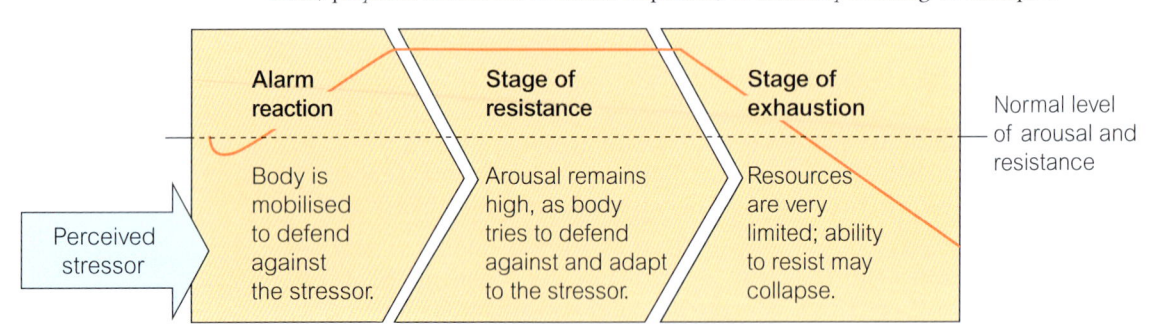

Figure 21.13 *GAS in three phases*

The physiological response to stress is controlled by two body systems.

- The autonomic nervous system is composed of two approximately antagonistic sub-systems, the sympathetic and parasympathetic branches. The autonomic nervous system acts rapidly to stimulate physiological changes such as breathing and heart rate as well as affecting the second element, the endocrine system.

- The endocrine system provides a slower communication route through the body using hormones released in response to signals from nerves or from other glands. In an emergency, the sympathetic branch of the autonomic nervous system responds quickly, preparing for 'fight or flight'. The sympathetic nervous system also sends impulses to the endocrine system, which responds by releasing hormones that enhance the preparation for action. This mechanism, which links the sympathetic nervous system to the adrenal medulla, is called the sympathetic adrenal medullary system.

Stress has a range of effects on health, including the following.

- Cardiovascular problems – these can include hypertension (high blood pressure), and atherosclerosis (the build-up of fat deposits in blood vessels), both of which increase the risk of having a heart attack.

- Gastrointestinal disorders – an increase in stomach acids can lead to ulcers and digestive problems; also, conditions such as irritable bowel syndrome can be made worse by stress.

Causes of stress

Life events (Holmes and Rahe, 1967)

Holmes and Rahe (1967) constructed a questionnaire called the Social Readjustment Rating Scale (SRRS), shown in Figure 21.14. The questionnaire is used to measure the amount of stress a person experiences over a certain amount of time (usually one year). Holmes and Rahe initially conducted research into how different life events are perceived in terms of how stressful they are. Each of the 43 life events were given a score out of 100, which were called the life change units

(LCUs). People simply had to add up all the LCUs they had scored over one year. This generated a total of LCUs that could be used as an indicator of the level of stress experienced. The researchers noted that people who scored more than 300 LCUs in a given year were much more likely to become ill due to the amount of stress they experienced.

The scale was created using the responses from 394 participants who were asked to rate the 43 life events. The life event of marriage was assigned a value of 500 and the participants were asked the following.

> 'The mechanics of rating are these: Event 1, Marriage, has been given an arbitrary value of 500. As you complete each of the remaining events think to yourself, "Is this event indicative of more or less readjustment than marriage?" "Would the readjustment take longer or shorter to accomplish?" If you decide the readjustment is more intense and protracted, then choose a proportionately larger number and place it in the blank directly opposite the event in the column marked "VALUES." If you decide the event represents less and shorter readjustment than marriage then indicate how much less by placing a proportionately smaller number in the opposite blank' (Holmes and Rahe, 1967: 213).

> **Challenge yourself**
>
> Explain at least one strength and one weakness of the SRRS to measure the causes of stress.

Rank	Life event	Mean value	Rank	Life event	Mean value
1	Death of spouse	100	23	Son or daughter leaving home	29
2	Divorce	73	24	Trouble with in-laws	29
3	Marital separation	65	25	Outstanding personal achievement	28
4	Jail term	63	26	Spouse begins or stops work	26
5	Death of close family member	63	27	Beginning or ending school	26
6	Personal injury or illness	53	28	Change in living conditions	25
7	Marriage	50	29	Revision of personal habits	24
8	Fired at work	47	30	Trouble with boss	23
9	Marital reconciliation	45	31	Change in work hours or conditions	20
10	Retirement	45	32	Change in residence	20
11	Change in health of family member	44	33	Change in schools	20
12	Pregnancy	40	34	Change in recreation	19
13	Sex difficulties	39	35	Change in church activities	19
14	Gain of new family member	39	36	Change in social activities	18
15	Business re-adjustment	39	37	Mortgage or loan less than $10 000	17
16	Change in financial state	38	38	Change in sleeping habits	16
17	Death of a close friend	37	39	Change in number of family get-togethers	15
18	Change to a different line of work	36	40	Change in eating habits	15
19	Change in number of arguments with spouse	35	41	Vacation	13
20	Mortgage over $10 000	31	42	Christmas	12
21	Foreclosure on mortgage or loan	30	43	Minor violations of the law	11
22	Change in responsibilities at work	29			

Figure 21.14 The SRRS questionnaire
Source: Holmes and Rahe (1967: 216)

Work (Chandola et al, 2008)

Chandola *et al* (2008) wanted to investigate which biological and behavioural factors link work stress to coronary heart disease (CHD). They ran a seven-phase study using civil servants from Whitehall, London (UK). A total of 10 308 participants started the study. The phases were:

1. 1985–1988 (recruitment)
2. 1989–1990 (postal questionnaire)
3. 1991–1993 (postal questionnaire + clinical examination)
4. 1995 (postal questionnaire)
5. 1997–1999 (postal questionnaire + clinical examination)
6. 2001 (postal questionnaire)
7. 2002–2004 (postal questionnaire + clinical examination).

Work stress was measured by a job-strain questionnaire. Participants were classified as being under work stress if they reported job strain, felt job control was low and felt socially isolated at work. Various follow-up measures were taken:

- fatal CHD and non-fatal CHD episodes
- biological risk factors: waist circumference, serum triglycerides, blood pressure, antihypertensive medication, morning rise in cortisol, low heart-rate variability
- behavioural risk factors: alcohol, smoking, activity, diet.

By phase 7 there were 9692 participants still alive and 6484 attended the final clinical examination. The results showed that greater reports of work stress were associated with higher risk of CHD. This was true for fatal CHD, myocardial infarction and definite angina. There was an age-related effect too. Participants who were younger showed a much stronger link between work stress and CHD. Those who reported greater work stress also had poorer diets and engaged in much less physical activity. All of this led the researchers to conclude '… cumulative work stress is a risk factor for CHD…' (Chandola *et al*, 2008: 643).

> **Challenge yourself**
>
> To what extent do you feel that the findings of the study are culturally biased? Justify your decision.

Strength	Weakness
The study was longitudinal so the researchers could track developmental changes (to do with stress and work) over time.	Stress was measured using a self-report technique so some of the workers may have given socially desirable answers, which could reduce the validity of findings.

Type A personality (Friedman and Rosenman, 1974)

Friedman and Rosenman (1974) observed that their coronary patients tended to sit on the edge of their seat, leaping up frequently to enquire how much longer they would be kept waiting for their appointments. The possibility of a connection between the heart conditions and the tense, frenetic behaviour of these individuals led to the proposal of 'hurry sickness', later renamed 'type A behaviour' (Friedman and Rosenman, 1974).

Type A individuals tend to be highly competitive, aggressive, impatient, and hostile, with a strong urge for success. Their behaviour tends to be goal-directed and performed at speed. In contrast, people with type B behaviour are relatively 'laid back', lacking the urgency and drive typical of type A individuals. Some individuals do not fall clearly into either category and are termed type X. The risk of stress-related illnesses, such as coronary heart disease, is greater for type A individuals than for type B due to the physiological strains placed on the body.

> **Challenge yourself**
>
> Look at the issue and debate tracker table on page 266. Create similar issue and debate commentaries for individual and situational explanations, reductionism versus free will, determinism versus free will, idiographic versus nomothetic, and generalisations from findings.

21.4.2 Measures of stress

Biological measures

Recording devices for heart rate and brain function (fMRI)

Wang *et al* (2005) used a functional magnetic resonance imaging (fMRI) scanning device to examine cerebral blood flow in participants under psychological stress. The perfusion fMRI uses arterial spin-labelling to 'follow' the pathway of stress. The study group consisted of 32 participants, 25 of whom (of average age 24.1 years; and 12 female) formed the experimental group. The other seven participants formed a control group. Within the experimental group, two participants were eliminated for having incomplete behavioural data and abnormally high salivary cortisol. None of the experimental group had a history of neurologic or psychiatric disease.

High-stress and low-stress tasks were devised as follows.

- For the high-stress tasks, mental arithmetic was chosen. The participants had to perform serial subtraction of 13 from a 4-digit number given to them. They had to respond verbally. As the task progressed, they were prompted to be quicker with their responses and to restart once an error occurred.

- Low-stress tasks were always given *before* the high-stress task. Participants had to count backwards from 1000 aloud.

These were the measures taken.

- Perfusion fMRI – there were scans in total, lasting eight minutes each, and then an anatomical scan for six minutes after all tasks had been completed.

- Self-report measures of stress and anxiety (on a scale of 1–9) were recorded as soon as participants entered the scanner, then after each scan had taken place.

- Salivary cortisol was also taken as soon as participants entered the scanner then after each scan had taken place. This was a two-minute procedure using a cotton swab.

- On a scale of 1–9, all participants had to rate effort, frustration and task difficulty after the low-stress then the high-stress tasks.

Heart rate was also taken.

The average subjective ratings, heart rate, and salivary cortisol are shown in Figure 21.15.

The ratings for the two tasks are shown in the Table 21.9.

Table 21.9 *Self-report of effort, difficulty, and frustration during the low- and high-stress tasks (scale 1–9)*

Stress	Effort	Difficulty	Frustration
Low-stress task	4.4 (0.5)	3.4 (0.4)	3.4 (0.4)
High-stress task	7.0 (0.3)	6.6 (0.3)	6.1 (0.4)

Data are presented as mean (standard error).
Source: Wang *et al* (2005: 17 806)

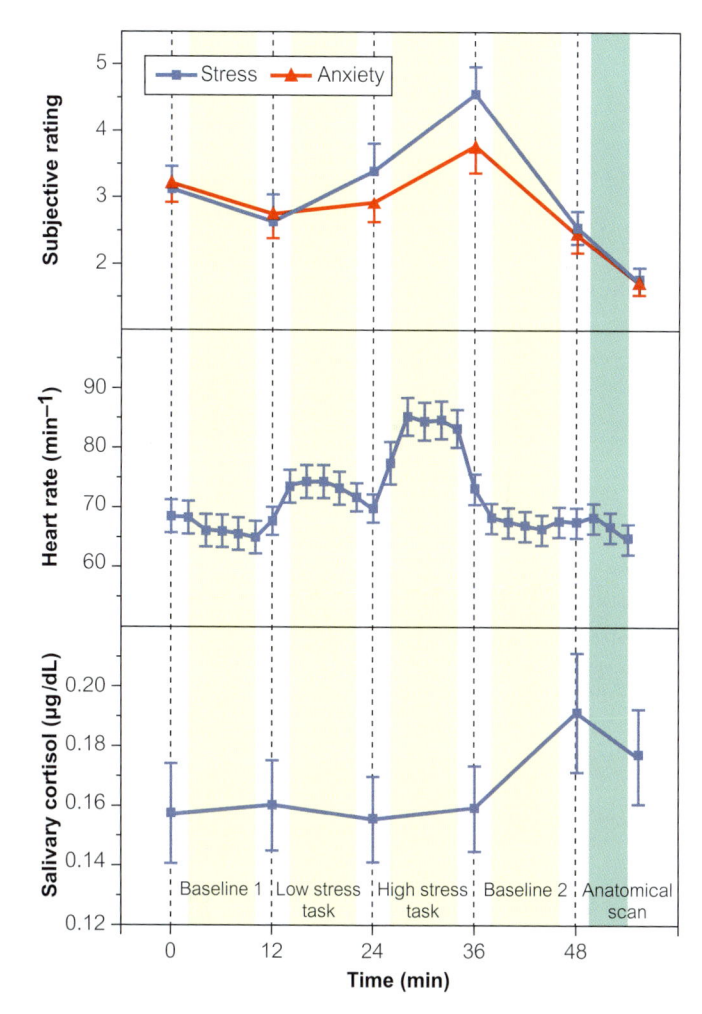

Figure 21.15 *Average subjective ratings of stress and anxiety, heart rate, and salivary-cortisol level during the time course of the stress experiment. Time 0 indicates the start of MRI experiments. The pale columns represent the perfusion fMRI scans (each 8 minutes) and the dark column represents the anatomical scan. Behavioural ratings and salivary-cortisol samples were taken between scans, whereas heart rate was continuously recorded every 2 minutes. Note that the peak in salivary-cortisol level lags behind other measures. The error bars indicate standard error.*

Source: Wang *et al* (2005: 17 805)

Overall, the subjective stress ratings mirrored the tasks given to them. The salivary cortisol peaked ten minutes after the end of the high-stress task, which was expected due to the time lag between physiological and subsequent behavioural measures. All of the measures of the tasks were significantly higher in the high-stress task than the low-stress task.

The main results for the fMRI scans were as follows.

- Cerebral blood flow was positively correlated with subjective stress ratings in the ventral right prefrontal cortex and left insula/putamen area.

- The ventral right prefrontal cortex along with the right insula/putamen and anterior cingulate showed sustained activity after the high-stress task.

- Variations in the baseline cerebral blood flow in the ventral right prefrontal cortex and right orbitofrontal cortex were found to correlate with changes in salivary-cortisol levels and heart rate caused by the stress tasks.

Strength	Weakness
The measurement technique is objective and scientific, meaning that no interpretation is needed and making the findings more valid.	The act of going through an fMRI may have an effect on cerebral blood flow which could be a confounding variable – this could cause more stress.

Sample tests of salivary cortisol

Evans and Wener (2007) used three indices of stress to examine what happens to commuters during rush hour on a crowded train. Participants were 139 adult commuters (54% male) who took part in the study during their commute from New Jersey to Manhattan. All had to have been taking this route for at least 12 months to qualify for participation. Three measures were taken from each commuter.

- A saliva sample was taken at the end of the journey and then analysed for cortisol levels.

- Motivation was measured by persistence with a proofreading task and the number of errors spotted.

- Mood was measured using two semantic differential items (a 5-point scale was used to rate mood from 'carefree' to 'burdened' and from 'contented' to 'frustrated').

The researchers measured carriage density (by dividing the number of passengers in a car with the number of seats available) and seat density (by dividing the number of people sitting in the same row by the number of seats on that row). It was only seat density that had a significant effect on all three stress measures. The higher the density, the higher the cortisol, the fewer the errors detected and the more negative the mood.

Strength	Weakness
The Evans and Wener (2007) study has some ecological validity as the train journey was something that participants did on a regular basis.	Some of the measures were subjective via the self-report techniques so the researchers could not know whether the train journey was causing the stress, or something else was causing it.

Psychological measures

Self-report questionnaires (Holmes and Rahe, 1967; Friedman and Rosenman, 1974)

For the Holmes and Rahe (1967) scale, see pages 256–257.

There is no set self-report measure that was used by Friedman and Rosenman (1974) but a type A structured interview has been used in some studies. However, the following was noted by Friedman and Rosenman (1974) about how to differentiate between type A and type B behaviour and it would have formed any self-report measure on the topic.

1. Type A people will forcefully note certain words in their speech and then finish off sentences quickly.
2. Type A people are always moving, walking, and eating rapidly.
3. Type A people feel impatient in most scenarios they encounter. One example is that they might try to finish other people's sentences.
4. Type A people tend to be polyphasic: they frequently want to be doing two or more things at the same time.
5. Type A people will always direct a conversation towards things they like or that intrigue them.
6. Type A people will feel guilty for relaxing.
7. Type A people do not appreciate their surroundings.
8. Type A people will attempt to do more and more in less and less time.
9. If two type A people meet they do not show compassion for their similarities but challenge each other to 'be the best'.
10. Type A people might use repetitive gestures.
11. Type A people will give themselves praise for good work just because they have done the work faster than others have, rather than based on its quality.

> **Challenge yourself**
>
> Create a questionnaire using a Likert-type scale that would measure the degree to which someone is a type A personality.

> **Challenge yourself**
>
> Look at the issue and debate tracker table on page 266. Create similar issue and debate commentaries for questionnaires, psychometrics, subjective and objective data, validity, and reliability.

21.4.3 Managing stress

Psychological therapy: biofeedback

Biofeedback is a technique that attempts to get people to take control of their own physiological state. Usually, people are connected to devices that measure key physiological processes such as heart rate, blood pressure, or muscle tension. The equipment gives individuals instant and continuous readings of these key physiological measures. The idea is that individuals take voluntary control of their physiology using the idea of rewards. If people are attempting to reduce their resting heart rate and they can see that deeper breathing and relaxation is doing this instantly then they are more likely to want to do the same next time. Sarafino (2006) noted that there is a lot of evidence for the usefulness of biofeedback techniques for stress-related illnesses such as tension headaches, even with children.

Biofeedback

Budzynski and Stoyva (1969) investigated the role of biofeedback in muscle relaxation. They developed an instrument that did the following.

- It continuously tracked the level of muscle action potential.
- It presented the patient with instant feedback from a given muscle.

- The information was given as a tone that varied in pitch depending on the level of muscle activity.
- The feedback loop could be adjusted to shape deep muscle responses.
- The instrument measured the performance of an individual in terms of relaxation attempts.

The researchers trialled the instrument on 15 people to see whether operant conditioning via information feedback would shape muscle relaxation. The participants were split into three groups.

1. The experimental group – participants in this group were told that the pitch would vary depending on the level of muscle tension in the forehead. They were told to keep the tone as low as possible.
2. The constant low tone group – members of this group were given irrelevant feedback because the tone always remained low. They were told to relax their forehead muscles as much as possible and that the constant low tone would help them to do this.
3. The silent group – no feedback was given to participants in this group and they were simply told to relax their forehead muscles.

Participants had to lie on a bed in a dimly lit room. There were 20 trials per session, which were automatically sequenced so that there was no experimenter interaction with participants during the trials.

Figure 21.16 shows the performances of the groups over the five sessions they all experienced.

These were the results in terms of decrease in muscle action potential from baseline to the end of the trial.

- The experimental group had decreased by 50%.
- The constant tone group by 28%.
- The silent group by 24%.

It would appear that using correct biofeedback can help people relax muscles more efficiently.

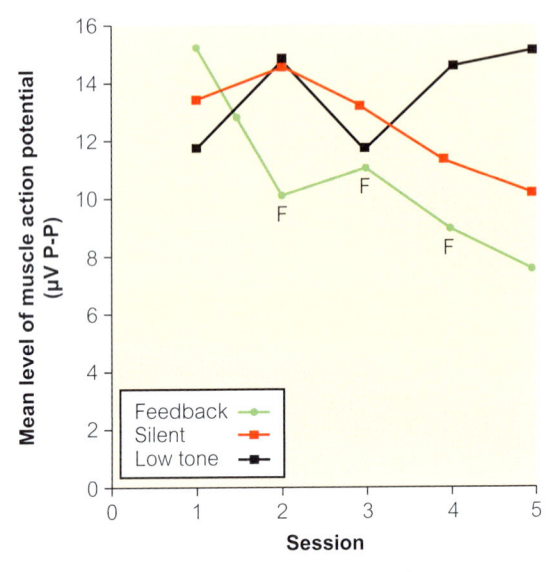

Figure 21.16 Mean levels of frontalis muscle action potential levels in feedback, no feedback (silent), and irrelevant feedback (low tone) groups. Each group consisted of five subjects.

Notes: 'F' indicates a feedback session; uV P-P signifies microvolts peak-to-peak.

Source: Budzynski and Stoyva (1969: 233)

Strength	Weakness
The procedure was standardised so that it could easily be replicated by other researchers to test for reliability. The feedback was standardised for each group.	It may be difficult to make generalisations because there were only five participants in each group and they might not represent a wider population.
The study showed that using correct biofeedback has good application for health professionals, especially in treating people with tension headaches.	

Use of imagery to reduce stress

Imagery can be used to reduce stress: mental imagery is used to distract people from thinking about any stressors they have. In addition, they may be taught relaxation techniques to help with the distraction. These may include visual imagery to take them 'away from their stressors' and deep-breathing exercises or even yoga and meditation. People using mental imagery will have to imagine a variety of situations that have nothing to do with the stresses they are currently experiencing. Ensuring that people are not focusing on current stressors allows them to calm down and take control of their own physiological state.

KEY STUDY: Bridge et al (1988)

Context and main theories/explanations

Previous research had attempted to find a link between stressful life events and cancer, but there had been no consistent results. However, it appears to be a logical argument that the process of being diagnosed and/or treated for cancer is stressful. In addition, some research had shown that the use of relaxation techniques and imagery had a positive effect on hypertension patients and people living with cancer.

Aim and hypotheses

Bridge et al investigated the effectiveness of a controlled randomised trial using relaxation and imagery with women who had Stage I or II breast cancer.

Design

Participants

The sample consisted of women who had been treated by either mastectomy or breast conservation for early breast cancer. Initially the sample was 183 but through refusals and some people being re-assessed as having late-stage breast cancer, the final sample was 139. All participants were having a six-week course of radiotherapy, were under 70 years of age, and could understand English. All participants had received a minimum of one radiotherapy session before the study.

Measures

There were two main measures.

1. Profile of Mood States questionnaire – this is a 65-item measure that has subscales for depression, vigour, fatigue, anger, and confusion. A total score is calculated.
2. Leeds General Scales for the Self-assessment of Depression and Anxiety – this has 12 items (six for depression and six for anxiety) and they are rated on a 4-point scale. An overall score of 7 or above indicates the presence of depression and/or anxiety.

Procedure

This was an experiment using a longitudinal design. The participants were told that the study was about investigating ways to alleviate stress during radiotherapy. They were told they would be randomly assigned to one of three groups.

1. Control group (n = 48) – participants in this group were encouraged to talk about themselves.
2. Relaxation group (n = 47) – members of this group were taught to concentrate on individual muscle groups.
3. Relaxation and imagery group (n = 44) – these participants were instructed in the same way as the other groups, but were also taught to imagine a peaceful scene of their own choice to aid relaxation.

All participants were reassured that refusal to participate would not affect their radiotherapy. The two relaxation groups were given a tape recording of instructions so that they could perform it at home every day for 15 minutes. They had 'official' sessions once per week for six weeks. Improvement in mood, depression, and anxiety were assessed using the measures noted above.

Results, findings, and conclusions

Initial scores on these measures did not differ between the three groups. However, at six weeks the mood scores were significantly lower in the two intervention groups with the women in the combined group showing the more favourable mood disturbance scores.

Table 21.10 shows the total mood disturbance scores at the initial time point and after six weeks.

This indicates that relaxation combined with imagery had the only reduction in overall mood disturbance scores.

There was also an effect of age of participant on mood disturbance scores. Table 21.11 shows these data.

When subscales were examined, those in either of the relaxation groups reported less tension, less depression, and less overall mood disturbance compared to the control group if their age was 55 years or above. Therefore, it would appear that using mental imagery in conjunction with relaxation can help to alleviate the stresses involved in breast cancer management.

Main discussion points

- The research team noted that the effectiveness of the relaxation plus imagery intervention could be due to the 'simplicity' of imagery. As the participant had to choose their own pleasant scene, it meant it was accessible to all. It was noted that during these sessions many of the participants smiled, which showed they were engaging with the pleasantness. Each participant could easily recall their pleasant scene. Other types of imagery could be aggressive, with patients visualising the symbolic destruction of cancer cells, which can be disturbing.
- The greater success with older women in the sample could be explained by them working less than the younger group and having fewer commitments. Therefore, it was hypothesised that they had more time to practise the relaxation and imagery.

Evaluation

- The study has good application as it shows that the technique works over time, meaning that practitioners can ensure that patients work through the entire programme. As the outcome of the study was positive, it could be used on other woman with breast cancer as part of their care package. It could also be tried with other types of cancer and other life-threatening conditions.

Table 21.10 Mean scores on profile of mood states at beginning and end of treatment (SD in parantheses)

Profile of mood states	Relaxation group (n = 39)	Relaxation plus imagery group (n = 43)	Controls (n = 46)
Tension:			
Initial	11.2 (7.0)	11.3 (7.9)	10.6 (7.0)
Six weeks	9.5 (7.7)	8.8 (5.0)	10.7 (8.1)
Depression:			
Initial	7.4 (7.2)	8.3 (9.2)	5.5 (6.5)
Six weeks	6.9 (8.5)	5.8 (5.2)	7.5 (10.8)
Vigour:			
Initial	18.5 (7.5)	16.6 (7.7)	17.3 (6.6)
Six weeks	18.5 (6.3)	17.4 (8.3)	18.9 (7.9)
Fatigue:			
Initial	9.2 (8.1)	8.7 (7.1)	8.7 (6.5)
Six weeks	11.9 (8.5)	10.4 (8.0)	11.9 (8.0)
Anger:			
Initial	7.9 (6.0)	7.8 (6.9)	5.6 (5.2)
Six weeks	7.8 (8.3)	5.9 (4.4)	5.5 (6.4)
Confusion:			
Initial	7.5 (4.9)	6.8 (5.4)	6.8 (4.2)
Six weeks	7.3 (5.0)	5.7 (4.1)	7.0 (5.2)
Total mood disturbance:			
Initial	61.7 (31.2)	59.6 (34.5)	54.4 (26.0)
Six weeks	61.9 (34.8)	53.9 (27.4)	61.4 (38.7)

Table 21.11 Mean scores on profile of mood states at end of treatment in the three study groups stratified by age

Profile of mood states	Relaxation group		Relaxation plus imagery group		Controls	
	Age < 55 (n = 29)	Age ≥ 55 (n = 15)	Age < 55 (n = 17)	Age ≥ 55 (n = 23)	Age < 55 (n = 22)	Age ≥ 55 (n = 24)
Tension	9.1	10.3	9.4	8.4	7.9	13.2
Depression	6.6	7.6	6.6	5.2	4.1	10.8
Vigour	18.0	19.4	20.5	15.0	17.7	20.0
Fatigue	12.6	10.6	13.7	7.9	10.9	12.8
Anger	8.8	5.9	6.9	5.1	4.9	6.0
Confusion	7.3	7.1	6.1	5.4	5.6	8.3
Total mood disturbance	62.3	60.9	63.1	47.0	51.0	71.0

- An independent groups design was used meaning that some individual differences (eg participant variable) may have affected the outcome measures as well as the technique. These could include motivation, previous experiences with cancer, knowledge about others who have also been through radiotherapy, or other cancer treatments. By chance, there could have been more motivated people in the relaxation and imagery group, or they could have been better at using imagery. This might mean that it was not the intervention directly affecting the mood measures.

- As it was an experiment using a longitudinal design, there is a baseline measurement that allows for a direct comparison of DV measures over time. This can allow an assessment if an intervention, for example, is working and/or when it began to work.

Preventing stress: three phases of stress inoculation training

Some techniques can be used that allow people not to be affected by stress and stressors. These are called preventive measures. One that has generated a great deal of research and following by therapists is stress inoculation therapy, which was proposed by Meichenbaum (1998). This therapy has three stages.

1. Conceptualisation phase – this is when a relationship is built between the trainer and clients. The trainer will educate clients about the nature and impact that stress has on their lives. The trainer may even show how clients may be currently making their stress worse without them even knowing they are doing it. Clients are then encouraged to see perceived stressors as problems to be solved rather than as a negative experience. They are introduced to different coping mechanisms and strategies they can then use. They are also taught to break down stressors into short-term, intermediate and long-term coping goals.

2. Skill acquisition and rehearsal phase – this is when the elements from stage 1 have been taught and clients have to put them into practice. The skills are initially practised with the trainer in the clinic but then clients are encouraged to try them in the real world. Some of the coping mechanisms could include relaxation training, cognitive restructuring, interpersonal communication skills and using social support to help clients in times of need.

3. Application and follow-through phase – this is when there are opportunities for clients to apply all of the coping skills to increasing levels of stressors. Additional techniques, such as imagery, modelling, role playing and rehearsal, are used in the form of 'personal experiments' so that clients can show that they can cope with any level of stressor. These help to consolidate the skills they have already learned. They are also given follow-up booster sessions to ensure that the entire process is working.

The whole technique is flexible and can be a simple 20-minute session for people who are just about to go into surgery, or 40 one-hour weekly sessions for people who cannot cope with any level of stress.

Test yourself

Explain at least one strength and one weakness of stress inoculation training. Make sure one of your points is about long-term effectiveness.

Challenge yourself

Look at the issue and debate tracker on the next page. Create similar issue and debate commentaries for determinism versus free will, individual and situational explanations, and generalisations from findings.

	Issue and debate tracker
Application to everyday life	Both the Budzynski and Stoyva (1969) and the Bridge *et al* (1988) studies have good application. Read the evaluation sections for these in this book. In addition, stress inoculation training can be used in the workplace to help employees deal with the stresses involved in working in an organisation. This training can be part of an appraisal system or can become part of the 'culture' of the organisation to ensure that employees know how to manage stress at work.
Ethics	The very nature of research into managing stress means that people are stressed during it at some point – otherwise there would be no need to manage it. In the Budzynski and Stoyva study there was additional stress of a tone playing that would only become comfortable once the person could control their muscles. This could have initially *increased* stress in participants. The study by Bridge *et al* highlights one of the moral dilemmas researchers face when conducting studies about managing stress. The findings showed that the imagery (and relaxation) group were managing stress much better than the control. However, the control group were still made up of people with cancer and they had been prevented for utilising techniques that probably would have helped them cope better. Placebo/control groups are needed in research but at an ethical and moral cost.

21.5 Health promotion

21.5.1 Strategies for promoting health

Fear arousal

The idea behind fear arousal is that if you 'scare people enough' they will change their thoughts and behaviour. Roberts and Russell (2002) noted that while fear-arousing methods may be effective, there are certain factors that can affect whether the person the message is aimed at does follow its advice. These are:

- the unpleasantness of the fear-arousing message
- the probability that whatever the message is warning about will occur if the person does not follow the advice given
- the perceived effectiveness of the recommended action portrayed in the message.

Therefore, ideally, the message should be relatively unpleasant; people must believe that what it is warning about will happen to them and that any 'evasive' action will be effective.

Fear arousal using varying messages

Janis and Feshbach (1953) showed three groups of participants a film about dental hygiene. Each group received either a strong fear message, a moderate fear message or a minimal fear message.

The group who received the minimal fear message showed the highest level of agreement with the advice (36%) compared to the strong fear group (8%). Therefore, the researchers reported that only minimal fear is effective.

Providing information: giving information so people know how to improve their health

'The Angina Plan' (Lewin *et al*, 2002)

Lewin *et al* (2002) assessed the effectiveness of 'The Angina Plan', a cognitive-behavioural disease management programme. Produced for patients newly diagnosed with angina pectoris, 'The Angina Plan' was a 70-page workbook and audio-taped relaxation programme. It contained information about:

- angina
- the role of frightening thoughts and misconceptions about the triggering adrenaline
- hyperventilation and panic attacks.

> **Ask yourself**
>
> What do you think are the best ways in which we can promote healthy eating?

> **Challenge yourself**
>
> Find out more about the Janis and Feshbach (1953) study. What was presented to each group?

Before patients took the book and audio-tape away, they were given information that tackled any misconceptions they had about angina pectoris. The audio-tape was to be used for 20 minutes per day. A nurse followed up the patients at weeks 1, 4, 8, and 12 after began the programme.

Surgeries in York (UK) were approached to take part in the study. Patients who were recruited were randomly assigned to a group following 'The Angina Plan' or an educational session led by a practice nurse. The sample consisted of 142 patients. There were no significant differences in baseline measures. At six months, however, patients following 'The Angina Plan' showed a greater reduction in anxiety, depression, the frequency of angina, the use of glyceryl trinitrate, and physical limitations. They were also more likely to have changed their diet and increased their daily walking distance. Therefore, it would seem that a carefully planned intervention programme of providing information alongside self-relaxation techniques can help people with angina pectoris.

Strength	Weakness
The study has good application – following 'The Angina Plan' was successful, which means other surgeries and health authorities can use it too.	Only surgeries in York were involved. It may be difficult to generalise beyond this geographical area as it could be unique.

Sarafino (2006) noted that one way in which people can engage in healthy behaviour is through information. This helps people make decisions about their own lifestyles. There are three main ways in which information can be provided:

- Mass media (eg television, radio, magazines, and newspapers) can be used. One popular approach is for health services and the government to inform the general population about the negative consequences of certain health-related behaviours such as smoking, and drinking alcohol. The following points should be considered:

  - This method appears to have limited success as many people misunderstand the messages. This is especially true if people are not all that motivated to change their behaviour anyway.

  - If people are motivated to change behaviour then this method of providing information can be useful.

  Sarafino (2006) gave the example of 'Cable Quit', a television show that helped people to prepare to quit unhealthy behaviours by giving out information from the first day they decided to quit. Around 17% of people had still quit a year after watching the programmes.

- The internet – there are thousands of websites that promote healthy behaviour and allow people to track their own progress and meet others online to help motivate them to change. An advantage is that there is a wealth of information for people to look at to see *how* they can change. However, not all information will be correct or checked by health professionals.

- Medical settings – having information displayed in a doctor's surgery or office might make people believe the messages more. As the information is in a professional setting, it could receive instant respect.

Challenge yourself

To what extent do you think that the findings from the study are culturally biased? Justify your answer.

Challenge yourself

Look at the issue and debate tracker table on page 275. Create similar issue and debate commentaries for individual and situational explanations, longitudinal studies, objective and subjective data, and ethics.

21.5.2 Health promotion in schools and worksites

Schools

Schools have a good opportunity to promote healthy living to students. Lessons where students are taught about the benefits of healthy living can be part of any curriculum.

Healthy eating at school

Tapper *et al* (2003) employed three techniques to increase healthy eating (with a focus on eating fruit and vegetables) in children at school.

- Taste exposure – the more a child tastes a novel food, the more the child learns to like the taste.
- Modelling – watching a role model eat certain foods can have an impact on whether a child is likely to imitate the behaviour.
- Rewards – when used appropriately, rewards can be useful in altering behaviour. Using them can be beneficial when: they are highly desirable; they are contingent on performance; and they convey a message that they are gained for desirable behaviours.

The researchers' initial study took place in a home environment. Participants were children five or six years old who were identified as fussy eaters by their parents or carers. There were four different intervention methods, which were:

- fruit and vegetable presentation only
- rewarded taste exposure
- peer modelling
- peer modelling with rewards.

The peer modelling was based around a video featuring the 'Food Dudes'. These characters were children who were slightly older than the participants and who gained super powers from eating fruit and vegetables. They were in battle against the 'Junk Punks' who wanted to take over the planet by destroying all fruit and vegetables. By doing this, the 'Junk Punks' would stop humans getting their 'Life Force' foods of fruit and vegetables. In addition, rewards (stickers, pens, erasers, etc) could be gained for eating set targets of fruit and vegetables. The peer modelling with rewards group showed dramatic increases in consumption of fruit and vegetables. Prior to the intervention, participants would eat only 4% of fruit presented to them and 1% of vegetables. After the intervention this rose to 100% for fruit and 83% for vegetables. A follow-up check showed that this had been sustained even when participants had not watched the video any more or received any of the rewards.

The researchers then produced a nursery school version of the 'Food Dudes' with characters called Jarvis and Jess. This had a major impact on the younger children targeted, with an increase from 30% to 71% for fruit consumption. This was being maintained at follow-up 15 months after the intervention. A similar increase was seen for vegetables (from 34% to 87% consumption) and this was also maintained at follow-up.

A further study was carried out at a primary school in North Wales. The intervention process happened as described above. At break time, participants were allowed to choose whatever food they wanted. The options included fruit and vegetables but also chocolate bars, cakes, and crisps. Fruit consumption rose from 28% to 59% while vegetable consumption rose from 8% to 32%. The number of other snacks being chosen fell.

Finally, the research team proposed a whole-school programme using the idea of 'Food Dudes'. Designed so that it could easily be implemented by school staff, this programme featured the elements described in Figure 21.17.

A variety of schools trialled the whole-school programme and all reported significant increases in participants' consumption of fruit and vegetables at break times. The researchers gave three reasons as to why the programme was so effective.

- Children discovered for themselves the intrinsic rewards of eating fruit and vegetables.
- The programme changed the culture of the school to one where it supports the eating of fruit and vegetables as being 'the norm'.

- A Food Dude video containing six 6-minute adventure episodes.
- A set of Food Dude rewards.
- A set of letters from the Food Dudes. These provide praise and encouragement and remind children of the reward contingencies.
- A Food Dude homepack to encourage children to eat fruit and vegetables in the home context as well as at school.
- A staff manual and staff briefing video to help teachers implement the programme correctly.
- A set of education support materials to help teachers meet curriculum targets using the Food Dude theme.

Figure 21.17 *The 'Food Dude' programme*
Source: Tapper *et al* (2003: 20)

- It changed the self-concept of children: they could label themselves as 'fruit and vegetable eaters'.

Strength	Weakness
The study has good application – the programme was successful, so other schools may want to introduce it.	Following the programme is time consuming. The commitment needed to make it work cannot be guaranteed in a school environment due to other pressures.

Worksites

Reducing accidents at work: token economy

Fox *et al* (1987) reported on the potential long-term effects of a token economy scheme on safety performances in open-pit mines. The token economy was based around the idea of trading stamps that could be redeemed at various stores in the locality. The employees earned stamps for:

- working without lost-time injuries
- being a member of a work group where all members had no lost-time injuries
- not being involved in equipment-damaging accidents
- making appropriate safety suggestions
- unusual behaviour that prevented an injury or an accident.

The employees could lose stamps:

- if they or a member of their group were injured
- for causing equipment damage
- for failing to report injuries or accidents.

The implementation of the token economy scheme had an immediate effect. There was a large reduction in the number of days lost from work due to injuries. There were also reductions in the number of lost-time injuries and the costs of accidents. Figures 21.18–21.20 show how these improvements were sustained for years after the scheme began.

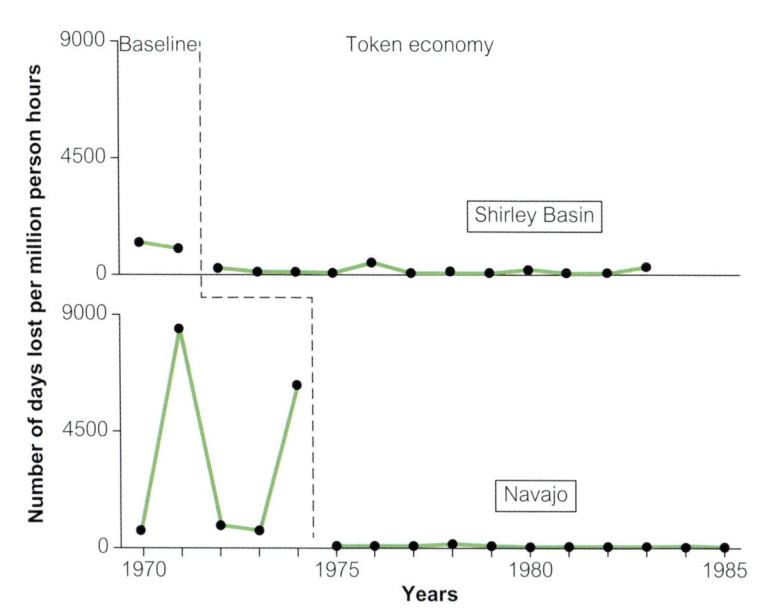

Figure 21.18 The yearly number of days lost from work, per million person hours worked, because of work-related injuries

Source: Fox et al (1987: 220)

> **Challenge yourself**
>
> Look at the issue and debate tracker table on page 275. Create similar issue and debate commentaries for use of children in research, experiments, longitudinal studies, quantitative and qualitative data, and generalisations from findings.

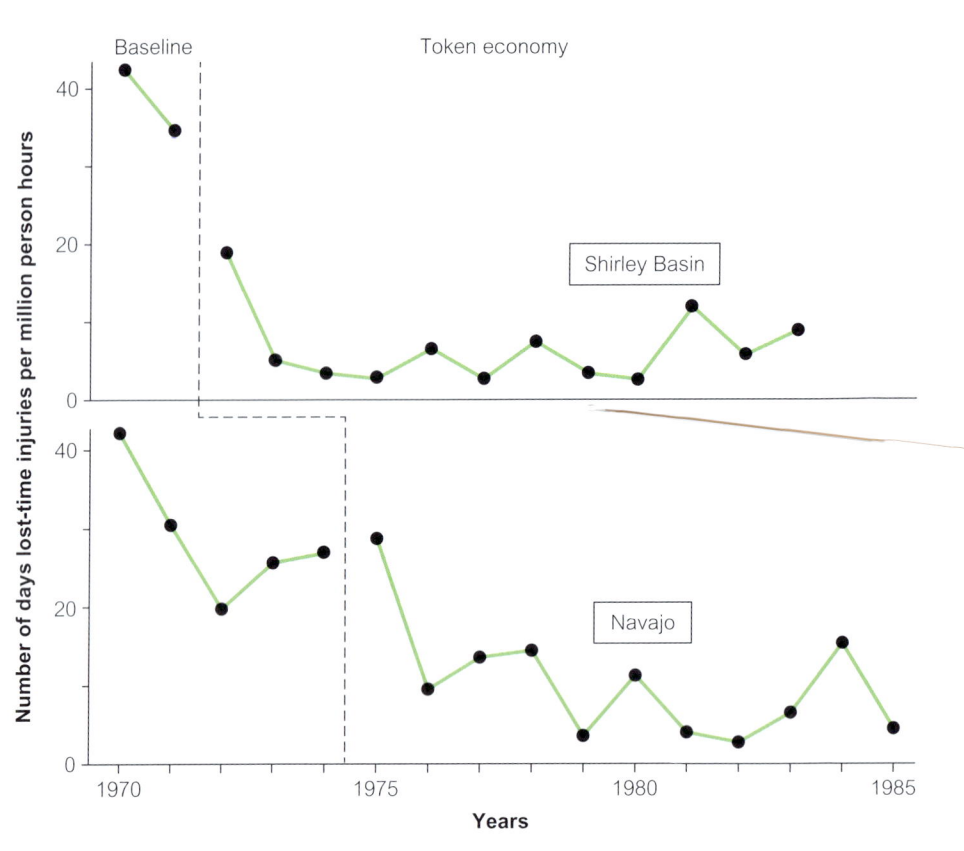

Figure 21.19 The yearly number of work-related injuries, per million person hours worked, requiring one or more days lost from work
Source: Fox et al (1987: 221)

> **Test yourself**
>
> Explain at least one strength and one weakness of the study by Fox *et al*.

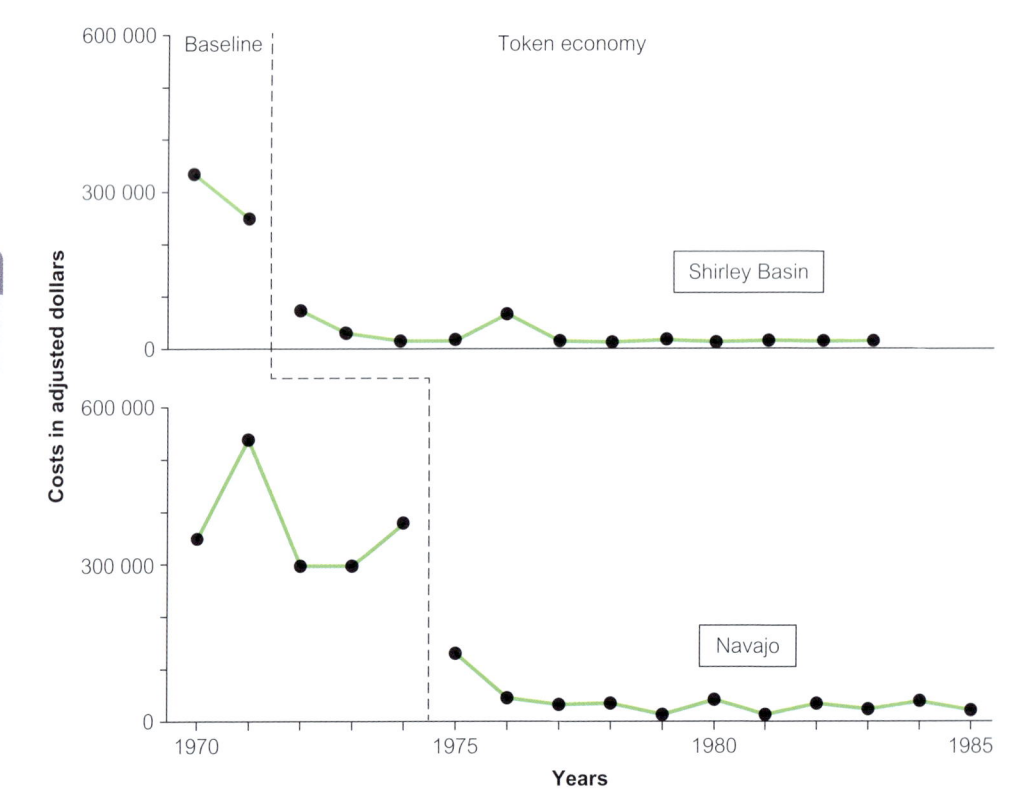

Figure 21.20 The yearly costs, adjusted for hours worked and inflation, resulting from accidents and injur[ies]
Source: Fox et al (1987: 222)

21.5.3 Individual factors in changing health beliefs

Unrealistic optimism: reason for disregarding positive health advice

Weinstein (1980) ran two studies that examined whether college students have unrealistic optimism about future life events.

Study 1

In this study 258 college students had to estimate their own chances of experiencing 42 different life events compared to their classmates. These were both positive (eg owning your own home, living past 80 years of age, receiving a good job offer after graduation) and negative (eg attempting suicide, being sterile, dropping out of college). Participants rated their own chances to be above average when the event was positive but below average when the event was negative. Factors such as the degree of desirability, the perceived probability of an event occurring, past personal experience, and perceived controllability appeared to influence this 'optimistic bias'.

Study 2

Students had to list what factors they thought influenced their chances of experiencing eight future life events. When these lists were read by a second group of students, the amount of unrealistic optimism shown by this group for the same eight life events decreased significantly. Therefore, as soon as people begin to compare their likelihood with what others' perceive, any optimistic bias is reduced significantly.

Positive psychology: defining positive psychology

Three focuses: pleasant life, good life, meaningful life

- The pleasant life is reached when we learn to appreciate and like basic human pleasures like some form of companionship, loving the natural environment, and attending to our bodily needs. This can be based on an assessment of our past, present, and future selves.
- The good life is reached when we discover our uniqueness and then use this to enhance our lives. This is all part of our self-esteem.
- The meaningful life is when we have reached a deep sense of fulfilment by using our uniqueness for the greater needs of others.

According to Seligman *et al* (2005), there are six virtues. Between them these virtues have 24 characters strengths that help us on our journey towards a pleasant, good, and meaningful life.

Positive psychology (Seigman *et al*, 2005)

All of the virtues and character strengths were part of the Seligman *et al* study to test the impact that positive psychology has on people. A total of 577 people were recruited using opportunity sampling from visitors to a website about positive psychology. The participants knew that they would be completing one of six exercises if they agreed to participate. One exercise was a placebo. An exercise was randomly assigned to them. They also knew that if they completed all follow-up sessions (the last one six months after their exercise) they could win $500 or $100. These were the six exercises.

1. Placebo control – participants had to write about their earliest memories every night for one week.
2. Gratitude visit – participants had to write a letter of gratitude to someone who had been kind to them and deliver it to the person.
3. Three good things in life – participants had to write down three things that went well each day for one week. They also had to identify the causes of these.

4. 'You at your best' – participants had to write about a time when they were 'at their best'. They then had to reflect on their personal strengths from the story every day for one week.

5. Using signature strengths in a new way – participants had to complete an online questionnaire that identified their five key strengths. They then had to use one of these key strengths in a new and different way every day for one week.

6. Identifying signature strengths – this was the same as above, but they were asked to use one of their key strengths more often for one week.

All participants completed a range of measures for depression and happiness at baseline then at one week, one month, three months, and six months after completing their assigned exercise.

Two of the positive psychology exercises, 'using signature strengths in a new way', and 'three good things in life', decreased depressive scores and increased happiness scores at six months. The 'gratitude visit' had the largest impact for the first month but at six months the positive effects had disappeared.

Application of positive psychology

> **Test yourself**
>
> Explain the findings of the Seligman et al (2005) study in relation to the three focuses of positive psychology. Also explain two strengths and two weaknesses of the study.

KEY STUDY: Shoshani and Steinmetz (2014)

Context

This century has seen a rapid rise in mental health disorders among children and adolescents. Estimations range from 8% to 20% of this population experiencing some form of negative mental health. Positive psychology has made significant progress and impacts on the wellbeing of children and students. However, there had been very few studies testing the impact of positive psychology prior to this study, including any long-term effects once a positive psychology programme has ended.

Main theories/explanations

Positive psychology is based around changing the subjective wellbeing of people. There are two components to wellbeing.
- The first is a cognitive component, which is about appraising your own satisfaction with life.
- The second is an affective component, which is about the presence of positive feelings and the absence of negative feelings.

There has long been an association between positive subjective wellbeing and academic functioning, social competence, physical health, general achievements, and engagement at school.

There can be many components to a positive psychology intervention programme (PPIP). These include writing gratitude diaries, writing about and sharing strongly positive experiences, focus on hope and self-worth, life satisfaction, all achievements, reframing so hurdles do not feel so difficult to overcome, and celebrating our strengths. PPIPs can be tailored for different age groups and different educational systems. However, six main factors must be part of any PPIP. These are:

1. positive emotions
2. gratitude
3. fulfilment of goals
4. optimism
5. strength of character
6. having positive relationships.

Aims and hypotheses

One aim was to investigate whether school children who participate in a PPIP would show improved mental health in the long term. Another aim was to investigate whether success in the intervention programme was affected by socio-demographic factors. These factors could be being part of a low-income or single-parent family.

One main hypothesis was tested: participants in the positive psychology intervention group will show a greater longitudinal increase in self-efficacy, optimism, life satisfaction, and lower levels of psychological distress and mental health symptoms compared to the control group.

Design

Participants

Table 21.12 shows the characteristics of the sample at baseline.

The PPIP was implemented in a school in Israel, with all of the student population and staff engaging in it. The PPIP lasted for one year and there was a two-year follow-up. Measures were taken pre- and post- PPIP intervention, so this was an experiment using a longitudinal design (repeated measures).

Table 21.12 Socio-demographic characteristics of the intervention and cotrol groups at baseline

	Control group (n = 501) Mean (SD)	Intervention group (n = 537)
Gender		
Girls, n (%)	257 (51.2 %)	268 (49.9 %)
Age (years)	13.75 (0.66)	13.61 (0.61)
Socioeconomic status		
Very good, n (%)	43 (8.58 %)	39 (7.26 %)
Good, n (%)	56 (11.18 %)	66 (12.30 %)
Average, n (%)	295 (58.88 %)	299 (55.68 %)
Low, n (%)	61 (12.18 %)	81 (15.08 %)
Very low, n (%)	46 (9.18 %)	52 (9.68 %)
Religious observance		
Orthodox, n (%)	23 (4.59 %)	16 (2.98 %)
Traditional, n (%)	105 (20.96 %)	118 (21.97 %)
Secular, n (%)	373 (74.45 %)	403 (75.05 %)
Family status		
Two-parent household, n (%)	332 (66.27)	335 (62.38 %)
Single-parent household, n (%)	169 (33.73 %)	202 (37.62 %)

Outcome measures

A total of five measures were used.

1. Brief Symptoms Inventory – this is a 53-item self-report symptom measure, using a 4-point Likert scale, designed for use with adolescents. There are ten subscales including depression, anxiety, and hostility.
2. Rosenberg Self-Esteem Scale – this is a ten-item measure that uses a 4-point Likert scale. A high score indicates high self-esteem.
3. General Self-Efficacy Scale – this is a ten-item measure that uses a 4-point Likert scale. A high score indicates high self-efficacy.
4. Satisfaction with Life Scale – this is a five-item measure that uses a 7-point Likert scale. A mean score across the five items is calculated.
5. Life Orientation Test (Revised) – this is a ten-item measure that has three positively phrased statements, three negatively phrased statements, and four filler statements. It uses a 5-point Likert scale.

The intervention group (PPIP)

There were two parts to this that ran simultaneously.

1. A teacher-training workshop, led by clinical psychologists, took place. There were 15, two-hour sessions throughout the school year.
2. Teachers administered age-appropriate programmes. These matched the timeframe for the teacher-training workshops being 15, two-hour sessions throughout the school year. The teachers had a textbook to use with additional multi-media material.

To ensure that the programme was being efficiently delivered, the school psychologist and counsellors completed reports after a series of random checks throughout the school year.

The activities for the students included discussions, poetry reading, and watching some movie clips that showed positive psychology. One specific example of an activity was to cover the gratitude component of the PPIP. Students were asked to list at least five things that they felt really grateful for over the past week. They were also encouraged to write gratitude letters to people who had affected them positively. These were shared among the class. Another example was to cover the goal-setting component of the PPIP. Students were asked to list all personal large-scale goals they wanted to achieve in life. They were then asked to break these goals down into smaller component goals. Every week they would list up to four methods that they planned to use that week to help move towards these smaller goals.

Control group

This group followed the typical school curricula with regular social science lessons. They did not participate in any of the activities used in the PPIP.

Procedure

Two ethical committees approved the study. Before the start of the study, letters that described the PPIP plus parental and student consent forms were sent to families. The PPIP ran from September 2010 until June 2011. The questionnaires were completed at four points: September 2010, June 2011, December 2011, and June 2012.

Results, findings, and conclusions

Baseline measures

There were some significant differences in the sample at baseline.

- Students classified as living in poverty reported higher levels of distress, depressive symptoms, and anxiety symptoms. This was also true for those in single-parent households when compared to two-parent households.
- Males reported lower levels of distress, depressive symptoms, and interpersonal sensitivity symptoms compared to females. Males reported higher levels of anxiety symptoms compared to females.

Longitudinal analyses

Figures 21.21 and 21.22 show the change in general distress, depressive symptoms, and self-efficacy over the period of the study. As can be seen, general distress and depressive symptoms appeared to decrease in the PPIP but increase in the control group. Self-efficacy increased in the PPIP but decreased in the control group.

These were the other main results.

- Participants in the PPIP reported significant decreases from baseline to final measure for general distress, depressive symptoms, anxiety symptoms, and interpersonal sensitivity symptoms. In the control group all of these measures, except for interpersonal sensitivity symptoms, increased significantly.
- Participants in the PPIP reported significant increases in self-esteem and self-efficacy from baseline to final measure. The control group reported significant decreases in both of these measures.
- With optimism, the participants in the PPIP reported significantly greater increases compared to the control group.
- The two family 'risk factors' were negatively associated with mental health from baseline to final measure, but none were statistically significant.

The main conclusion was that a PPIP benefited students' mental health even one year after it ended. Education for wellbeing should be an integral part of a school curriculum as the benefits far outweigh the costs.

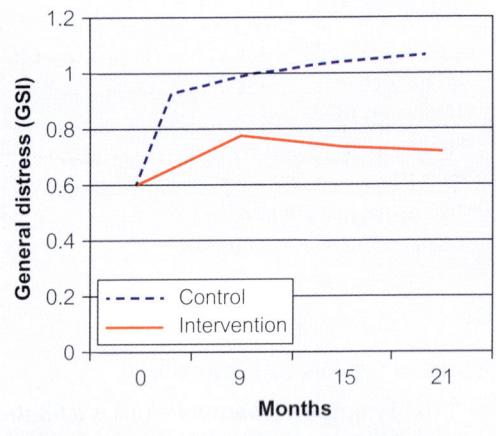

Figure 21.21 Changes in general distress from September 2010 to June 2012

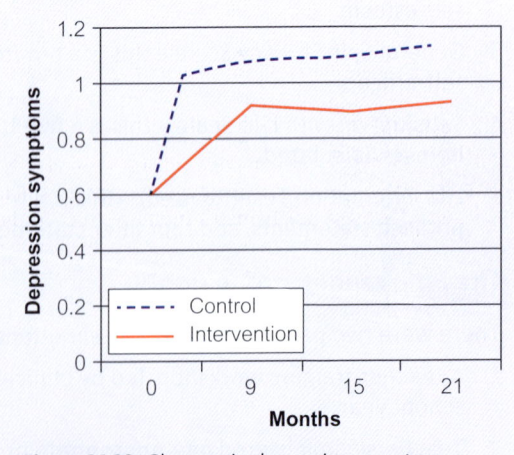

Figure 21.22 Changes in depression symptoms as a function of time and intervention type

Main discussion points

- The transition to middle school (in Israel when students are approximately 12 to 15 years old) can be a complicated process that impacts on the mental health of children. There are different environments and social interactions to deal with. However, a PPIP may help ease this transition.
- Student engagement in a PPIP is integral. The school in this study allowed students to decorate corridor walls with collages of positivity, images, quotes, etc. The school bell was used to play a popular self-empowerment Israeli song. Students also began to initiate community services activities.
- The whole-school approach to the PPIP was crucial to success as everyone felt part of it, whereas if only a few classes had followed the PPIP others may have felt apart from it.
- Overall life satisfaction did not differ between the PPIP group and the control group. The researchers were not expecting this. The measure used could have been the source of the 'no difference'. The researchers state that the life satisfaction measure is quite abstract and general whereas all other measures made students focus on day-to-day experiences.

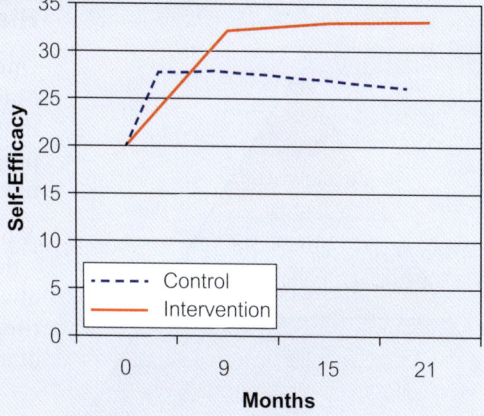

Figure 21.23 Changes in self-efficacy from September 2010 to June 2012

Evaluation

- The procedure used in the study was clear and standardised. The recruitment process, the PPIP, and measures used were clearly outlined so other researchers can replicate the study to test for reliability.
- The study has good application. The findings can be used to improve the mental wellbeing of many students especially those who have had to be educated during the COVID-19 pandemic. Having tasks for students to complete, either in the classroom, in virtual classrooms, or at home can maintain and improve many aspects of mental wellbeing.
- Generalisability may be low. Even though the sample size was large it was only conducted in one school in Israel. The PPIP may have worked here due to the nature of the school as well as the content of the programme. This could be unique. Other schools may not have the infrastructure or curriculum time to be able to introduce such a large programme. Schools in other countries may have different ideas and timetables so it needs to be replicated in other parts of the world to see whether the effectiveness is robust across different schools.

	Issue and debate tracker
Individual and situational explanations	This section is about individual factors in changing health beliefs. The study by Weinstein (1980) showed that people had their own ideas about unrealistic optimism, which may have been caused by their personality. However, we do not know whether some experiences that people had in a certain situation had influenced these unrealistic optimism beliefs. The chances of experiencing a certain life event that had to be estimated may have been based on a combination of individual factors (a pessimistic personality) and situational factors (experience of similar events or knowing about similar events). There is a similar argument for the three lives of positive psychology. Certain personality types may be drawn towards the journey involved in attaining the meaningful life, but these could be changed by experiences people have that allows them (or not allows them) to follow that journey, such as work commitments or financial obligations. It is difficult to know whether the Shoshani and Steinmetz (2014) study follows these explanations as there was no measure about health belief, just measures about quality of mental health.
Psychometrics	These types of measures tend to have had reliability and validity tests performed on them to make sure that they are measuring what they intend to measure and that they are stable over time. The study by Shoshani and Steinmetz used a range of psychometric measures such as the Rosenberg Self Esteem Scale and the General Self-Efficacy Scale. These allow a meaningful comparison across groups of people so that aspects of mental health and self-awareness can be discussed using standardised scores and descriptions. These can be seen as valid measures for a range of human behaviours examined in that study. This is the only example in this section that used psychometrics.

Challenge yourself

Create similar issue and debate commentaries for idiographic versus nomothetic, cultural differences, and generalisations from findings.

22 Psychology and organisations

22.1 Motivation to work

22.1.1 Need theories

Hierarchy of needs (Maslow, 1970)

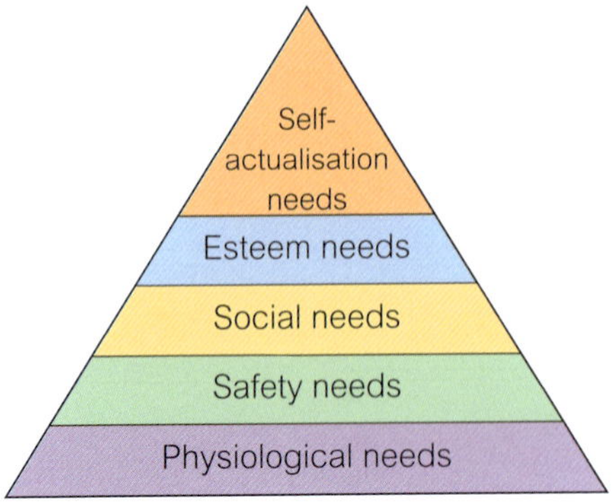

One idea from humanism that attempts to explain motivation was proposed by Maslow (1970, but based on his earlier research). He created a hierarchy of needs that starts at basic needs and moves up to higher level 'meta needs'. The hierarchy progresses from physiological needs to safety needs, to social needs, to esteem needs and finally to self-actualisation needs. The model is illustrated in Figure 22.1.

A human being must work up the hierarchy of needs to achieve self-actualisation – this is realising and reaching one's full potential. The basic (physiological) needs always have to be met (even if partially) before a person can consider working up the hierarchy towards self-actualisation. A worker has to be motivated and fulfilled at a physiological and safety level before attempting anything higher.

Figure 22.1 Maslow's hierarchy of needs

Maslow's hierarchy of needs in the workplace

Greenberg and Baron (2008) set out how Maslow's hierarchy of needs can be applied to the workplace in the following ways.

- To satisfy physiological needs, organisations can make sure that workers take breaks (eg for refreshments). Some companies, especially those where the workforce is quite sedentary in an office environment, provide exercise facilities for free. This can improve the health of workers and make them more productive.

- With regard to safety needs, organisations can ensure that workers have protective clothing if necessary and use specifically designed products, for example to reduce the strain of using computers and keyboards all day as part of a worker's job.

- To meet social needs, organisations can organise events that can build a 'team spirit' into the workforce. A company may have a 'family day' for everyone to get together out of the pressures of work. There is a company called The Picnic People that coordinates events to get the workforce together, for example.

- Esteem needs might be met through incentives organisations create such as 'employee of the month' or annual awards ceremonies for the workforce. They can also award bonuses for suggestions for improvements within the organisation.

- Self-actualisation needs are met when organisations nurture their workforce to allow people to reach their full potential (via things such as career progression and appraisals).

Challenge yourself

To what extent do you think that this theory is reductionist? Justify your answer.

Strength	Weakness
The theory is easy to test for validity as each level is clearly described.	The theory ignores other factors that might motivate people to work.

Mousavi and Dargahi (2013) investigated ethnic differences in workplace motivation in Iran, based on Maslow's theory. They wanted to know which levels of Maslow's theory had been fulfilled in a sample of employees at Tehran University of Medical Sciences. The random sample of 133 participants completed a structured questionnaire that collected information about demographics and Maslow's hierarchy of needs. Ethnic groups that were used in the overall analysis included Persians, Kurds, Turks, Lurs, and Mazandaranians. The main results included these findings.

- Irrespective of ethnic group, employees placed most emphasis on basic and self-esteem needs in the workplace and less emphasis on self-actualisation.
- Employees from Persian and Mazandaranian ethnic backgrounds tended to place most emphasis on basic needs.
- Employees from Lurs and Mazandaranian ethnic backgrounds tended to place the most emphasis on safety and security needs.
- Employees from a Mazandaranian ethnic background tended to place the most emphasis on social needs.
- Employees from a Persian ethnic background tended to place the most emphasis on self-esteem needs.
- Employees from a Mazandaranian ethnic background tended to place most emphasis on self-actualisation as being very important.

These findings shows that Maslow's hierarchy of needs is important to all employees in the university. However, ethnicity can affect which ones are seen as being more important to motivate employees at work. These need to be taken into consideration when setting goals, ensuring that employees feel needed and motivated to perform at their best.

Achievement motivation theory

Proposed by McClelland (1965), achievement motivation theory is based around the idea that people (and workers) are motivated by different needs and motives in different situations. There are three key needs and motives that people are driven by and they differ from individual to individual.

- People have a need for achievement. This is about having the drive to succeed in a situation. Therefore, workers driven by this will love the challenge of their job. They want to get ahead in their job and be excellent performers. They like to solve immediate problems swiftly and will go for challenges that offer a moderate level of difficulty (so that they feel challenged but know the goal is achievable). They also desire feedback about their efforts so will thrive on appraisals.

- People have a need for power. This is about having the drive to direct others and be influential at work. Workers in this category are status driven and are more likely to be motivated by the chance to gain prestige. They will want to solve problems individually and reach appraisal goals. The drive for power can be for personal gains or organisational gains.

- People have a need for affiliation. This is about having the drive to be liked and accepted by fellow workers in the organisation. People driven by this prefer to work with others and get motivated by the need for friendship and interpersonal relationships. Therefore, their main motivator is on cooperative tasks.

Workers can be assessed on these three key needs and motives by taking a thematic apperception test (TAT). To do this, workers have to look at a series of ambiguous pictures that tell a story. They have to tell whatever story they feel is behind the picture and their stories are then scored on a standardised scale that represents the three key needs and motives. From these, it can be seen whether a worker is driven by achievement, power, or affiliation.

Strength	Weakness
The theory has application as companies can use the information to help motivate staff via their appraisals.	The theory tends to be tested using the TAT, which is a subjective way of measuring motivation.

Test yourself

Explain at least one strength and one weakness of study by Mousavi and Dargahi (2013).

Challenge yourself

Look at the issue and debate tracker table on page 284. Create similar issue and debate commentaries for application to everyday life, individual and situational explanations, determinism versus free will, and validity.

22.1.2 Cognitive theories

Goal-setting theory

Goal-setting theory (Latham and Locke, 1984) appears relatively straightforward: it states that performance at work is affected by the goals that a workforce is set. The setting of these goals affects people's beliefs about whether they can perform a task or not.

However, goals need to be specific to an individual or group. Simply saying "Work harder" has very little effect on people as they may already feel that they are working hard. Setting specific and achievable goals allows workers to direct their attention towards achieving them while assessing how well they are doing. If workers feel that they may not reach a specified goal, they will be motivated to work harder to try to attain it. An organisation must set challenging but attainable goals, give workers the necessary equipment and support to attain the goals and give them feedback throughout the process as this will motivate them to attain each goal.

According to this theory, there are three main guidelines for setting effective goals.

- Assign specific goals. Goals have to have clarity, be measurable and achievable. An organisation cannot say "Do your best" and then hope the workforce gets motivated. Research has shown that workers may find the goal challenging but this motivates them to want to achieve it.

- Assign difficult, but acceptable, performance goals. Goals that are perceived as unachievable will demotivate the workforce, as will those that are seen as being 'too easy'. Therefore, a goal must be difficult, in order to get workers motivated, but not impossible to attain. There can be vertical stretch goals which challenge workers to achieve higher success in activities that they are currently involved with (eg sales). There are also horizontal stretch goals which challenge workers to perform certain tasks that are new to them.

- Provide effective feedback on goal attainment. Feedback throughout the process allows workers to know how far they are progressing and what is left to attain a goal. This keeps motivation at an optimal level. If feedback is used wisely, workers will believe even more that they can attain the goal and will be more motivated to achieve it.

Strength	Weakness
The theory has application as companies can use the information to help them set realistic goals to motivate people at work.	Not all goals are universal so setting a goal may not help to motivate workers if the goal is something they have no desire to achieve.

SMART goals

SMART is an acronym commonly used in organisations as a way of guiding goal setting. It stands for the following terms.

1. **S**pecific – this increases motivation to achieve the goal. It covers the '5Ws': what do I need to do, why is it important, who is involved with me, where is the goal located, and which resources are available for me to use?

2. **M**easurable – the progress and/or outcome must be measurable so the organisation can track progress over time.

3. **A**chievable – the goal(s) must be realistic and attainable given the resources available.

4. **R**elevant – to improve motivation, the goal must be relevant to you. It must mean something.

5. **T**ime-bound – this may include interim dates but there must always be an end date for completion.

VIE (expectancy) theory

This theory, devised by Vroom (1964), attempts to explain motivation more from a cognitive angle. Motivation is based on three factors that are multiplicative.

- Valence refers to the value that workers place on any reward they believe they will receive from the organisation. The overall reward must be one that reflects the efforts put into attaining a goal and therefore be *desired*.

- Instrumentality refers to any perceived relationship between effort and outcome that may affect motivation. This can be based around rewards as well. If any performance or motivation is not perceived as being instrumental in bringing about a suitable reward, then it is less likely to happen – motivation will be low.

- Expectancy refers to any perceived relationship between effort and performance that may affect motivation. If workers do not expect their efforts to make any difference to attaining a goal then their motivation will be low. If they do feel effort brings about reward then their performance will increase as they will be motivated.

This can be expressed as an equation:

$$M = V \times I \times E$$

Therefore, motivation is determined by how the three factors interact, so if one of them is low then motivation as a whole will be low as a result. All have to be reasonably high for motivation to be high too.

Managerial applications of expectancy theory

How can the above be used by managers in an organisation to improve motivation of its workforce? Riggio (1999), and Greenberg and Baron (2008) highlight the following practical ways.

- Managers need to define any goal-based work outcome very clearly to all workers. Clarity is the key to success. All rewards and costs of performance based around these rewards must be known and be transparent.

- Managers should get workers involved in the setting of any goals and listen to their suggestions about ways to change jobs and roles to help attain them. This should help to increase VIE levels.

- For the valence element, managers should ensure that the rewards are ones that employees desire and see in a positive light. These may need to be individually specific as not all workers are motivated by the same things. Greenberg and Baron (2008) highlight how many companies now use a 'cafeteria-style benefit plan' where employees can choose their own personalised incentives from items such as pay, additional days off and lower day-care costs for their children. The valence element for workers is very high if they are striving for something *they have chosen*.

- Progression from performance to rewards has to be achievable. Any performance-related goal (especially if workers have some performance-related pay) has to be attainable for all. Workers whose portion of their wage is based on performance need goals that are attainable but where motivation is the key to reaching them. Greenberg and Baron (2008) state that if there is a pay-for-performance method in the company then this should increase the instrumental motivation element of expectancy theory and motivation increases.

> **Test yourself**
>
> Explain at least one strength and one weakness of VIE (expectancy) theory.

> **Challenge yourself**
>
> Look at the issue and debate tracker table on page 284. Create similar issue and debate commentaries for individual and situational explanations, reductionism versus holism, determinism versus free will, and idiographic versus nomothetic.

22.1.3 Motivators at work

Intrinsic and extrinsic motivation

Extrinsic motivation is a desire to perform a task or behaviour because it gives positive reinforcement (eg a reward) or it avoids some kind of punishment. In terms of the workplace, this might mean workers gain extra pay or a day off for their efforts.

Intrinsic motivation is a desire to perform a task or behaviour because it gives internal pleasure or helps to develop a skill. In terms of the workplace, people will attribute success to their own desires (autonomy) and may be interested in simply mastering a task rather than focusing on something such as extra pay.

> **Challenge yourself**
>
> Design a study that investigates whether workers prefer intrinsic or extrinsic motivators at work.

Types of reward system

Pay, bonuses, profit-sharing, and performance related-pay

There are many reward systems that organisations can use with their workforce. They tend to be based around both extrinsic and intrinsic motivators. They can include the following.

- Pay – having some pay linked to a certain task or goal can increase the motivation of workers who want to have more money.

- Bonus – offering a bonus is are quite widespread in organisations linked to sales and finance. At the end of each year (maybe after an appraisal), workers will be given a bonus payment based on the performance of themselves and the company as a whole.

- Profit-sharing – a certain percentage of any profit a company makes can be 'ring fenced' to be shared by all workers. Therefore, everyone may be more motivated to attain goals and reach performance criteria so that there is a monetary reward.

- Performance-related pay – the explanation of VIE (expectancy) theory of motivation (above) discussed performance-related pay. In addition, sales organisations may set minimum targets that give workers basic pay and anything achieved above the target earns them commission. This should motivate workers to exceed minimum targets as they will gain a reward in the process.

Non-monetary rewards

Praise, respect, recognition, empowerment, and a sense of belonging

As we have seen, not all motivators have to be extrinsic. There are important intrinsic motivators in the workplace such as the following.

- Praise – simply gaining praise from a superior at work can motivate a worker to continue to work hard, and meet targets and goals. It is a form of positive reinforcement.

- Respect – gaining respect from superiors and fellow colleagues is also important in an organisation. This internal feeling of 'good' can motivate workers to continue to try hard at a task.

- Recognition – simply being recognised for any 'over and above' effort can motivate a worker to continue to work hard. For example, an 'employee of the month' scheme or being mentioned in a work newsletter can motivate people greatly.

- Empowerment – when workers succeed at a difficult task or achieve a difficult goal they may have a sense of empowerment. This may make them believe that the next task is attainable even if it looks difficult. It equips them to continually try hard at a task.
- A sense of belonging – making workers feel 'part of the team' and that their individual efforts are appreciated can motivate them to keep trying hard and reaching even difficult goals.

Self-determination theory (Deci and Ryan, 2008)

Deci and Ryan (2008) proposed this macrotheory of human motivation, development, and health. Some of the main ideas are presented in Table 22.1.

Table 22.1 Deci and Ryan's macrotheory of human motivation, development, and health (2008)

Main idea	Explanation
Motivation	There are three types. • Autonomous motivation has both intrinsic and extrinsic components which have been integrated into a person's sense of self. People believe they are their own motivator. • Controlled motivation tends to be regulated externally and affects our behaviour via rewards or punishment. It can also be internalised using factors such as avoidance of shame, protecting self-esteem, and the need for approval. This type of motivation forces people to behave, think, and feel in specific ways. • Amotivation is a lack of both intention and motivation. Deci and Ryan note that autonomous motivation tends to produce better psychological health and enhanced performance at tasks.
Basic psychological needs	Deci and Ryan state that, irrespective of culture (eg collectivist versus individualistic), there are many basic psychological needs for humans. These can directly affect autonomous and controlled motivation.
Individual differences	The needs for competence, relatedness, and autonomy are basic and universal. Individuals measure the degree to which a need is being satisfied or not satisfied ('thwarted'). This can be assessed in two ways. 1. Causality orientation, which itself has three variants: autonomous orientation, which means all three basic needs are satisfied; controlled orientation, which means competence and relatedness are satisfied but autonomy is not; and impersonal orientation, which means all three basic needs are not satisfied. 2. Aspirations or life goals: when needs have not been directly satisfied, people tend to follow extrinsic goals (eg money).
Mindfulness	See the AS-Level core study by Hölzel et al (2011) on page 51.

KEY STUDY: Landry et al (2019), study 1

(Note: Only study 1 of the research is covered here as the specifics of study 2 are not needed.)

Context

Organisations have used money as a prime motivator for its workforce for centuries. However, organisations can use a monetary reward system in many different ways. There could be a general bonus for the overall performance of the organisation, with the bonus linked to individually tailored goals that need to be achieved in order to gain the reward. How employees perceive the reward can affect the type of motivation shown to complete tasks related to their job.

Main theories/explanations

The study attempted to test self-determination theory (see above), in relation to motivation from cash rewards in organisation.

Aim and hypotheses

The aim was to investigate the potential impact of monetary rewards on motivation and performance in the workplace.

Two main hypotheses were tested.

'*Hypothesis 1*: Presenting rewards in an autonomy-supporting way so as to convey an informal meaning leads to greater performance than presenting them in a controlling way so as to conger a controlling meaning.

Hypothesis 2: The effect of informational rewards on performance is mediated by greater psychological need satisfaction, giving rise to greater intrinsic motivation, whereas the effect of controlling rewards on performance is mediated by greater psychological needs frustration, giving rise to greater extrinsic motivation' (Landry *et al* (2019: 3).

Design

Participants

The sample consisted of 123 students from an introductory organisational psychology course in Canada. They all volunteered. Of these, 65 were in the autonomy–supportive (informational) condition and 58 in the autonomy–threatening (controlling) group. All participants spoke French and had a mean age of 23 years with 60% female. The study was passed by an ethics board.

Procedure

At the beginning of this laboratory experiment, participants were asked to read a paragraph about what they were about to do. It differed depending on what condition the participant was in.

- Autonomy–supportive – participants in this group were given information about the reward bring offered for completion of the task. They were told that the reward was simply a token of appreciation. It was a $10 gift card to be used a local café.
- Autonomy–supportive – participants in this group were told that the reward was being used to reinforce performance standards for the task. It was also a $10 gift card.

Once they had read the information for their condition, there were several measures that each participant completed based on the variables being analysed. These are shown in Table 22.2.

Table 22.2 The three types of variables measured in the study

Type of variable	Description of motivation	How it was measured
Mediating	Psychological need satisfaction and frustration	This was measured using the Basic Psychological Needs Satisfaction Scale.
		Each need was measured for its satisfaction and frustration using four items.
		For example, for relatedness participants had to select from:
		'I feel part of a group right now OR I feel like other people dislike me right now.'
Outcome	Intrinsic motivation, extrinsic motivation, and performance	For both motivations, the Situational Motivation Scale was completed. A series of items were rated in a 7-point scale from 1 (does not correspond at all) to 7 (corresponds exactly).
		For performance, the participants had to solve 25 four-letter anagrams in two minutes. An overall performance score was generated using the formula:
		$$\frac{\text{Number of correct answers} - \text{Number of incorrect answers}}{\text{Total number of correct answers}}$$
Control	Perceived value of rewards plus positive and negative affect	Perceived value of rewards was rated on a three-item scale as to how valuable the particular reward was.
		For affect, the short-form Positive and Negative Affect Scale was completed. This generated a total for positive affect and a total for negative affect.

Results, findings, and conclusions

The differences between the two conditions on psychological need satisfaction, frustration, extrinsic motivation, intrinsic motivation, and performance were all significant. All the differences were in the direction predicted by the hypotheses.

However, more extensive analysis was conducted to produce a model as to how all of the mediating, outcome, and control variables were related. The model is shown in Figure 22.2.

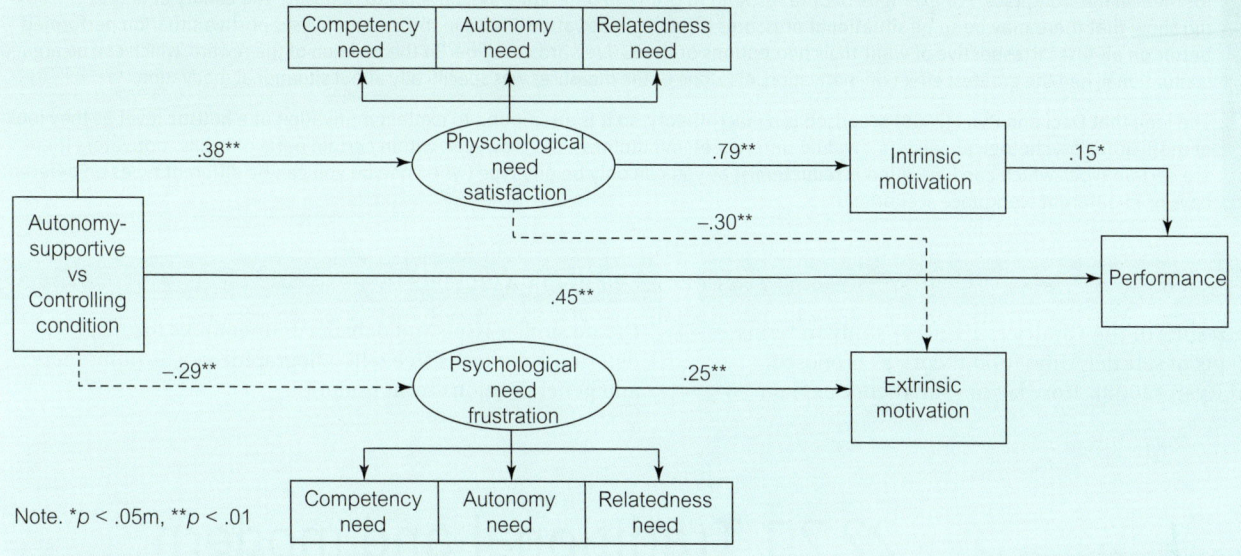

Figure 22.2 Results for study 1. Only the significant relations with their standardised path coefficients are shown. Continuous lines represent positive relations between the connect variables, and dotted lines represent negative relations between the connected variables.

Source: Landry et al (2019: 6)

The model supports these two hypotheses.

- Hypothesis 1: those in the autonomy–supportive (informational) condition performed better on the task compared to the autonomy–threatening (controlling) condition.

- Hypotheses 2: those in the autonomy–supportive (informational) condition reported greater psychological need satisfaction which in turn made for greater intrinsic motivation which then further predicted positive performance. Those in the autonomy–threatening (controlling) condition reported greater psychological need frustration which in turn predicted greater extrinsic motivation. However, this did not then have an effect on performance.

Landry et al concluded that rewards have a differential impact on an individual's performance in a task. This is based on the function of the reward (informational rather than controlling). Presenting rewards in a positive, informational way appears to have a stronger impact on performance.

Main discussion points

- This study gives support to organisations using extrinsic rewards to motivate employees to enhance performance.
- The beneficial effect of providing rewards with informational meaning on performance is not about people simply trying to output as much as possible without consideration of quality, as this study considered errors.
- The relationship between monetary rewards and performance is not a simple cause-and-effect model. There are linked pathways including type of motivation, need satisfaction, relatedness, and competence.

Evaluation points

- The task of solving anagrams lacks mundane realism. In a real-world situation in an organisation, the link between positive informational rewards and performance may not be as strong.
- The majority of the mediating, outcome, and control variables were measured using validated psychometric tests and so produced quantitative data that allowed for direct comparisons between conditions. Also, it can be argued that they measured what they were intending to measure.

	Issue and debate tracker
Individual and situational explanations	Both extrinsic and intrinsic motivators can be argued to be **individual** as people have differing perceptions on what is the best motivator for them in the workplace. For example, people respond to praise in different ways, but also to bonuses! The Landry *et al* (2019) study did show that there may be some **situational** pressures affecting motivation. Those in the autonomy–supportive situation performed better on all tasks irrespective of what their perceptions of the $10 reward could be. So the function of the reward, which can be argued is situational, had the greatest effect on motivation. Also, one of the measures was specifically about situational motivation.
Reductionism versus holism	The idea that Deci and Ryan (2008) proposed is a macrotheory, so it is attempting to explain motivation at a **holistic** level as they look at motivators, psychological needs, individual differences, mindfulness, etc. However, within certain parts of it, like motivators there are certain *types* which can be argued is **reductionist** as you can only be one type (when maybe you can be different types on different days or in different workplace scenarios).

Test yourself

Explain the results of the Landry *et al* (2019) study in terms of the concepts of self-determination theory as proposed by Deci and Ryan (2008). How far can the theory explain the results?

Challenge yourself

Create similar issue and debate commentaries for determinism versus free will, idiographic versus nomothetic, and generalisations from findings.

22.2 Leadership and management

22.2.1 Traditional and modern theories of leadership

Universalist and behavioural theories

This section looks at a range of psychological theories that attempt to explain what makes someone become a leader.

Universalist theories include great person theory and theories centred on charismatic and transformational leaders.

Behavioural theories include theories from Ohio State University studies (initiating structure and consideration) and University of Michigan studies (task-oriented and relationship-oriented behaviours).

Great person theory

This follows the idea that 'great leaders are born, not made'. Therefore, people are either 'natural leaders' or not. Their natural abilities allow them to 'rise to the top' of any organisation because of the skills they were born with. These leaders have special traits that allow them to progress up the managerial levels of an organisation and then lead the company effectively over time. These traits are stable and effective when they are used in a position of authority.

Charismatic and transformational leaders

Another idea is that certain leaders have the necessary charisma to become leaders. They possess first-class interpersonal skills. Charisma comes from the Greek for 'gift of grace' and it means that leaders possess a charismatic personality that allows them to lead a workforce effectively. These leaders tend to have very good public speaking skills, exude confidence, inspire people, captivate their audiences every time. As a result, the workforce is motivated to follow them and attain the goals set by them. In addition, Greenberg and Baron (2008) reviewed the field and produced a list of five 'agreed' traits shown by charismatic leaders.

- Self-confidence – they show high confidence about their own ability and the ability of their workforce to attain a goal.
- A vision – this usually takes the form of making working conditions or working life better.
- Extraordinary behaviour – they show some unusual or unconventional behaviours.

Ask yourself

What makes a good leader or manager at work? List all of the traits you think make someone a good leader or manager and then see how many appear in the following theories.

- Recognition as change agents – in other words, they are seen to make things happen.
- Environmental sensitivity – they show realism about what can be achieved given the resources they have available.

Transformational leaders, according to Riggio (1999), change how the workforce think, reason, and behave. They inspire workers using six different behaviours.

- Identifying and articulating a vision – they excite workers with a vision for the company.
- Providing an appropriate model – the leaders 'practise what they preach'.
- Fostering the acceptance of group goals – cooperation between all workers is promoted and a common goal is set.
- Maintaining high performance expectation – excellence is encouraged and work quality is improved.
- Providing individualised support – the leaders will show care and concern for all individuals.
- Providing intellectual stimulation – the leaders will challenge workers to rethink how they do things.

Behavioural theories

Researchers at Ohio State University collected data from self-reports and observations of leaders and their workers. From this they listed over 100 different behaviours shown by leaders. They conducted a factor analysis on the data (this looks for relationships between variables and clusters similar ones together) and found that there are just two broad categories of leaders.

- Initiating structure – this includes assigning specific tasks to people, defining groups of workers, creating and meeting deadlines, and ensuring that workers are working to a set standard.
- Consideration – this is shown by leaders who have a genuine concern for the feelings of workers and their attitudes. The leaders establish rapport with workers while showing them trust and respect. They will listen to workers more often than the other category of leaders and try to boost the self-confidence of their workforce.

Researchers at the University of Michigan examined many leaders of large organisations and also found two main types of behaviour in these leaders.

- Task-oriented behaviours – these were behaviours that focused on the actual task being conducted. The leaders are more concerned with setting up some structures within an organisation such as targets, standards, supervising workers, and achieving goals.
- Relationship-oriented behaviours – these were behaviours that had a focus on the wellbeing of the workforce. The leaders would look at interpersonal relationships between worker and worker, plus worker and manager. They would also take the time to understand the feelings of their workforce.

The researchers concluded that the relationship-oriented behaviours were more effective at motivating a workforce than task-oriented ones.

Heifetz's six principles in meeting adaptive challenges

Heifetz (1997) proposed the idea of adaptive leadership. Leaders have to mobilise their workforce to tackle whatever challenges happen and to then make them thrive. This can be done via being an adaptive leader, according to Heifetz. These are the basic assumptions of this idea.

- Leadership is about change that enables the workforce to thrive.
- Any change has to be built on the past.
- Organisational change can only happen through experimentation.

> **Test yourself**
>
> Evaluate all of these theories in terms of one strength and one weakness. Is there any empirical evidence for any?

- Leadership relies on diversity.
- Adaptive leadership can involve displacing, re-regulating, and rearranging 'old' structure in an organisation.
- Adaptive changes will take time.

To be an adaptive leader, the person must meet the following conditions.

- Get rid of the broken system's illusions that it is not broken.
- Differentiate between technical problems and adaptive challenges.
- Distinguish leadership from authority.
- Learn to live in a 'productive' zone even if it causes short-term disequilibrium.
- Observe, then interpret, then intervene.
- Engage above and below the neck.
- Connect to purpose.

There are other tips that Heifetz notes that can help someone to become an adaptive leader.

- Don't do it alone. Involve others in the organisation and distribute responsibilities according to each worker's strengths.
- Remember that the best way to learn is through life experiences.
- Resist leaping into action and try to stay reflective at all times.
- Make difficult choices but enjoy the experience.

Strength	Weakness
The theory has application as managers can train certain workers to become adaptive leaders.	The theory is subjective and has not been tested objectively by other researchers.

	Issue and debate tracker
Application to everyday life	The theories can be used in the workplace to help transform leaders and to help create new leaders. Training could help form better leaders like charisma training or running workshops on how to become a transformational leader. This could be part of a corporate training program to ensure that organisations recruit and maintain the better leaders for their company.
Nature versus nurture	The great person theory supports the idea of **nature** as people are born good leaders with traits already within them that are revealed when placed in leadership roles. The remainder of the theories appear to support the **nurture** side of the debate as it shows how we can learn (and change) our leadership styles to suit an organisation, a team or an event.

Challenge yourself

Create similar issue and debate commentaries for individual and situational explanations, reductionism versus holism, and generalisations from findings.

22.2.2 Leadership style

Muczyk and Reimann's four styles of leader behaviour

Muczyk and Reimann (1987) based their theory of leadership on two styles – permissive and autocratic – that can be combined to assess how a leader may be acting. In permissive leadership, workers are not told how to do their jobs and autocratic leadership means that workers are not allowed to participate in any decision making. Therefore, there can be four combinations.

- Permissive and autocratic – leaders will make decisions by themselves and let the workers 'get on with it'.
- Permissive but not autocratic – leaders will make decisions with others involved and will then let the workers 'get on with it'.
- Not permissive but autocratic – leaders will make decisions by themselves and then closely monitor how the workers are performing on the task.

- Not permissive or autocratic – leaders will make decisions with others involved and will closely monitor how the workers are performing on the task.

Strength	Weakness
The theory has application as different types of leader can be identified and used best within an organisation.	The theory could be reductionist as it only looks at factors in a given situation, overlooking other important leadership skills.

Scouller's levels of leadership

Scouller (2011) proposed a model of leadership that has three levels (see Figure 22.3). These are as follows.

- Public leadership is about the actions a leader takes in a group setting. These could be, for example, actions taken during meetings or trying to influence management. 'Togetherness building' is a technique that can be used. This encourages group-wide trust and respect while developing an atmosphere in which it is 'natural' for individuals to want to perform to their highest standard. This also nurtures the sharing of information and wanting to help colleagues.

- Private leadership is about how an individual handles group members. To achieve private leadership the leader needs to get to know people individually. Each member of a group needs to have individual targets to help support any group task that is set. The leaders need to help review individual task performances at appraisal, giving group members targets to help improve their performance where necessary. Selecting appropriate people for the job is part of this level of leadership, as is removing people who do not fulfil their roles or who underperform consistently.

- Personal leadership is about leaders' psychological, moral, and technical development that can affect their presence within a company and their behaviour. Therefore, it is about self-awareness, the progression to self-mastery, and technical competence (and updating knowledge) where applicable. It requires leaders to have a sense of connection with employees around them. It is the inner core of leadership.

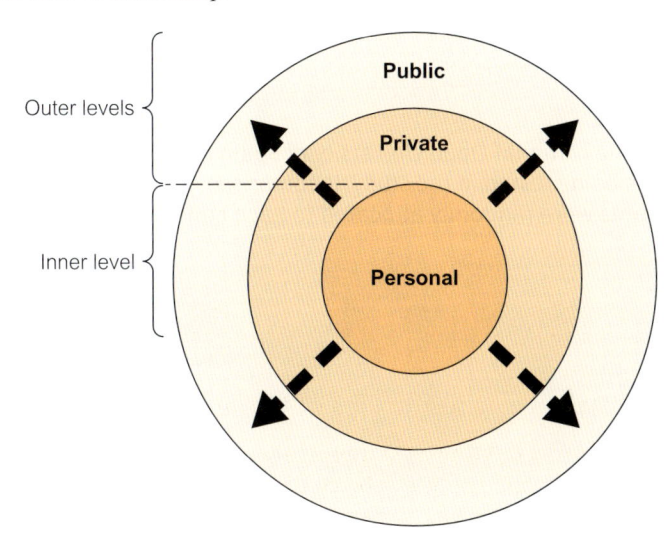

Figure 22.3 The three levels of leadership model
Source: Scouller (2011: 36)

Scouller (2011) believes that personal leadership is the most powerful of the three. He likens it to a pebble hitting the water where the personal leadership is the point of entry and this then 'ripples out' to the private and the public leadership levels. If the 'pebble' is positive, the ripples will be positive too. However, if the 'pebble' is negative then the ripples will also be negative.

Test yourself

Explain at least one strength and one weakness of Scouller's levels of leadership. Make sure one of your points is about real-world application.

Challenge yourself

Design a study to find out which type of Scouller's leadership levels is most common in a company.

Leadership style and gender

KEY STUDY: Cuadrado et al (2008)

Context

There has been a long-standing debate about whether males dominate leadership roles in organisations and how this affects leadership style. Some argue that female leaders are less common due to the glass ceiling effect: a social barrier that prevents women from reaching top management positions. Some people used to believe that females did not have the 'correct management styles and skills' to be able to lead an organisation. These stereotypical views are now challenged regularly in forward-thinking organisations.

Main theories/explanations

To test the 'role of congruity theory of prejudice toward female leaders' was the focus of this study by Cuadrado et al (2008). This focuses on the idea that when women have leadership roles in an organisation, they will be evaluated *less* favourably than a male equivalent when they show stereotypical male styles of leadership.

A stereotypical male style of leadership involves autocratic and task-oriented styles whereas a stereotypical female style of leadership involves democratic, relationship-oriented, and individualised consideration styles.

Aims and hypotheses

The investigate the role of congruity theory of prejudice toward female leaders.

Four hypotheses were tested.

> '*Hypothesis 1*: Female leaders will receive less favorable evaluations than male leaders when they adopt stereotypically masculine leadership styles (autocratic and task-oriented).
>
> *Hypothesis 2*: Male leaders will not receive less favorable evaluations than female leaders when they adopt stereotypically feminine leadership behaviors (democratic, relationship-oriented, individualized consideration).
>
> *Hypothesis 3*: Female leaders will receive worse evaluations from male evaluators than from female evaluators.
>
> *Hypothesis 4*: Male leaders will receive similar evaluations from male and from female evaluators' (Cuadrado et al, 2008: 58).

Design

Participants

The sample consisted of 136 psychology students from the National Open University of Spain in the second year of a social psychology course who were not familiar with the ideas being tested in the study. It comprised 53% women (mean age of 27 years) and 47% men (mean age 29 years). The participants were randomly allocated to each condition, as highlighted in the next section.

Conditions

There were four conditions in this experiment:

1. male leader – male stereotypical leadership style
2. male leader – female stereotypical leadership style
3. female leader – male stereotypical leadership style
4. female leader – female stereotypical leadership style

Design of materials

The study used a story. It was set in the emergency department of a public hospital. This setting was chosen as it had already been shown *not* to elicit gender stereotypes. The story was manipulated for each of the conditions. The following extracts from Cuadrado et al (2008: 59) show two of these conditions.

Female leader – female stereotypical leadership style

'Lucía called for a first meeting in which she presented all the information she had about the problem of user satisfaction. At this meeting, she encouraged the team members to express their opinions, to contribute their ideas, and to suggest possible actions to solve the problem. She appreciated and always took all the team members' suggestions into account. At this time, there were several internal arguments among various members of team, which Lucía tried to prevent. She offered encouragement and support when the situation became particularly difficult. Lucía allowed each team member to work with whomever they pleased, favoring the relations among the entire team. Lucía treated all the team members individually and made them feel that their contribution to the improvement of the service quality was important.'

Male leader – male stereotypical leadership style

'Carlos called for a first meeting in which he presented all the information he had about the problem of user satisfaction. At this meeting, he informed the team about the activities he had decided to carry out to solve the problem. Carlos explained at the beginning the new tasks the team would have to carry out and indicated how to perform them. He planned in detail how to achieve each task, and the responsibilities of each team member and the specific results he expected. He explained how to organize and coordinate the work activities to avoid delays, duplication of efforts, and wasting resources. Carlos treated all the team members like the components of a group and he made them feel that the contribution of the group in general to the improvement of the service quality was important.'

Procedure (including measures)

Each participant had to read the story narrative presented to them. Participants were told that they would be expected to evaluate the supervisor as they were in the position for a trial period. After reading the story narrative, they had to complete three measures, shown in Table 22.3.

Table 22.3 The measures used in Cuadrado et al (2008)

Measure	Description of the measure
Adjective choice	14 adjectives (half positive) were presented, and the participant had to rate how much it applied to the supervisor on a 7-point Likert-type scale (1 is never; 7 is always).
	Adjectives included 'honest', 'optimistic', 'careless' and 'bossy'.
Leadership capacity	4 items were rated on a 7-point Likert-type scale (1 is totally negative/disagree; 7 is totally positive/agree).
	An example item was 'Lucia is a competent supervisor'.
Leadership effectiveness	5 items were rated on a 7-point Likert-type scale (1 is totally negative/disagree; 7 is totally positive/agree).
	An example item was 'Carlos knows how to manage people effectively'.

Results, findings, and conclusions

The main results per hypothesis are shown in Table 22.4.

Table 22.4 Outcomes for the hypotheses

Hypothesis	Outcome
1 Female leaders will receive less favorable evaluations than male leaders when they adopt stereotypically masculine leadership styles (autocratic and task-oriented).	Independently of sex of leader, when a leader adopted a stereotypically female leadership style they obtained more favourable adjective ratings, leadership capacity scores, and leadership effectiveness scores. See Figure 22.4. Hypothesis rejected.
2 Male leaders will not receive less favorable evaluations than female leaders when they adopt stereotypically feminine leadership behaviors (democratic, relationship-oriented, individualized consideration)	Males did not receive less favourable evaluations if they adopted a stereotypically female leadership style. Hypothesis rejected.
3 Females leaders will receive worse evaluations from male evaluators than from female evaluators. 4 Male leaders will receive similar evaluations from male and from female evaluators.	The evaluation of leaders was virtually the same when male or female on all three measures. This was also seen when the sex of participant was analysed. Both hypotheses rejected.

Cuadrado *et al* concluded that a leader was considered more efficient, competent, and generally seen as being a more positive one if the leader adopted a stereotypically female leadership style irrespective of their own sex.

Main discussion points

- Contrary to popular beliefs, stereotypically male leadership styles are seen as being less popular, effective, and 'nice'.
- The role of congruity theory of prejudice toward female leaders appears not to have any support.
- This has implications for the choice of leaders in an organisation and their subsequent training and success.

Evaluation points

- Context was gender-neutral in terms of eliciting stereotypes. Would this be the same where the job *did* have gender stereotypes?
- The study had a standardised procedure. It could easily be replicated using different settings and narratives to check for reliability.
- The sample may lack some generalisability as we do not know if the sample were, or had been, in sustained employment so they could relate to the story narratives in the real-world.

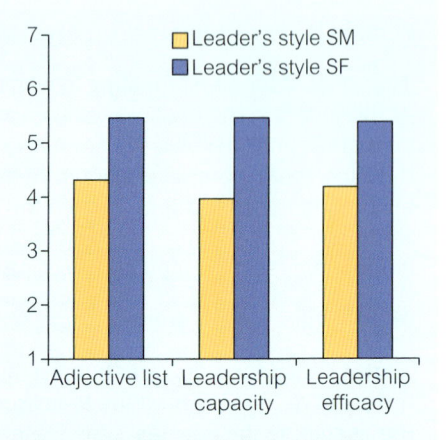

Figure 22.4 Effects of leadership style (SM = stereotypically masculine; SF = stereotypically feminine) on the adjective list, leadership capacity, and leadership efficacy

Source: Cuadrado et al (2008: 62)

Challenge yourself

Look at the issue and debate tracker table on page 286. Create similar issue and debate commentaries for individual and situational explanations, reductionism versus holism, idiographic versus nomothetic, and generalisations from findings.

22.2.3 Leaders and followers

Kouzes and Posner's Leadership Practices Inventory including five practices

Kouzes and Posner (1987) created the Leadership Practices Inventory (LPI) to allow leaders to see which of five core styles they think they use in their everyday working environment. The researchers called the five styles:

1. Model the way
2. Inspire a shared vision
3. Challenge the process
4. Enable others to act
5. Encourage the heart.

An individual completes an inventory of 30 items that cover these five core styles using the response scale shown in Table 22.5.

The inventory is also completed by a range of employees including managers and co-workers or via a direct report. Averages across all other raters is calculated. A Five Practices Data Summary sheet is produced, as shown in Table 22.6.

Table 22.5 Response scale used in this study

Response scale	
1 – Almost never	2 – Rarely
3 – Seldom	4 – Once in a while
5 – Occasionally	6 – Sometimes
7 – Fairly often	8 – Usually
9 – Very frequently	10 – Almost always

Source: Kouzes and Posner (2013: 1)

Table 22.6 Five Practices Data Summary

	Self	AVG	Individual observers							
			M1	D1	D2	D3	D4	C1	C2	C3	O1
1. Model the way	53	45.8	51	51	55	50	25	47	42	45	46
2. Inspire a shared vision	45	45.2	47	49	48	54	31	45	42	42	49
3. Challenge the process	54	49.2	49	54	58	54	29	48	51	44	56
4. Enable others to act	53	49.0	50	49	56	54	32	48	47	51	54
5. Encourage the heart	39	40.6	47	36	35	47	26	49	38	39	48

Source: Kouzes and Posner (2013: 2)

Psychology and organisations

A Leadership Behaviour Ranking chart is also produced. An example is shown in Figure 22.5.

	Practice	Self	AVG +/−	M +/−
14. Treats others with dignity and respect	Enable	8	9.6 +	6.0 −

- The AVG of all observers including manager
- LPI behavior number and statement
- Indicates the behavior is related to the practice of enable others to act
- The average observer response is more than 1.5 points higher than the self-response
- The manager response is more than 1.5 points lower than the self-response

	Practice	Self	AVG +/−	M +/−
14. Treats others with dignity and respect	Enable	8	9.2	7.0

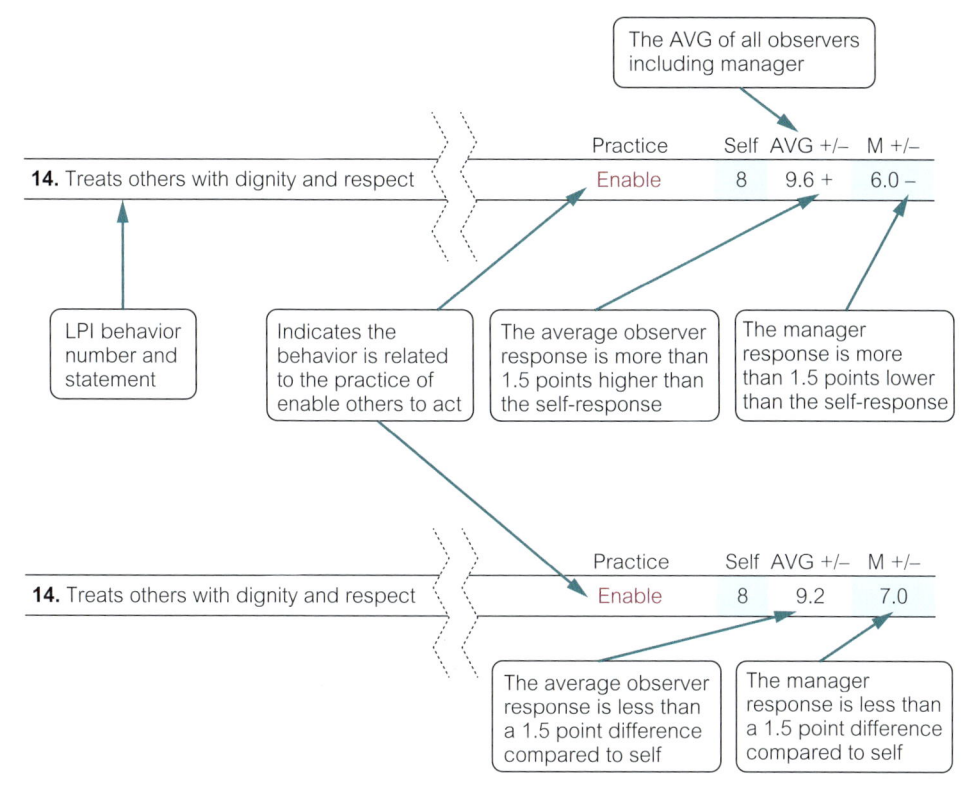

- The average observer response is less than a 1.5 point difference compared to self
- The manager response is less than a 1.5 point difference compared to self

Figure 22.5 *Leadership behaviour ranking*
Source: Kouzes and Posner (2013: 4)

Alongside many other charts and graphs, a full list ranking all 30 items based on the average score across all respondents is given, showing the most to least frequent leadership behaviours. Table 22.7 shows some examples.

Table 22.7 *Examples of leadership behaviour ranking*

Most frequent		Practice	Self	AVG +/−	M +/−
14.	Treats others with dignity and respect	Enable	10	9.6	10.0
4.	Develops cooperative relationships among the people he/she works with	Enable	8	8.4	8.0
8.	Challenges people to try out new and innovative ways to do their work	Challenge	9	7.9	8.0
26.	Is clear about his/her philosophy of leadership	Model	8	7.6	8.0
5.	Praises people for a job well done	Encourage	6	7.1	8.0 +
16.	Asks for feedback on how his/her actions affect other people's performance	Model	7	5.0 −	7.0
Least frequent					

Source: Kouzes and Posner (2013: 5)

This analysis can give leaders a clearer and more objective appraisal, helping them to pinpoint strengths and weaknesses of their current leadership qualities and behaviours. They may then wish to improve some of the weaknesses as necessary to fit in more with the ethos of their employer.

Strength	Weakness
The tool has good application as it can be used in an organisation to analyse what types of leader work there and then people can be given jobs that fit their skills.	The measurement is based on self-report and people may not always be honest about their own and others' behaviours.

Challenge yourself

To what extent do you think that the LPI is deterministic? Justify your answer.

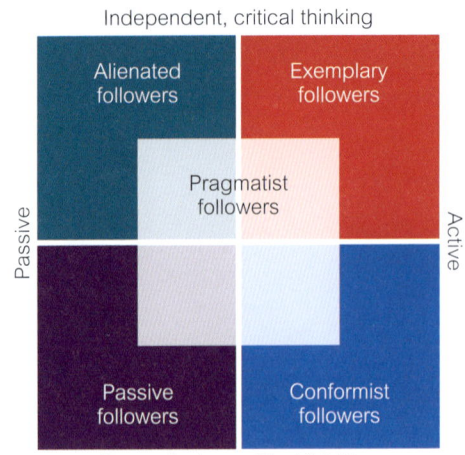

Figure 22.6 Two dimensions of followership style
Source: Based on Kelley (1988)

> **Challenge yourself**
>
> Look at the issue and debate tracker table on page 286. Create similar issue and debate commentaries for application to everyday life, idiographic versus nomothetic, self-reports, and psychometrics.

22.3 Group behaviour in organisations

Followership (Kelley, 1988)

Kelley (1988) noted five styles of followership.

- Alienated – these include people who are passive but independent. They have been effective before but may have experienced a lot of setbacks. They are capable in their jobs but always focus on the problems within an organisation. They remain cynical and do not contribute to any problem solving.

- Effective – these are people who are active and critical thinkers. They have the courage to initiate change (or help someone else who is initiating it). They are open to taking risks. They always serve the best interests of the organisation. They always work towards having a positive impact in any task given to them.

- Passive – these are people who are passive and uncritical thinkers. They lack any initiative and have no sense of responsibility. They always require supervision and always let the leader 'do the thinking' for them.

- Conformist – these people tend to be active but dependent thinkers. They happily carry out orders. They willingly participate in tasks. They are overly concerned with avoiding conflict.

- Pragmatic survivors – these people can have the qualities of the other four styles. They will change their style to suit the situation they find themselves in as long as it benefits them directly. They tend to avoid risk taking though.

The styles can be categorised on two dimensions:

- critical versus dependent thinking
- passive versus active behaviour.

Figure 22.6 shows the placing of each style on the two dimensions.

22.3.1 Group development and decision making

Stages of group development

The dynamics of a group can be assessed when we look at how groups form in organisations. Tuckman and Jensen (1977) noted a five-stage formation process.

1. Forming – members of a group get to know each other and ground rules are established in terms of conversations and appropriate behaviours. These are based around the job (the reason) that they are working but also around aspects relating to social skills (eg hierarchy).

2. Storming – this stage is characterised by group conflict. Members may want to resist any authority from whoever becomes the 'group leader' and there may be conflict between equals too (eg personality clash). If nothing can be resolved then the group dissipates. If the conflict can be overcome then the leadership stage is accepted and the group can move on.

3. Norming – this involves the group becoming more cohesive. Identification as a group member becomes stronger and the unit begins to work well on tasks. Group members begin to feel more comfortable in sharing feelings and responsibilities plus ways in which goals can be met. This stage is complete when all group members accept a common set of expectations of group behaviour.

4. Performing – the group is now set to work as a cohesive unit on tasks and to attain any goal or goals set. The group energy is diverted towards completing tasks to a high standard. The leader is now fully accepted.

5. Adjourning – there may be no longer any need for the group once the goals have been attained, so the group dissipates. This can happen abruptly (eg as a charity event ends) or take longer (eg new goals are formed that only some members of the group want to attain).

Some psychologists disagree about the nature of group formation and cohesiveness and that the order may differ between groups. This is tackled in a theory called punctuated-equilibrium model. There are just two phases that any group in an organisation goes through.

1. Phase 1 is when group members define who they are and what they want to achieve (eg goals). This phase usually lasts around 50% of the group's entire lifetime so new ideas tend not to be acted upon and the group is in a state of 'equilibrium' moving slowly towards its target.

2. Phase 2 is entered suddenly, when the group has a 'midlife crisis' and members realise that they will not achieve their goal. They recognise that they must change their outlook and pathway towards a target so they can take on new ideas and work harder to attain any goals. They move into a state of 'punctuating' to cope with these changes.

Group development (Tuckman, 1965)

Tuckman (1965) proposed a four-stage developmental procedure linked to the formation of groups.

1. Orientation to the task – group members must identify the task and then work out how best to use the group to solve it or work through it. They must decide on which type of information will be needed for the task.

2. Intra-group conflict – group members may begin to show their individuality by becoming hostile to other group members. This can easily polarise the group.

3. Development of group cohesion – the group accepts individual differences within it. Group members then 're-unite' as a force to work on the task given to them.

4. Functional role-relatedness – group members finally begin to tackle the task given to them, utilising the different strengths they have.

Belbin's nine team roles

Belbin (1981) proposed that there are nine different roles that people can take within a team. Each role category has certain strengths but also 'allowable weaknesses'. People can be in more than one team role. The roles are as follows.

1. Plant – these workers are creative, imaginative, and can solve difficult problems in a team. Their allowable weaknesses include not being able to communicate effectively as they get too pre-occupied in the task.

2. Specialist – these workers are dedicated, self-motivated, and provide much-needed knowledge and skills that could be rare. Their allowable weaknesses include sometimes dwelling on the technicalities of a task and so slowing the whole process down.

3. Monitor evaluator – these workers are strategic, seek opinions from all team members, and are accurate judges. Their allowable weaknesses include possibly lacking drive and the ability to inspire members of the team.

4. Implementer – these workers are reliable, efficient, and can easily turn ideas into practical action. Their allowable weaknesses include being somewhat inflexible and maybe too slow to respond to changing ideas.

5. Shaper – these workers are challenging and thrive on pressure. They are not afraid to take risks to complete a task. Their allowable weaknesses include being easily provoked into negative action and they may often offend the feelings of team members.

6. Completer finisher – these workers are anxious, conscientious, and are good at finding errors. They deliver projects on time every time. Their allowable weaknesses include worrying too much about tasks and being reluctant to delegate work within a team.

7. Teamworker – these workers are cooperative, perceptive, and somewhat diplomatic. They listen to other members of the team and try to avoid any friction. Their allowable weaknesses include being indecisive at crucial moments in a team task.

8. Coordinator – these workers are mature, confident, and good at being a chairperson of a team. They clarify goals and delegate tasks well within a team. Their allowable weaknesses include being manipulative at times and loading too much work onto other team members.

9. Resource investigator – these workers are extravert and enthusiastic about tasks. They like to explore opportunities for the team. Their allowable weaknesses include being overly optimistic at times and quickly losing enthusiasm if a task is not going well.

All of these types are measurable according to Belbin. He developed the Belbin Team Inventory (sometimes referred to as the Belbin Self-Perception Inventory or the Belbin Test) to show which category or categories workers fall into within a company.

Measuring team roles: the Belbin Team Inventory

The Belbin Team Inventory is a questionnaire (self-report) used to allow workers to answer a series of questions that then allocates them to one or several of the Belbin team roles outlined above.

The original inventory was split into eight sections featuring scenarios. For each of the sections there are eight answers that workers must read through and then tick a statement that describes themselves in that scenario. They can tick as many statements as they wish. Once they have completed a section, participants have to allocate a total of ten points across all of the items they have ticked to represent how often they think they react in that way. Obviously, if only one tick is present that item is given ten points. However, if more than one tick appears, participants have to divide the ten points between the items, ensuring that the total never exceeds ten for that section.

Once a participant has completed all eight sections, the points are transferred to the final grid which allows a total score to be generated for each of the team roles. Note that there were only eight categories on the original scale as 'Specialist' was added at a later date.

Strength	Weakness
The scale can be used to identify what type or types of team member a worker is, so that the person can be allocated particular tasks that require his or her skills. Therefore, it has real-life application.	As the scale is a self-report, we have to rely on workers being honest about their points allocation. Some results may not be valid as workers may want to look better than they really are.

Faulty decision making, explanations, and strategies to avoid it

Groupthink (Janis, 1971)

There may be other situations when a group decision may appear to be a good idea but it truly is not. There are two things that can happen to make the decision-making process go wrong: groupthink and group polarisation.

Groupthink is what happens when a highly cohesive group where all members respect each other's viewpoints comes to consensus on a decision too quickly without any critical evaluation. The group then makes a very poor decision as a result.

Riggio (1999) notes eight symptoms of groupthink.

- Illusion of invulnerability – as the group is so cohesive the members see themselves as powerful and invincible. They then fail to spot poorly made decisions.

- Illusion of morality – all group members see themselves as the 'good guys' who can do nothing wrong.

- Shared negative stereotypes – group members hold common beliefs.

- Collective rationalisations – group members easily dismiss any negative information that goes against their decision with no thought.

- Self-censorship – group members suppress any desire to be critical.

- Illusion of unanimity – group members can easily (and mistakenly) believe that the decision was a consensus.

- Direct conformity pressure – all those showing doubts have pressure applied to them to join the majority view.

- Mindguards – some of the group members buffer any negativity away from the group's decision.

Avoiding groupthink
Greenberg and Baron (2008) noted four different ways in which groupthink can be avoided.

- Promote open enquiry. A group leader could question all decisions made in order to get the group to think again and not go for the first, easy option. Leaders should also encourage members to question and be sceptical so that all decisions are thoroughly assessed.

- Use subgroups. Split the members of the main group up and set them exactly the same decision-making tasks. Get them to present their findings; differences between the subgroups can be discussed to form an overall group decision. If the subgroups agree then you can safely say that groupthink has not generated that decision.

- Admit shortcomings. You need to get members of the group to be critical and point out any *potential* flaws or limitations of the decisions being made. This should allow the group as a whole to discuss these to ensure that group members have not simply decided on the easiest option.

- Hold second-chance meetings. Allow group members to digest the original decision then get them back for a second meeting so they can discuss anything that is worrying them about the decision. This allows 'freshness' to be resumed; if a decision task is tiring group members they will go for the easy option. Having two 'fresh' attempts at the decision should reduce the probability of groupthink.

Forsyth's cognitive limitations and errors

Forsyth (2006) discusses the potential cognitive limitation and errors made by groups during decision-making processes. Prior to meetings, during meetings and after meetings, people have to think about ideas and potential consequences either by themselves and/or as part of a decision-making group. Forsyth notes the three types of 'sin' committed during group decision making, based on the work of MacCoun and Kramer in the mid-1990s.

- Sins of commission involve misusing information.
- Sins of omission involve overlooking information.
- Sins of imprecision involve relying inappropriately on mental 'rules of thumb' or heuristics that are inappropriate.

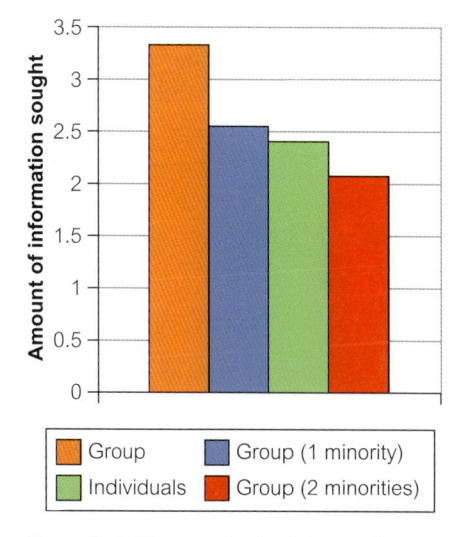

Figure 22.7 *The magnitude of the confirmation bias in groups and individuals*

Notes: 'Individuals, when they must make a decision, tend to seek out information that supports their initial preferences. This tendency is even stronger in groups, for groups showed a stronger preference for confirming information. Groups that include two members who initially disagree with the position taken by the majority of members, however, are somewhat less biased than individuals.'

Source: Forsyth (2006: 332)

Sins of commission have four sub-types:

- belief perseverance: when people rely too much on information that has already been reviewed by others and deemed inaccurate
- sunk cost bias: when people are reluctant to abandon a course of 'thinking action' once an investment has been made (even if it is clearly not the best option)
- extra-evidentiary bias: when people use information that they have been explicitly told to ignore
- hindsight bias: when people overestimate the accuracy of their knowledge of an outcome.

Sins of omission have two sub-types:

- base-rate bias: when people fail to attend to information about general tendencies
- fundamental attribution error: when people attribute the cause of behaviours to dispositional factors while overlooking potential situational factors.

Sins of imprecision have three sub-types:

- availability heuristic: when people base their decisions on information that is readily available and do not hunt for other useful information
- conjunctive bias: when people fail to recognise that the probability of two events occurring together will always be less than the probability of just one of those events occurring
- representativeness heuristic: when people excessively rely on salient but misleading aspects of a problem.

In addition, Forsyth notes that a confirmation bias can also cause errors in thinking within groups. This is when we have the tendency to seek out information that confirms our beliefs rather than disconfirms. This can become a major issue if individuals within a group continue to do this if it means that a unified solution cannot be reached. Forsyth noted research that showed that this bias is seen much more in a homogenous group than when individuals make decisions or when there are dissenters in the group.

22.3.2 Individual and group performance

Individual and group performance – social facilitation, social loafing, drive theory, evaluation apprehension, and social impact theory

Social facilitation

This follows the idea that the presence of others leads to an increase on a dominant response based on situational factors. There are two fundamental processes here.

1. When other people are around (and watching), we experience an increase in emotional arousal like feeling more excited or more tense.
2. Once this emotional arousal happens, people tend to perform what the most 'dominant' response is, based on the setting they are in. This is likely to be the correct response. However, if a behaviour is new and has not been established within the person then the 'dominant' response is more likely to be incorrect.

Therefore, the mere presence of others around us leads to increased motivation and effort and, in most cases, increased output.

> **Challenge yourself**
>
> Look at the issue and debate tracker table on page 300. Create similar issue and debate commentaries for application to everyday life, individual versus situational explanations, reductionism versus holism, idiographic versus nomothetic, and generalisations from findings.

Social loafing

This is based around the idea that individuals show *less* effort when working as part of a group on a task compared to if they were to complete the task individually. This is particularly true of 'additive' tasks, which are ones where all members of a group are performing similar tasks and so the overall output is pooled. Buchanan and Huczynski (2010) noted four reasons why social loafing occurs.

1. Negative effect of a group reward – the idea is that if everyone in the group will get the same reward, why should I put extra effort in?
2. Equity of effort – if other people don't contribute, why should I?
3. Problems of coordination – this could happen when group members get in the way of each other.
4. Dispersion of responsibility – when an individual is 'hidden' within a group, they believe no one will notice them putting in less effort.

Drive theory

This theory attempts to explain some of the effects of social facilitation. Zajonc (1980) used the term *compresence* to describe a state of responding when in the presence of others. It is a basic arousal response in social species. When tasks are easy, compresence elevates drive levels, and this then causes social facilitation. The theory also predicts that social facilitation will occur when all forms of social interaction and communication are blocked, due to compresence.

Evaluation apprehension

This theory also attempts to explain some of the effects of social facilitation. Cottrell (1972) believed that evaluative pressure is one of the reasons why people become more productive in the presence of others. As individuals we have learned, through experience, that other people are the source of most rewards and punishments we receive. Therefore, we begin to associate social situations with evaluations and as a result become apprehensive whenever people are around us. It actually helps with simple tasks but with complex tasks it can be devastating, and we easily fail to complete tasks.

Social impact theory

This theory attempts to explain some of the effects of social loafing. When there is a group task at work, there will be a number of forces acting upon that group. One force might be that a certain task requires completing by a certain date. These forces become divided equally by all members of the group. The larger the group, the lower any impact one of these forces will have on an individual group member. Also, responsibility for the task becomes easily diffused within the group.

> **Test yourself**
>
> Explain at least one strength and one weakness of each of these ideas about individual and group performance. Are there any similarities or differences?

Group performances across cultures – social loafing

A study by Clark and Baker (2011) examined culture and social loafing in ethnically diverse groups in New Zealand. Using a range of quantitative and qualitative methods, they collected data about social loafing in people categorised as being from individualistic-type cultures (eg Western students) and collectivist-type cultures (eg Chinese students living and studying in New Zealand). Questionnaires and semi-structured focus groups were used to collect data about *perceptions* of social loafing. When attitudes towards accountability in culturally diverse student groups were examined, concerns about social loafing and inequality within these groups were similar between individualistic-type cultures and collectivist-type cultures. The findings did not support an assumption that people from collectivist-type cultures are less likely to withdraw efforts in group work. The opposite was found; those from collectivist-type cultures were not only fully aware that they did not contribute 'equally' in group tasks, but they were aware that it was not in their best interest to do this. Clark and Baker suggest that this type of behaviour shown by people from collectivist-type cultures could be based on prior experiences, linguistic issues that inhibit full understanding of a group task, or different cultural values.

Strength	Weakness
A mix of quantitative and qualitative methodology was used to give a diverse set of data that could be used to help explain social loafing and its potential causes. This means that the overall conclusions have increased validity due to the in-depth analyses that were conducted on the data collected.	Research into socially sensitive concepts such as social loafing tend to produce ethical and moral dilemmas. While research is needed to help understand why people behave in the way they do, some areas can have ethical and moral implications that can lead to prejudice and other negative issues. When a particular culture is shown to be more likely to engage in social loafing, does the end justify the means? Could these findings be used in the 'wrong way'?

Performance monitoring of employee productivity

KEY STUDY: Claypoole and Szalma (2019), experiment 1

Context

Previous research had shown that electronic performance monitoring (EPM) could improve employee productivity and performance at work. However, the majority of this research has used a computer-based electronic 'presence' to test the effectiveness of EPM for clerical tasks that are brief. There had been little research testing the effectiveness of EPM on tasks that require vigilance for a sustained period of time.

Main theories/explanations

EPM is any electronic system that is used by an organisation to help monitor and then evaluate performance of employees. Vigilance, which is sometimes referred to as sustained attention, is a person's ability to maintain a concentrated level of attention over a sustained period of time. Social facilitation was also investigated in this study (see page 296).

Aims and hypotheses

There were two main overall aims of the study.

1. To examine the effects of EPM on vigilance.
2. To provide some evidence that video-based monitoring can be just as effective as EPM.

Claypoole and Szalma ran two studies, but you only need to know about experiment (study) 1.

Design

Participants

The sample consisted of 106 participants (65 female; mean age 20.57 years, range 18–37 years). All were undergraduates and recruited via volunteer sampling using a psychology experiment website at a large university. They all received course credit for participation. All responses remained anonymous and informed consent was taken. Once the study had finished, all participants were debriefed.

Conditions

There were two conditions.

1. Control – there was no social presence. The participant completed the task alone.
2. Electronic presence – there were two forms of social presence: a webcam and a video recorder. Both made noises and/or a light appeared to show participants that they were being watched.

The task

Participants were asked to look at a computer display of two-digit numbers. They were asked to only respond to a 'critical signal' by pressing the space bar. A 'critical signal' was when the difference between the two-digits was 0 or 1. So 45 was a critical signal but 62 was not. There were five critical signals per six-minute period. The entire task lasted 24 minutes, meaning there was a total of 20 critical signals per participant.

Results, findings, and conclusions

Figure 22.8 shows the proportion of correct detections of a critical signal, split by the four periods of six minutes.

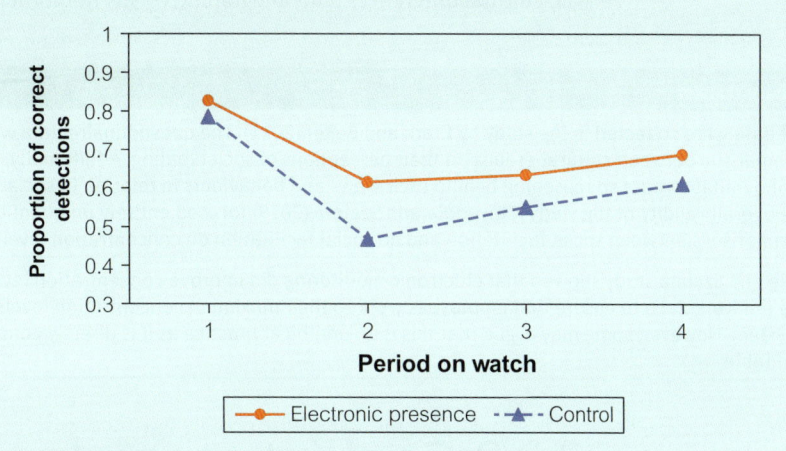

Figure 22.8 *The proportion of correct detections as a function of period on watch and experimental condition*

Overall, those with the electronic presence detected significantly more critical signals compared to the control condition. There was no significant difference between groups at any of the four periods of six minutes.

In terms of false alarms, those with the electronic presence produced significantly fewer compared to the control condition. There was no significant difference between groups at any of the four periods of six minutes. Also, irrespective of condition, the proportion of false alarms decreased significantly over time.

In terms of response times, those with the electronic presence detected critical signals faster compared to the control condition. There was no significant difference between groups at any of the four periods of six minutes. Also, irrespective of condition, median response times increased significantly over time.

In conclusion, the act of social facilitation via electronic presence appears to increase vigilance, decreases errors, and improves speed of accuracy compared to having no social presence.

Main discussion points

- EPM does seem to be successful at improving the vigilance of people who are engaging in cognitively demanding but boring tasks.
- The study lends support to social facilitation having a positive impact on workers engaged in these types of tasks.

Evaluation

- There were two forms of electronic presence used in the study: webcam and video. All we know is that the electronic performance group performed better and faster. We do not know if it was because one electronic presence was needed, or because both were needed. In terms of real-world applicability, based around cost, it would have been useful to know if just one type works.
- Generalisability is low for two reasons. The task may not effectively generalise to any monotonous, cognitively demanding process in the workplace. Also, the participants were all undergraduate students who are used to be evaluated under supervision (eg taking national and international examinations) so may have performed better and faster because of that, rather than the presence of a webcam or video. They may have not felt anxiety in the same way a worker might in an organisation.
- The procedure used in the study was clear and standardised. The recruitment process, the actual tasks, and the electronic presence equipment were clearly outlined so other researchers can replicate the study to test for reliability.

> **Challenge yourself**
>
> Evaluate this study based on ethical issues surrounding the procedure and its usefulness in the real world.

> **Challenge yourself**
>
> Create similar issue and debate tracker commentaries for determinism versus free will, cultural differences, and idiographic versus nomothetic.

	Issue and debate tracker
Quantitative and qualitative data	Both types of data were collected in the study by Clark and Baker (2011). The questionnaire data was quantitative which allowed a statistical comparison between cultural groups on their perceptions of social loafing. Additionally, the focus groups allowed for an exploration of qualitative data so reasoning behind their views and behaviours in relation to social loafing could be explored. This increases the overall validity of the study. Claypoole and Szalma (2019) focused entirely on quantitative data which also allowed statistical comparisons between social facilitation and no social facilitation on concentration levels.
Application to everyday life	The Claypoole and Szalma study showed that electronic monitoring did improve concentration levels in participants. This could be applied to the workplace to ensure that employees work to their maximum concentration levels by having an electronic monitoring system. However, some may argue that this is an unethical practice as it is directly controlling employees which can be seen as inequitable.

22.3.3 Conflict at work

There may be times in any organisation where there is group conflict. There are different types of conflict.

- Intra-group conflict is when people within the same group conflict and this interferes with the pathway towards a goal.
- Inter-group conflict is when there is conflict between different groups within an organisation.
- Inter-individual conflict is when two individuals within a group or organisation have a dispute.

Levels and causes of group conflict

Organisational and interpersonal

There can be any number of reasons why group conflict can happen within an organisation. According to Riggio (1999), there appear to be two broad categories of group conflict.

- Organisational factors form one broad category. For example, status differences within an organisation might cause friction. There could be conflict between people about the best pathway towards a goal. There may be a lack of resources such as money, supplies or staff which can cause conflict too. Also, when there are groups that form a 'chain of events' for a task to be completed, there are many opportunities for things to go wrong and hence conflict occurs.
- Interpersonal reasons make up the other broad category. These are things such as the personal qualities of two workers 'clashing', meaning they do not cooperate on tasks. It may be that individuals simply cannot get along with each other or due to a failed task may never want to work with each other again. Sometimes, if the conflict is between two heads of different departments, this can escalate into conflict between those departments as a result.

Positive and negative effects of conflict

Conflict that occurs within an organisation can have both negative and positive effects.

- There could be the following negative effects. Group cohesiveness may diminish as people do not get on. Communication can be inhibited as a result of people not talking. Workers may no longer trust each other due to conflict. Constant 'bickering' can reduce productivity and goal attainment.

- Here are some examples of positive effects. Conflict may get group members to rethink what they are doing. This improves creativity and innovation (and reduces the problems of groupthink). Workers may become less complacent with their work if conflict is occurring. If it means that the whole workforce is listened to and consulted then productivity may increase as all workers feel 'part of the organisation'.

Thomas–Kilmann's five conflict-handling modes

Thomas and Kilmann (quoted in Riggio, 1992) identified five different strategies that can be used to manage group conflict in an organisation.

- Competition – individuals may persist in conflict until someone wins and someone loses and then the conflict apparently, diminishes within the groups these individuals are from.
- Accommodation – this involves making a 'sacrifice' in order to reduce conflict and can help to cut losses and save the relationship between the two groups in conflict.
- Compromise – each group under conflict must give up something to help resolve the conflict. This can only be achieved if both sides can lose things that are comparable.
- Collaboration – the groups need to work together to overcome the conflict as long as resources are not scarce.
- Avoidance – this involves suppressing the conflict or withdrawing from the conflict completely. Neither side can truly resolve the conflict; the differences are still there and have not been worked through. This strategy can be used if the conflict is so aggressive that both sides need to 'cool off'.

Another technique might be for managers to create a superordinate goal. This is a goal that the conflicting groups are willing to work for together. This will focus them away from the original conflict. Also, managers can use their authority to call a vote on the conflict situation. As a result, the majority of workers will 'win' the conflict and managers then have to deal with the losing workers. Managers could also create opportunities for both groups to get a better understanding of one another through workshops, discussion, and presentations.

Bullying at work

Einarsen (1999) reviewed the nature and cause of bullying at work. There appear to be five types of behaviour that can be classified as bullying:

- work-related bullying, which can include changing work tasks or making them too difficult to perform
- social isolation
- personal attacks or some form of attack on someone's personal life
- verbal threats
- physical violence or the threat of it.

In terms of bullying at work, surveys tend to show that there are three main reasons behind it:

- competition concerning status and job positions
- envy
- the aggressors being uncertain about themselves.

When surveys have asked people which one of the above they think is the main reason for bullying at work, around 67% have answered 'envy'. However, Einarsen notes that there are also four factors that appear to be common in eliciting harassment at work:

Challenge yourself

Can you find any empirical evidence to support Thomas-Killmann's ideas?

Challenge yourself

You have been asked to help out a company that is experiencing group conflict. What advice would you give to the managers of the company as to the best ways they can manage group conflict? Justify your answer.

Challenge yourself

Design a study that investigates bullying at work.

> **Challenge yourself**
>
> Look at the issue and debate tracker table on page 300. Create similar issue and debate commentaries for application to everyday life, individual versus situational explanations, reductionism versus holism, idiographic versus nomothetic.

22.4 Organisational work conditions

- deficiencies in work design (eg having a heavy workload compared to an 'equal' colleague)
- deficiencies in leadership behaviour (eg a lack of constructive leadership and too much destructive leadership; also, predatory bullying may already be a common trait seen in leaders at a company)
- a socially exposed position of the victim
- a low moral standard within the department.

22.4.1 Physical work conditions

The Hawthorne studies (Wikstrom and Bendix, 2000)

In this review, Wikstrom and Bendix (2000) looked at what the original (1920s) Hawthorne studies actually showed. The 'Hawthorne effect' is a psychological term that refers to the effect when people know they are taking part in a study: they may change their behaviour as a result of being observed. As a result, any behavioural changes may be due to this effect rather than any manipulation such as an IV. Therefore, findings from such studies could be questionable.

The original studies into the Hawthorne effect were brought about by the managers of the Hawthorne Plant in Chicago, USA in the 1920s. They wanted to test the effects of lighting on the productivity of their staff. They systematically reduced the illumination levels for the experimental group, whereas the control had constant illumination. Workers in both groups increased their productivity levels over time (inspecting parts, winding coils, and assembling relays). When the light 'resembled moonlight levels' the workers in the experimental group began to complain that the light levels were affecting their work.

Light levels did not appear to affect productivity. However, as the workers knew they were in a study, it could have been this that made them work 'better' and therefore the light levels did not have the desired effect.

Wikstrom and Bendix concluded that while the original studies may have shown the Hawthorne effect, many subsequent studies probably haven't and they listed other factors that might be affecting the productivity of workers during a study:

- relief from a harsh supervisor
- having positive attention for their work
- having rest pauses different from a normal work session
- higher income
- thinking they may be influencing work procedures.

Open-plan offices (Oldham and Brass, 1979)

Oldham and Brass (1979) studied changes in employees' reactions to work when they were moved from a conventional office to an open-plan office (one without interior walls or partitions). The setting was a newspaper organisation with 21 different job roles, ranging from reporter and copy-editor to receptionist and clerk. At the beginning of the study, all employees worked in conventional offices and the company had been contemplating moving to an open-plan design for some years. There were three 'waves' of data collection.

1. T1 was approximately eight weeks before the planned move.
2. T2 was nine weeks after the move to an open-plan office.
3. T3 was 18 weeks after the move to an open-plan office.

The same questionnaire was given to employees at each time point. The researchers measured aspects of the job such as autonomy, skill variety, task identity, task significance and task feedback. Aspects such as intra-departmental and inter-departmental interaction were also measured. A measure of concentration was also taken. In addition, outcome measures were taken relating to:

- work satisfaction
- interpersonal satisfaction
- internal work motivation.

A total of 140 non-supervisory members of the company were invited to take part in the study and 128 participated. They were split into the following groups.

1. The experimental group (n = 76) were employees who moved to the open-plan office and completed measures at T1, T2, and T3.
2. The non-equivalent control group (n = 5) were members of the pressroom who did not move. They completed all measures at T1, T2, and T3.
3. The quasi-control group (n = 26) were chosen 'at random' and moved to the open-plan office but only completed measures at T2, and T3.

At T2 and T3, groups 1 and 3 did not differ significantly on all but one measure – supervisory feedback – meaning that the exposure to the measures at T1 was not responsible for any of the changes seen at T2 and T3. Therefore, the researchers focused on the experimental group to see whether the three main measures changed over time. The results showed significant changes, as shown in Table 22.8.

Table 22.8 shows that all measures decreased over time, meaning that the workers became less satisfied with work, experienced less interpersonal satisfaction at work and also reported less internal work motivation. Therefore, it would appear that open-plan offices do not help in giving workers satisfaction and motivation to perform their daily tasks. This may be due to a change in job characteristics accompanying the move to an open-plan office.

Strength	Weakness
The study followed a standardised procedure so it can be easily replicated to test for reliability.	The study used just one company changing its offices so generalisation is difficult.

22.4.2 Temporal conditions of work environments

Temporal conditions refer to the time conditions in which people work. There are many different work patterns that people follow around the world, from the 9am to 5pm work pattern, to shift-workers' hours, to those 'on call'. Below we look at some of the options an organisation has when choosing the temporal conditions for its workers.

Shift work

Rapid rotation (metropolitan rota and continental rota) and slow rotation

Shift work refers to when a worker does not do the same work pattern each week. Workers need to alternate the times they work so that an organisation can, say, operate on a 24-hour basis. Workers alternating between day and night shifts is a good example. However, more organisations run a rotation of three shifts per day: day shift (typically 6am to 2pm), afternoon or twilight shift (2pm to 10pm), and

Table 22.8 Median internal consistency reliabilities and intercorrelations among all variables (n = 76)

Variables	Internal consistency reliability	1	2
1 Work satisfaction	.86		
2 Interpersonal satisfaction	.85	.67	
3 Internal motivation	.82	.48	.38

Source: Oldham and Brass (1979: 278)

Challenge yourself

Look at the issue and debate tracker table on page 307. Create similar issue and debate commentaries for determinism versus free will, experiments, questionnaires, longitudinal studies, and quantitative and qualitative data.

night shift (10pm to 6am). Therefore, workers need to change their 'working day'. There are different options that an organisation can use for this.

- Rapid rotation – these are frequent shift changes that workers have to follow. There are two types:
  - A metropolitan rota is where workers complete two day shifts, then two twilight shifts, then two night shifts. This is then followed by two days off work.
  - A continental rota is where workers complete two day shifts, two twilight shifts, three night shifts, two days off work, two day shifts, three twilight shifts, two night shifts, then three days off work. After this, the rotation begins again.

- Slow rotation – these are infrequent changes of shift that workers have to follow. For example, they may work day shifts for three weeks or more, have a few days off, then work night shifts for three weeks or more. This type of shift pattern allows workers' circadian rhythm (their daily rhythm of sleep and wake) to adapt to a particular shift rather then it being 'out of sync' with work patterns, which can happen on a rapid rotation. Circadian rhythms need time to adapt to a change in shift pattern. If they do not there can be long-term health implications and some studies have even suggested that people who work shifts have higher rates of mortality. Also, when working at night, workers are attempting to go against their biological clock. During the night, humans are expected to sleep so our cognitive functioning decreases. This means we are more prone to accidents and making errors on tasks at night.

On-call working and flexitime

On-call working involves being available in case you are needed for work. So, workers can be contacted to provide a service, if necessary, even though they are not formally on duty. Flexitime is a system where workers have a set number of hours and can choose their start and finish time per day as long as by the end of the week they have worked all contracted hours. For example, employees might have a 35-hour week using flexitime. If allowed they could do ten-hour days on Monday, Tuesday, and Wednesday, have Thursday off and then work five hours on Friday. This would have to fit into the workplace system. For example, an office might not be open for ten hours per day. However, with more home working this is a feasible option for many.

Effects of shift work on health and accidents

Knutsson (2003) reviewed the effects of shift work on health. Here are the main findings given under the headings of six health issues:

- *Mortality* There was no evidence to suggest that shift work directly affects mortality rates.

- *Gastrointestinal diseases* These are much more common in shift workers than in day workers. Common complaints include changes to bowel habits, and ulcers.

- *Cardiovascular disease* Shift workers had a 40% excess risk of developing cardiovascular disease compared to day workers. Factors such as work schedules, noise, and chemical compounds used at work also affected cardiovascular disease rates.

- *Cancer* Knutsson states '…. there is no conclusive evidence that night work *per se* increases the risk of cancer' (2003: 105).

- *Diabetes and metabolic disturbances* Studies have shown that concentrations of potassium, uric acid, glucose, cholesterol, and total lipids increase during night

> **Challenge yourself**
>
> Explain the benefits and problems with each type of shift work pattern (including slow rotation), on-call working, and following flexitime. Which one is the best for a worker?

> **Challenge yourself**
>
> Design a field experiment that investigates whether the metropolitan rota or the continental rota is seen as being better by workers in a company.

work. However, they do return to typical levels upon return to day work. Some studies have indicated that the prevalence of diabetes increases with more and more exposure to shift work.

- *Pregnancy* There is some evidence to suggest that shift work leads to low birth weight and increased spontaneous abortion.

The review also suggested a pathway between shift work and disease. This is shown in Figure 22.9. Therefore, it would appear that shift work can have detrimental effects on health.

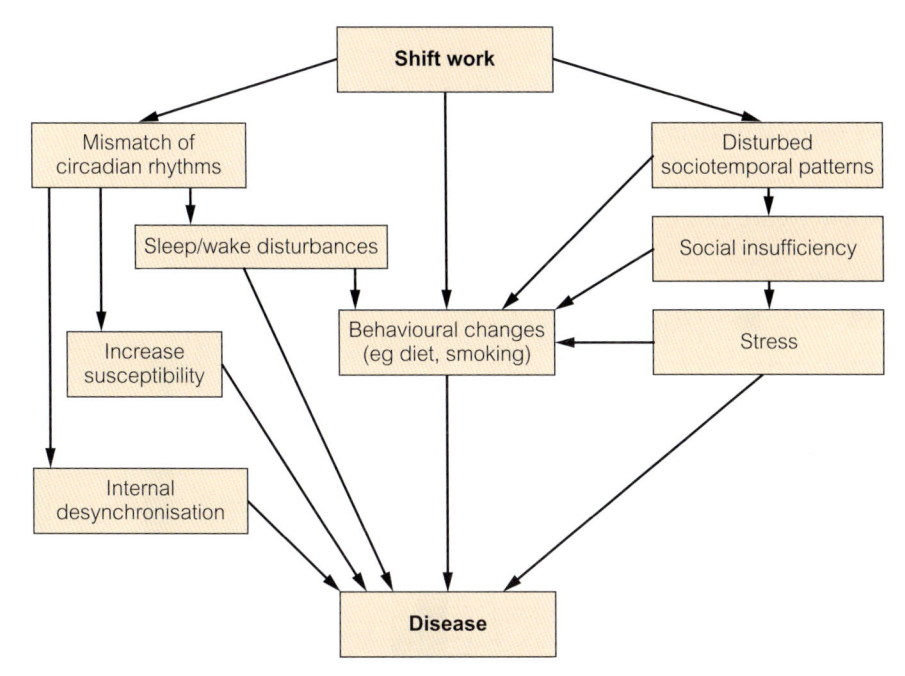

Figure 22.9 *Disease mechanisms in shift workers*
Source: Based on Knutsson (2003: 106)

Shift work and accidents

Gold *et al* (1992) examined the effect shift work had on sleep and accidents related to sleepiness in hospital nurses. The sample was of female nurses (n = 878) in a hospital in Massachusetts, USA. Participants completed a self-administered questionnaire that covered:

- current shift work patterns
- quality of sleep
- alcohol usage
- medication
- use of sleeping aids and/or drugs
- nodding off at work and while driving to and from work
- accidents, errors, and 'near-misses'.

The nurses were split into different work schedule categories, as shown in Figure 22.10.

Figure 22.10 *Work schedule categories of nurses surveyed*

Day/evening (n = 336): Within a month, working ≥ 4 day or evening shifts but no night shifts.
Night (n = 69): Within a month, working ≥ 8 night shifts and no day/evening shifts.
Rotator (n = 119): Within a month, working ≥ 4 day or evening shifts and ≥ 4 night shifts.
Day/evening, occasional night (n = 61): Within a month, working ≥ 4 day or evening shifts and 1–3 night shifts.
Night, occasional day/evening (n = 14): Within a month, working ≥ 8 night shifts and 1–3 day or evening shifts.
Part-time rotator (n = 17): Within a month, working 4–7 night shifts and 0–3 day or evening shifts.

Source: Gold *et al* (1992: 1012)

A total of 687 questionnaires were used in the analyses. The patterns of sleep are shown in Figure 22.11.

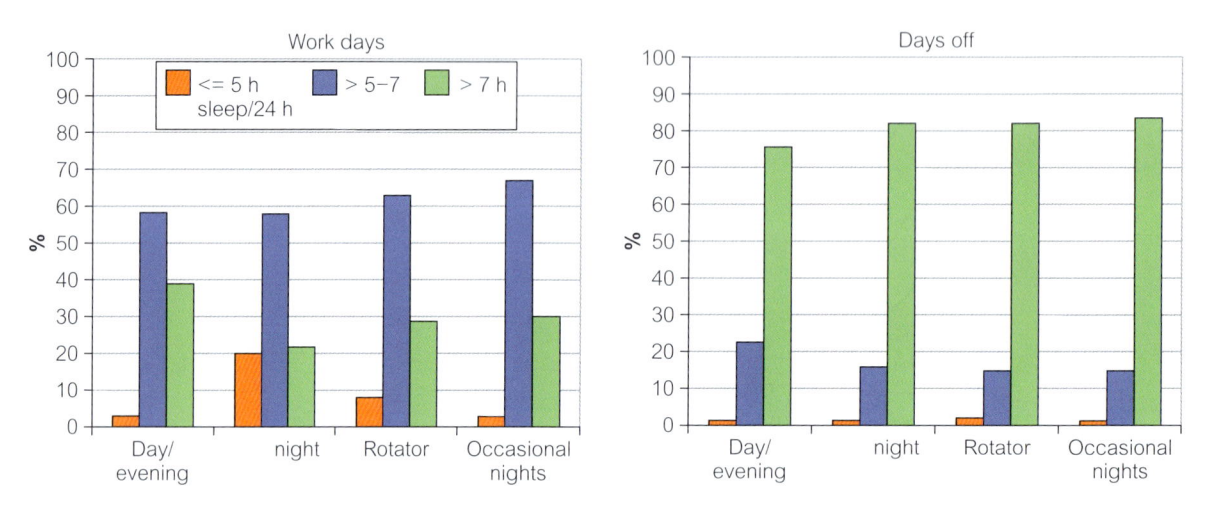

Figure 22.11 Hours of sleep per 24 hours on work days and on days-off by category of work schedule

Notes: Only 3% of day/evening nurses slept ≤5 hours/24 hours on work days, as compared to 8% of rotators and 20% of night nurses. Less than 50% of nurses from each of the work schedules slept >7 hours/24 hours on work days. On days-off greater than 75% of nurses from each of the work schedules slept >7 hours/24 hours.

Source: Gold *et al* (1992: 1012)

These were some of the other key results.

- Rotators and night nurses reported fewer hours of sleep than the other groups.
- Night workers were 1.8 times more likely to report poor-quality sleep compared to day/evening nurses. This rose to 2.8 times more likely for rotators.
- Nodding off at work occurred at least once per week for 35.3% of rotators, 32.4% of night nurses and 20.7% of day/night nurses.
- Compared to the day/night group, rotators were 3.9 times more likely and night nurses 3.6 times more likely to nod off driving to and from work.
- Two confounding variables were reported that could affect the type of relationship between shift work, accidents and type of accident: nurses who had worked for less than a year were more likely to have had an accident and an age of 35 years or younger predicted near-miss car accidents.
- Reporting any kind of accident was twice as high for rotators compared to day/night nurses.

It would appear that sleep deprivation that affects circadian rhythms during rotating shift work is clearly associated with errors in job performance and with accidents.

Strength	Weakness
A large, diverse sample was used in the hospital so it is likely that the findings can be generalised beyond the sample and have some validity.	The data was collected through questionnaires and participants may not have remembered things correctly or been honest in their answers, potentially lowering the validity of the findings.

	Issue and debate tracker
Questionnaires	The Gold *et al* (1992) study used questionnaires as the primary data collection method. This had the strength of people being able to accurately record aspects such as sleep patterns, medication use, and alcohol consumption in a non-invasive way. This should theoretically improve validity as they would be more likely to record truthful usage, etc. However, as some of the topics were socially sensitive (eg alcohol usage and falling asleep while driving), people may show some levels of social desirability and *not* reveal the full truth for fear of being judged by the research team, especially if it showed that the participant was the cause of a workplace accident.
Application to everyday life	The types of shift work can easily be used in everyday life by organisations, private or public, that require their business to be open 24/7. The different types of work design can be considered when creating new positions or opportunities within an organisation. Also, the findings from the Gold *et al* study can be used by organisations to improve the quality of working conditions for those positions where accident rates are higher due to work design patterns. This should then reduce the amount of accidents recorded within that organisation.

> **Challenge yourself**
>
> Create similar issue and debate commentaries for determinism versus free will, quantitative and qualitative data, and validity.

22.4.3 Health and safety

Accidents at work focusing on human errors and system errors

Operator–machine systems

Operator–machine systems are those where human workers have to interact with machinery to do their job. We will look at visual and auditory displays and controls. With technological advances still happening at a rapid pace, organisational psychologists need to help companies with the design of machinery to make the job more efficient but also to stop errors and accidents from occurring.

Visual displays and controls
There are three types of visual displays that can be used in organisational machinery.

- Quantitative – these are displays that project numbers giving data – temperature, time, speed, etc. Digital displays have taken over from, for example, 'clock-like' displays as they are much easier to read and fewer errors occur.

- Qualitative – these are displays that allow for a judgement using words as the tool. For example, a piece of machinery may not project temperatures as a number but have sections simply labelled 'cold', 'normal', and 'hot' – workers can then judge what to do based on this information.

- Check-reading – these are simpler displays where the information is limited but highly useful. For example, there may be a simple on–off button, or a light that comes on when something is not working correctly (or is working correctly).

Auditory displays and controls

In addition to a variety of visual displays noted above, auditory displays can be used. Buzzers, bells, or a constant pitched sound can alert workers to a potential problem or that a job is completed in a production line. Workers no longer have to be looking at a display to know what is happening; the sound tells them. The type of noise is what Riggio (1999) called 'psychologically effective'. That is, a really loud blaring horn or repetitive short beeps are usually perceived as danger so a worker will be alerted to something that is occurring.

Riggio (1999) noted when it was better to use either visual displays or auditory displays.

- It is better to use visual displays when: a message is complex, a permanent messuage is needed, the work area is too noisy, the workers' jobs involve reading information from displays, etc.

- It is better to use auditory displays when: a message is simple, the work area is too dark to see a visual readout, workers need to move about as part of their job, the message is urgent, information is continually changing, etc.

Errors and accidents in operator–machine systems

When a worker and machine are interacting, it is inevitable that at some point an error will be made. According to Riggio (1999), this can happen in four different ways.

- An error of omission is made. This refers to a failure to do something (eg a worker may fail to switch something on or off).

- An error of commission is made. This refers to performing a task incorrectly (eg a worker may simply not follow an instruction).

- An error of sequence is made. This refers to not following a set procedure for a task (eg a worker may work out of sequence, causing an error).

- An error of timing is made. This refers to performing a task too slowly or too quickly (eg a worker may press a button too quickly on a machine or not quickly enough to turn it off).

There are other factors that may well affect works and cause them to perform a task incorrectly.

- There may be lack of training on using a piece of equipment or the manual may be too complicated to understand.

- Some workers have a personality trait called accident proneness – the way the coordinate themselves both physically and psychologically makes them more likely to have an accident or make an error.

- Fatigue may be a factor. Workers who are having to cover a night shift are more likely to have accidents or make an error as they are working against their natural circadian rhythm – between 1am and 4am the human body is in a 'cognitive dip' as the body is promised for sleep and not, for example, working machinery.

See also Fox *et al* (1987) on pages 269–270. This study investigated the effect of a token economy scheme on reducing accidents at work.

Monitoring accidents

KEY STUDY: Swat (1997)

Context

Prior to the study, the reporting and documenting of occupational accidents in Poland was not effective. The limited documentation could not show the main causes of accidents, how they were monitored, and what risk factors could be involved in such incidents.

Aims and hypotheses

To investigate and develop a method of recording risk events in various industrial plants to help understand the causes of accidents and, subsequently, ways to prevent them.

Design

This was a three-year longitudinal study, using four plants involved in different industrial activities. These were foundry (cast iron parts), machinery (textile machines), meat processing, and furniture (mainly for residential use). All of the plants were 'rather old'. There were nearly 3000 workers employed across the four plants.

Two main measures were taken.

1. Accident frequency – this is the number of injury accidents resulting in sick leave, per 100 employees per year.
2. Accident severity rates – this is the number of sick leave days taken per accident.

In addition, minor incidents were logged in the meat-processing plant as a measure of workers' safety.

An accident was defined as one that had been formally reported by the safety supervisor in the plant. An incident was defined as any sudden event that resulted in some form of personal injury. Incidents were logged via first-aid reports and interviews with 96 workers in the meat-processing plant.

Results, findings, and conclusions

The average accident frequency (Figure 22.12) and average accident severity rates (Figure 22.13) are shown below.

There were five categories of accidents:

1. Falls and slips
2. Accidents that were connected to manual work
3. Accidents that were connected to coming into contact with working parts of a machine
4. Accidents that were connected to coming into contact with sources of energy
5. Other

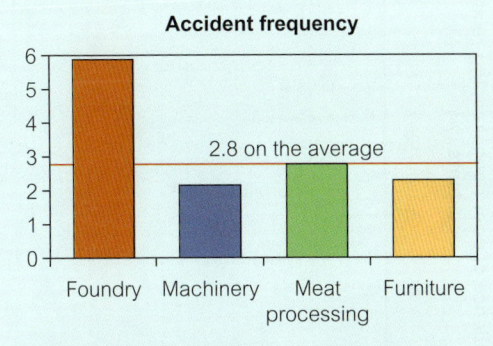

Figure 22.12 Average accident frequency in the individual plants versus the rate for all plants studied

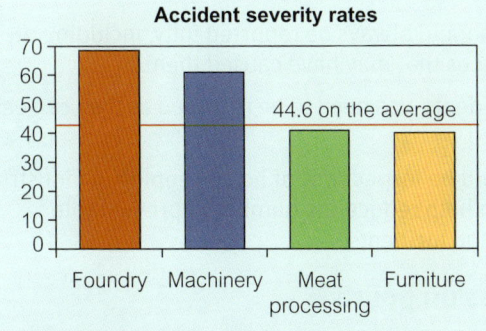

Figure 22.13 Average accident severity rates in the individual plants versus the rate for all plants studied

Figure 22.14 shows the distribution of these five categories across the four types of industrial plant.

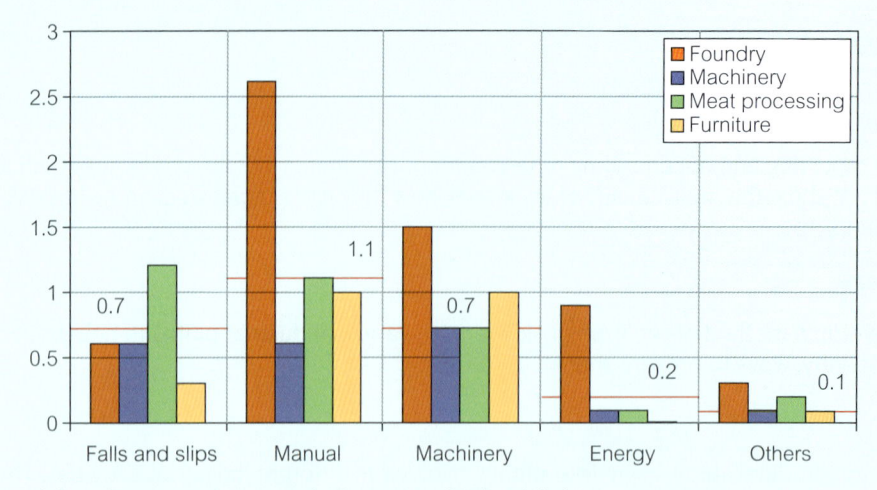

Figure 22.14 *The distribution of these five categories across the four types of industrial plant*

There were also four main causes of accidents and an accident could be a combination of one or more.

1. There is insufficient supervision of workers.
2. Workplace organisation is poor, including inadequate protective equipment and incorrect work procedures.
3. Technical factors cause accidents.
4. Worker inadvertence is the cause – this means individual error that no supervisor could predict.

Figure 22.15 shows the percentage of accidents attributed to each of the four main causes.

As there appeared to be a great deal of overlap between the four categories, Swat decided to analyse whether poor housekeeping was an overarching reason that could explain a lot of the accidents. Figure 22.16 shows the percentage of accidents Swat could attribute to poor housekeeping by type of plant.

When incidents were analysed in the meat-processing factory, it was seen that there had been an increase from 1993 to 1994, mainly through manual causes.

The main conclusions were as follows.

- Accidents should always be reported fully, including all circumstances that may have caused them.
- 'Lesser' incidents also need to be recorded as they can easily be remedied.
- There should be inspections of housekeeping in industrial factories to help reduce the number of preventable accidents and incidents.

Main discussion points

- Monitoring is both the first and last step in the process of potential accident prevention in industrial workplaces and factories.
- The categories of both accidents and incidents means that a more uniformed approach to monitoring can be used on a wider scale.

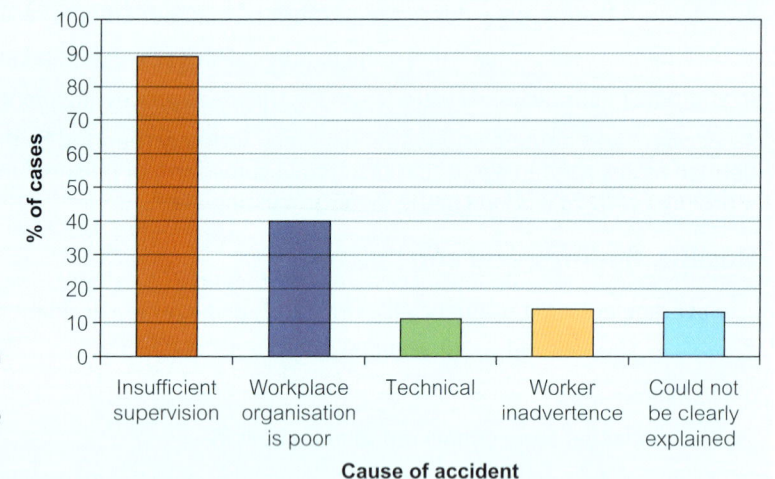

Figure 22.15 *The percentage of accidents across the four main causes*

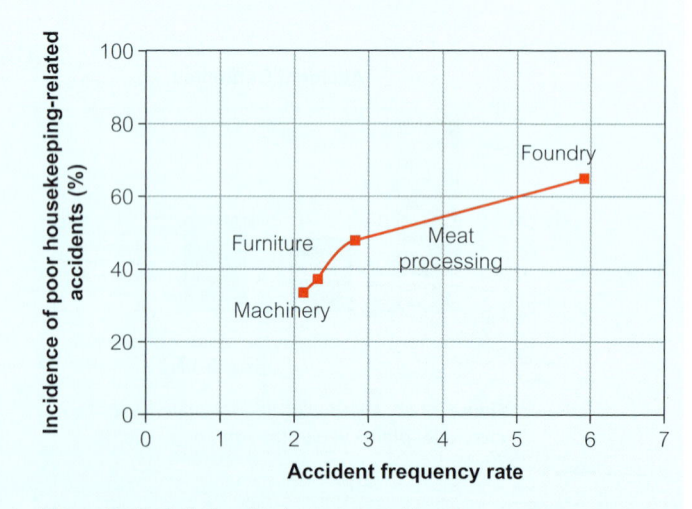

Figure 22.16 *Relationship between accident frequency rates and the incidence of poor housekeeping related accidents in the plants studied*

- Poor housekeeping appears to be a major cause of accidents and incidents and needs to be tackled, based on the findings from this study.

Evaluation

- The study probably lacks temporal validity. The research focused on accident and incident rates in industrial factories in the early 1990s in Poland. Many factories could now have more automated systems, meaning that some of the categories proposed by Swat may no longer be relevant.
- The study does have ecological validity and mundane realism. The four factories were real workplaces with no manipulation happening and the task involved in recording accidents and incidents is one that should be common practice in factories.
- The standardised categories for accidents and incidents can be used in other factories in other regions, countries, etc so we can compare causes directly.

Challenge yourself

Look at the issue and debate tracker table on page 307. Create similar issue and debate commentaries for individual and situational explanations, idiographic versus nomothetic, longitudinal studies, objective and subjective data, and generalisations from findings.

22.5 Satisfaction at work

22.5.1 Theories of job satisfaction

Two-factor theory (Herzberg, 1959)

Herzberg (1959) proposed the two-factor theory of job satisfaction. He believed that job satisfaction and job dissatisfaction are two independent things when it comes to the workplace. Prior to this, many psychologists believed there was a continuum from being satisfied to being dissatisfied at work. Herzberg surveyed many workers and asked them what made them feel especially bad or good about their job. He analysed the contents of these surveys and concluded that there are two main factors at work.

- Motivators – these are related to the content of the actual job and include:
    - level of responsibility within the job
    - how much workers had already achieved in the job
    - what recognition workers had received while doing the job
    - the content of work within the job
    - how much they had advanced (or could advance) within the job
    - how much they felt they had grown with the job.

These have to be present to achieve job satisfaction.

- Hygienes – these are related to the context of the job and include:
    - how company policies and administration affect the job
    - what level of supervision workers have in the job
    - what interpersonal relations are like within the job
    - what the working conditions are like within the job
    - salary.

These have to be absent or negative for job dissatisfaction to occur.

Therefore, workers need a range of motivators to be present to be satisfied with their job but when hygiene factors are absent this leads to dissatisfaction. Riggio (1999) notes that other organisational psychologists have tried to replicate Herzberg's findings but they keep failing to find these two distinct factors.

Job characteristics theory (Hackman and Oldham (1976)

Hackman and Oldham (1976) introduced us to the job characteristics model. Personnel staff, managers, leaders, etc can use it to devise and create jobs that will appeal to workers and keep them motivated. There are five critical decisions that have to be incorporated into any job design.

- Skill variety – does the job require different activities that utilise a range of the worker's skills and talents? It should.

- Task identity – does the job require the completion of a whole piece of work from its inception to its completion? It should.

- Task significance – does the job have a real impact on the organisation or even beyond that? It should.

- Autonomy – does the job allow the worker some freedom in terms of planning, scheduling, carrying out tasks, and organising teams? It should.

- Feedback – does the job allow for easily measurable feedback to assess the effectiveness of the worker? It should.

All of these added together bring about three critical psychological states, according to Hackman and Oldham (1980). Workers:

- experience meaningfulness at work
- experience responsibility in terms of the outcome of work
- have knowledge of the actual outcome of the job which can help employee growth.

All of this then makes workers much more motivated, their quality of work improves drastically, they become more satisfied and there is less absenteeism and fewer people leaving their job.

Figure 22.17 shows Hackman and Oldham's ideas about job satisfaction.

> **Test yourself**
>
> Explain at least one strength and one weakness of each of the theories of job satisfaction.

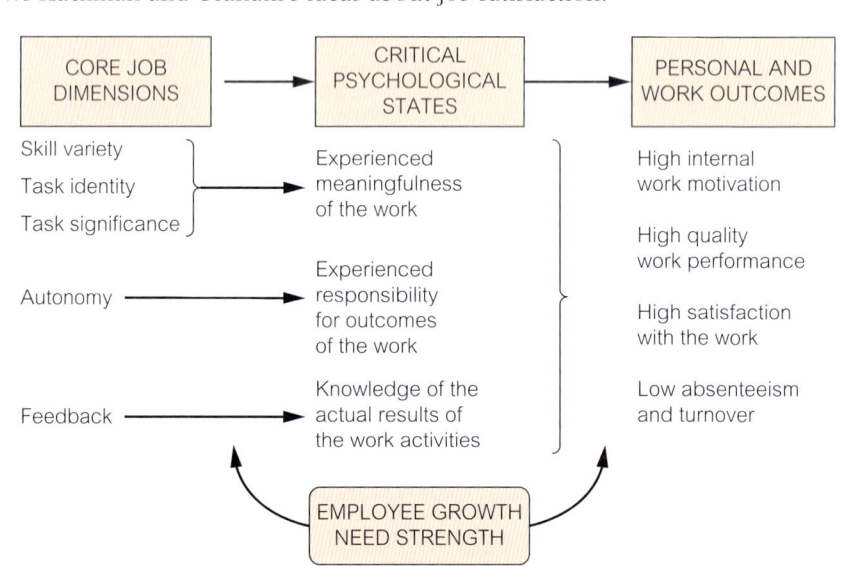

Figure 22.17 *The job characteristics model for work motivation*
Source: Hackman and Oldham (1976: 256)

Techniques for job design: enrichment, rotation, and enlargement

In addition to the job characteristics model, once a job has started there are other methods that can increase workers' satisfaction and motivation. Three of these are as follows.

- Job enrichment – this gives workers more jobs to do that involve more tasks to perform that are of a higher level of skill and responsibility. Workers can then have greater control over their job and it makes the job more interesting. Both of these increase satisfaction and motivation. One drawback is that this may be difficult to implement across many jobs within one organisation.

- Job rotation – this gives workers regular changes to tasks within their role at work. There may be daily, weekly, or monthly changes to the tasks that they are required to perform and this should keep them 'fresh' and highly motivated throughout their working day. This increases the workers' skills base too.

- Job enlargement – this gives workers more tasks to do but at the same level and usually as part of a team effort. There is no more responsibility or they are not required to learn new skills, rather they perform a wider variety of differing tasks during their working day.

> **Challenge yourself**
>
> Look at the issue and debate tracker table on page 315. Create similar issue and debate commentaries for application to everyday life, reductionism versus holism, idiographic versus nomothetic, and generalisations from findings.

22.5.2 Measuring job satisfaction

There are numerous ways in which workers' job satisfaction can be measured by an organisation. This allows the organisation's managers to assess how much they are allowing people to enjoy their work and be motivated.

Rating scales and questionnaires

There are some standardised rating scales and questionnaires that an organisation can use to measure the degree of satisfaction individual workers feel with their job. Two examples follow.

The Job Descriptive Index (Smith *et al* 1969)

Think of your present work. What is it like most of the time? In the blank space beside each word write:		Think of the pay you get. How well does each of the following words describe your present pay? In the blank space beside each word or phrase write:		Think of the opportunities for promotion the you have now. How well does each of the following words describe them? In the blank space beside each phrase write:	
Y	for "Yes" if it describes your work	Y	for "Yes" if it describes your pay	Y	for "Yes" if it describes your opportunities for promotion
N	for "No" if it does not describe it	N	for "No" if it does not describe it	N	for "No" if it does not describe them
?	if you cannot decide	?	if you cannot decide	?	if you cannot decide
Work on present job		**Present pay**		**Opportunities for promotion**	
— Routine		— Income inadequate for normal expenses		— Dead-end job	
— Satisfying		— Insecure		— Unfair promotion policy	
— Good		— Less than I deserve		— Regular promotions	
Think of the king of supervision your get on your job. How well does each of the following words describe this supervision? In the blank space beside each work or phrase write:		Think of the majority of people that you work with now or the purple your meet in connection with your work. How well does each of the following words describe these people? In the blank space beside each work write:		Think of your job in general. All in all, what is it like most of the time? In the blank space beside each word or phrase write:	
Y	for "Yes" if it describes the supervision you get on your job	Y	for "Yes" if it describes the people you work with	Y	for "Yes" if it describes your job
N	for "No" if it does not describe	N	for "No" if it does not describe them	N	for "No" if it does not describe it
?	if you cannot decide	?	if you cannot decide	?	if you cannot decide
Supervision on present job		**People on present job**		**Job in general**	
— Impolite		— Boring		— Undesirable	
— Praises good work		— Responsible		— Better than most	
— Doesn't supervise enough		— Intelligent		— Rotten	

Figure 22.18 *The Job Descriptive Index – the five dimensions*
Source: Smith *et al* (quoted in Riggio, 1999)

The Job Descriptive Index (JDI) devised by Smith *et al* is a self-report questionnaire for workers. It measures satisfaction on five dimensions: the job, supervision, pay, promotions, and co-workers (see Figure 22.118). Phrases are read and the worker has to answer 'Yes' or 'No', or '?' if undecided. Each answer to each phrase is already assigned a numerical value based on standardisation scoring. Therefore, the worker's satisfaction can be summed for the five dimensions to see whether all or just one or two dimensions are bringing about satisfaction or dissatisfaction.

Strength	Weakness
The questionnaire attempts to be holistic by measuring satisfaction on five different dimensions so it should have validity.	Many of the questions have fixed choices so workers may pick the one closest to their actual satisfaction rather than what they are actually feeling. This could reduce the validity of the index.

Quality of Work Life (QWL) questionnaire (Walton, 1974)

The QWL Evaluation Scale (Walton, 1974) allows workers to assess how they feel towards their job on eight different dimensions:

1. Salary (compensation) – four items
2. Working conditions – six items
3. Use of their capacities at work – five items
4. Opportunities at work – four items
5. Social integration at work – four items
6. Respecting the laws and rules at work – four items
7. The space work occupies in their life – three items
8. The social relevance and importance of their work – five items.

Each item is answered on a 5-point scale from 1 = very dissatisfied to 5 = very satisfied. Once the scale is completed, an overall score can be generated for each worker but also a score for each of the eight dimensions to see whether there are areas where workers are highly satisfied or highly dissatisfied with their work.

Example questions include those shown in Figure 22.19.

1.1	How satisfied are you with your salary (remuneration)?				
	Very dissatisfied	Dissatisfied	Neither satisfied nor dissatisfied	Satisfied	Very satisfied
	1	2	3	4	5
3.2	Are you satisfied with the importance of the task/work/activity that you do?				
	Very dissatisfied	Dissatisfied	Neither satisfied nor dissatisfied	Satisfied	Very satisfied
	1	2	3	4	5
4.1	How satisfied are you with your opportunity of professional growth?				
	Very dissatisfied	Dissatisfied	Neither satisfied nor dissatisfied	Satisfied	Very satisfied
	1	2	3	4	5
5.3	Regarding your team's and colleagues' commitment to work, how do you feel?				
	Very dissatisfied	Dissatisfied	Neither satisfied nor dissatisfied	Satisfied	Very satisfied
	1	2	3	4	5

Figure 22.19 QWL Evaluation Scale: example questions
Source: Reproduced in da Silva Timossi *et al* (2008: 14–16)

Psychology and organisations

Strength	Weakness
The questionnaire can be useful in appraisals to show managers what is good and not so good about the working life of the employee being appraised. Therefore, it has real-life application and usefulness.	The questionnaire is a self-report measure and workers may not complete each question accurately. For example, they may want to make themselves seem better than they actually feel at work because they believe that showing negativity restricts work opportunities.

	Issue and debate tracker
Psychometrics	Psychometric tests are useful as they enable direct comparison of workers based on their satisfaction scores and/or workers can be tracked over time to see how satisfaction changes in the workplace. They can also be used as a standardised, universal measure of satisfaction for large international organisations to see whether everyone across the world is happy at work. However, as a lot of the data is quantitative, it does not reveal the reasons for the satisfaction or dissatisfaction shown in workers' scores.
Reliability	Many measures of job satisfaction have reliability characteristics as they are psychometric measures with psychometric properties. This means that they would have been assessed via test–retest reliability to ensure that the measure is stable over time but can also measure variations over time when people begin to either increase or decrease in their motivation. This can be done if the same measure is used consistency across a workforce, with gaps in time long enough for employees not to remember how they answered it on a previous occasion.

> **Challenge yourself**
>
> Design a study that looks at two different groups of workers in the same company and finds out which group are more satisfied with their job.

> **Challenge yourself**
>
> Create similar issue and debate commentaries for individual and situational explanations, quantitative and qualitative data, and validity.

22.5.3 Attitudes to work

Workplace sabotage

Workplace sabotage is about rule breaking and workers making a conscious effort to stop themselves and others from working for an organisation. This can be caused by frustration as workers begin to feel powerless in their job. It can also be brought about as an attempt to make working conditions better, for instance to gain better wages or physical conditions in a factory. Finally, it can be an attempt to challenge authority as workers feel that their managers or leaders are not performing in their job. This is an extreme form of dissatisfaction so cannot be used to discover job dissatisfaction on a daily basis and in the majority of workers.

KEY STUDY: Giacalone and Rosenfeld (1987)

Context

It can be very difficult to investigate sabotage in the workplace. Workers may not want to report colleagues, and some sabotage can even involve criminal activities. However, there can be ways around this by using research methods that are anonymous (eg self-reports) and allowing employees to complete them away from their place of work.

Main theories/explanations

Organisational sabotage is defined as any type of behaviour that an employee who is on the payroll shows with the intention to ruin production or cause a financial loss to the organisation. Dubois (1980) proposed three general forms: destruction of machinery or goods, directly or indirectly stopping production, and slowing down production.

Aims and hypotheses

Giacalone and Rosenfeld (1987) conducted a study to investigate the reasons why organisational sabotage occurs.

Design

They used a volunteer sample of 38 electrical factory workers in the United States. A sabotage methods questionnaire was constructed. An ex-employee of the company was asked to list all of the different methods he had come across that those workers had used to sabotage their workplace. A list of 29 different methods was listed. They fell into four distinct categories.

1. Work – examples were slowing up feed and machine speed rates, going absent 'looking for parts', or carrying out management requirements word-for-word.
2. Destruction of machinery, premises, and products – examples were writing poetry on the wall of the bathroom, using glue to block tool lockers, or turning on a machine then walking away so it would damage itself.
3. Dishonesty – this included, for example, using company tools to complete personal work, changing the time on their clocking-in card, or taking tools home to use.
4. Causing chaos – this included, for example, calling on the union to help them at work, harassing the foreman, or throwing their timecards away.

A sabotage reasons questionnaire was also constructed. The same ex-employee had to list as many reasons as he had heard of where a worker had attempted to justify their sabotage actions. A total of eleven reasons were given.

1. Self-defence
2. Revenge
3. 'An eye for an eye'
4. To protect self from boss or company
5. To protect a friend or family from the boss or company
6. To protect own job
7. The company deserved the sabotage
8. The company had hurt the worker in the past
9. It does not matter as no one was hurt
10. A release for the frustrations at work
11. For fun

The participants were asked to rate each of the 29 methods on a Likert-type scale from 1 (not at all justifiable) to 7 (totally justifiable). The same scale was used when rating the 11 reasons. Each participant received a total score for the reasons questionnaire. These were ranked in order and then split via the median. This was so there would be a 'high reason accepter' group and a 'low reason accepter' group.

Results, findings, and conclusions

The top five differences between the groups for justification of methods used were as follows (all in the direction of the high reasons group seeing these as more justifiable).

1. Attempting to scare a foreman into quitting their job
2. Setting up a foreman to get them into trouble
3. Doing things too quickly to ensure the machine broke
4. Altering the dimensions of the goods being produced
5. Stealing as compensation for low wages

In terms of the four main categories, the high reason accepters were significantly more likely to justify work slowdowns, destruction, and causing chaos compared to the low reason accepters. However, there was no difference between the two groups on justifying dishonesty.

In conclusion, there are perceptual differences in the justification of many acts of organisational sabotage based around whether these acts are seen as being justifiable by an employee. However, this is not the case for sabotage by dishonesty.

Main discussion points

Giacalone and Rosenfeld focused their discussion around explaining the dishonesty result in three ways.

- Sabotage based on dishonesty could be qualitatively different from all other forms of organisational sabotage. This type of sabotage could mean monetary gain for an employee.
- Dishonesty does not serve the same sabotage function as all other types.
- Dishonesty is not justified as it is a threat to someone's self-esteem. All other forms of sabotage have no link to financial gain by the employee, so self-esteem cannot be affected.

> ### Evaluation points
>
> - The study was based around actual methods of sabotage and reasons for sabotage. Therefore, the findings do have application to the real world. It is useful for companies to know what the motives for sabotage are and what types occur to try to reduce incidences.
> - The study only took place in an electrical factory and so these reasons and methods may only apply to this one company. Generalisation may be difficult to other organisations that deal with cyber-sabotage, offices that are mainly administrative, or where sabotage levels are very low.
> - The 'justifiable' data, on a 7-point scale, is subjective. One employee's view of a 3 may not correspond easily with another employee's view of a 3. This can make comparisons across employees less valid.

Job absenteeism

Job absenteeism can be categorised as voluntary and involuntary. Voluntary absenteeism refers to instances where the worker has chosen to take the time off (eg the worker may choose to have an extra day for a long weekend or may have errands to run such as going to the vet). Involuntary absenteeism refers to times when the worker does not choose to be off work but is absent. The main reason for this is illness. Organisations have to be prepared for a certain number of instances occurring per worker and have policies in place to deal with it (eg use temporary workers or use an agency to find cover workers). Voluntary absenteeism may well be a measure of job dissatisfaction but, as with withdrawal above, the reasons vary so widely that it is another low validity attempt (people may just take the odd day off to do other things but really love their job). Therefore, as Riggio (1999) points out, there are problems with using this as any measure due to the complexity of reasons that people give for voluntary absenteeism.

Types of absence and categories of commitment

In addition, in studying absenteeism Blau and Boal (1987) provided another model that examined the role of the following aspects:

- job involvement – classified as high or low depending on how involved an employee is with the job and company
- organisational commitment – classified as high or low depending on how committed the employee is to the company and its vision for the future, etc
- individual task-related – how well the employee works by him- or herself on tasks
- group maintenance-related – how well the employee works in teams.

Table 22.9 highlights how these aspects interact according to Blau and Boal.

Ask yourself

Which of Blau and Boal's four categories is more likely to be absent from work? Justify your choice.

Challenge yourself

Look at the issue and debate tracker table on page 315. Create similar issue and debate commentaries for application to everyday life, individual and situational explanations, reductionism versus holism, idiographic versus nomothetic, and generalisations from findings.

Table 22.9 Job involvement; organisational commitment; individual task-related and group maintenance-related aspects

Cell (describing individual)	Effort focus	Salient satisfaction focus	Label
1 High job involvement and high organizational commitment	Individual task-related = higher; group maintenance-related = higher	Work itself Future with company Pay Co-worker Supervisor	Institutionalized stars
2 High job involvement and low organizational commitment	individual task-related = higher; group maintenance-related = lower	Work itself Working conditions Pay	Lone wolves
3 Low job involvement and high organizational commitment	Individual task-related = lower; group maintenance-related = higher	Co-worker	Corporate citizens
4 Low job involvement and low organizational commitment	Individual task-related = lower; group maintenance-related = higher	Reward	Apathetic employees

Source: Blau and Boal (1987: 293)

Exam centre: A Level

Paper 3

Clinical

1. James has recently been diagnosed with pyromania. Describe the diagnostic criteria (ICD-11) for this disorder. [4]

2. Javier has recently been diagnosed with schizophrenia. Explain how one biological treatment can help with his treatment. [4]

3. (a) Describe the study by Oruč et al (1997) about the genetics of depressive disorder. [6]

   (b) Evaluate the study by Oruč et al (1997), including a discussion about application to everyday life. [10]

4. (a) Suggest **two** ways in which psychological therapy can help Jeremy who has been diagnosed with obsessive compulsive disorder. [4]

   (b) Explain **one** strength of **one** of the therapies you suggested in part (a). [2]

Consumer

5. (a) Outline what is meant by the determinism versus free-will debate. [2]

   (b) Explain **one** strength of determinism, using brand recognition as an example. [2]

6. (a) Describe the study by Hall et al (2010) about choice blindness. [6]

   (b) Evaluate the study by Hall et al (2010), including a discussion about validity. [10]

7. (a) Suggest **two** ways in which an advertising company can write an effective slogan for a new type of biscuit. [4]

   (b) Explain **one** weakness of **one** of the ways you suggested in part (a) [2]

8. Explain **two** ways to close a sale, based on the ideas of Cialdini. [4]

Health

9. (a) Describe what psychologists have learned about misusing health services. [6]

   (b) Evaluate what psychologists have learned about misusing health services, including a discussion about case studies. [10]

10. (a) Suggest **two** ways in which a doctor could measure non-adherence in a patient who 'claims' to be taking all of his or her medication. [4]

    (b) Explain **one** strength of **one** of the ways you suggested in part (a). [2]

11. (a) Outline what is meant by the nature versus nurture debate. [2]

    (b) Explain **one** strength of nature, using types of pain as an example. [2]

12. Explain **one** way to improve healthy eating in a school. [4]

Organisational

13. Suggest **two** ways in which an organisation can use shift work with its employees. [4]

14. (a) Describe what psychologists have learned about need theories. [6]

    (b) Evaluate what psychologists have learned about need theories, including a discussion about individual and situational explanations of behaviour. [10]

15. (a) Suggest **two** reasons for sabotage in the workplace. [2]

    (b) Explain **one** weakness of **one** of the reasons you suggested in part (a) [2]

16. Company T has a poor record for health and safety at work. Explain **one** way in which Company T can reduce accidents in the workplace. [4]

Paper 4

Clinical

17. (a) Plan a study to investigate the effectiveness of psychological therapy for obsessive compulsive disorder. Your plan must include sampling technique and a directional/non-directional hypothesis. [10]

    (bi) For one piece of psychological knowledge on which your study was based: Describe this psychological knowledge. [4]

    (bii) Explain how you used two features of this psychological knowledge to plan your study. [2]

    (c) State two reasons for your choice of sampling technique. [2]

18. From the key study by Chapmann and DeLapp (2013):

    (a) Outline the aim of this study. [2]

    (b) Describe how the participant was assessed. [4]

    (c) Explain **one** strength and **one** weakness of this study in relation to how data was collected. [4]

Consumer

19. Outline **two** factors that can affect wayfinding in shopping malls. [4]

20. (a) Plan a study to investigate the how heuristics affect decision-making in consumers. Your plan must include sampling technique and a directional/non-directional hypothesis [10]

    (bi) For **one** piece of psychological knowledge on which your study was based: Describe this psychological knowledge [4]

    (bii) Explain how you used two features of this psychological knowledge to plan your study [2]

    (c) State **two** reasons for your choice of sampling technique [2]

21. You have learned about how product placement in films affects product choice in consumers

    (a) Describe the sample of participants used in a study about how product placement in films affects product choice in consumers. [4]

    (b) Explain **one** strength and **one** weakness of the study you have described in part (a). [4]

(c) Suggest **one** other way that product placement in films affects product choice in consumers can be studied, other than using the research method used in the study described in part (a). [2]

22. Explain **two** strengths of using field experiments to study choice blindness [4]

Health

23. From the key study by Savage and Armstrong on the effect of practitioner style on patient satisfaction: outline **two** results from this study. [4]

24. From the key study by Brudvik et al (2016) about measuring pain.

    (a) Describe how pain was measured in the younger children group (aged 3 to 8 years) the aim of this study. [4]

    (b) Outline **one** result of this study. [2]

    (c) Explain **one** strength and **one** weakness of this study. [4]

25. (a) Plan a questionnaire study to investigate whether patients understand a range of terminology used by their doctor. Your plan must include sampling technique and a directional/non-directional hypothesis [10]

    (bi) For **one** piece pf psychological knowledge on which your study was based: Describe this psychological knowledge [4]

    (bii) Explain how you used two features of this psychological knowledge to plan your study [2]

    (c) State **two** reasons for your choice of sampling technique [2]

Organisational

26. You have learned about a study linked to Maslow's hierarchy of needs.

    (a) Describe the procedure used in a study linked to Maslow's hierarchy of needs. [4]

    (b) Explain **one** strength and **one** weakness of the study you have described in part (a). [4]

    (c) Suggest **one** other way that Maslow's hierarchy of needs can be studied in the workplace, other than using the research method used in the study described in part (a). [2]

27. Suggest **two** ways in which a cognitive theory of motivation can be used to improve the motivation of employees in a factory that makes shoes. [4]

    (a) Plan a study to investigate cultural differences in group performance in the workplace. Your plan must include sampling technique and a directional/non-directional hypothesis [10]

    (bi) For **one** piece pf psychological knowledge on which your study was based: Describe this psychological knowledge [4]

    (bii) Explain how you used two features of this psychological knowledge to plan your study [2]

    (c) State **two** reasons for your choice of sampling technique [2]

Index

absenteeism from work 317
acceptance, persuasive communication 219
accidents at work *see* worksite accidents
achievement motivation theory 277
adaptive challenges, Heifetz's leadership principles 285–6
adherence/non-adherence to medical advice 238–46
advertising 219–27
    brand recognition/recall 206–7, 224–7
    digital media versus printed advertisements 220–2
    Lauterborn's 4 Cs marketing mix model 222
    media 219–22
    product placement 224–5
    retroactive and proactive interference with memory 206–7
    self-monitoring 222–3
    types and techniques 219–22
    Yale model of persuasive communication 219–20
affective disorders *see* mood disorders
agency theory 94
agentic state, agency theory 94
aggression in children 74–82
agoraphobia 153
aims in research 17
A Level issues and debates 128–9
alternative treatments, pain 255
ambience
    consumer psychology 179–80
    see also sound
amygdala 51, 102
anchoring, choice heuristics 198
anchors, suggestive/expansive selling 200
Andrade study (2009) 57–61
animal phobias 157–60
animal research
    elephant training 82–9
    ethical guidelines 25–6, 34
    toy preferences in rhesus monkeys 44–50
antidepressants 143
anxiety disorders and fear-related disorders 152–64
appraisal delays, recognising the need to seek treatment 235–6
approaches to psychology 35–6
arousal
    group behaviour 296, 297
    personal space 190
    pleasure-arousal-dominance model 179–80
    stress 256
AS Level issues and debates 33–4
Asperger syndrome (AS) 62–6
atmospherics, consumer psychology 179–80
attention 57–61
    diversion 255
    menus 187
    persuasive communication 219
    product shelf position 211–13
attitudes to work 315–18
attributional style, mood disorders 142
auditory displays and controls 308
autism 62–6, 169–70
autocratic leaders 286–7
autonomous state, agency theory 94
availability, choice heuristics 197
averages 29

Bandura *et al* study (1961) 74–82
bar charts 30
Baron-Cohen *et al* study (2001) 62–6
Beck Depression Inventory 139
Beck's cognitive triad 143
behavioural chaining 83–9
behavioural explanations of psychiatric disorders 148, 157–8, 168

behavioural leadership theories 284, 285
behavioural measures, pain 253–4
behavioural psychology 36, 74–93
behavioural techniques, improving adherence to medical advice 243–6
behavioural therapy
    fear-related disorders 159–60
    see also cognitive behavioural therapy
behaviour constraint theory, personal space 190
Belbin's nine team roles/Team Inventory 293–4
bias
    behavioural/cognitive 48
    cognitive limitations 296
    confirmation 295, 296
    cultural 141, 206, 213
    interviewer/researcher 12, 20
    optimistic 271
    overcoming 126
    subjective/qualitative data 20
BII *see* blood-injection-injury phobia
biochemical (drug) therapy, delivery changes improving adherence 242
biochemical factors *see* hormones; neurotransmitters
biochemical therapy (drugs)
    impulse control disorders 149–50
    mood disorders 139, 143–5
    obsessive-compulsive disorder 149–50
    OCD 169
    pain 254
    schizophrenia 135–6
biofeedback therapy 261–2
biological approaches 35, 37–56
biological explanations of psychiatric disorders 133–4, 139–41, 146, 157, 167–8
biological measures
    non-adherence to medical advice 242
    stress 259–60
biological treatments *see* biochemical therapy; electro-convulsive therapy
BIPI *see* Blood-injection Phobia Inventory
bipolar disorders 138, 140–3
blood-injection-injury (BII) phobia 161–3
Blood-injection Phobia Inventory (BIPI) 155–7
blood and injection phobias 155–7, 161–3
BPS *see* British Psychology Society
brain activity in sleep 37–43
brain areas
    localization of function 51–6
    obsessive-compulsive disorder 168
    OCD 167
    pain centre 248
    personal space 102
    pleasure centre 146
brain grey matter density 51–6
brain scans (MRI/fMRI) 53, 259–60
branding 173, 206–7, 224–7
British Psychology Society (BPS), guidelines 21–6
building design 173, 181–2
bullying at work 301–2
bystander behaviour 110–17

case studies, as research method 12–13
CBT *see* cognitive behavioural therapy
central gaze cascade effect 211–13
charismatic and transformational leaders theory 284–5
children
    aggression 74–82
    classical conditioning 157–8
    consumer psychology 224–6
    eyewitness testimony 67–73
    health promotion in schools 267–9

imitating adult behaviour 74–82
immunisation rates 243–6
improving adherence to medical advice 242
obsessive-compulsive disorder 168–70
pain assessment 250–3
phobias 90–3, 158–9
positive psychology applications 272–5
schizophrenia 135
social demands 71, 73
toy preferences 44, 48
use in research 23–4, 34, 73, 81, 93, 227, 246
choice *see* decision making
choice blindness 203–6
Cialdini's six ways to close a sale 215–16
CID *see* Comfortable Interpersonal Distance scale
classical conditioning 36, 90–3, 157–8, 160
clinical psychology 130–72
    anxiety and fear related disorders 152–64
    impulse control disorders 145–52
    mood disorders 138–45
    obsessive-compulsive disorder 164–72
    schizophrenia 130–7
closed questions 11–12, 233
closing a sale 215–16
Code of Human Research Ethics, BPS 21
cognitive approach, consumer behaviour 216–17
cognitive behavioural approaches, disease management 254–5, 266–7
cognitive behavioural therapy (CBT)
    fear-related disorders 160–4
    impulse control disorders 150–2
    mood disorders 143–5
    obsessive-compulsive disorder 171–2
    pain management 254–5
    schizophrenia 136–7
cognitive dissonance, consumer purchases 218–19
cognitive explanations of psychological disorders 135, 141, 148, 168, 278–9
cognitive limitations and errors in group behaviour 295–6
cognitive psychology 35–6, 54–73
cognitive redefinition 255
cognitive restructuring therapy 143–4
colour, packaging design 208–11
Comfortable Interpersonal Distance (CID) scale 105
communication 219–20, 228, 230–5
compensatory/non-compensatory decision making strategies 195–7
competitor-focused sales technique 214
comprehension, communication 219, 230–1
compulsions *see* obsessive-compulsive disorder
computer simulations, teaching resources 25
concentration study 57–61
conditioning
    classical 36, 90–3, 157–9, 160
    operant 36, 82–9, 168, 243, 262
confidentiality 24
confirmation bias 295, 296
conflict, at work 300–2
congruity theory of prejudice 288–90
consent to participation in studies 9, 22–4
construct validity 27
Consumer decision model 216–17
consumer profiling 182–6
consumer psychology 173–227
    advertising 219–27
    atmospherics 179–80
    decision making 195–207, 216–19
    food 176–9, 186–90
    online/virtual shopping 175–6
    personal space 190–5
    physical environment 173–80
    product packaging 201–2, 207–11
    psychological environment 181–95
    retail stores 173–6, 179–80, 182–6
    sales techniques 213–16
    shelf position 211–13
    shopping malls 181–2
    sound 176–9
contracts 243
control conditions in experiments 10
controlled observation 15
controlling variables, operational definition 18–19
correlational studies 15–16
cortisol 258, 259–60
cost-benefit analysis, adherence to medical advice 239
co-variables 16, 18
    see also dependent variable
covert observation 13
covert sensitisation therapy 150–1
criterion validity 27
cross-cultural differences 128
crowding 180, 191–3
cultural bias risk 141, 206, 213
cultural factors 36, 94, 128, 130, 236, 268, 297
customer-focused sales technique 213–14
customising treatment to improve adherence 243

data analysis 28–32
data types 19–20
debriefing 9, 23, 25
deception 9, 24, 60–1
decision making
    buying a product 216–19
    choice blindness 203–6
    choice heuristics 197–202
    cognitive approach 216–17
    cognitive dissonance 218–19
    consumers 195–207, 216–19
    giving reasons for choice 217–18
    mistakes 202–6
    models 195
    problem group behaviour 294–6
    strategies 195–7
    styles 201–2
defending place in a queue 193–5
delusions, schizophrenia 130–4
demand characteristics 8, 9, 27
Dement and Kleitman study (1957) 37–43
dependent variable (DV) 8, 9, 17, 18
depressive disorders (mood/affective disorders) 138–45
design of menus 186–90
destructive obedience 94–101
detecting manipulation, choice blindness 203–6
determinism versus free will 129
deviation from chance, null hypotheses 18
diagnosis, practitioner style 232–5
diffusion of responsibility 111, 116
digital media versus printed advertisements 220–2
directing style of consultations 233–5
directional (one-tailed) hypotheses 17
disclosure of information, patients describing symptoms 232
disgust 90–3
dispositional hypothesis, destructive obedience 94, 100, 101
disrupt-then-reframe (DTR), sales techniques 214–15
dizygotic twins, genetic studies 133–4, 140
doctor-centred style 232–3
doctors, practitioner–patient relationship 228–38
dominant response, social facilitation 296
doodling aiding concentration 57–61
dopamine 134, 146, 148
double-blind procedures 19, 104, 145–6
dreaming research 37–43
drive theory 297
drug therapy *see* biochemical (drug) therapy

DTR *see* disrupt-then-reframe
DV *see* dependent variable

ecological validity 8, 9, 27
electro-convulsive therapy (ECT) 136, 143
electro-encephalography (EEG) 37–43, 216–17, 221
electronic performance monitoring (EPM) 298–9
elephant training 82–9
emotional states, pleasure-arousal-dominance model 179–80
empathy 102–9, 115
enlargement and enrichment in job design 312–13
EPM *see* electronic performance monitoring
ethical issues 21–6
    animals in research 25–6, 34
    bystander behaviour study 117
    children in research 22, 24, 34
    laboratory versus field experiments 9
ethnicity/racial issues 112–16, 276–7
evaluation apprehension 297
evaluation of experiments 10
evaluative learning 90–3
event-sampling in observation studies 13
expectancy theory (VIE) 279
experiments
    design 9–10, 17
    longitudinal designs 17
    natural versus true experiments 38–9
    randomised control trials 126
    as research method 8–10
exposure and response prevention therapy 169–70
external validity 9, 127
extraneous variables 19
eye movements, sleep research 37–43
eyewitness testimony 67–73

faces pain rating scale for children 251, 252
face-to-face interviews 12
factitious disorders 237–8
Fagen *et al* study (2014) 82–9
false negative (type I) and false positive (type II) errors 232
false positive responses 67–73
fast thinking (system 1) 202
fear arousal, health promotion strategy 266
fear-related disorders 152–64
feeling-state theory 148
field experiments 8–9, 110–17
flexitime working 304
followership styles 292
food
    effects of name/description 189
    effects of sound/music 177–9
    menu design 186–90
    packaging design 201–2, 208–11
    post-purchase cognitive dissonance 218–19
forced/fixed choice questions 127
Forsyth's cognitive limitations and errors in group behaviour 295–6
free will versus determinism 129
Freud, Sigmund 158–9

gambling disorder 145–6
GAS *see* general adaptation syndrome
gate control theory of pain 248
gender
    distinction from sex 44
    leadership 288–90
    patient perception of doctors 228–30
    social sensitivity 62, 64
general adaptation syndrome (GAS) model of stress 255–6
generalisability of research 27
generalised anxiety disorder 152–4
genetic factors
    fear-related disorders 157
    mood disorders 140–1
    nature versus nurture 33
    obsessive-compulsive disorder 167–8
    schizophrenia 133–4
    twin studies 9, 133–4, 140
gift wrapping 207–8
goal-setting theory 278–9
graphical representation of data 30–2
great person theory of leadership 284
group behaviour 292–302
    conflict 300–2
    decision making 294–6
    group development 292–3
    maintenance focus of employees 317–18
    polarisation 294–5
    team roles 293–4
groupthink 294–5

Halls' zones of personal space 190, 191
Hassett *et al* study (2008) 44–50
Hawthorne effect 302
health belief model 236, 239, 240
health beliefs 271–5
health effects of shift work 304–5
health promotion 242–6, 266–75
health psychology 228–75
    adherence/non-adherence to medical advice 238–46
    changing beliefs 271–5
    patient–practitioner relationship 228–38
    promoting health 266–75
    stress 255–66
health and safety 307–11
    see also worksite accidents
healthy eating 267–9
Heifetz's six principles in meeting adaptive challenges 285–6
helping stranger in need 110–17
heuristics, decision making 197–202
hierarchy of needs 276
high-functioning autism (HFA) 62–6
histograms 31
holism versus reductionism 128
Holocaust 94, 101
Hölzel *et al* study (2011) 51–6
hormones 102–9, 164
    obsessive-compulsive disorder 168
    oxytocin 102–9, 168
    sex differences in behaviour 44, 45, 48
    social behaviour 102–9
hypotheses in research 17–18, 127

identical (monozygotic) twins 9, 133–4, 140
idiographic versus nomothetic 129
illness delays, time before seeking treatment 235–6
imagery 255, 262
imaginal desensitisation therapy 151–2
imitation, social learning 74–81
impulse control disorders 145–52
independent measures design 9
independent variable (IV) 8, 9, 18
individual and group performance 296–300
individual task-related focus of employees 317–18
inferential statistical tests 16
information provision for health promotion 266–7
informed consent 9, 22–4
internal versus external validity 9
interpersonal distance 102–9
interpersonal influence sales techniques 214–15
Interpersonal Reactivity Index (IRI) 103
interpersonal skills, patient–practitioner relationship 228–31
inter-rater or observer reliability 28

interviews 11–12, 240
IRI *see* Interpersonal Reactivity Index
IV *see* independent variable

job characteristics theory 312
Job Descriptive Index 313–14
job related issues
    absenteeism 317
    involvement of employees 317–18
    job design 312–13
    job satisfaction 311–18
    stress 258
    see also organisations and workplaces

kleptomania 145–7
Kouzes and Posner's Leadership Practices Inventory 290–1

landscaping, retail store design 173–4
Lauterborn's 4 Cs marketing mix model 222
leadership 284–92
    leaders and followers 290–2
    levels 287
    styles 286–90
    theories 284–6
Leadership Practices Inventory 290–1
learned helplessness, mood disorders 141–2
learning 36
    classical conditioning 36, 90–3, 157–9, 160
    elephant training 82–9
    evaluative 90–3
    leadership 186
    operant conditioning 36, 82–9, 168, 243, 262
    social learning theory 74–82
Likert-type scales 11, 53, 180, 190–2, 249, 273, 289, 316
longitudinal studies 16–17

McGill Pain Questionnaire (MPQ) 250
malingering 237
MAOIS *see* monoamine oxidase inhibitors
marketing mix model, Lauterborn's 4 Cs 222
Maslow's hierarchy of needs 276–7
matched pairs design 9–10
Maudsley Obsessive-Compulsive Inventory (MOCI) 165–6
mean/median/mode, measures of central tendency 29
measured variables *see* co-variables; dependent variable
media, advertising 219–22
medical consultations 228–36
medical terminology comprehension 230–1
Mehrabian and Russell's pleasure-arousal-dominance model 179–80
memory
    aids to concentration 57–61
    explicit versus implicit 224–5
    eyewitness testimony 67–71
    impulse control disorders 148
    mindfulness 51, 56
    products 220–2, 224–5
    retroactive and proactive interference 206–7
    social learning 74
menu design 186–90
metarepresentation, schizophrenia 135
methodological concepts in research 17–32
Milgram study (1963) 94–101
mindfulness 51–6
minimising harm (and maximising benefit), ethical guidelines for research 22, 25
MOCI *see* Maudsley Obsessive-Compulsive Inventory
money as a motivator at work 281–3
monoamine oxidase inhibitors (MAOIs) 143
monozygotic twins, genetic studies 9, 133–4, 140
mood, pleasure-arousal-dominance emotional states 179–80
mood (affective) disorders 138–45

motivation
    achievement motivation theory 277
    at work 276–84
    cognitive theories 278–9
    expectancy theory 279
    goal-setting theories 278–9
    hierarchy of needs 276
    intrinsic and extrinsic 280
    need theories 276–7
    punishments 26, 74, 82–3, 96–101
    rewards 26, 280–4
    self-determination theory 281
Muczyk and Reimann's four styles of leader behaviour 286–7
multi-unit pricing 198
Munchausen syndrome 237–8
mundane realism 8, 27
music, consumer psychology 176–9

natural experiments 38–43, 63–7
naturalistic observation 15
nature versus nurture 33
need recognition, buying products 216
need theories, motivation 276–7
negative correlation 15–16
neuropeptides (oxytocin) 168
neurotransmitters
    dopamine 134, 146, 148
    impulse control disorders 146, 148
    mood disorders 139–41
    norepinephrine 139, 143
    obsessive-compulsive disorder 168
    serotonin 139–41, 143, 168
nomothetic versus idiographic approaches 129
non-adherence to medical advice 238–46
non-directional (two-tailed) hypotheses 17
non-participant observation 14
non-verbal communication, patient–practitioner relationship 228
norepinephrine 139, 143
null hypotheses 18

obedience 94–101
objective data 19
objective measures, adherence to medical advice 241–2
objectivity, validity in research 26–7
observation
    inter-observer reliability 28
    as research method 13–15
    social learning theory 74
obsessive-compulsive disorder (OCD) 164–72
occupational accidents 305–11
OCD *see* obsessive-compulsive disorder
odours, consumer psychology 179–80
on-call working 304
online advertising 220–2
online face-to-face interviews 12
online questionnaires 10–11
online shopping 175–6, 196–7, 201–2
open-ended questions/statements 11, 12, 233
open-plan offices 302–3
operant conditioning 36, 82–9, 168, 243, 262
operational definitions of co-variables 16, 18
operationalisation in research 18
operator–machine systems 307–8
opiate antagonists 149–50
opportunity sampling 21
optimistic bias 271
organisational commitment of employees 317–18
organisational machinery 307–8
organisations and workplaces 276–318
    accidents 305–11
    conditions 302–11

325

group behaviour 292–302
job satisfaction 311–18
leadership 284–92
motivation 276–84
occupational accidents 305–11
sabotage 315–17
stress 258

overload theory, personal space 190
overt versus covert observation 13
oxytocin 102–9, 164, 168

packaging 201–2, 207–11
PAD *see* pleasure-arousal-dominance model
pain
    behavioural/objective measures 253–4
    management and control 254–5
    measures 249–54
    phantom limb pain 246–8
    self inflicted 237–8
    subjective measures 240, 249–53
    theories 248
    types and functions 246
pain behaviour scale 253
paper and pencil questionnaires 10–11
participant variables 19
participant versus non-participant observation 14
patient-centred style of practitioners 232–3
patient–practitioner relationship 228–38
permissive leaders 286–7
Perry *et al* study (2015) 102–9
persecutory ideation, schizophrenia 131–3
personal space 102–9, 190–5
persuasive communication 219–20
phantom limb pain (PLP) 246–8
phobias 90–3, 153, 155–64
physical environment effects 173–80, 302–3
physiological psychology 35, 37–56
physiology of stress 255–6
play, sex differences in toy choice 44–50
pleasure-arousal-dominance (PAD) model 179–80
plotting data 30–2
PLP *see* phantom limb pain
pluralistic ignorance 111
PMR *see* Progressive Muscle Relaxation
point of purchase decision making 198–200, 211–13
population sampling 20–1
positive correlation 15
positive psychology 271–5
positive reinforcement 148
postal questionnaires 126
post-purchase cognitive dissonance 218–19
Pozzulo *et al* study (2011) 67–73
practitioner errors 232
practitioner–patient relationship 228–38
prejudice 288–90
preventive measures, stress 265
price, multi-unit pricing effects 198
privacy, ethical issues 24–5
proactive interference with memory 206–7
product-focused sales technique 214
product placement 224–5
products
    advertising 219–27
    buying 216–19
    packaging 201–2, 207–11
    selling 213–16
    shelf position 211–13
Progressive Muscle Relaxation (PMR) 151
prompts, improving adherence to medical advice 243
prospect model, decision making 195

psychodynamic factors 158, 168
psychological explanations of disorders 135, 141–2, 148, 157–9, 168
psychological measures, stress 261
psychological therapies
    fear-related disorders 160–4
    mood disorders 143–5
    obsessive-compulsive disorder 169–72
    pain 254–5
    schizophrenia 136–7
    stress 261–2
psychometric tests 127, 315
punishments 26, 74, 82–3, 96–101
purchase quantity limits 199
pyromania 145

qualitative data 19
Quality of Work Life (QWL) questionnaire 314
quantitative data 18
questionnaires 10–11, 126–7
queue intrusions 193–5

racial/ethnicity factors 112–16, 276–7
random sampling 21
range of data 30
rapid eye movement (REM) and non-REM sleep 37–43
rapid rotation and slow rotation shift work 303–4
rating scales in self-reports 11, 126–7
rational emotive behaviour therapy (REBT) 144–5
rational non-adherence to medical advice 239
reading the mind in the eyes 62–6
REBT *see* rational emotive behaviour therapy
recognition, choice heuristics 197
recurrent episode mood disorders 138
reductionism versus holism 128
reframing, sales techniques 214–15
reinforcement
    secondary positive reinforcement training study 82–9
    see also operant conditioning
relaxation, stress reduction 261–5
reliability, job satisfaction measures 315
reliability of research 9, 28
REM *see* rapid eye movement
repeated measures design 10
replacement of animals in research 25
replicability of research 28
representativeness, choice heuristics 197
research methods
    A level 126–7
    AS level 8–32
restaurants 176–7, 186–93
retail stores
    atmospherics 179–80
    crowding 180
    exterior design 173–4
    interior design 174–6
    odours 179–80
    point of purchase decision making 198–200, 211–13
    spatial movement patterns 182–6
    store choice 217–18
    supermarkets 182–6, 198–9
retroactive interference with memory 206–7
rewards, motivation 26, 280–4
right to withdraw from studies 24
risk, ethical guidelines for research 22
rotation, job design 312–13

Saavedra and Silverman study (2002) 90–3
sales techniques 213–15
sampling 20–1, 27
satisfaction at work 311–18
satisficing model 195

scattergraphs 31
scents, emotional states 179–80
schizophrenia 130–7
schools, health promotion 267–9
Scouller's levels of leadership 287
secondary positive reinforcement (SPR) 82–9
selective serotonergic re-uptake inhibitors (SSRIs) 139, 143, 169
self-determination theory 281
self-monitoring theory 222–3
self-reports, as research method 10–12
self-selecting (volunteer) sampling 21
selling anchors 200
semi-structured interviews 12, 240
serotonin 139–41, 143, 168
sex differences 44–50
    see also gender
shape, packaging design 208–11
shaping, operant conditioning 83–9
sharing style of consultations 233–5
shelf position of products 211–13
shift work 303–7
shopping *see* consumer psychology; retail stores
signage 181–2
single episode mood disorders 138
situational hypothesis, destructive obedience 94, 100, 101
situational variables 19
six principles in meeting adaptive challenges 285–6
sleep and dreaming research 37–43
slow thinking (system 2) 202
SMART goals 278–9
social cues, oxytocin and empathy effects 102–9
social demands, children 71
social facilitation 296, 297
social hormones 103
    see also oxytocin
social impact theory 297
social interactions, interpersonal distance 102–9
socialisation 44
social learning theory 74–82
social loafing 297
social pressure, destructive obedience 94–101
social psychology 36, 94–117
social salience hypothesis 102, 108
social sensitivity 62–6
sound, consumer psychology 176–9
spatial behaviour, shoppers in a supermarket 182–6
spatial zones, interpersonal distance 102–9
Spearman's Rank Order Correlation Coefficient 16
specificity theory of pain 248
specific phobias 90–3, 153, 155–64
SPR *see* secondary positive reinforcement
SSRIs *see* selective serotonergic re-uptake inhibitors
standard deviation 30
standardisation of procedure, controlling variables 18
stores *see* retail stores
stress 255–66
    cortisol 259–60
    inoculation training 265
    management 261–6
    measures 259–61
    physiology 255–6
    related illness 258
    sources 255–8
structured interviews 11
structured observation 14–15
subjective data 19
subjective measures
    non-adherence to medical advice 240
    pain 249–53
subjectivity, validity in research 26–7
supermarkets 182–6, 198–9

system 1 (fast thinking) 202
system 2 (slow thinking) 202
systematic desensitisation, fear-related disorders 159–60
tabulation of data 28–31
take-the-best, choice heuristics 198
target population (TP) 20–1, 27
Team Inventory 293–4
telephone interviews 12
temporal validity 127
temporal work conditions 303–7
test-retest reliability 28
theory of mind 62–6
thinking error, obsessive-compulsive disorder 168
thinking fast and thinking slow 202
Thomas–Kilmann's five conflict-handling modes 301
time-sampling, observation studies 13
token economy scheme, reducing accidents at work 269–70
toy preferences, sex differences 44–50
TP *see* target population
tricyclic antidepressants *see* selective serotonergic re-uptake inhibitors
twin studies 9, 133–4, 140
two-factor theory of job satisfaction 311–12
type A/type B personalities, stress 258, 261
type I (false negative) and type II (false positive) errors 232

UAB *see* University of Alabama at Birmingham
ultradian rhythms 38
uncontrolled variables 9, 19
unipolar depressive disorder 138
universalist leadership theories 284–5
University of Alabama at Birmingham (UAB), pain behaviour scale 253
unrealistic optimism 271
unstructured interviews 11
unstructured observation 14, 15
utilisation delays, time before seeking treatment 235–6
utility model, decision making 195

valid consent 22–4
validity in research 9, 26–7, 127
variables 8, 9, 16–19
victim's responsibility, perception 112
VIE (expectancy) theory 279
virtual shopping 175–6
visual analogue scale for pain 250
visual displays and controls 307
Volunteer (self-selecting) sampling 21

wayfinding in a shopping mall 181–2
websites *see* online
window displays, retail stores 173–4
Wong-Baker face scale 251, 252
work, *see also* job related issues; organisations and workplaces
workplace conditions 302–11
workplace sabotage 315–17
worksite accidents 269–70, 305–11
    errors 307–11
    operator–machine systems 308
    recording and monitoring 309–11
    reduction using token economy scheme 269–70
    shift work 305–7
work stress 258

Yale-Brown Obsessive Compulsive Scale (Y-BOCS) 166–7
Yale model of communication 219–20

Gottesman, I: "A Critical Review of Recent Adoption, Twin and Family Studies of Schizophrenia", *Schizophrenia Bulletin*, **Volume 2, Issue 3, 1976, Pages 360 – 401**, https://doi.org/10.1093/schbul/2.3.360 used by permission of Oxford University Press.

Hall et al: Reprinted from Cognition, vol.117, no.1, pp.54–61, Hall, L, Johansson, P, Tärning, B, Sikström, S and Deutgen, T, "Magic at the marketplace: Choice blindness for the taste of jam and the smell of tea" © 2010 with permission from Elsevier.

Hassett, J M, Siebert, E R and Wallen, K: Reprinted from Hormones and Behaviour, 54(3): 359–64, Hassett, J M, Siebert, E R and Wallen, K, "Sex differences in rhesus monkey toy preferences parallel those of children", © 2008 with permission from Elsevier.

Hodgson, R.J. and Rachman, S: Reprinted from "Obsessional-compulsive complaints" Behaviour Research and Therapy. Volume 15, Issue 5, 1977, Pages 389-395, © 1977 with permission from Elsevier.

Holmes, T H and Rahe, R H: Reprinted from 'Journal of Psychosomatic Research', vol.11, no.2, pp.213–18, "The social readjustment rating scale", © 1967 with permission from Elsevier.

Hölzel et al: Reprinted from Psychiatry Research, 191(1): 36–43, Hölzel, B K, Carmody, J, Vangel, M, Congleton, C, Yerramsetti, S M, Gard, T and Lazar, S W, "Mindfulness practice leads to increases in regional brain gray matter density", © 2011 with permission from Elsevier.

Jedetski, Adelman & Yeo: "How Web site decision technology affects consumers," in IEEE Internet Computing, vol. 6, no. 2, pp. 72-79, March-April 2002, doi: 10.1109/4236.991446. Reprinted by permission.

Kardes, F. R. et al: "The Role of the Need for Cognitive Closure in the Effectiveness of the Disrupt-Then-Reframe Influence Technique" from Journal of Consumer Research, October 2007, Oxford University Press. Reprinted by permission of Oxford University Press.

Kouzes, J. M. and Posner, B. Z: *Leadership practices inventory: LPI®*. Jossey-Bass. © Copyright 2013 by James M. Kouzes and Barry Z. Posner, www.leadershipchallenge. com. All rights reserved. Reprinted by permission of John Wiley & Sons Inc.

Landry, A T, Zhang, Y, Papachristopoulos, K and Forest, J: "Applying Self-Determination Theory to understand the motivational impact of cash rewards: New evidence from lab experiments". International Journal of Psychology, 55(2): 487–98. 2019. John Wiley and Sons Reprinted by permission.

Lovell, K. et al: "Telephone administered cognitive behaviour therapy for treatment of obsessive compulsive disorder: randomised controlled noninferiority trial", BMJ Publishing Group Ltd, October 26, 2006. Reproduced with permission of BMJ Publishing Group Ltd.

McKinlay, J. B: "Who is really ignorant – physician or patient?" *Journal of Health and Social Behavior*. Vol. 16, number 1, 1975, pp. 3–11 American Sociological Association and J. B. McKinlay. Used by permission.

McKinstry, B. and Wang, J. X: "Putting on the style: what patients think of the way their doctor dresses". *British Journal of General Practice* July 1991; 41(348): 270, 275–278. Reprinted by permission.

Mehrabian: "Pleasure-arousal-dominance: A general framework for describing and measuring individual differences in Temperament". Current Psychology, vol.14, p.261-292, 1996. Reprinted by permission from Springer Nature.

Oldham, G.R. and Brass, D.T: Table from p.278 Administrative Science Quarterly. Vol. 24, number 2 1979. Reprinted with permission.

Pavesic, D: "The Psychology of Menu Design: Reinvent Your 'Silent Salesperson' to Increase Check Averages and Guest Loyalty", in Hospitality Faculty Publications, paper 5, 2005, Georgia State University.

Perry, Anat; Mankuta, David: "OT promotes closer interpersonal distance amonghighly empathic individuals", Social Cognitive and Affective Neuroscience, 2014,10, 1, pp. 7, by permission of Oxford University Press.

Pozzulo, Joanna D. et al: "The Culprit in Target-Absent Lineups: Understanding Young Children's False Positive Responding". Journal of Police and Criminal Psychology, 27(1): 55–62, 2011. Reprinted by permission from Springer Nature and Copyright Clearance Center.

Porublev, E. et al: "To wrap or not wrap? What is expected? Some initial findings from a study on gift wrapping", ANZMAC: Sustainable management and marketing conference. Melbourne, Australia. December 2009.

Robson SKA, Kimes SE, Becker FD, Evans GW: "Consumers' Responses to Table Spacing in Restaurants". *Cornell Hospitality Quarterly*. 2011;52(3):253-264. doi:10.1177/1938965511410310. Reprinted by permission of Sage Publication.

Roth, H P and Caron, H S: 'Accuracy of doctors' estimates and patients' statements on adherence to a drug regimen', in Clinical Pharmacology & Therapeutics, vol.23, no.3, pp.361–70, 1978, John Wiley and Sons Reproduced by permission.

Saavedra, L M and Silverman, W K: Reprinted from Journal of the American Academy of Child & Adolescent Psychiatry, 41(11): 1376–79, Case Study: Disgust and a Specific Phobia of Buttons/Lissette M. Saavedra,Wendy K. Silverman © 2002 with permission from Elsevier.

Savage, R. and Armstrong, D: "Effect of a general practitioner's consulting style on patients' satisfaction: a controlled study". *BMJ: British Medical Journal*. Vol. 301, No. 6758. Reproduced with permission of the BMJ Publishing Group Ltd.

Swat, K: "Monitoring of Accidents and Risk Events in Industrial Plants". Journal of Occupational Health,

39(2): 100–04, 1997. Reproduced by permission of John Wiley & Sons.

Tapper, K., Horne, P. J. and Lowe, C. F: "The Food Dudes to the rescue!" *The Psychologist*. Vol. 16, No. 1, 2003. British Psychological Society.

Vrechopoulos et al: Reprinted from Journal of Retailing, vol.80, no.1, pp.13–22, Vrechopoulos, A P, O'Keefe, R M, Doukidis, G I and Siomkos, G J, "'Virtual store layout: an experimental comparison in the context of grocery retail" © 2004 with permission from Elsevier.

Wang, J. et al: "Perfusion functional MRI reveals cerebral blood flow pattern under psychological stress". *PNAS*. Vol. 102, No. 49. Copyright (2005) National Academy of Sciences, U.S.A. Reprinted by permission.

Wansink B, Kent RJ, Hoch SJ: "An Anchoring and Adjustment Model of Purchase Quantity Decisions". *Journal of Marketing Research*. 1998;35(1):71-81. doi:10.1177/002224379803500108. Reprinted by permission of Sage Publication.

Wansink, B., van Ittersum, K. and Painter, J. E: "How Descriptive Food Names Bias Sensory Perceptions in Restaurants" *Food Quality and Preference*, 16:5, 2005, 393- 400. Reprinted by permission.

Watt, P M, Clements, B, Devadason, S G and Chaney, G M: 'Funhaler spacer: improving adherence without compromising delivery', in Archives of Disease in Childhood, vol.88, no.7, pp.579–81, 2003.

WHO: Reproduced from ICD-11 International Classification of Diseases 11th Revision, 25 May 2019 World Health Organization.

Yokley, J M and Glenwick, D S: "Increasing the immunization of preschool children; an evaluation of applied community interventions". Journal of Applied Behavior Analysis, 17(3): 313–25, 1984. Reproduced by permission of John Wiley & Sons.

Cover illustrations: Chris Madden / Getty Images

Photos: p4: vectoriart/iStockphoto; p6:Kubko/Shutterstock; pp6-7,p124-125: Robert Szymanski/Shutterstock; p39: Hank Morgan/Science Photo Library; p46(t): Don Mammoser/Shutterstock; p46(bl): MeteeChaicharoen/Shutterstock; p46(br): lookas.camera/Shutterstock; p53(t): Leah-Anne Thompson/Shutterstock; p53(b): SpeedKingz/Shutterstock; p64: tugol/Shutterstock; p69(l): Allstar Picture Library Ltd. / Alamy Stock Photo; p69(r): Everett Collection Inc / Alamy Stock Photo; p82: Neijia/Shutterstock; p86: Tracey Whitefoot/Alamy Stock Photo; p106: Perry, Anat; Mankuta, David, "OT promotes closer interpersonal distance amonghighly empathic individuals", Social Cognitive and Affective Neuroscience, 2014,10, 1, pp. 7, by permission of Oxford University Press.; p117: Photographee.eu/Shutterstock; p174: Jana Krizova/Shutterstock; p181(t): lettett/Shutterstock; p181(m): Boyo Ducks/Shutterstock; p181(b): Dogu and Erkip (2000: 745); p187(l): Marchie/Shutterstock; p187(r): mountain beetle/Shutterstock; p191: Stephani Robson, PhD, Senior Lecturer Emerita, Cornell University; P201: del Campo, C., Pauser, S., Steiner, E. et al. Decision making styles and the use of heuristics in decision making. J Bus Econ 86, 389–412 (2016). https://doi.org/10.1007/s11573-016-0811-y; p204: Petter Johansson/Lund University; p208: Elizabeth Porublev, et al: "To wrap or not wrap? What is expected? Some initial findings from a study on gift wrapping", ANZMAC: Sustainable management and marketing conference. Melbourne, Australia. Dec. 2009. Reprinted by permission.; p209: University of Twente(UT); p210: University of Twente(UT); p229: Brian McKinstry.

Artwork by Q2A Media, Greengate Publishing Services Ltd., and Oxford University Press.

Every effort has been made to contact copyright holders of material reproduced in this book. Any omissions will be rectified in subsequent printings if notice is given to the publisher.

Although we have made every effort to trace and contact all copyright holders before publication this has not been possible in all cases. If notified, the publisher will rectify any errors or omissions at the earliest opportunity.

Links to third party websites are provided by Oxford in good faith and for information only. Oxford disclaims any responsibility for the materials contained in any third party website referenced in this work.